D1596974

Objectivity Is Not Neutrality

Objectivity Is Not Neutrality

EXPLANATORY SCHEMES IN HISTORY

Thomas L. Haskell

THE JOHNS HOPKINS UNIVERSITY PRESS

BALTIMORE AND LONDON

© 1998 The Johns Hopkins University Press
All rights reserved. Published 1998
Printed in the United States of America on acid-free paper

07 06 05 04 03 02 01 00 99 98   5 4 3 2 1

The Johns Hopkins University Press
2715 North Charles Street
Baltimore, Maryland 21218-4319
The Johns Hopkins Press Ltd., London

Library of Congress Cataloging-in-Publication Data will
be found at the end of this book.
A catalog record for this book is available from the British
Library.

ISBN 0-8018-5681-7

For Dorothy,
with love and gratitude

CONTENTS

Objectivity Is Not Neutrality

History, Explanatory Schemes, and Other Wonders of Common Sense

> It is, in no case, the real historical Transaction, but only some more or less plausible scheme and theory of the Transaction, or the harmonised result of many such schemes, each varying from the other and all varying from truth, that we can ever hope to behold. . . .
>
> Such considerations were truly of small profit, did they, instead of teaching us vigilence and reverent humility in our inquiries into History, abate our esteem for them, or discourage us from unweariedly prosecuting them.
>
> —Thomas Carlyle, "On History" (1830)

These essays span twenty years of teaching and writing, from the 1970s to the 1990s. The earliest one, originally published when I was in my mid-thirties, was a contribution to a debate over the efficiency of slave labor. No obvious thread of continuity connects that work with an essay I was working on recently about "responsibility," a word with seemingly timeless resonance that turns out to be no older than the United States, having first appeared in the 1780s, during the debate over the adoption of the Constitution. The seeming remoteness of these two topics from each other is characteristic of the way I have proceeded. Over the past two decades my path has meandered among topics as diverse as the cultural concomitants of capitalism, John Stuart Mill's youthful "mental crisis," the rising authority of professional experts in nineteenth-century America, and the cognitive preconditions that set the stage for antislavery and other humanitarian reforms during the century following 1750.

Various as these topics may seem, my work has never strayed far from three interlocking interests. I trust that I am not merely succumbing to vanity in thinking that these recurring interests give the collection a definite center of gravity, in spite of its topical diversity. One of my abiding preoccupations is signaled by the book's title: a long-standing curiosity about the *explana-*

tory schemes on which we humans rely to make sense of our experience. Like Thomas Carlyle, I am impressed both with the apparent frailty of these ordering devices and with the utterly indispensable, world-making role they play in our thinking. As will be seen, this interest turns out to entail another, in the seemingly arcane subject of causal attribution. Another prime interest is the *history of ethics*, which for me has less to do with great thinkers and their teachings than with collective shifts of moral sensibility that occur over a period of decades or centuries. A third interest could, for the sake of symmetry, be labeled the *ethics of history*. That phrase takes less for granted and is less weighed down by philosophical baggage than the word "objectivity," but it does much the same work, by calling attention to the intricate network of constraints (cognitive, ethical, and institutional) that we professional historians tacitly rely on whenever we distinguish history from fiction, scholarship from propaganda, or good history from bad. I suppose that it goes without saying that this interest brings us full circle, for insofar as historical understanding depends on explanatory schemes, the question of their reliability inevitably looms large. That, I suppose, is what is at stake when questions of objectivity arise.

Of these three interests, the first, our unavoidable dependence on explanatory schemes, is most ubiquitous. Some of the essays in this volume showcase my interest in the history of ethics, others my interest in the ethics of history, but all reflect my preoccupation with problems of interpretation, explanation, and causal attribution. Because that theme runs through the entire volume, it seems wise to begin the book with a concrete illustration of what I mean by it. That is supplied by part 1, "Slavery and the Historical Profession," which consists of two essays I wrote about *Time on the Cross,* a controversial 1974 book about slavery published by two historically minded economists, Robert Fogel and Stanley Engerman. Their book serves my purpose well because it jarred widespread assumptions about the ethical import of slavery, was assailed as "bad history," and sparked a controversy centered on rival explanatory schemes. Thus their work involved all three of my paramount interests.

Those interests also dictate the contents of parts 2 and 3 of this book. Essays concerned with the ethics of history are grouped together in part 2, "Objectivity and Its Institutional Setting." Those devoted mainly to the history of ethics will be found in part 3, titled "The Shifting Conventions of Human Agency and Responsibility." Needless to say, these interests and others yet to be mentioned do not define separate compartments and are by no means mutually exclusive. On the contrary, my interests seem to me to overlap extensively and even to entail one another, thus giving the volume a good deal more in-

ternal coherence than the essay titles alone might suggest.[1] At the head of each
of the three sections the reader will find brief introductions to the essays presented there. What follows here stresses themes that cut across sections and
particular essays, to orient the reader to the volume as a whole.

Somewhere Robert Frost says that even the most successful poem can be no
more than a "momentary stay against confusion." I am content to say the same
of historical interpretations. Thomas Carlyle was conceding as much when he
observed that it is only the "more or less plausible scheme and theory of the
Transaction [not the events themselves] that we can ever hope to behold."[2] We
historians weave words into explanatory schemes and throw them like fisher-
men's nets into the unfathomable depths of the past. What we catch depends
as much on the shape, weave, and texture of our conceptual nets as on what
the sea contains. No doubt much eludes us, for beneath its tranquil surface the
past contains things stranger than any surface-dweller can readily imagine.
But any scheme is better than none. Without a net we would catch nothing at
all. Whatever its limitations, this effort to harvest the past's bounty has been
going on too long and has too often yielded useful knowledge for any serious
person even to contemplate abandoning it now.

That we never behold the past itself and must rely on understandings of it
mediated by explanatory schemes is no cause for dismay. The historian's aim
is to make sense of the past, not to reexperience it in what William James
called its unmediated, "buzzing confusion." In fact, the cataclysmic panic that
would be our lot if explanatory schemes and other mediating structures were
to release their hold on us, even for an instant, is not adequately conveyed
by such a mild word as "confusion." Without mediation there is no experience. Except perhaps in the case of outright insanity, we enculturated human
beings never encounter the world in a manner so direct and primitive as to
be unaffected by the ordering influence of explanatory schemes, paradigmatic
assumptions, frames of reference, presuppositions, expectations, narrative traditions, memories, and other mediating mental structures. To reserve the word
"real" for that which precedes all mediating influences, as some contemporary
theorists have tried to do, is to play games with words, transforming "reality"
from that which all need to know and some know better than others, into
something that no one either could know or has any need to know.

Many laypeople and some scholarly theorists imagine that historical knowledge is especially suspect because its object, the past, no longer exists and is
unavailable for direct inspection. But the reality of the past is no more likely
to elude understanding than the reality of the present, for our experience of

present events is no more "immediate" in the requisite sense—no more *unmediated*—than our experience of past events. The army general scrutinizing his battle map and the soldier awaiting orders in the trench experience as directly as anyone can the events in which they are involved. Yet neither the soldier nor the general can be said to experience more than a tiny fragment of the battle—to say nothing of the larger campaigns and wars and geopolitical developments of which the battle is but one part. "Direct" eyewitness testimony based on that which has been experienced firsthand carries special authority, and justifiably so. But even it is no more than the raw material out of which generals and soldiers alike make sense of their lives.

This they accomplish by employing the cognitive tools that nature and culture make available to them. Where nature leaves off and culture begins is a moot point, irrelevant for present purposes. One of the most elementary cognitive tools is that imaginative power that enables soldiers and generals to step back from their own direct experience and think of it as belonging to some larger project, such as a battle or a war, in which others have a part. Generals, soldiers, and all the rest of us also make sense of our lives by narrating causal stories, linking past to present, so as to get our bearings in time and explain how things came to be as they are. In a more active mode, we carry out an activity whose resemblance to narration is inadequately appreciated: we formulate *plans* that link present acts, not to the past, but to an imagined future, in hopes of selecting a course of conduct that will bring about desirable changes. What is common to both our retrospective stories and our prospective plans is causal reasoning, which, as we shall see, figures centrally in the explanatory schemes on which historians and laypersons alike rely.

To say that the past is not intrinsically any harder to understand than the present is not to say that we understand either past or present as well as we would like. Measured against our aspirations, the accomplishments of all forms of human understanding are pathetically inadequate. But we do manage, generation after generation, to muddle through. Making fateful choices and embarking on irrevocable courses of action under the shadows of doubt and uncertainty is part of what it means to be human. That our prospective plans and retrospective explanatory schemes succeed as well as they do is an amazing and insistent fact of life, one that skeptics deny at peril of being held in contempt of common sense. If our explanatory schemes were altogether misguided, as some contemporary skeptics fear (and others hope), then the elaborate cultural worlds we sustain and share would have come crashing down about our collective ears long ago.

Carlyle was right. Although cognizance of the mediating role played by explanatory schemes in all historical understanding should teach us "vigilence" and "humility," it should not discourage inquiry. Least of all should it be allowed to breed discouraging fantasies of a noumenal "reality," logically prior to all the needs, purposes, and presuppositions that scheming humans bring to life's endeavors. That which is prior to mediated experience is beyond the possibility of being experienced by humans at all. It is not the Real, finally exposed to view after all appearances have been stripped away. It is an irrelevant will-o'-the-wisp.[3]

Common sense is a high tribunal, never ignored with impunity. And yet its limitations are deservedly notorious, partly because of its commonness, but also because it is in motion. Far from being the fixed standard it always pretends to be, common sense is a historical phenomenon, about which histories can and should be written. And as common sense changes, so do the explanatory schemes it authorizes. As the philosopher Louis Mink once wrote, "nothing is more wonderful than common sense."

> The comfortable certainties of "what everybody knows" have been since Socrates a more natural field for philosophical reflection than eclipses, prophecies, monstrosities, and the irruption of unintelligible forces. The common sense of an age, we recognize when we compare that age with others, may well be for different times and places beyond the limits of comprehension or even of fantasy. A primary reason for this is that common sense of whatever age has presuppositions which derive not from universal human experience but from a shared conceptual framework, which determines what shall count as experience for its communicants. For experience centered on one conceptual framework, there are literally sermons in stones or vengeance in the thunderbolt. But for other experience these perceptions seem poetic fancies, and for yet other experience they are simply unintelligible.[4]

If Mink is right, as I believe he is, that not only philosophical reflection but even the smallest details of everyday experience can depend for their meaning on "shared conceptual frameworks" that vary from one era to another, then it follows that explanatory schemes should interest us in two distinct ways. They are, as I have already asserted, cognitive instruments upon which all of us, historians and laypersons alike, necessarily rely every time we attempt to understand our own or anyone else's past. They also are, or ought to be, a subject for historical inquiry. They are not only the means by which we make sense of history, they are historical phenomena in their own right that have a history, although one that historians have scarcely begun to investigate systematically.

Much more can and should be done. Within a population, modes of explanation rise and fall like empires, and tracing their career in time can shed light on every other branch of historical investigation.

Like Mink, I proclaim my sincere respect for common sense and the explanatory schemes it sponsors, partly in hopes of loosening their grip upon us. Uncritically received, those "comfortable certainties" that "everybody knows" can imprison us within our own era and distort our understanding of other times, places, and forms of life. Alas, when it comes to overestimating the authority of common sense and expecting more than it can deliver, my fellow historians are sometimes among the worst offenders. On this score I have a long-standing quarrel with the mainstream of my profession, many of whose members pride themselves on a tough-minded, archive-based empiricism and openly disdain everything that smacks of "theory" or "abstraction."

When historians indulge their aversion to theory they have no choice but to fall back on common sense. In doing so, they risk introducing a fatal anachronism into their work, because the common sense they unreflectively rely on will almost certainly be that of their own times. One elementary prerequisite of historical understanding is an appreciation of the meaning events had for the actors of the past, and this entails imagination and a readiness on the part of the historian to suspend or bracket the common sense of his or her own era. The meaning historical actors attached to their acts and decisions will not always, or even usually, be the same as the meanings we formulate in retrospect from our own moment in time, but we cannot begin to understand who they were and why they acted as they did until we have acknowledged differences between the presuppositions that prevailed in their time and the ones that prevail in ours.

To acknowledge this is not only to confess the historicity of common sense but also to admit the necessity of "theory," by which term I mean nothing more than a freewheeling recognition that events are interrelated in more ways than are immediately apparent or carry the sanction of common usage. The theory wars that have laid waste to some fields of literary criticism these past two decades are something I would not wish on my worst enemies. But when historians disdain theory in the modest sense that I am recommending, I believe they betray their calling as intellectuals. History need not be a flat-footed report from the archives that smugly prides itself on factual completeness and accuracy while remaining conceptually thin and unimaginative. The best history has always been that which combines empirical rigor with deep and adventurous thinking about the best way to conceptualize and frame the events being related. Yet professional education in history does little to cultivate awareness of the theoretical dimension of human affairs, and less than it could to sharpen students' skills in conceptualization.

Venturing outside the mainstream of one's profession is not without hazards, of course. Because my principal curiosities as a historian concern problems of explanation, interpretation, and the conceptualization of change, my professional colleagues have often remarked on what they regard as the unusually abstract, philosophical cast of my writing. Some find it tolerably illuminating, even refreshing; others denounce it as "ahistorical." During a visit many years ago to Princeton's Davis Center Seminar, when a paper of mine was criticized because it was not pitched at the matter-of-fact level that historians take to be natural, I was so bold as to shrug and suggest that from the standpoint of the profession I might well be a "recruiting error." The center's director and its senior members stiffened in stony silence, taking my words to be a gauche confession of personal delinquency, too embarrassing to be uttered in public. The graduate students, not yet fully socialized, understood that it was no confession and laughed uproariously.

My interest in theoretical questions has made it seem necessary, or at least natural and fitting, to enter into controversy with specialists on what commonly passes as "their" turf. Although limitations of competence have confined nearly all of my work to nineteenth century American (or at most Anglo-American) sources, within that large and extraordinarily rich field — probably more intensively cultivated than any other area of historical studies ever has been — my choice of topics has been dictated largely by an agenda of interpretive and analytical questions. That kind of question is, by nature, not very closely tied to particular times, places, or episodes. It lends itself more readily to analysis than storytelling. Pursuing such questions has led me into what are conventionally designated as separate areas of specialization, such as the histories of slavery, of higher education, and of professionalization, each of which is a distinct subfield populated by its own tribe of historical specialists, most of whom devote their entire career to it and are more familiar with the local terrain than I could ever hope to be. In their eyes I figure at best as an outsider and interloper, at worst as a gadfly and dilettante. That my trespasses have generally been forgiven testifies to an admirable spirit of openness and tolerance that usually prevails in the historical profession. That they have been seen as trespasses at all testifies to the continuing reluctance of historians (virtually alone among all the practitioners of the humanities and social sciences) to acknowledge that their discipline has a non-empirical, "theoretical" dimension, as worthy of specialized attention as any other.

Although complacency about the theoretical dimension of historical practice is deeply entrenched in the professional training and recruitment of historians, it has become harder and harder to sustain over the past two decades, as various forms of epistemological radicalism have swept through literary criticism and other adjacent disciplines. Change is imminent. That genres are blurring and disciplinary walls tottering has become a cliché, one repeated so often that it may yet come true. The once staid and resolutely empirical *American Historical Review* now occasionally opens its pages to debates over theory; social and political historians emerge from the lonely gloom of the archives, blinking in the sunlight and asking what all the fuss over "historicism" is about. Meanwhile, intellectual historians, whose labors have always drawn them into the borderlands between history and adjacent disciplines, suddenly find themselves in demand as go-betweens and translators, on the assumption that they are better equipped to understand what neighboring tribes of philosophers or literary critics are up to.

My own reaction to "postmodernism," to use a convenient catchall label for this multifaceted explosion of interest in theoretical and epistemological issues in the human sciences, has necessarily been ambivalent. I unreservedly admire the broadly epistemological questions postmodernists have raised. These are questions that deserve answers. They have a long and honorable history, having originated in a quarrel between Reason and History that goes all the way back to ancient Greece. They erupted with special force in the late-nineteenth-century "crisis of historicism," the repercussions of which figured prominently in my early formation as an intellectual historian.

I first encountered a version of them in Karl Mannheim's *Ideology and Utopia*, which I read in 1959 while preparing to write an undergraduate thesis at Princeton entitled "Relativism and the Reform Impulse in American Thought." I grappled with them again in the late 1960s while writing a doctoral dissertation at Stanford on the rise of social scientific thinking in this country and the decline of an earlier, more formalistic mode of explanation rooted in small-town life and the Christian tradition (published as *The Emergence of Professional Social Science*).[5] Although the story I told in that book focused on developments on this side of the Atlantic, the tacit background against which I naturally projected American events was the great methodological controversy in the social sciences, or *Methodenstreit*, of the 1880s and 1890s, which had been provoked in large part by Continental speculation about the implications of historicism. Finally, from graduate school on, my thinking has been deeply influenced by Thomas Kuhn's elegantly argued *Structure of Scientific Revolutions*, a remarkable demonstration of the power of historicism, without which the questions of postmodernism could scarcely have achieved their current salience.

Given my long-standing interest in problems of explanation, interpretation, and epistemology broadly speaking, I can hardly help welcoming the postmodern revival of these questions and feel, in common with many "postmodernists," that many of the answers historians and others standardly give to these questions are evasive and unsatisfying. On the other hand, even the standard answers are better than the answers given by some of those who most eagerly wear the label "postmodernist." I much prefer the sober fallibilism of the generation of intellectuals who rose into prominence in the 1890s, men such as William James in this country and Max Weber in Germany, to the extravagant hyperbole of Michel Foucault and Jacques Derrida. I am not among those who believe that, on a certain day in the 1960s, the path of human development darted off in an unprecedented new direction, producing a so-called linguistic turn that relieves us of any further need for words such as "objectivity," "rationality," "logicality," or "truth." It is mere presumptuousness to think that ours is the first generation to see how things really are, and presumptuousness on stilts to think that how things really are is that nothing but language or discourse is real. Although I have no quarrel with those who remind us that history and fiction are not easily separable, I do resist those who glibly dismiss the distinction, as if it made no difference to the conduct of life or scholarship. The fallibility of all truth claims I readily concede, but I have little patience with those who go beyond fallibility to attack the idea of truth itself.

In its moderate form, historicism dignifies everyday life and sustains the pluralism without which liberal democracy is unthinkable. In its most radical forms, historicism levels everything of value, discrediting right and leaving might as the only arbiter of human affairs. No one saw this more clearly than the patron saint of postmodernism, Friedrich Nietzsche, who resolutely carried historicism to its absurd limit. Confronted in the mid-1980s with what I regarded as foolhardy attempts by neo-Nietzscheans to set up domestic housekeeping in a criterionless wilderness, I began doing the obvious thing, which was to cry "Wolf!" Several of the essays in part 2, "Objectivity and Its Institutional Settings," take to task various forms of epistemological radicalism, and sometimes in a decidedly polemical way. Readers alert to the difference between the polemical posture of a writer and the ideological location of the turf he or she is trying to defend will see, however, that this is a polemic on behalf of moderation.

The moderate historicism I mean to defend (most explicitly in "The Curious Persistence of Rights Talk") admits the fallibility and contestability of truth claims without abandoning the idea that some claims are, from virtually any defensible human perspective, more belief-worthy than others. The notion of objectivity I advocate is so social, so much a matter of institutional arrangements and collective judgmental processes, that I hesitate to speak of a lone individual or single opinion as "objective." My position owes much to Kuhn and is more or less congruent with the teachings of pragmatism's founders, Charles S. Peirce, William James, and John Dewey. Although I differ with contemporary pragmatists such as Richard Rorty about some important issues (see especially "Justifying Academic Freedom in the Era of Power/Knowledge"), I endorse just as heartily as he does one of the cardinal principles of the pragmatic tradition, which holds that what truth requires is not unassailable foundations but self-correcting social processes. Whether the mutual criticism that actually goes on in the existing professions qualifies as a truly self-correcting social process is a question I take very seriously. To that question several of the essays in part 2 are devoted, especially "Professionalism versus Capitalism" and the review essay, "Power to the Experts."

The attack on truth, to which Rorty has sometimes given ambivalent encouragement, has become one of the most distinctive and disturbing features of our era. It is often prompted by a sincere sympathy with one or another subaltern class, whose members, it is said, will benefit from greater toleration as stiff-backed confidence in "truth" gives way to relaxed acceptance of multiple perspectives. I agree, of course, as the best minds of the 1890s did, that perspective must be given its due. More than that, a plurality of legitimate perspectives must, up to a point, be welcomed as constitutive of what we mean by "liberal democracy," a form of government that forswears from the outset any claim that there is any one right way to live. But the fulfillment of liberal democratic ideals will not be furthered by blurring the difference between truth and falsehood, any more than it will be furthered by abandoning distinctions between good and evil.

In the absence of truth, the moral difference between villains and victims collapses into nothing more than a clash of incommensurable perspectives, beyond any possibility of adjudication. Justice becomes an incoherent ideal when one rules out in advance the possibility that the victim's complaints may be *true* as to the facts alleged and *right* as to the relevance of the moral obligations invoked. When push comes to shove, I am convinced, it is the villains who have the most to gain by truth's demise. To insist as radical historicists do upon the indeterminacy of all interpretation and to subsume history and law indiscriminately under rhetoric, is to dissolve the concept of injustice and render its victims incapable even of naming their plight. Sharpening the boundary between radical and moderate forms of historicism has therefore seemed to me to be an important project, one to which most of the essays in part 2 are meant to contribute.

The essays gathered in part 3, "The Shifting Conventions of Human Agency and Responsibility," are, in my own opinion, the most important I have written so far and the ones I am most eager to follow up in future work. Given the words "agency" and "responsibility" in the section heading, the reader will instantly recognize that this is where my interest in the history of ethics and moral sensibility moves to center stage. What may surprise and puzzle the reader is that this is also the section in which causal reasoning moves to center stage. The reader will not, I trust, be wholly taken aback by this unexpected development, for I have already mentioned (a) that causal reasoning figures vitally in all explanatory schemes, (b) that those schemes are part and parcel of what we call common sense, and (c) that the history of common sense could and should be written more systematically than it has been. These considerations all come to a focus in the essays of part 3, which are, among other things, preliminary forays into what I regard as a veritable *terra incognita,* the history of causal attribution.

But what, the reader may ask, does causal attribution have to do with ethics or moral sensibility? Everything, for they are they two sides of the same coin. To be an agent is to be causally efficacious, a producer of intended consequences. To hold people responsible is to presume that they are causally efficacious agents and therefore capable (within limits) of choosing which consequences to produce. Judgments of praise, blame, responsibility, liability, courage, cowardice, originality, deliberateness, and spontaneity are just a few of the quintessentially ethical qualities that ride piggyback on perceptions of cause and effect. In the words of the philosopher Bernard Williams, causation is the "primary" element in all judgments of responsibility. "The other issues can only arise in relation to the fact that some agent is the cause of what has come about. Without this, there is no concept of responsibility at all." [6]

Although the essays in part 3 are explicitly about agency and moral responsibility and only obliquely about causal attribution as such, the reverse is true of these introductory remarks, which focus on the place of causal reasoning in history and in everyday life, leaving the relationship between causal reasoning and ethical judgment off to one side. I have chosen this strategy partly because causal reasoning is so prominent in everything I have to say about ethics and moral sensibilities, and partly because interest in causation per se is sufficiently rare among historians that it requires some justification.

But more important, I know from responses to my previous work that the likelihood of misunderstanding is immense when the discussion is about causation. Philosophers and theorists of history have debated to a fare-thee-well the place of causal reasoning in the writing of history. The results of these debates, which most historians have followed only intermittently if at all, have been disappointing. Practicing historians today are, I believe, badly confused about the role of causal reasoning in the writing of history. My aim in these introductory remarks about part 3 is to frame the essays that follow in a way that will ward off misunderstandings. This I hope to accomplish by (a) briefly reviewing some of the consequences of the "covering law" debate, (b) highlighting the little-appreciated difference between attributive and nomological modes of causal reasoning, and (c) reexamining the supposed chasm of difference separating narration from causation.

Any reader of history knows that historians are not shy about assigning responsibility or imputing the causal status upon which responsibility rests. Historians routinely bestow praise and assign blame; they talk incessantly about change and presume that acts have consequences; they tell stories showing how one thing leads to another, how things came into being and go out of being. Professional historians are, in sum, deeply preoccupied with relations between particular causes and their effects, and yet they seldom display any interest in causation per se. Indeed, in many professional circles today the very word "causation" is tainted by its association with hard science and regarded as an alien import, unwisely introduced into historical discourse by misguided practitioners eager to ape the authority of chemists and physicists. The business of the historian, it is often said, is nothing so rigid or mechanical as cause and effect linkages, but instead the subtler, more refined, more contingent interrelationships disclosed by hermeneutic technique and narrative art.

The supposed contrast between narrative art and causal inquiry has become especially stark since the mid-1970s, when Carl Hempel's covering law thesis came under sharp and sustained attack by able narrativists such as Hayden White and Louis Mink. The narrativists' commendable goal was to rescue the philosophy of history from philosophers who were content to regard the discipline as an immature form of science. That contention, though never without cogent critics, had thoroughly dominated the terms of debate in Anglo-U.S. philosophy of history ever since the 1940s, when Carl Hempel published his landmark essay, "The Function of General Laws in History." Crisp and elegant though Hempel's formulation of the covering law thesis was, it was nothing more than an elaboration and formalization of the claim, already familiar to nineteenth-century philosophers and social theorists, that explaining an event means construing it as a manifestation of nomological (lawlike) regularities.

In renewing that claim, Hempel was not moved by curiosity about history as such. His principal concern was to show that historical understanding was not, as some believed, fundamentally different from scientific understanding — that it was not, in the vocabulary of the times, an exception to the "unity of science." To advance that thesis he maintained that the logical form of explanation remains the same whether we are trying to explain the bursting of an automobile radiator in subfreezing temperatures or the decisions of a farmer to abandon Dust Bowl Oklahoma and head for California in the midst of a depression. In the first instance, explanation relies explicitly on a law relating the temperature, volume, and pressure of H_2O in closed containers; in the second it depends (implicitly) on a lawlike regularity regarding the tendency of human populations to migrate to regions that offer superior living conditions. Whether we speak of natural science or human affairs, Hempel insisted, the same logic of explanation is at work: To explain an event — any event at all — is to subsume it under (treat it as an instance of) a "covering law," such that the occurrence of the event can be deduced, given certain initial conditions and a law linking the event to its cause.[7]

Historians were not mistaken to think that Hempel's argument was scandalously indifferent to their practice and incapable of shedding light on their most pressing concerns. But a curious thing happened. After decades of debate, some scholars seem to have concluded that since the covering law model proved to be a blind alley in matters historical, the same must be true of causation itself. The polarizing dynamics of the contest between narrativists and Hempelians appear to have fostered the impression that causal explanation in history, if it were to be adequate, would indeed have to entail explicit reference to covering laws so as to meet the criteria for scientific adequacy that Hempel specified. Since doing that is obviously out of the question, the richly causal language that historians have always used — and that they have wisely continued to use, all through the covering law debate and after — is tacitly demoted to a "manner of speaking," convenient and acceptable, but philosophically unjustifiable and unworthy of systematic examination or thoughtful development.

Thus we have what might be called Hempel's secret revenge on the discipline that spurned his thesis: Although his argument fell before sustained and trenchant criticism, historians, of all people, have ceded to covering law theory the entire domain of causation. So one hears it taken for granted that narration and causation are polar opposites; that in spite of all appearances to the contrary, causal reasoning plays only a peripheral role in history; that in the last analysis the relation denoted by "cause" and "effect" is only another poetic trope; that what we want from history is not explanation, but something entirely different, "understanding." In the words of a prominent narrativist, Hans Kellner, "Cause . . . which can be seen as merely the product of narrative structures once the world is considered as a text, is a trap, always to be questioned." [8]

All this smacks of overreaction. The time is ripe for second thoughts about causation. Whatever else history may be, it cannot but be about the ways things come into being and go out of being, which is to say about cause and effect, broadly and untechnically speaking. Instead of pitting narration against causation, we would do better to acknowledge their close kinship. The resemblance between the productive sequence "cause-and-effect" and the equally productive "beginning-middle-end" of narrative form goes beyond superficial appearances. Even so rigorous a narrativist as Louis Mink had to concede that when it comes to defining the criteria for deciding what to include in a proper narrative, we have little to go on besides causal relevance. [9]

There may be room to argue about which is more fundamental, narrative form or cause-effect relations. For now I am content simply to say that narration is an especially supple form of causal reasoning. Not the most rigorous or conclusive form, perhaps, but one whose genial tolerance for simple sequence and noncommittal ambiguity about the necessity or contingency of the linkages it depicts between one event and the next is well suited to the frailty of our reasoning powers and the elusiveness of much that we humans aspire to know. Once causation is disentangled from universalizing covering laws and treated as a context-dependent and largely convention-governed attributive practice, it loses its scientistic pretensions and can be appreciated for what it plainly is: The "cement [or glue] of the universe," as a British philosopher once called it—the most fruitful and indispensable of all the cognitive instruments by means of which we humans construct explanatory schemes and make what sense we can of the world we inhabit. [10]

The historians' narrational mode of causal reasoning, which does not differ from that of everyday common sense in any deep structural way, is very different from that of the scientist working in a laboratory, conducting experiments. It was exclusively the laboratory setting that supplied Hempel with his image of causal reasoning—and blinded him to the significance of everyday practices of causal attribution. A key difference between the laboratory and life in the world at large has to do with whether causal knowledge is treated as the

means or the end of knowledge. A half century before Hempel began muddy-
ing the waters, Max Weber understood that causal reasoning has not one form
but two, both of which are intellectually indispensable.

It is ironic that Weber, who came to intellectual maturity during the *Methodenstreit,* already knew in 1904 what it took decades of academic debate to
reestablish a half century later: that it is not oversight or disciplinary immaturity that keeps history from offering "full" explanations on Hempel's covering law model, but rather history's interest in "concrete relationships" among
"cultural events." Historical explanations are not mere "explanation sketches,"
as Hempel called them. They are complete explanations of a certain kind. They
differ from those of the working scientist in that they do not aim at the accumulation of new knowledge about invariant causal relationships, but instead
use existing knowledge of causal relations (some, no doubt, of debatable validity) as a means to other ends.

What Weber said about causation in his famous 1904 essay, " 'Objectivity'
in Social Science," could have been written seventy years later in direct refutation of Hempel's covering law thesis:

> Where the individuality of a phenomenon is concerned, the question of cau-
> sality is not a question of laws but of concrete causal relationship; it is not a
> question of the subsumption of the event under some general rubric as a rep-
> resentative case but of its imputation as a consequence of some constellation
> [of conditions]. *It is in brief a question of imputation. Wherever the explanation
> of a "cultural phenomenon" — a "historical individual" — is under consideration,
> the knowledge of causal laws is not the end of the investigation but only a means.
> It facilitates and renders possible the causal imputation to their concrete causes of
> those components of a phenomenon the individuality of which is culturally signifi-
> cant.* So far and only so far as it achieves this, is it valuable for our knowledge
> of concrete relationships. And the more "general" (i.e., the more abstract) the
> laws, the less they can contribute to the causal imputation of individual phe-
> nomena and, more indirectly, to the understanding of the significance of cul-
> tural events.[11]

Undoing the distortions inflicted on historians' self-understanding, first by
the excesses of the Hempelians and then by the overreaction of the narrativists, is a large task, to which I hope to return on another occasion. My present
concern is simply to make a case for the legitimacy and importance of historical studies that give serious attention to human practices of causal attribution,
whether in moral and ethical matters or in any other dimension of human affairs. That is what I was trying to do in "Capitalism and the Origins of the

Humanitarian Sensibility" and the other essays of part 3. It is also what I have been trying to do in this introduction, by relating all of my interests to "explanatory schemes," for, as the reader will have gathered by now, explanatory schemes are ipso facto causal ones.

The crux of the misunderstanding into which historians have been led by the covering law thesis and the narrativists' overreaction to it is the notion that there is only one interesting form of causal reasoning, the nomological-deductive. There is, as Weber knew, another mode of causal reasoning, the *attributive* mode, which we take so much for granted that we fail to recognize it for what it is: the very bone and sinew of which common sense is constituted. To show the difference between Hempel's kind of causal analysis and that authorized by common sense, I return to Hempel's own illustration, the cracking of an automobile radiator on a cold night. Recall that Hempel's claim is that all scientific explanations take the form of two sets of statements, the first identifying the "determining conditions" for the event to be explained (including its "initial and boundary conditions"), and the second setting forth the "universal hypotheses" or "covering laws" from which the occurrence of the event can be deduced, given the specified conditions. In the first part of his radiator illustration, Hempel lists as conditions facts that are predominantly natural: for example, that the radiator was made of iron, that its bursting pressure was such and such, that the cap was screwed down tight, that the temperature declined from 39° to 25°F, and so on. But included in the list is one distinctly cultural fact to which he attached far less importance than it deserved: "The car was left in the street all night."

Now from the standpoint of everyone except, perhaps, the scientist working in the laboratory, whose career depends on priority in formulating new universal "laws of nature," the fact that the car was left in the street one winter night goes further toward explaining why the radiator cracked than all the other conditions put together. Indeed, this single cultural fact has a stronger claim to explanatory adequacy than would a learned disquisition on the covering laws governing the expansion of water as it freezes or the tensile strength of iron under pressure. For the purposes of laypersons, knowing that the car was left unprotected while the temperature fell below freezing is enough to explain the burst radiator and satisfy curiosity. Leaving a car outside in freezing weather without antifreeze violates a norm of prudent behavior in our society. And in the commonsense game of causal attribution, conditions that are abnormal—whether in the sense of statistical rarity or deviation from behavioral prescriptions endorsed by convention—are prime candidates for being designated "causes."

Revisiting Hempel's example calls attention to another important difference between the attributive and the nomological modes of causal reasoning, one that Weber did not mention. The two modes differ not only as to whether causal knowledge is treated as an end or a means, but also in regard to the context of explanation and the rhetorical posture of the person doing the explaining. Context counts for nothing in the nomological mode, which in its attempt at universality becomes radically abstract, ignoring all contextual details except those that qualify as necessary conditions of the event to be explained. Thus for Hempel the list of initial and boundary conditions that must be spelled out in order for the explanation to be "complete" is potentially very long indeed, because nothing can be taken for granted.

In sharp contrast, the commonsense mode of causal attribution proceeds in a kind of shorthand, taking it for granted that since people have a common context of needs, opportunities, conventions, and experiences, there is much that can be left unsaid. Thus to explain why the barn burned down it is enough to say, "Someone dropped a lighted cigarette." There is ordinarily no need to specify the presence of hay on the floor, or wood in the walls, much less oxygen in the atmosphere. The salutory brevity of commonsense explanations held no interest for Hempel, but it is one of the "wonders," as Mink put it, that follows from reliance on a shared conceptual framework. Anyone who in everyday conversation disregarded that tacitly understood framework and felt obliged to provide his interlocutors with complete explanations on the Hempelian model would be thought not merely boorish or deficient in the arts of rhetoric, but daft.

Hempel's claims about the supremacy of covering law explanations collapse without the prop of radical abstraction. Because the failure to shelter the car is only one in a list of mainly natural, material conditions, readers of Hempel's essay are unlikely even to notice it. But if we refuse to fly along with Hempel at his stratospheric level of abstraction and choose instead to reinsert the radiator into an automobile, the automobile into the lives of those who own and use it, those lives into a human economy of scarce resources, and that economy into a culture that expects of its members elementary prudence in regard to the use of such resources—if, in short, we take cultural context into account—then we will immediately understand that Hempel's preferred mode of explanation, far from being the best, would be considered flagrantly evasive if put forward, say, by a college freshman calling his or her parents to announce that the car needed a new radiator. In the everyday discourse of history and common sense, the prime cause of the cracked radiator is not the decline in temperature, but negligence by the car's operator. For the negligent party to shrug off personal responsibility for the event and construe it simply (or even mainly) as the result of universal laws governing the behavior of fluids in closed containers would be outrageous. And it is common sense against which the outrage would be committed.

Hempel of course knew that "incomplete" explanations were often acceptable in everyday conversation. One example he mentioned was the dropped cigarette that "explains" the burning of the barn. Another was leaving the car out in the cold, which "explains" the cracking of the radiator. Although these explanations fell far short of adequacy in his eyes, he explicitly acknowledged their acceptability in everyday conversation and admitted that full explanations were seldom set forth. But common practice held no theoretical interest for Hempel. Any acknowledgment that the attributive mode of causal reasoning had either significance or legitimacy might have compromised his argument for the unity of science.

Hempel's taste for abstraction went still further. He even insisted that history was no different from astronomy, in that explanation is "not complete unless it might as well have functioned as a prediction": "If the final event can be derived from the initial conditions and universal hypotheses stated in the explanation, then it might as well be predicted, before it actually happened, on the basis of a knowledge of the initial conditions and the general laws. Thus, e.g., those initial conditions and general laws which the astronomer would adduce in explanation of a certain eclipse of the sun are such that they might have also served as a sufficient basis for a forecast of the eclipse before it took place."[12]

Bizarre and profoundly wrongheaded though this analogy (not to say equation) was between historical explanation and astronomical prediction, it was strictly in keeping with the framework within which Hempel cast his entire discussion. In the two opening sentences of his essay, he simply took it for granted that the aim of historians, like astronomers, was — or ought to be — to establish the scientific laws that governed the phenomena within their field, thus ruling out as "unscientific" any inquiry of the attributive sort that attempts to apply existing causal knowledge as a means to other ends, such as "making sense" of what happened. "It is a rather widely held opinion," he wrote, "that history, in contradistinction to the so-called physical sciences, is concerned with the description of particular events of the past rather than with the search for general laws which might govern those events. As a characterization of the type of problem in which some historians are mainly interested, this view probably cannot be denied; as a statement of the theoretical function of general laws in scientific historical research, it is certainly unacceptable."

Hempel would have been on strong ground if he had confined himself to the claim that historians cannot avoid relying, at least tacitly, on "general laws." That claim might have provoked resistance in some quarters, but not from Weber and many others of his generation who explicitly recognized that historians rely on general laws, or at least lawlike regularities, whenever they attribute causal status to people, institutions, or events. Weber never took the position that explanation in history was wholly unrelated to scientific explanation, or that it was noncausal. Instead, Weber's point, which would have been lost on Hempel, was simply that for history "knowledge of causal laws is not the end of the investigation but only a means. It facilitates and renders possible the causal imputation to their concrete causes of those components of a phenomenon the individuality of which is culturally significant."

It was not only Hempel's infatuation with the image of the laboratory scientist as the sole exemplar of causal reasoning that gives his project its bull-headed quality. His image of laboratory science was itself faulty. Anyone even remotely familiar with the post-Kuhnian literature of the history of science will know that not even physicists or chemists confine themselves exclusively to causal explanations of the covering law variety. Scientists do not become illogical or unscientific when they do (occasionally) what historians do (almost always) — set aside the "search for general laws" and instead make use of whatever knowledge of lawlike regularities they have at their disposal so as to explain a particular event.

That, for example, is what Richard Feynman and other scientists did when they agreed to serve on the presidential commission convened to investigate the causes of the *Challenger* space shuttle disaster in 1986. In that setting, Feynman and his colleagues proceeded much as historians, lawyers, or indeed any layperson would. They construed the explosion as an effect and inquired into its causes. What interested them was that particular explosion in all its detailed and unrepeatable uniqueness, not explosions in general; and their interest had to extend far beyond the laboratory world of chemical reactions and mathematical formulas to take into account the entire institutional and even political and cultural context in which the launch occurred. Their aim was not to discover new laws or to develop more elaborate knowledge about the functioning of old ones, but instead to use existing knowledge of causal connections as a means to the very different end of explaining why the shuttle exploded, thereby fixing responsibility for the tragedy. The commission's task was fundamentally a matter of distinguishing causes from necessary conditions, and this is the task of common sense and attributive reasoning. In the *Challenger* inquiry, then, we have a convenient closing illustration of the force and legitimacy of attributive as opposed to nomological causal reasoning.[13]

When it comes to explaining particular events, Hempel's highly abstract covering law model offers little guidance. Indeed, by treating the distinction between causes and conditions as if it were effortlessly transparent, the model oversimplifies the task of explanation and obscures its most difficult and interesting phases. The inquirer who knows only general laws of the sort that figure so prominently in Hempel's thinking can do no more than identify the necessary conditions *but for which* the event in question could not have happened. That merely sets the stage for most sorts of causal inquiry in the attributive mode: Given a particular event and the conditions necessary for its occurrence, which of those conditions deserve to be singled out as "causes"? That is the important question. *Distinguishing causes from conditions and ranking them in importance is the central problem in causal reasoning that historians, commissions of inquiry, and ordinary people face.* Here knowledge of covering laws, however vital it may be in setting the stage for inquiry, is of no avail.[14]

That is not to say that nomological knowledge is irrelevant to causal explanation; only that it cannot tell us where to draw the line between causes and conditions, or how much weight to give particular causes. In the case of the *Challenger* explosion, knowledge that declining temperature causes many materials to lose their elasticity presumably prompted Feynman and his colleagues to think that a defective seal, the now notorious O-ring, could have been involved in the disaster. But that item of nomological-deductive knowledge suffices only to identify the defective O-ring as one condition without which the disaster would not have occurred. That gives the O-ring the same uninteresting status as the presence of oxygen in the atmosphere, which was no less necessary to the *Challenger* explosion.

The necessity of oxygen for combustion can be demonstrated in the most rigorous and scientific manner; so indispensable is it, in fact, that we can be far more confident that oxygen was involved in the *Challenger* explosion than we can about the involvement of a defective O-ring. Yet it would have been ridiculous for the commission to rank the presence of oxygen among the significant "causes" of the disaster. Neither the necessity of a condition, nor the certainty of its causal involvement in the event to be explained, is enough to qualify it for causal status. Had the commission been so foolish as to attribute the explosion to the presence of oxygen, it would have been disbanded in disgrace. Its members would have been guilty of flagrantly disregarding the tacit rules of the game we humans play as we sort through the contingent factors in our lives, imputing cause-effect status to some so as to achieve explanatory understanding. Among those rules, one with very wide application dictates that *abnormal* conditions, such as the defective seal, are the ones most eligible for causal attribution; conditions that are omnipresent, such as oxygen in the atmosphere, scarcely ever qualify.

Learning to play the game of causal attribution requires much more than memorizing a list of rules, however. One must know how to apply them and for this no rule book suffices. The commission would also have been ridiculed if it had blamed the explosion primarily on cold weather. The day of the *Challenger* launch was, in fact, the coldest launch date in the history of the shuttle program, and that abnormal circumstance presumably contributed to the inflexibility and ultimate failure of the O-ring. So cold weather quite properly loomed large in the commission's account of the disaster—larger, certainly, than the presence of oxygen, which was normal and could be taken utterly for granted. But cold weather was not the only departure from normality that figured in the disaster. Neither oxygen nor cold weather seemed to the investigatory commission as causally relevant as the conduct of NASA administrators and suppliers.

A prime candidate for causal status was the decision of a manufacturer to make the O-ring of material that would become inflexible at low temperatures —low by the standard of Florida's mild climate, but not so low as to be off the scale of prudent expectations. Manufacturers are expected to know that seals must function across a wide range of temperatures and to manufacture them accordingly. Also relevant were funding anxieties that made NASA administrators so fearful of disrupting a scheduled launch that they failed to observe standard operating procedures. Engineers who warned against the launch found themselves expected to prove that it was unsafe to fly, even though aeronautical convention always places the burden of proof on those who think it safe.

These attributions of responsibility to human actors rank high in the commission's report, not just because human scapegoats needed to be found (although that motive can never be discounted when things go wrong) but because each of these acts, decisions, and omissions constitutes—just as the defective O-ring did—a deviation from a norm. Trumping them all, quite possibly, is the purely natural but non-normal fact of a sudden wind shear that *Challenger* encountered shortly after takeoff, which could have helped unseat the seals. But for that abnormality of nature, the explosion might never have occurred, in spite of all the other natural and cultural conditions that were in place and conducive to its occurrence.

My discussion of the *Challenger* inquiry need not go any further for present purposes. Although it has been organized around analytical considerations rather than aesthetic ones, the reader will have no difficulty in reimagining it in conventional narrative form, with a proper beginning, middle, and end. In either form, I submit, it would constitute an exercise in causal reasoning. That is why, contrary to what narrativists would have us believe, I contend that narration and causation are close kin.

Narration can be construed as a supple form of causal thinking. The inner order of narrative derives not merely from sequence — one thing after another — but also from productivity. Beginnings do not merely precede middles and ends; they prepare them, help produce them. If one thing does not *lead* to the next, the narrative fails. Although narrative is eclectic about the form productive relations may take, the form most characteristic of narrative (because it presumes least about the necessity of causal linkages) is "stage setting." Setting a stage imposes limits on the sort of dramatic action that can plausibly occur there, but does not prevent action from unfolding along a variety of different paths, including ones that are unexpected and unpredictable. The possibilities are finite, however. If the action that occurs on stage is unsuited to the setting, the narrative will not persuade. Appropriateness of scene to action is therefore one element the narrator must "get right."

Narrators must also get right an inner structure of narrative that is much more detailed and constraining than is suggested by the classic tripartite Aristotelian schema of beginning, middle, and end. The structure of narratives is shaped primarily, though not exclusively, by causal relevance, for at every stage of an effective narrative account the reader must be informed of that, without which, the next stage or scene would not follow. Most narratives have many more stages than three; it is not enough for a beginning to precede a middle and a middle to precede an end. If the reader is to accept narrative's generic claim to constitute a unity that extends through time, connecting events that occurred at different moments, certain needs must be met. Those needs have much to do with causal relevance and they must be met not just section by section (beginning, middle, end) but paragraph by paragraph and sentence by sentence.

Every sentence of a successful narrative text is located *where* it is and is *what* it is because of its capacity to follow from what went before and lead toward that which follows. "Leading toward that which follows" means setting the stage in such a way as to encourage the reader to grant the plausibility of subsequent events. "Following from what went before" means reporting events of the sort that seem plausible, given the stage on which they occurred. Narratives seek to persuade us that a particular past, present, and future are so densely interrelated that they can best be comprehended as a unity. It won't do merely to report what happened at T^1, T^2, T^3, T^4. The reader must learn what it was about the event at T^1 that helped *cause* the one at T^2 (or, as the case may be, produce it, bring it about, pave the way for it, conduce to its occurrence, remove obstacles to its happening). What is needed is not a rigid chain of cause-and-effect relationships of the necessitarian variety, such that each event mandates the occurrence of the next, like so many falling dominoes lined up in a row; instead, what narrative supplies is a much looser sequence of stage-setting observations, such that the reader who knows what happened at T^1 will respond to what happens at T^2 with a tacit nod of understanding, rather than a scowl of befuddlement. "Yes," the reader must think, "given what went before, and given all the contrariety of human motivation and the cunning of fate, that is one possible/likely outcome." It is not predictability that is signified by this nod of understanding, but plausibility—no small thing in a world as short on truth and certainty as ours.

I gave my readers fair warning that these introductory remarks about part 3 would deal directly with the place of causal attribution in history and only obliquely with the section's titular subjects, "agency" and "responsibility." My aim has been twofold: to narrow the gap between narrative art and causal inquiry and to liberate causal inquiry itself from two equally acute dangers— the overardent embrace of the Hempelians and the scorn of the narrativists. If I have succeeded, the reader who now turns to the essays of part 3 will find nothing off-putting in my conviction—which underlies everything I have written on the subject—that the history of human agency and moral responsibility cannot be understood apart from the shifting conventions through which common sense enables the practices of causal attribution by means of which we humans make sense of our experience.

Recognizing the dependence of moral judgment on prevailing practices of causal attribution is indispensable for anyone interested in the history of agency and moral responsibility. It is important to see why. The conventions that shape our judgments of responsibility are deeply embedded in social practice and profoundly influenced by the material circumstances, historical experiences, and technological capabilities of the people who employ them. That means that as circumstances, experiences, and capabilities change, the limits of responsibility are liable to change as well. If we would understand how and why moral sensibilities change from one era to another, we would do well to begin by tracing major shifts in habits of causal attribution. And the best place to look for such shifts is in dimensions of life that at first seem to lack moral significance altogether, for that is where change is likely to encounter least resistance and therefore proceed most rapidly.

Insofar as the conventions that govern moral responsibility are influenced by changing practices in other, seemingly nonmoral dimensions of life, those conventions mark the pale beyond which morality remains irredeemably historical in spite of its endless and necessary efforts to achieve universality. Here at the pale, where civilization is left behind and the criterionless wilderness begins, is just where we should be working if, as appears to be the case, our generation is destined to test itself against the same question that the generation of Nietzsche, James, and Weber grappled with a century ago, during the "first" crisis of historicism: Within what limits can the historicity and "situatedness" of that which we value be acknowledged without discrediting valuation itself? We cannot deny that moral judgment varies historically. The explanatory scheme that construed variation as progress has obviously fallen on hard times. The path ahead is unclear. We can be sure, however, that abandoning all distinctions between beauty and ugliness, truth and falsehood, good and evil would be to exhibit the symptoms of our problem, not its cure.

PART ONE

Slavery and the Profession of History

Time on the Cross, a book about the history of slavery in the United States by economists Robert Fogel and Stanley Engerman, took the country by storm in the spring of 1974. My criticism of that book, together with my account of a conference devoted to it at the University of Rochester, were the first things I ever published. That they appeared in the pages of the *New York Review of Books* was a stroke of good fortune that owed much to the sensational political implications of the book and the high-powered publicity campaign accompanying it. The episode illuminates some of the dynamics of specialization and professional authority that operate in the modern academy and serves as an illustration of the role that explanatory schemes necessarily play in historical interpretation.

My involvement began when the *Houston Chronicle* sent an early review copy of the book to a Rice University colleague who taught diplomatic history. Knowing of my interest in methodological issues and the historiography of slavery, he generously passed the book on to me. By the time I was halfway through it I suspected that the authors had committed a blunder. Untrained in economics and having received my Ph.D. in history only a year earlier, I knew it would seem absurdly presumptuous of me to accuse two of the nation's most distinguished economic historians of misusing a tool of their trade, the "index of total factor productivity." Yet that index seemed logically incapable of justifying the conclusion they drew about the superior productivity of slave labor. That conclusion, in turn, was the linchpin of the explanatory scheme on which their entire study was based.

After consulting with colleagues in economics and poking around in the relevant economics literature, I became convinced that my objections had a basis in fact and could win at least grudging support from economists. From the beginning I envisioned, or rather fantasized, the *NYRB* as the ideal place to publish my criticism, even though a respectful review by C. Vann Woodward, dean of southern historians, had already appeared there. My first telephone contact was with a young editorial assistant who could barely conceal her mirth at the thought of some unknown fellow in Texas sending in an "over-the-transom" submission about a book that had already been reviewed. But the next day another assistant called to say that the editor, Robert Silvers, was interested and would contact me as soon as he returned from a trip abroad.

If *Time on the Cross* had been addressed exclusively to a scholarly audience, or if the *NYRB* had been bound by the standard peer-review procedures characteristic of scholarly journals, my essay might never have seen the light of day. After all, the issues looked imposingly technical, and I lacked the appropriate credentials. On the other hand, my argument had plain logic in its favor and was readily accessible to lay readers. The book I was attacking was already generating excitement outside the academy in such places as the *Today* show, *Time, Newsweek,* and the *Wall Street Journal.* When a scholarly book garners headlines, its flaws become newsworthy. Still, the *NYRB* had nothing to gain by publishing criticism that specialists would think incompetent. Its editor, Robert Silvers, made it the most influential intellectual organ of our generation precisely by striking a fine balance between accessibility and respect for expertise. He accordingly sent my essay off by express mail to a half-dozen historians and several prominent economists (including Evsey Domar, the originator of the productivity index, then traveling in Australia) before satisfying himself that I was right—or, I suppose, at least close enough to the mark to advance the public debate.

An avalanche of criticism would soon descend on the book, but the *Review*'s rapid publication schedule made my essay, "Were Slaves More Efficient? Some Doubts about *Time on the Cross,*" the first serious criticism to appear in print. Publication in September gave me instant, if evanescent, celebrity among academics. I was, as my wife kept fondly reminding me, the *New York Review*'s "token unknown for 1974." Not that everyone was impressed. A month after my article appeared, when some one hundred historians and economists gathered at the University of Rochester to discuss the book, I was not among those invited. Robert Silvers was; I tagged along as his guest to write up my report of the conference, which later appeared as "The True & Tragical History of *Time on the Cross.*"

Another lesson in the prickly solidarity of specialists was delivered shortly after the conference when I approached a group of economists and other critics of Fogel and Engerman about including my essay in a collection they were planning. In it they presented their own studies confirming, among other things, the validity of my doubts about the way Fogel and Engerman used the efficiency calculation, but to my essay they gave the cold shoulder. I was chagrined, but they were not being unfair. A person untrained in economics, reading my analysis alongside that of the economists, might have found my text equally persuasive, or maybe even more so, precisely because of its lack of technical complications and refinements. But mine, being the work of a rank amateur in economics, was inattentive to considerations that would occur naturally to anyone with professional training. Broadly speaking, my conclusions were correct (unusually intense demand for cotton does indeed render the meaning of the productivity index doubtful in the case to which Fogel and Engerman applied it), but for reasons that I understood imperfectly and articulated in a manner that could only seem clumsy to specialists.

Stanley Engerman, a saintly controversialist who somehow manages not to take criticism personally, told me at the time that the opposition to *Time on the Cross* had more to do with politics than the book's methodological flaws. My own opposition was not, I think, politically motivated, but he had a point. Having swum upstream against political currents within the profession on several later occasions, I can testify that on this one I was swimming downstream and that it makes for a nicer ride. As for the political wisdom of Fogel and Engerman's effort to supply the nation with a "positive" interpretation of slavery, one in which blacks would presumably pride themselves on their contributions to an unusually productive agricultural enterprise, I remain skeptical. But unlike some historians at the time, I have never doubted that the authors' motives were honorable. The broad line of interpretation that won out over Fogel and Engerman's — an interpretation that credits African-Americans with creating a rich and resilient family-oriented culture, even while depicting the system that enslaved them as relentlessly oppressive — has left the nation with an ambiguous legacy that is logically evasive and heavily freighted with lessons of black rage and white guilt.[1] Neither lesson has proved to be an unmixed blessing. Whether this interpretive legacy has done the nation more good than harm is less clear than most members of the profession are ready to admit. Nor is it certain that the prevailing interpretation of slavery's place in the history of the nation has an evidentiary base any more secure than that of *Time on the Cross.*

1. Peter Novick alludes to this problem obliquely in observing that historians of the 1970s sometimes seemed to be depicting "Teflon slaves, all but immune to the system that oppressed them." *That Noble Dream: The "Objectivity Question" and the American Historical Profession* (Cambridge: Cambridge University Press, 1988), 487.

What seems most dated in the story told by these two essays (which I have not revised) is the triumphal scientism of the publicity campaign that launched *Time on the Cross*. The cohort of historians who entered graduate school with me in the mid-1960s was impressed by the heightened rigor and statistical sophistication that quantitative methods seemed to promise. But this flirtation with a form of "scientific history" in the late 1960s was short-lived. Whether the repudiation of *Time on the Cross* helped trigger the change or was merely one manifestation of it, I do not know, but by the mid-1970s the pendulum was swinging the other way, as mainstream historians rushed to disavow scientific aspirations and reaffirm the kinship of history with narrative art. That impulse within the profession was soon reinforced from without by "poststructuralism," an ill-defined movement of thought originating in literary studies and anthropology that has generally tended to undercut the authority of "science" and to repose unprecedented trust in literary theory as the polestar of humanistic inquiry. How far these tendencies are compatible with the practice of history remains to be seen.

In 1994, twenty years after the publication of *Time on the Cross*, Robert Fogel was awarded the Nobel Prize for Economics, mainly for his work in economic history. By that time the field of economic history had become almost exclusively the preserve of economists. Few among the younger generation of historians knew Fogel's name or had read his work. Among those who were old enough to remember the chilly reception given to the book, many were shocked by the Nobel Committee's choice, but as Eugene Genovese wisely observed at the Rochester conference, the book was a "creative failure." Fogel and Engerman accomplished "all that they should have dared hope: they have thrown the burden of proof back upon their opponents."

It is the fate of all explanatory schemes to provoke criticism and die. Some die slowly and fruitfully; others are stillborn. A few, like Max Weber's *Protestant Ethic and the Spirit of Capitalism,* are resilient enough to draw fire decade after decade without ever being destroyed, stimulating in the process the creation of shelf upon shelf of first-rate critical literature. Others are spared criticism only because no one cares enough to finish them off. The test of success in scholarly inquiry is not immunity to criticism, not popularity (often the product of political happenstance), nor even longevity, as such, but fruitfulness in provoking critical responses.

The process is inescapably ironic. For an explanatory scheme to succeed is for it to provoke thoughtful and well-informed criticism that exposes its frailties and limitations. Whether this is done by hostile critics who condemn its inadequacy, or by admirers who try to expand upon it — inexorably revising the original formulation in the process—makes little difference. Either way, the academic world at its best is a spectacle of mutual criticism and creative destruction. As Max Weber put it, "the history of the social sciences is and remains a continuous process of passing from the attempt to order reality analytically through the construction of concepts—the dissolution of the analytical concepts so constructed through the expansion and shift of the scientific horizon—and the reformulation anew of concepts on the foundations thus transformed."[2] By that standard, *Time on the Cross* was not an insignificant achievement.

2. Weber quoted in H. Stuart Hughes, *Consciousness and Society: The Reorientation of European Social Thought, 1890–1930*, rev. ed. (New York: Vintage, 1977), 314.

CHAPTER ONE

Were Slaves More Efficient?

Some Doubts about *Time on the Cross*

The carnival of publicity attending the publication of *Time on the Cross* suggests that the authors, Robert Fogel and Stanley Engerman, desire an audience embracing not only econometric historians but all reasonable people. I am not an econometric historian or a specialist in the history of slavery, but I am a reasonable man and, as such, entitled to judge the plausibility of the authors' argument. Fogel and Engerman contend that slave labor was more efficient than free labor. This contention appears to rest on a dubious inference that vitiates several of the book's most striking conclusions.

The most troublesome phase of any quantitative study is the translation of numerical procedures into plain English. In their research and calculations, Fogel and Engerman may have considered all the objections raised below. But even if their conclusions turn out to be procedurally well founded, their presentation still fails, for they have not exposed to the reader's view any process of reasoning adequate to justify their conclusions.

The crux of the problem is that Fogel and Engerman appear to have drawn unjustifiable inferences from data based on the "geometric index of total factor productivity"—inferences which that index is inherently unable to support. The index is essentially a ratio of output to input. They use it to compare the "efficiency" of southern (slave) agriculture with northern (free) agriculture. They conclude that in the single year tested, 1860, "southern agriculture as a whole was about 35 percent more efficient than northern agriculture."[1]

First published in *New York Review of Books,* Sept. 19, 1974, 38–42. Reprinted with permission from *The New York Review of Books.* Copyright © 1974 Thomas Haskell.

One would never know from the authors' discussion of this index that economists are not entirely sure what it measures, or what causal factors it reflects, even in its most conventional applications. Fogel and Engerman's interpretation of it as a measure of efficiency is defensible, but it would have been delightfully frank of them to tell their readers that Evsey Domar, the economist who formulated the "geometric" version of the index, was so wary of misinterpretation that he called it simply the "Residual," rather than an index of efficiency. Commenting on a comparative study of the relative efficiency of the USSR and the United States, Domar noted that "if the Index shows that the average factor productivity in one country is markedly inferior to another, greater efficiency of the latter is not an unreasonable hypothesis. But there may be other explanations as well." Another economist referred to the entire class of aggregate productivity indices as a "measure of our ignorance."[2]

But let us grant that the index can be construed as a measure of efficiency in some sense. What does it mean in the particular case—a static comparison of northern and southern agricultural production in the year 1860—to which Fogel and Engerman apply it? The critical difficulty arises from the fact that the index, which is basically a ratio of output to input, states output not in physical units—bushels, bales, or pounds per worker—but in total market value of the product. It is, therefore, as much a measure of *profitability* as of the intrinsic *technological efficacy* of the production process. The authors explain in their technical supplement that the figures for northern output are derived from estimates of "*income* originating in agriculture for the year 1860," and that the figures used for southern output are computed from a sample of physical output data "weighted by *prices*."[3] Both procedures permit the index to vary with the market value of the product. Indeed, there would appear to be no other way to aggregate total output—barrels of tobacco, plus pounds of chicken, plus bushels of peas, plus bales of cotton—except by reducing everything to dollar value.

Because the index expresses output in market value, the "efficiency" it measures has an Alice-in-Wonderland quality under certain unusual conditions. If the demand for a product and therefore its price are sufficiently high, its producers may appear to be very "efficient," according to this index, even if their work habits are slovenly and their mode of production irrational. Since there was an extraordinary international demand for the dominant southern agricultural product, cotton, it is possible that this exceptional demand situation explains (in part or even wholly) the so-called efficiency of southern agriculture. The possibility may prove ephemeral, but it should be explored. At no point in their presentation, either in the expository volume or in the supplementary volume devoted to evidence and method, do the authors openly entertain this possibility. On the contrary, they attribute the "efficiency" gap primarily to "the combination of the superior management of planters and the superior quality of black labor."[4] This is not a permissible inference, given the limitations of the index.

If the index measured economic output in physical units—bushels or bales per worker—then it could serve as a basis for inferences about the comparative diligence of workers and skill of managers in the two regions. If workers on one farm produce eight bales per hand and workers on another farm using similar inputs of capital and land produce only four, there can be no doubt that the first farm is more efficient (although before assigning merit to workers and managers we will want to know more about the role of impersonal factors such as climate, soil quality, economies of scale, etc.). But since the index used by Fogel and Engerman measures output by the price the product brings in the market, rather than its physical volume or quantity, the index is necessarily influenced not only by the behavior of producers but also by the behavior of consumers.

Price, after all, is a function of both supply (efficiency of producers) and demand (eagerness of consumers). If a southern farm produces cotton worth $800 per hand and a northern farm using similar inputs produces wheat worth only $400 per hand, the index used by Fogel and Engerman will unhesitatingly rate the southern farm more "efficient." But does this superior "efficiency" reflect superior productive performance—greater energy, perseverance, rationality of organization, more pounds per man-hour? Or does it reflect merely the different intensities of consumer demand for cotton and wheat? The index used by Fogel and Engerman cannot distinguish between these two quite different sources of "efficiency."[5]

Some economists have recognized this limitation of the index, but the literature on productivity often ignores it because what finally counts, from the economists' most common perspective, is "the bottom line"—profit. To a businessman wondering where to invest his money, or an economist looking for the sources of growth, the efficiency of an enterprise is adequately expressed by the ratio between income taken out and investment put in. The diligence of the work force and the rationality of management are, in the last analysis, irrelevant if intensive consumer demand for the product creates a large income relative to a given investment of resources.

But there are situations in which the limitations of the index become critical. Thus, to take a fanciful case, if one applied the economists' index of efficiency to various enterprises in Holland during the Great Tulip Craze, even the most slovenly tulip producer might look highly "efficient," compared to other agriculturists, simply because of the booming market for tulip bulbs. Here the index would not be a true measure of the energy of the producer or the rationality of the production process, but would merely register the extraordinary value placed on the product by consumers. Likewise, to take another case equally hypothetical but not dependent on transitory boom conditions, it is conceivable that Turkish opium growers, using primitive agricultural methods, might consistently be more "efficient" than highly mechanized, scientifically trained wheat farmers in the United States. Again, strong demand can create high "efficiency," especially when producers are partially shielded from competition by legal or natural barriers to production.

The economists' index of efficiency is a perfectly good guide to economic growth and profit maximization. I do not deny the validity or usefulness of the index itself, I challenge only the careless use to which Fogel and Engerman put it. The question is: What kinds of inferences can the index justify in this particular case? The answer is clear: If an unusual demand situation exists, the index cannot serve by itself as a basis for inferences about the quality of the labor force or the rationality of the process of production. Yet this is exactly the inference that Fogel and Engerman draw from the "efficiency" gap between slave and free agriculture. The advantage of slave over free labor, they say, was due to the "special quality of plantation labor."[6] Nowhere do the authors acknowledge that international consumer demand for cotton might have helped create the observed advantage. Instead they assert,

> The advantage of plantations, at least that part which has been measured thus far, was due to the combination of the superior management of planters and the superior quality of black [*sic*] labor. In a certain sense, all, or nearly all, of the advantage is attributable to the high quality of slave labor, for the main thrust of management was directed at improving the quality of labor. How much of the success of the effort was due to the management, and how much to the responsiveness of workers is an imperative question, but its resolution lies beyond the range of current techniques and available data. (210)

Neither the slaves nor their masters deserve this kind of credit if their apparent "efficiency" is merely an incidental result of extraordinary demand for the crop they produced.

Pointing to the inferior "efficiency" of the North, Fogel and Engerman cast aside the image of the South as a comparatively traditional, noncommercial culture. Southern planters, they say, were "on the whole a highly self-conscious class of entrepreneurs . . . steeped in the scientific agricultural literature of the day" (201). With decisive aid from black overseers and drivers, slaveowners fashioned the "first large, scientifically managed business enterprises." These work forces were made up of functional gangs and teams that worked at a level of intensity comparable to that of modern assembly lines (208). The authors recognize that such impersonal factors of collective discipline and specialization contributed to the superior "efficiency" of slave plantations, but they lay greatest stress on the effort and ingenuity displayed by the average slave. This moral dimension is what most impresses them. Slaves typically were "diligent and efficient workers"; they were even "imbued like their masters with a Protestant ethic." The average slave field hand was "harder working and more efficient than his white counterpart" (263, 231, 5).

The primary evidence for this portrait of the achievement-oriented slave is the index of "efficiency"—which, as shown above, may say more about the behavior of cotton consumers than about the diligence of producers. Fogel and Engerman also use the "efficiency" gap as a launching pad for their most spectacular polemic, the attack on the "myth of black incompetence" (223). This regrettable phrase, which might be rendered more accurately as "the myth (if such it is) of slave apathy," is a catchall rubric under which the authors lump together virtually all previous observers and analysts of slavery. Both Stanley Elkins's "Sambo" thesis and Kenneth Stampp's thesis of "day-to-day resistance" are condemned by Fogel and Engerman as mere variations on a myth fabricated, ironically, not by slaveowners but by abolitionists: "What bitter irony it is that the false stereotype of black labor, a stereotype which still plagues blacks today, was fashioned not primarily by the oppressors who strove to keep their chattel wrapped in the chains of bondage, but by the most ardent opponents of slavery, by those who worked most diligently to destroy the chains of bondage" (215).

Fogel and Engerman declare that the myth has been perpetuated principally by "racism" and "racist myopia" (223, 215). But there may be a simpler explanation for the myth's persistence. It may conform to the observed facts— not of black incompetence, certainly, but of slave apathy. It is no racial slur to suppose that self-interest evokes a sense of task and dedication that the whip cannot impose. What Fogel and Engerman seem not to realize is that a considerable degree of slave apathy—indeed, even psychological trauma or a measure of deliberate sabotage—is perfectly compatible with their finding of high "efficiency." This follows from the inherent limitations of the index. One can grant that slavery was a profitable institution and that the southern economy was thriving as a whole. One can also grant that southern agricultural production was "efficient" in the narrow economic sense measured by the index.

All three of these conditions are compatible with indifference and even "day-to-day resistance" by slave laborers. If the demand for cotton was sufficiently strong, even the most cumbersome production process might have yielded a net profit for planters, economic growth for the region, and a favorable "efficiency" rating for slave labor.

How intense was the demand for cotton? All the objections I have raised thus far hinge on this question. If the demand for cotton was not significantly stronger than the demand for northern agricultural products, then Fogel and Engerman are correct to infer a superior quality of southern labor from the "efficiency" gap (though one would still need to distinguish between the role of individual work habits on the one hand and impersonal factors like collective discipline and economies of scale on the other).

But the reputation of King Cotton is well known, and Fogel and Engerman build upon it. Although they never relate the question of cotton's profitability to the subject of efficiency, they take great pains to show that the demand for cotton was insatiable in real life as well as legend. Even though the long-term trend in cotton prices was downward throughout the antebellum period,

> the 1850s constituted a period of sustained boom in profits for cotton planters. It was an era that outstripped even the fabled prosperity of the 1830s. Nearly every year of the decade was one of above-normal profit. What is more, profits remained high during the last four years of the decade, with prices averaging about 15 percent above their trend values. No wonder cotton production doubled between 1850 and 1860. It was clearly a rational economic response to increase cotton production by over 50 percent between 1857 and 1860. If planters erred it was not in expanding cotton production by too much. Quite the contrary—they were too conservative. Their expansion had not been adequate to bring prices down to their trend values and profits back to normal (equilibrium) levels. (93)

If supply lagged so far behind demand as this, surely we have a prima facie case for attributing at least part of the "efficiency" gap to the extraordinary demand for cotton. If the index is influenced by demand at all, Fogel and Engerman are obliged to ascertain the influence of the demand for cotton before they can claim to know what caused the "efficiency" gap.

The case for King Cotton as a source of the "efficiency" gap is not limited to the contention that 1860 was an atypical year in which the output of cotton producers was artificially inflated by a transitory lag between demand and supply. There was such a lag, and the authors ought to have taken it into account. But more important, what makes the authors' calculations suspect is the continuing high demand for cotton throughout most of the nineteenth century and the inability of producers outside the South to respond effectively to that growing demand. Even if there had been no lag at all between demand and supply in 1860, there still would be grounds for attributing part of the "efficiency" gap to cotton because the South enjoyed a semimonopoly in the production of the crop. On the eve of the Civil War 80 percent of the cotton consumed by Great Britain's voracious textile mills came from the South. The South grew all but a third of the world's total crop.[7] No conceivable margin of advantage of slave over free labor could account for such a gargantuan share of the world market. Instead, the South's dominance in large part must be attributed to the region's natural advantages of soil and climate.

The South's competitors in cotton production were notoriously weak by comparison. India's short-staple cotton accounted for 18 percent of world production, but it was so inferior to "American Upland" that it was seldom used alone, even in the coarsest cloth.[8] In spite of repeated British efforts, Egypt's fine, long-staple cotton did not become a serious competitor until much later because the crop required extensive irrigation and posed special problems of ginning and spinning.[9] The South's natural advantages are demonstrated by its recovery after the Civil War. In spite of extensive devastation that prevented the region from matching its prewar production record until 1878, by the turn of the century the South was again supplying well over half of the world's cotton—without the supposed benefits of slave labor.[10] No wonder a recent econometric study concludes that although the South did not exploit its position by deliberately restricting production, it "did indeed possess substantial monopoly power in world cotton markets."[11]

Although the South faced little international competition, there was of course competition among producers within the South. No planter or combination of planters controlled the price of cotton. But it is essential to recognize that this domestic competition did not reach the mode of production. All large planters relied on the same basic mode of production: slave labor. As a result, slavery as a system of cotton production faced little competition either at home or abroad. Fogel and Engerman note the total absence of large free farms in the South and attribute it to the superior efficiency of slave labor.[12] But it might just as well be attributed to the shortage of free laborers and the ideological opposition that slaveowners no doubt would have mounted against an alternative mode of production which, if proved successful, would have undermined the value of their investment in slaves. If an entrepreneur wished to produce cotton on a large scale in the antebellum South, he probably had to use slave labor, whether or not it was efficient.

Given these semimonopoly conditions of mild competition and strong demand, the southern labor force did not need to be efficient in order to achieve
a high ratio of dollar output to input. Just as in the case of Turkish opium,
even primitive production methods might rank high in measured "efficiency"
if demand was strong and competition was limited by legal or natural barriers.
Under such circumstances producers would have no compelling incentive to
adopt new methods because the old ones—strongly sanctioned by cultural or
ideological values—would continue to yield adequate profits.

In conclusion, two puzzles in Fogel and Engerman's presentation can be
resolved handily if one adopts the view that cotton demand has something
to do with the superior "efficiency" of southern agriculture. First, the authors
fail to ask why, if slave labor was so efficient, did northern businessmen not
make stronger efforts to import it, not only into the disputed territories, but
into the North itself? What moral scruple could have persuaded entrepreneurs
to forgo a 35 percent margin of advantage, in an era when even abolitionists
were "racists"? If southern planters were rational enough to overcome "racist
myopia" and acknowledge the efficiency of slave labor, why weren't northern
businessmen? Perhaps the answer is that although slave labor was potentially
mobile, the crop that made it "efficient" was not.

Second, Fogel and Engerman find striking differences of efficiency within
the slave South: "The slave plantations of the Old South exceeded the efficiency of free northern farms by 19 percent, while the slave plantations of the
newer southern states exceeded the average efficiency of free northern farms
by 53 percent."[13] Again the authors fail to ask themselves an obvious question:
Why was slave labor so much more "efficient" in the new states—the heart of
the cotton belt—than in other parts of the South? Are we to believe that slaves
grew stronger and more diligent as they moved from Virginia to Mississippi?
Or that their masters gained in entrepreneurial skill under the hot Alabama
sun? Occam's razor would suggest that it was not the special qualities of slave
labor per se that made for "efficiency," but unusually favorable conditions for
cultivating cotton.

Are Fogel and Engerman correct to believe that the special quality of slave
labor made southern agriculture 35 percent more efficient than northern agriculture? What has been said here does not settle the question, but only holds
it open. I have not tried to prove that slave labor was of low quality, but only
to show that the opposite contention is unproved. The question now is one of
degree—how much of the observed "efficiency" gap is attributable to the diligence and rationality of producers, how much to the impersonal advantages of
large-scale collective discipline, and how much to consumer demand for cot-

ton?[14] To settle the question will require the techniques of the cliometricians, and I will gladly defer to their final judgment. As a start, we need to do for cotton what Professor Fogel has already done for the railroad — imagine it out of existence and thereby ascertain the consequences of its presence.

Perhaps this has already been done. Perhaps all the considerations proposed here already have been taken into account and are incorporated into the final conclusions of *Time on the Cross*. If the authors can show that this is the case, then we can accept their conclusions and find fault only with their unconvincing manner of presentation. Given only the evidence presented in the book, however, a reasonable man must conclude that the "efficiency" gap is probably more the result of extraordinary consumer demand than extraordinary producer performance. But there may be more to this matter than meets the eye. It may be that the emperor is in reality fully clothed, in which case he now needs only to make his full outfit visible to reasonable men.

CHAPTER TWO

The True & Tragical History
of *Time on the Cross*

Anyone who recalls the uncritical enthusiasm that greeted the publication of *Time on the Cross* a year and a half ago will be shocked by the three volumes of criticism under review. Their combined effect is devastating. A study of slavery that at first seemed exceptionally important, if contentious, now appears at least to be severely flawed and possibly not even worth further attention by serious scholars. This is hardly the fate one would have predicted for a book that the Harvard historian Stephen Thernstrom called "a remarkable achievement," "absolutely stunning, quite simply the most exciting and provocative book I've read in years." Or that inspired the Columbia economist Peter Passell, in his review for the *New York Times,* to declare: "If a more important book about American history has been published in the last decade, I don't know about it." It has, he said, "with one stroke turned around a whole field of interpretation and exposed the frailty of history done without science."

The enthusiasm of the book's initial reception and the intensity of the attack now being mounted against it leave one uncertain what questions to ask about *Time on the Cross* — should we ask how such an important book can be so severely flawed, in spite of its importance? Or how a book with such deep

This review of Herbert Gutman, *Slavery and the Numbers Game: A Critique of Time on the Cross* (Urbana: University of Illinois Press, 1975); Gary Walton, ed., "A Symposium on *Time on the Cross,*" *Explorations in Economic History* 12 (Fall 1975); and Paul A. David, Herbert G. Gutman, Richard Sutch, Peter Temin, and Gavin Wright, *Reckoning with Slavery: Critical Essays in the Quantitative History of American Negro Slavery,* with an introduction by Kenneth M. Stampp (New York: Oxford University Press, 1976), originally appeared in the *New York Review of Books,* Oct. 2, 1975, 33–39. Reprinted with permission from *The New York Review of Books.* Copyright © 1975 Thomas Haskell.

flaws could ever have been thought important? To understand these wildly contradictory judgments we must return to the puzzling book itself.

Time on the Cross was written by two scholars trained primarily as economists, Robert W. Fogel and Stanley Engerman. The book advances two major themes. The first dramatically revises the history of slavery; the second is a polemic on behalf of scientific method in history. Fogel and Engerman contend that slavery in the United States was far more successful economically and far less vicious in its impact on the personality and culture of blacks than most historians have thought. Their view contrasts sharply with the interpretations formulated by such conventional historians as Kenneth Stampp, Stanley Elkins, and Eugene Genovese. These scholars differ markedly among themselves, but each finds in the history of the peculiar institution ample grounds for both white guilt and black rage.

Although the authors of *Time on the Cross* grant the immorality of slavery, they depict it as a rational business enterprise in which the interests of master and slave often converged. Precisely because the master was a rational businessman and the slave his valuable property, there could exist no general incentive for abusive treatment. The authors condemn harsher views of slavery as a "perversion of the history of blacks" that serves to "corrode and poison" race relations by making it appear that blacks were deprived of all opportunities for cultural development for their first two and half centuries on American soil. Like Genovese's *Roll, Jordan, Roll* and most other recent contributions to the history of slavery, *Time on the Cross* is intended to soften the stark image of the concentration camp that Stanley Elkins so subtly superimposed over the plantation in *Slavery* (1959).[1] But it overshoots the mark.

To support their own benign interpretation, the authors present masses of computer-digested quantitative evidence purporting to show, for example, that slaves were rarely whipped, seldom sold, and usually able to maintain a stable family life. Food, housing, and medical care, they claim, were good by contemporary standards. Under these favorable conditions slaves became imbued with the work ethic and adopted the prudish sexual mores of the Victorian era. The typical slave as represented by *Time on the Cross* is reminiscent of a Horatio Alger figure in his eagerness to rise from field hand to artisan to slave driver or even overseer. These were the major steps in an occupational hierarchy within slave society that the authors describe as being remarkably well differentiated and open to talent.

Inspired less by the whip than by positive inducements and the values favoring achievement they had internalized, the typical slave, according to *Time on the Cross,* worked so diligently that the South was 35 percent more efficient in agricultural production than the North. Without denying the injustice of slavery, the authors calculate that the economic benefits of the plantation's large-scale and elaborate organization were so great that blacks actually received more income as slaves than they would have as free farmers. And although a share of their earnings was expropriated by the master, his share was only about 10 percent, "well within the modern tax rate on workers." The master's modest rate of expropriation did not prevent him from making a healthy profit or the South from being among the most economically advanced regions of the world.

In short, Fogel and Engerman contend that the slave experience is a fitting object of modern black pride — not merely to the limited extent that slaves resisted or evaded the coercions of the system, but more importantly because slavery was an unusually efficient productive system in which slaves willingly participated, feeling they had a genuine stake in its success. How could previous historians of slavery have failed to see these things? How could the historical profession have so misled the American public about what is, after all, the most fateful chapter in the nation's past? The methodological argument of *Time on the Cross,* which at times threatened to dominate the book, emerged in response to this often repeated question, with its arch connotations of disciplinary competition and institutional rivalry. The answer was simple: previous students of slavery, Fogel and Engerman said, exaggerated the severity of the system, in part out of neo-abolitionist sentimentality and in part out of a covert racism that refuses to attribute the work ethic to nonwhites. But mainly their methods failed them. They erred because they employed the unscientific methods of conventional historical scholarship.

The authors of *Time on the Cross* are proponents — missionary is the more apt word in Fogel's case — of our generation's version of scientific history, known as "econometric history" or the "new economic history" or, more broadly, "cliometrics." As exponents of the cliometric approach, Fogel and Engerman characteristically (though not uniformly, as we shall see) disdain impressionistic judgments based on diaries, correspondence, newspaper accounts, and other merely literary sources that are the mainstay of conventional history. Instead they and dozens of their research assistants scoured the country to gather information on slave life from manuscript census returns, probate records, and other sources of quantitative data. These data were then fed into computers and analyzed by means of sophisticated statistical techniques and the elegant mathematical equations of modern econometric theory. The authors claim to have amassed more data on slavery and dealt with it in a more scientific manner than any previous investigator.

Appearances to the contrary, the principal feature of the cliometric approach is neither its preference for hard, quantitative data nor its reliance on computer technology and mathematics. Rather, it is the effort to specify explicitly the usually implicit assumptions about causation that underlie and make possible any explanation of human behavior. When formally stated and systematized, these theoretical assumptions constitute the cliometrician's "model," and in the ideal case the model should be clear enough to express in the perfectly unambiguous form of an algebraic equation. The mathematical aspect of the method derives from this effort to specify assumptions rigorously.[2]

Conventional historians tend to dismiss all this painstaking specification of assumptions as misplaced precision or, worse, a futile aping of scientific method. If a cliometrician were to write the history of the Crucifixion, he would, according to a current historical joke, begin by counting the nails. But the cliometricians are on strong ground when they reply that conventional historians often get away with fuzzy thinking by leaving their theoretical assumptions implicit or, as is often the case, simply unexamined.

On the surface, cliometrics is an austere and rigorous discipline that minimizes the significance of any statement that cannot be reduced to a clear empirical test ("operationalized"). But beneath the surface one often finds startling flights of conjecture, so daring that even the most woolly minded humanist might gasp with envy. The soft, licentious side of cliometrics derives, paradoxically, from its reliance on mathematical equations. Before the cliometrician can use his equation to explain the past, he must assign an empirical value to each of its terms, even if the relevant empirical data have not been preserved or were never recorded. When an incomplete historical record fails — as it often does — to supply the figures that the cliometrician's equations require, it is considered fair play to resort to *estimation,* just so long as one specifies the assumptions underlying the estimates. And although cliometrics requires that these and all other assumptions be made explicit, it sets no limits at all on the number of assumptions one may make, or how high contingent assumptions may be piled on top of each other — just so they are explicit.

Pyramiding assumptions in this manner is an art-within-a-science whose finest practitioners achieve brilliant results without forgetting the ethereal nature of the medium in which they work. But inherent in the art is a temptation to see how high one's assumptions can be stacked before they begin to topple. That temptation brings out the daredevil in all cliometricians occasionally, and the Evel Knievel of the profession is Robert Fogel. His now classic "counterfactual" study of the railroad perfectly exemplifies the daredevil impulse that lurks just beneath the austere surface of cliometrics. It is precisely this impulse that has gotten *Time on the Cross* in such deep trouble.

Fogel's aim in *Railroads and American Economic Growth* (1964) was austere: to test empirically the widespread notion that the coming of the railroad contributed greatly to the industrial growth of the United States. But to carry out this aim Fogel shifted into his daredevil mood: he concocted a railroadless United States in 1890. After all, to say that the railroad helped to cause economic growth is to say that if the railroad had not existed, economic growth would have been retarded. So Fogel built a counterfactual world by estimation: he estimated how much it would have cost in the absence of railroads to expand the canal system to its maximum potential; how much more shippers would have paid if they had been forced to rely on wagons and boats alone; how much income would have been forgone by steel manufacturers and other suppliers of the railroad if they had lost their best customer—and so on, at great length.

All historians bemoan the incompleteness of the historical record, but Fogel's problem was quite different: he needed data that had never existed and could only be estimated. This is a game for which the rules have yet to be written. Each estimate introduced a new chain of assumptions—all explicit, of course, to anyone who cared to burrow through them. The difficulties of making reliable estimates were compounded by his choice of the year in which to test the railroad's impact, 1890, six decades after the railroad's introduction, when the entire society had adjusted to its presence in the most subtle ways. No surgeon struggling to excise a malignant growth from a living body ever faced so difficult a task.

The result of this painstaking projection was a fabulous pyramid of assumptions and estimates that was plausible (as well as highly debatable) in its parts, but exceedingly fragile as a whole. Fogel crowned his careful conjectures with the conclusion that the railroad contributed less than 5 percent of the gross national product in 1890. Thus he rejected the "myth" of the railroad's indispensability to economic growth. Out of a series of conjectures, it seemed, he made an argument of empirically warranted scientific exactitude.[3]

Although *Time on the Cross* is not a counterfactual exercise, it relies on chains of assumption and estimation that are no less daring than the ones Fogel employed in the railroad study. But there is a difference. In the railroad study the conjectural elements of the work are plainly exposed to view, as cliometric doctrine requires. In *Time on the Cross* they are hidden from all but specialists. Most readers of *Time on the Cross* see only the silk purse of apparent scientific exactitude; the authors spared them the sight of the sow's ear from which it all came.

This neat trick the authors accomplished by splitting *Time on the Cross* into two volumes, one for general readers, the other for specialists. Volume one is written in a brisk, declarative style that achieves terrific argumentative force by eschewing the tedious tasks of qualification and substantiation. It has no footnotes; much less, extensive specification of assumptions. It "announces" findings in the way an astronomer might announce the discovery of a new planet, and it heaps scorn on previous interpretations, especially those of Kenneth Stampp of Berkeley, as if they were astrological gibberish written by people unequipped with a telescope. But the tiresome qualifications, discussion of evidence, and specification of assumptions—the things that give cliometrics its rigor—were relegated to volume two.

Or at least they were supposed to be. Volume two is indeed jammed with tables and equations and cryptic descriptions of procedure, but in fact it often fails to substantiate the story told so simply in volume one. One cannot even find in volume two the citations for quotations presented in volume one. The authors have been apologetic about this failure in documentation, which they explain as a result of the haste with which volume two had to be thrown together at the last minute—they originally planned to publish the undocumented popular volume alone![4]

Of course the authors' motive in adopting the unprecedented two-volume format was not to deceive, but to popularize. They evidently believed that their topic was so sensitive and their reinterpretation of it so dramatic that the book might be used to advertise cliometrics, bringing to public attention for the first time a discipline that is in constant need of money for computer time and research assistants, but whose literary products the average undergraduate is not eager or able to read. Fogel did not hide this motive: he told a reporter, "We're using the book like a red flag to get attention."[5]

The same aim was pursued after publication by arranging for the first review to appear in the *Wall Street Journal,* by setting up a debate between author Fogel and black psychologist Kenneth Clark on the *Today* show, and by arranging numerous interviews. It was no accident, one supposes, that the starry-eyed *Time* magazine reviewer came away from his interview believing that "traditional 'impressionistic' historians persistently wrote about American slavery in delusive and polemical stereotypes," and that "historians who do not have these [cliometric] tools could grope for another hundred years in subjective confusion and never be able even to evaluate or rebut the work of the cliometricians." Popularization made *Time on the Cross* a weapon of methodological and institutional rivalry.

Now a year and a half has passed since the publication of *Time on the Cross*. No one is surprised that the book has generated controversy, but what is startling and ironic in view of the authors' aims is the identity of the book's critics. *Time on the Cross* is being torn apart by cliometricians. The conventional historians to whom Fogel and Engerman threw down the gauntlet have hardly been able to get their word in. That this would be the likely pattern of the book's downfall became apparent late last October at a much publicized conference held at the University of Rochester.

Most of the leading scholars in the history of slavery and many prominent historians, economists, and sociologists in other fields — nearly one hundred participants in all — gathered at Rochester to subject *Time on the Cross* to careful scrutiny. Participants included Eugene Genovese (who as chairman of the Rochester history department was co-organizer of the conference with Engerman), Kenneth Stampp, Stanley Elkins, David Brion Davis, C. Vann Woodward, Winthrop Jordan, Oscar Handlin, Albert Fishlow, Peter Laslett, and R. M. Hartwell. Few black scholars attended because the conference coincided with the meeting in Philadelphia of the Association for the Study of Afro-American Life and History.

Whatever the ultimate fate of *Time on the Cross,* Fogel and Engerman will be justified in feeling a certain pride in the Rochester conference. For a single study to rivet the attention of an entire field of scholarship is rare enough, and it is even more astonishing considering that *Time on the Cross* had been published only six months before. But after paying *Time on the Cross* the scholar's highest tribute of undivided attention, a great many of those who attended the Rochester conference felt ready to consign the book to the outermost ring of the scholar's hell, obscurity. Rarely has such an important book proved so vulnerable, not only to attack — but to dismissal.

Fogel and Engerman set out to save history from the historians, but at Rochester they were waylaid by a campaign to save cliometrics from Fogel and Engerman. The great *Methodenstreit* that the authors had hoped to generate was a bust, because *Time on the Cross,* judged on its own premises, proved to be too severely flawed to sustain any sort of profound controversy. At Rochester serious methodological questions were crowded offstage by such prosaic queries as "Have Fogel and Engerman gotten their facts straight?" and "Can this formula even in principle answer the questions they ask of it?" The conventional historians generally sat in bemused silence as the most telling blows were struck by Fogel and Engerman's cliometric colleagues.

The most devastating criticisms leveled against *Time on the Cross* at Rochester are now reproduced in the three volumes under review. All but one of the contributors to these volumes were participants at Rochester, and two of the essays (by Richard Sutch and Gavin Wright) were originally prepared for the conference. Of the seven contributors, five are trained econometric historians whose professional standing is as high as that of Fogel and Engerman. The other two contributors are Kenneth Stampp, author of *The Peculiar Institution,* probably the most widely read history of slavery, and Herbert Gutman, whose two-volume history of the black family is scheduled for publication next year and whose work uses much quantitative data even though he is not known as a cliometrician.

Gutman's book, *Slavery and the Numbers Game,* first appeared last winter as an issue of the *Journal of Negro History.*[6] It shows some signs of hasty and angry preparation, but it inflicts great damage on the nontheoretical parts of *Time on the Cross,* those concerned with labor incentives, slave work habits, sexual mores, slave sales, and the slave family. It is all the more striking because Gutman shares Fogel and Engerman's aim of illuminating the "record of black achievement under adversity." Yet he concludes, shockingly, that *Time on the Cross* "really tells us nothing of importance about the beliefs and behavior of enslaved Afro-Americans."

"A Symposium on *Time on the Cross*" is a special issue of *Explorations in Economic History,* one of two major organs of the new economic history. The most important piece in the collection, by the Berkeley econometrician Richard Sutch, is a lengthy criticism—almost as long as Gutman's—of Fogel and Engerman's novel claims about the treatment of slaves. Sutch's paper was the sensation of the Rochester conference because it exposes, as we will see, blunders so obvious that they would make a sophomore blush with shame. Sutch's conclusion is as damning as Gutman's: "*Time on the Cross* is a failure."

Reckoning with Slavery is an imposing collaborative effort that consolidates the closely related criticisms of Gutman and Sutch and brings them together with the more theoretical econometric work of Paul David of Stanford, Peter Temin of MIT, and Gavin Wright of the University of Michigan. David and Temin, in two jointly written essays, expose many conceptual confusions in *Time on the Cross* and also do much to clarify the inherent limits of cliometric method and its proper relationship to conventional history.[7] They predict that *Time on the Cross* "will be remembered as an unsatisfactory and profoundly disappointing book . . . [because it] pressed behaviorist social science to its natural limits, and then beyond."

Gavin Wright's important essay in *Reckoning with Slavery* goes beyond the particular failings of *Time on the Cross* to locate the real cause of the prosperity and apparent efficiency of the southern economy in consumer demand for cotton rather than the virtues of slave labor cited by Fogel and Engerman. Wright contends that the booming demand for antebellum cotton was an "inherently impermanent foundation" for prosperity which, in fact, collapsed in the 1860s, for reasons essentially unrelated to the Civil War. His rigorously cliometric evidence undermines *Time on the Cross* at many points and injects new life into the old thesis, especially dear to Eugene Genovese, that the slave regime was destined to face a severe economic crisis even without the Civil War.[8]

The authors of *Reckoning with Slavery* showed their respect for conventional historical scholarship by inviting Kenneth Stampp to write the introduction to their volume. He admires some cliometric work and concedes that his book on slavery would have benefited from computer analysis of some of the data; but he remains skeptical of any methodological approach that is intolerant of the ambiguities of human experience.

To convey in a short space the reasons for the disenchantment felt by those who participated in the Rochester conference, we can begin with a sampling of the most egregious blunders made in *Time on the Cross* and then turn to the fragility of the book's central argument, the claim that slaves were more efficient workers than free men. Although many of Fogel and Engerman's errors are attributable to nothing but carelessness, others suggest an extreme overindulgence in the heady art of pyramiding assumptions.

Consider first Fogel and Engerman's discovery that "the houses of slaves compared well with the housing of free workers in the antebellum era. . . . The 'typical' slave cabin of the late antebellum era probably contained more sleeping space per person than was available to most of New York City's workers half a century later." Upon trying to reproduce this finding, Sutch discovered that it was based on a comparison of whole slave cabins to the bedrooms of workers' tenements. It is also of passing interest that the free worker's living space was measured in 1893, not just a random year, but at the lowest point of one of the country's worst depressions prior to the 1930s. Far worse, the authors exaggerated the size of the average slave cabin, according to their own sources, by about 50 percent. They also understated the size of the average worker's tenement (bedroom) by presenting figures drawn from a study that expressly set out to find the very worst slums in all of New York City. Using data drawn from neighborhoods containing the most downtrodden 1.8 percent of the city's population, Fogel and Engerman concluded that slave dwellings compared favorably with those of "*most* of New York City's workers."[9]

Another error that caused much discussion at Rochester was Fogel and Engerman's contention, which came as a great surprise to historians of the South, that most plantation overseers were black slaves. This is an important point for the authors because the black overseer neatly symbolized their theme of an essential convergence of interests between master and slave, and also strengthened their portrait of a full occupational hierarchy within slave society by showing that there was room for slaves even at the top. When the shouting was over it was clear that *Time on the Cross* had gone astray again. First, the authors had virtually no positive evidence about the racial identity of overseers. They surmised that at least 70 percent of overseers were slaves on the basis of strictly negative evidence: if no free overseer was listed for a plantation in their sample of census data, they leaped to the conclusion that (1) there must have been an overseer, and (2) he must have been a slave. They discounted the likelihood, especially great on small holdings, that the master or his sons supervised the plantation. They ignored other census data in which thousands of free whites listed their occupation as "overseer."

Still worse, the authors failed to recognize that the census data they used did not even record the presence of an overseer unless he happened to live in the same house as the plantation owner—hardly the usual arrangement. The authors conceded at Rochester that their estimate of the number of white overseers needs to be raised by about 100 percent, but even this radically revised estimate is ephemeral, because it is still based on strained assumptions about negative evidence.[10]

Fogel and Engerman's unfamiliarity with the pitfalls awaiting users of nineteenth-century census data is reflected in many more of their claims—for instance, that there were no slave prostitutes in Nashville in 1860. They adduced this arcane fact to support their larger thesis that masters were not likely to exploit their female slaves sexually. But Gutman shows that their source was a census that recorded the occupations only of the free population, so even if the census taker had been surrounded by slave prostitutes he would not have recorded their presence.

Even when Fogel and Engerman have their facts straight, their deceptive presentation breeds distrust. Sutch discovered through correspondence with the authors that their sweepingly revisionist portrait of an elaborate occupational hierarchy within slave society is based on information from only thirty plantations, all of which were located in a single, decidedly untypical sugar and rice parish of Louisiana. Gutman argues on the basis of a larger collection of data that Fogel and Engerman overestimated the number of slave artisans by at least half, and perhaps much more. Of 20,576 blacks who enlisted in the Union Army of Kentucky, for example, only 1.6 percent identified themselves as artisans, as contrasted with Fogel and Engerman's estimated average of 15.4 percent.[11]

Fogel and Engerman published an imposing bar graph purporting to show the "prudishness" of slave morality by the high age of slave mothers when they first gave birth. The graph proves nothing of the kind. Actually it is based on the mother's age at the birth of her first *surviving* child, a very different figure in an age of high infant mortality. Their calculation also disregards the possibility that some children were separated from their mothers, or simply not listed with their mothers in plantation records once they reached a certain age. Under pressure from Sutch, Gutman, Peter Laslett, and Edward Shorter, Fogel seemed to concede on the final day of the Rochester conference that the average age-at-first-birth of American slaves is one of the lowest of known populations—yet he still professed to see in the data evidence of "prudishness." But of course it could be argued that the authors commit an even more elementary error by equating high morality with the observance of a taboo on adolescent intercourse.[12]

Sometimes Fogel and Engerman cast statistical data in misleading form. Readers cannot help but be impressed with the infrequency of slave sales when told that only 1.92 percent of all slaves were sold each year. But the authors, being mathematically adept, must have known—and should have told their readers—that the same data mean that in the course of a thirty-five-year life-time the average slave had a fifty-fifty chance of being sold at least once himself and was likely to witness the sale of at least eleven members of his immediate family (parents, siblings, spouse, children).[13] Expressed in this form, the figures take on a different meaning.

Similarly, as Gutman points out, readers of *Time on the Cross* are inclined toward a benign view of slavery when they read that the average slave on the Barrow plantation received only 0.7 whippings per year. In the first place the figure is too low because it is based on an erroneous count both of the number of slaves Barrow owned and the number of times he whipped them. But more important, the figure is not the most relevant measure of the importance of whippings. A whipping, like a lynching, is an instrument of social discipline intended to impress not only the immediate victim but all who see or hear about the event. The relevant question is, "How often did Barrow's slaves see one of their number whipped?"—to which the answer is every four and a half days. Again, the form in which the figures are expressed controls their meaning. If one expressed the rate of lynchings in the same form Fogel and Engerman chose for whippings, it would turn out that in 1893 there were only about 0.00002 lynchings per black per year. But obviously this way of expressing the data would cause the reader utterly to misunderstand the historical significance of the 155 Negro lynchings that occurred in 1893.[14]

Anyone who cares to see how outrageous Fogel and Engerman's pyramiding of assumptions can become ought to read Sutch's and Gutman's exposé of their treatment of the slave trade and its impact on the slave family. The chain of aberrant reasoning in *Time on the Cross* is too long and convoluted to reproduce entirely, but some of its weakest links may be noted. Fogel and Engerman claim that of the multitudes of slaves who were taken from the Old South to the fertile cotton lands of the New South in the period 1820–1860, only 16 percent were conveyed by means of the slave trade — i.e., sold on the open market — the vast majority instead moving with their owners in whole plantations.

Narrowing their attention to the small (16 percent) proportion of all migrating slaves who were sold on the open market, Fogel and Engerman further claim that the vast majority of these were unmarried adults — so their sale imposed no great strain on the integrity of slave families. Indeed, the authors calculate, on the basis of what appears in volume one to be direct evidence from New Orleans slave market records, that no more than 13 percent of interregional slave sales broke marriages. Combining these two "small" proportions, they conclude that "it is probable that [only] about 2 percent of the marriages of slaves involved in the westward trek were destroyed by the process of migration."[15] Clearly, then, even during one of the world's largest forced migrations, masters managed to protect the integrity of the slave family.

The basis for this conclusion is a web of assumptions that are individually implausible and cumulatively preposterous. In the first place slave "marriages" had no legal standing. The bills of sale in the New Orleans slave market do not record the marital status of the slave sold. How, then, could Fogel and Engerman determine that only 13 percent of sales broke marriages? By assuming that all men sold alone were unmarried. By assuming that all women sold alone were unmarried. And by assuming that only those women who were sold with children but without a man represent marriages broken up by sales. These assumptions, unwarranted in themselves, rest on the further assumption that masters were highly averse to separating mothers from children. No empirical evidence is offered for this assumption which, in fact, begs the question, since the master's attitude toward the slave family is one of the questions at issue.

We have not yet reached the muddy bottom of this pyramid. Underlying

their calculation of marriages broken by sale is Fogel and Engerman's earlier
calculation of the proportion of migrating slaves who entered the slave trade
in the first place—16 percent. Neither volume of *Time on the Cross* tries to
explain how this figure was calculated. By writing to Engerman, Sutch discovered its origins: Fogel and Engerman do not really know what proportion of
migrating slaves entered the slave trade throughout the South—their figure of
16 percent represents only one state, Maryland. Nor do they even have hard
evidence for Maryland. They arrived at 16 percent by combining two estimates
made by other scholars. These estimates do not jibe with each other, and Sutch
could find no way to combine them to yield 16 percent, and had to conclude
that this whole sorry business may rest on an error in long division.[16]

Taken singly, most of these blunders and distortions and unwarranted assumptions fall within the ordinary range of fallibility. Every scholar has made
some mistakes. But it was the cumulative impact of these and numerous similar gaffes that left many Rochester conferees wondering if *Time on the Cross*
deserved to be taken seriously at all. The flaws of *Time on the Cross* are not confined to its parts but extend to its conceptual heart: the efficiency calculation.
No finding raised more eyebrows than the dramatic claim that slaves, through
their personal diligence and enthusiastic commitment to the work ethic, made
southern agriculture 35 percent more efficient than the family farms of the
North. My own nonspecialist's doubts about this contention, published in
these pages last September, have been amply confirmed (and superseded in
expertise and weight of evidence) by the work of a half-dozen economic historians.[17]

Fogel and Engerman should have known from the beginning that any
comparison of regional efficiency in the antebellum period was fraught with
breathtaking difficulties. The basis for their comparison, a rather controversial
economist's tool known as the "geometric index of total factor productivity,"
gives results whose interpretation is debatable in even the most conventional
applications. The index is essentially nothing more than a ratio of output to
input: it ranks as most efficient that region, or other economic entity, which
achieves the highest output with the lowest inputs of capital, labor, and land.
The fatal limitation of the index, given the uses to which Fogel and Engerman wished to put it, is that it measures output in market value, rather than
physical units (contrary to the impression given in volume one of *Time on the
Cross*). There is no escaping this limitation, for one cannot aggregate a total
output composed of bales of cotton, bushels of peas, pounds of pork, and so
on, without reducing everything to dollar value.

Since the index is based on market value, it reflects not only the performance of producers (which is what we have in mind when we talk about productive efficiency) but also the behavior of consumers, whose eagerness for the product helps to determine its market value. Consumer behavior is clearly irrelevant to productive efficiency, and the index is misleading to the extent that it is influenced by this factor.[18] In short, the index is sensitive to demand: if two producers organize their work in equally rational ways, work equally hard, and even produce equal amounts of physical output, the so-called efficiency index may nonetheless rank one producer more "efficient" than the other because his product is in greater demand. As David and Temin observe, this is not the accepted meaning of "efficiency."

Given the sensitivity of the index to demand and the heavy demand for the South's principal crop, cotton, the index by itself is utterly incapable of justifying the chief inference that Fogel and Engerman drew from it—that slaves must have been hardworking Horatio Alger types and their masters skilled scientific managers. Gavin Wright confirms that the efficiency gap has more to do with voracious consumer demand for cotton than with any Herculean feats of productivity by southern producers. He is at particular pains to show that the differing efficiency ratings Fogel and Engerman observed within the South, between slave and free farms, are attributable to the differing abilities to specialize in cotton rather than to the economies of scale or other virtues of slave labor cited by Fogel and Engerman.

The bias introduced by cotton demand is only the most obvious of the flaws in the efficiency calculation. Even apart from the inherent frailties of the index in this especially difficult application, Fogel and Engerman's use of it rests on some extremely dubious assumptions. The choice of 1860 as a typical year for measurement has been sharply questioned. So has the authors' proposition that an acre of northern farmland was on average 2.5 times better in quality than southern farmland. This extraordinary assumption alone is enough to guarantee a finding of southern superiority in productivity.

The originator of the geometric version of the efficiency index, Evsey Domar of MIT, has in the past gone out of his way to condemn simplistic interpretations of its meaning. Indeed, he once declared that "however tempting, it would be just as well not to treat the index as a measure of efficiency, or even as an approximation to it."[19] The authors of *Time on the Cross* heaved a visible sigh of relief at Rochester when Domar, in his remarks there, confined himself to a brief, cautious, and rather enigmatic statement. Instead of "flunking" his onetime student, Fogel, for misusing the index, Domar gave him "about a 'C,'" as Peter Laslett wryly observed.

Domar did not defend the efficiency calculation as presented in *Time on the*

Cross; on the contrary, he accepted the main criticism of it. But granting the frailty of the index, he insisted that rival arguments ought to be couched in its terms as long as economists have no better tool for the job. Many economists at Rochester preferred simply to concede that the index is not up to the task of comparing the antebellum North and South.

Lance Davis of the California Institute of Technology, a prominent clio-metrician, singled out the efficiency calculation as the least plausible argument of a generally unpersuasive book. He estimated that Fogel and Engerman's chances of successfully defending the efficiency finding were about one in ten. This is a telling judgment from the man who introduced the term "New Economic History," who once called Fogel's railroad study a "great book," and who even crowned Fogel himself as "the best" of the cliometricians nine years ago. The efficiency calculation has been closely scrutinized not only by Davis, Wright, Temin, and Paul David but also by Stanley Lebergott of Wesleyan, Harold Woodman of Purdue, Jay Mandle of Temple, and Frank B. Tipton Jr. and Clarence E. Walker, both of Wesleyan. No one has a kind word to say for it.[20]

Friends of *Time on the Cross* have suggested that the authors might do well to try to ride out the storm by jettisoning the efficiency calculation altogether. But this is plainly impossible. Fogel explained to a stunned audience on the last day of the Rochester conference that the efficiency calculation is the pro-pelling idea behind the whole book. The efficiency calculation was the initial discovery that led the authors to conceive of a book on slavery in the first place. The surprising superiority of slave to free labor is by their own account the puzzle they set out to solve, and all the other research presented in *Time on the Cross* — on slave treatment, diet, living conditions, and so on — was developed in the course of their effort to show how and why slave labor was so efficient.[21]

Moreover, the generous grants from the National Science Foundation which have supported Fogel and Engerman's vast research establishment for the past five years — grants totaling $362,300 — were allocated specifically for research on "Factor Productivity in American Agriculture" — i.e., efficiency.[22] The en-tire book and the ongoing research effort behind it, probably the largest and most costly enterprise in historical scholarship ever undertaken, rest squarely on what now appears to be the book's most vulnerable argument. Of course the raw data assembled by Fogel and Engerman with this grant money con-stitute a permanent acquisition for all scholars. Nonetheless it is staggering to think how much effort has already been expended — vainly — in hopes of find-ing support for this exceedingly ephemeral calculation.

The foregoing discussion of criticism of *Time on the Cross*, it must be added, is incomplete. I have not touched on the extensive work that Sutch and others have devoted to overturning Fogel and Engerman's findings on slave nutrition and health. I have not discussed the withering attack that Vedder, David, and Temin have launched against Fogel and Engerman's findings on the rate of expropriation, or Gutman's use of the notorious Barrow diary to show that slaves were whipped precisely because they lacked an internalized "work ethic," or David and Temin's criticism of the moral obtuseness built into the questions that Fogel and Engerman asked. If Fogel and Engerman cleared themselves of all the charges I have discussed, they would raise our estimate of the quality of scholarship that went into *Time on the Cross,* but the book would still be shrouded in controversy.

Can *Time on the Cross* survive? So far, the book and its authors are prospering, notwithstanding Fogel and Engerman's failure to respond convincingly to their critics. The book has already appeared in English, Spanish, and Italian editions. The trustees of Columbia University bestowed upon it the prestigious Bancroft Prize, albeit by a hesitant, divided vote.[23] Fogel will be visiting Pitt Professor at Cambridge during the academic year 1975–1976; upon his return to this country he will take up a new joint appointment in both economics and history at Harvard.

Even when the criticism discussed here reaches print and is fully disseminated, one cannot predict that *Time on the Cross* will promptly disappear from view. There are at least two reasons. First, the authors are resourceful and talented scholars. They encouraged a vigorous debate by trying to make their assumptions explicit — they did try, I believe — and, as C. Vann Woodward said at Rochester, they deserve respect for exposing themselves to a degree of scrutiny from which no scholar could emerge unscathed. Moreover, they repeatedly described *Time on the Cross* as an "interim report" on a continuing research project of which volumes three and four are already in preparation ("I wish I'd waited for volume four," was one response to this news at Rochester). In the long run, Fogel and Engerman may salvage arguments that now appear lost. Even if they do not, these "interim reports" may serve the unintended function of decoys, exhausting the critics before the "final" report is made public.

The book may have a longer life than it deserves because of the awesome financial and institutional apparatus that stands behind it. *Time on the Cross* is a product of factory scholarship, and we know what happens to artisans who compete with factories. The production line for *Time on the Cross* was subsidized by government grant money and manned by dozens of graduate research assistants who are now fiercely loyal to their company and its prod ucts. Without so much as a Ph.D. to hide behind, they threw themselves into battle at Rochester, fearlessly controverting scholars twice their age and eminence. Can we be confident that the life or death of this book's ideas depends, as scholarly ideas should, solely upon their intellectual merit?

Eugene Genovese closed the Rochester conference with the careful opinion that *Time on the Cross* was a "creative failure." Given his Sisyphean view of scholarship it was, as he intended, a sincere compliment, though a fragile one. Earlier, when the book first came out, Genovese generously conceded that the authors "accomplished all that they should have dared hope: they have thrown the burden of proof back upon their opponents." Now, though only a year and a half has passed, it is not too soon to suggest that the burden of proof has passed back again to Fogel and Engerman. And it is a far heavier burden, for now they must prove, before any of their particular contentions, that their book merits further scholarly attention.

PART TWO

Objectivity and Its Institutional Setting

The rise of the modern American university is part and parcel of an explosive proliferation of expertise that got under way in the decades following 1870. When the resulting edifice of professional authority came under vigorous attack a century later, the academic critics of my generation who led the assault seldom paused to consider how hard it is to challenge the knowledge claims of overbearing physicians, lawyers, and engineers, without also raising questions about the authority of the university and all who inhabit it, including the critics themselves. Not for nothing is the university known as the gatekeeper of the professions.

Among the critics of the 1970s, none were more skeptical of the knowledge claims that professionals make than Burton Bledstein. Unlike many other critics, however, he candidly acknowledged that professors themselves are deeply implicated in the "culture of professionalism." In his view, the professionalizing movement of the late nineteenth century was a far-reaching collective project of self-promotion, in which the members of a rising middle class sought to bolster their self-esteem by laying claim to esoteric knowledge and cultivating the dependency of a gullible public. He construed the university as the primary vehicle of their ambition, the esoteric knowledge it cultivates as little more than a means to their self-gratification. From Bledstein's standpoint, the knowledge claims of neurosurgeons are no less suspect than those of "professional" tree surgeons or hairdressers.

In "Power to the Experts," a review-essay of Bledstein's book, *The Culture of Professionalism,* I take issue with the extraordinary productivity and historical force that he imputed to bourgeois careerism and argue for a less cynical and more discriminating view of professional authority. Assuming that many professional knowledge claims are valid, I locate the decisive causes of professionalization not so much on the supply side of the equation as on the demand side — not, that is, in the self-serving arrogance of middle-class professionals so much as in the rising incomes, urban residence, and hunger for reliable opinion of their clients (also predominantly middle class), who willingly deferred to expertise when the opportunity presented itself.

The deep and nontrivial roots of the public's growing reliance on experts also figure significantly in "Professionalism versus Capitalism." That essay draws on the writings of Charles S. Peirce, Emile Durkheim, and R. H. Tawney to explore the assumption so characteristic of the late Victorians that involvement in a professional community enhances the disinterestedness of its members, enabling them both to grasp the truth and to subordinate their own self-interest to the needs of their clients and the good of the public. Tawney in England and Durkheim in France both ranked the breakdown of community among the most pressing social problems of their era and saw in the collegial solidarity of professional communities a promising antidote to the excesses of individualism and self-aggrandizement that industrial capitalism brought in its wake. They were not alone, for many intellectuals during the years 1880–1929 saw professionalization as a kind of cultural reform, one that often modeled itself after the disciplinary communities then taking shape in the academic world.

Peirce prized community no less highly than Tawney and Durkheim, but more for its epistemological virtues than its moral ones. Although he set forth a thoroughly communal theory of truth, thereby strengthening the conventional association between professionalism and disinterestedness in the sense of objective knowledge, he was much more ambivalent about the community's supposed capacity to foster disinterestedness in the sense of unselfishness. Instead, beneath the surface of his communitarian rhetoric one finds a countercurrent of recognition that professional communities of the sort he knew best, in natural science, were arenas of competition that succeeded in promoting the discovery of truth only by intensifying criticism, a form of interpersonal conflict that is indispensable to the work of intellectuals. In the last analysis, I contend, Peirce's truth-seeking "community of inquiry" functions as a countervailing market that succeeds in offsetting some of the degrading consequences of capitalism only by fostering another (equally ego-driven) sort of competition in which the stakes are reputation and honor rather than pecuniary reward. I conclude that such a community, although seen as a potential remedy for market-driven selfishness as late as the 1920s, could at best be no more than a "capitalist solution for the problems of capitalism."[1]

1. Two other essays that examine the cultural concomitants of capitalism and/or market culture will be found in part 3: "Capitalism and the Origins of the Humanitarian Sensibility [parts 1

The next essay, "The Curious Persistence of Rights Talk in the Age of Interpretation," was prepared for a special volume of the *Journal of American History* devoted to "rights consciousness," published in 1989 to commemorate the 200th anniversary of the adoption of the Constitution. If the institutional preconditions of reliable knowledge loom large in the first two essays of part 2, objectivity and its defense take center stage here. It falls more nearly into the "history of ideas" tradition than most of my work, and it marks a shift in my concerns — away from the shortsighted cynicism of the antiprofessional critics of the 1970s to the much more focused and formidable epistemological radicalism of the poststructuralists, who by the 1980s were calling into doubt not merely the truth claims of overbearing experts but truth itself. Begun in the mid-1980s, before "poststructuralism" had made much of a splash in historical circles, my essay was meant to call the attention of historians to the developing debate and urge upon them the virtues of a moderate historicism. The essay's central claims are (1) that the discourse of human rights (which, I assume, most of us rely on and would be loath to give up) implies an objective or at least intersubjective moral order, and (2) that although such an order can be defended on the fallibilist premises of moderate historicism, it can receive no support at all from more radical varieties of historicism. From Nietzsche's standpoint, rights talk can be no more than a masked assertion of interest.

The essay begins by contrasting Nietzsche with Leo Strauss to establish the poles within which the debate has proceeded, and then turns to contemporary philosophers whose work exemplifies the high quality and internal diversity of what I call the moderate camp of historicists — figures such as Alasdair MacIntyre, John Rawls, and Thomas Kuhn. Although the essay has a polemical edge, I have been gratified by the comparatively friendly reception it has received from scholars standing both to my left and to my right on the spectrum of cultural politics.

The last two essays in part 2 take up where "Curious Persistence of Rights Talk" left off, in that they, too, defend a version of objectivity and thereby take a contested position in the great debate that has come spinning out of literary criticism these past couple of decades. "Objectivity Is not Neutrality" is an essay-review of Peter Novick's *That Noble Dream,* a wonderfully provocative history of the historical profession in this country that takes historians' endless quarrels about objectivity as its central theme. The essay was solicited by *History and Theory* and first published there. Much as I admire Novick's book, which is the most ambitious history of the historical profession yet written, I

and 2]" and "Persons as Uncaused Causes: John Stuart Mill, the Spirit of Capitalism, and the 'Invention' of Formalism."

contend that he oversimplifies and misrepresents the debate on objectivity by virtually equating objectivity with neutrality. He is not the first to blur the two terms, of course, but it is surprising that so sophisticated a writer would fail to register, not merely the presence, but the prevalence among twentieth-century historians of a concept of objectivity that does not aspire to self-effacement and that is, within wide limits, perfectly compatible with strongly held convictions. When it comes to interpretation, sophistication does not consist in thinking there is nothing to "get right," or that one interpretation is as good as any other.

What I champion under the rubric "objectivity" is not neutrality or passionlessness but that "vital minimum of ascetic self-discipline that enables a person to do such things as abandon wishful thinking, assimilate bad news, and discard pleasing interpretations that cannot pass elementary tests of evidence and logic." Most important, objectivity requires the ability to "suspend or bracket one's own perceptions long enough to enter sympathetically into the alien and possibly repugnant perspectives of rival thinkers." These mental acts require a degree of detachment, an ability to achieve some distance from one's own spontaneous perceptions and convictions. But they do not require indifference. On the contrary, the finest fruit of detachment is the powerful argument, which anticipates opposing lines of argumentation and reveals by its every twist and turn the force—even the respectability—of the positions it rejects. Without a saving degree of detachment, scholarship becomes indistinguishable from propaganda, which through deliberation or a calculated negligence obscures opposing lines of argumentation in its passion to manipulate. Ironically, in practice Novick generally lives up to my ideal of objectivity, even as he derides it as a hopeless and mean-spirited illusion.

The second section's last essay, "Justifying Academic Freedom in the Era of Power/Knowledge," adopts much the same strategy as "Persistence of Rights Talk." Supposing that the reader cherishes the rights of academic freedom, just as I do, it asks what sorts of resources the radical epistemologies of the day provide for the justification of those rights. The answer is that on postmodern premises the resources are few and far between. Here the themes developed in previous essays—the meaning of professionalization, the question of objectivity, the significance of the swift current of historicism in which we now find ourselves—all come together. Their convergence is sure to be controversial.

When John Dewey, Arthur O. Lovejoy, and the other founders of the American Association of University Professors met in 1915 to institutionalize the defense of academic freedom, they took it for granted, as Dewey put it, that "the university function is the truth function."[2] They were fallibilists who had no quarrel with the idea of truth itself, yet insisted that the adequacy of any particular representation of the real was in principle always open to question. From the standpoint of their generation, as it was most fully articulated by Charles Peirce (and here I borrow extensively from what I have already written about Peirce's community of inquiry in "Professionalism versus Capitalism"), the disciplinary communities comprising the university had an epistemological function that benefited the entire society: By putting inquirers into direct competition with one another, such communities facilitated the winnowing of truth from error, a task that could be successful only to the extent that the pursuit of knowledge was sheltered from the exercise of power. When confronted with questions such as "Why should university trustees tolerate the teaching of doctrines they find reprehensible?" the confident reply of Dewey's generation centered on the long-term advantages to all society of allowing truth claims to be sorted out by open competition among scholars, rather than by the dictates either of powerful individuals or of majority opinion.

That rationale has been eroded at many points during the past half century. Michel Foucault asks us to believe that knowledge, far from being the enemy of power, is ordinarily its handmaiden. Thomas Kuhn knocks the realist props out from under Peirce's conception of the community of inquiry by denying that there is any fixed reality for inquirers to converge upon. Richard Rorty, donning the mantle of pragmatism, brushes aside Dewey's allusions to "truth" as a condescension to the vulgar public.[3] In committing philosophy to the task of "edification" rather than accurate representation, Rorty is explicitly attacking a project for professionalizing philosophy that Arthur Lovejoy set forth not long after he helped found the AAUP. Stanley Fish grants that disciplinary communities have vast powers to define the life-world of their members, but he would never identify the opinion of the community with truth in any deep sense — or concede that the right of free speech can ever be anything more than a rhetorical ploy on behalf of some political project. Hayden White suggests that the entire process of disciplinization embodied in the modern American university has worked against the wretched of the earth, by imposing a normalizing influence that discredits all varieties of visionary thought and favors the complacent center.

2. Dewey, "Academic Freedom," *Educational Review* 23 (1902): 3. Reprinted in *The American Concept of Academic Freedom in Formation: A Collection of Essays and Reports,* ed. Walter P. Metzger (New York: Arno Press, 1977).

3. Richard Rorty, "Does Academic Freedom Have Philosophical Presuppositions?" *Academe* 80 (Nov.–Dec. 1994): 59.

Failing to see how academic freedom can be justified on premises such as these, I close on an interrogatory note: Which will win our loyalty, if push comes to shove? The practices that have been institutionalized under the banner of academic freedom, or the radical epistemologies that leave those practices without a leg to stand on? My hope is that once theorists are confronted with such a dire choice, they will go back to their drawing boards and take practice as their guide. Here Rorty and I reach the same conclusion, though by different routes: "Dewey," he speculates, "would say that if it should ever come down to a choice between the practices and traditions which make up academic freedom and anti-representationalist theories of truth and knowledge, we should go for academic freedom."[4] We agree on the priority of practice over theory, but unlike Rorty I think the time for choice has arrived.

4. Ibid., 60.

CHAPTER THREE

Power to the Experts

A Review of Burton Bledstein's
Culture of Professionalism

In 1967, Paul Goodman tried to teach a course entitled "Professionalism," at the New School for Social Research. The course failed. Goodman watched with mounting embarrassment as the journalist, the physician, the engineer, the architect, and other friends he brought to speak to the class were dismissed as "liars," "finks," and "mystifiers." If any teacher could count on receptive students in the 1960s it ought to have been the author of *Growing Up Absurd,* yet Goodman could not persuade his class even to take seriously what he thought was the premise of the course: That "professionals are autonomous individuals beholden to the nature of things and the judgment of their peers, and bound by an explicit or implicit oath to benefit their clients and the community."[1]

He knew, of course, that these words express an ideal and do not correspond in any simple way to the corrupt reality of professional life. But admitting that did him no good. The students were intent on showing that "every professional was co-opted by the System," that "every decision was made top-down by the power structure," and that professions were "conspiracies to make more money." Puzzled by their refusal to acknowledge the sincerity of his own critical standpoint, Goodman tried to get them to concede that however corrupt the professions might be, the tasks they performed were indispensable in any imaginable social order. The students replied that "it was important only to be human and all else will follow." "Suddenly," said Goodman, "I realized

First published in *New York Review of Books,* Oct. 13, 1977, 28–33. Reprinted with permission from *The New York Review of Books.* Copyright © 1977 Thomas Haskell.

that they did not really believe that there was a nature of things. Somehow all functions could be reduced to interpersonal relations and power. There was no knowledge, but only the sociology of knowledge." He knew then that he could no longer get through to them.[2]

The historian Burton Bledstein gives the ideal of the professional little more credence than did Goodman's students in the 1960s. His book *The Culture of Professionalism* is a history of the very ideals that Goodman took so seriously, but Bledstein believes that they were never anything more than a self-serving myth. After the sorry spectacle that lawyers presented during the Watergate affair, and a decade of Medicaid scandals and spiraling malpractice insurance costs for physicians, it becomes difficult to believe anything better of professionalism. Certainly within the university the snarling underside of professional scholarship is more plainly exposed to view in this era of retrenchment than it was a few years ago.

Whether organized professionals really help us to achieve insight into the "nature of things," as Goodman believed, is the question of paramount importance, but it holds little interest for Bledstein. What does interest him, almost to the exclusion of anything else, is the self-satisfaction that people derive from becoming "professional." His tendency to let the whole range of critical inquiry collapse into the single implicit question, "Are professions compatible with the ideal of equality?" is distinctly reminiscent of the cast of mind that Goodman found so frustrating in the 1960s. The resemblance ends there, however, for unlike Goodman's students Bledstein is a careful and sophisticated scholar. His argument is original, he builds it intelligently, and the result is a formidable reinterpretation of recent American history. He may go too far when he compares his interpretation with Charles Beard's account of the rise of industrial civilization or Frederick Jackson Turner's frontier thesis, but his confidence that he has hit on a new and important theme is not misplaced.

When reduced to a few sentences his thesis is deceptively simple. Bledstein believes that in America today life is organized by the habits and attitudes appropriate to a "culture of professionalism" that came into existence during the last half of the nineteenth century. The agent of this cultural transformation was a new middle class bent on making the world safe for its own characteristic obsessions with self-discipline, social control, and rational order. The main instrument of reform was the modern university, which began developing after the Civil War under the inspiration of German models and the leadership of such men as Daniel Coit Gilman of Johns Hopkins, Charles William Eliot of Harvard, and Andrew Dickson White of Cornell. Much of the book is devoted to these and other Victorian university presidents who Bledstein believes laid the institutional foundations for modern culture.

The "culture of professionalism" itself defies quick definition, but we all know people who exemplify it. They identify life with work and career, confident that merit will always find its true reward. They take what Bledstein feels is inordinate pride in the cool self-mastery that enables them to bring their talent and training to bear on challenging problems, thereby advancing themselves and serving society at the same time. What seems to puzzle Bledstein most about the adherents of this culture is their stern conviction that no matter how hierarchical their society may be, it is a just social order if it springs from an initial condition of formally equal opportunity.

If we set aside for the moment Bledstein's strictures against meritocracy, we find that his basic contention involves a relationship among the university, the middle class, and the professions so commonplace that at first glance it seems impossible to refute and hardly worth writing a book about. Everyone already knows that the university—whatever loftier purposes it may also serve—earns its keep by catering to middle-class students and acting as gatekeeper for the professions. All Bledstein wants to do is show historically how this quid pro quo among the middle class, the university, and the professions came about and examine its cultural implications. But customary social arrangements often take on a startling new aspect when seen in historical perspective, and the shock value of Bledstein's inquiry is doubly magnified by his insistence on the primacy of class. By treating both the university and the professions largely as expressions of class interest, he achieves a surprisingly fresh and unsettling perspective on higher education and professional life today. Even if Bledstein's argument finally is not entirely convincing, it is close enough to the mark that no one with a professional degree on the wall or a Ph.D. after their name will read this book without feeling uneasy.

The origins of the culture of professionalism date from the appearance of the middle class itself.[3] In the eighteenth century Americans spoke loosely of "middling classes" or "the middling sort," terms that referred to a broad range of farmers, artisans, shopkeepers, and other small property holders comprising perhaps 70 percent of the white population. These were people whose work changed little from one year to the next and whose social standing was likely to remain constant for a lifetime. Only in the nineteenth century did the more exact term, "middle class," come into use to reflect what Bledstein believes was a quite different social reality. Although the Oxford English Dictionary records the first use of the term in 1812, Bledstein argues that the watershed in America was in the 1830s and 1840s. By then the urban-industrial transformation was well under way, per capita income was rising steeply, and glaring inequalities in wealth were becoming a regular feature of the social landscape. The spread of labor-saving machinery was opening up new occupations in which wit and ingenuity counted for more than experience. Static rank in a local community no longer sufficed to define the identity of people who took mobility for granted and conceived of life as a series of ascending stages of wealth and prestige. It is immaterial for Bledstein's purposes that statistically mobility may have fallen short of expectations. In the popular imagination, "middle" no longer meant a fixed position; rather, says Bledstein, "it referred to the individual as 'escalator,' moving vertically between the floors of the poor and the rich."

As far as middle-class Americans could see, nothing prevented them from rising into the highest reaches of society but hard luck or their own inertia or lack of potential. By the same token, there was nothing to prevent them from plummeting to the bottom but their own anxious striving, for the same forces that swept away the old barriers of privilege also robbed people of the security of established status. Freer to make their own way in society than their ancestors had ever been, they were at once exhilarated and frightened. In this fluid and boundless social world the attribute most conducive to survival was a preoccupation with self so intense that there was little precedent for it in history. "The middle-class person was not merely self-reliant," says Bledstein, "he was absorbed in his own egoism." He desperately needed legitimation for his self-centeredness and got it from intellectuals such as Ralph Waldo Emerson, who gained fame on the lecture circuit by being a spokesman, as Bledstein puts it, "for the moral management of a calculated life."

The Victorian ideas of "character" and "career," to which Emerson contributed, were, according to Bledstein, middle-class inventions with a single purpose: to provide individual lives with the structure that tradition and community could no longer supply. The man of "character" so admired by the middle class possessed an inner psychological firmness that enabled him to resist pressure and rise above circumstance. In Bledstein's apt formulation, "Character was the deepest self of the man that bound together the whole of the individual." Corresponding to the inward coherence of character was the outward continuity of career, which ideally meant a "pre-established total pattern of organized professional activity, with upward movement through recognized preparatory stages, and advancement based on merit and bearing honor." People of strong character naturally dedicated themselves to careers, for they possessed what Bledstein calls a "vertical vision of life." The vertical vision blurred and attenuated all human relationships except those relevant to one's anticipated promotions and future professional development. It prevailed at the expense of human sympathy and communal solidarity. For example, in the everyday "horizontal" world the young university instructor and the policeman might live side by side in an eastern city and earn the same income; but as an aspiring professional scholar, the instructor thought "vertically" and identified himself not with his neighbor but exclusively with the successful senior people in his field—even if they ignored him or abused his trust or loaded him with drudge work at low pay. Eventually the policeman would adopt the vertical perspective and struggle to define his work as a profession too.

Having established the existence of a strong middle-class predisposition to overcome disorder and create structure, both within the person and in the world at large, Bledstein then tries to show how the university and the professions served this end. Professions did so, of course, by being consummate careers. More than any other occupation they offered the rootless middle-class person a strong sense of identity and an ample field for self-fulfillment in regular, ascending stages appropriate to the "vertical vision." By becoming professional, a person set himself apart from the crowd and gained the ability, within his specialized field, to look beneath surface appearances to the fundamental order of things. The pleasures of belonging to an elite were nicely tempered by the thought that his expertise was an unselfish, even democratic, service to the community.

Bledstein believes that the post–Civil War culture of professionalism embodied a more radical idea of individual autonomy than even Jacksonian democracy had dared to imagine. Yet even as professional careers released individual energy, they also crystallized it and gave definite form to a force that might otherwise have been anarchic. The conservative implications of professionalism were most obvious in the growing dependence of clients on professional advice. Bledstein presses hard on the theme of exploitation, emotional more than economic. "Professionals," he says, "succeeded by playing on the weakness of the client. . . . Perhaps no Calvinist system of thought ever made use of the insecurities of people more effectively than did the culture of professionalism." The tendency of professional practitioners to undermine their clients' self-confidence leads Bledstein to conclude that the culture of professionalism has taken "an inestimable toll on the integrity of individuals," even while it has fattened the ego of the professional expert himself.

Given the existence of vulnerable clients and a middle class destined to exploit them, it appears only natural from Bledstein's perspective that there should have occurred in the last third of the nineteenth century a vast multiplication of professional careers—as indeed there did. For reasons that will appear below, I doubt that clients were the passive victims that Bledstein's theory requires, or that bourgeois careerism was potent enough by itself to produce the startling expansion of professional expertise that followed the Civil War. But the fact of explosive growth is indisputable. By the 1880s and 1890s a renaissance was under way within the traditional professions of law and medicine, and new fields of expertise proliferated at an astounding rate. During these years, for example, the modern division of labor within the medical profession took shape as practitioners organized themselves according to specialties such as neurology, dermatology, laryngology, pediatrics, and so on. In the academic world the professional associations that still function today were formed in modern languages, history, economics, mathematics, physics, geology, forestry, chemical engineering, electrical engineering, and other fields. In these decades, as Bledstein says, "the citizen became a client whose obligation was to trust the professional. Legitimate authority now resided in special spaces, like the courtroom, the classroom, and the hospital; and it resided in special words shared only by experts." This was the dawn of what Ivan Illich calls "the age of professional dominance." Behind all these epoch-making events, Bledstein sees the restless ambition of the rising middle class:

> The professions as we know them today were the original achievement of Mid-Victorians who sought the highest form in which the middle class could pursue its primary goals of earning a good living, elevating both the moral and intellectual tone of society, and emulating the status of those above one on the social ladder.

Concerning the actual mundane details of building new professions and renovating old ones, Bledstein has surprisingly little to say. The man who almost single-handedly organized the American Bar Association in 1878, Simeon E. Baldwin of Yale Law School, is never mentioned in this book; neither are most of the other notable professionalizers, such as William H. Welch, who put American medicine on a scientific footing at Johns Hopkins, or Robert Thurston, first president of the American Society of Mechanical Engineers and organizer of the engineering curriculum at Cornell. Instead Bledstein concentrates on the men who presided over the creation of the modern American university, for it served as nursery for all the major professions. In addition to the three most famous university presidents, Gilman, Eliot, and White, he also discusses James McCosh of Princeton, Noah Porter of Yale, Frederick A. P. Barnard of Columbia, and Presidents Angell, Bascom, and Folwell of Michigan, Wisconsin, and Minnesota, respectively. These men were the ideologues of professionalism. In fact, what we have been calling the "culture of professionalism" is in essence little more than the utopian vision of a meritocratic society run by university graduates that these men projected in order to win support from prospective patrons, legislators, and popular audiences.

The Victorian university presidents remembered with special horror their own experiences as students in the "old-time colleges" before the Civil War. It was not only dull recitations and a stale curriculum that they were reacting against as they embarked on their movement to reform higher education; Andrew Dickson White also recalled

> the student brawl at the Harvard commons which cost the historian Prescott his sight, and the riot at the Harvard commencement which blocked the way of President Everett and the British minister . . . the fatal wounding of Tutor Dwight, the maiming of Tutor Goodrich, and the killing of two town rioters by students at Yale . . . the monstrous indignities to the president and faculty at Hobart of which I was myself a witness, as well as the state of things at various other colleges in my own college days.

Pandemonium swept through American college campuses time after time during the early decades of the nineteenth century, and Bledstein sees in this puzzling phenomenon telling evidence of a disjunction between the needs of the first generation of middle-class students and the strained capacities of institutions attuned to an older social order.

The old colleges offended the new class both by the unfocused, impractical character of the education they offered and also by their reliance on an external, authoritarian mode of discipline, erratically enforced. In contrast, the new university succeeded by taking advantage of the student's "vertical vision." It played on his ambition, grouped him exclusively with students of his own age, subjected him to regular tests, and reported his class standing or grade average to his parents at stated intervals. These devices had not been common in the old colleges. In 1790, when Harvard tried to introduce a required examination, students went on a rampage that emptied the examination room. Students became docile and took higher education seriously in the closing decades of the nineteenth century because by then they saw the college years as a vital stage in the most desirable careers. This was the student's prime opportunity to discipline himself for the competitive trials ahead, sharpen his mind, conquer laziness, learn to be patient.

Most important, the variety and rigor of the university experience helped the young person identify his special "strengths"—which is to say, the experience helped him decide within which career he might expect to rise highest.

Again Bledstein believes that Emerson (who was enormously popular among college students) articulated the guiding thought: "Nature arms each man with some faculty which enables him to do easily some feat impossible to any other, and this makes him necessary to society." Therefore, "each is bound to discover what his faculty is, to develop it, and to use it for the benefit of mankind." A similar dictum was put forward in France by Emile Durkheim in grimmer and more revealing language: "The categorical imperative of the moral conscience is assuming the following form: *Make yourself usefully fulfill a determinate function.*"[4]

Bledstein's analysis thus substitutes the university for the Chamber of Commerce as the representative institution of bourgeois society, and self-esteem for profits as the driving force of modern historical development. These curious twists become especially clear near the end of his book when he contrasts his view of the university to Thorstein Veblen's. Veblen attributed the failings of the American university to the corrupting influence of the industrial tycoons who held it in trust and the businesslike "captains of erudition" who administered it. Their sin was to market education like a commodity and to judge scholarship by its cash value.

Bledstein puts the matter in a different light by erasing the line that Veblen drew between cynical business practices and high-minded professional ones. In his view the tragic flaw of the American university is not the commercialism that seeps in from outside, but the professionalism that is deliberately cultivated within. "On the basis of the present study," says Bledstein, "it would surely seem obvious that Veblen and his followers grossly overestimated the idealistic disinterestedness of professional behavior in American life, including that of the 'scholarly' American professor. . . . Neither praise nor blame for the direction of higher education in America can be leveled at the traditional villain, the business community . . . . No, a far more powerful element is at work here. From the beginning the ego-satisfying pretensions of professionalism have been closer to the heart of the middle-class American than the raw profits of capitalism."

It is easy, and not inaccurate, to complain that this book is one-sided. Bledstein shows little interest in the genuine benefits professionalism sometimes has brought, and he never seriously considers what it would mean for us today to try to do without professional experts. His animus against things professional is so sweeping that it leads him to the brink of hypocrisy. One cannot help wondering what undisclosed loophole permits this professional teacher and historian to escape from his own strictures against the innately parasitic and self-inflating ways of professional people. The work of lawyers, physicians, engineers, and architects can hardly be any more egotistical than "giving" lectures or writing books. In fact, if we readers were to take Bledstein's very severe ethical standpoint to heart, there would be nothing to prevent us from condemning *The Culture of Professionalism* as a self-serving display of scholarly virtuosity, designed, all too obviously, to advance its author's professional career. To do so would be most unfair, but for reasons that Bledstein is loath to examine.

On the other hand, the existing literature on the rise of the university and the "achievement of professional standards" in various fields is larded with self-congratulation; by stressing the costs of professionalization, Bledstein may help to right the balance, even though he does not tell the whole story. Who among us does not know someone who is too professional? In every field one finds people obsessed with the pursuit of arcane professional honors, intolerant of all disciplines but their own, cut off by their expertise from basic human interests and sympathies, or perhaps even intellectually crippled by premature loyalty to the doctrines of an overpowering mentor. The costs of professionalism have been real, and Bledstein exposes them brilliantly.

A more serious criticism must be directed against the extraordinary historical creativity and force that Bledstein assigns to the new middle class of the nineteenth century. His thesis rests heavily on this point. What he professes to explain is the rise of the modern university, the emergence of the culture of professionalism, and the origins of the towering edifice of institutionalized expertise that looms over contemporary society. The cause of all these developments he finds in the hunger for order, discipline, and self-fulfillment that he believes was characteristic of the new middle class. Even though Bledstein opens his book with a definition of "middle class," I have put off mentioning it until now because his thesis appears strongest as long as one relies on a loose, commonsensical understanding of the term. Closer examination reveals it to be untenable. Bledstein reviews the many and generally incoherent uses to which the term has been put by American historians, takes note of sociological surveys like the one in *Fortune* magazine in 1940, which found that 79.2 percent of Americans regarded themselves as middle class, and then, just as one hopes that he is about to introduce some clear thinking into this farrago, he offers the following sequence of progressively vaguer definitional statements:

> The middle-class person in America owns an acquired skill or cultivated talent by means of which to provide a service . . . he does not view his "ability" as a commodity, an external resource, like the means of production or manual labor. . . .
>
> Historically, the middle class in America has defined itself in terms of three

characteristics: acquired ability, social prestige, and a life style approaching an individual's aspirations. Neither restrictions of income nor even differences between occupations have delimited the scope of the middle class in America.

Finally, as if to confirm that this drift into the haze is deliberate, he says:

> Being middle class in America has referred to a state of mind any person can adopt and make his own. It has not referred to a person's confined position in the social structure, a position delimited by common chances in the market and by preferred occupations.

By adopting a mainly subjective and psychological definition of "middle class," Bledstein allows his thesis to approach perilously close to perfect circularity. Since the "culture of professionalism" is itself largely a state of mind, we cannot get very far in explaining its emergence and historical significance by saying that the people who brought it forth are identifiable only by virtue of another state of mind that they share — especially if the two states of mind, one defining "middle class" and the other defining the "culture of professionalism," overlap extensively. The explanatory power of the concept of class ordinarily derives from the reduction of complex thought and behavior to economic interest. But Bledstein expressly denies that his "middle class" is composed of people who share a certain relationship either to the market or to the mode of production. They are, in fact, simply the neither-rich-nor-poor who labor in what economists call the "service sector" of the economy.

It is no mere oversight that leads Bledstein into these difficulties of definition. Anyone who wishes to write about the new middle class must contend with the possibility that the subject is an empty category with no real existence outside the minds of academicians. This possibility was not denied even by Emil Lederer and Jakob Marschak, the social theorists who gave prominence to the idea of a "new middle class" in a well-known 1926 essay. They, like Bledstein, wished to account for the salaried white-collar employees, ranging from mere clerks and salesmen to lawyers and industrial managers, whose growing numbers upset the original socialist expectation that society would be split between propertied entrepreneurs and unpropertied proletarians. No one doubts that such middling people exist, only whether they are sufficiently bound together by mutual interest and sympathy to constitute a class. Lederer and Marschak conceded at the outset that the group's membership was so diverse that it could be "comprehended as an entity only in contra-distinction to the other classes."[5] In his book *White Collar* (1951), C. Wright Mills described it as a passive and fragmented group, lacking any independent way of life, ordinarily too disorganized to act, and capable of no more than a "tangle of unconnected contests" at best. "Whatever history they have had is a history without events; whatever common interests they have do not lead to unity; whatever future they have will not be of their own making."[6] Eight years later, Ralf Dahrendorf concluded that in spite of all the efforts of sociologists to clarify the position and significance of the class, "there is no word in any modern language to describe this group that is no group, class that is no class, and stratum that is no stratum. . . . It neither has been nor is it ever likely to be a class in any sense of this term."[7] Far from refuting these weighty opinions, Bledstein never mentions them.

In order to hold this heterogeneous mass of people together long enough to write a book demonstrating their inconsequentiality, Mills let the lowest and most numerous ranks of the new middle class, the mere clerks and salespeople, stand for all the rest. An incautious reader of his account is likely to forget that prosperous lawyers and corporate vice presidents wear white collars too. Bledstein, who is eager to create the opposite impression that the class has historical force and a coherent culture, turns Mills's white-collar group on its head, letting the professional elite stand for the whole. He defines "professional" so broadly that almost everyone is included, and those who are not are assumed to be busily upgrading their occupation so as to become professional someday.

By treating all claims to professional status with equal seriousness, Bledstein hopelessly entangles whatever may be culturally valuable in the idea of a profession with what is patently pretentious and fraudulent. In these pages neurosurgeons are not distinguished from tree surgeons; "professional" football players and beauticians stand on an equal footing with chemists, architects, and aeronautical engineers. The first profession mentioned, on page 4, is mortuary science. Pinkerton detectives are said to exemplify the intimidating authority that a profession can wield. Incongruously interspersed with these pseudo professions are an equal number of references to authentic ones, whose work possibly does require the extended training, mastery of esoteric bodies of knowledge, and mutual discipline and support that the professional mode of occupational organization affords. Bledstein seems unwilling to admit such differences, lest his idea of the middle class fall apart.

Nor is this the only contortion Bledstein goes through in order to give the middle class a commanding position. He gives as leading examples of "professional trends" in the late nineteenth century such curious developments as the mass distribution of books by subscription, the organization of the nation's first lecture bureau, the formation of the first pro baseball team, and the first running of the Kentucky Derby. He also understands professionalization to include certain "novel uses of space and protective boundaries to regulate the social experience of the individual." By this elastic standard almost everything exemplifies the professional trend. Specifically, he has in mind the division of space into public parks, private homes, and civic buildings; the allocation of leisure time to special places like baseball diamonds, golf courses, and football gridirons; and the sorting out of words into specialized publications like *Bicycling World,* or technical vocabularies like that of bridge building. This "structuring of space and words," he says, "belonged to a larger process: the professionalization of American lives."

Now all these things certainly happened; they were vital elements in an important cultural transformation, and Bledstein's account of them is extremely perceptive — quite possibly the best we have. But we gain nothing by calling them examples of "professionalization." It would be far more accurate to say that all of these developments *and* professionalization are manifestations of a still larger process, which Max Weber called "rationalization," the ominous tendency in European civilization for impersonal calculations of least cost and maximum efficiency to enter, and finally dominate, every sphere of life. The only thing the founding of the American Bar Association has in common with the running of the first Kentucky Derby or the sale of books by subscription is that all three represent steps toward the systematic exploitation, or rationalization, of nationwide markets for particular services that previously had been confined to local markets by the slow speed and high cost of transportation. Bledstein's awkward efforts to stretch "professionalization" to embrace every new refinement of the division of labor — and, for that matter, every advance of rational order of any kind — is obfuscating, and merely testifies to the superiority of Weber's formulation. There would be no need for this inflation of terms if Bledstein were not trying to make professionalism serve as the cultural keystone of the entire middle class.

Still another difficulty arises from Bledstein's conception of the middle class. Because he stresses the class interest underlying professionalism so heavily, his discussion of exploitation has a robust Marxian flavor to it. But in Marxian theory the concept of exploitation derives its force from the clear separation of the exploiters and the exploited into two different, mutually exclusive, classes. If we ask whom Bledstein's middle-class professionals exploit, the answer is their clients, who obviously do not constitute a distinct class. Nor are clients likely, on the average, to stand much lower in the social order than the professional people who "exploit" them, for the most common criticism of professionals has always been that they confine their clientele to the affluent. No doubt professional people do overcharge clients, intimidate them, and cultivate emotional dependencies, and we may wish to call these practices "exploitation." But contrary to the impression conveyed by Bledstein, this form of exploitation is not typically a class phenomenon. The most objectionable offense remains denial of services to the poor, which certainly is a class phenomenon, but about which Bledstein's analysis is silent.

The way out of these difficulties is not to abandon Bledstein's important achievement, but to modify it in two major ways. The first is to demote the middle class to a lesser position and look instead to the most dynamic elements within it. The struggle to modernize higher education and extend the orbit of institutionalized expertise in American culture did not pit the middle class against the rest of the population: it pitted a small, cultivated, forward-looking gentry elite against the inert middle class and nearly everyone else. The university presidents Bledstein discusses were important spokesmen for this elite, and historians have only recently begun recovering the names of others.[8]

The second way one might modify Bledstein's analysis is simply to recognize that professional people are not exempt from the laws of supply and demand. They cannot derive an income from their expertise unless there is a demand for it. Like any producer of goods or services, of course, they have a limited ability to stimulate the demand for their work; but it would be fatuous to suppose that they can create demand out of thin air. Consequently, any major expansion of professional services such as the one we are concerned with could not have happened without an intensification of the demand for those services. Moreover, the increase of demand must have preceded or at least been concurrent with the increase of supply: while it is possible for increases of demand to occur first and bring about increases of supply, the reverse is inconceivable.

This means that the central question Bledstein poses in *The Culture of Professionalism* needs to be supplemented, or perhaps even replaced, by another. Bledstein asks, in effect, "What happened in the nineteenth century to increase the supply of professional services?" He finds the answer in the emergence of a new class of people who are psychologically predisposed to seek the order and other gratifications of a professional career. But it is easy to imagine that an ample supply of people eager to pursue remunerative and prestigious careers existed long before the nineteenth century. The decisive changes probably occurred on the side of demand, rather than supply, and the pertinent question for the historian is: What happened in the nineteenth century to increase the number of people willing and able to pay for professional advice? The answer in part is obvious: urbanization and the rising level of income associated with the industrial revolution made the advice of specialists accessible and affordable to more people. Demand was also stimulated by real advances of knowledge in some fields. The germ theory of disease, for example, produced a quantum leap in the utility of the advice that physicians and surgeons sold to their patients.

Finally, and most generally, it must be recalled that modern society involves the individual in relationships both with other human beings and with physical nature that are vastly more complex than those his ancestors before the nineteenth century ever had to contend with. If modern man displays an alarming tendency to defer thoughtlessly to expert opinion, it is largely because alternative guides to conduct such as common sense and the customary ways of his local community have long since failed him in important areas of life. The Victorians treasured Emerson's advice to "trust thyself," but they could not live by it and neither can we. The conditions of modern society place a high premium on esoteric knowledge, especially when it comes stamped with the special authority of an organized community of practitioners who police each other's opinions and thereby create something approaching a consensus of the competent. To explain fully the special authority that now inheres in a consensus of the most competent investigators would require a general inquiry into the intellectual consequences of the vast social and economic transformation that occurred in America during the nineteenth century, but nothing less will explain the rise of the expert to his present position of dominance.

Few developments from the Civil War to the present stand out so vividly or account for so much of the shape of modern America as the growth of the professions and the steady retreat of the lay public before the ever-expanding claims of professional expertise. Bledstein is right to insist on the extraordinary significance of this course of events, and his evocation of the subjective meaning that professionalism held for people of the Victorian era is an extremely important contribution to historical understanding. But by attributing this major cultural transformation merely to the careerist ambitions of the middle class, he obscures its most important causes and underestimates the degree to which the objective conditions of life that prevail in modern society make us dependent on expert knowledge. One may lament this fact, but not ignore it.

The point is the same one Paul Goodman tried to defend in the 1960s. Bledstein belatedly acknowledges its force at the very end of his book. "The question for Americans," he says, should be "How does society make professional behavior accountable to the public without curtailing the independence upon which creative skills and the imaginative use of knowledge depend?" That question implies what the preceding three hundred pages of *The Culture of Professionalism* seem to deny: that professionalism can be highly conducive to creativity, and that the public demand for what is created under its auspices is, for the most part, genuine. The professions today are corrupt and deserve unrelenting criticism and reform, but their claim to be mankind's best means of cultivating and preserving insight into the "nature of things" ought to be taken seriously.

CHAPTER FOUR

Professionalism versus Capitalism

Tawney, Durkheim, and C. S. Peirce on the Disinterestedness of Professional Communities

Consider these two statements about the disinterestedness of professional people. The first was published by R. H. Tawney in *The Acquisitive Society* (1920):

> A profession may be defined most simply as a trade which is organized, incompletely, no doubt, but genuinely, for the performance of function. It is not simply a collection of individuals who get a living for themselves by the same kind of work. Nor is it merely a group which is organized exclusively for the economic protection of its members, though that is normally among its purposes. It is a body of men who carry on their work in accordance with rules designed to enforce certain standards both for the better protection of its members and for the better service of the public.

The second statement was published by Randall Collins in *The Credential Society* (1979):

> The rise of the professions in America, then, is an extension of the age-old struggles of self-interested groups using refinements of traditional tactics. They do not represent the technical needs of a new technocratic society.
>
> What of altruism? . . . The altruistic professions, in fact, are among the high-

I gratefully acknowledge receipt of very useful criticism from Martin Wiener, Patrick Leary, Dorothy Ross, David Hollinger, and two anonymous referees—none of whom, of course, is responsible for the final form of this essay.

First published in *The Authority of Experts: Studies in History and Theory*, ed. Thomas L. Haskell (Bloomington: Indiana University Press, 1984), 180–225.

est paid, and their "altruism" gives a further payoff in the form of status and deference.

A better explanation of professional's altruistic codes of ethics is that they are defenses against the potential distrust of their clients. . . . Esteem is a goal like any other. Usually it goes along with a desire for power, especially over the reality-constructing activities of other people's minds. . . . Altruism per se is just as much a part of the conflicts that make up most of history as violence and property.

Only sixty years separate Tawney's *The Acquisitive Society* from Collins's *The Credential Society,* yet the form of the title is all the two books of social criticism have in common. In their diagnoses of what ails society they are poles apart. Tawney thought the root social problem was acquisitiveness. To cure it he proposed the professionalization of all occupations. Tawney's cure is now Collins's problem. Tawney thought he saw in the professions a way of life that lifted people out of their baser selves and enabled them unselfishly to serve their fellow human beings. Collins regards the professional credentialing process as only another form of self-aggrandizement and proposes to abolish it. So complete is the failure of communication that Collins never mentions Tawney and is apparently unaware that his analysis exactly reverses that of an earlier generation of reformers.

It is difficult today to take seriously Tawney's premise: the idea that people in professions characteristically subordinate self-interest to higher ends — the truth, the public interest, the welfare of individual clients, the quality of the work itself — and thereby stand on a higher moral plane than those who merely truck and trade in the marketplace. The image of the disinterested professional lingers on, but reactions to it range from mild skepticism to curt dismissal.[1] Some modern writers regard it as a harmless myth, possessing like all myths a grain of truth and serviceable as an ideal, perhaps, but certainly not an adequate representation of the actual motives of most professionals, most of the time. Others share Collins's hostile conviction that professionals are wolves in sheep's clothing, monopolists who live by the rule of Caveat emptor, but lack the integrity to admit it.

The skepticism that Tawney's benign view of the professions arouses in modern readers reflects more than the limitations of one man's vision or the flaws in a particular scheme of reform. It reflects also the decay and, within the past several decades, the virtual extinction among serious thinkers of a set of assumptions about the moral superiority of professional careers that once enjoyed extremely wide acceptance. Why have these once prevalent assumptions fallen into disrepute? How can our generation dismiss out-of-hand convictions that a recent generation, no more foolish than ours, found so compelling? Can we in fact confront and demonstrate the inadequacy of the strongest theoretical justifications of professionalism advanced by Tawney and his contemporaries? What exactly was it that sustained their faith?

These are the questions this essay is meant to answer. I pose them in connection with a close reading of the relevant writings of three men who took the idea of professional disinterestedness with utmost seriousness. The first of these is, of course, R. H. Tawney, British economic historian and member of the Fabian Society from 1906 to 1933. The second is the French sociologist Emile Durkheim, whose independently formulated plan for reforming society through professionalization bears a surprisingly close resemblance to Tawney's. The third figure is the American "pragmaticist" philosopher, Charles S. Peirce, whose communal theory of truth emerged from much the same context as Tawney's and Durkheim's ideas, and who shared many of their assumptions, but who put those assumptions to decidedly different uses and never conceived of professionalization as a general remedy for greed. I have tried sympathetically to reconstruct the thought of these three men and the circumstances that shaped their perspective. My aim in doing so is not to gain a fresh hearing for their claim of professional disinterestedness, which I think is more nearly wrong than right, but to explore the meaning and implications of an important discontinuity in the history of intellect.

These three figures were not isolated or idiosyncratic thinkers. Although Tawney and Durkheim drew out of the premise of professional disinterestedness a bold program of social reform to which comparatively few people subscribed, and although Peirce put a version of the same premise to careful philosophical uses that only small numbers of people read, the premise itself was very widely accepted in the late nineteenth and early twentieth century. Among sociologists, the scholars most concerned about the nature of professions and their relation to other occupations, it was an unchallenged article of faith. My search of American sociological literature beginning in the 1890s reveals no direct challenge to the idea that professional people were less selfish than businessmen until 1939, when Talcott Parsons published his first essay on the subject.[2] As late as 1933, when A. M. Carr-Saunders and P. A. Wilson published their magisterial volume on the professions in England, their supreme confidence in the disinterestedness of the professions did not seem in the least controversial, for within the academic world the professions had no enemies, nor even critics worth mentioning. The authors took Tawney's premise for granted and asserted without any fear of contradiction that "the family, the church, the universities, certain associations of intellectuals, and above all the great professions, stand like rocks against which the waves [of uninformed public opinion] beat in vain."[3]

Since our three figures chose to articulate and explore the ramifications of a presupposition about the moral superiority of professional careers that was widely shared in their day, the question naturally arises, For whom were they speaking? It is a difficult question and does not admit of any incontrovertible answer. Precisely because I do not wish to be detained by the controversies that swirl about it, my own assumptions had better be spelled out at the beginning. One way to answer the question is to say that Tawney, Durkheim, and Peirce were spokesmen for a class of "brain workers," or intellectuals in the broadest sense. The invidious distinction they drew between the morality of businessmen and that of their own, largely professional, class then appears as an ideological weapon, an instrument of class rivalry. From this vantage point, the myth of professional disinterestedness can be seen as a classic expression of the claim made by every ascending class that its values are universal and its triumph will serve the interests of all mankind. One can even argue that the antagonism between capitalists and intellectuals is essentially a conflict between two types of capital, the one monetary, the other cultural in character. The antecedents of this interpretation can be traced all the way back to Marx, and it has been greatly strengthened in recent years by scholars such as Eric Hobsbawm, Harold Perkin, Alvin Gouldner, Barbara Ehrenreich and John Ehrenreich, and George Konrad and Ivan Szelenyi, some of whose work will be touched on in the following discussion.[4]

I find this interpretation very tempting and think that historians ought to pay far more attention to it than they have. But in this essay I do not adopt it, or in any case the argument I present is such a severely modified version of it that its proponents will quite properly wish to disown me. I have two major reservations. The first is familiar to anyone who has ever tried to use the concept of class. On what grounds can we lump together such diverse social types as poets and technicians, professors and white-collar corporate managers, engineers and government bureaucrats, lawyers and chemists, and treat them all as a single entity with identifiable interests and a common destiny? Alvin Gouldner's answer, that "classes as such are never united" but serve instead as "cache areas" in which elite organizations recruit support and build legitimacy, almost persuades me, but only because it leaves such a thin line between class analysis and conventional studies of elite leadership.[5]

My second objection is that this assemblage of social types has not displayed the minimal instinct for self-preservation that one would expect of a class. Its path is not upward toward supremacy, but sideways toward fragmentation and dispersal. The feeling of kinship and solidarity among the various groups said to compose it was far greater during the first three decades of the twentieth century than at any time since, and its internal cohesion plummeted to a nadir in the 1970s that seems beyond remedy. Not even a class with a distinctively critical culture of the sort that Gouldner describes can be expected to survive internal criticism as severe as that which university scholars directed at the other professions during the 1960s and 1970s.[6]

Rather than seek out the subtle bonds that link poets to technicians, or the exotic strategies that advance a class toward dominion through an orgy of self-criticism, I am content to treat Tawney, Durkheim, and Peirce simply as spokesmen for a movement, with all the temporal boundedness and uncertainty of social origin that word suggests. The movement may also have been a chapter in the history of a class, but that remains to be proven, and it is not the task I have undertaken here.

The common thread that I see running through the work of Tawney, Durkheim, Peirce, and many other intellectuals of the period 1850–1930, which justifies us in speaking of a movement, is a deep-felt revulsion against certain libertarian excesses that they thought were inherent in the culture of capitalism. In a manner that Philip Rieff argues is typical of pre-Freudian cultural elites, these intellectuals defined their public role not in terms of release and liberation, but in terms of control and the maintenance of institutional constraints on individual choice and action.[7] Their role was traditional, but they carried it out with the legendary zeal that we now identify with the Victorian generation because they felt the cultural balance tipping rapidly against them. The principal destabilizing force, I suggest, was the relentless advance of the capitalist market, with its rule of uninhibited competition and celebration of each competitor's right to be the sole proper judge of his own interests. In spite of strenuous efforts by even its most ardent friends to restrict the principle of laissez-faire to economic affairs alone, that philosophy tended continually to spill over into adjacent areas of life, where its message seemed only too clear: now everything is permitted. Where would liberation stop if the entire social universe was given over to competing selves, none acknowledging any standard higher than his or her own desires?

In response to this alarming prospect, there developed among intellectuals a phenomenon whose less intellectual manifestations were described by Karl Polanyi in *The Great Transformation* — a "countermovement," directed against the market and against the radical subordination of society and politics to economic priorities that the policy of laissez-faire entailed. Polanyi argued that "for a century the dynamics of modern society was governed by a double movement":

The market expanded continuously but this movement was met by a counter-movement checking the expansion in definite directions. Vital though such a countermovement was for the protection of society, in the last analysis it was incompatible with the self-regulation of the market, and thus with the market system itself.

That system developed in leaps and bounds; it engulfed space and time. . . . By the time it reached its maximum extent, around 1914, every part of the globe, all its inhabitants and unborn generations, physical persons as well as huge fictitious bodies called corporations, were comprised in it. A new way of life spread over the planet with a claim to universality unparalleled since the age when Christianity started out on its career, only this time the movement was on a purely material level.

Yet simultaneously a countermovement was on foot. This was more than the usual defensive behavior of a society faced with change; it was a reaction against a dislocation which attacked the fabric of society, and which would have destroyed the very organization of production that the market had called into being.[8]

The countermovement Polanyi described was profoundly ambiguous. It was directed against the harshest consequences of the rule of the market, not against capitalism itself. In aiming only to check the excesses of market society, it domesticated the market and ensured its survival. At one extreme Polanyi's countermovement took shape as revolutionary socialism, but he realized that it also took the form of centralized banking measures designed to save little capitalists from big ones. Polanyi did not regard it as a class contest: "the fate of classes," he observed, "is much more often determined by the needs of society than the fate of society is determined by the needs of classes." The general tendency of the countermovement was collectivist, yet its advance depended not on the spread of a preference for socialism or nationalism, but simply on the widening circle of vital interests throughout society that were endangered by the utopian principle of laissez-faire. The major institutional outcome of the countermovement was the welfare state, which characteristically opposes capitalism just enough to make it electorally acceptable.[9]

The intellectual phase of the countermovement that Tawney, Durkheim, and Peirce spoke for was equally ambiguous in its attitude toward capitalism. It seldom aimed at the destruction of the existing economic order, or even a return to premarket conditions. The more common aim is best described in Rieff's terms: simply to throw weight on the side of control, so as to restrain what was felt to be a headlong plunge toward release. Efforts among intellectuals to right the cultural balance took the form of a nagging preoccupation with the problem of self-interest and a quest for some means of *establishing authority*, of finding some sound basis on which to erect a criterion superior to individual desires and capable of passing judgment on them. The goal, in short, was to do what utilitarianism, as interpreted first by orthodox "Manchester" economists, and then after the 1870s by the marginal utility theorists, said could not be done—dethrone the principle of self-interest in human affairs, bringing it back into relation with the demands of morality.[10]

This was the context within which professionalism appeared to be a promising corrective, or even antithesis, to capitalism. Stunned by the suddenness of economic change, the reformers depicted the backdrop of commerce and industry as a scene of such unrelieved selfishness that once the professional was thrust into the foreground he could hardly fail to look selfless in comparison. Because it was economic novelty against which they were reacting, they virtually confined the meaning of self-interest to pecuniary accumulation, and averted their eyes from the nonpecuniary forms of self-aggrandizement more characteristic of the professions. Since the market "released" individuals from what were perceived as healthy and proper social obligations, the reformers identified capitalism with individualism, and morality with the restoration of communal bonds. On all counts, the professions seemed to offer solutions to the problem of self-interest, and for that reason professionalization could seem a cultural reform of vital importance.

Some of the friendliest things any serious scholar has ever said about the professions were set forth by the economic historian R. H. Tawney in *The Acquisitive Society* in 1920. That this extravagant praise of professionalism should appear in the most influential (though untypical) English-language socialist tract of the 1920s is warning enough that Tawney's views are easy to misunderstand when removed from their context. What do socialism and professionalism have in common? Precious little today, but everything of consequence for Tawney: Both promised to contain economic individualism and thereby to rescue industrial society from impending moral bankruptcy.

Tawney was a moralist whose deepest roots were religious. When he graduated from Oxford in 1903 he went to live in Toynbee Hall in London's East End. Several years of charity work convinced him that structural change, not preaching or philanthropy, was what the workingman needed, but he never abandoned a Christian framework of values.[11] Unlike many English radicals of his generation, he was not attracted to communism in the 1930s. What disturbed him most deeply, even in the depression decade, was "idolatry of wealth," that "chief enemy of the life of the spirit," which had itself been elevated into a "religion" in capitalist society.[12] Like Matthew Arnold, he felt himself to be surrounded by confusion and anarchy, and he searched for new and more compelling sources of authority. "Modern industry," he said, "has no body of ethical doctrine to control our crude instinct to believe that success is its own justification. . . . The existing social order is Macchiavellian [*sic*] in the sense of rewarding successful and unscrupulous cunning. It is inhuman in the sense of using men as means—'hands'—not as ends. It is pagan in its exaltation of strength, its contemptuous crushing of the weak. . . . They [the capitalists] are essentially a conquering race." [13]

In all of Tawney's thinking, there is no sharper division than that which separates the pursuit of Mammon from service to one's fellow man. His horror of the banality and selfishness of life in capitalist society was intensified by the experience of World War I. Declining a commission, he spent the war years in France and was impressed with a certain transcendent quality in the French which he attributed to the "charm of the opening years of the revolution," that brief moment when "masses of Frenchmen were really disinterested enthusiasts." In the words of his biographer, the mobilization for war and the sight of an entire population working for the common good instead of self-aggrandizement provided Tawney with a "paradigm, however imperfect, of the principle of social function at work." [14]

For Tawney the industrial problem was fundamentally a moral one, "a problem of learning as a community to reprobate certain courses of conduct and to approve others." He conceded that his trust in the power of values to shape behavior would be thought "moonshine" by some, but he took heart from the extraordinary change of sensibility wrought by the antislavery movement at the beginning of the nineteenth century. To help bring about a similarly radical shift of public sentiment regarding the new "immoralities of modern industry" was the aim of his extensive labors before the war as a writer and activist for the Worker's Education Association and the Labour Party. [15] At war's end he was catapulted into national prominence and given an opportunity to pursue the same goal in a much larger arena by his appointment along with Sidney Webb and several others to represent the labor point of view on the Royal Commission on Coal Mines. The commission was created in response to a threatened strike, and its every session was followed closely by the press. Tawney performed brilliantly, cutting through the mineowners' arguments and pounding away on the theme of "functionless property," which he was simultaneously developing in *The Acquisitive Society*.

The argument of *The Acquisitive Society* was built on a distinction between rights and functions. "A function," wrote Tawney near the beginning of the book, "may be defined as an activity which embodies and expresses the idea of social purpose. The essence of it is that the agent does not perform it merely for personal gain or to gratify himself, but recognizes that he is responsible for its discharge to some higher authority." For the idea of function to control behavior, individuals must believe in collective purposes that embrace and transcend all private interests. During the eighteenth century both Church and State abdicated their traditional roles in the maintenance of such a sense of purpose, leaving behind only corrupt and repressive institutional shells that were visibly obsolete and cried out for the destruction that was soon visited upon them. Into the vacuum created by their collapse moved the principle of individual rights. Rights had once been understood to be contingent privileges, granted for the sake of carrying out functions related to the divine will or the national welfare. But now rights, including especially the rights of property, were held to derive from Nature and to be unconditional in character. "The essence of the change," said Tawney, "was the disappearance of the idea that social institutions and economic activities were related to common ends, which gave them their significance and served as their criterion."[16]

The consequence of divorcing rights from social functions and treating rights as the constitutive force that brought the social organism itself into being was the emergence of the "acquisitive society." The acquisitive society is one devoted to nothing higher than the material happiness of individuals, one in which those who possess property are seen as the natural governors of those who do not, one that "has the whole modern world under its spell" because it assures people that "there are no ends other than their ends, no law other than their desires, no limit other than that which they think advisable." To end what he regarded as a monstrous refusal to acknowledge human limitations, Tawney called for people once again to regard themselves "not as the owners of rights, but as trustees for the discharge of functions and the instruments of a social purpose" (30–31, 51).

To reintroduce purpose into people's lives, weld rights back onto functions, and stem the tide of acquisitiveness, Tawney proposed the remarkably simple solution of professionalizing all occupations. That was the point of the passage with which we began:

> The application to industry of the principle of purpose is simple, however difficult it may be to give effect to it. It is to turn it into a Profession. A Profession may be defined most simply as a trade which is organized, incompletely no doubt, but genuinely, for the performance of function. It is not simply a collection of individuals who get a living for themselves by the same kind of work. Nor is it merely a group which is organized exclusively for the economic protection of its members, though that is normally among its purposes. It is a body of

men who carry on their work in accordance with rules designed to enforce certain standards both for the better protection of its members and for the better service of the public. (92)

Tawney was not naive. He knew that the power of corporate bodies, professional or otherwise, was susceptible to abuse. Before the war he had expressed concern about the inegalitarian consequences of the "existing monopoly of higher education." Oxford, Cambridge, and the bar all exemplified, he said, "how syndicalist management fosters corporate selfishness." The consequence of state management of the Church of England, he felt, was a deadening of spiritual life.[17] Still, he put all his bets on the professions as a model of occupational autonomy and responsible self-management that everyone should imitate. His willingness to take this risk testifies to the extreme revulsion he felt toward the uninhibited pursuit of self-interest. It also testifies to a confidence in the power of ideals to shape behavior that is rare in our more cynical era, however common in Tawney's.

> The difference between industry as it exists today and a profession is, then, simple and unmistakable. The essence of the former is that its only criterion is the financial return which it offers to its shareholders. The essence of the latter, is that, though men enter it for the sake of livelihood, the measure of their success is the service which they perform, not the gains which they amass. They may, as in the case of a successful doctor, grow rich; but the meaning of their profession, both for themselves and for the public, is not that they make money but that they make health, or safety, or knowledge, or good government or good law. They depend on it for their income, but they do not consider that any conduct which increases their income is on that account good. . . .
>
> So, if they are doctors, they recognize that there are certain kinds of conduct which cannot be practised, however large the fee offered for them, because they are unprofessional; if scholars and teachers, that it is wrong to make money by deliberately deceiving the public, as is done by makers of patent medicines, however much the public may clamor to be deceived; if judges or public servants, that they must not increase their incomes by selling justice for money; if soldiers, that the service comes first, and their private inclinations, even the reasonable preference of life to death, second. Every country has its traitors, every army its deserters, and every profession its blacklegs. To idealize the professional spirit would be very absurd; it has its sordid side, and, if it is to be fostered in industry, safeguards will be needed to check its excesses. But there is all the difference between maintaining a standard which is occasionally abandoned, and affirming as the central truth of existence that there is no standard to maintain.[18]

Tawney's use of the professions as a scourge against businessmen was anything but original. The polemic bite of *The Acquisitive Society* derived not
from its novelty but from its conformity to a set of cultural conventions that
had flourished in England for nearly a century and that has been amply inves-
tigated by Raymond Williams, Harold Perkin, Martin Wiener, Sheldon Rothblatt, and others.[19] As early as 1825, *Blackwood's* magazine complained that "the
Philosophers . . . are getting up what they are pleased to call a New Aristocracy—an Aristocracy of Science [which] is to be the enemy and ruler of the old
one." Coleridge identified all that was civilized with "the *Clerisy* of the nation,"
comprehending "the learned of all denominations," and Carlyle called attention to a new "Aristocracy of Talent" made up of pamphleteers, journalists,
politicians, and political economists.[20] Matthew Arnold could discern by 1868
a major split within the English middle class between its professional and business components, the former embracing intellectuals, proud of its "governing
qualities," disdainful of business, and eager to identify itself with the aristocracy. When Ruskin wanted to chastise businessmen, it was the professions he
held out as a model. In words that strongly anticipate Tawney he argued that
the merchant's or manufacturer's task, properly understood, was "to provide
for the nation": "It is no more his function to get profit for himself out of
that provision than it is a clergyman's function to get his stipend. This stipend
is a due and necessary adjunct, but not the object of his life, if he be a true
clergyman, any more than his fee (or honorarium) is the object of life to a true
physician."[21]

The professional man's claim of moral supremacy appears in Harold Perkin's analysis as a weapon in a complex rivalry of classes, a contest in which
professionals initially were spokesmen for other interests but then asserted
with mounting confidence a social ideal of their own. "Their ideal society
was a functional one based on expertise and selection by merit," says Perkin.
"For them trained and qualified expertise rather than property, capital or
labour, should be the chief determinant and justification of status and power
in society." Their vision increasingly brought them into opposition to laissez-
faire policies, and Perkin credits them with setting in motion the tectonic shift
that would eventually transform the world's first industrial nation and showcase of entrepreneurial success into a collectivist society.[22]

The universities were the chief staging areas for this prolonged struggle
against entrepreneurial values. Sheldon Rothblatt has demonstrated the remarkable degree to which Cambridge excluded the sons of the commercial
and industrial bourgeoisie. Over half of all Cambridge undergraduates in the
nineteenth century were the sons of professional men. Still more revealing,

one out of every three students was the son of a clergyman, even in the last half of the century. Businessmen's sons constituted only 6 percent of the students from 1800 to 1850, and only 15 percent from 1850 to 1900. Even when the gates swung open, the meaning of a Cambridge education remained at odds with the ethos of the marketplace. In the 1930s, by which time 46 percent of Cambridge students came from business families, only a third went into business upon graduation. Cambridge dons, reports Rothblatt, "so closely tied being capable and cultivated to the ideal qualities of the professional man, that it was obvious a man of character could not remain a man of character unless he avoided business and the pursuit of wealth."[23]

Thus it was that the entire weight of the gathering critique of bourgeois society in England, from Carlyle and Coleridge to Arnold, Ruskin, and Morris (not to mention lesser lights such as T. H. Green, F. D. Maurice, John Robert Seeley, or an anonymous army of country clerics), could be brought to an effective point in the idea that the best safeguard against the snares of self-absorption was a career in the professions. In opening to everyone the opportunity to realize what Arnold had called "one's better self" — by making professionals of them — Tawney was drawing on a rich heritage and wrapping the pill of socialism in the sweetest coating imaginable for the educated Englishman of his day.

Although he never mentions Tawney, Eric Hobsbawm has suggested one useful way of understanding what Tawney and other Fabians were doing. In his essay, "The Fabians Reconsidered," he brings into sharper focus the question of the class identity of professional people. Stressing the anomalous quality of Fabian socialism, decidedly antiliberal yet aloof from its only probable source of mass support in the working class, Hobsbawm proposes that the Fabians be seen in fairly classical Marxian terms as representatives not of a class, properly speaking, but of a new social stratum of salaried professionals and managers. They are from this point of view an "accidental" rather than "essential" chapter in the history of British socialism. The cultural background that helps explain the peculiarities of Fabian socialism, Hobsbawm says, is "the need to find some alternative to laissez-faire, the readiness to define any such alternative as 'socialism,' and the capacity of Britons in this period to separate 'socialism' from the working class movement." When Sidney Webb and other Fabians described the socialist professionals of the future, they drew a portrait based on the professional ideals of their day: in Hobsbawm's words, they were to be "sufficiently comfortable not to need to pursue money for material reasons, sufficiently secure in an accepted and respected social rank to be genuinely without envy of the idle rich or the business profiteers, sufficiently at one with society to feel themselves to be of social use." The unavoidable conclusion, of course, is that Fabian socialism was an ideology well suited to the particular needs of the British professional-managerial stratum at the turn of the century.[24]

There is much support for this interpretation in the concluding chapter of *The Acquisitive Society*. Tawney titled it "The Position of the Brain Worker," and in it he displayed a keen awareness of the growing separation between ownership and management that later came to be identified with James Burnham's *The Managerial Revolution*. One of Tawney's principal aims was to arouse to self-consciousness the "intellectual proletariat to whom the scientific and managerial work is increasingly intrusted." He assured the managers, who he thought were often worse paid than the workers, that the professionalization of industry was to their advantage, that their authority would remain intact, that there was no danger of the "obliteration of the brain workers beneath the sheer mass of artisans and laborers." Indeed, Tawney went on, "under such an organization of industry the brain worker might expect, as never before, to come into his own."[25]

The sincerity of Tawney's commitment to equality is beyond question. He wanted to enhance "the opportunity for self-direction," not put citizens under the thumb of a centralized hierarchy manned by technocrats and intellectuals. Yet it is accurate to say that Tawney was—among many other things—a spokesman for professional and managerial types in his society, and that the reforms he proposed assigned to such people positions of great power and responsibility. This is not to "unmask" him, but simply to summarize what he says explicitly. Even in his book *Equality* (1931) he was very careful to acknowledge the need for certain levels of centralized authority, and he bent over backwards to show that his reforms would not allow the layman to override the expert. In the concluding chapter of *The Acquisitive Society* he sounded the same theme: "Public ownership does not appear to confront the brain worker with the danger of unintelligent interference with his special technique, of which he is, quite naturally, apprehensive. It offers him, indeed, far larger opportunities of professional development than are open to all but a favored few today."[26]

If, in disgust at what he has learned to call "profiteering," the consumer seeks an alternative to a system under which product is controlled by "Business," he can hardly find it except by making an ally of the managerial and technical *personnel* of industry. They organize the service which he requires; they are relatively little implicated, either by material interest or by psychological bias, in the financial methods which he distrusts; they often find the control of their professions by business men who are primarily financiers irritating in the obstruction which it offers to technical efficiency, as well as sharp and close-fisted in the treatment of salaries. Both on public and professional grounds they belong to a group which ought to take the initiative in promoting a partnership between the producers and the public. They can offer the community the scientific knowledge and specialized ability which is the most important condition of progress in the arts of production. It can offer them a more secure and dignified status, larger opportunities for the exercise of their special talents, and the consciousness that they are giving the best of their work and their lives, not to enriching a handful of uninspiring, if innocuous, shareholders, but to the service of the great body of their fellow-countrymen.[27]

Hobsbawm criticizes the Fabians for their failure to examine the nature and the historical basis of their model of the social elite, but one wonders whether this criticism is applicable to Tawney. He knew what he was doing. He was aware that he and his kind of people, "brain workers," stood to benefit from the reforms he proposed; that they would, in fact, become the leaders of society, checked of course by democratic majorities; and he felt that they deserved such positions of leadership precisely because they were, compared to their capitalist rivals, disinterested. That an interest in gaining power or influence might be just as ugly as pecuniary lust seems not to have occurred to him. What seems dated in Tawney came not from a simple failure of self-awareness, but from a peculiarly narrow and conventionalized definition of self-interest produced by the headlong confrontation of capitalism with the Christian ethical tradition in the nineteenth and early twentieth century.

Hobsbawm asks why the Fabian ideology should have arisen at this time in Britain and not elsewhere, and finds the answer in the late emergence of bureaucratic elites in England as compared to France or Germany. But minor differences of timing aside, Fabianism can be viewed as a local instance of a broad movement of reform in the West. Certainly many American reformers in the Progressive Era felt a strong kinship with the Fabians. Herbert Croly's *The Promise of American Life* (1910) is strongly reminiscent of Tawney in its protest against the ascendancy of rights over duties, and its enthusiasm for disinterested expertise.[28] Hobsbawm himself mentions the indebtedness of Shaw and the Webbs to the American economist Francis A. Walker. Hobsbawm also takes note of the crucially important role of the *Methodenstreit* in the thinking of Walker, the Fabians, and a host of similar reformers in Germany, France, and the United States. This far-reaching and long-extended controversy over method in the social sciences originated on the Continent in the 1880s as a contest for supremacy between the rising Austrian marginal utility school and the reigning German historical school of economists. The central issues concerned the place of ethical considerations in economic thinking and the theoretical adequacy of the utilitarian or hedonistic model of "economic man" as a being propelled entirely by calculations of self-interest. The Webbs in England, even more strongly than Walker in America, identified themselves with the antihedonistic, "ethical" or historical school and with its principal institutional stronghold in Europe, the Verein für Sozialpolitik. The members of the *Verein* bear a strong resemblance to the English Fabians, and the *Verein* served as a model for Richard T. Ely, Edmund J. James, and other young reform-minded economists when they launched the American Economic Association (with Walker as its first president) amid a parallel, though derivative, controversy in America.[29]

The nonrevolutionary, quasi-socialist, professionally oriented movement of opposition to capitalism that Hobsbawm treats as a uniquely English phenomenon had a wider appeal than he cared to claim. This essay is not intended to carry out the extensive investigation that would be required to demonstrate conclusively the kinship of reformers in England, the United States, France, and Germany at the turn of the century. But to see that Tawney's reform proposals were not unique to England one need only examine the remarkably similar program put forward in France by Emile Durkheim, a program that, in turn, Durkheim's contemporaries recognized as being analogous to that of the "socialists of the chair" headquartered in the Verein für Sozialpolitik.[30] Durkheim spelled out his vision of the good society in his lectures entitled "Professional Ethics and Civic Morals," first given in the 1890s at Bordeaux, then at the Sorbonne in 1904, 1912, and again shortly before his death in 1917. At his direction, they were published posthumously in 1937. We have no evidence that Tawney knew of these lectures, so the strong parallel between them and *The Acquisitive Society* can only be attributed to common reading and similarities in the objective social situation to which each man reacted independently.

Like Tawney, Durkheim felt that his society was suffering a momentous moral crisis precipitated by the transformation of the economy. "For two centuries," he said, "economic life has taken on an expansion it never knew before. From being a secondary function, despised and left to inferior classes, it passes on to one of the first rank." So sweeping has this turn toward economic concerns been, says Durkheim, that there has even "been talk, and not without reason, of societies becoming mainly industrial." As the economic function has grown in importance, "we see the military, governmental and religious functions falling back more and more in the face of it." There is but one barrier left to its expansion. "The scientific function"—a category in which Durkheim undoubtedly included sociology and probably most other university disciplines—"alone is in a position to dispute its ground." And even the prestige of science, he lamented, was increasingly dependent on its material usefulness to businessmen.[31]

Quite apart from his regrets over the spread of materialistic values and the disruption caused by the displacement of traditional elites, the growing centrality of the economic function alarmed Durkheim, as it did Tawney, because he believed that industry and trade impoverished ethics. In these spheres of life he believed relationships were singularly unsteady and inconsequential, often consisting of no more than the transient enmity of competition. Businessmen and industrial workers, he thought, had no life in common and lacked any experience of a corporate body, set above them, embracing all their interests. "Now, this lack of organization in the business professions has one consequence of the greatest moment," claimed Durkheim. "That is, in this whole sphere of social life, no professional ethics exist. Or at least, if they do, they are so rudimentary that at the very most one can see in them maybe a patterning and a foreshadowing for the future" (9).

Because France lacked the Anglo-American heritage of free and independent professions, proudly standing apart from the rest of the occupational order, Durkheim was able to use the phrase "professional ethics" so inclusively as to be nearly synonymous with "occupational ethics." Nevertheless, the reform he proposed was not only comparable but quite similar to that advocated in England by Tawney. What Durkheim had in mind when he spoke of improving "professional ethics" was what Tawney meant when he spoke of transforming occupations into professions, namely, the establishment or reinforcement of a collegial mode of occupational control. Since it was a mode of control rather than a kind of occupation, both men assumed that it could be applied (at least in principle) to a wide variety of occupations. But, wherever applied, it meant an intensification of collegial discipline and a struggle for autonomy against patrons, clients, and other forces outside occupational ranks.

Tawney's and Durkheim's conception of professions as collegially governed occupations is similar to that of the modern sociologist Terence Johnson.[32] Yet their conception differs from Johnson's in one crucial respect. For them the virtue of professionalism lay not primarily in the *autonomy* but in the *collegiality* that it entailed. Their principal aim was not to free the members of the occupation from the influence of consumers, patrons, and other outside parties (for the sake of either income or self-direction) as Johnson's generally perceptive analysis would lead us to expect, but to *constrain the individual members of the occupation by more intense exposure to each other*. We shall see that this is also the principal function of Charles Peirce's "community of inquiry." Their confidence that almost any strengthening of a collectivity would elevate the morality of the individuals composing it came very naturally to a generation that saw economic individualism as the principal social problem and that could not anticipate the threat to individuality that twentieth-century totalitarianism would soon unleash. In their eyes the most pressing problem was atomization, and the corporate, collegial character of the professions held out the hope of a proven remedy.

Durkheim was characteristically explicit in spelling out assumptions that I believe underlay not only his thought but that of Tawney and perhaps Peirce as well. In the absence of corporate life and the moral discipline that it generates, he said, "nothing remains but individual appetites, and since they are by nature boundless and insatiable, if there is nothing to control them they will not be able to control themselves." The only rule of conduct Durkheim could see at work in the sphere of trade and industry was that of acting on one's clear self-interest. But "morality" meant for Durkheim restraint of the self and sacrifice of its interests. So if the sphere of trade and business continues to expand, "how can we keep the springs of morality from going slack in us? . . . how should we get the habit of it? . . . how should we acquire a taste for any disinterestedness or selflessness, or sacrifice?" (11, 12).

The solution was not merely to improvise a set of a priori ethical rules. Durkheim believed that authentic moral rules could only emerge as a natural expression of group integration. "In general," he asserted, "all other things being equal, the greater the strength of the group structure, the more numerous are the moral rules appropriate to it and the greater the authority they have over their members." It followed logically, then, that the true cure for the evil was to "give the professional groups in the economic order a stability they so far do not possess." Already certain occupations that in France had been absorbed into the state bureaucracy—the army, education, the law, and civil service are the examples Durkheim gives—appeared to him to be adequately unified and organized. The task Durkheim urged on his generation was to extend the same stability and collegiality into the "moral vacuum" that was trade and industry (7, 13, 12).

His confidence in the transformative power of this simple measure of "professionalization," as we might call it, was no less sweeping than Tawney's. When people sharing the same interests, ideas, sentiments, and occupations come into contact, Durkheim argued, they will be socialized, and to be socialized is also—in the most literal sense—to be civilized, for socialization and civilization come to virtually the same thing. People coming together in corporate groups, he argued, will be carried along by the current of their similarities, as if under an impulsion; they feel a mutual attraction, they seek out one another, they enter into relations with one another and form compacts and so, by degrees, become a limited group with recognizable features, within the general society. *Now, once the group is formed, nothing can hinder an appropriate moral life from evolving.* . . . this adherence to some thing that goes beyond the individual, and to the interests of the group he belongs to, is the very source of all moral activity. . . . *the more highly and the more profoundly men are socialized, that is to say, civilized— for the two are synonymous—the more those joys* [of peace and harmony] *are prized.* (23–25; emphasis added)

Aware that he might be accused of nostalgia for the guilds of the hated ancien régime, Durkheim took pains to insist that these "*collegia* of craftsmen," as he called them, met human needs so fundamental that their antecedents extended back even to the prehistoric era. He also admitted the possibility that revived guilds might merely replace individual egoism with corporate egoism, but he did so only for the sake of reasserting that the traditional guilds had functioned as an authentic "moral sphere" and that, in general, "when individuals who share the same interests come together, their purpose is not simply to safeguard those interests. . . . It is, rather, just to associate, for the sole pleasure of mixing with their fellows and of no longer feeling lost in the midst of adversaries . . . in short, of being able to lead their lives with the same moral aim" (23, 25).

To these reform proposals Durkheim assigned the highest importance. No change in the ownership of the means of production could do as much to rectify the existing "state of anarchy"; neither the scientist nor the statesman could accomplish anything further until the groups concerned had organized themselves into strong collegial bodies. "I believe that no reform has greater urgency," he declared. He closed his discussion of professional ethics with a brief sketch of how the entire nation might be reorganized around clusters of related industries with an administrative council, or "miniature parliament," presiding over each, regulating wages, conditions of work, and so forth, and beneath them a succession of parallel regional and local bodies. Employers and employees would be separately represented at every level. He was not troubled by the thought that membership in the new guilds would have to be compulsory, because in the existing state of things membership in one's local parish or commune was not voluntary either. The guilds were to have an equally fundamental and taken-for-granted place in the social life of the future (30–31, 39).

Durkheim's good society is sufficiently insensitive to individual liberties that some readers have seen in it the foreshadowings of twentieth-century totalitarianism. His biographer, Steven Lukes, strongly defends him against this misreading. An ardent Dreyfusard and in many ways a not untypical twentieth-century liberal, Durkheim assigned a nearly sacred quality to a certain kind of individualism that he associated with Rousseau and Kant, one that stresses creativity, independent mindedness, and a broad sphere of immunity against state intrusions into matters of conscience. He extolled this individualism even as he condemned the "utilitarian egoism" of Spencer and the economists.[33] The difficulty he experienced in keeping these two forms of individualism distinct, so that one could be honored and the other condemned, was not unique to him. The necessity of trying to maintain this important but inherently awkward distinction was forced upon him (as it has been forced upon many twentieth-century liberals) by his perception of himself and his fellow professional practitioners of the "scientific function" as the last effective barrier to the expansion of the anomic sphere of trade and industry. As the anti-Dreyfusards were quick to point out, the professors and "intellectuals" (a term that first came into use during the Dreyfus affair) despised only the individualism of the businessmen, and thought very highly indeed of an individualism that was well suited to their own needs, interests, and values as "brain workers."[34] Although Durkheim does not specify the powers and privileges of managers, experts, and administrative elites in his projected society, one suspects that he differs from Tawney in this regard only because in France he could take it for granted that practitioners of the "scientific function" would be employed by the state and would naturally have access to its highest councils.

If we shift our gaze across the Atlantic, we find a quite different picture, for capitalism and its bearers met with far less resistance in America than in England or on the Continent. In a population whose orientation to the market began early and was unchecked by powerful proponents of antilibertarian values such as Crown and Church, the problem of self-interest seemed less urgent and therefore elicited, even from those most worried about it, less radical solutions. For these reasons, there is no exact counterpart in America to Tawney and Durkheim, no major thinker who advocated a systematic program of "professionalization" as a general remedy for the individualistic excesses of capitalism. To be sure, there were Americans who saw in professionalism an Arnoldian cultural reform of the first importance, and of course in the Progressive Era a host of reformers cultivated expertise as a counterweight against both the cupidity of business interests and the foolishness of an uninformed electorate.[35] Moreover, before the 1930s virtually all thinking Americans shared the basic premise underlying Tawney's and Durkheim's reform program: the assumption that professionalism offered a way of life morally superior to that of the marketplace. As we have seen, there was no challenge to this assumption even in academic circles before Talcott Parsons's 1939 essay. In America as in England, no one of Tawney's generation needed to read *The Acquisitive Society* to grasp the moral antithesis between business and the professions, but that antithesis did not necessarily lead to the radical conclusions that he and Durkheim teased out of it.

In contrast to Tawney, American critics of economic individualism found themselves in a weak position that dictated a more defensive strategy. In a culture that retained in rhetoric many traditional taboos against self-assertion, but did not carry them into practice with anything like the stringency that obtained in England or on the Continent, critics of individualism had to be content with the creation and preservation of what they perceived, accurately or not, as institutional exemplars of disinterestedness. That function was first served by the Church and then increasingly by the university after the 1860s. One might even say, with some irony, that the closest American counterpart to Tawney's and Durkheim's reform proposals was Thorstein Veblen's *The Higher Learning in America* (1918), which aimed to set limits to the sway of economic individualism, not by the offensive tactic of projecting the university's collegial way of life outward to other occupations, but defensively, by securing the principal fortress of the disinterested against those who would universalize pecuniary competition and divert even the "idle curiosity" of the intellectual to the service of Mammon.[36] No one was more deeply repelled by the pecuniary lust of businessmen than Veblen, and no one divided the world so radically between the selfish and the unselfish — traits that he thought were rooted in instinct and derived from remote stages of human evolution.[37] Though he seems to have looked forward to the possibility that predatory businessmen would botch things so badly that a "soviet of technicians" might someday take over the reins of industrial society, he was fundamentally skeptical of the claims of disinterestedness made by professionals working outside the walls of the university. Only true scientists and scholars met his stringent criteria of idle curiosity, and even their commitment to the "disinterested pursuit of unprofitable knowledge," with "no ulterior motive beyond the idle craving for a systematic correlation of data" was precarious in a business culture. Veblen felt himself to be living in the embryonic stages of a "civilization of disinterested intellectual achievement," but being an American he could feel no certainty that the embryo would survive. "Nothing more irretrievably shameful," he warned, "could overtake modern civilization than the miscarriage of this modern learning, which is the most valued spiritual asset of civilized mankind."[38]

If Tawney and Durkheim had been compelled, as American critics of self-interest were, to fall back on their last line of defense, it is the university around which they, too, would have ringed their forces. Its centrality in their vision of the good society was not limited to the role it performed in recruiting, training, employing, and reproducing "brain workers," or the opportunity it afforded of arming students with high ideals and characters steeled to resist the temptations of the market. More important, the university, or more precisely the scholarly disciplines that it sustains and houses, supplied Tawney and Durkheim with a vivid personal illustration of the beneficial effects of communal discipline and governance by peers. It is no coincidence that the principal critics of self-interest and enthusiasts for collegial discipline were all university professors. Nor was this simply because capitalism is intellectually vulnerable, and professors, being intellectuals, are apt to challenge it. The movement to contain individualism for which Tawney and Durkheim spoke was led by professors and took professional collegiality as its model for relationships throughout society because professors knew from personal experience what it meant to join a community, to transcend one's self, and to subordinate one's desires to higher authority. They did these things in the course of becoming professional scholars.

That Tawney's and Durkheim's enthusiasm for collegial association was inspired by their personal experience of submission and achievement within their own scholarly disciplines is more evident in what they omitted to say than in what they said. A modern reader of *The Acquisitive Society* or *Professional Ethics* cannot fail to be struck by how much the authors took for granted. What they especially took for granted was the very heart of the matter—the disciplinary mechanism or process by which the collegial community induces good behavior in its members. Neither Tawney nor Durkheim supplied more than the most rudimentary explanation of how this takes place. They left unexamined and undefended, in other words, the pivotal assumption around which their entire reform program had to revolve and which alone could justify the underlying popular faith that professional people are morally superior to others. Durkheim's assertion that "once the group is formed, nothing can prevent an appropriate moral life from evolving" is typical of the surprisingly cursory treatment they gave this critical question.[39]

When systematizing intellectuals leave assumptions as large as this one unexamined, we are entitled to conclude that their convictions were buoyed up by the force of personal interest and firsthand experience. They knew professional communities made better men of their members because they felt that their own recruitment, training, and mature participation in the invisible republic of scholars and scientists had brought forth their own better selves. Like riders astride bicycles, they felt no need to explain how the community keeps its members upright; they said in effect, "Watch us and you'll see how."

Being congenitally immune to utopian projects, Veblen did not aspire to extend the benefits of collegiality to everyone, but he fully shared Tawney's and Durkheim's extravagant faith in the disinterestedness of scientific communities. His faith may well have been learned at the feet of Charles S. Peirce, with whom he studied briefly while a student at Johns Hopkins in the fall of 1881. Peirce was the author of the boldest claims for the communal character of intellectual achievement ever written. His communal theory of truth and reality supplies a most revealing parallel to the views of Tawney and Durkheim and exposes to view a major confusion in their thinking.

It is conceivable, though not necessary for my argument, that his writings were known to Tawney and Durkheim. Durkheim taught a course entitled "Pragmatism and Sociology" in 1913–14 and knew enough about Peirce's place among the originators of pragmatism to know that William James had misinterpreted him.[40] Tawney acknowledged no debt to Peirce, but the following passage from his commonplace book could stand as a fair summary of Peirce's conclusions on the social, indeed self-abnegating, character of inquiry: "The secret of growth is self-surrender, and as much so in matters of intellect as in matters of morals. If a man wants to do serious scientific work in any sphere, he must become impersonal, suppress his own fancies and predilections, and try to listen to reason speaking in him. But whatever the cause, religion, science, faith in social progress, the elevation of a man out of himself into a world where there is no rivalry but only service, is the supreme good."[41]

The triumph of capitalism repelled Charles Peirce just as deeply as it did Tawney, Durkheim, or Veblen. During the tense decade of the 1890s, when labor violence and agrarian agitation sent a shock of alarm through the upper reaches of American society, he expressed his fears in the *Monist* essay, "Evolutionary Love." The issue, he declared, was a choice between Christianity and the "Gospel of Greed." On the one side was the Christian teaching "that progress comes from every individual merging his individuality in sympathy with his neighbors." On the other side was the teaching of the political economists "that progress takes place by virtue of every individual's striving for himself with all his might and trampling his neighbor under foot whenever he gets a chance to do so." Saint John taught that God was love and that "self-love was no love," but political economy had a new "formula of redemption," said Peirce, one that not only legitimated the love of self but loudly proclaimed it to be more beneficent in the long run than love of others. The economist's formula teaches that "intelligence in the service of greed ensures the justest prices, the fairest contracts, the most enlightened conduct of all the dealings between men, and leads to *summum bonum,* food in plenty and perfect comfort." But it was the "greedy master of intelligence," thought Peirce, who actually got the food and comfort.[42]

Freely adopting the "sentimentalist" label that the economists turned against their foes, and also making what was for him the very significant concessions that political economy was an authentic science and that his criticism of it would "probably shock my scientific brethren," Peirce set himself firmly against the mainstream of what he called the "Economical Century." In a tone reminiscent of his Puritan ancestors he trumpeted a warning against the "Gradgrind banner . . . long flaunting in the face of heaven with an insolence to provoke the very skies to scowl and rumble." He predicted that a day of reckoning was near at hand. "Soon a flash and quick peal will shake economists quite out of their complacency, too late. The twentieth century, in its latter half, shall surely see the deluge-tempest burst upon the social order — to clear upon a world as deep in ruin as that greed-philosophy has long plunged it into guilt" (VI-292).

Temperamentally unsuited to the role of practical reformer, this erratic genius poured all his misgivings about the individualizing direction of nineteenth-century social change into a philosophy that made the very possibility of knowing what is real contingent upon self-transcendence and involvement with others. As if to repudiate Emerson's romantic advice to "trust thyself," Peirce contended that no individual, least of all one's self, could ever be worthy of trust. "The individual man, since his separate existence is manifested only by ignorance and error . . . is only a negation" (VI-317). Peirce's advice was to trust instead the "community of inquirers."[43]

Peirce insisted even more strongly than Durkheim on the frailty and incompetence of the individual apart from his fellows. But unlike both Durkheim and Tawney, who admired community for the higher moral character it supposedly induced in its members, Peirce admired it mainly for the closer approach to truth he believed it permitted. He did not doubt that the community of scientists exacted a high standard of "self-control" and "righteousness" from its members, just as Tawney and Durkheim believed, and he often stressed that "the logically good is only a particular species of the morally good" (V-108, 130). But what makes Peirce's conception of community still a lively source of debate and even inspiration today, when Durkheim's and Tawney's conceptions have fallen into obscurity, is that the principal function he claimed for community was epistemological, not moral.[44]

Peirce of course denied the moral adequacy of utilitarian doctrines of self-interest just as Tawney and Durkheim did: "If it were in the nature of a man to be perfectly satisfied to make his personal comfort his ultimate aim," said Peirce, "no more blame would attach to him for doing so than attaches to a hog for behaving in the same way." But the greatest flaw Peirce saw in individualist doctrines was that the pursuit merely of selfish interests is incompatible with the very possibility of making logical inferences. In matters of statistical proba-bility, for instance, individual cases mean nothing, and to be logical one must imagine what would happen in an indefinitely large number of cases, experi-enced by an indefinitely large number of people with a multitude of interests. "Logicality," Peirce insisted, "requires that our interests shall *not* be limited. They must not stop at our own fate. . . . Logic is rooted in the social principle" (V-130; II-654).

Peirce believed that every phase of thinking was pervasively influenced by the social dimension of human existence. What provokes inquiry in the first place is doubt, and doubt is an eminently social phenomenon: it originates in a clash of opinions. "No matter how strong and well-rooted in habit any ratio-nal conviction of ours may be," wrote Peirce, "we no sooner find that another equally well-informed person doubts it, than we begin to doubt it ourselves." Since we necessarily influence each other's opinions, "the problem becomes how to fix belief, not in the individual merely, but in the community." The only respectable way to accomplish this is through the method of scientific in-vestigation, which is inherently communal. As both doubt and the effort to escape it through inquiry are social, so must be the object of inquiry, truth itself (V-378).[45]

"What anything really is," argued Peirce, "is what it may finally come to be known to be in the ideal state of complete information." Since informa-tion cannot be complete in my lifetime or yours, our best conceptions are riddled with error, and the truth can only be known by the last survivors of a community of inquirers that includes the yet-to-be-born as well as the living, and extends indefinitely far into the future. "The real, then," said Peirce in a famous passage, "is that which, sooner or later, information and reasoning would finally result in, and which is independent of the vagaries of me and you. Thus, the very origin of the conception of reality shows that this concep-tion essentially involves the notion of a **COMMUNITY**, without definite limits, and capable of a definite increase in knowledge" (V-316, 311).

It may have been his status as an outsider who never found permanent employment in the academic world that sensitized Peirce to the social, consensual quality of all that passes for truth among human beings. Yet there is no trace of cynicism in his conception. The ultimate consensus to be reached by his community of inquiry is of a very special kind, and his theory of reality, though indubitably social, is not at all relativistic, as twentieth-century analogues have tended to be. Like Thomas Kuhn, he regarded science as the practical accomplishment of a community of researchers. Unlike Kuhn, however, he supposed that the universe was so made that an ultimate convergence of opinion was virtually predestined and that the reality toward which opinion converged was utterly independent, not of thought in general, but of what any finite number of human beings might think. When pressed by a critic, he allowed that the ultimate convergence of opinion might be incomplete in some matters and that convergence was a "hope" rather than an inevitability, but the hope was of the same indispensable character as the expectation of survival that a man struggling for his life must feel. To live is to hope; similarly, to inquire is to suppose that opinions ultimately converge toward the real.

> This activity of thought by which we are carried, not where we wish, but to a fore-ordained goal, is like the operation of destiny. No modification of the point of view taken, no selection of other facts for study, no natural bent of mind even, can enable a man to escape the predestinate opinion. This great hope [originally he wrote "law"] is embodied in the conception of truth and reality. The opinion which is fated to be ultimately agreed to by all who investigate, is what we mean by the truth, and the object represented in this opinion is the real. That is the way I would explain reality.

Peirce conceded that "perversity" might delay the emergence of a consensus, or "even conceivably cause an arbitrary proposition to be universally accepted as long as the human race should last. Yet even that would not change the nature of the belief which alone could be the result of investigation carried sufficiently far" (V-407, 408; VI-610).

Peirce was no ideologue. He had no intention of supplying existing communities of inquiry in physics or chemistry or biology with a philosophical warrant for their authority. Much less did he intend his communal theory of reality to buttress the claims of quasi sciences like law or medicine. He expressly rejected the "method of authority" as a means of fixing belief, and he equated that method with the claims of priesthoods, aristocracies, guilds, and other "association[s] . . . of men whose interests depend . . . on certain propositions" (V-379). As long as we interpret his words strictly, as he no doubt

wished us to do, his theory bundles truth and reality off into an infinite progression where it is too remote to serve any interest or strengthen any particular claim to knowledge. Indeed, one might even ask what value there can be in
a truth that is known only in the indefinitely remote future.[46]

But if his theory undermines all existing authorities and courts radical
skepticism when strictly interpreted—offering us no guidance when we ask
"Which *present* claim is true?" or "What belief shall I *now* act on?"—it performs the opposite function of building bulwarks against skepticism when
loosely interpreted. And how can we resist interpreting it loosely? As John E.
Smith has said, "Reality in the end for Peirce is future experience, and this is
not enough."[47]

No one can claim to know the final opinion of a community that extends
indefinitely into the future, but once we accept Peirce's identification of truth
as the outcome of a community's striving, then if a community of inquiry
exists in a field that interests us, surely its *current best opinion* is, in practice,
the closest approach to the truth we can possibly hope for. We live now and
need now to distinguish between true and false propositions. If we take our cue
from Peirce, sound opinion becomes that opinion which wins the broadest and
deepest support in the existing community of inquirers; certainly Peirce does
not suggest any higher test of reality that is actually within our reach. Strictly
interpreted, this philosopher who inspired a notoriously action-oriented philosophy seems to be preaching a curiously fatalistic lesson. It might read:
"Truth cannot be known till eternity, so for purposes of choosing our present
course of action, all truth claims are equally unreliable." But loosen the interpretation even the least bit, and the message takes dramatically different form:
"Recognizing the fallibility of all truth claims, act in accord with the current
best opinion of the existing community of inquirers"—at least if there are
any inquirers in the relevant field, and if the field is one that promises "convergence" or is, in other words, a science. Given a choice between these two
interpretations, it may well be that the strict one is closest to Peirce's own intentions. But the most important thing to observe about Peirce's communal
theory of reality is that the more persuasive we find it, the more likely we are
to live by the loose interpretation of it. Identifying truth with the community,
but lacking the community's final opinion, we are bound to prefer its current
best opinion to a chaos of indistinguishable truth claims, which is the only
other alternative Peirce's line of reasoning leaves us.

However strictly we interpret Peirce's conception of the community of inquiry, the likelihood that its genesis lies in the actual scholarly and scientific
institutions of Peirce's day requires more careful attention than scholars have

given to it. There are in fact many reasons to suppose that his communal theory of truth was an idealized extrapolation from the professionalizing tendencies that were transforming the intellectual world in his lifetime. Peirce knew these tendencies at first hand, in spite of his exclusion from the universities, because of his own work as a scientist for the Coast Survey, and because his father, the eminent astronomer and mathematician Benjamin Peirce, was one of the foremost professionalizers of science in America. The elder Peirce, member of a self-selected elite circle of American scientists known as the Lazzaroni, organized the Lawrence Scientific School at Harvard, helped write the constitution of the American Association for the Advancement of Science, and helped push through Congress the bill creating the National Academy of Sciences. In the late 1870s, as his son was writing about the indispensability of the community of inquiry in "The Fixation of Belief" and "How to Make Our Ideas Clear," the two essays that William James later identified with the origins of pragmatism, the elder Peirce was an officer of the American Social Science Association, a gathering place for forward-looking professionalizers and proponents of established authority. In that role he drafted a bold plan in 1878 that would have united the ASSA with Daniel Coit Gilman's fledgling university in Baltimore, the first authentic university in the United States, to regulate public opinion in every field from physics to economics and politics. The ASSA had already played a part in the civil service reform movement in the 1870s, and for two decades after 1880 it was closely involved with the origins of professional scholarly associations such as the American Historical Association and the American Economic Association, which were organized at its annual meetings in 1884 and 1885, respectively.[48]

There is at least a relationship of mutual suggestiveness between Benjamin Peirce's institution-building activities and his son's insistence that truth is a communal enterprise. It is well known that Benjamin Peirce took charge of his son's early education in the same extraordinarily intense manner one associates with the fathers of other Victorian intellectuals such as Margaret Fuller and John Stuart Mill. It would be a mistake to link the younger Peirce's ideal philosophical constructs too closely with any concrete professional association of scholars or scientists, but on the other hand it would require a remarkable faith in people's capacity to compartmentalize their lives to suppose that his ideal community of inquirers was unrelated to the actual institutions of inquiry that his father was working so hard to create. However indirect and unintentional the relationship may have been, Charles Peirce's communal theory of truth and reality had the effect of supplying an elegant epistemological rationale for just the sort of scholarly and scientific institutions that his father and a host of other academic professionalizers were bringing into existence in late-nineteenth-century America. They were the creators of the American university system, which Veblen fretfully defended and whose venerable European counterparts inspired Tawney's and Durkheim's admiration for collegial discipline as a general remedy for greed.

Charles Peirce's writings throw into bold relief a fundamental ambiguity in the thinking of Tawney and Durkheim and others who implicitly took the collegial community of scholars as a model for human relations throughout society. Although Peirce's conception of the community of inquiry arose from the same context of anticapitalist sentiment that motivated Tawney and Durkheim, and although he, like them, deplored atomistic individualism and incautiously expected moral improvement from almost any strengthening of communal bonds, he stands apart from them in one decisive respect: For him, as we have seen, the primary effects of membership in the community of inquiry were epistemological, not moral. Although he shared enough of their assumptions to insist that the "logically good" is only a "species of the morally good," what mainly interested him about the community of inquiry was its power to produce logical goodness, or truth. The central theme of his argument is that involvement in the community encourages disinterestedness in the sense of unbiased perception of reality. That it might also produce disinterestedness in the sense of selfless concern for others, or love, was incidental to the advancement of science.

Thus Peirce's understanding of what membership in the community does to and for its individual members renders the community inappropriate as a model for the general reform of society—at least if greed, selfishness, and raw ambition are the social problems wanting a cure. According to Peirce's analysis, transforming coal mining or salesmanship into collegially governed occupations might rid the workers of job-related idiosyncrasies and ensure their conformity to acceptable technical standards of performance, but one would not expect it to make them more altruistic. Had Tawney and Durkheim accepted Peirce's stress on the epistemological consequences of communal organization, they might not so quickly have brushed aside the possibility that their reforms promised only to replace individual selfishness with corporate selfishness. Indeed, once it is conceded that the community's principal virtue is epistemological, its relevance to reformers bent on limiting self-aggrandizement becomes highly doubtful. If this was all there was to say about Peirce's views on community relations, we would be left in as deep a state of puzzlement as when we began, still unable to account for the extravagant hopes that Peirce, Durkheim, Tawney, and so many others of their generation attached to professionalization. But there is more to Peirce's conception of community, and our next task is to force into view what he implied but left unsaid.

The place of love in Peirce's ideal community is even more precarious than our analysis has thus far revealed. We have already seen that Tawney and Durkheim were oddly silent on the exact means by which they expected their communities to elevate morality. Peirce, carried along in the same swift current of opposition to economic individualism, was not much more forthcoming about the means by which he expected his community to generate a warranted consensus among inquirers. But he said enough about the inner workings of the community of inquiry to make it clear that rivalry and competition play in this regard a much larger role than love or affection. Indeed, upon close examination it appears that Peirce's community reproduces within itself the perpetual conflict and struggle for supremacy of a competitive market society. After all, love and criticism do not sit well together, and although he wanted it to be both, Peirce's community is finally more critical than loving. With this ironic discovery, we return to the central problem of this essay, the relation of professionalism to capitalism, and begin to see how astute observers like Tawney and Durkheim could accept the popular judgment that professional morality was profoundly at odds with that of the marketplace, even though professional institutions have proved in the long run to fit into capitalist society like hand in glove.

The few clues Peirce supplies about the inner workings of the community imply that relations between its members are far from peaceful. Although he contrasted capitalism's "Gospel of Greed" with his own gospel of love and formulated, as R. Jackson Wilson says, the most "radical ideal of community in American or European letters," his communitarian rhetoric does not jibe with his combative vision of scientific inquiry. He seems to have meant by community intense "communication," rather than neighborliness or avoidance of conflict, a *Kommunikationsgemeinschaft,* as Karl-Otto Apel calls it, that implies an attitude of respectful *attention* between members, but not *affection.*[49] Peirce expected the inquirers comprising his community to behave pretty much as intellectuals actually behave: they quarrel and contend with one another. They interact mainly by setting forth claims and counterclaims, rival interpretations and arguments that pit one inquirer against another. They smite their opponents hip and thigh when they err, and stand ready to defend their own ideas against all challengers. For them to turn the other cheek would be a cowardly betrayal of the quest for truth.

There is, of course, a tendency toward consensus in Peirce's community, and this might seem enough in itself to provide the expected quality of *agapē.* But

Peirce's consensus lies in the infinitely remote future. Nor is there any reason to think he expected it to develop frictionlessly. Most intriguing, he evidently thought of the ultimate consensus as something brought about by the influence of a force outside the community, in nature itself, that operated over the heads of individual inquirers. The convergence of opinion within the community therefore does not depend upon its members' benevolence any more than the provision of our dinner depends upon the benevolence of the butcher, the brewer, or the baker.

Indeed, the entire process that causes what Peirce called "the most antagonistic views" (V-407) to converge in the ultimate consensus is strongly reminiscent of the price mechanism in economic markets.[50] There, in accordance with the natural laws of supply and demand, the jockeying of rival consumers and producers looking out for their own interests generates for each commodity a convergence toward its "natural price." Similarly, in the community of inquiry the clash of erring individuals produces eventually a convergence of opinion about reality. No one in Peirce's community need feel love toward the other members, nor even love of the truth, strictly speaking (since no individual's present ideas can be said to correspond with that opinion which the community will ultimately settle on). What inquirers must love, as Peirce made plain, is their own ideas:

> Everybody can see that the statement of St. John is the formula of an evolutionary philosophy, which teaches that growth comes only from love, from I will not say self-*sacrifice*, but from the ardent impulse to fulfill another's highest impulse. Suppose, for example, that I have an idea that interests me. It is my creation. It is my creature; for as shown in last July's *Monist*, it is a little person. I love it; and I will sink myself in perfecting it. It is not by dealing out cold justice to the circle of my ideas that I can make them grow, but by cherishing and tending them as I would the flowers in my garden. The philosophy we draw from John's gospel is that this is the way mind develops; and as for the cosmos, only so far as it yet is mind, and so has life, is it capable of further evolution. Love, recognizing germs of loveliness in the hateful, gradually warms it into life, and makes it lovely. That is the sort of evolution which every careful student of my essay "The Law of Mind" must see that *synechism* calls for. (VI-289)

Although no one in Peirce's community needs to be benevolent, it is absolutely necessary in order to bring about the ultimate convergence that some members engage in the sort of competitive struggle that is entailed in *criticism*. It did not trouble Peirce that mutual criticism might divide the community and produce strife among its members. The pursuit of pecuniary self-interest had no place in the community, but the pursuit of glory and reputation evidently was to provide its motive force. No ideologue of entrepreneurial values ever wrote of self-advancement in language any more passionate or, indeed, grandiose than that which Peirce used to close his famous essay "The Fixation of Belief." Granting that the method of science was a hard taskmaster, he insisted that "we should not desire it otherwise."

> The genius of a man's logical method should be loved and reverenced as his bride, whom he has chosen from all the world. He need not contemn [*sic*] the others; on the contrary, he may honor them deeply, and in doing so only honor her the more. But she is the one that he has chosen, and he knows that he was right in making that choice. And having made it, he will work and fight for her, and will not complain that there are many blows to take, hoping that there may be as many and as hard to give, and will strive to be a worthy knight and champion of her from the blaze of whose splendors he draws his inspiration and his courage. (V-387)

Imagery of combat and struggle punctuates Peirce's discussion of truth seeking, and we know that he had every reason to appreciate the role of criticism and conflict in science. His father's elite circle of friends, the Lazzaroni, were severe critics who zealously took upon themselves the task of denouncing error and chastising mediocrity in their respective fields of science. Peirce's own attitude toward rival scientists could be gladiatorial. The very essay we have been examining, although entitled "Evolutionary Love," was actually an expression of hatred, directed not only against the abstract "greed philosophy" of political economy but also at the tangible person of Simon Newcomb, an astronomer and economist who had played a part in Peirce's expulsion from both Johns Hopkins and the Coast Survey, and whose textbook on political economy was the unnamed source of the passages Peirce used to ridicule political economy.[51]

Readers familiar with the existing scholarly literature on Peirce may well be uncomfortable with my claim that his ideal community tolerates — indeed requires — such self-aggrandizing behavior in its members. But if we ask what exactly it is about life in the scientific community that produces the gradual convergence of opinion toward the real, what can the answer be if not criticism, competition, impassioned confrontations between error-ridden individuals, each seeking to advance his own flawed conception of truth? There is no other dynamic element at work in the community Peirce envisioned, unless we credit truth itself with the power of a final cause, capable of drawing qualified inquirers to it like a magnet. If there is anything more substantial than this (and I think there is) to his idea that involvement in a community of peers lifts the individual to a higher epistemological plane, in the sense of heightening the chances that his opinions will approximate the truth, surely the crux of the matter has to be that community involvement entails exposure to criticism, and that in things of the mind, criticism purifies. If the members of the community were related to one another in a predominantly affectionate, uncritical way, the epistemological efficacy of the community would fall toward zero. The philosopher Nicholas Rescher has observed that if we press Peirce, asking him just why the long-term acceptance of a thesis—its mere ultimate survival in the community of scientific inquirers—betokens the *truth* of the thesis, "the only convincing line of reply takes 'survival' to mean survival of tests: the thesis has successfully frustrated all experiments or observations designed to prove it false." Rescher likens Peirce's conception of scientific method to Karl Popper's model of "conjecture and refutation"—a process of claim and counterclaim that implies perpetual conflict and draws explicitly on an evolutionary scheme to explain why some truth claims survive and others do not.[52] In the last analysis, criticism is all that *could* make the community of inquirers epistemologically efficacious, and criticism requires that the community's members engage in conflict and pursue goals in which each self must be profoundly interested, though in a nonpecuniary way.

Now of course there are definite limits to self-aggrandizement in the community that Peirce envisioned. I stress its competitive character because previous commentators, misled by Peirce's own deeply ambivalent statements about it, have seen only its harmonious, self-abnegating features. The community's achievement of "logical goodness" depends not only on conflict and competition but also on its members' adherence to such collegial values as honesty, a degree of tolerance (given one's own susceptibility to error), dedication to the resolution of conflicts, willingness to be persuaded by evidence, logic, and reason, and so on. But if self-aggrandizement is carefully hedged and channeled in Peirce's community, the same can be said, at least as a matter of degree, of the capitalist marketplace. For as Max Weber observed, "unlimited greed for gain is not in the least identical with capitalism, and is still less its spirit. Capitalism may even be identical with the restraint, or at least a rational tempering, of this irrational impulse."[53]

At bottom, Peirce's confidence in the disinterestedness of scientists relies, at least in part, on the same two dubious assumptions that Tawney and so many others of their generation embraced: first, the stereotypical and oversimplified notion that the capitalist marketplace is a moral vacuum, lacking any ethical constraints of its own; and second, that selfishness consists exclusively of the pursuit of material gain and therefore cannot be present in the pursuit of nonpecuniary goods such as intellectual influence or reputation. Only these implausible assumptions permitted Peirce to accentuate the cooperative element in the life of the scientific community, contrasting its members' self-transcendent, truth-seeking behavior with the greediness of the larger society, while at the same time describing scientific method as a profoundly critical, combative process, in which each fallible individual, pitifully sure of his own version of the truth, struggles to expose the errors of his peers, thereby contributing his infinitesimally small part to the eternally incomplete consensus. Who today, being familiar with the conduct of scholars and scientists, could deny that they are in competition with one another? Or that exposing the errors of others and winning recognition for one's own views brings self-gratifications every bit as intense as those a businessman feels when he clinches a deal or expands his market share? To say that the scholar-scientist's pleasure comes from "advancing the truth" does not lift it cleanly out of the sphere of self-interest, as Peirce's and Tawney's generation believed, but only specifies the dimension of performance that the scholar-scientist finds most salient, given his own temperament and the structure of rewards within his occupation.

Halting and ambivalent though he was about it, Peirce did at least partially recognize the critical, competitive character of the community of inquiry. This insight distances his conception from those of Tawney and Durkheim, and shows that the latter two theorists' hope of modeling all society on the collegial pattern of the scholarly disciplines was even more misguided than it initially appeared. Not only is the scholarly or scientific community's efficacy confined to the production of "logical goodness," or truth, rendering it largely irrelevant to the reformer's mission of moral improvement; now we also discover that these communities rely on the same motive power of self-interest (albeit nonpecuniary) that propels the larger society. If, as Peirce suggests, the community requires its members to advance their own desires for glory and eminence as truth-seekers at the expense of others, it reproduces—though on a small scale and in a nonpecuniary sphere—the competitiveness of market society, and its value as a moral exemplar becomes doubtful. How can a community composed of professional specialists competing against one another for reputation serve as a counterweight to the competitive excesses of capitalism? How can a market-in-miniature, as it were, do anything to remedy the demoralization created by the intrusion of market relations into all spheres of life?

There is no denying that these questions create serious embarrassment for the reform programs of Tawney and Durkheim, neither of whom ever managed even in Peirce's halting manner to acknowledge the competitiveness of scholarly communities or the self-seeking behavior of the brain workers who constitute them. Yet on the whole, Peirce's acknowledgment that the scientific community is an arena of competition has the effect of heightening one's respect and sympathy for Tawney's and Durkheim's plans. It does so because it discloses a plausible mechanism by which the community might influence its members' moral conduct. By stressing the competitiveness of the community, Peirce enables us to see how it influences its members' behavior. He thereby gives us a sociological purchase on the otherwise puzzling confidence his generation felt in the improving power of professional institutions. Even though Tawney and Durkheim were unable or unwilling fully to articulate it, and even though they tried to make it carry more weight than it can bear, we are now in a position to see that there was a rational basis for their confidence that professionalization enables people to lead "more moral" lives.

To grasp the rational kernel at the heart of Tawney's and Durkheim's extravagant faith in the power of professional communities to elevate morality, we must not think of professions in the currently fashionable imagery of economics, according to which they are *monopolies*. Monopolies aim to *maximize* pecuniary gain by *minimizing* competition through the *exclusion* of outsiders. Instead, taking our cue from Peirce, we must think of professions as special communities (more accurately, intense communicative networks) that deliberately *intensify* competition among *insiders* in *nonpecuniary* dimensions of achievement, such as glory and reputation. From this angle of vision, which highlights crucially important realities of professional life that the monopoly model routinely obscures, a professional community is indeed a miniature market. It is a market in which people compete not for money, but for the affective currency of criticism: fame instead of disgrace; honor in place of shame; compliments, not complaints, about the technical worth of one's work. What each competitor strives to accumulate in this special "countervailing" market is not capital, but reputation, a stock of favorable impressions of himself and his work in the minds of his peers. Since people do not necessarily lose self-esteem when they bestow praise on others, the competitors in this market are not playing a strictly zero-sum game, and the spirit of their competition is consequently often relaxed and friendly. But esteem is not limitless in supply, and the deeply personal character of the productions and performances being criticized can charge the competition in this market with explosive emotional force.

Now of course this is not the only market in which professionals compete. Everyone in a capitalist regime necessarily competes in another market, a society-wide market in which the stakes are monetary. Professionals are no exception. They sell expert advice and services in the general economic market and aim to maximize their incomes just as businessmen do. Like everyone else in this market, they must adapt their economic behavior to the laws of supply and demand, as expressed in fluctuating price and wage levels, or risk impoverishment. He who ignores what the sovereign consumer demands, no matter how elevated and scrupulous his reasons, goes under. If the market is a true one, a "free" one, no buyer or seller is able to control prices, but all contribute infinitesimally to the wage and price levels that each experiences as an impersonal objective reality. It is in fact capitalism's proudest boast that any Tom, Dick, or Harry able to pay for a good can do so, thereby contributing his mite to the state of demand that implacably controls economic behavior throughout society.

This is at once capitalism's pride and its fatal flaw, for the perpetual danger is that dumb Tom, frivolous Dick, and uninformed Harry, collectively occupying the role of sovereign consumer that capitalism so recklessly bestows upon them, will drag all standards of judgment and performance down to their own mediocre level. Neither the producers of tangible goods nor the suppliers of professional services have any way to resist this descent toward the standards of the uninformed as long as they confine their transactions to the ordinary economic market, for in such a market those who ignore the promptings of demand and the preferences of consumers face a loss of income, or even extinction, because their competitors will fill any demand they neglect.

Or at least competitors will do so if they are not restrained by the fear of incurring nonpecuniary costs. This is how the competitive collegial community helps its members to lead lives that may be at least marginally more scrupulous than those of laymen: It functions as a "countervailing market," structuring a set of inducements and sanctions that can pull the path of self-interest up out of the rut of purely pecuniary advantage. The involvement of professional people in a nonpecuniary market does not make them altruistic, but it does compel them to calculate self-interest twice: once in pecuniary terms that are shaped by the consumer sovereignty of an uninformed mass public, and again in nonpecuniary terms dictated by their struggle for eminence within a body of specially competent consumers, their professional peers. Sometimes the two calculations converge, but often they do not. The resulting fragmentation of consumer sovereignty liberates each member of the community by restraining his or her competitors. The more each competitor feels constrained by the nonpecuniary demands of his or her peers, the more confident all become that their competitors feel similarly constrained. The greater the confidence all feel in the constraining power of the professional community, the freer each becomes to uphold whatever the community defines as "high standards" in spite of the pecuniary inducements created by the existence of an uninformed mass of consumers.

The grain of truth in the myth of professional disinterestedness, then, is that the professional person, because he competes simultaneously in pecuniary *and* nonpecuniary markets, finds his interests running in nonpecuniary channels more often than the businessman, who competes in the pecuniary market alone. This may seem a frail distinction today, when the pursuit of Mammon has lost its status as a sin, and pecuniary accumulation has become for most of us merely one among many kinds of self-indulgence. But it made a world of difference to Tawney's generation, and not only because they still felt the full force of traditional religious proscriptions. Beneath the surface of the biblical convention that permitted them to condemn the pursuit of "filthy lucre" while ignoring nonpecuniary forms of self-aggrandizement was the very substantial reality of two different markets, two different sets of sovereign consumers, two fruitfully opposed configurations of supply and demand in a society being rudely reshaped by the invisible hand.

By fragmenting consumer sovereignty in what was rapidly becoming a mass society, professionalization really did supply at least a mild antidote against the demoralization and the subordination of social, political, and ethical affairs to economic relations that attended the rise of the market. It was, as Magali Larson points out, an authentic part of Polanyi's countermovement to repair the damage done by the irruption of competition in spheres of life previously immune to it.[54] But that is not to say that professionalization could ever have become the anticapitalist measure Tawney and Durkheim wanted it to be. Professionalization held out some promise of minimizing idiosyncrasy and stimulating the production of warranted consensuses about technical standards of work—but there was little basis for the reformers' hope that it would rid people of selfishness. Professionalization was capable of giving producers a leg to stand on as they tried to resist the temptations of an uninformed mass market—but it offered no guidance about a wide range of ethical issues that attended the rise of capitalism. Professionalization may have diverted the path of interest into nonpecuniary channels, but self-interest remains self-interest whether pecuniary or not. Moreover, although the economists' category of monopoly obscures much that is important in professional organizations, professions are monopolies too, and once consumer sovereignty is fragmented, the opportunity to extract monopoly profits will not go unnoticed.

The ironic epilogue to Tawney's utopian vision of a professionalized and unacquisitive society is visible on all sides today. The professionals have turned out to be no less acquisitive than businessmen, and the businessmen have turned out to be much more "professional," in exactly Tawney's sense, than he ever expected they could be. The distinction between pecuniary and non-pecuniary interest has become a mere formality, and the line between professional and nonprofessional is growing hazier every day. The reasons are fairly obvious. On the one hand, the marketplace was never so lacking in moral restraints as Tawney's generation imagined. Tawney's brilliant contemporary, Max Weber, saw (as Benjamin Franklin and many others of an earlier generation had seen) that although the culture of capitalism legitimates many forms of self-interest, greed is not the capitalist's definitive trait, and success in the market requires a good deal of striving after nonpecuniary goals like honor and reputation. And on the other hand, a somewhat diluted professionalism did not need the help of cultural reformers to spread to one occupation after another in the twentieth century. Trade magazines, the pleasures of shoptalk, and tipsy conventions at company expense have brought to many occupations the collective spirit and stress on reputation that Tawney and Durkheim identified exclusively with the professions. Dependence for self-esteem on the judgment of one's closest competitors and peers is probably still stronger in the professions, especially the scholarly and scientific professions, than anywhere else in the occupational order. But that is only to suggest the deeply ironic conclusion that competitiveness may be more pervasive (and therefore reliance on the social discipline generated by competition may be more complete) in the modern professions than in the business world.

Here lies the most fundamental limitation of Tawney's and Durkheim's vision. They failed to recognize that, as a remedy to the problem of self-interest in market society, professionalization was very much a matter of fighting fire with fire, competition in one dimension with competition in another, self-interest of one kind with self-interest of a different kind. It was, to paraphrase words James Madison used in a political context, a capitalist remedy for the defects of capitalism. Far from being antithetical, capitalism and professionalism can best be understood as two sides of a single coin: rationalization, that ominous tendency in the West to universalize competition and introduce into all spheres of life the harsh but productive tests of least cost and maximum efficiency.

CHAPTER FIVE

The Curious Persistence of Rights Talk in the Age of Interpretation

Talking about rights, as Americans are wont to do, implies something highly controversial: the existence of an objective moral order accessible to reason. To be conscious of a right is at least tacitly to lay claim to a kind of knowledge that is not merely personal and subjective but impersonal and objective. When I say that I have a *right* to do something—whether it is to exercise dominion over a possession, to enjoy equal employment opportunities, or to express controversial opinions in public—I am not merely saying that I want to do it and hope that others will let me; I am saying that they *ought* to let me, have a *duty* to let me, and will be guilty of an *injustice,* a transgression against established moral standards, if they fail to do so.[1]

Does the objective (or at least intersubjective) moral order implied by words such as "ought" and "duty" and "injustice" really exist? Can there be any intellectually respectable justification for the claim "I have a right"? Or is rights talk nothing more than a fancy cloak for the interests of individuals and groups?

My own view is that rights talk, for all its liabilities, refers to something real (what I will call "rational conventions") and is a valuable cultural practice, one we ought to encourage. That is the viewpoint this essay is meant to advance, and I have not hesitated to press my case with a good deal of polemi-

This essay was written for a conference on rights consciousness organized by the *Journal of American History* and sponsored by the University of Massachusetts at Amherst, November 1986. In addition to helpful comments from the symposium's other participants, and valuable editorial advice from David Thelen and his staff, the essay has benefited greatly from readings by Thomas Cole, David Hollinger, Martin Wiener, and Richard Wolin. All responsibility remains mine.

First published in *Journal of American History* 74 (Dec. 1987): 984–1012. Also available in *The Constitution and American Life,* ed. David Thelen (Ithaca: Cornell University Press, 1987), 324–52.

cal intensity. I may as well confess from the outset, however, that beneath the polemical surface of my text the reader will find a darker current of ambivalence and anxiety, for the plain truth is that no one at present can offer any entirely satisfactory justification for the idea of a right, or for the larger and even more vital notion on which it depends, the idea of objective moral obligation. My polemical zeal arises from my concern and the very high stakes of the argument, not from any calm assurance that rights consciousness can be shown to have sound foundations in this post-Nietzschean world. Although I choose to stand with those who admire rights consciousness, my aim is less to bolster their morale than to alert them to a present danger and encourage them to pay closer attention to the problem of justification.

The background against which we must evaluate rights consciousness today, and against which it will almost certainly appear to lack any adequate foundation, is the far-ranging debate over "interpretation" that riveted the attention of literary critics during the 1980s and then began sweeping through philosophical, legal, and social scientific circles as well. Although one pole of this debate is often labeled "historicism" and the entire controversy grows out of a rivalry between History and Reason that goes all the way back to ancient Greece, professional historians have, with few exceptions, failed to take any active part in the debate and seem, for the most part, to be oblivious of its existence.[2] The aloofness of historians today is very different from the active role that Carl Becker and Charles Beard played in an earlier round of what was essentially the same debate. Whether the absence of historians from the current field of battle testifies to the imperturbable good sense of a discipline that has both feet firmly planted in empirical inquiry, or signifies instead the dullness of a discipline smugly unaware of its own theoretical commitments and so busy sifting through its own overspecialized and underconceptualized scholarly productions that its members no longer have time to be intellectuals, is an open and important question—but not one I plan to answer here.[3]

By arguing, as I do in this essay, (1) that rights refer to something real and ought to be valued as rational conventions, and (2) that they neither have nor need any deeper sort of justification, in nature or anywhere else, I stake out a position (not at all original with me) that is situated at neither of the extreme ends of the spectrum of possibilities defined by "History" and "Reason." Being located somewhere in the middle, the moderate variety of historicism that I am recommending has to anticipate attacks coming from opposite directions and is perpetually liable to be mistaken for one extreme by partisans of the other. Despite those discomforts and the ambivalent stance they induce, it is a position that seems to me especially suitable for historians, people who spend much of their lives struggling to make sense of change. Given our professional interest in change, we historians are not likely to feel comfortable at the Reason end of the spectrum, often identified with Plato, because from that standpoint reality is what never changes and change cannot be expected to make sense. Anyone who trusts logic and distrusts appearances as much as Plato would be unlikely to become a historian in the first place, for if reason is the sole and sufficient route to understanding, history is only a vain chase after the fleeting shadows of reality.

On the other hand, the moderate historicism that I admire (and that I think promises a safe haven for rights talk) must also be sharply distinguished from the more radical varieties of historicism that are commonly identified as Nietzschean. We historians can hardly help being attracted to the historicist end of the spectrum in this debate, but that need not prevent us from recognizing that historicism harbors within itself radical possibilities that are deeply antagonistic not only to ideas of natural right but also to all hopes of expanding the sway of reason and moral order in the world. Friedrich Nietzsche saw with uncanny clarity just where the most extreme forms of historicism lead — not just away from Plato's universal Truth and timeless forms, which we can all do without, but beyond the very ideas of truth and falsehood, or good and evil, toward a heroic but brutal world in which nothing counts but will and the power to carry it out. Committed though I am to a moderate historicism, if forced to make a painful choice between the extremes of Nietzsche and Plato, it is Plato I would unhesitatingly choose.

Since the essay was written in a predominately anti-Nietzschean mood and then revised in a quite different mood as Allan Bloom's belligerently anti-historicist tract, *The Closing of the American Mind,* soared to the top of best-seller lists in this country and abroad, the necessity of defending two flanks at once has been the overriding consideration, and I have accepted help wherever I could find it. No one saw the dangers of radical historicism more clearly than Bloom's mentor, Leo Strauss, and so I have drawn freely on Strauss's *Natural Right and History* (a more substantial work than Bloom's) to set the stage and to unfold the basic issues of the debate — even though Strauss's indiscriminate hostility to historicism would have led him to reject out of hand even the moderate variety that I am recommending.[4] Having set the stage, I then draw on the work of Alasdair MacIntyre, who has done as much as anyone to develop and clarify the implications of a moderate form of historicism. The third and final section of the essay examines some of the strengths and limitations of rights understood as conventions and points to some of the most impressive achievements of moderate historicism, the work of John Rawls and Thomas S. Kuhn.

In the Walgreen lectures at the University of Chicago in 1949 (later published as *Natural Right and History*), Leo Strauss argued that the outcome of World War II was paradoxical. The United States and its allies had won the war militarily but lost it culturally. "It would not be the first time," he said, "that a nation, defeated on the battlefield and, as it were, annihilated as a political being, has deprived its conquerors of the most sublime fruit of victory by imposing on them the yoke of its own thought." The German yoke that Strauss thought Americans had unaccountably accepted was historicism, and what it threatened to strangle was the idea of natural rights, which Strauss took to be the mainstay of American democracy. A generation earlier, he claimed, "an American diplomat could still say that 'the natural and the divine foundation of the rights of man . . . is self-evident to all Americans.'" In prewar Germany, by contrast, the idea of natural rights had become almost incomprehensible under the influence of a historicist mode of thought that set all fixed values adrift on the stormy sea of relativism. Now, said Strauss, in spite of the Allied victory, the German attitude toward natural rights had spread to leading intellectual circles in the United States.

> Whatever might be true of the thought of the American people, certainly American social science has adopted the very attitude toward natural right which, a generation ago, could still be described with some plausibility, as characteristic of German thought. The majority among the learned who still adhere to the principles of the Declaration of Independence interpret those principles not as expressions of natural right but as an ideal, if not as an ideology or a myth. Present-day American social science, as far as it is not Roman Catholic social science, is dedicated to the proposition that all men are endowed by the evolutionary process or by a mysterious fate with many kinds of urges and aspirations, but certainly with no natural right.[5]

There is, I believe, a genuine paradox about rights in twentieth-century America, and Strauss's attack on German historicism can help us understand what it is. But Strauss misconstrued the cultural landscape of postwar America, and the paradox I want to bring into focus is not the same one he had in mind. Skepticism about natural rights thinking was not the recent arrival in America that he made it out to be, and it has not always spoken with a German accent.[6] The impeccably American sociologist William Graham Sumner (a sturdy liberal who prided himself on having "never caught the Hegelian fever" during his two years at Göttingen) taught Yale students in the 1880s that the whole natural rights tradition was a dangerous illusion in a world governed by the Darwinian struggle for survival. Even before Charles Darwin, thinkers as little tainted by German ideas as Jeremy Bentham had declared natural rights to be no more than "nonsense upon stilts." Neither the rights tradition nor criticism of it has been as unitary as Strauss thought. Indeed, if Garry Wills is correct about the influence of the Scottish moral sense school on Thomas Jefferson, not even the author of the Declaration of Independence imagined the rights he called "self-evident" to have quite the Platonic qualities of timelessness and universality that Strauss claimed for them in *Natural Right and History.*[7]

The puzzle about rights, then, is not why the West allowed Germany to sabotage the intellectual foundations of democracy just at the moment of Allied victory; instead, it is why talk about rights should continue to flourish in the West after well over a century of widespread (and not exclusively German) skepticism about the soundness of its foundations. The paradox deepens dramatically as we shift our attention to the past four decades. After a brief respite in the 1950s, the tide of relativism that Strauss sought to check has continued to swell. Today the most radical of the German historicists, Nietzsche and Martin Heidegger, are not only being given a respectful hearing in America, they are riding a wave of intellectual fashion. One could hardly imagine a setting less hospitable to the idea of natural rights, yet in the practical domains of law and politics, rights have a stronger hold on the public imagination than ever before. The years since Strauss spoke include, after all, the era of the civil rights movement. Under the banner of "equal rights," blacks and other ethnic minorities made major gains and decisively transformed the shape of public life. In spite of the failure of the Equal Rights Amendment, rights for women expanded steadily. During these years, not only has the routine business of the courts continued to revolve around rights, but, moreover, thousands of Americans have challenged existing law and pressed for the establishment of new laws because of their perception that their own rights, or someone else's, were being violated. As Ronald Dworkin reported in 1977, "The language of rights now dominates political debate in the United States."[8]

Even more remarkable (though perhaps less for its present accomplishments than for what it presupposes) is the growing respect paid in these years to the idea that human rights should sometimes determine policy even in international affairs, where amoral judgments of national interest have traditionally held sway. To assert the existence of rights common to all human beings, regardless of nationality—rights that transcend and override all the polyglot differences of culture and historical situation that we see around us in the world today — is quite astonishing, for it seems to presuppose a confidence in the power of reason to identify the essential nature and universal destiny of man that owes more to Plato than to German historicism.

It was precisely such confidence that Strauss sought to bolster in *Natural Right and History*. He argued that "disastrous consequences" would follow from basing rights on anything less stable than the essential nature of man and the world. Rejecting natural right was "tantamount to saying that all right is positive right, and this means that what is right is determined exclusively by the legislators and the courts of the various countries." If legislators and judges create the only rights there are, then it is not clear what we mean by speaking of "unjust" laws and "unjust" decisions, for such words imply the existence of a standard higher than any statute or court. "In passing such judgments we imply that there is a standard of right and wrong independent of positive right and higher than positive right: a standard with reference to which we are able to judge of positive right." The standard, he thought, could not be merely conventional in character, arising from society itself, or from culture, or from a "way of life," because we do, after all, condemn certain ideals even though they are well established in our society. "The mere fact that we can raise the question of the worth of the ideal of our society shows that there is something in man that is not altogether in slavery to his society, and therefore that we are able, and hence obliged, to look for a standard with reference to which we can judge of the ideals of our own as well as of any other society."[9]

In contrast to the natural rights tradition, as Strauss correctly observed, historicism denies the possibility of establishing any transhistorical or transcultural standard. Stressing the irreducible uniqueness of all events in human history and therefore the artificiality of all the concepts and categories that mankind invents to impose order on the flux of experience, historicism leaves little or (in its radical form) no room for a mental faculty capable of transcending time and place. Historicism teaches that we never stand in the same river twice, and that the quintessentially Platonic aspiration to reach behind the shifting appearances of things to grasp immutable truths is futile. Man himself, all his faculties, and all the standards and values to which he might possibly refer are understood by historicism to be deeply immersed in an endlessly changing stream of circumstances from which no thought escapes. There are no eternal values or universal standards, only contingent and relative ones. There is no Archimedean point, independent of time and place, for reason to occupy. In Strauss's apt summary, the central thesis of historicism is that

> all understanding, all knowledge, however limited and "scientific," presupposes a frame of reference; it presupposes a horizon, a comprehensive view within

which understanding and knowing take place. Only such a comprehensive vision makes possible any seeing, any observation, any orientation. The comprehensive view of the whole cannot be validated by reasoning, since it is the basis of all reasoning. Accordingly, there is a variety of such comprehensive views, each as legitimate as any other: we have to choose such a view without any rational guidance.[10]

To say, as historicism does, that all our efforts to grapple mentally with the world are shaped by a frame of reference, and that we do not have any rational basis for choosing between frames of reference, is to suggest that reason is indeed enslaved by (or at least confined within) the particular social and historical context in which it finds itself. And if that is the case, it is difficult to see how rights and the other insights proclaimed by reason can be anything more than mutable social conventions. They evidently cannot be natural or possess any other sort of ultimate foundation. They become, at best, merely agreed-upon fictions, and their value, if any, becomes merely instrumental, open to negotiation, subject to change. Under a historicist dispensation, rights cannot be understood to possess the deep and certain epistemological basis that Strauss thought they needed if democracy was to thrive.

Once we confront the question as to whether historicism leaves us with anything worth calling a right, Strauss and a moderate historicist like myself have to part company; I say yes, he says no. From my standpoint, Strauss exaggerates the damage that historicism does to the idea of rights, and his discussion of democracy, insofar as it seeks to identify democracy exclusively with transcendent reason and epistemological certainty, is plainly tendentious. Democracy is not an offspring of Reason alone: it not only can tolerate, it even requires a rather large dose of historicism's uncertainty, for if we felt that our knowledge of the good was epistemologically beyond question, there would be no occasion for cultivating the democratic habits of tolerance and pluralism.[11]

But if Strauss exaggerates the dangers of historicism, there are many participants in the current debate over interpretation who greatly underestimate them. One would not know from the laid-back, happy-go-lucky tone of much contemporary historicist writing that the doctrine even had teeth, much less fangs. Virtually all shades of historicists must feel some degree of skepticism about what Strauss took to be the indispensable foundation for natural rights: namely, confidence that by employing our reason we can acquire "genuine knowledge [as opposed to opinion, whether idiosyncratic or conventional] of what is intrinsically good or right." But this need not be alarming, it is calmly observed, for after all, we live today in an "age of interpretation." If any single story can stand for the mood of the times, it is Clifford Geertz's tale about the

Englishman in India who, "having been told that the world rested on the back of an elephant which rested in turn on the back of a turtle, asked . . . what did the turtle rest on? Another turtle. And that turtle? 'Ah, Sahib, after that it is turtles all the way down.' "[12]

Clearly if it's "turtles all the way down," there is nothing on which to rest rights claims but the slippery back of yet another turtle. But what needs explaining is how we are to reconcile this lighthearted image with the heaviness of heart we all feel upon reading, say, the reports prepared by Amnesty International. Do our objections to torture have no better foundation than this? Are the torturer's practices just the product of a particular cultural and historical situation incommensurably different from our own? How can we label them "inhuman"—implying cross-cultural standards of humane behavior—unless reason actually has some of the power that Strauss attributes to it of transcending time and place, so as to grasp what is essentially human?

The supposed impossibility of ever reaching an essential or foundational level of thought or perception closely parallels another theme of contemporary historicism, the claim that since there is no simple object of thought that exists "out there," independent of our thinking, the entire intellectual ethic calling for accuracy in representation is fundamentally misguided. " 'Accurate representation,' " philosopher Richard Rorty rather glibly declares, "is simply an automatic and empty compliment which we pay to those beliefs which are successful in helping us to do what we want to do."[13] Accordingly Rorty urges his fellow philosophers to abandon the entire enterprise of epistemology, stop worrying about justifying their beliefs, and confess that philosophy and similar efforts of intellect are merely extended conversations that, although edifying, can never hope to represent the world "as it really is." Far from requiring any drastic change in the way we live, Rorty seems to regard the breakthrough to an epistemology-free world as an easy progression from where we already stand—easy at least for those of us who favor the welfare state, are in tune with the vaguely antiformalist trends of contemporary culture, and subscribe to a litany of good causes that would be familiar on any American college campus.

One doubts that the transition, if it were to occur, would really be so innocuous. As historicist criticism converts the world of so-called facts into an evanescent mirage and puts in doubt the very possibility of grounded argument, more apocalyptic scenarios inevitably heave into view. The primordial intellectual enterprise of interpretation, fed by an imagination that no longer meets resistance in any direction and thus has learned to scorn the very idea of objective reality, now throbs and swells in hopes of filling the entire cosmos. In the much-quoted words of Michel Foucault, "What has emerged in the last ten or fifteen years is a sense of the increasing vulnerability to criticism of things, institutions, practices, discourses. A certain fragility has been discovered in the very bedrock of existence."[14] The high priest of interpretive liberty and archenemy of intellectual foundations of all sorts is, of course, deconstructionist philosopher Jacques Derrida, for whom all attempts to cultivate "presence"—the sense that one has been brought by argument, logic, rationality, or any other mode of thought or communication into the intimate vicinity of what is essential, or fundamental, or truthful—are illusions, tricks with words, and nothing more. For him the target is not merely epistemology, but the very heart of philosophy, the "logocentric" ambition to see behind appearances. With Derrida and other contemporary relativists, human discourse becomes free at last—free, one fears, even of the chastening thought that there is a real world to which our minds ought to become adequate.[15]

Nietzsche cut closer to the quick and put his finger on the heart of the problem—the absence of natural limits to interpretation. "Whatever exists," he said in *The Genealogy of Morals*, "having somehow come into being, is again and again reinterpreted to new ends, taken over, transformed, and redirected by some power superior to it; all events in the organic world are a subduing, a becoming master, and all subduing and becoming master involves a fresh interpretation, an adaptation through which any previous 'meaning' and 'purpose' are necessarily obscured or even obliterated. . . . Only that which has no history is definable."[16]

The boundlessness of interpretation—implying, as it does, the absence of any but self-imposed constraints upon thought, the fluidity of the boundary (if any) between reason and the imagination, and the impossibility, therefore, of objective judgment—is the quintessential premise of the more radical forms of historicism. And from it Nietzsche drew the necessary conclusion concerning not only natural rights but also law and moral order generally. All, he thought, are of a piece with religion and kindred superstitions. All are futile gestures, in which man flees from the world as it *is,* and tries vainly to impose upon his experience an otherworldly *ought.* By imputing to this figment of his own imagination a specious quality of externality and tenacity—of objective reality, in other words—man merely betrays his deep and "nihilistic" hatred of himself and the profane world of his actual experience.

"Just" and "unjust" exist, accordingly, only after the institution of the law (and *not,* as Duhring would have it, after the perpetration of the injury). To speak of just or unjust *in itself* is quite senseless; *in itself* of course, no injury, assault, exploitation, destruction can be "unjust," since life operates *essentially,* that is in its basic functions, through injury, assault, exploitation, destruction and simply cannot be thought of at all without this character. One must indeed grant something even more unpalatable: that from the highest biological standpoint, legal conditions can never be other than *exceptional conditions*, since they constitute a partial restriction of the will to life, which is bent upon power, and are subordinate to its total goal as a single means: namely, that of creating *greater* units of power. A legal order thought of as sovereign and universal, not as a means in the struggle between power complexes but as a means of *preventing* all struggle in general—perhaps after the communistic cliché of Duhring, that every will must consider every other will its equal—would be a principle *hostile to life*, an agent of the dissolution and destruction of man, an attempt to assassinate the future of man, a sign of weariness, a secret path to nothingness.[17]

The heart of the antagonism between historicism and the concept of natural right can be summed up in a single question. What is the difference between saying, "I have a *right* to *x*," and saying simply, "I want *x*"? If Nietzsche is correct, there is no substantial difference. The language of natural rights, like the puffing up of a mockingbird's feathers as it hops and screams in defense of its territory, is just for show. The first statement ("I have a *right* to *x*"), while speciously making appeal to an objective notion of the good, is just a grandiose form of the second. Honesty would require us to abandon the puffed-up language of rights and confine our conversation to all that is really at stake—our conflicting wills. Whatever course of action wins the contest thereby demonstrates its superiority. There are no objective grounds on which the loser can stand to impugn the victor; there is no fourth dimension, as it were, in which defeat is counterbalanced by being "in the right." Sour grapes there can certainly be in Nietzsche's world, but no injustice, save that pale formality defined by statute. In a world of ceaseless change, evolving toward nothing, might makes right. There is no higher standard by which to judge might. Whatever outrage we may feel on reading the reports of Amnesty International must dissipate downward, slipping and sliding forever over the back of one damn turtle after another.

Strauss contends, of course, that there is a vital difference between the two statements; that its basis can be found in the essential nature of man and the world he occupies; and that reason, a faculty potentially available to all human beings, though not fully developed in all, is capable of revealing the natural basis to us. In Strauss's world, rights claims are subject to rational assessment. They can be mistaken. Some are stronger than others. Some deserve our support; others do not. In contrast, there is no such thing as a "mistaken" rights claim in Nietzsche's world. Such claims are understood by Nietzsche in strictly instrumental terms. All appeals to "objective" standards are merely rhetorical moves in a contest of wills. Rights have no real existence for Nietzsche, but if claiming a right furthers the realization of one's will, the claim passes the only test he recognizes. Mockingbirds, after all, have come a long way by puffing themselves up, and the practice will continue as long as it fools sparrows.

The chasm that yawns between Strauss and Nietzsche is as deep and wide as any known to mankind. Yet there is one thing they agree on. They both assume that the only acceptable basis for rights would be metaphysical. Nietzsche hitches rights talk to metaphysics for the purpose of discrediting it; Strauss, because he thinks reason can vindicate the connection. Both hold that right must refer to something timeless and universal, something that transcends the mundane world of human experience, something, in Strauss's words, that "is wholly independent of any human compact or convention."[18] That is the assumption that moderate historicism fruitfully rejects.

No one can remain indifferent in the face of a choice as momentous as that posed for us by Strauss and Nietzsche. As a historian, however, I am for the moment less concerned to resolve the ultimate question of the objectivity of rights than to understand the significance of the paradox evidenced by current talk about rights. Whether or not we have objective knowledge of natural rights, we continue to talk as if we did. What are we to make of the paradoxical persistence of rights talk in an age of interpretation?

One answer, Nietzsche's answer, is that on closer inspection, there is no paradox. If rights talk is nothing but a puffed-up form of the will to power, then there is nothing surprising in the persistence of such talk so long as it serves some manipulative purpose. Indeed, from Nietzsche's perspective, one might predict the intensification of rights talk as more and more people shed their illusions about objectivity and come to see in the old superstitions about natural rights a useful device for manipulating the gullible. Only in the far distant future, when no one any longer believes in metaphysical things, when everyone has learned Nietzsche's lesson that "there is *only* a perspective seeing, *only* a perspective 'knowing' " — in short, when there are no more sparrows for mockingbirds to intimidate — only then will the language of rights fade away.[19]

Uncongenial though Nietzsche's vision is, it cannot be lightly dismissed. The antimetaphysical tilt of modern culture is very strong, and there is much in contemporary rights debates that rings hollow and suggests that the debaters often see their opponents, and even themselves, in a predominantly cynical light. If nothing were at stake but the possibility that some elements of the traditional vocabulary of law and politics have become obsolete, then it might make sense, as some members of the critical legal studies movement have recently suggested, to modernize the vocabulary, to search for alternative ways of talking that do not imply anything objective about rights.[20] But the paradox is not confined to rights. It extends across the entire spectrum of ethics and morality. The idea of a right, after all, is only one variation on the claim to objective knowledge about morality. Our awkward silence when asked to specify the difference between "I want *x*" and "I have a *right* to *x*" is duplicated when we are asked to distinguish *any* form of moral utterance from statements of merely personal preference. Certainly we feel no more sure of ourselves when we try to explain the all-important difference between "You *ought* to do *y*" and "I want you to do *y*."

Having begun by noticing something paradoxical about the persistence of rights talk in modern society, we have now apparently stumbled across a fragment of a ruin so extensive that it stretches to our farthest cultural horizon. It is as if we found ourselves standing before an ancient building, visibly weathered and beginning to tumble down, which squatters inhabit and even use ceremonially, but whose founders have vanished, and whose true function and purpose becomes hazier in the minds of each succeeding generation. The ruin is the very idea of moral obligation. We are the squatters.

The irrelevance of the effort merely to patch up our legal and political vocabulary about rights is made manifest by the brilliant opening chapters of Alasdair MacIntyre's *After Virtue*. Although, as we shall see, MacIntyre ultimately segregates rights from other claims to objective moral knowledge and treats them dismissively, that gambit is very much at odds with the main thrust of his argument, which is to encourage us to take very seriously the possibility of objective knowledge about morality—including, as I see it, knowledge of rights. MacIntyre launches his argument with an imaginative exercise. In a metaphor less physical than the one I have employed, but equally archeological, he likens the way we use the language of morality today to the way the language of science might be used in a civilization whose scientific institutions had been catastrophically disrupted. Imagine, he proposes, that all scientific instruction is brought to a complete halt, that all scientists are put to death and their books and instruments destroyed. Eventually a reaction against the wave of destruction occurs, and a countermovement strives to restore science to its former glory, but its members scarcely remember what science was, and all they possess are fragments: parts of theories, instruments whose purpose is unknown, books with missing chapters. From the fragments they reconstruct what purports to be a systematic scientific enterprise and train their children in its rituals and incantations. But so disordered is their knowledge that the result is without substance. They can only go through the motions.

MacIntyre's arresting hypothesis is that "in the actual world which we inhabit the language of morality is in the same state of grave disorder as the language of natural science in the imaginary world which I described." "What we possess, if this view is true, are the fragments of a conceptual scheme, parts which now lack those contexts from which their significance derived. We possess indeed simulacra of morality, we continue to use many of the key expressions. But we have—very largely, if not entirely—lost our comprehension, both theoretical and practical, of morality." [21] What persuades MacIntyre of the incoherence of contemporary moral discourse is the very same paradox we have already encountered in rights talk: the coexistence in our culture of moral language implying objectivity and of a deep skepticism about the theoretical possibility of achieving such objectivity. By standing on MacIntyre's shoulders, we can situate the paradox in the broader moral context where it belongs, and we can unfold further implications of our obstinate tendency to continue striving for objective knowledge of rights and other moral matters, even in the face of our own skepticism.

The most striking feature of contemporary moral debate, MacIntyre argues, is its literally interminable character. "There seems to be no rational way of securing moral agreement in our culture." Whether we debate abortion, arms control, or affirmative action, we quickly find the exchange petering out as each party falls back on premises that seem incommensurable. "The rival premises are such that we possess no rational way of weighing the claims of one as against another." In addition to its interminable character, however, contemporary moral debate has a second characteristic that is equally striking in a contrasting way. It is the tendency of all parties to formulate moral injunctions in terms like duty or general social utility, considerations that "presuppose the existence of *impersonal* criteria, the existence, independently of the preferences or attitudes of speaker or hearer, of standards of justice or generosity or duty."

> This second characteristic of contemporary moral utterance and argument, when combined with the first, imparts a paradoxical air to contemporary moral disagreement. For if we attend solely to the first characteristic, to the way in which what at first appears to be argument relapses so quickly into unargued disagreement, we might conclude that there is nothing to such contemporary disagreements but a clash of antagonistic wills, each will determined by some set of arbitrary choices of its own. But this second characteristic, the use of expressions whose distinctive function in our language is to embody what purports to be an appeal to objective standards, suggests otherwise. (6, 8, 9)

Forthrightly rejecting the Nietzschean or (as MacIntyre calls it) the "emotivist" interpretation of the paradox, according to which the language of objectivity is nothing but a mask for personal feeling and preference, MacIntyre insists that the entire paradox—the obstinate persistence of the appeal to objective standards, as well as the skepticism aroused by such appeals—deserves to be taken with the utmost seriousness: "For even if the surface appearance of argument is only a masquerade, the question remains, 'Why *this* masquerade?' What is it about rational argument which is so important that it is the nearly universal appearance assumed by those who engage in moral conflict? Does this not suggest that the practice of moral argument in our culture expresses at least an aspiration to be or to become rational in this area of our lives?" (9–10).

Taking the paradox seriously does not mean that we must treat all claims to objective moral judgment as sincere, much less as valid. MacIntyre acknowledges that emotivism has become embodied in our culture, so that under present conditions the assertion of rights and other moral principles does often function as a mask for personal preferences (22). Our suspicion about moral claims is often justifiable. In a culture such as ours, there is no skulduggery that cannot be carried out in a righteous manner and no inhumanity that cannot be perpetrated under the banner of humanitarianism. All MacIntyre denies is that what is true of our culture and our era must be true of all cultures and all eras. Taking the paradox seriously, then, means two things: recognizing that even in our emotivist culture, some claims to objective moral judgment may be valid, however degraded the idiom in which they are expressed, and recognizing also that the confusion we experience between morality and mere personal preference is not a timeless feature of the human condition, but the product of particular historical conditions. In effect, MacIntyre proposes to historicize historicism. Instead of dismissing claims to moral objectivity as inherently fraudulent, he treats them as evidence of a deeply human "aspiration to be or become rational in this area of our lives" and asks what it is about recent historical and social development that frustrates that aspiration.

His answer to that distinctively historical question combines two interwoven strands, the first of which I find fruitful, but open to question, and the second fascinating, but finally unconvincing. The first strand of his answer is that our present dilemma results from the breakdown of the "Enlightenment project of morality." That project aimed to lift morality off the Christian and Aristotelian foundations on which it had been erected and to graft it, little altered, on a new secular, rational foundation, incorporating a naturalistic conception of human nature. The key figures in the grafting project were Thomas Hobbes, John Locke, David Hume, and Immanuel Kant. As a first approximation to what MacIntyre has in mind, one can say that the "state of grave disorder" in which we find morality today results from the fact that the graft did not take, and so our expressions of moral judgment today are little more than "linguistic survivals from the practices of classical theism" (2, 60). Deprived of the pre-Enlightenment cultural context that gave it its original meaning, the language of morality, like the language of science in MacIntyre's imaginary civilization, lingers on in our lives, but it is incapable of sustaining more than a flat and vulgarized form of moral practice.

MacIntyre is not just repeating the old fear that no system of moral obligation can be made sufficiently binding without a divine being to command human obedience. He traces the moral frailty of emotivist culture not to a particular belief or its absence, but to a cultural condition, a relationship between ideas and institutionalized practices that is reciprocal and self-sustaining. What is distinctive about emotivist culture is a cluster of beliefs and practices that tends to obliterate the distinction between manipulative and non-manipulative social relations. We treat people manipulatively when we disregard Kant's maxim and construe them as a means to our own ends rather than as ends in themselves. But in order to treat others as ends, one must offer them "good reasons" for acting one way rather than another while leaving it up to them to evaluate those reasons. If there are no impersonal objective criteria for reason to appeal to, then the distinction between "good reasons" and other inducements wavers and the very idea of morality loses substance. In the individualistic and bureaucratic environment characteristic of emotivist culture, people tend in fact to encounter one another as means rather than ends. The result is a blurring of the categories on which moral judgment depends and a growing suspicion, seemingly confirmed by everyday experience, that all human relations are indistinguishably manipulative (23, 24).

It is at this point that MacIntyre picks up the second and less convincing thread of his argument. Striving to ascertain what cultural transformation would be required to overcome emotivism and to enable people to deal with one another as ends rather than means, he finds the key in a reaffirmation of a teleological conception of the self. The difference between manipulative and nonmanipulative social relations would not be difficult to discern if we could all agree that man has an essence that defines his true end, or *telos*. Classical theism, the Christianized version of the Aristotelian worldview that the Enlightenment project sought to supersede, conceived of man in just that way. It understood morality to consist of dynamic relations among the parts of a tripartite scheme: first there was man-as-he-happens-to-be, then there was man-as-he-could-become-if-he-realized-his-essential-nature. The third element in the scheme was the science of ethics, which showed man how to make the transition from the former state to the latter. Within that inherently teleological scheme, morality was not so much a matter of *interpretation* as of *fact*, and therefore moral claims were not merely a matter of perspective but could be said to be either *true* (if they furthered the realization of man's essence) or *false* (if they did not) (52–53).

The fatal mistake of the Enlightenment, then, was its abandonment of a teleological conception of man. Hobbes and his eighteenth-century successors, the heirs of the extensive critique of reason carried out by the Protestant Reformation, did not have sufficient confidence in the power of reason to impute to man any true and universal end. Deprived of any general end inherent in human nature, the classical image of man was inadvertently transformed by the Enlightenment into the modern *individual,* whose only "essence" is his lack of essential qualities, and whose only destiny is the barren "freedom" to choose arbitrarily between an infinity of private and particular ends. From start to finish, claims MacIntyre, the Enlightenment project was incoherent. Beginning, as it did, with a conception of human nature deeply influenced by Christianity, the project could have no hope of finding in that conception a rational basis for morality, for Christianity had always understood human nature and morality to be fundamentally antagonistic. Nor, since the Enlightenment lacked any conception of what-man-could-be-if-he-realized-his-telos, could its moral scheme have any *destination* for man's ethical aspirations. Consequently, the science of ethics, which had once shown man how to move from a lower state to a higher one more in accord with his essential nature, quite literally lost its point (53–55).

Schematic though it is, MacIntyre's account undeniably deepens our understanding. By insisting on the relevance of sociology and history to philosophy, and vice versa, he points the way to a genuine history of morality, as opposed to the histories of moral philosophy that we already possess in abundance. By historicizing historicism, he rescues our curiously persistent claims to objective moral knowledge from the oblivion to which radical historicism would consign them, forcing us not only to take them seriously but also to search for new practices and forms of communal existence better able to sustain them.

My reservations about his thesis take two forms, the first methodological, the second substantive. The first, unsurprisingly, is that as a historian I think we must do even more than MacIntyre has already done to put history and philosophy in each other's intimate service. Eager though he is to give history its due, MacIntyre's account remains (as perhaps it must) the great-man style of history that one would expect of someone trained primarily as a philosopher. In the postscript to the second edition of *After Virtue,* responding to a historian's criticism, MacIntyre acknowledges that "from the point of view that I am taking theoretical and philosophical enterprises, their successes and failures, are far more influential in history than academic historians generally have taken them to be. The issues that need to be settled in this area are questions of fact concerning causal influence" (272).

I find it difficult to believe that factual inquiry could sustain MacIntyre on that point. By trying to justify the mutual relevance of philosophy and history in terms of the *influence* of great thinkers, he seems to me to weaken his case and stifle his own best instincts, which are to construe the great thinker's role mainly in terms of reflecting and articulating the presuppositions of a particular form of life, practiced by an entire community. MacIntyre seems at times to forget his own lesson, the lesson history always wants to teach philosophy, namely, that "moral philosophers, however they may aspire to achieve more than this, always do articulate the morality of some particular social and cultural standpoint." As MacIntyre himself says, it is for exactly that reason that "the history of morality and the history of moral philosophy are a single history" (268). If the significance of figures such as Hobbes, Hume, and Kant lies largely in what their work *reflects* about the cultural systems, or moralities, within which they did their thinking, then we cannot understand the course of historical development by constructing narratives that cast them in predominantly causal roles, as if they were generals whose decision to attack this doctrine, or defend that one, implied an obedient response by armies of followers.

Although MacIntyre's best instincts in this regard often prevail over his worst ones, some of the most vital turns in his argument rest on serious exaggerations of the causal significance of great thinkers and their decisions. Here my methodological objection becomes a substantive one as well, for it is precisely such exaggeration that leads MacIntyre to conclude that the only way out of our present emotivist difficulties is to go all the way back to Aristotle and a teleological conception of man. It is not just a manner of speaking, I suggest, that prompts him to dramatize our present dilemma as a stark choice between Nietzsche and Aristotle, and to commit himself to the plainly hopeless task of vindicating the latter—a task in which MacIntyre could succeed only if he managed to shoulder aside upwards of three centuries of historical development, to the satisfaction of an audience profoundly shaped by that development.

This is the daunting task he sets himself:

It was because a moral tradition in which Aristotle's thought was the intellectual core was repudiated during the transitions from the fifteenth to the seventeenth centuries that the Enlightenment project of discovering new rational secular foundations for morality had to be undertaken. And it was because

that project failed, because the views advanced by its most intellectually powerful protagonists, and more especially by Kant, could not be sustained in the
face of rational criticism that Nietzsche and all his existentialist and emotivist
successors were able to mount their apparently successful critique of all previous morality. Hence the defensibility of the Nietzschean position turns *in the
end* on the answer to the question: was it right in the first place to reject Aristotle? . . . And thus the key question does indeed become: can Aristotle's ethics,
or something very like it, after all be vindicated? (117–18) [22]

MacIntyre cannot have it both ways. If we endorse his views that the history of morality and moral philosophy are one and that the moral philosopher
can at best hope only to articulate the morality implicit in his or her community's form of life, then we cannot endorse his attempt to explain the most
important turning point in the recent history of morality, the emergence of
emotivist culture, as the result (even *"in the end"*) of a philosophical *mistake,*
a failure to recognize the merits of Aristotle's teleological views. The first set
of commitments requires us to regard any such epochal development as the
downfall of Aristotelianism as a broadly social and cultural development, in
which the debates of philosophers played a part more reflective than causal.
And if that is so, many of the factors sustaining the culture of emotivism today
are far beyond the reach of philosophical argumentation. MacIntyre acknowledges as much in an extended discussion of practices and the dependence of
the virtues upon practice, but I find nothing in his discussion quite capable
of overcoming the initial impression that a philosophical error is at the root
of our problems — that if we rectified the mistake about Aristotle, morality
might now be returned to a more desirable path. MacIntyre's own sense of futility becomes painfully clear in the last pages of the book, where he expresses
an almost bottomless pessimism about the future and can think of nothing
more hopeful to recommend than the construction of "local forms of community within which civility and the intellectual and moral life can be sustained
through the new dark ages which are already upon us" (263).

Not the least of the anomalies in *After Virtue* is MacIntyre's dismissive attitude toward the rights tradition. Having begun by insisting that we ought to
take claims to moral objectivity very seriously, as evidence of a deeply human
aspiration, regrettably thwarted by mutable historical conditions, he seems to
undercut his own argument when he later declares flatly that "the truth is
plain: there are no . . . [natural or human] rights, and belief in them is one
with belief in witches and unicorns" (69).

Why should rights talk be dismissed while other claims to objective moral
knowledge are treated sympathetically? I do not quarrel with MacIntyre's la-

ment over the ritualistic cycle of indignation, protest, and reciprocal unmasking that is so characteristic of public debate in a rights-conscious emotivist culture; it can be tiresome, and it no doubt breeds sanctimoniousness by the barrelful, as all sides to a dispute cast their opponents in the role of the willfully blind, who refuse to see what is supposed to be self-evident. And it is true that the rights tradition and its principal rival in moral philosophy, utilitarianism, together constitute the main legacy of the Enlightenment project, against which MacIntyre's book is written. Rights also incur his wrath because they are so prominent in the vocabulary of individualism and private property. But it is curiously inconsistent of him to dismiss rights on the grounds that they are "fictions."

Saying that rights are fictions need not mean anything more than that they are human creations, *conventions,* as opposed to natural or metaphysical objects. And it is not at all clear how MacIntyre, a moral philosopher with a singularly strong historical orientation, could object to a moral claim simply because it is conventional. In the classic polar opposition between nature and convention, one would expect anyone as deeply influenced by historicism as MacIntyre to locate moral obligation in the category of convention, and there, on that comparatively low-lying ground, to build the strongest defense for it he can. MacIntyre is committed, after all, to the view that moral philosophy is a matter of articulating the (conventional) practices of a community's form of life. For both Strauss and Nietzsche, rights have to be based on the high ground of man's essential nature, or to lack any adequate basis at all. But MacIntyre, like me, is presumably a moderate historicist, trying to thread his way between Strauss and Nietzsche. Once we embark on that middle path, admitting that rights talk has a fictive element loses its dismissive implications and, as we shall see, even gains some potentially constructive ones.

In the last analysis, MacIntyre's dismissal of rights talk arises from the same acute ambivalence about history that we find in his quixotic attempt to revive Aristotle as a guide for the twentieth century. Having first used history to historicize Nietzsche's radical historicism, MacIntyre then tries to use history one last time as a springboard to launch himself into an empyrean orbit, alongside Aristotle (and Strauss), where reason securely prevails over history, and where fictive rights are no longer needed, since morality has become (once again?) immune to time and cross-cultural variation, a matter of fact rather than of interpretation.

What harm would there be in regarding rights (and other claims about moral obligation) as conventions? We have already encountered the two most basic kinds of objections. Strauss would say that if rights are no more than conventions, they cannot have the desired qualities of timelessness and universality and hence cannot serve as standards against which to judge positive law. Nietzsche would say that once we have acknowledged their merely conventional character, there is no stopping: Not only do conventions obviously lack the otherworldly qualities that alone could allow them to serve as standards for the judgment of this world, they are in fact deeply mired in the same endless struggle for worldly dominance that they pretend to judge. They are just another form of the will to power.

The Straussian objection seems to me adequately refuted by our historical experience. Rights not only survive but flourish after more than a century of skepticism about their timelessness and universality. The plainest meaning of the paradoxical persistence of rights in an age of interpretation is that Strauss was wrong: neither rights nor the practices they authorize need foundations sunk deep into the heart of nature. They evidently are so amply supported by the prevailing form of life that our inability to formulate an entirely satisfying theoretical justification for them has no direct bearing on their staying power.[23]

The Nietzschean objection requires a more extensive response, but it, too, can be, and often has been, rebutted. The question is whether there is a stopping place: Once we admit that rights are in history and a product of human construction, are we compelled to discard them, and to slide all the way down the slippery slope of relativism, into Nietzsche's brutal world, where there is nothing to check one will but another of greater force and ruthlessness? Having given up timelessness and universality, are we left with nothing but the will to power? The principal argument for drawing that conclusion appeals to our sense of intellectual honesty. Having inspected our practices, which imply (or declare) the existence of rights, and having then noticed that on theoretical reflection no one is able to come forward with a fully satisfying account of what the rights are, where they come from, or why we should pay any attention to them, honesty compels us to discard them. Reasonable people do not cling to illusions, no matter how alarming the prospect of giving them up. If the unexamined life is not worth living, it is because some minimal agreement between theory and practice is vital to our sense of personal integrity.

But that is a line of argument that no honest and consistent proponent of radical historicism could pursue. Radical historicism is a standpoint from which it makes little sense to say that anyone *ought* to give up an illusion, or *ought* to adopt a new practice. The relativist cannot, with consistency, claim that his own view is true, but only that it is one of a number of perspectives between which there are no rational grounds for choice. To the extent that the relativist concedes that his view lacks the privileged character that we convey by the use of the word "true," the force of whatever recommendations he may be making will obviously be diminished. Another way of saying the same thing is to observe that if the world is as radically open to interpretation as Nietzsche says it is, there cannot be any such things as illusions, since illusions are *mistaken* interpretations, a category that implies some ground for objective judgment.[24]

More specific and still more damaging is a second liability of relativism. When the relativist says, "*Since* the world is as I describe it, you/we *ought* to do *x*," he is doubly inconsistent, for not only is he implicitly asking us to act as if his view were true, thus at least partially exempting himself from his own assumptions about the limitations of reason, he is also silently reversing the priorities of theory and practice in which historicism originates. Bringing practice into line with theory makes no sense unless one supposes that theory has priority over practice, and the rejection of that supposition is constitutive for historicism. If reason could supply the incontestable truths that Strauss claimed it could, then reason's first product, theory, could indeed be brought into play as a tool to correct practice—any hesitation to apply theory to practice would then be "unreasonable" in the most literal sense. But if one begins, as the historicist does, by denying reason such power, by insisting that reason is irretrievably embedded in time and place, then to turn around and recommend the correction of practice by theory is to lay claim to the very Archimedean point that historicism has already negated. Historicism begins by humbling reason out of respect for the irreducible singularity of every time, place, and situation; for it then to grab up the fallen mantle of theory and try to bring everyday existence under the sway of a generalized and atemporal conception of how things *ought* to be done is, at best, a bad joke.

David Hume set a good example for all those who are unimpressed with the power of reason. Writing in a tradition that located the frailty of reason less in the flux of temporality than in the difficulty of ascending from particular sensations to general conceptions, Hume glimpsed limitations of reason even more disturbing than those Nietzsche so theatrically trumpeted. Nietzsche's world, where there is nothing to counterbalance might, is terrifying enough. But there, at least, power has its result, like causes reliably produce like effects, and our past experience is a trustworthy guide to present and future action— brutal though it may be. Hume's theoretical ruminations led him to conclude that the confidence that common sense teaches us to feel about those matters has no anchorage in reason. We have no direct knowledge of any necessary connection between cause and effect. Nor do we find any warrant in reason for our commonsense assumption that the future will resemble the past. For all logic can infer, Hume argued, the bread that nourished us yesterday could poison us today, and the flame that once burned may next time be cool to the touch. From those ruminations Hume did not conclude that mankind should tailor practice to theory. He did not try to devise a new mode of life, free of the "illusions" of causality and inferential predictability. Instead he resigned himself to the imperfections of reason, shifted some of his trust to social custom and common sense, and sought out convivial company for a game of back-gammon.[25] Would that Nietzsche had done the same.

These considerations are meant to show only that there is a stopping place, that having declared rights and other kinds of moral obligation to be conventions, we do not thereby expose ourselves to an inexorable logic that will ultimately pull us down into Nietzsche's world. We are not on a frictionless slope, but on level ground, free to decide where to stand. Once we have ventured out into this sparsely settled land, far from the seductive, but unreal, comforts of Reason, and uncomfortably close to the maelstrom of History, the next question is whether the ground is stable enough to build on.

To that question a cautiously optimistic answer can be given. If convention were indistinguishable from fashion, varying kaleidoscopically in ways impossible for us to understand, then it could not provide the stable ground we seek. Rights need not be either eternal or universal, but if they are to do us any good, they must be rooted deeply enough in the human condition to win the loyalty of more than a single culture or generation.[26] Conventions obviously possess the requisite durability. We are all familiar with their power to project an aura of incontestable givenness into the most contingent arrangements, thus imposing a burden of proof on anyone seeking change. But if rights are to command rational allegiance, they must be not only durable but also open to rational criticism and deliberate change. The two requirements of durability and rationality do not sit easily with each other. The more durable a convention is, the more it becomes a matter of tradition, and the less rational human allegiance to it is likely to be. Conversely, the more open to rational criticism a convention is perceived to be, the greater the likelihood of change or abandonment. There is nothing to be gained in trying to paper over this inescapable tension.

Clearly rights as rational conventions will lack some of the qualities that have traditionally been claimed for rights. They will not be self-evident or eternal. And every attempt to apply them beyond the boundaries of one's own culture will carry grave risks of injustice through the unwitting effects of parochialism and ethnocentrism. Far from being fixed once and for all in a constitution or a bill of rights, the definition of rights will be a perpetual object of contention between rival groups with strong vested interests, both ideal and material. Far from allowing us to escape from interpretation into a realm in which moral judgment becomes a matter of fact, rights understood on the model of rational conventions promise only a continuation of the endless, but usually bloodless, wrangling to which bourgeois societies are already well accustomed. Few changes would accompany a general acceptance of the idea that rights are conventions, because much of our everyday practice already implies that they are no more than that. At best one might hope that if the conventional nature of rights ever became widely understood, rights debates might take on a less sanctimonious character, as people recognize that their differences concern conventions, rather than Truth.

Can rights that do not pretend to be eternal provide public life with sufficient order and continuity? Consider the splendid hypothetical case that Mark Tushnet devised for a purpose exactly contrary to my own. Tushnet's aim was to show that rights are irredeemably historical and, therefore, not a fit basis either for law or for morality. His exercise concerns the right to abortion, and it hinges on our recognizing that today, when a woman decides to abort a pregnancy, she chooses not one, but two things: to remove the fetus from her body and, by so doing, to terminate the life of the fetus. As Tushnet observes, the two choices seem inseparable, but only the first is the subject of rights talk, and, indeed, "all the arguments that support the right to reproductive choice apparently implicate only the first decision."

> The technology of reproduction, however, has now neared the point where the two choices are independent. If the choices were independent, there would no longer be a right to *reproductive* choice in the sense that interests us today. No one would care about a woman's decision merely to *remove* a fetus from her body, because that act would not have the consequence (*i.e.,* the death of the fetus) that troubles many people today. If the removed fetus had some caretaker available to it, the mere act of removal would be morally inconsequential.[27]

Not only would technological advance make this first choice "inconsequential" (or at least less consequential), Tushnet also points out that it would decisively alter the conditions surrounding the second choice. For once the technology was in place, a statute requiring the removal, rather than the destruction, of the fetus would probably meet with no significant resistance, on grounds of privacy or anything else. Thus technological innovation could produce a major discontinuity in the rights tradition.

For those who think of the right to abortion as an eternal verity, long neglected and only recently recognized, Tushnet's hypothetical exercise is a useful corrective. What he has shown, I take it, is that rights can more plau-sibly be construed as historical conventions than as timeless verities or meta-physical objects. I concur with him, at least in principle, that this and other rights are "contingent on social and technological facts," and that "the set of rights recognized in any particular society is coextensive with that society," so that social conditions define "what kind of rights talk makes sense, and the sort of rights talk that makes sense in turn defines what the society is." I can also agree with Tushnet that although rights debates are formally about what already exists (whether a right to do x exists or not, for example), in substance they often involve an effort to change what exists, to bring about conditions in which doing x will no longer be resisted. Although I can agree with Tush-net about each of the preparatory points, I am baffled by the generalization he intends them to support: "Once one identifies what counts as a right in a specific setting," he claims, "it invariably turns out that the right is unstable; significant but small changes in the social setting can make it difficult to claim that a right remains implicated."[28]

Tushnet's imaginary case seems to me to suggest just the reverse. Instead of showing that rights, being historical products, are hopelessly ephemeral, it suggests that such rights are likely to be quite durable, stabilizing expectations in ways that would be thought desirable in almost any conceivable society, and yet also flexible, so that when conditions change radically a right rendered obsolete might pass painlessly out of existence. The invention of a technology routinizing the care of the fetus outside the womb may be a "small change" in the sense that we can imagine it happening soon, but it would be a gigantic change in its moral implications: It would fundamentally transform the con-ditions of human existence and thereby moderate, or perhaps even avert, the most tragic collision of rights in our era, that between the right to life of a being unquestionably on the path to personhood, and the right of an adult person to control the uses made of her body.[29] Tushnet's case supports my argument better than it supports his own because it suggests that rights need not become arbitrary just because they are conventions; some conventions are better than others, more rational, more in accord with our values, better suited to the problems we face. The alacrity with which the members of Tushnet's imaginary society abandoned the right to abortion as it is defined today and adopted statutes guaranteeing the preservation of the fetus by the new tech-nology is no cause for lamentation. It is reassuring testimony that even when rights are admitted to be conventions, they retain a kind of objectivity: debates concerning them can be rational; there is a basis for discriminating between better and worse conventions. Evidently in giving up the Straussian search for a basis in Nature and Reason, we do not relinquish rationality or pass beyond good and evil. In other words, the case suggests that the supposed no-man's-land between Reason and History is a terrain suitable for human habitation.

Tushnet's hypothetical case is but one of many examples that could be marshaled to show that moral judgment, although it can never escape the coils of history and convention, need not on that account be written off either as empty rhetoric or as a devious form of the will to power. I have argued elsewhere that conventions play such a large and indispensable role in judgments of moral responsibility that, without reference to them, we could not even begin to explain the tacit choices that each of us makes every day about aiding or not aiding the world's many suffering strangers. Even such a large-scale change in moral sensibility as the rise of humanitarianism in the eighteenth century can, I believe, be best explained as the result of an outward shift in conventions governing causal attribution. That shift expanded the horizon within which people applied traditional rules of morality such as the Golden Rule, thereby exposing them to sensations of guilt and responsibility for evils that had previously appeared to be "necessary," beyond remedy. Those changes in the basis of moral judgment are ultimately traceable, I believe, to what might very broadly be labeled "technological" change, a proliferation and elaboration of everyday knowledge of cause-and-effect relations that was encouraged, among other things, by the increasing force of market relations.[30] In all these arguments, I am committed to the view that moral choices cannot be understood without reference to historical conventions.

There is fear in some quarters that by assigning convention and history such a large role in moral thinking, we open the door to all the worst excesses of the neo-Nietzscheans.[31] In my view, that fear is misplaced. By mapping more precisely the pale beyond which morality is irredeemably historical, we do concede some territory to the criterionless wilderness and bring a regrettable measure of satisfaction to the radical wing of historicism. But we also demarcate a domain—spacious, even if not as expansive as we might like—within which rights and other claims to objective moral knowledge can enjoy something like "universal" sway. That historically defensible sense of objectivity, that *provisional* immunity to incursions of time, place, and circumstance, is all we can realistically hope for.

More important, it is also all we need. We have already observed that rights talk has long flourished without deep epistemological foundations, that much of our practice in the field of rights already implies an awareness that they are conventional and historical in character, and that they are acceptable as such. That is also the status assigned them in the most important recent theoretical discussions. Philosophers John Rawls, Robert Nozick, H. L. A. Hart, and Ronald Dworkin can be called "natural rights" philosophers, but only in a very modern sense of "natural," one with few of the epistemological connotations that Strauss had in mind.[32] None of the major contemporary theorists subscribes to what Rawls calls "rational intuitionism," the classic contention descending from Plato that there is a fixed moral order given in the nature of things, which presents itself to a suitably receptive mind in the form of self-evident truths. In contrast to that Straussian position, Rawls characterizes the standpoint of his own book *A Theory of Justice* as "Kantian constructivism," which, as the name implies, specifically accepts the conventional nature of rights.[33]

> What justifies a conception of justice is not its being true to an order antecedent to and given to us, but its congruence with our deeper understanding of ourselves and our aspirations, and our realization that, given our history and the traditions imbedded in our public life, it is the most reasonable doctrine for us. We can find no better charter for our social world. Kantian constructivism holds that moral objectivity is to be understood in terms of a suitably constructed social point of view that all can accept.[34]

The "constructive" aspect of Rawls's theory of justice is vividly embodied in his conception of "the original position," a hypothetical exercise in which we imagine what sort of social arrangements would be chosen by free, rational people operating behind a "veil of ignorance." The veil of ignorance is what makes the original position a suitable position for choosing the first principles of a just society, for it guarantees that the choices made will possess something approaching a universal character. What the original choosers must be ignorant of in this exercise is knowledge of their own particular place in society. By depriving our hypothetical choosers of any inkling of their race, their gender, their age, their abilities, their wealth, their religion, their conception of the good, and so on, we gain a reasonable assurance that the arrangements they choose will be fair. There is, of course, room to argue that in working through his argument, Rawls uses the veil of ignorance to filter out too much of what is human (e.g., our conceptions of the good) or silently to introduce as premises controversial assumptions (e.g., regarding the relative priorities of the individual and the community).[35] But in the present context these are quibbles. Rawls would be the last to pretend that no other interpretations are possible, or that his method could ever hope to make moral judgment a matter of fact rather than interpretation. At a minimum the acclaim for *A Theory of Justice* testifies to his success in formulating an approach that imputes to some conceptions of justice and right a very considerable measure of objectivity, without relying on self-evident truths, Kant's leap into the noumenal realm, or any of the other "otherworldly" stratagems that even a moderate historicism must consider discredited.

Rawls's demonstration that justice can live in the borderlands between Reason and History is one more powerful argument for settling there. The most powerful of all, however, is Thomas S. Kuhn's remarkably influential book, *The Structure of Scientific Revolutions*. What Kuhn deployed in the history of science was a moderate historicism of the sort that I expect will shed much light on the history of morality in the coming decades. In spite of repeated efforts by more radical relativists to claim Kuhn as one of their own, it is increasingly clear that his own cautious historicization of science was not intended to diminish its cultural authority over matters genuinely scientific and need not have that effect, when properly understood. Scientific thinking is for Kuhn a thoroughly social and historical enterprise, and the state of opinion within any scientific community is, in his view, inescapably conventional in character, for he firmly rejects the idea that the history of scientific theorizing can be understood as series of closer and closer approximations to an objective antecedent reality, independent of time and human consciousness. His "paradigms" are a variation on the "frames of reference" that Strauss identified with historicism: within them reason functions in familiar ways, but between them we find varying degrees of incommensurability. The problem of translation therefore looms large, and we often lack any straightforwardly rational basis for choice. But Kuhn's rationalist critics as well as his most ardent historicist admirers have sometimes failed to notice that when he stresses the incommensurability of rival paradigms (or asserts that scientists ordinarily work within the confines of a normalizing paradigm that is destined one day to perish in revolution; or says that there is no higher authority in scientific matters than the present opinion of the relevant scientific community; or acknowledges that even the community's most trustworthy opinions result from struggle between competing professional factions), his point has never been to diminish the authority of science or to question the value of the customary scientific procedures of rational debate and validation. On the contrary, his aim has been to stress the reasonableness and profoundly authoritative character of certain sorts of conventions that are at once sponsored by, and constitutive of, communities. For all his stress on convention, Kuhn does not doubt that scientific thought grapples with a real world and can be more or less adequate to it. He does not hesitate to say that "scientific behavior, taken as a whole, is the best example we have of rationality."[36]

The heat of the recent debates over interpretation has brought to the surface historicist claims of a truly extravagant nature, claims so extreme in their pessimism about human reason that they threaten, by provoking a justifiably indignant and skeptical reaction, to bring all varieties of historicism under an indiscriminate cloud of suspicion.[37] If the moderate form of historicism that Kuhn exemplifies is not to be discredited by the recent excesses, its proponents had better come forward and define with some precision the difference between their position and that of the neo-Nietzscheans.

The line that needs to be drawn between radical and moderate historicism was sketched by Kuhn himself in a brief paper prepared for a symposium on rhetoric at the University of Iowa. Regrettably, the paper remains unpublished. Responding to an essay by Richard Rorty, to whom he feels close intellectually (and whose historicism is in truth only a few vital shades more radical than his own), Kuhn chose to play the role of Cassandra. Alarmed by Rorty's sweeping rejection of objectivity and warm embrace of solidarity as an adequate standard of correct belief, Kuhn warned of a "profound misconception of the human condition, a misconception here manifest in an insufficient respect for the intrinsic authority of language."

> Rorty opens his paper by attempting to drive a wedge between objectivity and solidarity. At the end of his paper, hammering the last nail into the coffin of objectivity, he writes: "The best argument we partisans of solidarity have against the realistic [*sic*] partisans of objectivity is Nietzsche's argument that the traditional Western metaphysico-epistemological way of firming up our habits simply isn't working anymore." . . . I agree that it is not. But in that foundational sense, solidarity isn't working either. The very proliferation and divergence that Rorty and Feyerabend invoke to rid us of our gods, of the other-worldly concept of objectivity, testify to the decline of solidarity as well. That, however, is as it should be, for the two are, I think, opposite sides of a single coin. Like solidarity, objectivity extends only over the world of the tribe, but what it extends over is no less firm and real for that. When that reality is threatened, as it sometimes is by exposure to other solidary groups, solidarity is necessarily threatened as well. Both "solidarity" and "objectivity" are, if you will, names for a character in a myth. But they name a single character; their myth is the one we live; and I can imagine no human life without it.
>
> I said I would speak as Cassandra, and I have been doing so. What I fear are attempts to separate language or discourse from the real and to do so in the name of freedom.[38]

This sharp-edged response may surprise readers who assume that Kuhn and Rorty share essentially the same position. Certainly Rorty is no nihilist, and other historicists have adopted much more radical positions than he has. The area of overlap between the views of the two men no doubt remains extensive. But if I understand Kuhn correctly, he wants to rescue epistemology, along with all the justificatory concerns that epistemology traditionally embodies, from the oblivion to which Rorty would consign them. And that, in my opinion, is precisely where the distinction between moderate and radical historicism has to be drawn. Historicism can, and ought to, revise our traditional understanding of what it means to be "objective" "rational," and "scientific," but historicism does not show any promise of leading us into a brave new world where those qualities can be merrily dispensed with. Why would anyone but a narcissist want a world free of the constraints of epistemology? The effort to justify our beliefs by reference to realities that extend beyond language and communal solidarity is a wholesome discipline and a deeply human practice, the value of which is quite independent of the likelihood that it will ever yield incontrovertible Truth.

The same can be said for rights talk. Just as the historicity and conventionality of science can be fully acknowledged without making science unreal, irrational, arbitrary, or irrelevant to the conduct of life, so the conventionality of rights and other claims to objective moral knowledge can be recognized without concluding that such claims are an empty ritual or a devious form of the will to power. Giving up naive forms of the correspondence theory of truth does not require us to stamp out rights talk or to jettison the ideal of the rule of law. No historicist can be confident that any right is eternal or universal, but historicism need not identify itself with the view that all rights claims are indistinguishably weak. Even if it is "turtles all the way down," some turtles are less slippery than others. Understanding rights as more or less rational conventions cannot render rights immune to skepticism or eradicate the aura of paradox and suspicion that surrounds claims to objective moral knowledge in a culture beset by the twin plagues of emotivism and illimitable interpretation. But uncertainty, skepticism, paradox, and suspicion are familiar and inescapable aspects of the human condition; historicism does not betray us in failing to cure them.

From a moderate historicist point of view, mankind's persistent effort to achieve impersonal and intersubjective knowledge about morality, even in the face of perpetual and predictable disappointment, is nothing to regret. The effort to "be objective" constitutes a very deeply rooted practice, and it therefore deserves the respect of all who claim to appreciate in a balanced way both the strengths and the limitations of theoretical reason. As MacIntyre concedes, we can have no assurance that rationality and objectivity are not just masks we

wear when engaged in moral conflict. But his questions, why *these* masks?—
"Why *this* masquerade?"—point to a practice of rational argumentation that
it would be absurd to abandon just because its outcome is not guaranteed. As
long as there is a chance that we have "got it right"—no matter how historical
and conventional getting it right may be—we must keep trying, for the game
itself is quintessentially human and the stakes are beyond measure.

CHAPTER SIX

Objectivity Is Not Neutrality

Rhetoric versus Practice in Peter Novick's
That Noble Dream

In general, I believe that skepticism is revealing and not refutable, but that it does not vitiate the pursuit of objectivity. It is worth trying to bring one's beliefs, one's actions, and one's values more under the influence of an impersonal standpoint even without the assurance that this could not be revealed from a still more external standpoint as an illusion. In any case, we seem to have no choice but to make the attempt. . . .

Objectivity and skepticism are closely related: both develop from the idea that there is a real world in which we are contained, and that appearances result from our interactions with the rest of it. We cannot accept these appearances uncritically, but must try to understand what our own constitution contributes to them. To do this we try to develop an idea of the world that includes an explanation of why it initially appears to us as it does. But this idea, since it is we who develop it, is likewise the product of interaction between us and the world, though the interaction is more complicated and more self-conscious than the original one. If the initial appearances cannot be relied upon because they depend on our constitution in ways that we do not fully understand, this more complex data should be open to the same doubts. . . . However often we may try to step outside of ourselves, something will have to stay behind the lens, something in us will determine the resulting picture, and this will give grounds for doubt that we are getting any closer to reality.

I am indebted to Peter Novick for several very open and informative letters sent in response to my initial reactions to his book. Although the essay was materially improved by the advice of Sandy Levinson, its tone and conclusions are my responsibility alone. Subsequent page references to *That Noble Dream* appear in parentheses.

First published in *History and Theory* 29 (1990): 129–57. Copyright © Wesleyan University.

The idea of objectivity thus seems to undermine itself. . . .

I want both to defend the possibility of objective ascent [that is, the possibility of developing an impersonal standpoint, the "view from nowhere," a view of the world in which the self is not at the center but is included as merely one among many objects] and to understand its limits. We should keep in mind how incredible it is that such a thing is possible at all. We are encouraged these days to think of ourselves as contingent organisms arbitrarily thrown up by evolution. There is no reason in advance to expect a finite creature like that to be able to do more than accumulate information at the perceptual and conceptual level it occupies by nature. But apparently that is not how things are. Not only can we form the pure idea of a world which contains us and of which our impressions are a part, but we can give this idea a content which takes us very far from our original impressions. . . .

The search for objective knowledge, because of its commitment to a realistic picture, is inescapably subject to skepticism and cannot refute it but must proceed under its shadow. Skepticism, in turn, is a problem only because of the realist claims of objectivity.

—Thomas Nagel, *The View from Nowhere*

When it comes to debates over objectivity and relativism, appearances can be deceiving, not just in the world the debaters strive to comprehend, but also in the relation between a debater's position and the rhetoric he or she employs to defend it. For example, as I sift through my reactions to Peter Novick's important and provocative book, *That Noble Dream: The "Objectivity Question" and the American Historical Profession* (Cambridge: Cambridge University Press, 1988), I find it necessary to distinguish the moderate position he actually seems to occupy on the objectivity question from the rather more radical rhetorical posture he adopts in defense of that position. All things considered—that is, taking into account not only what he *says* about the ideal of objectivity, but also what he *does* as a practicing historian, writing about historians' quarrels over that ideal—I conclude that he and I occupy pretty much the same, moderate, position. We admire the same sorts of historical judgments and feel about the same degree of confidence in the end product of the historian's labors. We agree that representing the past is a far more problematical enterprise than most historians realize, and that there are more ways to represent it than the guild currently acknowledges. Certainly I do not believe any more than he does that facts speak for themselves, that political neutrality is a virtue in itself, that scholarship is a wall-building exercise in which each scholar con-

tributes his brick to a steadily accumulating edifice of unchallengeable knowledge, or that the best history is that which provokes no controversy. Nor am I
any more sanguine than he about the likelihood that disagreements over historical interpretation will one day fade away in some grand convergence.

Yet I regard objectivity, properly understood, as a worthy goal for historians. Novick, on the contrary, says the ideal is "essentially confused" (6), and
the text he has written—which, ironically, passes all my tests for objectivity
with flying colors—is in the main designed to persuade readers that the ideal
of objectivity is all washed up. We seem not to differ greatly in what we admire
and wish to defend in terms of historical practice, but our rhetorical postures
vis-à-vis the ideal of objectivity are decidedly at odds.

That two people sharing the same position should say different things about
it need not be surprising. One obvious reason is the difficulty of forecast-
ing audience response. We all occasionally polemicize on behalf of our own
version of the good, the true, and the beautiful, and the posture we assume
in public is shaped by our estimate of where our audience already stands on
these issues and which way it needs to be moved in order to strengthen the
position we admire. Two authors may say very different, even opposite, things
in defense of the same position, simply because they have different estimates
of where their audience currently stands, or what its members need to hear
in order to be moved in the desired direction. For the same reason a single
person may, without any inconsistency, adopt different rhetorical postures on
different occasions. If, for example, a proponent of the welfare state were to
deliver exactly the same speech to the National Association of Manufacturers
and the Young Socialist League, we would not applaud the speaker's consistency, but lament the insensitivity of the performance, the failure to anticipate
objections coming from different directions. Estimating the composition and
likely reaction of the audience for a book is notoriously difficult, so it is easy
to see how Novick and I might share much the same position on substantive
issues, and yet adopt opposing postures and appear for all the world as if we
were completely at loggerheads.

Two further reasons help explain why I want to endorse much of Novick's
analysis of objectivity even as I draw what may seem opposite conclusions
from it. The first is a matter of strategy. He and I agree that objectivity was the
charter under which professional history was inaugurated, in his words, "the
rock on which the venture was constituted, its continuing raison d'être" (l). We
also agree that the ideal is currently viewed with considerable skepticism, especially by scholars impressed by recent developments in literary criticism; that
historians eager to counter that skepticism have sometimes done so naively

and ineffectively; and that although attacks in the past have come and gone cyclically, the overall trend has been one of declension. The ideal of objectivity just does not grip us as powerfully as it did the founding generation of the 1880s. Given this state of affairs, Novick's advice to the profession evidently is to cut loose from the ideal, declaring it obsolete — even while silently perpetuating many of the practices associated with it. In contrast, my inclination is to protect those practices by continuing to honor the ideal, meanwhile ridding it of unwanted connotations. Fatefully dissimilar though the two strategies may be, they do not aim at very different outcomes in terms of historical practice.

That difference of strategy immediately points to crucial differences in the way Novick and I use the term "objectivity." My impression, unlike Novick's, is that among the influential members of the historical profession the term has long since lost whatever connection it may once have had with passionlessness, indifference, and neutrality. Eugene Genovese, a much-honored member of the profession and a self-proclaimed Marxist whom no one will think dispassionate or politically neutral, passes my test of objectivity with plenty of room to spare, just as Novick himself does.[1] In my view, what sophisticated historians mean by the term today has precious little to do with neutrality, but a great deal to do with a cultural orientation in which neutrality, disinterestedness, and like qualities did indeed figure prominently in the nineteenth century: that complex of values and practices which Nietzsche contemptuously called "asceticism."[2] If objectivity could be reduced simply to neutrality, I would not bother to defend it; but insofar as it is the expression in intellectual affairs of the ascetic dimension of life, it deserves a defense, for asceticism is not only "common to all culture," it is "the 'cultural' element in culture. . . . Where there is culture there is asceticism."[3]

I regard Nietzsche's attack on asceticism as a cultural calamity, all the more regrettable because of his high seriousness and the brilliance of the assault. Had he directed his wrath merely against Victorian passionlessness there would be no room for complaint, but his ridicule of ascetic values and practices became reckless and indiscriminate, reaching far beyond the foibles of a generation to renunciation itself. Morality is what suffers most from the devaluation of ascetic practices, but such practices are also indispensable to the pursuit of truth. The very possibility of historical scholarship as an enterprise distinct from propaganda requires of its practitioners that vital minimum of ascetic self-discipline that enables a person to do such things as abandon wishful thinking, assimilate bad news, discard pleasing interpretations that cannot pass elementary tests of evidence and logic, and, most important of all, suspend or bracket one's own perceptions long enough to enter sympathetically into the alien and possibly repugnant perspectives of rival thinkers. All of these mental acts—especially coming to grips with a rival's perspective—require *detachment,* an undeniably ascetic capacity to achieve some distance from one's own spontaneous perceptions and convictions, to imagine how the world appears in another's eyes, to experimentally adopt perspectives that do not come naturally—in the last analysis, to develop, as Thomas Nagel would say, a view of the world in which one's own self stands not at the center, but appears merely as one object among many.[4] To be dissatisfied with the view of the world as it initially appears to us, and to struggle to formulate a superior, more inclusive, less self-centered alternative, is to strive for detachment and aim at objectivity. And to turn thus against one's most natural self—to engage in "this uncanny, dreadfully joyous labor of a soul voluntarily at odds with itself"—is to commit that very sin against the will to power that Nietzsche so irresponsibly condemned.[5]

Detachment does not promise access to any transcendental realm and always remains, as Nagel says, "under the shadow" of skepticism.[6] Although it is an ideal and holds out a standard higher than any of us routinely achieve, acceptable performance under its regulative influence does not require superhuman effort. It is that frail and limited but perfectly real power that, for example, permits conscientious scholars to referee one another's work fairly, to acknowledge merit even in the writings of one's critics, and successfully to bend over backwards when grading students so as not to penalize those holding antagonistic political convictions. We try to exercise this capacity every day; sometimes we succeed, sometimes we fail, and we assign praise and blame to ourselves and others accordingly. It is of course true that we sometimes delude ourselves, developing a pseudo-objective standpoint that functions mainly to obscure choice, so responsibility for what we want to do shifts to a seemingly impersonal state of affairs. But to shrug off the capacity for detachment as entirely illusory—to claim that since none of the standpoints the self is capable of imagining are *really* that of "the other," but are self-produced (as is certainly the case), and to argue that all viewpoints therefore are *indistinguishably* contaminated by selfishness or group interest or the omnipresent Nietzschean will—is to turn a blind eye to distinctions that all of us routinely make and confidently act upon, and thereby to blur all that distinguishes villainy from decency in everyday affairs. Not to mince words, it is to defame the species. Fairness and honesty are qualities we can rightfully demand of human beings, and those qualities require a very substantial measure of self-overcoming—more than could exist if Nietzsche's hyperbolic and indiscriminate war on asceticism were permitted to triumph. Objectivity is not something entirely distinct from detachment, fairness, and honesty, but is the product of extending and elaborating these priceless and fundamentally ascetic virtues.[7]

If I am correct in thinking that these virtues of self-overcoming already rank high in historians' practice, that should suffice to show that my strategy of keeping alive the term "objectivity" while ridding it of unwanted connotations is not a matter of appropriating a traditional name as a dignified cover for new practices. The tendency of past generations to associate objectivity with "selflessness," and to think of truth seeking as a matter of emptying oneself of passion and preconception, so as to become a perfectly passive and receptive mirror of external reality, has, for good reason, become notorious.[8] But in valuing (as even Nietzsche did, in his calmer moments) the elementary capacity for self-overcoming, we need not aspire to the unrealistic and undesirable extreme of extinguishing the self or denying that its situation in time and space limits the perspectives available to it.[9] Likewise, in making detachment a vital criterion of objective thinking, we need not make the still greater error of confusing objectivity with neutrality.

I see nothing to admire in neutrality. My conception of objectivity (which I believe is widely, if tacitly, shared by historians today) is compatible with strong political commitment. It pays no premium for standing in the middle of the road, and it recognizes that scholars are as passionate and as likely to be driven by interest as those they write about. It does not value even detachment as an end in itself, but only as an indispensable prelude or preparation for the achievement of higher levels of understanding—higher not in the sense of ascending to a more spiritual plane, where the concerns of the soul displace those of the body, as an earlier generation might have understood it, but higher in Nagel's sense of being more complete, more cognizant of life's most seductive illusion, which is that the world centers on me (or those with whom I choose to identify) and that what matters to me (or us) is paramount.

Detachment functions in this manner not by draining us of passion, but by helping to channel our intellectual passions in such a way as to ensure collision with rival perspectives. In that collision, if anywhere, our thinking transcends both the idiosyncratic and the conventional. Detachment both socializes and de-parochializes the work of intellect; it is the quality that fits an individual to participate fruitfully in what is essentially a communal enterprise. Objectivity is so much a product of social arrangements that individuals and particular opinions scarcely deserve to be called objective, yet the social arrangements that foster objectivity have no basis for existence apart from individual striving for detachment. Only insofar as the members of the community are disposed to set aside the perspective that comes most spontaneously to them, and strive to see things in a detached light, is there any likelihood that they will engage with one another mentally and provoke one another through mutual criticism to the most complete, least idiosyncratic, view that humans are capable of. When the ascetic effort at detachment fails, as it often does, we talk past one another, producing nothing but discordant soliloquies, each fancying itself the voice of reason. The kind of thinking I would call objective leads only a fugitive existence outside of communities that enjoy a high degree of independence from the state and other external powers, and that are dedicated internally not only to detachment but also to intense mutual criticism and to the protection of dissenting positions against the perpetual threat of majority tyranny.

Some hypothetical examples may clarify what I mean by objective thinking and show how remote it is from neutrality. Consider an extreme case: a person who, although capable of detachment, suspends his or her own perceptions of the world not in the expectation of gaining a broader perspective, but only in order to learn how opponents think so as to demolish their arguments more effectively—who is, in short, a polemicist, deeply and fixedly committed as a lifelong project to a particular political or cultural or moral program. Anyone choosing such a life obviously risks being thought boorish or provincial, but insofar as such a person successfully enters into the thinking of his or her rivals and produces arguments potentially compelling, not only to those who already share the same views, but to outsiders as well, I see no reason to withhold the laurel of objectivity.[10] There is nothing objective about hurling imprecations at apostates or catechizing the faithful. But as long as the polemicist truly engages the thinking of the enemy, he or she is being as objective as anyone. In contrast, the person too enamored of his or her own interpretation of things seriously and sympathetically to entertain alternatives, even for the sake of learning how best to defeat them, fails my test of objectivity, no matter how serene and even-tempered.

The most common failure of objectivity is preaching to the converted, complacently presupposing the pieties of one's own coterie and making no effort to appreciate or appeal to the perspectives of outsiders. In contrast, the most commonly observed fulfillment of the ideal of objectivity in the historical profession is simply the *powerful argument*—the text that reveals by its every twist and turn its respectful appreciation of the alternatives it rejects. Such a text attains power precisely because its author has managed to suspend momentarily his or her own perceptions so as to anticipate and take account of objections and alternative constructions—not those of some straw man, but those that truly issue from the rival's position, understood as sensitively and stated as eloquently as the rival could desire. Nothing is rhetorically more powerful than this, and nothing, not even capitulation to the rival, could acknowledge any more vividly the force and respectability of the rival's perspective. To mount a telling attack on a position, one must first inhabit it. Those so habituated to their customary intellectual abode that they cannot even explore others can never be persuasive to anyone but fellow habitués.

That is why powerful arguments are often more faithful to the complexity and fragility of historical interpretation — more faithful even to the irreducible plurality of human perspectives, when that is, in fact, the case — than texts that abjure position-taking altogether and ostentatiously wallow in displays of "reflexivity" and "undecidability." The powerful argument is the highest fruit of the kind of thinking I would call objective, and in it neutrality plays no part. Authentic objectivity has simply nothing to do with the television newscaster's mechanical gesture of allocating the same number of seconds to both sides of a question, or editorially splitting the difference between them, irrespective of their perceived merits.

This conception of the ideal of objectivity, stripped as it is of any association with neutrality and offering no metaphysical guarantees of truth, is not terribly different from that "future 'objectivity'" that even Nietzsche grudgingly acknowledged in the midst of his slashing attack on asceticism. He spoke without malice of an objectivity "understood not as 'contemplation without interest' (which is a nonsensical absurdity), but as the ability *to control* one's Pro and Con and to dispose of them, so that one knows how to employ a variety of perspectives and affective interpretations in the service of knowledge."[11] Even in one of his fits of hyperbole, as Nietzsche gathered up the last hope of objective knowledge and threw it out the window along with the bathwater of a literal-minded notion of disinterestedness, he let slip a crucial concession. This often-quoted passage proclaims the impossibility of disinterestedness so stridently that it is easy to ignore the second half of the lead sentence and the important qualification that Nietzsche there inserted against the grain of his own thought:

> There is *only* a perspective seeing, *only* a perspective "knowing"; and the *more* affects we are allowed to speak about one thing, the *more* eyes, different eyes, we can use to observe one thing, the more complete will our "concept" of this thing be. But to eliminate the will altogether, to suspend each and every affect, supposing we were capable of this — what would that mean but to *castrate* the intellect?[12]

What needs rescuing here is the thought that some conceptions are more "complete" than others and that by doing what we can to multiply the perspectives brought to bear on a problem, we can achieve higher levels of completeness. Once it is acknowledged that conceptions differ in this way, it is but a small additional step to say that the more complete a conception is, the greater its claim upon us—opening the possibility that we are sometimes *obliged to* give up incomplete conceptions for more complete ones. The ideal of objectivity requires no more of a foothold than this.

The possibility of distinguishing baby from bathwater is lost the moment we confuse objectivity with neutrality. And my most serious reservation about Novick's uncommonly intelligent and wide-ranging history of the objectivity question—the most complete history of the American historical profession ever written for any purpose—is that he virtually equates objectivity with neutrality. Subtle and perceptive though his analysis is, much of his text reads like an exposé. His aim is to show, often through passages selected from personal correspondence, that in spite of all their high-minded public rhetoric about the importance of "being objective," historians have bristled with likes and dislikes and have often conceived of their work as a means of striking a blow for what they liked, be it reunification of North and South in the founding generation, or racial integration in a later one.[13] All this is presented to the reader in a tone of bemused shock and wide-eyed dismay, as if by discovering connections between their scholarship and their likes and dislikes, we were catching the mighty with their pants down. That tone is justifiable in a few sad and striking cases in which prominent historians' dislikes turn out to have been ethnic and ugly. But on the whole, who will be either surprised or disappointed to discover that historians who praised objectivity and thought of themselves as objective had strong preferences about mobilization for World War I, isolationism, responsibility for the cold war, Vietnam, racial segregation, and the like, and wrote books and articles meant in part to advance their side of these major public debates? These commitments betray a lack of objectivity only if we define objectivity as neutrality, and to do that would be to trivialize both the ideal and those who have striven to realize it.

Novick generally construes active political commitment by historians who subscribe to the ideal of objectivity as evidence of either personal insincerity or, more often, the incoherence and emptiness of the ideal. I wonder. Perhaps Novick has defined objectivity too narrowly. Perhaps historians who advocated objectivity and worried, say, about the relativism of Charles Beard and

Carl Becker meant neither to claim neutrality for themselves nor to impose it on others. Perhaps instead, by defending what they called "objectivity," they meant, as I do, to sustain that minimal respect for self-overcoming, for detachment, honesty, and fairness, that makes intellectual community possible. Perhaps they were not naive to sense in snappy slogans like "Everyman his own historian," not only the useful corrective to scientism that Novick appropriately sees there, but also the harbinger of a remissive cultural movement corrosive of all constraints upon the will, a movement that over the course of the twentieth century has in fact succeeded in putting on the defensive the very idea of obligation, whether moral ("You ethically *ought* to do *x*") or epistemological ("You rationally/logically *ought* to believe *y*").[14] The upshot, as a new century looms, is that many wonder if "ought" statements capture anything important about human beings and the world they live in, or are merely grandiose masks for preferences that are ultimately personal and self-serving ("I *want* you to do *x* or believe *y*").[15] Some will see in this cultural shift a welcome retreat of authoritarianism; others, a tragic breakdown of authority. Those who lament it as a breakdown will by no means be found only on the political right, for insofar as the left trades on ideas of moral obligation (for example, to the poor, to minorities), or distinguishes between policies that are well or ill suited to the "realities" of our situation, it too has a vested interest in objectivity. Without entering into the debate here, we can simply observe that the stakes in this cultural contest are extremely high, and while the possibility of objective knowledge is a central point at issue, neutrality is not.

Yet in Novick's definition of objectivity, neutrality looms very large indeed. In two key definitional paragraphs near the beginning of his text, Novick spells out in abbreviated form the principal tenets of the ideal of objectivity to which he believes historians have subscribed with little change for the past hundred years.[16] I place the second of the sequential paragraphs first because it strains hardest to identify objectivity with neutrality.

> The objective historian's role is that of a neutral, or disinterested, judge; it must never degenerate into that of an advocate or, even worse, propagandist. The historian's conclusions are expected to display the standard judicial qualities of balance and evenhandedness. As with the judiciary, these qualities are guarded by the insulation of the historical profession from social pressures or political influence, and by the individual historian avoiding partisanship or bias—not having any investment in arriving at one conclusion rather than another. Objectivity is held to be at grave risk when history is written for utilitarian purposes. One corollary of all this is that historians, as historians, must purge

themselves of external loyalties: the historian's primary allegiance is to "the objective historical truth," and to professional colleagues who share a commitment to cooperative, cumulative efforts to advance toward that goal. (2)

Although there is much in this sketch that strikes me as accurate, on the whole I find it impossible to reconcile with my impression that most historians, certainly the abler and more influential ones, recognize full well that fine history can be and routinely is written by politically committed scholars. Most historians just do not assign to "neutrality" and "disinterestedness" the inflated value that Novick suggests. Most, I think, would be aghast at the thought that historians must "purge themselves of external loyalties" in order to do their job well. Seeing an analogy between the role of the judge and that of the historian does not imply any overestimation of the value of neutrality: judges, like historians, are expected to be open to rational persuasion, not to be indifferent about the great issues of their day or — bizarre thought — to abstain from judgment. What we demand of them is self-control, not self-immolation. Bias and conflict of interest do indeed arouse our suspicion, not only of judges and historians, but of whomever we depend upon to be fair. The demand is for detachment and fairness, not disengagement from life. Most historians would indeed say that the historian's primary commitment is to the truth, and that when truth and "the cause," however defined, come into conflict, the truth must prevail. But to say that is not to prohibit political advocacy; it is only to set intellectually responsible limits to it — limits without which advocates would discredit not only scholarship but their own cause. Who will trust a scholar-advocate who claims the privilege of lying or obscuring the truth for good causes?

By the same token, Novick is no doubt right that historians see a world of difference between politically committed scholarship, which I think they accept, and propaganda dressed up as history, which they certainly do not, and should not, accept. Historians do indeed become wary, but not necessarily dismissive, when scholarship is performed as a means to exogenous, "utilitarian" ends; they do regard scholarship as a collaborative effort, requiring a great deal of mutual trust, and most no doubt regard a degree of insulation from external influence as indispensable. (The latter point seems impossible to doubt as I write these lines in the summer of 1989, just as the Chinese government rewrites the history of the Tiananmen Square killings and as intellectuals in the USSR and central Europe put their lives on the line by publicly challenging state-sponsored orthodoxies in historical interpretation.) None of these beliefs require historians to "purge themselves of external loyalties," or to be "neutral," or to be "disinterested" in any extravagant sense. What is required is at most a modicum of ascetic detachment.

Does Novick think that even this modicum is too much to ask? It is not easy to tell, either from his two definitional paragraphs or from the 600-plus pages that follow, how much of the ideal of objectivity he actually means to reject. Consider both the passage quoted above and the more general of his two definitional paragraphs (which in his text appears first):

> The principal elements of the idea [of objectivity] are well known and can be briefly recapitulated. The assumptions on which it rests include a commitment to the reality of the past, and to the truth as correspondence to that reality; a sharp separation between knower and known, between fact and value, and above all, between history and fiction. Historical facts are seen as prior to and independent of interpretation: the value of an interpretation is judged by how well it accounts for the facts; if contradicted by the facts, it must be abandoned. Truth is one, not perspectival. Whatever patterns exist in history are "found," not "made." Though successive generations of historians might, as their perspectives shifted, attribute different significance to events in the past, the meaning of those events was unchanging. (1–2)

Since Novick is evidently out to show that the ideal of objectivity is "essentially confused," one might think that he is prepared to abandon each of the "elements" of the ideal he lists in these two paragraphs. But considering the text in its entirety, and, again, taking into account both his statements about objectivity and his practices as the author of this particular historical narrative about historians' debates, I conclude that his rejection of the ideal is far from total.

Let us examine the elements he lists. What precisely it would mean for a historian or anyone else to doubt the "reality of the past" is not obvious, but surely anyone whose doubt was more than a rhetorical gambit would think twice before writing a 600-page book about it. "Correspondence" as a metaphor for the hoped-for relation between thought and reality has notoriously fallen on hard times, and mention of dualisms such as "knower and known," "fact and value," "history and fiction," will call up important debates familiar to the readers of the journal *History and Theory*. Without slighting in the least either Novick's performance as a historian, or the significance of those debates, I find it difficult to see how the debates influence the performance. Rhetorically his epistemological anxiety is acute, but it has little effect on the way he writes history. The fault is not Novick's. Knowing that correspondence is an inadequate metaphor, how are historians to conduct themselves differently?

Novick gives no answer, either explicitly or implicitly, and was probably wise not to try. As for the ostensible benefits of recognizing the kinship of history and fiction, Novick seems at best half-persuaded. His treatment of Hayden White, the scholar most closely identified with those benefits, is respectful (he calls him our "philosopher of freedom" and laments his scapegoating by objectivists looking for an embodiment of "nihilistic relativism" [601, 599]), but decidedly guarded: White's "trivializing of questions of evidence was in the service . . . above all of his existentialist quasi obsession with the historian's liberty of choice," says Novick, and it requires only a "moderately careless reading," he continues, to conclude that White's relativism is that of the proverbial freshman "for whom any view was as good as any other" (601). These are not the attitudes one expects of a radical on the objectivity question.

"Fact" is another word that has fallen on hard times. Just as there are many historians out there who need to be reminded that, for all their differences, the writing of history and the writing of fiction are kindred activities, so there are also historians who still need to learn that facts only take shape under the aegis of paradigms, presuppositions, theories, and the like. There are even historians who might benefit from writing on the blackboard twenty times, "facts are just low-level interpretive entities unlikely for the moment to be contested." That said, it must also be observed that one of the virtues of Novick's book is that it is jam-packed with such low-level entities. I would be very surprised if he really thought that the value of his higher-level interpretations was independent of their ability "to account for" the lower ones, and I would be still more surprised if he retained in his book any higher-level interpretations that he really thought were flatly "contradicted" by the lower ones. He is much too good a historian for that.

As for Novick's questions about the oneness of truth and the origin of the patterns historians "find" in history, his subsequent discussions make perfectly clear his sensible refusal to grasp either horn of such either-or dilemmas. He appears in practice to believe, as I do, that some truth claims are irreducibly perspectival, while others lend themselves to rational resolution. His practice seems compatible with my view (not at all unusual among historians) that historical patterns are "found," but not without a process of imaginative construction that goes far enough beyond the intrinsic properties of the raw materials employed that one can speak of their being "made" — though certainly not out of whole cloth. Once again, sweeping though Novick's abandonment of objectivity sometimes sounds, in practice he is usually what I would call a sensible moderate.

Although the most conspicuous struggle under way in this text is between the author's practice and his rhetorical posture, the rhetorical posture itself is also conflicted. Novick claims, interestingly, that he is more concerned to report the debate over objectivity than to take a position: "What I can't do," he says, "is hope to satisfy those who exigently demand to know if I am 'for' or 'against' objectivity." Having said this, he then proceeds in the next two paragraphs to speak of the ideal and the distinctions it gives rise to as "confused," "dubious," "naive," "unreal," "empty," and "incoherent" (6). Summing up this uniformly critical commentary, he says, "Another way of describing my stance is to say that, in general and on the whole, I have been persuaded by the arguments of the critics of the concept; unimpressed by the arguments of its defenders" (6). Clear though his rejection of objectivity seems at this point, he reasserts two paragraphs later his role as nonjudgmental reporter: "Above all, the reason why I cannot take a position for or against objectivity is my historicism, which here means simply that my way of thinking about anything in the past is primarily shaped by my understanding of its role within a particular historical context, and in the stream of history" (7).

Novick's characterization of his own views seems most promising to me when he likens objectivity to a myth that, while resisting classification as either "true" or "false," indubitably sustains valued practices and thus comes to possess many of the qualities of tenacity and inescapability that we associate with truth. In the same vein he likens objectivity to the inalienable and self-evident rights of the Declaration of Independence: hopelessly ambiguous, philosophically indefensible, even "nonsense," perhaps, but, in Novick's words, "*salutary nonsense*" (7), in view of the form of life they have fostered.[17] On balance, however, Novick is not content to regard the ideal of objectivity as salutary: "it promotes an unreal and misleading invidious distinction between, on the one hand, historical accounts 'distorted' by ideological assumptions and purposes; on the other, history free of these taints" (6). Nor does the idea of myth provide much shelter, for in Novick's eyes the valued practices sustained by the myth of objectivity are strictly those of historians striving to professionalize their discipline, enhance their dignity, and maximize their incomes. He would evidently give little credence to my own view, which is that although the ideal of objectivity has been most fully and formally developed by scholars and serves importantly to legitimize their work, it was not invented by them and in fact pervades the world of everyday affairs. As I see it, the ideal is tacitly invoked (sometimes as a test, sometimes in a gesture of blind faith) every time anyone opens a letter, picks up a newspaper, walks into a courtroom, or decides which of two squabbling children to believe. All of us, professional or not, invoke the ideal every time we choose between conflicting interpretations with confidence that they are not simply different, but that one is *superior* to the others, superior as a representation of the way things are. No wonder Novick is less concerned than I about the fate of the ideal: for him the consequences of abandoning it are confined to the academic professions; for me the cultural ramifications are incalculably wide.

Although I disagree with many of Novick's judgments, I have high confidence in his objectivity as a historian. He sees little connection between the scholar's ideal and the humble virtues of fairness, honesty, and detachment, and therefore assumes a posture vis-à-vis objectivity that seems to give those virtues short shrift. In practice, however, he takes them seriously enough. It would be tedious to recite many examples, but even his introductory comments about the near-fatal inadequacy of the ideal of objectivity are interspersed with declarations of respect for the homier virtues that constitute the very taproots of that ideal as I would define it. Thus, having declared himself persuaded by the critics of objectivity, he expresses the hope, in the very next sentence, that he has succeeded in setting forth "fairly" (12) both sides of the argument. I wonder how he could explain the high value we place on fairness — or even explain what fairness means in this context — without resorting eventually to the language of objectivity. Similarly, in defense of his self-conscious tendency to give rather more explanatory weight to extrarational factors than most historians do, Novick hastens to assure the reader that he has done his best "to extend such treatment evenhandedly: as much to the thought of those with whom I am in sympathy as to those whose views I dislike" (15). Again the practice he promises is not something other than objectivity, but a facet of it.

He even aspires to detachment. Noting that most historians write about their profession "the way Arthur Schlesinger, Jr., writes about the Kennedys," he fears that "what I think of as my attempt at detachment may be read as hostility" (13). In the narrative account that follows, he seems to me generally to live up to the promise of these declarations. If we could be sure that abandoning the ideal of objectivity meant that all the professions' members would continue (or begin) to go about their work as scrupulously as Novick, we could rest easy. But we cannot.

If there is any aspect of the objectivity question about which Novick and I are truly opposed, substantively as well as rhetorically, it is the degree of solicitude the profession owes to scholars whose zeal for advocacy carries them up to, or across, the border between politically committed scholarship and propaganda. Novick is more tolerant of border violations than I am, more reluctant, in fact, to believe that any border can be defined that is not itself an artifact of political perspective. His sensitivity on this issue may well reflect painful personal experiences. He describes himself in the book as a member in the mid-1950s of the " 'Schachtmanite' Young Socialist League" (419). More important, he also describes himself as a mentor and good friend of David Abraham, a young Marxist scholar teaching at Princeton whose dissertation on the role of big business in the rise of Hitler became a *cause célèbre* in the mid-1980s when it was attacked by Professors Henry Turner of Yale and Gerald Feldman of Berkeley. Turner and Feldman did not merely criticize Abraham's arguments, but alleged "outright invention" of "nonexistent archival documents" (614). They also took the unusual step of contacting departments where Abraham was under consideration for employment; Feldman, in addition, although uninformed about an effort within the University of Chicago history department to rescind Abraham's Ph.D., said that he would have favored such a measure if Abraham had been his student. Abraham replied to his critics, publicly apologizing for some errors that he called "inexcusable" (616), but denying any inventions. Some historians found his reply persuasive; some did not. The pivotal issues, on which the leading lights of the profession publicly split and about which I, to my embarrassment, remain undecided, are whether all of Abraham's errors could have been excusably accidental (the result, as he put it, of "hasty and niggardly note taking" [616]) and whether the "facts" that have been contested play a vital or a peripheral role in supporting the conceptual structure of the book (612–21).

Novick construes the outcome — Abraham's departure from the profession and enrollment in law school — as "a striking demonstration of the continued power of the empiricist-objectivist alliance" (621). Traumatic as the incident obviously was for him and for the profession (not to mention the immediate protagonists), Novick does not pretend that Abraham was laid low by the ideal of objectivity pure and simple. Abraham was, of course, accused of far more than a lack of objectivity or neutrality. Novick characterizes the standpoint of his critics not only as "neo-objectivist" but as "hyperobjectivist" and "hyperempiricist." Novick's account of the episode is impassioned. I would not expect it to please Abraham's critics, and I concede that their displeasure may be justifiable. But even if it is, I would contend that Novick's account is manifestly the work of someone who prizes detachment and makes a serious effort to bracket his own perspective long enough to enter sympathetically into the thinking of others, even under trying circumstances. Indeed, although Novick regards the case as another black mark for objectivism, his principal complaint about Abraham's critics is that, in their zeal for their own, non-Marxist perspective they exaggerated the importance of details and failed to grapple with the conceptual heart of Abraham's position, thereby themselves violating accepted standards of scholarly conduct. Without trying to pass judgment on the merits of the accusation, we can note that the standard he tacitly invokes—an obligation to enter sympathetically into rival perspectives—is that of objectivity, much as I have defined it.

Novick's silent loyalty to the practices I would identify with objectivity is also evident in the accounts he gives of other rancorous episodes in the recent history of the profession. In fact, a surprisingly pained, elegiac tone creeps into his last four chapters, in which he traces what he regards as the virtual demise of the ideal of objectivity in our own time. Chapter and section titles tell the story: "Objectivity in crisis," "The collapse of comity," "Every group its own historian," "The center does not hold," and finally, "There was no king in Israel; every man did that which was right in his eyes." These titles are hard to reconcile with the tone of the first twelve chapters, which display little sympathy for the ideal of objectivity or those who rallied to it.

In the chapter titled "Every group its own historian," Novick recounts the rise of black history and women's history since the 1960s. Among the people attracted to these highly politicized fields were many for whom academic employment and scholarly performance were means to what they perceived as political ends, and who, far from seeing any danger in the subordination of scholarship to politics, sometimes looked with considerable disdain on their more conventional colleagues who had no more elevated mission in life than to teach and write well—goals easy to dismiss as "privatistic" or "careerist." Moreover, the internal wars over doctrine that were waged within activist circles during these years often stirred up intensely particularist currents and explicit repudiations of the universalistic values that had eased the none-too-smooth assimilation into the profession of Jews and left-leaning dissenters during earlier decades, and that continued to underwrite arguments for academic freedom and toleration of dissent during the McCarthy era. By the late 1960s there were in activist circles many who, in the arena of national politics, were not willing to settle for reforms aiming at race-and gender-blind treatment. For similar reasons, many also were not willing to think of themselves merely as historians who happened to be black and/or female. The demand for objectivity, whether defined my way or Novick's, was from these particularistic standpoints often construed as one more link in a chain of oppression.[18]

Novick is more patient with these assaults on universalistic values than I am, but if I understand him correctly, he does not finally accept the key contention: that each gender and ethnic group has its own truths, inaccessible to outsiders. He tells harrowing stories about black history, mentioning, for example, that black militants told Kenneth Stampp that he had no right, as a white man, to write *The Peculiar Institution.* In a tone of stern disapproval Novick reports that at meetings of the Association for the Study of Negro Life and History, Herbert Gutman, an ex–Communist Party member whose "left" credentials could hardly have been in dispute, was shouted down, as were other white historians. One of those shouted down was Robert Starobin, whose support of black liberation had extended even to the Black Panthers. Devastated by that experience and no doubt much else, Starobin committed suicide the following year (475–76).

Novick also traces the less dramatic but equally sad intellectual sequence that begins with Stanley Elkins's 1959 book, *Slavery,* likening the psychological impact of slavery to the trauma of incarceration in Nazi concentration camps. In 1965 came the ill-fated Moynihan Report, which, drawing on Elkins and other scholars, many of them black, argued that government policy ought to focus on the breakdown of the black family. Amid simplistic cries of "racism" and "don't blame the victim," what amounts to a political taboo was erected against the "damage thesis," and a whole generation of historical work, capped by Herbert Gutman's 1974 book, *The Black Family in Slavery and Freedom,* set out to show that blacks had managed to create a rich and resilient family-oriented culture even in the grip of slavery. "At its extreme," Novick observes, "work in this vein suggested Teflon slaves, all but immune to the system which oppressed them" (487). In the 1980s, as the NAACP (which had chastised Moynihan severely for his emphasis on family breakdown) reversed its ground and placed the "precipitous slide of the black family" at the top of its agenda, and as black sociologists took the lead in reopening questions about the black family—questions highly reminiscent of those raised by W.E.B. Du Bois as far back as 1908—a generation of historians was caught flat-footed. The episode does not reflect well on the independent-mindedness of historians, let alone their objectivity. Novick admits to the "troubling thought . . . that insofar as the new black historiography of the seventies had discernible social impact, it was to divert attention from the urgent needs of the constituency which those who produced it were dedicated to serving" (485, 489). He stops just short of the conclusion that seems inescapable to me: when scholar-advocates put advocacy first, exempting "their" group, however defined, from detached, critical examination, they deprive that group and the larger society of the one authentic contribution scholars can make in public affairs.[19]

Although the field of women's history experienced nothing as traumatic as the events in black history, there, too, what Novick calls an "assertive particularism" holds sway and there, too, the social dynamics of a "more militant than thou" attitude has created a professional subculture in which detachment, far from being encouraged, is likely to be construed as a betrayal of the cause (470). Much of Novick's discussion of women's history revolves around the 1986 case *Equal Employment Opportunity Commission v. Sears, Roebuck and Company*, in which Barnard College historian Rosalind Rosenberg was accused by her professional colleagues of precisely that—"betrayal"—when she testified as an expert witness for Sears. The subsequent campaign of intimidation mounted against her calls to mind C. Vann Woodward's warning that political orthodoxies of the left can have the same "chilling effect" on scholarship as those of the right: in the 1960s and 1970s, Woodward observed, just as in the McCarthy period, "there is no reckoning the number of books not written, research not done, and the standards, values, and ideals besmirched or trashed." [20]

The Sears case reveals with exceptional clarity the difference between politically committed scholarship and advocacy that is intellectually indefensible. In my opinion—anything but neutral, since I am the joint author of an essay defending Rosenberg against her assailants and drawing out the distressing implications of the episode for academic freedom—the EEOC's case against Sears was so deeply flawed that once historians were called into the courtroom, their testimony, if faithful to the complexity of the problems at issue, could hardly help favoring Sears. [21] The pivotal issue was whether the undenied predominance of males in Sears' higher-paying commission sales positions was evidence of a systematic pattern and practice of discrimination against women, or was compatible with gender-blind hiring practices and attributable to the greater interest of men in a type of sales job long associated with career commitment and the aggressive hard-sell. For reasons that have never been adequately explained, the EEOC chose to rely almost entirely on a high-tech statistical "proof" of Sears' guilt and did not present in court either victims or witnesses of the alleged offense. The task of the EEOC statisticians was to estimate the number of women who would have been hired by a truly gender-blind recruitment policy. In the absence of complainants or even of known applicants for the jobs in question, the statisticians had to base their esoteric calculations on some very bold hypothetical assumptions, one of them being that in choosing between commission and noncommission sales jobs, women have interests and preferences that are identical to those of men. On that unlikely assumption (possibly built into the EEOC's argument inadvertently by statisticians, without the knowledge of the agency's lawyers) the statisticians calculated that Sears should have given four out of every ten jobs to women.

The firm had in fact given women *three* out of ten. Sears defended itself by calling Rosenberg and many other witnesses to testify that the interests and job-related experience that men and women bring to the workplace are not identical — seemingly a truism, but one sharp enough to puncture the Achilles heel that the EEOC's litigators had fashioned for themselves.

Novick's account of the case (written entirely independently of the one I helped write) is understandably thin on the legal setting, and it underestimates the role played by statistics, but we concur entirely on one vital point: the historian called by the EEOC to rebut Rosenberg, Alice Kessler-Harris of Hofstra University, found her dual roles as scholar and as political activist in dire conflict. Her published work provided so much support for Sears' argument that one wonders what induced her to appear as a witness for the EEOC. Rosenberg, testifying for Sears, had quoted extensively from Kessler-Harris's book, *Out to Work: A History of Wage-earning Women in the United States,* to show not only that women's job interests were distinguishable from men's but, in Novick's words, that "women's own attitudes were an important factor limiting their full and equal participation in the work force" (504).

> Until quite recently, she had said in her book, "the ideology of the home still successfully contained most women's aspirations." Elsewhere Kessler-Harris had expressed the view that women "harbor values, attitudes, and behavior patterns potentially subversive to capitalism," an assertion that Rosenberg, in surrebuttal, found "at odds with her testimony . . . that women are as likely as men to want Sears' most highly competitive jobs, those in commission sales."
>
> Embarrassed at having her own work used against her, Kessler-Harris tried to talk around the narrowly posed question, and to advance broader arguments, but the format defeated her. She found herself offering testimony in which as she later acknowledged, "subtlety and nuance were omitted . . . complexity and exceptions vanished from sight." It was, in fact, a bit worse than that. The rules of the game were such that Rosenberg had only been required to show that women's values and attitudes played some role in their choice of jobs; Kessler-Harris was required to assert that they played no role. In an impossible situation Kessler-Harris advanced impossible arguments. "Where opportunity has existed," she told the court, "women have never [*sic*] failed to take the jobs offered. . . . Failure to find women in so-called non-traditional jobs can thus only [*sic*] be interpreted as a consequence of employer's unexamined attitudes or preferences, which phenomenon is the essence of discrimination." (504)[22]

Novick quite properly brushes aside Kessler-Harris's claims that she was misquoted and that the court misconstrued the legal significance of her work, and leaves practically no doubt about the intellectual superiority of Rosenberg's testimony.[23] Rosenberg's central claims, that women cannot simply be assumed to want exactly the same jobs as men, and therefore that "disparities in the sexual composition of an employer's workforce, as well as disparities of pay between men and women in many circumstances, are *consistent with* an absence of discrimination on the part of the employer," are virtually impossible to contest.[24] Sears needed little more than truisms from its expert witness on women's history because of the extraordinary vulnerability of the EEOC's statistical argument and because the government agency, as plaintiff in the case, bore the burden of proof. In contrast, Kessler-Harris's central contention (quoted above by Novick) — that gender-typing in the workplace has *nothing* to do with the preferences of employees and is attributable entirely to employer discrimination — is patently implausible.

But the two historians' testimony was seldom judged on intellectual merit. Within the professional subculture of women's history, in widely circulated letters, public meetings, and nationally published magazine interviews, Rosenberg was subjected to scathing verbal abuse, much of which Novick duly reports. In print she was accused of "class bias" and her decision to testify was labeled "immoral," "stupid," "unethical," and "unscholarly." Although she is a feminist who differs with other feminists mainly over the advisability of blanket denials of gender difference, she was said to have "betrayed" feminism by collaborating in "an attack on working women and sexual equality." At an annual convention of the American Historical Association, two organizations of women's historians jointly adopted a resolution declaring that "as feminist scholars we have a responsibility not to allow our scholarship to be used against the interests of women struggling for equity in our society." The resolution was widely understood as a condemnation of Rosenberg's interpretation of "the interests of women," and a suggestion that by espousing that interpretation in a court of law, she had compromised her status as a "responsible" feminist scholar. In what I regard as the nadir of the whole affair, the feminist journal *Signs* published an "Archive" ostensibly documenting historians' involvement in the case, that omitted — and thus effectively consigned to silence — one of the three documents the historians prepared for the trial. The document omitted was Rosenberg's devastating response to Kessler-Harris's testimony, in which she displayed many contradictions between Kessler-Harris's published views and what she had said in court — contradictions often as transparent as the ones Novick mentions in the passage quoted above.[25]

Novick describes the attack on Rosenberg but expresses no clear disapproval of it, and although he is eager for us to understand how little deceived he was by Kessler-Harris's testimony (for her, he observes, Sears was "guilty until proven innocent, inherently complicit in the discrimination endemic to the capitalist system"), he is not critical of her effort, under oath, to persuade the judge that her testimony represented the collective judgment of the profession (506). His attitude, if I understand him correctly, is that Kessler-Harris, as a politically committed feminist scholar, was entitled to walk into court and describe the world from whatever perspective the movement required and say about the history of gender typing whatever feminists currently found it convenient to believe. Conventional scholarly standards, not to mention objectivity, detachment, or even simple candor, weigh very little for Novick, it appears, against the claims of a good cause.[26] Reverting, oddly enough, to the starchy neutrality of the television news commentator, Novick wraps up his account of the case by coolly splitting the difference between the two historians: "Neither of the two opposing expert witnesses was 'disinterested.' Neither had taken a 'tell the truth though the heavens fall' posture. Both decided to testify based on their respective evaluations of the political consequences of the verdict . . . [and] a priori beliefs about Sears' guilt or innocence which in neither instance seemed very well grounded" (506).

Unsubstantiated though they are, let us assume, just for the sake of argument, that Novick is right on each of these three points: both witnesses were at the outset equally "interested," their decisions to testify were equally "a priori," and they were equally oriented to "political consequences." These stipulations boil down to the assertion that Rosenberg was no more *neutral* than Kessler-Harris.

That banal observation evidently suffices to persuade Novick that the only basis on which scholars can evaluate the two historians' testimony is political: feminists will find Kessler-Harris's testimony true, the rest of the world will not, and never the twain shall meet.[27] Although he has already acknowledged immense differences of intellectual merit and elementary plausibility between the two historians' statements, those differences now fade out of sight, all matters of degree become incalculable, and the only thing that finally counts is that neither witness attained a "God's eye view" — neither was neutral. Since neither witness's statement was immaculately conceived, Novick concludes that one is intrinsically as good as the other, leaving political affiliation as the only basis for preference. Notice that Novick throws in the towel and treats intellect as an abject slave of political alignment, not because he has any difficulty distinguishing which historian's testimony was more intellectually compelling, but simply because he hesitates, even in the affairs of scholars, to assign intellectual criteria priority over political considerations. The possibility that intellect might give direction to political commitments — that a movement with an ill-conceived agenda might revise it beneficially out of a concern for intellectual respectability—is left with no purchase.

Novick's relativistic rhetoric is usually counterbalanced by de facto moderation on the objectivity question, but here the rhetoric carries the day. His aim, I assume, in treating political commitments with kid gloves, is commendable: it is to make the academic world safe for politically committed scholarship. We must remind ourselves that on his assumptions, unlike my own, that task appears to require reforms root and branch, because he is convinced that the central ethical tradition of the scholarly world calls for neutrality, and neutrality, of course, would outlaw commitment. He actually says at one point that historians today face "a choice between either relaxing traditional objectivist criteria or reading important constituencies [that is, black and feminist historians] out of the discipline" (596). If the question were whether to purge the profession of activists, I would of course side with Novick, for in spite of the lapses he describes, important work is being done in both fields, and activists have undeniably and valuably widened the scope and variety of the profession's interests. But the idea that political activists might be read out of the profession is laughable: several recent presidents of the Organization of American Historians would have to be placed high on the list of deportees.[28] On the contrary, as I have said, it appears to me that there is widespread recognition within the profession that political commitment need not detract from the writing of history—not even from its objectivity—as long as honesty, detachment, and intelligence are also at work.

Perhaps overreacting to the traumas of the Abraham incident, Novick closes his discussion of the Sears case by speaking sketchily of "dual citizenship," a doctrine that would evidently elevate the claims of political loyalty to co-equal status with the traditional intellectual imperatives of the scholarly community (510). Dual citizenship would mean, if I decode his rather cryptic reference to it correctly, that sometimes we would understand ourselves to be acting in our capacity as scholars, sometimes as political partisans; the laws of neither domain would be allowed to overrule those of the other. Or, at any rate, no one would ever be under any very weighty obligation to adhere to scholarly standards if doing so encroached on political loyalties. Whether Novick is really prepared to go this far I am not sure, but it is certainly too far. Although he questions the ethic of objectivity precisely because of the intellectual hubris he thinks it breeds, and although he appears at heart to be a skeptic, a person who believes little and doubts much, in the end Novick allows his solicitude for advocacy to subvert his skepticism: he hands to any scholar who can claim membership in a political movement a blank check, a license to believe whatever the movement requires and to assert it with all the authority of scholarship. Instead of trimming pretentious claims to certainty, he inadvertently multiplies them. As so often happens, the relativist ends up by championing self-indulgence, for if moral and epistemological obligations are nothing more than ghostly superstitions, then mistakes and unethical choices (departures from obligation) become phantasmagorical as well, and we can literally do no wrong. All the while, of course, the relativist claims that "anything goes" is *not* the intended message, and the claim is sincere in the sense that most of us cannot avoid construing the world in terms of right and wrong, no matter what our formal views on objectivity and relativism. But the status of these intuitive judgments is what is at stake, and here obligation is the keystone: if in principle no opinions and courses of action can be obligatory or "right," then none can be "wrong," and everything is permitted, notwithstanding the annoying static of intuition. Saying that there is such a thing as obligation does not, of course, commit us to a metaphysical account of foundations, or to the idea that any particular bundle of claims and practices adequately defines truth or morality.

Within the scholarly community, the characterological values that we associate with the intellectual vocation—respect for logical coherence, fidelity to evidence, detachment, candor, honesty, and the like—must not only compete on equal terms with other values, they must prevail. When the members of the scholarly community become unwilling to put intellectual values ahead of political ones, they erase the only possible boundary between politically committed scholarship and propaganda and thereby rob the community of its principal justification for existence. John Q. Public would be sensible and well within his rights to terminate his support for the university and the academic disciplines it houses if the scholarly world were nothing more than its most cynical and shallow members now say it is: an ancient, tumble-down fortification, constructed by other generations for purposes no longer intelligible, valued today only for the territory it controls, and devoid of any character apart from the political coloration supplied by whichever band of ideological warriors happens by hook or crook to occupy its battlements at the moment. The university, in my view, does control valuable territory, and it is an arena of conflict. But the contest is vitally constrained by the ascetic values we associate with objectivity. Those constraints, in turn, give the institution an identity radically distinct from, and far more durable than, any of the various partisan bands that struggle for influence under its auspices. There is nothing in the nature of things that guarantees the perpetuation of this unique and priceless institution. It lives only insofar as we choose to live by the values that sustain it.

My concern about Novick's near equation of objectivity with neutrality, and his willingness sometimes to subordinate intellectual priorities to political ones, may create the wrong impression. So let me say as plainly as I can that this is no run-of-the-mill piece of work. The range of Novick's research is staggering, and the story he tells is gracefully constructed and wittily presented. *That Noble Dream* is an exceptionally important book. I do not know of any other work by a historian that, if read by everyone in the profession, could do more to raise the general intellectual level of the guild. Even where the lessons it teaches are, in my view, wrong, its power of provocation is immense and all to the good. Epistemological issues about which historians have long remained oblivious, even as debate has raged like brushfire through adjacent disciplines, are here shown to be relevant to every historian's daily labors. Novick's next-to-last chapter, fifty pages long, could serve as a fine crash course on contemporary debates among intellectuals and should be read by every graduate student in history, regardless of field. But like all texts, even the best, this one is open to many interpretations, and some are, I think, potentially hazardous to the health of the profession. Two dangers — throwing off the reins of objectivity just because no one is neutral, and endorsing political commitment uncritically, without erecting any fences against propaganda — have been sufficiently attended to. It remains to show that there is something to regret about the apocalyptic tenor of Novick's rhetorical posture, even though he usually, if unaccountably, couples that posture with admirably moderate practices.

The academic air is thick nowadays with sensational pronouncements about the failures of reason. Given Novick's silent loyalty, in practice, to the ascetic values that I associate with objectivity, I do not think that he can be counted among those who imagine that we stand at the threshold of a new epoch of endless interpretative play, in which words like reason, logic, rationality, truth, and evidence can be merrily and painlessly dispensed with. The tone of his concluding chapters is more suggestive of the breaking of the seventh seal than the dawning of a brave new world, and like all authentic skeptics he extends his skepticism at least intermittently to the claims of skepticism itself. He understands that relativism predicts its own relativity; he knows that if one supposes historicism to be "right," one must suppose it to be so only during a passing phase of history — observations that have, of course, never been enough to silence doubt about reason.

Tempered though his skepticism is, he does believe that the ideal of objectivity, the "founding myth" of the profession, is more or less defunct, presumably leaving the practice of historical representation foundationless, adrift in the cosmos. Toward the end of the book, in a discussion that slides back and forth between talk of cognitive crisis and concrete institutional conundrums such as the growth of specialization, decay of the academic job market in the 1970s, the exponential growth of the literature each of us tries to stay abreast of, and the inherently dispersive character of a discipline that, unlike English and Philosophy, lacks even the possibility of defining a single canon familiar to all practitioners, Novick repeatedly suggests that history is today so fragmented — politically, institutionally, and intellectually — that it "no longer constitute[s] a coherent discipline" (577, also 592). He even concludes that a sense of "dismay," "disarray," and "discouragement" is more prevalent among historians than among the members of any other discipline (578) — hardly likely in view of the state of numb exhaustion that prevails in the literary disciplines after a decade of theory wars that make historians' quarrels look like family reunions.[29] Whether he intends it or not, all this gloom and doom might well lead the reader to conclude that writing a history of anything — even a history of historians' quarrels about objectivity — is a preposterous undertaking that only a fool would attempt. As if to encourage that reading, Novick closes the book with a rather portentous passage from Sartre: "In the domain of expression . . . success is necessarily failure. It is impossible to succeed, since at the outset you set yourself the goal of failure (to capture movement in immobile objects, for instance). . . . So there it is. You never quite grasp what you set out to achieve. And then suddenly it's a statue or a book. The opposite of what you wanted" (629).

Coming from an author who is (at least in practice) as securely wedded to conventional modes of representation as Novick, this display of epistemological angst is harmless enough. It is, however, strongly reminiscent of the distinctively "postmodern" syndrome a literary critic had in mind when he observed that many scholars influenced by deconstructionist doctrines seem to feel that they "live upon inevitable but somehow invigorating failure."[30] This characteristically postmodern authorial stance in which the author cheerfully acknowledges that what he or she is saying is unsubstantiable or worse, and then goes on to assert it exactly as if it were "true" — always ready, if challenged, to fall back on the initial disclaimer — has the undeniable advantage of allowing an author to indulge in quite ordinary forms of communication and common sense while preserving a reputation for sophistication and undeceivability.[31] The benefits are obvious at a time when strife over epistemological questions is so intense that only the debater with no recognizable position is unassailable. In an age of guerrilla scholarship, the thing to do is stay always on the offense and unburden oneself of any convictions, lest they require a defense. The ancient military advice of Sun Tzu applies: "Subtle and insubstantial, the expert [warrior] leaves no trace; divinely mysterious, he is inaudible. Thus he is master of his enemy's fate." [32]

The most striking example of what might be called "the undeceivability ploy," and one that by its very extremity sheds light on the much more modest gap between Novick's rhetoric and his practice, comes straight from the author of *The Postmodern Condition,* Jean-François Lyotard himself. In his latest book, Lyotard fondly recalls an old friend, Pierre Souyri, a comrade-in-arms with whom he served for many years on the barricades of the Parisian left. Together they helped publish radical Marxist organs with titles such as *Socialisme ou Barbarie* and *Pouvoir Ouvrier.* What is immediately noteworthy about this reminiscence, or "memorial," as Lyotard calls it, is not so much its deceased subject as the display of epistemological anxiety and contrition with which it begins. The author's first words announce the unworthiness of his efforts. "The only testimony worthy of the author of *Révolution et Contre-révolution en Chine,*" worries Lyotard, "is the one I cannot give him: it would be to write the history, in Marxist terms, of the radical Marxist current to which he belonged." But this is impossible, says Lyotard, for "I am not a historian." [33]

Lyotard hesitates to take up the historian's pen not because he feels untrained or insufficiently talented. Nor is it simply that, having lost faith in Marxism, he fears that even his best efforts to represent his friend's life will embody terms and assumptions that Souyri himself, whose own devotion to the cause never faltered, would find unacceptable. Rather, Lyotard explains, what makes it impossible for him to write the history his friend deserves is that he lacks faith of another sort, shared by Marxist and non-Marxist historians alike: faith in the reality of the past and the possibility of representing that reality in words:

> Obviously, I lack the expertise, the knowledge, the fine tuning of the mind to the methodology; but above all I lack a certain way of interrogating and situating what is spoken of in relation to what one is saying. To be brief, let us call this the postulate of realism. That which the historian recounts and explains had [sic] to be real; otherwise what he is doing is not history. As in legal rhetoric, everything is organized in order to explore the clues, produce proofs, and induce the belief that the object, the event, or the man now absent were indeed there just as they are being depicted. The opposing party against whom the historian argues with all his force is not easy to beat; it is the forgetting which is the death of death itself.

He cannot subscribe to such hubris and naiveté:

However, I cannot manage to make this pious activity my own, to share the historian's confidence in its ends, to believe in the fidelity or the plausibility of that which is, in any case, only a representation. I cannot manage to forget that it is I, the historian, who makes my man speak, and speak to men he did not know and to whom he would not necessarily have chosen to speak.[34]

Once an author has carried skepticism to this extreme, one might expect him or her simply to fall silent: better to say nothing than to soil one's hands in the shabby illusions of historical representation. Or alternatively one might expect these words to introduce an experimental form of communication, a text designed to overcome the conventional limits of representation, or at least to acknowledge those limits with greater candor and precision. But none of these expectations is borne out.

Having warned his readers of the inescapable futility of all efforts to represent the past "as it was," Lyotard then embarks upon the very course he has just declared to be impossibly naive. Having shown that the historian's pious, death-defying claim to know "how things really were" does not deceive him in the least, Lyotard proceeds to tell us . . . well, how it really was with his friend Souyri. In spite of himself, Lyotard commits a historical representation. He makes Souyri speak. And, by all appearances, he puts his representational pants on pretty much the same way the rest of us do. He informs us that he sent his friend a letter announcing his resignation from the *Pouvoir Ouvrier* group in 1966. Souyri answered him in October. "He affirmed that our divergences dated from long before . . . he considered it pointless to try to resolve them. . . . He attributed to me the project of. . . . He added. . . . He knew himself to be bound to Marxist thought. . . . He prepared himself. . . . We saw each other again. . . . I felt myself scorned. . . . He knew that I felt this. . . . He liked to provoke his interlocutor. . . . [He was] a sensitive and absent-minded man in daily life."[35] And so on. The representation is unexceptional. It is successful enough as representations go—we feel that we have learned something of Souyri and of the relation between the two men—but there is nothing to distinguish it from representations each of us hear, read, and produce dozens of times every day, not just in writing history but in the conduct of the most mundane affairs of life. Nor, in spite of all the cautions Lyotard has urged upon us, do we know any better how to assess the trustworthiness of this portrait of Souyri than we would if its author had simply set it forth as a "true account."

Does Lyotard believe in the "postulate of realism"? Certainly not, if we judge from what he says on the subject. But if we take into account what he *does* as well as what he says, he seems in the end, in practice, unable to escape it. Notwithstanding all his skeptical rhetoric, in telling us about his deceased friend he acts as if the past is real, as if some representations of it are prefer-able to others, and as if the criteria of preference are far from idiosyncratic. We are reminded of Thomas Nagel's suggestion, which stands at the head of this essay, that objectivity and skepticism are not opposites but complementary ideas; that every effort to get beyond appearances postulates the real. The gap between Lyotard's hyperskeptical rhetorical posture and run-of-the-mill real-ist practice is immense and evidently unbridgeable. What is to be gained from it? Nothing that I can see, except a reputation for undeceivability and possibly (as Denis Donoghue said of deconstruction) a "Pyrrhic victory of angst over bourgeois liberalism."[36]

What, then, are we to think when able people like Novick tell us that the effort to represent the past, and "get it right," is bound to fail—and then do a rather good job of getting it right? The obvious answer is to do as they do, and not as they say. But in closing allow me to suggest, in the compact form of a parable, the outlines, at least, of a more expansive answer. It is as if we are lost in the French countryside, trying to find our way to Paris with maps that do not agree. We happen upon a native philosopher, Jean, whom we ask for help in deciding which map to believe. He examines the maps and frowns, saying, "None of these documents will do. They give only a two-dimensional repre-sentation of a path that is at least three dimensional, even disregarding what Einstein says . . . no, they won't do at all. These are mere pieces of paper, and they fail utterly to convey any sensation of movement, of passage from one town to another, of what the scenery along the route looks like, the feel of the road beneath one's feet, the aromas, the sounds of the birds as you pass by! And look at this! Why, these pieces of paper rely on mere round black dots to represent whole cities of people: families, complex souls, individuals full of life and variety and mystery, all absurdly compressed into a dot!" Stretching him-self to his full height, Jean, exasperated, hands the maps back to us, and asks, incredulously, "How can anyone ever have thought that anything so sublime as getting to Paris could be represented by a few marks on a sheet of paper?"

Confronted with such radically misplaced expectations, we can only walk on, in hopes of finding a more discriminating philosopher. What Jean wants, maps cannot supply.[37] But we want to go to Paris, we know perfectly well that maps can help us get there, and we also know that some maps are better suited to the purpose than others. (Why that should be so is the really interesting question, though it seems not to arouse much curiosity nowadays in Paris.) Take with a grain of salt Novick's distress over the supposedly insuperable dif-ficulties of mapmaking; be glad that, in spite of them, he has helped us find our way into this past so effectively.

CHAPTER SEVEN

Justifying Academic Freedom
in the Era of Power/Knowledge

A hundred years ago, when the old-time colleges seemed to have lost their way and the modern university system was still struggling to be born, American academics worried about an entire range of questions that hardly anyone asks today. Broadly speaking, the questions lay at the intersection of epistemology and intellectual authority. How is knowledge best cultivated? What institutional setting is most conducive to intellectual authority? How is the professoriate to justify its existence to those who pay the bills? What is the university *for?*

Questions of this kind, which carry no special charge today, seemed urgent indeed at the turn of the century, when less than 4 percent of the college-age population was attending college and the university had not yet become securely ensconced as gatekeeper to the professions. The Victorian reformers whom we now remember as the architects of the modern American University—Charles William Eliot of Harvard, Andrew Dickson White of Cornell, Daniel Coit Gilman of Johns Hopkins, and many others whose names are less well known—confronted questions of intellectual authority every day and did not have the luxury of suspending judgment. They had to get on with the practical business of building universities, for expanding enrollments and lavish

I am indebted to more people for advice about this essay than I can mention here. Special pains were taken by Steven Crowell, Sanford Levinson, Randall McGowen, Louis Menand, Walter Metzger, Robert Post, and Carol Quillen. Advice sometimes took the form of vigorous dissent, so no one is to be blamed for the final product but me. The essay was originally prepared for the conference "Paradoxes of Rights" at Amherst College in November 1992. Subsequent working versions were given at the annual meeting of the American Association of University Professors in June 1993, at the History Department of the University of Oregon in October 1993, at the Swedish infusions of capital from a burgeoning industrial economy were opening up a world of new possibilities in higher education.[1]

The same developments also brought crude demands for orthodoxy. State legislators and wealthy private donors alike took it for granted that "he who pays the piper, calls the tune," an assumption strongly seconded by the prevailing legal doctrines of the era. Faced with contradictory possibilities and pressures, Victorian reformers thought long and hard about authority and professional autonomy. They drew inspiration from ancient precedents of faculty self-governance in England and from the full-bodied traditions of academic freedom that many of them had seen at first hand during their own student days in Germany. Their thinking and worrying bore practical fruit during the decades following the Civil War, and we who teach and work in the American university system today are the beneficiaries of what they wrought. Nowhere is the success of their handiwork more evident than in the easy complacency with which we take for granted the intellectual authority of the university and those who work within it.

My aim is to dispel that complacency, at least momentarily, by doing what historians so often do: tell stories about how things came to be the way they are. The story I will tell draws heavily on the work of Walter Metzger, Mary Furner, William Van Alstyne, and other scholars. I will have little to say about either the captains of industry who financed the modern university, or the educational entrepreneurs, such as Eliot, White, and Gilman, who superintended its construction. Nor will I say much about martyrs to academic freedom, with the single exception of Edward A. Ross. His case deserves special attention because it illustrates the late emergence and fragility of the rights we take for granted, and helps us recall the circumstances under which the American Association of University Professors (AAUP) was founded. The focal point of my story is the emergence of the disciplines, such as History, Chemistry, Sociology, Mechanical Engineering, and so forth, in which we academics do our work today. These "communities of the competent" were, I believe, the seed crystals around which the modern university formed. Defending their authority is, in my view, what academic freedom is principally about. What concerns me are two things that imperil that authority: the decay of the epis-

Collegium for Advanced Study in the Social Sciences in September 1994, and at the History Department of Rice University in September 1994. The essay was initially published under a slightly different title in Austin Sarat and Thomas R. Kearns, eds., *Legal Rights: Historical and Philosophical Perspectives* (Ann Arbor: University of Michigan Press, 1996), 113–76. An abbreviated version of the essay appears in Louis Menand, ed., *The Future of Academic Freedom* (Chicago: University of Chicago Press, 1996), 43–90.

temological assumptions that originally underwrote the founding of disciplinary communities, and a growing assimilation of academic freedom to First Amendment law, a development that has brought immense benefits, but at the expense of obscuring both the function of the disciplinary community and its intimate relation to academic freedom. My aim is not to put forth a new justification for academic freedom, but to call attention to the limitations of the old one and hold up for critical examination some of the obstacles that stand in our way as we seek a formulation more adequate to our needs.

Appearances to the contrary notwithstanding, the comfortable state of affairs in which we find ourselves today was not foreordained. What brought it about was a process of institutional development that proceeded in two overlapping phases, each vital to the success of the other. The first created communities of competent inquirers, the second used them to establish authority in specialized domains of knowledge. The history of the community of the competent is long and honorable but only sketchily documented. It has roots that go far back into the history of ecclesiastical establishments, on the one hand, and science, on the other, and that intertwine at every stage with controversies over heresy and communal autonomy. The rudiments of an always edgy and competitive communal solidarity among competent inquirers date back to the founding of the first European universities. By the eighteenth century, the changing technology and economics of print culture had decisively surpassed personal acquaintance and private correspondence as a means of knitting inquirers together, giving rise to a nascent division of intellectual labor and prompting much speculation about the growing influence of the "republic of letters."[2]

The nineteenth century brought changes of scale so great as to constitute a qualitative transformation of the conditions of intellectual endeavor.[3] Population growth, rising literacy rates, growing per capita income, and the rapid spread of a predominantly urban form of life joined with immense improvements in the ease and speed of communication to make the fruits of specialized intellectual competence relevant and accessible to a larger public than ever before. Architects of the modern American university such as Daniel Coit Gilman at Hopkins capitalized on these changes, not only by constructing ivy-covered classrooms and dormitories to house an expanding clientele of students, but also by founding academic journals, reshaping undergraduate libraries to the needs of research, funding graduate fellowships, and encouraging their faculties to seek reputations of national and international scope. The most visible manifestation of the maturing communities around which the university formed were the specialized disciplinary associations that began organizing on a national basis in the 1880s: the Modern Language Association (1883), the American Historical Association (1884), the American Economic Association (1885), and many others in succeeding years. By the time of World War I, a new intellectual division of labor had taken shape as college and university campuses all over the country reorganized themselves around "departments," local outposts of the fields of learning established by the national specialist associations. Neither the departments nor the national professional associations they represented were of any great consequence in themselves, but the maturing communities of the competent for which they stood had profound effects on the lives of their members and utterly transformed the character of higher education in this country.[4]

The importance of these newly defined communities lay in the opportunity they provided for professors to divide their loyalties, thereby complicating their identity and enhancing their authority. Professors would, of course, continue to be teachers, dependent as always on a particular college or university for a salary and for provision of the mainly undergraduate classrooms in which they earned their keep. But they would also become something new: research scholars. As such, their employment credentials, even in their traditional role as teachers of undergraduates, would become contingent upon membership and reputation within trans-local communities made up of fellow research specialists. By keeping up a constant exchange of communications in the form of journal articles and books, as well as private correspondence and face-to-face conversations at periodic conventions, the members of these far-flung communities, or *Kommunikationsgemeinschaft*, as Karl-Otto Apel calls them, would police each other's opinions and thus provide, in theory at least, a collective warrant for one another's authority.[5] Knit together not by affection, but by the respectful attention that experts owe to their peers, these densely interactive communities effectively constitute the specialized universes within which scholarly discourse proceeds today.[6] Although they have undeniably generated their share of ponderous mystifications over the years, when all is said and done they created a space for originality and critical thinking without which modern culture would almost certainly be the poorer.

The second phase of reform harvested what the first planted. Insofar as a distinct community of competent investigators could be said to exist in a given field, the keystone of professional autonomy was already in place, for the individual members of such a community were empowered by its very existence to speak in a quasi-corporate voice. Having acknowledged one another as peers, and thus relieved one another of the heavy burdens of anonymity and idiosyncrasy, they were well situated to deflect criticism originating outside the community's borders and deflate truth claims unable to win communal support. The result of the sharpened identity and growing solidarity of specialists was an effective monopoly on "sound opinion" within their domain. The cardinal principle of professional autonomy is collegial self-governance; its inescapable corollary is that only one's peers are competent to judge one's performance. "Monopoly" is not an inappropriate term to describe the resulting advantage enjoyed by communally sponsored opinion, yet it carries implications that tend to obscure the defining feature of the community. It is vital to remember that this sort of monopoly comes about by *intensifying* competition between producers (in this case, of ideas), not by sheltering them from it, as in the classic case of economic monopoly. *The price of participation in the community of the competent is perpetual exposure to criticism.* If there is anything at all that justifies the special authority and trustworthiness of community-sponsored opinions, as I believe there is, it lies in the fact that these truth claims have weathered competition more severe than would be thought acceptable in ordinary human communities.[7]

All that remained was to reach an understanding about the practical limits of solidarity. What degrees and kinds of politically sensitive expression would the professoriate be willing actually to defend through collective action? Where was the pale beyond which the outspoken individual would be left to twist in the wind? That understanding gradually took shape in the political turbulence of the Populist and Progressive eras as young social scientists, in particular, espoused unpopular views that triggered explosive controversies on campus after campus. Out of this crucible of controversy a tacit set of standards and expectations finally crystallized in 1915, with the founding of the American Association of University Professors and its publication of the first Report on Academic Freedom and Tenure.

Although the AAUP code would be severely tested in the patriotic fervor of World War I and placed under heavy strain again in the loyalty controversies of the McCarthy period, it served as a kind of capstone, bringing to completion the institutional edifice the Victorians planned and built out of their concern to provide safe havens for sound opinion. Today, although the professoriate is less influential (and less affluent) than it would like to be, it speaks with unchallenged authority in many spheres of life and is substantially free to play whatever tunes it likes, without begging permission from those who pay the piper. Some recent Supreme Court decisions might even be taken to indicate that professional autonomy, suitably garbed in the lofty language of rights and academic freedom, is today not only secure, but as close to sacred as a secular society can make it. Our Victorian predecessors never dared hope that academic freedom had been high on the agenda of the nation's Founding Fathers. Yet in 1967, speaking for the majority of the Supreme Court in *Keyishian v. Board of Regents,* Justice Brennan did not hesitate to say that "academic freedom . . . is of transcendent value to all of us and not merely to the teachers concerned. That freedom is therefore a special concern of the First Amendment, which does not tolerate laws that cast a pall of orthodoxy over the classroom." [8]

Ironically, even as Justice Brennan crowned the Victorian project with a victory more complete than its architects had envisioned, the tide was running out on the intellectual premises that had sustained it in the first place. None of us today are likely to feel entirely comfortable with the assumptions on which our ancestors built the modern academic order. The problem is most severe for those among us who unreservedly identify themselves as "postmodern," from whose vantage point the assumptions that propelled the Victorians are likely to seem at least naive, and possibly sinister. Consider, for example, the familiar Foucauldian notion that power and knowledge, far from constituting a natural opposition, are locked in a mutually supportive embrace so tight that they should be written "power/knowledge," as if two sides of a single coin. [9] Nothing could be more alien to the thinking of our Victorian predecessors, for whom the whole point of academic freedom was to expand the sphere of disinterested knowledge and fence it off from power. [10] Obvious questions present themselves. If a day should come when the premises of academic freedom no longer seem plausible even within the academy, how long can they be expected to prevail in the world at large? And if, as I have contended, academic freedom is but the exposed cutting edge of the drive toward autonomy that every community of the competent must undertake if it is to do its work of authorizing sound opinion, what does the decay of those premises portend for the university?

Turning up the level of magnification a bit will help us gauge the chasm that is opening between the Victorians and ourselves. In 1896, at the height of Populist agitation against the gold standard, Edward A. Ross, a young economist recently hired by Stanford, made several speeches in support of William Jennings Bryan and published a campaign pamphlet titled *Honest Dollars.* At a time when respectability and Republican party loyalty were expected to go hand in hand, Ross became the first academic economist to openly endorse the idea of free silver. He was no lightweight. Trained at the University of Berlin and the Johns Hopkins University, Ross was married to the niece of social theorist Lester Frank Ward and had recently become secretary of the American Economic Association. Although only thirty years old, he had already

achieved high visibility in his field, both as a scholar and as an outspoken reformer at Indiana University and Cornell. When David Starr Jordan left the
presidency of Indiana to take over the new university Leland Stanford was
building in California, he invited Ross to come along. With Indiana, Stanford,
Northwestern, and Cornell all courting him, Ross put Jordan off twice before
accepting his third offer.

Jordan's admiration for Ross was soon put to the test by Mrs. Jane Lothrop
Stanford, who had been left in sole command of the university after her husband's death. Offended by Ross's activism, she demanded that Jordan dismiss
him. Stalling for time, Jordan persuaded Mrs. Stanford to give Ross a sabbatical leave in 1898–99 with the understanding that he would look for another
position and resign a year later if still considered unsuitable. Simultaneously
Jordan transferred Ross out of economics and made him professor of sociology.

Although he was professionally well connected and had a friend in power,
Ross had good reason to wonder how much support he could count on. San
Francisco newspapers reported that six out of every seven Stanford faculty
members supported McKinley and the gold standard. Leading economists
viewed Ross's activism with mixed feelings at best. Frank Taussig of Harvard
cautioned Ross that flamboyant popular pronouncements on economic issues
were "undignified and objectionable." Taussig was a man of conservative temperament, but even fellow radical Simon Nelson Patten asked: "Have you not
been giving a little too much time to politics lately? . . . That miserable money
problem gets much more attention than it deserves and I never see an article
of yours on it but what I feel that intellectual force has been wasted which
might have produced far greater results in other directions."[11]

There was no such thing as tenure at Stanford in 1896, and no one could
say just how far an outspoken scholar could go. A colleague of Ross's, H. H.
Powers, clearly went too far when he had the misfortune not to notice Mrs.
Stanford, an orthodox Catholic, sitting in a predominantly student audience
as he spoke on religion. The "pessimism and heterodoxy" of his remarks offended her. When Powers added insult to injury by challenging the gold standard as well, she demanded his resignation. Comparatively unpublished and
not nearly so well connected as Ross, Powers understandably regarded publicity as a profound threat to his career. He had little choice but to accept his
fate in silence. Ross showed him no great sympathy and in fact helped the ad-
ministration smooth his departure by taking over some of his assignments. By
the end of 1897, Ross felt confident that his own safety was assured, as long as
he confined himself to questions "about which it was my business to know."[12]

Sure enough, at the end of his cooling-off sabbatical, Jordan notified him that in spite of Mrs. Stanford's threats, his annual appointment would be resumed in 1899–1900.

By this time, Mrs. Stanford had issued a total ban on faculty political activity. Her aim, she said, was to preserve the neutrality of the institution. Ross flouted the ban so brazenly on his return that one cannot rule out the possibility that he had, perhaps, already made up his mind to leave. Speaking before a group of San Francisco labor leaders in 1900, he condemned coolie immigration and issued a plea for Anglo-Saxon racial purity, going so far as to assert, according to some reports, that vessels bringing Asian laborers to these shores should be fired on to prevent their landing. Ross's ugly racial chauvinism was unexceptional in the context of the times. What made his comments inflammatory was the fact that the Stanford fortune had been built on coolie labor. In another address at about the same time, Ross predicted that in the twentieth century all natural monopolies, including railroads, would pass into public ownership. Outraged once again; concerned about the "socialistic" elements that Ross seemed to be courting; and feeling pressure from her late husband's business associates, Mrs. Stanford ordered Jordan to fire Ross, giving him six months to wrap up his affairs.[13]

Not one to play the passive victim, except when doing so in public might work to his advantage, Ross carefully timed the announcement of his firing to coincide with publication of his major book, *Social Control.* At a well-managed press conference in November 1900, Ross turned on his friend in power, depicting himself as the victim not only of Mrs. Stanford and Big Money but also of a university president who lacked the courage to defend free speech.[14] His self-conceived role was that of the scientific expert, duty-bound to announce truths arduously wrested from nature and corporately sanctioned by a community of peers. "I cannot with self-respect decline to speak on topics to which I have given years of investigation," he said. "It is my duty as an economist to impart, on occasion, to sober people, and in a scientific spirit, my conclusions on subjects with which I am expert. . . . The scientist's business is to know some things clear to the bottom, and if he hides what he knows he loses his virtue."[15]

George Howard, head of the Stanford History Department, went before his French Revolution class two days later and likened the university's termination of Ross to the tyrannies of the ancien régime. When subsequently Howard refused to apologize for this outburst, he, too, was ousted. In the ensuing turmoil, thirty-seven of forty-eight senior faculty members pledged their loyalty to Jordan, but all those in the social sciences who could afford the gesture resigned, virtually wiping out the fields of economics, history, and sociology.

Frank Fetter, a prominent economist who had just come from Cornell to take over economics, asked for assurances of free inquiry and expression for all faculty in the future; when it was not forthcoming, he resigned. So did Arthur Lovejoy, Stanford's first and, at the time, only philosopher. Ross may well have shaped the encounter in self-serving ways, but there is no denying that his flair for the dramatic gesture achieved what no other academic-freedom case of the era did: it overrode political differences, galvanized opinion, and produced united action by the professoriate to defend one of its own.[16]

At the annual convention of the American Economic Association in December 1900, Edwin R. A. Seligman, one of the most widely respected American economists of his generation, stage-managed a quasi-formal vindication of Ross. The president of the AEA at the time was Richard T. Ely, whose own radicalism had triggered an academic-freedom case at Wisconsin in 1894, during which he received only lukewarm support from the profession. Still thought by some to be too much the Chautauqua speaker and Christian socialist, and too little the scholar, Ely would have had to put his name at the top of the list of signatures if the association had officially declared its support for Ross. Apparently in hopes of avoiding that outcome and bringing together both ends of the political spectrum in defense of Ross, Seligman preferred to act informally, even though that meant not having the official imprimatur of the AEA. Accordingly, Ross made a dramatic appearance before a meeting of about forty economists and then sat silently as Seligman read excerpts from Jordan's letters to show that he was being unjustly persecuted. The AEA members present then created a committee to investigate the case. "With this declaration," says Walter Metzger, "the first professorial inquiry into an academic freedom case was conceived and brought into being — the predecessor if not directly the parent of Committee A of the AAUP."[17]

Given the cold shoulder by President Jordan and many members of the Stanford faculty, the inquiry rapidly bogged down in futile efforts to unravel Mrs. Stanford's motives. Lacking the imprimatur of the AEA, its report was fair game for critics. Magazines and newspapers that were unfavorably disposed dismissed it as a partisan document. Thus, in spite of receiving strong support even from conservative economists, the inquiry fell flat. Seligman and others tried to organize a boycott of Stanford. They succeeded in persuading several job candidates to withdraw from consideration, but when it came to a choice between professional solidarity and placing one's graduate students advantageously, solidarity evaporated. Much to the chagrin of Harvard social scientists, new Ph.D.s from Harvard promptly filled the empty slots in Stanford's History Department. Although efforts were made to find a desirable post for Ross, he left Palo Alto for the academic wilderness of Nebraska, where another martyr to academic freedom, E. Benjamin Andrews, was president. Five years later, as memories faded, Ross moved to Wisconsin, where his career flourished for the next thirty years. The warmhearted historian of the ancien régime, George Howard, went to Nebraska for good.[18]

The Ross case was a happy fluke that enabled Ross and his supporters to publicize the issues of academic freedom in uncharacteristically stark, black-and-white terms. The imperious "Dowager of Palo Alto," as sociologist Albion Small called her, could not have played her role better if Ross had been writing the script.[19] Yet even in convenient caricature, the issues of academic freedom are sufficiently murky that the case also illustrates the fragility of intellectual authority and the difficulty of mobilizing effective support on behalf of a scholar confronted with demands for political conformity. Rescuing Ross was no piece of cake. In the absence of a well-organized and highly self-conscious community of the competent, forearmed with values appropriate to the task, there would have been no one to come to Ross's rescue, and she who paid the piper would have called the tune — or hired another piper.

Some may imagine that with the resources of the First Amendment at his disposal, Ross and the cause of academic freedom were bound ultimately to prevail. Those resources were not yet available, however. Justice Oliver Wendell Holmes did as much as anyone to make them available, but not until after World War I. Holmes's famous dissent in *Abrams v. United States* came in 1919: "The best test of truth is the power of the thought to get itself accepted in the competition of the market. . . . We should be eternally vigilant against attempts to check the expression of opinions that we loathe and believe to be fraught with death, unless they so imminently threaten immediate interference with the lawful and pressing purposes of the law that an immediate check is required to save the country." In contrast, back in 1892, while still a justice of the Massachusetts Supreme Court, Holmes had no compunctions about making freedom of expression contingent upon contractual obligations. In keeping with legal doctrines that prevailed at the time, he then construed the First Amendment only as a prohibition on prior restraint, not a guarantee of immunity against the consequences of expression. In the case of a policeman who had been fired after criticizing his department, Holmes held that "the petitioner may have a constitutional right to talk politics, but he has no constitutional right to be a policeman. There are few employments for hire in which the servant does not agree to suspend his constitutional right of free speech, as well as of idleness, by the implied terms of his contract. The servant cannot complain, as he takes the employment on the terms which are offered him."[20]

The Ross case not only was a trial run for the investigative *modus operandi* that the AAUP would later make its stock in trade, it also brought together the two men who, more than anyone else, brought the AAUP into existence. Arthur Lovejoy, the Stanford philosopher who resigned in protest over Ross's ouster, would become secretary of the organization at its founding in 1915. E. R. A. Seligman, the Columbia economist who arranged for Ross's quasi-official vindication, wrote the first draft of the 1915 Report on Academic Freedom and Tenure. Lovejoy then rewrote the text so extensively that Walter Metzger, our premier historian of academic freedom, credits him with being virtually co-author. Both men later served as president of the organization. It was Lovejoy and a group of seventeen colleagues at Johns Hopkins University who hosted the first intercollegiate meeting aimed at the construction of a national association of university professors. Since Hopkins men had also founded the MLA, the AHA, the AEA, and most of the other specialist organizations that defined the new intellectual division of labor, it was only fitting that they would take the lead in adding this capstone to their professionalizing labors.

The word "capstone" needs stressing. This is how I, as a historian, would *define* academic freedom: as the capstone of the institutional edifice that Victorian reformers constructed in hopes of establishing authority and cultivating reliable knowledge. The metaphor implies a stronger linkage between academic freedom and professionalization than is commonly recognized today. The connection often goes unacknowledged, partly because in our generation professors have been extremely loath to admit their kinship to lawyers, physicians, and other fee-for-service professionals. Here etymological common sense should be our guide: "Professor" could hardly help being a variety of "professional."[21] The founders of the AAUP were not so skittish about their professional aspirations. They explicitly identified their organization as a complement to the specialist societies and deliberately modeled it on the American Bar Association and the American Medical Association:

> The scientific and specialized interests of members of American university faculties are well cared for by various learned societies. No organization exists, however, which at once represents the common interests of the teaching staffs and deals with the general problems of university policy. Believing that a society comparable to the American Bar Association and the American Medical Association in kindred professions, could be of substantial service to the ends for which universities exist, members of the faculties of a number of institutions have undertaken to bring about the formation of a national Association of University Professors.[22]

Still more important, the linkage between professionalization and academic freedom has been obscured by the stupendous growth of First Amendment law over the past half century. The incoming tide of First Amendment protections has undeniably lifted academic freedom to new heights, and today it does indeed make good sense, legally speaking, to think of academic freedom as a subset of First Amendment liberties. But academic freedom and free speech overlap and reinforce one another only at certain points. Any effort to completely assimilate the former to the latter would be disastrous. Historically speaking, the heart and soul of academic freedom lies not in free speech but in professional autonomy and collegial self-governance. Academic freedom came into being as a defense of the disciplinary community (or, more exactly, the university conceived as an ensemble of such communities), and if it is to do the work we expect of it, it must continue to be at bottom a denial that anyone outside the community is fully competent to pass judgment on matters falling within the community's domain. From my standpoint, no justification for academic freedom can succeed unless it provides ample resources for justifying the autonomy and self-governance of the community. For this task, the First Amendment is ill suited.[23]

One way to highlight the difference is simply to observe that the founders of the modern university were not so much libertarians as communitarians. They wanted to liberate individual practitioners such as Ross from the dictates of their employers, not as an end in itself, but as a way of enhancing the authority of the entire community of practitioners.[24] This was a generation whose members, like Matthew Arnold, were not much impressed by the freedom merely to do (or say) whatever one pleases. They looked askance at individualistic values and felt no embarrassment about imposing a wholesome discipline on the crude, market-driven society that was growing by leaps and bounds around them. They set out to professionalize higher education because they wanted to establish the good, the true, and the beautiful on a firmer base. Of all the institutions they founded, none are more characteristic or more aptly named than the "disciplines," which even today define the division of intellectual labor within the university.

To sharpen the contrast still more, consider the continuing controversy over the teaching of Darwin's evolutionary theory. If our point of departure were free speech alone, it would not be at all easy to justify the exclusion of "creation science" from the curriculum. After all, when biblical literalists say that evolution is "only a theory," they are not wrong. Like all scientific theories, Darwin's is contestable and will one day be superseded. Why give it a privileged place in the curriculum? The only persuasive answer lies in the authority that inheres in a well-established disciplinary community. Darwin's theory deserves a privileged place because it, unlike "creation science," enjoys the support of a strong consensus of competent biological investigators, who have organized themselves in such a way as to foster mutual criticism and drive out of circulation truth claims that cannot take the heat.

We academics are prone to hide from ourselves the degree to which we ourselves rely on authority and count on others to do the same. I once heard a prominent sociologist blithely announce that "authority has no place in the classroom." He meant that teachers should encourage discussion, tolerate dissent, and bend over backwards to avoid silencing or penalizing students whose politics offend them. These are admirable values, too often honored in the breach, but it would be the height of naiveté to think that authority plays no role in the classroom, or that professors and students meet on a level playing field. We professors walk into a classroom and the students cease their chatter, get out pen and paper, and wait dutifully for us to begin. Surely no one dreams that this effect is produced merely by personal charisma or sheer mental power. Teachers occupy one role and students another in an institution cunningly designed to make it in the student's interest to pay attention, to listen up, to defer to our authority. We appear before them not as mere citizens, but as delegates of a community of inquiry, made up of members who earn their keep by engaging in mutual criticism. When we defend academic freedom, we are defending that authority.

The very mention of authority makes late-twentieth-century academics nervous, yet we all routinely defer to the authority of experts. Deference undergirds even our most fundamental assumptions about ourselves and the world we inhabit. For example, I believe in evolution with nearly the same degree of confidence I feel about the existence of the table I am writing on, or the accuracy of an account I might give of some episode in my own life, based on personal experience and recollection. Yet my belief in evolution rests on no firmer basis than deference to expert authority. I have not inspected the fossil record for myself, or worked my way through the intricate details of Darwin's argument in *On the Origin of Species*. Much less have I followed the tangle of debates that lead up to the present version of the theory. Many imagine that the story of divine creation is *intrinsically* less plausible than evolution. They claim to find in the idea of one-celled primeval slime gradually evolving into complex forms of life under the directionless pressure of natural selection a virtually self-evident truth. I am not persuaded. The compelling quality they attribute to the idea of natural selection itself, I would attribute instead to the institutional arrangements that have succeeded in making belief in evolution a recognized badge of intelligence and educational attainment in our culture. We nonfundamentalists who are not trained in biology believe in evolution, not because we are more rational than biblical literalists, not because we can recite the "good reasons" that a fully rational judgment would require, and not because we have in mind the evidence and the experience it would take to envision the process and grasp it in the way biologists do. We believe because we trust biologists.[25]

Our trust is not blind, of course. We willingly defer to the judgment of biologists in large part because we feel sure they have good reasons for their beliefs and could display those reasons to us if we were willing to take the time. But my confidence that good reasons exist does not alter the plain fact that my present acceptance of the theory of evolution is based not on those uninspected reasons but on deference to authority. What shapes my belief is as much psychological and sociological as logical. And although I think the thought process that leads me to my belief is far sounder than the one that leads the creationist to his, the difference is not a matter of his clinging to authority while I rely on reason: we both submit to authority, but to different authorities. For this no apologies are needed. Up to a point, we are better off for our willingness to defer to experts. Even though deference to authority short-circuits the quintessentially rational processes of personally weighing the evidence and following out a chain of logic to one's own satisfaction, deferring to experts brings real advantages insofar as it enables us to gain vicariously from others' experience and compensate for the limited range of our own. Sometimes deferring to expert authority is the rational thing to do.

If, as I have been arguing, academic freedom was the capstone of an effort to establish authority by fostering the development of communities of the competent, we should expect to find evidence supporting that claim in the AAUP's charter document, the 1915 Report on Academic Freedom and Tenure. The expectation is amply borne out. As we shall see, Seligman and Lovejoy, in writing that document, addressed themselves most explicitly to the rights of scholars, the duties of trustees, and the needs of the lay public—the nuts and bolts, as it were, of academic freedom—but at every stage they self-consciously advocated deference to expert authority and took for granted the epistemological efficacy of disciplinary communities. Notice that in doing so they were already moving far beyond any simple correspondence theory of truth. However much they may differ from us, the late Victorians were not epistemologically naive. After all, the first "crisis of historicism" occurred during their watch, and no one since has plumbed the crisis any more deeply than that renegade Victorian, Friedrich Nietzsche. The generation of the 1890s, of which the founders of the modern university were a part, was already energetically embarked on what H. Stuart Hughes has called a "revolt against positivism." The lessons of fallibilism and the unavoidable subjectivity of perception were widely appreciated at the turn of the century. The insight that truth was a collective, communal enterprise, rather than a solitary, culturally unmediated one — the enabling idea behind the community of the competent — was itself one of the products of the Victorians' struggle to come to terms with the uncertainties that historicism notoriously breeds.[26] The words of the AAUP's 1915 report testify to greater confidence in the power of reason than is commonly acknowledged today, and may seem to some readers quaint. But it remains to be seen whether the radical forms of historicism in circulation today will prove as durable as the more moderate varieties that were already firmly in place at the beginning of the century.

In drafting the 1915 report, Seligman and Lovejoy most certainly did not proceed on the Foucauldian premise that power and knowledge were two sides of a single coin. They took the possibilities of disinterestedness and objectivity with utmost seriousness, not as results easily attained, but as ideals well worth pursuing. The university, they said, should be an "intellectual experiment station" and an "inviolable refuge" against the equally dangerous tyrannies of public opinion and political autocracy (400). If scholars were to solve the problems of society, "the disinterestedness and impartiality of their inquiries and their conclusions [would have to be], so far as it is humanly possible, beyond the reach of suspicion" (399). Warding off suspicion meant that the line between authentic scholarship and political propaganda would have to be sharp and clear (the implication again being "so far as it is humanly possible"). They warned against teachers who would take "unfair advantage of the student's immaturity by indoctrinating him with the teacher's own opinions" (402). They associated the right of academic freedom with a duty on the part of the academic profession to police its ranks and rigorously uphold standards. "If this profession," they wrote, "should prove itself unwilling to purge its ranks of the incompetent and unworthy, or to prevent the freedom it claims in the name of science from being used as a shelter for inefficiency, for superficiality, for uncritical and intemperate partisanship, it is certain that the task will be performed by others" (402). Although they specifically moved beyond the German model of academic freedom by claiming protection for extramural as well as intramural utterances, they never doubted the desirability of teachers having "minds untrammeled by party loyalties, unexcited by party enthusiasms, and unbiased by personal political ambitions" (404).

The first section of the 1915 report bears a revealing title: "The Basis of Academic Authority." The section is in its entirety organized around a distinction between real universities, engaged in the pursuit of truth, and "proprietary school[s] . . . designed for the propagation of specific doctrines." The latter are bound by their founders "to a propagandist duty" (394). Seligman and Lovejoy grudgingly acknowledged the legitimacy of proprietary schools (usually religious), but only for the sake of relegating them and their propagandistic function to the lowest ranks of post-secondary education. "Any university which lays restrictions upon the intellectual freedom of its professors," they asserted, "proclaims itself a proprietary institution, and should be so described when it makes a general appeal for funds." By their standard, any institution that withheld from its faculty the rights of academic freedom in the interest of serving a propagandistic function could not claim the authority of a true university and would deserve the support only of fellow sectarians, not that of the general public (395).

The central thrust of the 1915 report was to displace trustees as sole interpreters of the public interest and put forth a strong claim for the corporate authority of professional communities. As Seligman and Lovejoy put it, "the responsibility of the university teacher is primarily to the public itself, and to the judgment of his own profession" (397).[27] In a nutshell, they were defining the university as a loose-knit family of specialized disciplinary communities and making the family's integrity conditional on the degree of self-governance attained both by the whole and by its constituent parts. The role of the community looms largest in the second section of the report, titled "The Nature of the Academic Calling," where they spelled out the "distinctive and important function" of the professional scholar:

That function is to deal at first hand, after prolonged and specialized technical training, with the sources of knowledge; and to impart the results of their own and of their fellow-specialists' investigations and reflection, both to students and the general public, without fear or favor. The proper discharge of this function requires (among other things) that the university teacher shall be exempt from pecuniary motive or inducement to hold, or to express, any conclusion which is not the genuine and uncolored product of his own study or that of fellow-specialists. Indeed, the proper fulfillment of the work of the professorate [*sic*] requires that our universities shall be so free that no fair-minded person shall find any excuse for even a suspicion that the utterances of university teachers are shaped or restricted by the judgment, not of professional scholars, but of inexpert and possibly not wholly disinterested persons outside their ranks. (396)

Notice that the authors of the 1915 report did not imagine that the problem of intellectual authority was to be solved merely by appeals to disinterestedness. In common with other members of their generation they did of course take it for granted that scholars would display a large measure of that self-denying quality of asceticism that Nietzsche so merrily skewered in the third essay of *On the Genealogy of Morals*. But if scholars were to speak without "fear or favor" — and, equally important, be *seen* as speaking thus, so as to earn the deference of the general public — they would not only have to purge themselves of interest, insofar as possible, but generally distance themselves from all influences extrinsic to their work. The latter task was understood by Seligman and Lovejoy as inherently collective: accomplishing it required the existence of a community so energized that its internal relations would overshadow external influences, as members strove above all to earn and retain one another's respect according to standards specifically tailored to the work at hand. Their vision of the ideal community differs little from that of Jürgen Habermas, who defines the "ideal speech situation" as one in which "no force except that of the better argument is exercised; and, . . . as a result, all motives except that of the cooperative search for truth are excluded." [28]

Thus Seligman and Lovejoy's discussion in "The Nature of the Academic Calling" continues:

> The lay public is under no compulsion to accept or act upon the opinions of the scientific experts whom, through the universities, it employs. But it is highly needful, in the interest of society at large, that what purport to be the conclusions of men trained for, and dedicated to, the quest for truth, shall in fact be the conclusions of such men, and not echoes of the opinions of the lay public, or of the individuals who endow or manage universities. To the degree that professional scholars, in the formation and promulgation of their opinions, are, or by the character of their tenure, appear to be, subject to any motive other than their own scientific conscience and a desire for the respect of their fellow-experts, to that degree the university teaching profession is corrupted; its proper influence upon public opinion is diminished and vitiated; and society at large fails to get from its scholars, in an unadulterated form, the peculiar and necessary service which it is the office of the professional scholar to furnish. (396–97)

In the vision set forth by Seligman and Lovejoy, the psychological, institutional, and legal dimensions of the problem of intellectual authority fit together and reinforce one another like the nested boxes of a Chinese puzzle. To speak with authority, one must visibly enjoy the respect of one's peers, organized as a self-governing community. In order for the community to exist and be self-governing, its members must, in the work at hand, defer only to one another and be ready to resist the influence of nonpractitioners in matters intrinsic to the community's domain. The legal rights of academic freedom stake out the vital boundary between matters intrinsic and extrinsic, distinguishing those who are competent to judge a practitioner's work from those who are not. In the words of Seligman and Lovejoy, it would be "inadmissible that the power of determining when departures from the requirements of the scientific spirit and method have occurred, should be vested in bodies not composed of the members of the academic profession. Such bodies necessarily lack full competency to judge of those requirements" (402). The proper relationship, then, between professors and trustees is not that of employees to employers. The relation should instead be analogous to that of federal judges and the chief executive who appoints them, but then has no authority over their decisions. Leaving unchallenged the power of trustees and administrators to appoint faculty, Seligman and Lovejoy denied that those exercising that power could properly retain any control over the intellectual productions of those whom they appointed, and insisted that appointment itself be based on criteria established within the community, by the candidate's peers (397, 402).

There is no single author who can be said to have exhaustively conceptualized the widespread assumptions about truth and inquiry that Seligman and Lovejoy were trying to distill in their 1915 report. But Charles Sanders Peirce, arguably the most original of the pragmatists and the author of the strongest claims for a communal theory of truth ever written, did more than anyone else of his generation to articulate the presuppositions that I believe underlay Victorian reform. My claim is not that his philosophical writings influenced any large number of people or served as a blueprint for action. Peirce's writings on community and the social basis of scientific endeavor were, as a matter of fact, influential among Harvard philosophers while Lovejoy was a graduate student there, but professionalization was a social process with great momentum in late-nineteenth-century life: it did not wait upon theoretical articulation. It is, I believe, no coincidence that Charles Peirce was the son of one of the foremost professionalizers of science in the antebellum period, the eminent Harvard astronomer and mathematician Benjamin Peirce. Member of a self-selected elite of scientists known as the Lazzaroni, the elder Peirce helped organize the Lawrence Scientific School at Harvard, helped write the constitution of the American Association for the Advancement of Science, and helped push through Congress the bill creating the National Academy of Sciences.[29] Charles Peirce's communitarian theory of truth can stand on its own philosophical legs, but for my purposes it would suffice to regard the theory as an idealized extrapolation from the practical processes of professionalization that were transforming society during his lifetime. Peirce's theory suits my needs especially well because it invites comparison with the communitarian theorizing of recent writers such as Thomas Kuhn, Richard Rorty, and Stanley Fish.[30] These three authors share Peirce's basic conviction that communal solidarity among inquirers can function epistemologically, and thus their differences with him — substantial, as we shall see — give us a way of gauging the gap between the Victorians and ourselves.[31]

Charles Peirce believed that the very possibility of attaining truth depended on transcending one's self and entering into intensely communal relations with other competent investigators. As if to repudiate Ralph Waldo Emerson's advice to "trust thyself," Peirce contended that no individual, least of all one's self, could ever be worthy of trust. "The individual man, since his separate existence is manifested only by ignorance and error . . . is only a negation."[32] Peirce's advice was to trust instead the community of inquirers. "What anything really is," argued Peirce, "is what it may finally come to be known to be in the ideal state of complete information." Since information cannot be complete in my lifetime or yours, our best conceptions are riddled with error, and the truth can only be known by the last survivors of a community of inquirers that includes the yet-to-be-born as well as the living, and extends indefinitely far into the future. "The real, then," said Peirce in a famous passage, "is that which, sooner or later, information and reasoning would finally result in, and which is independent of the vagaries of me and you. Thus, the very origin of the conception of reality shows that this conception essentially involves the notion of a COMMUNITY, without definite limits, and capable of a definite increase in knowledge" (V-316, 311).

It may have been his prickly personality and status as an outsider who never found permanent employment in the academic world that sensitized Peirce to the social, consensual quality of all that passes for truth among human beings. Yet in his conception there is no trace of cynicism. The ultimate consensus to be reached by his community of inquiry is of a very special kind, and his theory of reality, though indubitably social, is not at all relativistic, as twentieth-century analogues have tended to be. Like Kuhn, Rorty, and Fish, modern thinkers who have advanced arguments that sound quite Peircean, Peirce himself clearly regarded science and scholarship as the practical accomplishment, not of individuals, but of a community of researchers. Unlike Kuhn, Rorty, and Fish, however, Peirce was a philosophical realist: he supposed that the universe was so made that an ultimate convergence of opinion was virtually predestined and that the reality toward which opinion converged was utterly independent, not of thought in general, but of what any finite number of human beings thought about it. For him reality was socially discovered, but not socially constructed. When pressed by a critic, he allowed that the ultimate convergence of opinion might be incomplete in some matters and that convergence was a "hope" rather than an inevitability. But he insisted that the hope was of the same indispensable character as the expectation of survival that a person struggling for his life must feel. To live is to hope: similarly, to inquire is to suppose that opinions ultimately converge toward the real. The following passage catches the spirit of Peirce's discussion of the community better than any other I know.

> This activity of thought by which we are carried, not where we wish, but to a fore-ordained goal, is like the operation of destiny. No modification of the point of view taken, no selection of other facts for study, no natural bent of mind even, can enable a man to escape the predestinate opinion. This great hope [originally he wrote "law"] is embodied in the conception of truth and reality. The opinion which is fated to be agreed to by all who investigate, is what we mean by the truth, and the object represented in this opinion is the real. That is the way I would explain reality. (V-407, 408; VI-610)

Peirce was no ideologue. He had no intention of supplying existing communities of inquiry in physics, chemistry, or biology with a philosophical warrant for their authority. Much less did he intend to buttress the claims of quasi sciences like law, medicine, or historical studies. He expressly rejected the "method of authority" as a means of fixing belief, and he equated that method with the claims of priesthoods, aristocracies, guilds, and other "association[s] . . . of men whose interests depend . . . on certain propositions" (V-379). As long as we interpret Peirce's words strictly, as he no doubt wished us to do, his theory bundles truth off into an infinite progression where it is too remote to serve *any* interest, or strengthen any particular claim to knowledge. But if his theory undermines all existing authorities and courts radical skepticism when strictly interpreted—offering no guidance at all when we ask, "Which present claim is true?" or "What belief shall I now act on?"—it performs the opposite function of building bulwarks against skepticism when loosely interpreted. And how can we resist interpreting it loosely? As the philosopher John E. Smith has said, "Reality in the end for Peirce is future experience, and this is not enough."[33] Peirce conceived of the truth in such a way as to make it literally useless, for no one can claim to know the truth, once it has been defined as the final opinion of a community that extends indefinitely into the future. However, once we accept Peirce's identification of truth as the outcome of a community's striving, then, if a community of inquiry exists in a field that interests us, it is difficult to resist the implication that its *current best opinion* is, in practice, the closest approach to the truth we can possibly hope for. Given a choice between these two interpretations, it may well be that the strict one is closest to Peirce's own intentions. But even if this is so, the most important thing to observe about Peirce's communal theory of reality may be that, the more persuasive we find it, the more likely we are to live by the loose interpretation of it. Identifying truth with the community, but lacking the community's final opinion, we are bound to prefer its current best opinion to a chaos of indistinguishable truth claims, which is the only alternative Peirce's line of reasoning leaves us.

No writer today would dare attribute to the community of inquiry quite the same truth-finding power that Peirce assigned it. Of the writers I mentioned above, Kuhn comes closest to Peirce. Certainly, in Kuhn's world there, is no standard higher than the current best opinion of the relevant scientific community. If one asks, "Why should taxpayers foot the bill for professors who devote more time to research than to teaching?" or "Why should trustees tolerate the expression of views they loathe?" Kuhn supplies us with a compelling answer: The community is epistemologically efficacious. Without it, our grasp of reality would be immeasurably weaker. Yet Kuhn's community is not nearly as efficacious as Peirce's, for Kuhn is not nearly the realist Peirce was. The relationship between the community's current best opinion and anything that deserves the name "truth" becomes problematic in Kuhn's treatment. He retains a trace of realism by holding that the sequence of conceptions espoused by a scientific community takes the shape of an irreversible branching tree. A kind of development not altogether different from progress is, therefore, involved—but this is "progress" away from confusion, rather than toward any antecedent reality existing "out there," independent of human consciousness, awaiting our apprehension of it. How much epistemological comfort we are entitled to draw from this sort of development, especially in fields other than natural science, is an open question.[34]

If the Peircean rationale for disciplinary autonomy is left looking a bit frayed around the edges by Kuhn, it is left in tatters by others who have been inspired by Kuhn's writings. Rorty and Fish both pay homage to Kuhn, but their own posture is that of uncompromising antirealism. Unlike Kuhn, who is ambivalent and who frankly confesses that, although he is disenchanted with the realist view, no existing alternative seems an adequate replacement for it, Rorty and Fish flatly deny that there is any important sense in which ideas can be said to converge on, approximate, correspond to, or be adequate to the real. For them, the real is socially and linguistically constructed, through and through. Rorty declares the entire enterprise of epistemology to be wrong-headed. He joins Derrida in recommending that we overcome our nostalgic longing for "foundations," and throw overboard the entire "metaphysics of presence." Even Derrida's most notorious antirealist sally, "There is nothing outside the text," wins from Rorty a blithe nod of approval. Rorty asks us to believe that the tradition inaugurated by Plato and called "philosophy" has quite simply lost its usefulness and ought to be discontinued in favor of conversations that aim at nothing more than "edification." "The notion of 'accurate representation,'" he says, "is simply an automatic and empty compliment which we pay to those beliefs which are successful in helping us do what we want to do."[35]

The immediate target of Rorty's campaign on behalf of edifying conversation is none other than Arthur Lovejoy, one of the heroes of the Ross case and a founder of the AAUP. It was Lovejoy who, in his presidential address to the American Philosophical Association in 1916, called upon philosophers to choose between edification and verification, hoping they would choose the latter. In picking up the banner of edification, Rorty seeks to turn Lovejoy's Victorian project upside down. Lovejoy epitomizes for Rorty the antipragmatic disciplinarian who spurns the gentle delights of edification and makes a fetish of rigor and circumspection. "Echoing what was being said simultaneously by Russell in England and Husserl in Germany, Lovejoy urged the sixteenth annual meeting of the APA to aim at making philosophy into a science," reports Rorty. "Lovejoy insisted that philosophy could either be edifying and visionary *or* could produce 'objective, verifiable, and clearly communicable truths,' but not both." William James agreed that the two aims were incompatible, Rorty observes, but wisely preferred edification to science. To Rorty's dismay, "Lovejoy . . . won this battle." The mainstream of the philosophical profession chose the analytical path over edification.[36]

There is no denying that Lovejoy was a devotee of rigor. His belief that philosophy's family quarrels were a "standing scandal" that threatened to bring "discredit upon the entire business" seems to me misguided, and his plan for the production of a *catalogue raisonné* of "considerations" pertaining to all important issues in philosophy—a modern *Summa Metaphysica,* as he himself called it—seems both misguided and grandiose.[37] I readily confess that if I were choosing books for a year's sojourn on a desert island, Rorty's *Mirror of Nature* would be a more likely choice than Lovejoy's *Great Chain of Being,* important though the latter is.

These things said, there remains room to argue that Lovejoy was not the Dr. Strangelove that Rorty makes him out to be. In calling for philosophy to become a science, Lovejoy meant only that it should be a *Wissenschaft*, an "organized body of knowledge," not that it should mindlessly imitate physics or chemistry.[38] Lovejoy's essays on pragmatism are, in my view, the sort of close, respectful criticism that any school of thought should count itself lucky to receive. One of them, titled "William James as a Philosopher," is as warm, generous, and open-minded a tribute as any scholar ever rendered to a rival.[39] Lovejoy's point about edification was not that it was an unworthy goal, but that philosophy may not be the best way to achieve it. He acknowledged that "the philosopher's reasonings" may only be his "peculiar way of uttering the burden of his soul and of edifying the like-minded," but, he continued, if edification is the goal, "poetry is surely a happier medium."[40]

Convinced, just as Peirce was, that "philosophizing is a collective process," Lovejoy thought philosophers should never concede the incommensurability of rival positions at the start of an argument, but should instead obstinately hold out the "possibility of unanimity" as a regulative ideal. After all, he observed, the prospect of really achieving unanimity was "scarcely so imminent as to justify alarm." As these words suggest, Lovejoy was not naive about the likelihood of convergence. His aim was to strengthen the community of inquiry by making communication between its members more complete and harder to evade, thus intensifying the half-competitive, half-cooperative exchange of opinions that constitutes the life process of such communities. He shared Walter Bagehot's admiration for a "polity of discussion," in which the obligation to talk things over and seek agreement would always act as a check on precipitate action. Like most Victorians, including Peirce (whose essay "Evolutionary Love" is a sermon on the subject), Lovejoy blamed human ignorance largely on "subjective sources of error" and looked to socialization for the cure. We guard against the snares of subjectivity, he wrote, by "seeking the complementary and correcting action of other minds upon our own; and not of dead men's minds, alone, but of contemporaries with whose thoughts ours may establish genuine and vital contact, to whom we may explain and re-explain our own thoughts, who will patiently 'follow the argument' with us, who will drive their meanings into our consciousness with friendly violence if necessary, and will gladly submit to like violence in return."[41]

Rorty has little use for either Peirce's communal theory of truth or Lovejoy's "friendly violence." The problem with both, apparently, is that by holding out the possibility of rational convergence, they breed confrontation. Unlike the Victorians, who prized criticism and accepted the need for confrontation, Rorty looks forward to a culture devoted to edifying conversation, which he specifically likens to Kuhn's "abnormal" or "revolutionary" science and associates with the perpetual incommensurability of rival vantage points. Since the contributors to Rorty's conversation would by definition share few common presuppositions, their contributions would be largely incommensurable, leading no doubt to an abundance of divergent opinions, but seldom to confrontation in the classic sense of a rigorous encounter from which only the truth can emerge unscathed. Everyone's views would be different; no one's would be right or wrong. Most important, no view would qualify even potentially as "normal." Lacking foundations, absent any hope of rational convergence or correspondence with the real, confrontation loses its point and becomes difficult to distinguish from aimless aggression.

Rorty's aversion to convergence-oriented confrontation (perfectly compatible with polemical brilliance, as we shall see) most often manifests itself in his frustrating habit of sidestepping bothersome questions. As Stefan Collini has remarked, Rorty frequently announces "with a studied off-handedness that some find exhilarating and others infuriating, that a large number of time-honoured questions just are not interesting questions any more." Granting the exceptional range and brilliance of Rorty's contribution, Collini nonetheless complains that "the range of questions which 'we pragmatists' would say there is no point in asking threatens to shrink the horizons of intellectual inquiry," possibly encouraging a kind of "anti-intellectualism." [42]

Rorty assigns top priority, not to the characteristically Victorian task of pruning back error in hopes of expanding the domain of reliable knowledge, but instead to the distinctively post-Holocaust task of encouraging respect for otherness and cultivating sensitivity to the lush multiplicity of human perspectives. Rorty's priorities are eminently decent and readily understandable in view of the ethnic clashes and seemingly endless dilemmas of difference that beset the world today. I have no quarrel with those priorities, except insofar as they block historical understanding and tempt us to think we can get away without having any adequate justification for academic freedom. Rorty evidently believes that we academicians have it in our power to help reduce bloodshed and brutality in the world at large simply by adopting a kinder and gentler mode of intellectual exchange within the academy. I demur because I doubt that the academy's influence takes quite that form, and because I feel that the intellectual price Rorty is prepared to pay is too high. If I read Lovejoy correctly, he understood full well that many of the great debates in philosophy originate in incommensurable premises and are unlikely ever to yield consensus. What he opposed was a premature abandonment of consensus as an *ideal,* a target one aims at without expecting to reach. That ideal is as indispensable as ever, for the community of the competent cannot do its work of cultivating and authorizing sound opinion unless its members confront one another and engage in mutual criticism. Unless I miss my guess, Lovejoy could have said about philosophy what Clifford Geertz said of anthropology: that it is "a science whose progress is marked less by a perfection of consensus than by a refinement of debate. What gets better is the precision with which we vex each other."[43] Still, Lovejoy would have added, Peirce was right: to inquire at all is to hold out the *possibility* of convergence.

Although Rorty (unlike Fish, as we shall see) is not the sort of person to treat ideals dismissively, this particular ideal gets short shrift in his "conversation of the West." Conversation and consensus figure prominently in his thinking, but their role is therapeutic rather than rigorous, remissive rather than exacting. Conversation he recommends not as a means of exposing error, but rather as an opportunity to savor the kaleidoscopic variety of the human experience. He values consensus less as a regulative ideal, the pursuit of which may provoke confrontation and inflame passion, than as our last hope of solace in a world that lacks foundations. Threatened as we all are by the eruption of violence, he judges the sacrifice of rigor a small price to pay for greater solidarity.

Given Rorty's aversion to confrontation, we should not be surprised that his revival of pragmatism, unlike those of Richard Bernstein, Hilary Putnam, or Jürgen Habermas, pointedly excludes Peirce from the front ranks of the tradition.[44] A "tendency to overpraise Peirce," he says, is the first symptom of a mistaken conception of what pragmatism is all about. One might think that Peirce's perpetually postponed truth, never accessible in any human "present," would be sufficiently remote and impractical to at least seem harmless, but Rorty detects within it the bitter seeds of tyranny. "The pragmatist must avoid saying, with Peirce, that truth is *fated* to win. He must even avoid saying that the truth *will* win." So deep is Rorty's distaste for this aspect of Peirce's thinking that he appears to sympathize even with an imaginary antipragmatic interlocutor of his own devising, the "traditional philosopher," who asks rhetorically, "When tyrants employ Lenin's blood-curdling sense of 'objective' to describe their lies as 'objectively true,' what is to prevent them from citing Peirce in Lenin's defense?"[45]

At first, arguments like these seem to sound a death knell for the dream of epistemological efficacy that Charles Peirce articulated at the dawn of the modern American university system. If convergence is unacceptable, even as an ideal, the disciplinary community cannot serve as a crucible of criticism and so cannot claim any special authority for the ideas it sponsors. Indeed, if

Rorty really believes that the very idea of "truth" is dangerous, because of the encouragement it gives tyrants, then it is not just Peirce we need to renounce, but the university itself, for the university has always been and is likely to remain a hotbed of aspirations for truth, sound opinion, and other invidious distinctions between better and worse ways of thinking. In the words of John Dewey, whom of course Rorty holds in very high regard, and whose conception of truth was not naive, "the university function is the truth function."[46] Dewey published these words in 1902, two years after Ross's dismissal from Stanford and thirteen before taking office as the founding president of the AAUP. In his AAUP inaugural address in 1915, Dewey spoke in the same vein, calling for the "judgment, the courage, and the self-sacrifice commensurate with reverence for our calling, which is none other than the discovery and diffusion of truth."[47]

Rorty's conflation of Peircean fallibilism with Leninist objectivism need not be taken as his last word on the subject. Clearly Peirce's theory of truth is not acceptable to him, and the community of the competent does not, as such, play a prominent role in his thinking. Still, there are important similarities. The philosopher whom William James credited with founding pragmatism and who wanted to write on every wall of the city of philosophy, "Do not block the way of inquiry," cannot truly be a dangerous man in Rorty's eyes.[48]

One might argue that the two pragmatists differ more sharply at the level of tactics than ultimate goals. Both want to substitute persuasion for force. Whether to aim at that goal directly and try to extend its benefits to an entire society at once, or approach it obliquely, relying for the foreseeable future on an elite vanguard of inquirers, is where they seem to differ most concretely. Rorty's "conversation of the West" is conceived in an inclusive spirit of Romantic egalitarianism that embraces an entire *ethnos* and all who partake of it, leaving no specified role for intellectual elites or disciplinary institutions. In effect, Rorty's vision of the ideal liberal society tacitly anticipates the extension to everyone of the life of inquiry and persuasion that Peirce assigned to a scholarly elite. Rorty's utopia, in short, looks rather like Peirce's community of inquiry writ large—larger than Peirce would have thought appropriate or feasible.[49] Having given up all foundationalist hopes, and having expanded the circle of the "we" to embrace all willing recruits, Rorty would in his version of the good society presumably downplay degrees of competence, extending to all citizens the opportunity of engaging as equals in the "conversation" through which reality is socially constructed. Rorty's utopia could even acknowledge a pale surrogate for Peirce's objectivity, defining it as that which wins "unforced agreement."[50] And although Rorty's liberal utopia would most assuredly not be devoted to the pursuit of Truth, he assures us that it would honor "truth," decapitalized and safely quarantined within quotation marks:

> It is central to the idea of liberal society that, in respect to words as opposed to deeds, persuasion as opposed to force, anything goes. This openmindedness should not be fostered because, as Scripture teaches, Truth is great and will prevail, nor because, as Milton suggests, Truth will always win in a free and open encounter. It should be fostered for its own sake. A liberal society is one which is content to call "true" whatever the upshot of such encounters turns out to be.[51]

Here it is tempting to think that Rorty and Peirce come within hailing distance, for Peirce, too, was content (at least on the "loose" interpretation of his doctrine) to call "true" the upshot of the community's debates—true for now, anyway. Yet the differences remain fundamental. The reality-discovering task that Peirce assigned to the community of the competent, Rorty assigns to liberal society as a whole, and he adds the antirealist proviso—fatal, from Peirce's standpoint—that reality is something we construct, not discover. For much the same reason, relaxed "conversation" replaces confrontational debate. The disciplinary function disappears; the free expression of ideas no longer serves as a means of winnowing truth, for Rorty redefines it as an end in itself. Intellect is dethroned and takes its cue from sociability. In the last analysis, our choice between the two visions is likely to hinge on our estimate of the feasibility and desirability of Rorty's effort to extend to everyone the essential features of a form of life thus far inhabited only by scholars.[52] Not only is it uncertain that all aspire to such a life, many are not well suited for it, making their opportunity to contribute to the conversation merely formal. The history of professionalization over the past century and a half suggests that dense, fast-paced scholarly "conversations" of the sort Rorty admires have greater momentum and will be more difficult for novices to break into than he acknowledges. Indeed, they have proved to be formidable sources of privilege and authority for those who possess the skills to excel in them: democratizing them would be no easy matter.

The most intractable difference between Peirce and Rorty appears to lie in the question of realism. There are of course many versions of realism, and it is not inconceivable that a version making the right sort of concessions to history, perspective, and social convention might earn Rorty's grudging acceptance. But as long as there is no respectable sense (not even a largely social and conventional one) in which we are entitled to say that there is a "nature of things" for inquirers to "get right," then one cannot help wondering what the community of inquiry is for.[53] If nothing at all constrains inquiry, apart from the will of the inquirers and whatever value they may assign to the traditions of their *ethnos*, why should anyone defer to the community's judgment, pay its expenses, or tolerate its "findings" when they offend? Peirce's fallibilistic realism had ready answers to such questions, because it acknowledged other constraints, clinging fiercely to the possibility of truth even as it admitted truth's elusiveness and hammered home the lesson of fallibility. Antirealism, even Rorty's comparatively domesticated version of it, necessarily annihilates error along with its opposite, truth, making fallibilism an untenable posture: Where no opinions can be right, neither can any be wrong.

Disregard for the moment the deep questions of ontology and episte-mology. Even focusing on the rhetorical consequences alone, the death of fal-libilism has ominous implications, for it narrows the number of argumentative positions available to us, threatening to reduce all intellectual exchanges to a naked clash of wills. If there is no such thing as truth, but only a variety of incommensurable perspectives in criterionless competition with one another, then force and persuasion become indistinguishable, cutting the ground out from under any politics based on consent and representation. If nothing is true, then giving up one's own initial perspective and adopting that of an interlocutor can signify nothing more than submission. The honorable option of bowing to reason and willingly renouncing error for the sake of imper-sonal truth drops out, leaving only me versus you, or us versus them. Down this path lies Nietzsche's world, where not only power and knowledge blur together, but might and right as well.

It is seldom recognized that three quarters of a century ago, when William Butler Yeats wondered what new thing "slouches toward Bethlehem" and warned of a time when "The best lack all conviction, while the worst are full of passionate intensity," the state of the debate was very different from what it is today. Nietzsche's influence was slight; no one of consequence contended that there is nothing outside language for us to represent. The relativism that worried Yeats in "The Second Coming" was a comparatively mild variety that stemmed from the excesses of fallibilism. Fallibilists took the reality of the world for granted but acknowledged that it perpetually eludes our grasp, leaving us with tokens, fragments, and intimations of the real rather than its substance. The danger, as Yeats saw it, was that those with refined intellects, being most likely to acknowledge the frailty of their knowledge, were also likely to be paralyzed by doubt and uncertainty. Meanwhile, the mean and opinionated, taking their own perspective to be the only one possible, would be full of conviction and rule the world with the passionate intensity that only conviction can sustain.

The first lesson of fallibilism is indeed humility. Although it need not be carried to excess, fallibilists must be suspicious of their own convictions. Why? Because those convictions may turn out to be inadequate to the real. Take away the very idea of the real, as Rorty's antirepresentational stance does, and the lesson ceases being humility and becomes very nearly its opposite. If there is nothing real for one's convictions to represent, then they *cannot be inadequate* and may as well be asserted with all the force one can muster. For the question is no longer whether they are right, or even how they stack up against other people's convictions, but simply which will prevail, for everyone's convictions are equally arbitrary. On this model, convictions differ not in intrinsic merit or in the degree of their correspondence with the real, but only in the degree of influence they achieve by extrinsic means: the power exerted in their behalf. The characteristic danger that will be perceived by the denizens of an antirepresentationalist era is not the paralyzing excess of humility that Yeats warned of, but an acute shortage of the brute force needed to make sure things go one's own way.

Thus, in the end, antirepresentationalism promotes escalation of conflict — just the opposite of the virtue commonly claimed for it. Fallibilism, in sharp contrast, authentically promotes de-escalation. If there is a reality and we possess some ability to "get it right" — but can only hope to do so fallibly and thus are never entitled to feel *certain* we are right — then all of us, friends and foes alike, are equal in our deprivation, similar in our ignorance. The reality that eludes us all dwarfs us all; we share our inferiority to it even when we share nothing else. But if nothing is real, if there is nothing to "get right," then there is nothing of which we are equally ignorant; nothing greater than ourselves; nothing that all acknowledge, but none possess. The fallibilist's banner, "Let's talk," presupposes an option not available on antirepresentational premises: the possibility of convergence, not on the home territory of either party (which would represent defeat for the other), but on the common ground of reason and reality. In the absence of anything real, convergence becomes capitulation to some "other."

The consequences of doing away with truth (or shrinking it to a vestigial synonym for whatever we want to believe, which comes to the same thing) do not all point in the same direction. The problem is not simply that the rhetorical consequences are escalatory; nor is it simply that Rorty has retreated too far from Peircean claims of epistemological efficacy and thus called into question the cognitive *raison d'être* of the community of the competent. As Stanley Fish has seen as clearly as anyone, there is a curious sense in which the historicist standpoint, if carried far enough, also makes it possible to impute to such communities an authority more august than Peirce would have dared to claim even in his most extravagant moments. For in keeping with the "linguistic turn" one can argue that if there is no reality with a capital "R," then the conversation of inquirers can be regarded, not merely as approximating knowledge of the real, but as actually *constituting* the only small "r" socially constructed reality that human beings can ever hope to know. Thus antirealism points paradoxically in two opposed directions, neither reassuring. It is not easy to say which we should think more worrisome: the retreat from Peircean claims of epistemological efficacy or the imperious claim that academic conversations actually constitute reality.[54] Either way, we lack any adequate rationale for the autonomy academic freedom is meant to defend. If we take the modest tack, admitting that our communities aim at nothing more than edification, it becomes unclear why anyone should defer to our judgment. Alternatively, if reality comes to be seen as entirely a social construction, incapable of representing or corresponding to anything outside language, the lay public would have to be incredibly trusting, even gullible, to let us academics retain the disproportionate voice we now have in the language games that are said to make the world what it is.

Whether the greater danger is timidity or hubris, the question we must face about academic freedom today is why, on antirealist premises, trustees and legislators should ever consent to the propagation of a reality not to their taste. Indeed, in the hands of antirealists more radical than Rorty, the pertinent question becomes: *How in good political conscience could anyone who has the resources to shape the very construction of reality—say, by changing the curriculum or influencing the selection of teachers or regulating the discourse of students about gender, ethnicity, or other sensitive issues—pass up such an opportunity? Is not abstention from the use of power on behalf of the good an abdication of responsibility?* The fate of academic freedom cannot be disentangled from prevailing conceptions of the good and the real. Insofar as reality is understood to be a malleable collective construction, political at its core, no person or group in a democratic society could be entitled to any sort of privileged voice—that is, an autonomous and authoritative voice—in its definition. We have seen that the founders of the modern university were not wedded to a naive correspondence theory of truth, and they made important concessions to truth's historicity, to its conventionality, and occasionally even to its cultural variability. Fallibility they accepted. But they did not doubt that some interpretations were better than others, better in a strong sense that did not necessarily depend on correspondence and yet was not reducible to perspective. If they were wrong about this — if "truth" is so much a matter of perspective that it belongs always inside quotation marks, as befits a claim made only half-seriously — must not the "rights of academic freedom" be enclosed within quotation marks, too?[55]

Here we must step back from Rorty's rhetorical posture and begin taking into account his practice, for although he has delivered powerful blows against the assumptions that have traditionally been used to justify the rights of academic freedom, anyone familiar with the whole tenor and spirit of his writings will know perfectly well that he means no harm to the university or to the disciplinary communities it harbors. If circumstances should warrant, he is among the first I would expect to find in the foxholes, risking his own safety in defense of academic freedom. The point of my discussion has not been to indict Rorty as a reckless nihilist, which he most certainly is not, but to highlight the tendency of his antirealist rhetoric to generate implications that spill beyond the limits he evidently intends. Between his words and his intentions a touch of hyperbole often intrudes. There is, for example, room to suspect that, as a recent president of the APA, he may not be altogether serious about doing away with philosophy. His writings, after all, are from a layman's point of view not something other than philosophy, but a delightfully lucid example of it, and one that could never have been produced were he not the member of a thriving and well-disciplined community of the competent. His pages bristle with all the telltale name dropping, alliance building, and allusive arm wrestling of a scholar whose every thought is conditioned by the network of rivalrous relationships in which the professional community inserts him. Against confrontation? Why, Rorty thrives on it, even as he impugns the epistemological assumptions that would distinguish it from aimless aggression. Like the biblical David with his sling, he has taken on the entire analytical mainstream of his profession at once, as if to prove how fruitful confrontation can be. His own words to the contrary notwithstanding, Rorty is too much the virtuoso of the community of the competent to knowingly contemplate any reduction in its authority.

What, then, are we to make of his antiprofessional posture? A useful corrective to Rorty's underestimation of the role that disciplinary influences play in shaping the way we think can be found in Stanley Fish's witty and perverse defense of professionalism. As will become clear, I have grave reservations about Fish's conception of the professional community, but no one has displayed a keener awareness of the ways in which the community defines the life world of its members. Drawing on Kuhn's portrait of revolutionary science as a clash between rival groups whose professional worldviews are defined by the paradigmatic, world-making assumptions of their members, Fish argues that in an era of illimitable interpretation such as ours, it is the professional community that prevents opinion from becoming merely arbitrary. To be sure, not even the professional community can provide a firm foundation for interpretation. Fish would be the last to suggest that membership in the community enables anyone to transcend time and place, or attain Truth. Still, the current state of opinion within the professional community, even though ultimately a matter of fashion, is all he thinks we need for intelligibility. Just how impressed the public should be with the level of intelligibility currently being sustained in the academy is debatable, but in any event Fish accords to the disciplinary community an important and at least quasi-epistemological function in fixing collective opinion.[56]

Fish sees in antiprofessionalism a posture that serves distinctly professional ends. The relationship he has in mind between individuals and institutions appears to be broadly Freudian. Just as civilization breeds discontent by thwarting instinctual gratification, so on Fish's conception the disciplinary community unavoidably breeds resentment among its members in the course of defining their life world. The result is a state of consciousness that is not only "false," but inverted, as the community's members conceal from themselves their utter dependence on it by indulging in fantasies of solitude and self-sufficiency, all the while complaining about the shallowness and parochialism of communal life. Far from suggesting the imminent breakdown of the community, these complaints and escapist fantasies may signify that a healthy balance has been achieved between individual initiative and communal constraint. Fish construes his own profession of literary criticism as one that depends vitally on imagining itself to be something other than it is. "Antiprofessionalism," he says, "is a form of professional behavior engaged in for the purpose of furthering some professional project." That is how Fish would explain what he calls the "virulence" of antiprofessionalism among literary critics: "While most professions are criticized for betraying their ideals," Fish observes, "this profession betrays its ideals by being practiced at all, by being, as a professor of medicine once put it to me, 'a parasite on the carcass of literature.' "[57] Thus it becomes obligatory within some academic circles to present oneself to the world as a free spirit, spontaneous to the point of idiosyncrasy, who disdains everything that smacks of calculation and self-advancement and lives only for the love of art and justice. Successfully managing such a self-presentation can be the key to professional advancement, precisely because it prominently displays a disposition to subordinate self-advancement to other, higher values.

Fish's point, however, is not simply that conspicuous renunciation of careerist aims can be an effective strategy for their attainment. The larger and less cynical point is that in order for such a community to function effectively, its members may have to imagine that they are boldly improvising, even when they are playing roles the community defines for them. Antiprofessionalism in this largest sense, says Fish, is the "founding gesture of the profession" (201–2), in that it supplies members with a "vocabulary of transcendence" (179) and enables them to ward off fears of heteronomy. "A professional must find a way to operate in the context of purposes, motivations, and possibilities that precede and even define him and yet maintain the conviction that he is 'essentially the proprietor of his own person and capacities.' *The way he finds is anti-professionalism*" (244).[58] "To be a professional," says Fish, "is to think of oneself as motivated by something larger than market conditions" (177). From this standpoint, the community not only can tolerate a high level of antiprofessionalism, but needs it to offset the pressures for consensus and rigor (and perhaps also scholasticism and conformity) that are bred by communal life. Antiprofessionalism of the sort that Rorty displays thus becomes an ironic but integral part of the ideology of professionalism. At the end of his essay titled "Anti-Professionalism," Fish admits that "in my efforts to rehabilitate professionalism, I have come full circle and have ended up by rehabilitating anti-professionalism too" (246).

Alas, Fish's admirable insight that the community must, *for its own good,* leave a niche for personal autonomy is squandered by his insistence that this niche can never be anything more than a mirage. Freedom for Fish is a myth to which we cling out of hunger for self-esteem. If Rorty's view of the professional scholar is "undersocialized" in its failure to acknowledge the immensity of the intellectual debt each of us owes to the disciplinary matrix within which we work, Fish's view is, in the last analysis, "oversocialized," for in the end his professionals turn out to be nothing more than passive reflexes of their professional surroundings, incapable of voicing any opinion not prefabricated by the community. Taking thought; putting one's affairs in a larger perspective; heightening one's awareness of one's place in the world; attaining higher stages of self-consciousness—all these inward operations performed by the thinking self he dismisses as illusory. "The demand for self-consciousness," he says, "is a demand for a state of consciousness in which nothing has yet been settled and choices can therefore be truly rational" (394). No such state of mind exists. "If you are a finite being, and therefore situated, you are wholly situated, and no part of you or your experience is asituational; your every capability is positive, a reflection and extension of the system of belief that bespeaks you and your possibilities, and there is nothing negative (detached, independent, free) to nurture" (430). Careening over the edge, Fish concludes that "freedom, in whatever shape it appears, is another name for constraint" (459).[59]

Surely this goes too far. It does not follow that since we are situated (constrained by circumstance) we must be "wholly situated" (fated, incapable of authentic choice). The idea of freedom is riddled with paradox and there is plenty of room to criticize commonsense understandings of it, but our vivid everyday experience of choice and decision has to be taken more seriously than this. Nor is it enough to add, as Fish so characteristically does, that perceptions of freedom, although illusory, are built into the human condition, and so cannot finally be doubted or set aside, any more than mortality itself. Fish's own doubts about the authenticity of freedom are on record, and he carries them out in practice. Caught up in the exuberance of his own rhetoric, he is not content to describe scholars as independent agents, or even as participating members of a community whose every thought bears traces of its corporate origins. Instead, they are mere "extensions" and "reflections" coughed up by a soulless socio-cognitive machine that "bespeaks" them and their possibilities—not a promising place to begin if one is trying to justify academic or any other variety of freedom (246).

What if the customary rights and privileges of academic freedom were to come under attack: Would Fish defend them? I have no doubt that he would, but only because he is utterly fearless when it comes to incurring charges of inconsistency and expediency. As a self-identified member of the species *homo rhetoricus,* who is used to being accused of a morally paralyzing relativism, Fish is quick to insist that we are *always* entitled to assert our interests and resist actions that have deplorable consequences (482–83). The adequacy of our justification would not concern him: we defend academic freedom because it is in our interest to do so, and the justificatory rhetoric we employ is adequate insofar as it carries the day—no internal or logical criterion of adequacy applies. Some readers may wonder how anyone who sees so little difference between freedom and unfreedom, and who has so much disdain for the "vocabulary of transcendence," could defend academic freedom with a good intellectual conscience, but from Fish's perspective this is not only a tender-minded response but also an obfuscating one, because of its easy distinction between those who act on conscience and those who do not. This being a Darwinian world, motives unmindful of the self promise extinction. Us versus them, me versus you:

that's life. Nietzsche's slippery slope holds no terror for Fish. We have been there all along; there is no other place to be.

In a recent essay impishly titled "There's No Such Thing as Free Speech and It's a Good Thing, Too," Fish shrugs aside the conventional wisdom that free speech is a right of "independent value" — that is, a value we should uphold for its long-term benefits regardless of whose speech is in question and how well our own immediate interests and preferences are served by it. The alternative, one gathers, is to regard free speech as a *dependent* value, and what it most depends on is whether or not it serves one's own personal or political interests. Fish observes, accurately enough, that no society ever has or ever could protect any speech whatsoever, that a limit must always be set somewhere. From this familiar and uncontroversial fact he brings forth the astonishing non sequitur that, all pretenses aside, free speech has never been anything more than a dependent value and therefore we would be fools to honor the right of free speech when it does not serve our interests. If, in a particular instance, acknowledging a right of free speech would be inconvenient, or suit the other fellow's interests better than your own, well then, says Fish, just don't acknowledge it. In the essay's introductory paragraph he lays out its lesson without a trace of embarrassment: "Free speech is not an independent value but a political prize, and if that prize has been captured by a politics opposed to yours, it can no longer be invoked in ways that further your purposes for it is now an obstacle to those purposes. This is something that the liberal left has yet to understand and what follows is an attempt to pry its members loose from a vocabulary that may now be a disservice to them." [60]

Fish spells out the lesson again near the essay's end. "My counsel is therefore pragmatic rather than draconian: so long as so-called 'free speech principles' have been fashioned by your enemies, contest their relevance to the issue at hand; but if you manage to refashion them in line with your purposes, urge them with a vengeance" (26). In short, free speech, being a privilege, is best reserved for oneself and one's allies. When in the presence of those who mistake free speech for an "independent value," demand it as a right; but do not be so naive as to extend reciprocal rights to them, or anyone else, as long as you can get away without doing so. Fish's Machiavellian advice transforms free speech from a matter of obligation that may constrain us to act against our own wishes, into a rhetorical ruse that liberates us to take advantage of suckers, including all who believe in such ephemeral things as "independent value." Here the message is delivered in a soothing context of concern about the harmful effects of hate speech, but Fish has delivered similar messages before, and, whatever the occasion, his basic assumptions remain the same. These assumptions, widely shared in the era of power/knowledge, are not hard to enumerate: It's a jungle out there. Politics is the only game in town, all appearances to the contrary notwithstanding. Playing politics means being rhetorical, at least until the violence begins. Only the tender-minded take ideals, principles, and procedural scruples to be actual rules of conduct; everyone else knows them to be nothing more than masks, means of persuasion, moves in a struggle that aims always at dominance. The only operative rules are catch as catch can, winner take all, dupe or be duped.

Given these assumptions, all the agonizing complexities posed by hate speech evaporate into thin air:

> When someone observes, as someone surely will, that anti-harassment codes chill speech, one could reply that since speech only becomes intelligible against the background of what isn't being said, the background of what has already been silenced, *the only question is the political one of which speech is going to be chilled,* and all things considered, it seems like a good thing to chill speech like "nigger," "cunt," "kike," and "faggot." And if someone then says, "But what happened to free speech principles?" one could say what I have now said a dozen times, free speech principles don't exist except as a component in a bad argument in which such principles are invoked to mask motives that would not stand close scrutiny. (25; emphasis added)

Although the raw examples Fish lists seem potentially to qualify as "fighting words," and thus to be actionable under the principle adopted by the Supreme Court in *Chaplinsky v. New Hampshire* (1942), not even that principle carries any weight with him, for "every idea is an incitement to somebody" (23).[61] Against the dangers of the jungle, principle is powerless, the resort to force inescapable.

It is not hard to imagine what would become of academic freedom if trustees took to heart Fish's lesson that free speech is inescapably a "dependent value," to be honored or ignored depending on how well it serves one's own interests. I argued above that academic freedom could not be fully assimilated to free-speech protections without grave loss, but the two obviously overlap extensively, and the fate of academic freedom can no more be disentangled from free-speech protections than it can from epistemological assumptions. If free speech is not an "independent value," then neither is academic freedom. Fish claims merely to be refining our understanding of free-speech conventions, which he admits usefully "channel" political debate and "protect society against over-hasty outcomes," but in truth widespread adoption of his "refinements" would reduce those conventions to rubble (26). Insofar as free speech and academic freedom are selectively applied and made "dependent" on political consequences, they lose their independent status as "values" and become incapable of channeling debate. Deprived of independence, they exert no force of their own and merely augment whatever political interest has over-powered them.

Defining academic freedom as a "dependent value" would carry us back to the state of affairs that existed in the 1890s, at the time of Edward A. Ross's dismissal. By Fish's Orwellian standard, Mrs. Stanford committed no sin against academic freedom; she just construed it realistically, as a dependent value. Her decision to fire Ross depended on his politics, which Fish recognizes as a good and sufficient reason for withholding free speech protections. Of course Fish might disapprove of her politics and therefore accuse her of violating Ross's rights, but only as a theatrical ploy on behalf of his own politics. The goal of the Victorian project that was brought to completion by the founding of the AAUP in 1915 was to ensure that politics and other influences deemed extrinsic to intellectual work would not be the sole, the primary, or even the major determinants of scholarly expression. For Fish, such a project can be one of two things: an exercise in futility (if the projectors are sincere about their intentions) or deception (if not). Not that deception would be out of bounds. "The only question," as he says, "is the political one of which speech is going to be chilled."

> People cling to First Amendment pieties because they do not wish to face what they correctly take to be the alternative. That alternative is *politics*, the realization . . . that decisions about what is and is not protected in the realm of expression will rest not on principle or firm doctrine, but on the ability of some persons to interpret — recharacterize or rewrite — principle and doctrine in ways that lead to the protection of speech they want heard and the regulation of speech they want silenced. (That is how George Bush can argue *for* flag-burning statutes and *against* campus hate-speech codes.) When the First Amendment is successfully invoked the result is not a victory for free speech in the face of a challenge from politics, but a *political victory* won by the party that has managed to wrap its agenda in the mantle of free speech. . . . In short, the name of the game has always been politics, even when (indeed, especially when) it is played by stigmatizing politics as the area to be avoided. (25)

The primacy of the political: Here is an article of faith so rich in implications as to be virtually constitutive of the era of power/knowledge. It is deeply inimical to academic freedom, presumably another of the "pieties" like free speech to which Fish says the timid "cling." For those who subscribe to this web of assumptions, politics extends seamlessly into every nook and cranny of life, making unthinkable the very ideas of the unpolitical and the nonpartisan (not to mention the disinterested). Even the thought that politics is a matter of degree, that some decisions or motives are *less* political than others, is taken by the faithful to be an evasion of this all-revealing truth about the universal sway of political motivation. The pervasiveness of the political is commonly presented as a plain and palpable fact of the sort that only fools or knaves could deny, but in fact it is the predictable outcome of a hermeneutics of suspicion to which all of us resort in our most cynical moments, when we are eager to project our own aggression outward into the world. The presumption that everything is political reproduces at the level of policy the character ideal specific to a "therapeutic" culture, in which the goal of personal autonomy has resolved itself into the crass problem of knowing how to use others without being used by them. Just as the inhabitants of a therapeutic culture, in Philip Rieff's words, "cannot conceive of an action that is not self-serving, however it may be disguised or transformed," neither can they imagine anything standing outside the struggle for political advantage. "This is a culture in which each views the other, in the fullness of self-knowledge, as 'trash.'"[62] One's guard instinctively goes up in the presence of those who mutter "It's a jungle out there!" and for good reason. One never knows whether this incantation is, as it pretends, the prayer of innocents, who fear becoming prey; or is instead the curse of predators, eager to dilute their guilt by universalizing it.

The "politics" that is said to be so ubiquitous is a thin, one-dimensional affair, bearing little resemblance either to the bookish subject taught by political science, or to the turbulent panorama of horse trading, arm twisting, rule making, and rule bending—by turns ennobling and degrading—that is on display daily in legislatures, courthouses, and town councils across the land. "Politics" stands simply for the lawlessness of the jungle. It is a nightmare vision, devoid of empirical substance and animated by bruised innocence. There is little room in it for the rich assortment of institutions, devices, and strategies by which wise statesmen have tried to deflect power, diffuse antagonisms, out-wait confrontations, and set baffles in the way of force. From the vantage point Fish occupies all these measures (like academic freedom) smack of otherworldliness, of the *flight* from the political, of vain attempts to make of ourselves something more than creatures of the jungle.

Thus in the long passage quoted above Fish characteristically identifies politics with the stark "realization" (no mere "supposition" or "hypothesis," contingent on the facts of the case) that our *principles* and *doctrines* count for nothing; that the only important question is who gets to *interpret* them. He thereby obscures the elementary political lesson that principles and doctrines can usefully narrow an officeholder's range of personal discretion; that personality, principle, and doctrine *all* have a hand in shaping political outcomes; that neither the interpreter nor that which is interpreted determines everything. In the same vein, he dismisses the argument that the short-run benefits of silencing haters might be offset by the detrimental long-term consequences of chilling free expression. He does so archly, on the grounds that such an argument "could be seen" as the mask that hate wears. Even when not a mask, he contends, the argument is just the secular residue of the "Puritan celebration of millenarian hopes," plausible only to those who put their faith in the "Holy Spirit" and the indefinite future, instead of this world and the present (25). When it comes to regulative ideals, Fish simply has a tin ear. He would no more pursue a goal that he knew in advance could only be imperfectly attained than go shopping in a museum. Shopping is for malls, where dollars count and consumers get what they ask for. Why want something that eludes your grasp, that you cannot wrap up and take home with you?

Some of the premises underlying academic freedom are open to serious objections, but the Victorians were not wrong to distinguish between motives more and less political. Those who see ominous political implications lurking beneath every bed and hiding behind every door, do so not because "that is the way the world is"—an impermissible formulation on their own premises, after all—but because of assumptions they deploy as a matter of choice. The skillful deployment of these assumptions is a kind of game. Foucault was past master and Fish a world-class practitioner, but anyone can play. Here's how: First, acknowledge no limits to interpretation. Second, acknowledge no difference between intended and unintended consequences. Third, disregard all distinctions between acts of commission and omission. Fourth, firmly embrace (as if true) the logical fallacy of supposing that whoever is not for your cause is against it.

These axioms constitute a blank check for tendentiousness. Adopt them and you, too, will find that politics has expanded to fill your entire universe. Threatening agendas and scandalous breaches of responsibility will rear up on all sides; masks will fall away and sordid motives leap into view. Advocates of speech codes will be revealed (in the eyes of their opponents) as stealthy Stalinists; advocates of free speech will be revealed (in the eyes of *their* opponents) as covert bigots. Actions and inactions, words and silences, choices and accidents, things done and things left undone—all acts and omissions to act will testify to the universality of self-aggrandizement and the pervasiveness of political machination. Anyone who rebuffs your idea of a proper solution will be "part of the problem"; anyone who argues for an understanding of events more complicated than your own will be guilty of "blaming the victim." Once these strategic premises are in place, responsibility will have been transformed from a concrete relation into a diffuse quality that floats freely through all relations, ready to be imputed to anyone, anytime. If it suits your needs, you can find fault with the person who sends his annual charitable donation to Amnesty International for not caring enough about world hunger, while simultaneously accusing the person who sends her contribution to Oxfam of being indifferent to torture—for from this standpoint, nothing evil "just happens." Remember: good acts omitted are no less incriminating than evils committed; the indirect consequences of a person's acts signify unconscious wishes, even if not conscious intention; moral liability extends as far as interpretation can carry it. And interpretation knows no bounds.[63]

Once this perspective is adopted, Fish's description is undeniable: politics floods the world, leaving, as he says, "no safe place."[64] It is a perspective from which academic freedom can be seen as an enviable political prize, well worth hanging onto; it is also one from which all efforts at justification have to be interpreted as self-serving rhetoric. Illogical though the assumptions underlying this perspective plainly are, their appeal today is great. Rieff may be right; we may already live in a culture that cannot conceive of acts that are not self-serving and can only define autonomy as the opportunity to use without being used. If so, the "safe place" the Victorian founders of the university tried to create under the banner of academic freedom is beyond any possibility of justification. One can only hope and trust that this is not the case.

I have examined the views of Rorty and Fish at some length because, in their very different ways, they (along with Kuhn) are heirs of the tradition in which Peirce, Lovejoy, and Seligman stood. The fragility and inconclusiveness of the support they render the community of the competent is therefore all the more revealing of the chasm that has already opened between the Victorians and ourselves. If those who share in the traditions of the community can speak of it only in the equivocal manner of Rorty and Fish, what of critics who subscribe to rival traditions? In particular we should ask how the autonomy of the disciplinary community can continue to be defended in the face of sweeping doubts about "disciplinization," such as those advanced by Hayden White, to whose arguments I now turn, in conclusion.

Up to this point my purpose in this essay has not been to weigh the substantive merits and demerits of the disciplinary community, but rather to trace the shifting fortunes of its rationale at the level of "rights talk," which of course marches under the banner of academic freedom. That the community is but a flawed and imperfect means of attaining reliable knowledge was conceded even by its greatest champion, the fallibilist Charles Peirce. In this closing section, I will briefly rehearse some of its limitations and liabilities, partly for the sake of presenting a balanced picture, but also to sharpen the contrast between moderate and radical forms of criticism. I have no quarrel with those critics who remind us of the community's limitations or its susceptibility to misuse in unskilled hands. What concerns me are criticisms such as those voiced by White that if widely accepted would leave disciplinary communities without a justificatory leg to stand on, either epistemologically or ethically. White's doubts about "disciplinization" are more far-reaching than any we have yet considered; to assess them we need first to mention the warts and blemishes that even the strongest friends of the community should be prepared to admit.

The most common complaint today about disciplinary communities concerns the underrepresentation of women and minorities. These complaints sometimes oversimplify the question of responsibility and exaggerate the ease of reform—ignoring, for example, the wide acceptance by women themselves of the now hated gender conventions of the not-so-distant past, or failing to acknowledge the continuing shallowness of the pool of qualified applicants from some minority groups, even after two decades of energetic efforts to deepen it. But there is no denying that white males are disproportionately represented. Reform is well under way. It will not be complete in our lifetimes; there will be tarnished standards, travesties of justice, and much hypocrisy along the way. But fulfilling the community's own ideal of admitting to membership all who demonstrate competence reaffirms its deepest commitments and can only strengthen it in the long run.

A more troubling criticism has been set forth by critics who lament the demise of the "public intellectual" and blame that complex development largely on the rise of academic professionalism. Louis Menand, for example, justly complains that the very existence of a professionally organized community imposes hardships and disabling restrictions on amateurs, outsiders who in some cases are more talented than those who flourish professional credentials.[65] The community obviously desecrates its own deepest commitments when it rewards mediocre "insiders" over talented "outsiders," but the problem is hard to address because the vice of premature closure is not easily disentangled from the virtue of professional autonomy. Even insiders become victims of professional closure when the quest for autonomy becomes so inward-turning and self-enclosing that it shrinks the ethical or intellectual horizons of its members. Thomas Bender has issued eloquent warnings against the "mystified but determined careerism" that "animates and supplies a pattern to contemporary academic intellect." He calls for a shift of priorities, away from autonomy, to "the opening up of the disciplines, the ventilating of professional communities that have come to share too much and that have become self-referential."[66]

These liabilities are authentic and largely irremediable. In the absence of countervailing forces, it is probably true that all human organizations tend to devolve into country clubs and fraternal lodges. Unchecked, the republic of letters becomes a republic of pals. The only remedy for this degenerative tendency is for individuals deliberately to embrace values that offset and counterbalance it. The importance and fruitfulness of countervailing values is what Richard Rorty had in mind when he singled out the *ethnos* of the West as one that "prides itself on suspicion of ethnocentrism" and therefore stands out as a model worthy of respect and even emulation around the globe.[67] Rorty was not saying that the West has overcome the dangers of ethnocentrism; his point was that the culture of the West has made suspicion of ethnocentrism a "norm," or "value," or "ideal," powerful enough to significantly influence conduct, thus giving it a limited but hopeful capacity for self-correction. It is in the same spirit that I endorse the community of the competent: not because it is all we might desire, but because insofar as its members genuinely engage in mutual criticism and pride themselves on suspicion of professional closure, they make it, too, a partially self-correcting enterprise.

To make the need for countervailing values clearer, we might do well to think of disciplinary communities as dangerous tools designed to fight fire with fire. In their effort to establish authority, Victorian reformers embraced a broadly Tocquevillian analysis of democracy, taking it for granted that democracy's great liability was the tyranny of the majority and its great strength the art of "voluntary association." The community of the competent is, after all, a special kind of voluntary association, one that offers its members (and through them, indirectly, the entire culture) a degree of protection against the tyrannous tendencies of unchecked public opinion. What usually escapes notice is that it achieves this laudable end only by exposing them to a rival source of majoritarian pressures, internal to the community. When individuals become members of such a community, they are elevated above laypersons and made somewhat independent of public opinion, but at the same time they are made more dependent on their professional peers and less able to resist the consensus of the competent.[68] Their heightened susceptibility to peer-group majorities is what gives them both the incentive and the ability to resist the majoritarian excesses to which the larger society is prone.

Thinking of the disciplinary community in this way might help us remem-

ber that it is a potential engine of orthodoxy, which uses the tyrannical proclivities of an *internal* majority to offset and counterbalance the even more
dangerous proclivities of an *external* majority. This is, to paraphrase what
James Madison said about the Constitution, a majoritarian remedy for the defects of majoritarianism. The use of such a toxic remedy can be justified only
by the greater dangers of stultification and conformity that might result from
the unchecked majoritarian tendencies of the larger democratic culture, which
are no more benign today than they were in Tocqueville's time. Although
suspending individuals between two rival centers of conformity opens up opportunities for independence, that outcome is by no means guaranteed. This
intricate system of checks and balances is not complete unless it extends to the
conscious preferences and values of the individuals who constitute the community, for in the last analysis what keeps the community from becoming a
tyrannical fount of orthodoxy in its own right are the countervailing values of
the individuals who work within it. When individual scholars lose their suspicion of professional closure, become impatient with dissent against their own
views, or cease going out of their way to encourage originality and diversity of
opinion within the community, especially in matters political, then they themselves generate the orthodoxy that academic freedom was created to resist.

Some of the thorniest academic-freedom issues of recent years have been
produced by demands for political orthodoxy coming not from powerful outsiders, as in the classic case of Edward A. Ross, but from a politically mobilized
faction of peers *within* the scholarly community, relentlessly pursuing its own
vision of righteousness.[69] President Kingman Brewster of Yale once suggested
that the principal threats to academic freedom at major universities come
from within faculty ranks. Some of the glaring failures of the academy to defend endangered members during World War I and the McCarthy era might
be similarly explained in terms of the community's susceptibility to waves of
majoritarian excess — not just *external* waves that overwhelm the community's
defenses, but also internal, self-generated ones that permit an incensed political faction to assume for a time the mantle of truth intended for those who
articulate the community's "current best opinion."[70]

The sobering truth is that, acting collectively and employing the routine
mechanisms of peer review established by their professional disciplines, academicians have it in their power (through hiring decisions, selective admission
of graduate students, refereeing of one another's work, allocating grants, controlling professional associations, and so on) to impose on one another an
orthodoxy more complete than Mrs. Stanford could have imagined. This perversion of the community's purpose will be perpetrated with a clear political

conscience as long as scholars continue to embrace the self-indulgent illusion that their own efforts to enforce political orthodoxy—originating inside the community and unaccompanied by the administrator's direct threat of job termination—simply do not count as offenses against academic freedom. On the contrary: The enemies of academic freedom are those who try to enforce orthodoxy, whether inside or outside the community. The danger will be averted only insofar as the members of the community conduct themselves with the caution and restraint appropriate to people who understand that they share in the operation of a risky instrument, one that if carelessly employed can be every bit as hazardous to independent thinking as the majoritarian tyranny it is meant to hold in check.

The truths of the disciplinary community are perishable, its side effects are regrettable, and when misused it compounds the very problems it is meant to rectify. These blemishes remind us that a significant gap exists between the community's ideals and the reality of its operation, but few readers will think imperfections of this sort weighty enough to discredit the disciplinary enterprise itself. The same cannot be said of Hayden White's very different criticism, in which the assumptions of power/knowledge might be said to reach their logical conclusion. In a brilliant and controversial 1982 essay, "The Politics of Historical Interpretation," White confined his attention to a single discipline, history, but set forth an argument that takes as its target "disciplinization."[71] His argument seems to me to confirm the improbability that any justification of academic freedom could ever be reconciled with the highly skeptical epistemological views that have gained currency in recent years. White never speaks of the community of the competent as such and displays little interest in the social or institutional mechanisms by which "disciplinization" was accomplished, but the process he has in mind is obviously produced by the community of the competent.

White's thesis claims to unmask the deep political significance of disciplinization and therefore of the disciplinary community itself. Its central claim is easily stated: The nineteenth-century transformation of historical studies into an empirical discipline, distinct from both belles-lettres and speculative philosophy, came about because of the "ideological benefits to new social classes and political constituencies that professional, academic historiography served and, *mutatis mutandis,* continues to serve down to our own time." The ideological function of disciplinization boils down, in White's view, to the development of a "standard of realism in political thought and action," a standard that dignifies history as a superior alternative to fiction and distinguishes sharply between verifiable "facts," on the one hand, and speculative philosophies or theories of historical development on the other. The very existence of such a standard, White believes, favors the political center by enshrining common sense and marking out for repression "utopian thinking in all its forms (religious, social, and above all political)." Utopian thinking he further defines as "the kind of thinking without which revolutionary politics, whether of the Left or the Right, becomes unthinkable" (61–63).

Disciplinization thus brings about a "domestication of historical consciousness" that narrows the political spectrum and, in White's view, tragically deprives oppressed peoples of the opportunity for "visionary politics" (75, 73). He never specifies exactly who has been deprived or what a "visionary politics" might consist of, but presumably he has in mind "the wretched of the earth" and a politics that would enable them to cope with the mounting demographic and economic crises of the third world. This supposed tendency of professional historiography to repress visionary politics is not a function of the individual historian's preferences or ideological convictions. Marxist historiography is as guilty as Liberal. Not only have both schools of thought aspired to a "science" of history, even more fundamentally both have shared the conviction — unwarranted and presumptuous in White's eyes — that "history is not a *sublime spectacle* but a *comprehensible process* the various parts, stages, epochs, and even individual events of which are transparent to a consciousness endowed with the means to make sense of it in one way or another" (73; emphasis added).[72]

It is precisely the success of disciplinization in rendering the past comprehensible that White deplores. After all, he argues, "the conviction that one can make sense of history stands on the same level of epistemic plausibility as the conviction that it makes no sense whatsoever." Following Schiller and other early Romantic theorists of the "sublime," he suggests that many of the world's peoples would be better off to regard their own past as a terrifying and incomprehensible spectacle of confusion, uncertainty, and moral anarchy, for only this would provoke them to take command of their lives and forge from their miseries a more satisfying future. White contends that

> the theorists of the sublime . . . correctly divined that whatever freedom and dignity human beings could lay claim to could come only by way of what Freud called a "reaction-formation" to an apperception of history's meaninglessness. . . . Modern ideologies [such as Liberalism or Marxism] impute a meaning to history that renders its manifest confusion comprehensible to either reason, understanding, or aesthetic sensibility. To the extent that they succeed in doing so, these ideologies deprive history of the kind of meaninglessness that alone can goad living human beings to make their lives different for themselves and their children. (72)

One might expect that anyone expressing concern about the anti-utopian, antirevolutionary bias of disciplinization would do so in hopes of reopening revolutionary options, but White denies having any such motive. "I am against revolutions," he disarmingly announces. Even more surprisingly, he expresses the "wish" that politicians and political thinkers might continue to be guided by "the kind of realism to which a disciplined historical consciousness conduces." The only motive he imputes to himself is intellectual curiosity: a concern to resolve differences of opinion at the level of "interpretative theory" (63). He thus credits himself with a level of scholarly detachment and independence from political considerations that is strikingly at odds with the central thrust of his argument, which is to construe disciplinization as an epiphenomenon of political domination and scholarship itself as the willing handmaiden of power.

There is no satisfying a critic who prefers his history incomprehensible. Tempting though it is for historians to dismiss White's concerns out of hand, the brilliance of his provocation is undeniable, and there are lessons to learn from it. The controversy that has swirled about his essay since its publication, much of which is not germane to my immediate purposes, centers on the Holocaust and the extreme limits of representation. Passion has run high because White chose—out of intellectual honesty, I believe, not malice—to tackle head-on the question always put to relativists: "What about the Nazis?" He also candidly admitted that his own fascination with the "historical sublime" bears more than a passing resemblance to that of fascist theorists such as Giovanni Gentile. So far as I can tell, White is as horrified by the Holocaust as anyone, but he is also unwilling to duck the implications of his own epistemological commitments. Those commitments he has spelled out in *Metahistory* and other writings, and they define him as a thoroughgoing ironist and antirealist, one for whom the writing of history and the construction of political ideologies necessarily blur into a single enterprise. There is, in his view, nothing stable and independent about the past for the historian to "get right"; nothing for historical interpretation to "correspond with" or to which it might "be adequate." All attempts to distinguish between scholarship and propaganda, or to array knowledge against power, are doomed merely to manifest the political passion they pretend to circumscribe. When historians set out to discover the meaning of the past, all they can possibly find, in White's view, are the tropological artifacts of their own will and imagination, more or less consciously projected onto a medium that is, in itself, shapeless and unresisting. A certain notoriety has been achieved by White's far-reaching and highly characteristic claim that "the best grounds for choosing one perspective on history rather than another are ultimately aesthetic or moral rather than epistemological" (74).[73]

Confronting critics who have accused him of promoting a "debilitating relativism" that permits, as he says, "even a Nazi version of Nazism's history to claim a certain minimal credibility," White unflinchingly turns in "The Politics of Historical Interpretation" to what he calls the "bottom line," the claim of revisionists that the Holocaust never occurred. "Do you mean to say," he asks himself rhetorically, "that the occurrence and nature of the Holocaust is only a matter of opinion and that one can write its history in whatever way one pleases?" (76).

Common sense and old-fashioned "positivist" historiography answer with a forthright "No." In contrast, White's response is extremely roundabout. He finally gives his grudging assent to the judgment of a professional historian, Pierre Vidal-Naquet, who says that Holocaust revisionists are quite simply putting forth a "total lie."[74] But White observes that Vidal-Naquet was not content to distinguish lies from truth. Having done that, he then invoked the authority of the professional historical community to carve out a third category, situated somewhere between "historical truth" and outright "lies," a category made up of "ideological distortions" and "untruths" that do not go so far as to deny the very occurrence of the Holocaust, but twist its meaning farther than the facts will allow. These interpretations, spurned by professional historians, are produced by passionately interested parties; Vidal-Naquet's own example was Zionists who contend that "Auschwitz was the ineluctable, logical outcome of life lived in the Diaspora, and all the victims of the death camps were destined to become Israeli citizens" (77).

The claim that ideologically driven history is "distorted" and can be relegated to the inferior category of "untruth," even though not an outright "lie," provokes from White a crucial objection that goes to the very heart of his quarrel with disciplinization:

> Vidal-Naquet is inclined—too hastily, I think—to consign the Zionist interpretation of the Holocaust . . . to the category of untruth. In fact, its truth, as a historical interpretation, consists precisely of its *effectiveness* in justifying a wide range of current Israeli policies that, from the standpoint of those who articulate them, are crucial to the security of and indeed the very existence of the Jewish people. . . . Who is to say that this ideology is a product of a distorted conception of history? . . . The effort of the Palestinian people to mount a politically *effective* response to Israeli policies [some aspects of which White believes are themselves "totalitarian, not to say fascist"] entails the production of a simi-

larly *effective* ideology, complete with an interpretation of their history capable of endowing it with a meaning that it has hitherto lacked. (80; emphasis added)

Highlighting White's repeated use of the word "effective," just as I have done above, the historian Carlo Ginzburg has exposed to view the deeply disturbing implications of White's position. Having concluded that "there are no grounds to be found in the historical record itself for preferring one way of construing its meaning over another," White, like Nietzsche before him, seems tacitly to have accepted in the notion of "effectiveness" a criterion with appalling implications. By assuming that the only truth a historical interpretation can ever have is relative to the ideology it serves (one more instantiation of the assumption that power and knowledge are two sides of a coin), he gives up any defensible basis for passing moral judgment on historical developments and makes "right" the passive reflex of "might." For, as Ginzburg says, if the historical interpretation advanced by Holocaust revisionists were ever to prove *effective,* in the sense, say, of winning a strong popular following or being incorporated into the official policy of a state, then White would presumably regard it as being no less "true" than the Palestinian and Zionist interpretations that he endorses above. Even the revisionists' "total lie" could become historically "effective" in White's sense, and once it did it would presumably "justify" current policies deemed "crucial" by those who articulate them, and endow history with "a meaning that it has hitherto lacked" (75).[75]

White's understanding of the politics of interpretation is, I think, deeply flawed, but I give him full credit for following his skeptical assumptions to honest conclusions. It appears to me, as it does to him, that skepticism this radical deprives the disciplinary community of any basis whatsoever for claims of epistemological efficacy.[76] It thereby also appears to me to cut the ground out from under all existing justifications for the rights of academic freedom. If I am right in this, it will not do just to paper the matter over, expecting the general public to continue accepting the traditional rationale for academic freedom, even though we undeceived sophisticates have come to regard it as poppycock. If the old rationale has lost its power to convince, then we need a new one, in which both we and the educated public can believe. If no such rationale can be formulated, then the right should be allowed to perish, along with other unjustifiable practices. Needless to add, I neither desire nor expect that the rights of academic freedom will be abandoned. Much more likely, the practice will continue to generate deeper convictions and stronger loyalties (both among academics and the public) than any of the theoretical considerations that tell against it. Should that be the case, presumably our theoreticians will take a cue from common sense, as theory has so often done in the past, and return to their epistemological drawing boards.

But of course my inability to formulate an adequate justification on the basis of *au courant* epistemologies may signify nothing more than my own personal limitations, of which the writing of this essay has made me more than usually aware. Insofar as this is the case, one can only hope and trust that my errors, now in the public domain, will provoke a corrective response from others. Fortunately for my generation, even if the autonomy of disciplinary communities currently lacks any adequate justification, such communities do still exist, and their very existence gives some assurance that no one's incompetence is likely to hold the floor for long. In spite of all the sound and fury of the current *Kulturkampf,* the minimalist case for the authority of the disciplinary community remains hard to gainsay. Timothy Garton Ash set it forth unguardedly in a review of the controversial films *Heimat* and *Shoah.* Like White, Ash sees in the Holocaust an acid test of disciplinization, but he draws the opposite conclusion.

> The one conclusion to which [both films] lead me is: Thank God for historians! Only the professional historians, with their tested methods of research, their explicit principles of selection and use of evidence, only they can give us the weapons with which we may begin to look the thing in the face. Only the historians give us the standards by which we can judge and "place" Heimat and Shoah. Not that any one historian is necessarily more impartial than any one film director. But (at least in a free society) the terms of the historian's trade make them responsible and open to mutual attack, like politicians in a democracy.[77]

The "terms of the historian's trade" are those of all disciplinary communities, whatever their subject. A full description of those terms would fill volumes and require the skills of an ethnographer, but at their heart are some elementary provisions: that practitioners should constitute a professional community; that they should be in competitive communication with one another ("open to mutual attack"); that their decision-making process should be as public as possible (a matter of "tested" methods and "explicit" principles). The truths that such communities generate fall short of being universal or "foundational." Anyone who relies on such truths takes a calculated risk, not only that the community's current opinion may not be right, but that the community's own internal dynamics may render it obsolete tomorrow. In many parts of the world these truths will seem too frail to be valued, and even where valued they may prove too lacking in charismatic authority to compete against other, more visceral sources of conviction. Whether Ash's confidence in the truth claims of disciplinary communities is sustainable today, in a world very different from that faced by the Victorians, is the great question before us. I for one believe it is, but not until we reestablish through candid debate a plausible relationship between, on the one hand, our epistemological convictions, and on the other, our claims to authority and the rights of academic freedom.

PART THREE

The Shifting Conventions of
Human Agency and Responsibility

In the closing pages of the introduction to this volume the reader will find a discussion of the role of causal reasoning in history that is meant to stand as the backdrop to all the essays of this section. By reexamining Hempel's covering law thesis, the narrativist reaction it provoked, and the tendency of both to obscure the critically important distinction between attributive and nomological modes of causal reasoning, I hope to have warded off misunderstandings of the sort that routinely plague the discourse of causality in our generation. In view of the fullness of that backdrop, which I urge every reader to consult, this preface will be brief and businesslike. My aim here is to do little more than report how these essays came to be written and highlight some of their inter-relationships.

The five essays in part 3 are more closely related than those in the preceding section. They need to be read together, for in effect they are progress reports on a single continuing project. The section begins with a long essay, "Capitalism and the Origins of the Humanitarian Sensibility," that was divided in half for publication in consecutive issues of the *American Historical Review* in April and June 1985. (Here it appears as two distinct chapters, 8 and 9). In that two-part essay, as a means of highlighting the distinctive elements of my own interpretation, I systematically contrasted my views with those of David Brion Davis in *The Problem of Slavery in the Age of Revolution, 1770–1823*. Two years later, in October 1987, the same journal carried a reply from Davis, another reply independently submitted by John Ashworth, and my rejoinder to both writers. Toward the end of my 1987 rejoinder, there appeared a free-standing

225

discussion of formalism that I have included here in revised and expanded form as chapter 11, "An Excursus on Formalism."[1]

That accounts for three of the five essays in part 3. The other two essays are driven by much the same set of problems and display the influence of the same interpretive rivalry. "Responsibility, Convention, and the Role of Ideas in History" is a synthetic meditation that borrows several key paragraphs from my original two-part essay, placing the issues, however, in a quite different and more philosophical frame. The last essay, "Persons as Uncaused Causes: John Stuart Mill, the Spirit of Capitalism, and the 'Invention' of Formalism," was originally prepared for the 1990 Tulane University conference "The Culture of the Market" and then published in a conference volume of the same title.[2] It had already gone through several drafts when I began writing my response to Davis and Ashworth, so although it is by no means a reply to them, it was written at about the same time and should help illuminate the differences between us. "Persons as Uncaused Causes" is not the most accessible of my essays, but from my own perspective it is the most ambitious. Its main thrust is to show how much is lost when historians fail to take into account the changing conventions that unavoidably underlie all judgments of agency and responsibility.

But of course that is the overarching aim of all five of the essays in this section. When I embarked on this project back in the late 1970s, I had a methodological agenda in mind. In my first book, I had argued that the emergence in the late nineteenth century of professional social scientists — full-time specialists who earned a living by claiming special insights into the nature of man and society — marked a profound cultural shift in the conditions of adequate explanation. That shift I traced back to the novel habits of remote casual attribution encouraged by the increasingly interdependent character of social relationships in a society being transformed by urbanization and industrialization. Although the book was generally well received, the silence of reviewers about what I took to be a promising new approach persuaded me of three things: that the methodological virtues of my concern with attributive practices were less obvious than I had imagined; that the best way to call attention

1. Needless to say, anyone wishing to explore the entire controversy triggered by "Capitalism and the Origins of the Humanitarian Sensibility" needs to read all of my rejoinder and all the contributions of Davis and Ashworth, which include not only their replies to my original essay but also counters to my rejoinder which they prepared for publication in *The Antislavery Debate: Capitalism and Abolitionism as a Problem in Historical Interpretation,* ed. Thomas Bender (Berkeley: University of California Press, 1992). The Bender volume contains all contributions to the controversy, as well as several chapters from Davis's *Problem of Slavery.*

2. *The Culture of the Market: Historical Essays,* ed. Thomas L. Haskell and Richard F. Teichgraeber III (Cambridge: Cambridge University Press, 1993).

to them was by demonstrating their efficacy in a point-by-point contrast with more familiar approaches; and that this should be done in a subject area about which historians cared more deeply than they do about the history of the social sciences. That is how "Capitalism and the Origins of the Humanitarian Sensibility" came to be written.

At first I titled my project "The Blameworthiness of Criminals." David Rothman's *Discovery of the Asylum* was generating considerable interest at the time, and although it was about treatment of the insane, many of its protagonists were also active in prison reform. Foucault's formidable and frustrating *Discipline and Punish* came out in English translation in 1977. Like Rothman, Foucault disapproved of reformers' motives in ways that seemed to me anachronistic. I, like the two of them, had been struck by the comparatively unsympathetic attitude toward criminals expressed by the prison reformers of the late eighteenth and early nineteenth century. Unlike prison reformers of the twentieth century, the early reformers seldom expressed any doubts about the blameworthiness of incarcerated felons or about the justice of punishing them, as long as punishment was not arbitrary but was closely geared to the reform of character. Indeed, as I worked through archival material on prison reform, what especially intrigued me was abundant evidence that it was not until much later, in the 1880s and 1890s, that significant numbers of prison reformers began speaking of convicts in the manner that has become common among twentieth-century intellectuals (though never prevalent in society at large) — as victims of circumstance, who live under such oppressive and degrading social conditions that they are not fully blameworthy, however criminal their acts might be.

This finding resonated with earlier impressions I had formed about mid-century reformers such as Samuel Gridley Howe, who did much to inaugurate and institutionalize humane treatment of the poor in the 1840s and 1850s. Although a pioneering humanitarian, Howe did not hesitate to blame the poor for their limitations and to attribute their miseries largely to character flaws, much as a rock-ribbed Republican might today. In both "charity" and "corrections," then, the last three decades of the nineteenth century seemed to mark a transition between two quite distinct phases of humane sentiment. The key difference had to do with perceptions of blameworthiness. It was unlikely to be coincidental, I thought, that those years also marked the onset of the "revolt against formalism," well known to intellectual historians as a watershed in social thought and the seedtime of the social sciences.[3]

3. Morton White, *Social Thought in America: The Revolt Against Formalism* (Boston: Beacon Press, 1957).

The discovery that humanitarianism's founding figures held attitudes and opinions now regarded as inhumane prompted both Rothman and Foucault to adopt variations on the "social control" scheme of explanation, in which the ostensibly humane motives of the reformers are revealed to have been masks for something less admirable. Indeed, in Foucault's case it prompted overwrought speculations about the birth of a "carceral society," a sinister development of global proportions, dedicated in all dimensions of life to the meticulous extraction of labor and obedience from a hapless citizenry.

In contrast, my interest in causal attribution alerted me to the possibility that the shift in attitudes from early to late humanitarianism resulted from changes in conventional ways of perceiving agency and responsibility. In order to account for the chronological pattern the evidence displayed, such changes would have had to proceed in two principal phases. First, in the years 1750–1850 something gave reformers unprecedented confidence that they could and should intervene in other people's lives to diminish crime and alleviate needless suffering of many different kinds. What seems counterintuitive to us about this escalating sense of agency and responsibility (coupled with the well-known outburst of practical reform activity to which it gave rise), is that "common sense"—that of our own times, at least—would lead us to expect an accompanying rhetorical flood of compassion and sympathy, which did not immediately occur. What distinguished the early humanitarians from their parents' and grandparents' generation was evidently not a deeper sympathy for the destitute, or unease at the thought of their own privileged place in society, but a more expansive estimate of their own ability (and therefore obligation) to alleviate suffering. What earlier generations had perceived as necessary evils, the humanitarians of the period 1750–1850 perceived as remediable, even though there was initially little or no change in the long standing perception of paupers and criminals as ne'er-do-wells, who by their ineptitude and willfulness brought about their own suffering.[4]

Only later, in the 1880s and 1890s, did a second phase get under way, in which paupers, criminals, and other "clients" of reform came regularly to be seen as victims of circumstance, not fully responsible even for deliberately chosen actions in violation of the law. Among the new breed of settlement-house workers, exemplified by Jane Addams, aid for the poor was motivated not by religious duty or simple generosity, whereby the strong condescended to "lend a hand" to the weak; instead, aid for the poor came from a spirit

4. Much evidence for this view can be found in Martin Wiener's important work, *Reconstructing the Criminal: Culture, Law, and Policy in England, 1830–1914* (Cambridge: Cambridge University Press, 1990).

of guilt, a sense that the reformers themselves were causally implicated in poverty, since social arrangements had "made" them affluent and others poor. Correspondingly, the techniques of aiding the poor shifted away from the effort to inculcate thrift, prudence, and the other elements of self-mastery so essential to nineteenth-century humanitarianism, to direct redistribution of wealth or the design of institutional devices such as social security to shelter the poor from life's worst hazards. These changes — first, an enlargement of the agency and responsibility that reformers imputed to themselves; then, decades later, the adoption of an increasingly circumstantial mode of explanation that diminished the degree of agency and responsibility that reformers' imputed to paupers, criminals, and other objects of reform — seemed very likely to be associated with the intellectuals' "revolt against formalism," which tended systematically to elevate circumstantial modes of explanation at the expense of voluntaristic ones. This I knew to be the case from my own earlier research into the growing plausibility of social scientific modes of explanation in the 1880s and 1890s.

By 1979–80, when a year's leave at the Institute for Advanced Study gave me my first opportunity for sustained work on the project, prison reform had come to seem too restrictive a topic. The entire phenomenon of humanitarianism interested me because parallel questions of causal attribution seemed to arise in all fields of reform. Before reformers can feel obliged to go out of their way to alleviate the suffering of strangers, they must impute to themselves far-reaching powers of intervention. Before they can know which of the world's many suffering strangers have the strongest claim on their intervention, they must (at least tacitly) take into account not only degrees of immiseration and the ease or difficulty of various kinds of intervention but also a judgment of how complicit both the reformer and the suffering stranger are in the stranger's misery. All of these issues lend themselves to analysis in terms of shifts in the habitual modes of causal attribution by which people assign praise, blame, and responsibility to themselves and others.

Meanwhile, the topics of slavery and antislavery, having attracted many of the most able historians of the generation ahead of mine, continued to rivet the attention of the entire profession. I knew from my own involvement in the controversy over *Time on the Cross* how sensitive interpretive issues in this area could be. And although my interest in attributive practices had led me toward an interpretation of prison reformers distinctly at odds with those of Rothman and Foucault, many of my reservations about their interpretations had nothing to do with attributive practices, the methodological issue I wanted to highlight.

So, instead of writing about prison reform, I decided to launch my project with an essay on the history of antislavery. That field's most eminent historian, David Brion Davis, had written a celebrated interpretation that I could endorse in every way but one: his inattentiveness to the historicity and conventionality of the attributive practices that shape perceptions of agency and responsibility —both ours, at the end of the twentieth century, and the quite different perceptions of the antislavery reformers themselves, a century and a half earlier.

Like Rothman and Foucault, Davis told a story about humanitarian reformers whose compassion, though much heralded, fell short of late twentieth century expectations. The abolitionists poured their energy into efforts to abolish chattel slavery, but paid little attention to the suffering of formally free "wage slaves" whose misery they often regarded as self-inflicted through imprudence and incompetence. Davis deplored this "selectivity" of abolitionist vision and attributed it to class interest. He was keenly aware, however, of the pitfalls of the social control mode of interpretation and skirted them far more carefully than either Rothman or Foucault did. His interpretation was not only scrupulously and elegantly crafted, it also had the advantage for me of being about that phase of humanitarianism that seemed least susceptible to disillusionment. The emancipation of the slaves, after all, comes closer to being an unqualified good than anything accomplished by reformers working on prison reform, poverty, or care of the insane. If I could show that a historical interpretation as strong as Davis's, about a subject as vital as antislavery, could be improved by attending to conventions of causal attribution, my methodological agenda would have been accomplished. Or so I hoped.

When I entered the debate over antislavery, it was taken for granted by all parties that the rise of antislavery agitation had been concomitant with the rise of capitalism and that this fact, paradoxical on the face of things, demanded explanation. Eric Williams had taken the most direct explanatory route, claiming that by the late eighteenth century, slave labor was becoming unprofitable, making the lofty rhetoric of the antislavery movement little more than a cloak for a transition to free labor that was fundamentally advantageous to capitalist interests. Davis drew on the spirit of Williams's argument, but rid it of all conspiratorial implications by suggesting that antislavery reformers were sincere in their rhetoric of human rights, but unconsciously drew back from pressing their case as far as disinterested moral judgment would have required—into the burgeoning and often sordid world of wage labor, where it was members of their own class (and sometimes their own fathers, uncles, and nephews) who exploited nominally free workers behind a facade of formalistically defined freedom.

My own tack was to contend that class interest was not the sole link between economic change and ideas:

Whatever influence the rise of capitalism may have had generally on ideas and values through the medium of class interest, it had a more telling influence on the origins of humanitarianism through changes the market wrought in *perception* or *cognitive style*. And it was primarily a change in cognitive style—specifically a change in the perception of causal connection and consequently a shift in the conventions of moral responsibility—that underlay the new constellation of attitudes and activities that we call humanitarianism. What altered cognitive style in a "humanitarian" direction was not in the first instance the ascendancy of a new class, or the assertion by that class of a new configuration of interests. It was, rather, the expansion of the market, the intensification of market discipline, and the penetration of that discipline into spheres of life previously untouched by it. In an explanation of humanitarianism, then, what matters in the capitalist substructure is not a new class so much as the market, and what links the capitalist market to a new sensibility is not class interest so much as the power of market discipline to inculcate altered perceptions of causation in human affairs.[5]

My argument was exceedingly well received, but to my surprise, issues other than causal attribution dominated readers' reaction to it. Although in retrospect I would do nothing differently, there can be no doubt that the prime significance I attached to two concepts, "interest" and "market," account for much of the controversy that followed. My challenge to Davis's extremely ambivalent reliance on class interest persuaded some readers that my aim was not merely to supplement explanation-by-interest, but to supplant it—a bizarre project I never dreamed of undertaking. By assigning the market an important role in the development of the cognitive style upon which humanitarianism depends, I evidently convinced some readers that I must be a pro-capitalist booster, out to credit capitalism with being the wellspring of humane values. Nothing could have been farther from my intention, or from the meaning of my words, as I read them today.

The crux of my argument was that the market heaps rewards on people who (whether for selfish or unselfish reasons) systematically take into account the most remote consequences of their actions. The discipline of the invisible hand thereby tends to expand causal horizons and set the stage for the appearance of what Nietzsche called "sovereign individuals," people who act out of conscience, "think causally," and strive to "ordain the future in advance," thereby expanding the boundaries of responsibility far enough potentially to include for the first time perfect strangers, people for whose suffering no one in traditional society felt responsible. All this I summed up in two mental exercises of

5. "Capitalism and the Origins of the Humanitarian Sensibility," 238–39 (this volume).

a sort familiar to philosophers but never before seen in the pages of a major historical journal. The most important was the "case of the starving stranger," a hypothetical exercise meant to delineate the perceptual and cognitive preconditions that had to be satisfied before humanitarianism could emerge on the stage of history; the other asked readers to imagine the displacement of our carnivorous way of life by a triumphant movement of vegetarian reform, comparable to the nineteenth-century crusade against slavery. Both exercises were meant to highlight the inescapable role that causal conventions play in imputations of moral responsibility.

The replies by Davis and Ashworth to my original two-part article alerted me to the need for a fuller specification of the difference between the formalism of the mid-nineteenth-century reformers and the antiformalism that began displacing it toward the end of the century. Both the "Excursus on Formalism" and "Persons as Uncaused Causes" address this need. In the excursus I explore the contrast between Wendell Phillips's formalist perspective on wage labor in the 1840s and the antiformalist views he was expressing by the 1870s, treating him as a harbinger of the revolt against formalism. Here the central question is about the relation between capitalism on the one hand and formalism/antiformalism on the other. Both Ashworth and Davis are committed to the view that formalism is an ideological stance that, by no coincidence, served the interests of the bourgeoisie. While conceding a grain of truth to their claim, I contend (a) that there is a deeper affinity between capitalism and *anti*formalism; (b) that the deepest affinity of all is that between formalism and Christianity; and (c) that we would do well, therefore, not to look to interest alone for the connection between ideas and economic development. Specifically, I claim that we can learn more about the limits of humanitarian reform by inquiring into the cognitive style induced by the market—the modes of explanation and attribution it encourages—than we can by construing reform priorities as a reflex of economic interest.

"Persons as Uncaused Causes" develops in greater detail my claim about the affinities linking capitalism, religion, and formalism/antiformalism, taking as case in point yet another, still earlier, harbinger of antiformalism, John Stuart Mill. At the age of twenty in the year 1826, Mill experienced the onset of a debilitating "mental crisis" that continued off and on for several years, convincing him for a time that he was not authentically the cause of anything, since he and all his choices and acts could all be construed as the effects of prior events and influences. This agonizing episode, to which he devotes much space in his autobiography and during which he was literally persuaded of his own inconsequentiality, I interpret as a crisis of causal attribution, personal in its incidence, but culturally significant for its implications about the future. Moreover, the episode brings into view two vitally important and hitherto unexamined aspects of the game of causal attribution we all play: first, that the conventions that allocate causation between the self and the circumstances that impinge upon it are constitutive of personhood; and second, that every attribution of causal status to persons, acts, choices, or events is subject to dissolution in the acids of *transitivity,* by which term I refer to the fact—well known but hitherto assigned scarcely any importance—that everything we might wish to call a "cause" of subsequent events can, by an elementary shift of perspective, be construed as an *effect* of antecedent events, thereby emptying it of its originary status. From this curiosity of causal reasoning, I argue, arise many of the paradoxes of freedom and fate.

Also included in part 3 is "Responsibility, Convention, and the Role of Ideas in History." Although it is not an entirely original production (an inadvertently ironic disclaimer, in the context of Mill's mental crisis), I have positioned it right after "Capitalism and the Origins of the Humanitarian Sensibility." It is a synthesis of other work I have done in this area, and its occasional repetitiveness is offset by three virtues. First, it summarizes arguments developed at greater length elsewhere, offering to readers the opportunity of an overview. Second, it is my most explicit defense of causal conventions as a subject for historical inquiry. Third, it picks up the entire constellation of questions by a different handle: not humanitarianism, not capitalism, not causal attribution or formalism or the history of slavery, but the history of responsibility. That different framing of the issues may help clarify them for some readers.

This essay also gives me the opportunity to discuss and comment on the recent writings of a philosopher whose extensive writings on moral responsibility I greatly admire, Bernard Williams. In *Shame and Necessity,* Williams challenges the widespread assumption that there is something premoral or childlike in the ancients' attitude toward responsibility. Aristotle's notoriously irresolute discussion of the morality of slavery is Williams's case in point. Since Williams shares both my aversion to anachronism and my conviction that causal perceptions of causal relations are the seed crystals around which judgments of responsibility take shape, we have much in common. All the more reason to hope that the differences spelled out here will be of interest to our readers.

Capitalism and the Origins of the Humanitarian Sensibility, Part 1

An unprecedented wave of humanitarian reform sentiment swept through the societies of western Europe, England, and North America in the hundred years following 1750. Among the movements spawned by this new sensibility, the most spectacular was that to abolish slavery. Although its morality was often questioned before 1750, slavery was routinely defended and hardly ever condemned outright, even by the most scrupulous moralists. About the time that slavery was being transformed from a problematical but readily defensible institution into a self-evidently evil and abominable one, new attitudes began to appear — on deterring criminals, relieving the poor, curing the insane, schooling the young, and dealing with primitive peoples.[1] The resulting reforms were, by almost any reasonable standard, an improvement over old practices that were often barbarous. Even so, twentieth-century historians have not been satisfied to attribute those reforms either to an advance in man's moral sense or to a random outburst of altruism. In explaining the new humanitarianism, historians have repeatedly pointed to changes in what Marxists generally call the economic base or substructure of society, that is, the growth of capitalism and beginnings of industrialization. Tracing links between humanitarianism and capitalism has been a major preoccupation of historians, and the enter-

So many people have given me advice about an earlier and briefer version of this essay that I can scarcely call it my own, except insofar as it errs or offends. My principal debt is to David Brion Davis, whose extraordinarily generous and thoughtful correspondence saved me from many errors of fact, taste, and judgment. The essay was first presented to the Social Science Seminar of the Institute for Advanced Study, Princeton, N.J., in April 1979. Since then I have benefited from discussions with members of the Social Science Seminar at Rice University and the Department of History and Philosophy, Carnegie-Mellon University. For especially thorough and helpful comprise has succeeded, I believe, in greatly extending our understanding of the new sensibility. We know now that the reformers were motivated by far more than an unselfish desire to help the downtrodden, and we see more clearly now why their reforms went no farther and took the particular form they did.[2] Historians are never again likely to believe, as did W. E. H. Lecky in 1876, that Britain's campaign against slavery was "among the three or four perfectly virtuous acts recorded in the history of nations."[3]

But these advances in understanding have been achieved only at the expense of a growing ambivalence as we try to acknowledge two things at once: that humanitarian reform not only took courage and brought commendable changes but also served the interests of the reformers and was part of that vast bourgeois project Max Weber called rationalization. This ambivalence reached painful heights in Michel Foucault's *Discipline and Punish,* in which he questioned whether there really was a new humanitarian sensibility and argued that, though a new sensitivity to suffering did exist, its aim in prison reform was not humane. Its real aim, Foucault concluded, was "not to punish less, but to punish better; to punish with an attenuated severity perhaps, but in order to punish with more universality and necessity; to insert the power to punish more deeply into the social body."[4] Foucault's position contains much truth, yet in contemplating it, we must not lose sight of another truth, namely, that to put a thief in jail is more humane than to burn him, hang him, maim him, or dismember him.

The inadequacy of prevailing modes of explanation tempts scholars to migrate toward two extremes: either to abandon the very idea of humanitarianism, lest it veil the play of domination, or to reassert the classical liberal view that humanitarian ideas belong to a transcendent realm of moral choice, which no inquiry into social or economic circumstances can hope to illuminate. The latter strategy, essentially one of compartmentalization, finds considerable support in Roger Anstey's sophisticated effort to refurbish the traditional image of British abolitionists as moral giants. Even more decisive encouragement comes from Seymour Drescher's *Econocide,* which seeks to show, contrary to the thesis of Eric Williams, that slavery was a profitable and important

ments, I am grateful to Seymour Drescher, Stanley Engerman, Ira Gruber, Albert Hirschman, Jay Hook, Jackson Lears, Elizabeth Long, George Marcus, Lewis Perry, Andrew Scull, Quentin Skinner, Peter Stearns, Richard Teichgraeber, Larry Temkin, Mark Warren, Roger Wertheimer, Morton White, and Bertram Wyatt-Brown. Martin Wiener's encouragement and advice have been especially valuable. The work was made possible by leaves funded by the Institute for Advanced Study, The Rockefeller Foundation, and the Dean of Humanities, Rice University.

First published in *American Historical Review* 90 (Apr. 1985): 339–61.

part of the British economy and that the decision to abolish it ran directly counter to Britain's economic interest.[5]

The present historiographical dilemma has been aptly described by Howard Temperley. To argue that "abolition had nothing to do with economics except insofar as economic interest was a factor to be overcome," he observed, leads to conclusions that are "to put it mildly, a little odd."

> Here we have a system—a highly successful system—of large-scale capitalist agriculture, mass producing raw materials for sale in distant markets, growing up at a time when most production was still small-scale and designed to meet the needs of local consumers. But precisely at a time when capitalist ideas were in the ascendant, and large-scale production of all kinds of goods was beginning, we find this system being dismantled. How could this happen unless "capitalism" had something to do with it? If our reasoning leads to the conclusion that "capitalism" had nothing to do with it, the chances are that there is something wrong with our reasoning.[6]

I believe that a real change in sensibility occurred, and that it was associated with the rise of capitalism. The way out of the current historiographical impasse is to find a way to establish the connection without also reducing humane values and acts to epiphenomena. To do this we must begin by reexamining the ways in which substructural developments like the rise of capitalism might have influenced superstructural developments like humanitarianism. There is more than one way in which these phenomena might be linked, and the purpose of this essay is to bring into focus a kind of linkage that historians have sometimes tacitly assumed but never explored in a deliberate and systematic way.

Today the most popular way to formulate the linkage between capitalism and the humanitarian sensibility goes under the banner of "social control" or "class hegemony." Reduced to its basic outlines, this scheme of explanation rests two assumptions. The first concerns what we really have in mind when we use the umbrella phrase "rise of capitalism," which, after all, covers a large cluster of quite diverse concrete developments, any one of which we might think more important than others. When social control theorists use this phrase, they usually mean only one of the elements hidden under the umbrella—the ascendancy of a new, entrepreneurial class, the bourgeoisie. This new class is understood to have distinctive interests deriving from its control over the society's predominant means of production. Those interests are understood to be such that the class will favor any measure that ensures the docility of the less advantaged sectors of the population, that enhances the discipline and productivity of the work force on which the economy depends, that strengthens its own morale or weakens that of other groups, or that contributes in any other way to the maintenance of its own supremacy.

The second assumption basic to the social control interpretation flows naturally from the first: class interest is the medium — and, presumably, the only important medium — through which substructural change influences developments in the superstructure. Given these assumptions and the bourgeois origins of almost all humanitarian reformers of the late eighteenth and early nineteenth century, the strategy of explanation becomes obvious: the way for the social control historian to explain humanitarianism is to show how supposedly disinterested reforms actually functioned to advance bourgeois interests. To state the explanatory schema so baldly makes it sound simpler and more vulnerable than it really is. The social control thesis, like any other, is capable of sophisticated as well as crude applications, as the following discussion of a very refined application of the thesis should make clear. But however indirectly and subtly reform may be said to have served class interest, the historian employing the social control schema is strongly predisposed to look to class interest alone for the connecting link between capitalism and humanitarianism, base and superstructure.

The alternative interpretation that I shall present rejects both assumptions of the social control thesis. Without questioning the great importance of self-interest and class interest in human affairs, and while fully recognizing that interests exert an important influence on belief through what Weber called "elective affinity," I shall argue that in this particular inquiry the concept of class interest has obscured almost as much as it has revealed.[7] Stated plainly, my thesis is this: Whatever influence the rise of capitalism may have had generally on ideas and values through the medium of class interest, it had a more telling influence on the origins of humanitarianism through changes the market wrought in *perception* or *cognitive style*. And it was primarily a change in cognitive style — specifically a change in the perception of causal connection and consequently a shift in the conventions of moral responsibility — that underlay the new constellation of attitudes and activities that we call humanitarianism. What altered cognitive style in a "humanitarian" direction was not in the first instance the ascendancy of a new class, or the assertion by that class of a new configuration of interests. It was, rather, the expansion of the market, the intensification of market discipline, and the penetration of that discipline into spheres of life previously untouched by it. In an explanation of humanitarianism, then, what matters in the capitalist substructure is not a new class so much as the market, and what links the capitalist market to a new sensibility is not class interest so much as the power of market discipline to inculcate altered perceptions of causation in human affairs.

This approach has certain advantages. Instead of prompting the historian to unmask the interestedness of ostensibly disinterested reforms, the explanatory approach advocated here would lead the historian to demonstrate the "naturalness" of these reforms, given the historical development of certain cognitive structures that were formed in the crucible of market transactions. Because these cognitive structures underlay *both* the reformers' novel sense of responsibility for others and their definition of their own interests, there is indeed a certain congruence between the reforms they carried out and the needs of their class. The social control argument errs not in stressing the existence of this congruence but in the account given of its origins. The approach recommended here does not aim to turn the social control argument on its head, retaining its opposition of ideas and interests while reversing their causal relationship; instead, the purpose is to overcome this dualism altogether by acknowledging that ideas and interests are interwoven at every level and in fact arise from the same source—a certain way of perceiving human relations fostered by the forms of life the market encouraged.

In another respect, however, the reader will note that my argument does reverse what is commonly thought to be the proper order of things. The pervasive, if diffuse, influence of the neo-Freudian tradition has prepared us to accept without much question the idea that feelings influence perception, that our emotional needs shape the way we see and experience the world around us. Although I do not doubt in the least that emotion has the power to influence perception, and often does, the present study shows, I believe, that the reverse can also be true. The rise of antislavery sentiment was, among other things, an upwelling of powerful feelings of sympathy, guilt, and anger, but these emotions would not have emerged when they did, taken the form they did, or produced the same results if they had not been called into being by a prior change in the perception of causal relations.

The argument is roughly as follows. To specify more exactly the dilemmas inherent in the social control interpretation, I will examine the most penetrating and sophisticated example of that approach—David Brion Davis's *Problem of Slavery in the Age of Revolution*. My aim is to show that, although this book's sophistication has many sources, one is the tendency to play down class interest (even while finally embracing it) by stressing the concept of self-deception; that, in trying to avoid making class interest the exclusive or overpowering link between substructural and superstructural change, Davis naturally moved in the direction of cognitive style; and that, by going one step further in the same direction, we can clarify some residual ambiguities in his analysis. Once the need has been established, a new formulation can be attempted.

Davis moved so far beyond the ordinary limitations of the social control thesis that one is tempted to credit him with having superseded it. Certainly much of the alternative approach that I wish to recommend is implicit in Davis's analysis. He never denied the authenticity of the reformers' good intentions and never claimed that their "actual" aim was to achieve social control. He was, however, content to depict the antislavery movement as peculiarly susceptible to efforts to convert it into a "vehicle for social control," and, even after all of his many qualifications are taken into account, class interest is the only link between base and superstructure that he specifically recognized.[8] For Davis, "the key questions concern the relationship between antislavery and the social system as a whole."

> Why did a seemingly liberal movement emerge and continue to win support from major government leaders in the period from 1790 to 1832, a period characterized by both political reaction and industrial revolution? How could such a movement be embraced by aristocratic statesmen and yet serve eventually as a vehicle for the triumphant middle class, who regarded West Indian emancipation as the confirmation of the Reform Bill of 1832, and who used antislavery rhetoric and strategy as models for their assault upon the Corn Laws? How could antislavery help ensure stability while also accommodating society to political and economic change? Antonio Gramsci defined "hegemony," in the words of his biographer [John M. Cammet], as "the predominance, obtained by consent rather than force, of one class or group over other classes"; or more precisely, "the 'spontaneous' loyalty that any dominant social group obtains from the masses by virtue of its social and intellectual prestige and its supposedly superior function in the world of production." The paramount question, which subsumes the others, is how antislavery reinforced or legitimized such hegemony. (348–49)

Unlike Foucault, Davis was confident that humanitarianism, or at any rate its antislavery component, represents an authentic and "remarkable shift in moral consciousness . . . a momentous turning point in the evolution of man's moral perception and thus in man's image of himself." Like Foucault, however, Davis insisted that the new sensibility "did not spring from transcendent sources." Rather its origin, he said, lies in "the ideological needs of various groups and classes" (41–42). Davis achieved a highly nuanced view of the reformers' motivation by creating in the reader's mind a tense double image in which reformers appear not only as free moral actors, moved by ethical considerations of which they are fully conscious, but also as unwitting agents of class interest, moved by social needs that worked "over their heads" and were scarcely (if at all) accessible to consciousness. As long as one assumes, as Davis apparently did, that class interest is the only important link between base and superstructure, this juxtaposition of contradictory images is perhaps the only way to ward off reductionism and to do justice to the insolubility of the old problem of free will and determinism.

In an earlier book, *The Problem of Slavery in Western Culture,* Davis identified four major intellectual transformations that set the stage for an antislavery movement. Primitivist currents of thought permitted at least a momentary ambivalence about the superiority of European civilization. The evangelical movement in Protestantism dramatized the dangers of moral complacency even as the latitudinarian reaction against Hobbesian and Calvinistic views of man popularized an ethic of benevolence. Secular social philosophers from Hobbes to Montesquieu stripped away many of the previous sanctions for slavery and moved closer to a rejection of the institution, though Bodin was the only one who actually condemned it. These developments came to a practical focus in the affairs of the Quakers, the only perfectionist sect spawned by the revolutionary turmoil of seventeenth-century England that found a way to compromise and thus to survive and prosper. By the mid-eighteenth century, the Quakers were both representatives of the most radical strand of the Protestant tradition and figures in the vanguard of the development of capitalism and industrial society. The Quakers supplied a natural pivot for Davis's analysis as he turned, in his second book, away from the history of ideas to "more material considerations which helped both to shape the new moral consciousness and to define its historical effects" (48).

Here in the material substructure Davis found the two principal threads of argument that he followed throughout his second volume. First, he explored "the ideological functions and implications of attacking this symbol of the most extreme subordination, exploitation, and dehumanization, at a time when various enlightened elites were experimenting with internalized moral and cultural controls to establish or preserve their own hegemony" (49). The second theme, less relevant to the purposes of this essay, traced the geopolitical and international economic considerations that led Great Britain to tolerate the annihilation of a species of property within its imperial borders and to exert military force against the slave trade, whether conducted by foreign nationals or its own citizens.

Davis turned away from the history of ideas, in his second volume, and opened the door to a much less voluntaristic and rationalistic mode of explanation than that tradition has thought acceptable. Yet his conversion was incomplete and uncertain. Characteristically, his strongest assertions explaining superstructural developments by reference to substructural ones are immediately followed by reservations that accumulate nearly to the point of contradiction. For example, Davis attributed receptivity to antislavery ideology to "profound social changes" connected with "the rise of new classes and new economic interests." But in the following sentence he declared that "this ideology emerged from a convergence of complex religious, intellectual and literary trends—trends which are by no means reducible to the economic interests of particular classes, but which must be understood as part of a larger transformation of attitudes toward labor, property and individual responsibility" (82). Davis in this passage came closer than anywhere else to a recognition of the role played by cognitive style, yet, having almost said that class interest cannot be the exclusive link between humanitarianism and capitalism, he named no alternative link.

Davis's interpretation is not reductionist. He forthrightly rejected the argument that "Quaker abolitionists were governed by 'economic interest' in the sense that they stood to profit from the destruction of the slave trade or a weakening of the plantation system" (251). Instead of direct profit, the relevant interests were those of an entrepreneurial class preoccupied with problems of unemployment and labor discipline. And Davis was acutely aware that even this argument "must be developed with considerable care to avoid the simplistic impression that 'industrialists' promoted abolitionist doctrine as a means of distracting attention from their own form of exploitation" (455).

Although Davis denied the existence of any crude cause-and-effect relationship between the needs of capitalists and the attack on slavery, he assigned great importance to a more subtle linkage based solidly on class interest. The heart of his analysis lies in the claim that "as a social force, antislavery was a highly selective response to labor exploitation. It provided an outlet for demonstrating Christian concern for human suffering and injustice, and yet thereby gave a certain moral insulation to economic activities less visibly dependent on human suffering and injustice" (251). Elsewhere, speaking of long-range consequences rather than immediate intentions, he concluded that the abolitionist movement helped "clear an ideological path for British industrialists," and he noted that, by exaggerating the harshness of slavery, abolitionists "gave sanction to less barbarous modes of social discipline." In the same breath Davis credited the abolitionist movement with breeding "a new sensitivity to social oppression" and providing a "model for the systematic indictment of social crime" (466–68).

The tendency of protests against chattel slavery to overshadow the evils of "wage slavery" had special significance for Davis because of the extraordinary role that Quakers played in the early antislavery movement. The Quaker reformers who were so prominent in antislavery and every other humanitarian endeavor of the age were often fabulously successful businessmen who epitomized the Protestant ethic and the capitalist mentality. Either directly or through close family connections, they were deeply involved in industry, shipping, banking, and commerce; they knew firsthand the task of devising new modes of labor discipline to replace older methods of social control. As members of an entrepreneurial class confronted by an "unruly labor force" prone to "uninhibited violence" and not yet "disciplined to the factory system," late-eighteenth-century reformers had strong incentives to formulate an ideology that would "isolate specific forms of human misery, allowing issues of freedom and discipline to be faced in a relatively simplified model" (241, 252, 254).

As these statements illustrate, Davis relied heavily on the explanatory power of class interest as the driving force behind ostensibly disinterested reforms. Apart from explicit denials of reductionism, what prevents his account from reducing the humanitarian sensibility to a reflexive instrument of the class struggle is his often repeated conviction that the reformers were generally unaware of the interested character of their ideology and unable to see that it played a role in furthering the hegemony of their own class. The reformers, wrote Davis, "*unwittingly* drew distinctions and boundaries which opened the way, under a guise of moral rectitude, for unprecedented forms of oppression." He said of David Barclay and other Quakers that it was "*inconceivable* [to them] that English servants were in any sense unfree," and it was "*unthinkable* that an attack on a specific system of labor and domination might also validate other forms of oppression" (253, 350; emphasis added). In Davis's opinion, the formalistic conception of human freedom that enabled people militantly opposed to slavery to ignore the plight of the impoverished factory laborer and to turn their back on the ex-slave once he was legally free was powerful enough to constrain the vision even of the more radical abolitionists. "At issue, then," Davis concluded, "are not conscious intentions, but the social functions of ideology" (266n, 350).

By insisting that the reformers were unaware of the hegemonic function served by their ideology, Davis opened a crucially important space between their intentions and the long-term consequences of their ideas and activities. It is mainly this zone of indeterminacy and free play that keeps his account clear of the reductionist and conspiratorial overtones that have so often plagued the social control argument. Yet it is also indispensable to Davis's purpose that the gap between intentions and consequences not grow too wide, for, if the aid and comfort that abolitionism gave to capitalist hegemony was utterly unrelated to the intentions of the reformers, or if it was related only in an incidental or accidental way, Davis would have to abandon his conclusion.[9] In order to conclude (as he did) that the attack on slavery was crucially shaped by the needs and interests of the rising class to which the reformers belonged, capitalist hegemony cannot be merely one among the many unintended consequences of reform. The category of unintended consequences is too loose to supply either the ethical or the causal quality that his explanation requires. After all, when Hank Aaron hit a home run, one of the consequences of the act was to put a new baseball into the hands of some lucky spectator. But this was not what Aaron intended by swinging at the ball, and we do not credit him with generosity because of the "gift" he bestowed on the spectators (nor would we have blamed him if the ball had struck one of them on the head). If the aim of furthering capitalist hegemony entered into the intentions of the abolitionists no more significantly than the aim of gift giving figured in Aaron's mind as he swung at the ball, we would not feel that humanitarianism had anything important to do with the rise of capitalism — not, at least, as long as we assume that class interest is the only way to link the two. To say that a person is moved by class interest is to say that he *intends* to further the interests of his class, or it is to say nothing at all.[10]

The intention need not be simple, of course. What is wanted, as Davis himself put it, is a way to show that the reformer's thinking was "rooted . . . in the needs of a social group" yet not "reducible" to them (349). The problem (faced by Davis and anyone else striving to formulate a nonreductive explanation based on class interest) is that interest explains the conduct of reformers only by reducing it, revealing beneath the pretty surface of laudable intentions another layer that better accounts for their reforms. Interest explains much, but it explains by reduction. To shy away from the reductive step is to sacrifice explanatory force. No amount of cautious language can overcome the trade-off built into the logic of this kind of explanation.

Unwilling to give up the explanatory force of class interest, yet uncomfortable with its tendency to undercut the authenticity of stated intentions, Davis, like many other recent scholars, resorted to the "soft" form of intentionality embodied in the notion of self-deception. By so doing he adopted a concept that bids fair to become the keystone of an imposing historiography constructed by Raymond Williams, E. P. Thompson, Eugene Genovese, and many other scholars who have drawn theoretical inspiration from the work of

Gramsci. The notion of self-deception or some close equivalent of it has played an important role in the efforts of the "cultural school" to escape the criticism that doomed an earlier and more "positivist" tradition in Marxian historiography. The question I wish to raise is whether this conception can bear the explanatory weight thus thrust upon it.[11]

Davis observed that "ideological hegemony is not the product of conscious choice and seldom involves insincerity or deliberate deception." He then quoted the sociologist Peter Berger, who said that "deliberate deception requires a degree of psychological self-control that few people are capable of. . . . It is much easier to deceive oneself." In a passage that Davis did not quote but that would have suited his purposes equally well, the Marxist art critic Arnold Hauser made a similar point: "What most sharply distinguishes a propagandistic from an ideological presentation and interpretation of the facts is . . . that its falsification and manipulation of the truth is always conscious and intentional. Ideology, on the other hand, is mere deception — in essence self-deception — never simply lies and deceit. It obscures truth in order not so much to mislead others as to maintain and increase the self-confidence of those who express and benefit from such deception."[12] Unquestionably the concept of self-deception represents a major advance over the mechanistic formulations for which it substitutes. It virtually banishes the implication of conspiracy that so marred the work of Eric Williams, for example, and, if it does not grapple with the problem of free will at a very deep level, the concept at least does not pretend to have solved that problem by the discovery of an all-encompassing theory of determinism. In short, self-deception has the distinct merit of occupying the space between intention and consequence, precluding any rigid coupling of the two while maintaining a connection between them. The notion is, however, very slippery and, in spite of all its virtues, is not the best way to formulate the relationship between the abolitionists' intentions and the hegemonic consequences of their actions.

The problem with self-deception is not that it is a rare mental state or an overly technical term. All of us can recall episodes in our lives when we ignored or denied what now seems the plain and reprehensible meaning of our action — moments when, to paraphrase what Sigmund Freud said about dreams, we knew what the consequences of our actions would be but did not know that we knew.[13] But the usefulness of the concept of self-deception to the historian is limited by two considerations. The first has to do with the ambiguous ethical import of acts committed by a person said to be deceiving himself; the second concerns the difficulty of distinguishing between cases of true self-deception and cases in which a person simply is either ignorant of some of the consequences of his actions or convinced that those consequences are incidental to his aim. Let us examine each problem in turn.

The ambiguity inherent in the idea of self-deception appears immediately when we ask what degree of ethical responsibility a person bears for acts the consequences of which he has deceptively concealed from himself. If we construe the term in a Freudian manner, knowledge of the unpalatable consequences is presumably hidden in the unconscious. Can a person will that what is unconscious become conscious? If not, he cannot be held responsible for acting on knowledge he does not know he possesses. Although a moralist in many ways, Freud had no patience with the idea that psychic events were undetermined or with the glib confidence that reason could master the unconscious. Making the unconscious conscious was for him the world-historical task of psychoanalysis, not the personal responsibility of ordinary individuals unaided by therapeutic intervention.[14]

But we also use the term "self-deception" to describe situations in which the actor is thought to be blameworthy. When we decide that an episode in our own past was a case of self-deception, we are embarrassed and feel regret. The implication of our embarrassment is that we suspect we could have done other than we did, that by trying harder we could have become cognizant of the self-concealed consequences of our action and changed course accordingly. And of course the blame we attach to our own actions in such cases applies with at least equal force to the self-deceptions we think we see others commit.

What does it mean, then, to say that the abolitionists deceived themselves? That they could and should have overcome their self-imposed blindness? Or that they did all that could be expected, given the limitations of the only perspective available to them? The concept of self-deception is ambiguous enough to sustain either reading. More specifically, was Davis saying that chattel slavery and "wage slavery" were so similar that anyone opposing one ought to have opposed the other, that the formalism confining prevalent nineteenth-century definitions of freedom (among abolitionists and many others) to the mere absence of physical or legal constraint was so transparent that anyone who tried could have seen through it? This seems to be the clear implication of Davis's contention that abolitionism was a highly "selective response to labor exploitation." Yet as we have seen, Davis was not at all comfortable with this implication; he also said that the reformers contributed to capitalist hegemony only "unwittingly" and that it would have been "unthinkable" and "inconceivable" for them to adopt less formalistic conceptions of liberty. These are strong words, and they play an important role in Davis's account. They imply a far less voluntaristic image of the reformers, one that holds them essentially blameless for the limitations of their ideology — even though those limitations are said to have been self-imposed.[15] Without pursuing these conundrums any further, we can see that self-deception is an exceedingly spacious concept. I suspect that some readers welcome Davis's use of the term precisely because it seems to insist on a fairly high degree of intentionality and responsibility, while others welcome it because it seems to let the abolitionists entirely off the hook. Life has irreducible ambiguities, but this is a case in which there may be greater ambiguity in the terms of representation than in the reality we seek to represent.

Now let us turn to the second and more serious limitation on the usefulness of the concept of self-deception. Although the ethical import of self-deception is ambiguous, the intentionality of it is not. Self-deception implies intention, although not of the conscious variety. If it did not imply intention, it would not have served Davis's purpose, which was to treat humanitarianism as a product in part of a specific kind of intention — advancing the interests of one's own class.[16] The intentions implied by self-deception presumably operate unconsciously, and, as we have seen, this complicates their ethical significance. But it does not turn them into something other than intentions. Freudian theory is quite clear on this point: what resides in the unconscious are intentions (relegated to that nether region precisely because of their ugly character) that compete with and sometimes overwhelm the conscious intentions of the actor.[17] One might argue that there are degrees of intentionality and that the self-deceiver's is less than the deliberate actor's, but in the last analysis the person deceiving himself must be said to know basically what the outcome of his action will be and to desire it (even though he may not be aware that he knows and desires it). Otherwise, the person who deceives himself would be no different from the person who through incomplete knowledge simply fails to anticipate all the consequences of his acts. That would make the term utterly vaporous. The person who deceives himself about the consequences of his actions knows a great deal more about them than the person who is ignorant of them.

Underlying any explanation built on the notion of self-deception, then, is an implicit claim to have successfully reconstructed the historical actor's unconscious intention. The claim is a bold one. Even conscious intentions are notoriously difficult to nail down in the absence of explicit statements of purpose (or even in their presence, for that matter), and unconscious intentions are much more problematical. By definition, they leave no direct empirical trace. One can only hypothesize their existence from the "goodness of fit" between the actor's interests (as reconstructed by the analyst) and certain consequences that follow from his actions. The reasoning process behind such hypothesizing is treacherous. After all, every act (or failure to act) has consequences both proximate and remote that are potentially infinite in number and extension. This is the stuff of which debates about the influence of horseshoe nails and Cleopatra's nose are made. It is altogether too easy to pluck from the ever-widening stream of consequences some that fit our reconstruction of the actor's interests and then repackage these as his unconscious intention. Even if we assume that we know his interests, a question remains: what empirical evidence could, even in principle, confirm that the observed "goodness of fit" is more than coincidental?[18]

The impossibility of confirming our hunches about the existence of unconscious intentions is only an aspect of a larger problem: the absence, even in principle, of any empirical evidence that would permit us to distinguish between the *unconsciously intended consequences* that the self-deception explanation requires and the *unintended consequences* that make up so much of what happens in human affairs. To return to an earlier analogy, when Hank Aaron hit a home run, we felt confident that the spectator's acquisition of a baseball was not Aaron's intention, even though it was unquestionably a consequence of his action. Our confidence might have yielded to confusion, however, if we had grounds for believing that Aaron had an incentive for currying the favor of fans by giving them gifts in this manner. In that unlikely circumstance, we might suspect, but could never confirm, that gift giving was a significant, even though unconscious, part of his intention. Even if we could be sure that he was aware of the gift-giving consequences of his home run (say, by having called it to his attention as he strode to the plate), we could not confirm our suspicion, for all of us are always aware (or can easily be made aware) of consequences of our actions that fall outside intention in spite of our awareness of them. Knowing that a certain consequence will follow from one's actions does not necessarily make the production of that consequence part of one's intentions. The immense category of unintended consequences includes not only events of which the actor is completely ignorant but also events of which the actor may be aware but which social convention nonetheless classifies as unintentional—as incidental concomitants of his action (like Aaron's "gift" to the spectator) rather than the aim of it. Given the immensity of this category of events, and the absence of any empirical means by which unintended consequences can be distinguished from unconsciously intended consequences, one may well doubt that the social control argument gains anything of substance by relying on the notion of self-deception.

Among all these liabilities, the fatal flaw of the self-deception argument is its obliviousness to the paramount role played by convention in all judgments of moral responsibility. Once we understand the inescapable part that conventions play in channeling and limiting responsibility, it becomes apparent that imputations of unconscious intention (empirically unverifiable anyway) are gratuitous in the case of abolitionists. What I aim to show in the next section of the essay is that abolitionists did not need to hide anything from themselves. All of us, no matter how humane, disown responsibility every day for known consequences of our own acts (and omissions) that are far more horrifying than those the abolitionists disowned when they chose to help slaves rather than wage workers. Keeping a clear conscience in spite of being causally involved in the suffering of others does not require self-deception. There was nothing distinctively selective about the abolitionists' preoccupation with chattel slavery: all humane action entails "selectivity." What enables us all — the abolitionists in their day, and you and me in ours — to maintain a good conscience, in spite of doing nothing concretely about most of the world's suffering, is not self-deception but the ethical shelter afforded to us by our society's conventions of moral responsibility. These conventions allow us to confine our humane acts to a fraction of suffering humanity without feeling that we have thereby *intended*, in any way, or *caused*, in any morally significant way, the evils that we do not relieve.

The reader may well suspect sleight of hand at this stage of my argument. Are not these social conventions merely collective forms of self-deception? And might they not conceal widely held unconscious intentions of the sort that Davis and many other historians have postulated? I think even a skeptical reader will be persuaded by the following arguments that the burden of proof rests heavily on anyone who makes these claims. The conventions I have in mind are always open to criticism from the vantage point of rival conventions (we certainly need not admire those of any earlier generation), but they are not the transient reflexes of any social interest, and not even the most extraordinary feats of moral gymnastics would permit a person to transcend the limits of all such conventions, thereby becoming perfectly humane and invulnerable to the charge of "selectivity."

To show that this is so, I ask the reader to participate in two mental exercises, which have a twofold purpose. First, they explore the problem of "selectivity" and highlight the role that conventions play in judgments of moral responsibility, thus wrapping up my criticisms of the self-deception argument and the social control thesis that it supports. Second, the longer of the two exercises, the "case of the starving stranger," brings into view the crucial anatomical features of the historical process that I believe gave rise to the modern humanitarian conscience. It thereby paves the way for an alternative to the social control explanation, one that does not rely on class interest as the link but nevertheless firmly connects capitalism with the emergence of the humanitarian sensibility.

First, to illuminate the charge of "selectivity" and self-deception, we can imagine ourselves to be in a situation analogous to that of the abolitionists, men and women living in the midst of a great change in moral sensibility. The crux of the analogy addresses the intriguing problem to which Davis returned again and again: why were the abolitionists so slow, at best, to concern themselves with the misery of free workers? That they *could* have been quicker to see through the formalism so characteristic of nineteenth-century liberalism and *could* have acknowledged the similarity of chattel slavery to wage slavery is sufficiently demonstrated by those contemporary reformers, such as Owen, Fourier, Marx, and Engels, who actually did so. But the fact that abolitionists could have been more concerned with the plight of the free laborer does not justify the speculation that they really knew they should be and only failed to be because they deceived themselves.

Imagine that fifty or a hundred years from now the world is swept by another great shift in moral sensibility—this time a wave of revulsion against man's carnivorous way of life. The possibility is not, after all, so far-fetched: philosophers have long debated what duties man owes to other sentient beings; antivivisection is an issue that has moved many; hard-boiled legislators pass statutes protecting endangered species; prominent publications like the *New York Review of Books* occasionally run articles on the problematical ethics of eating flesh. Dietary regulations occupy an important place in many religions, and whole Asian cultures have for extended periods regarded vegetarianism as a prerequisite to the ethical life. Moreover, we have in our midst many people who practice vegetarianism, providing a living model to those of us (including myself) who continue to eat meat.

If vegetarianism should someday become the mainstream point of view, how would the historians among our vegetarian descendants view us, their carnivorous ancestors? I suppose they would ask much the same questions about us that Davis asks about the abolitionists. How can we draw such an arbitrary line between human misery and the misery of nonhuman, but certainly sentient, creatures? Is not our comparatively intense concern for oppressed human beings a highly selective response to the general problem of predation, one that provides an outlet for demonstrating concern for suffering yet thereby gives a certain moral insulation to even more ruthless predatory practices in our society? Surely it would be tempting from the vegetarian point of view to say that all our busy efforts to alleviate human misery serve to isolate specific forms of suffering, thereby allowing issues of moral responsibility to be faced in a relatively simplified model. And they might even say that exaggeration of the harsh consequences of poverty, the pain of discrimination, the penalties of class, and the horrors of human warfare allows our most dedicated reformers to give tacit sanction to the systematic slaughter of nonhumans.

Readers who refrain from eating meat on ethical grounds may wish to endorse this interpretation insofar as it is an embodiment of their own anti-carnivorous values. But I think even they would agree that the vegetarian historian's interpretation is flatly wrong on two counts. First, it errs in tacitly assuming that, because some twentieth-century people are ethically opposed to eating meat, others must know in their hearts that it is wrong and can only maintain a clear conscience by deceiving themselves. It is conceivable to me that I may someday become convinced that eating meat is wrong, but by no stretch of the imagination can I persuade myself that in some way I already know that it is wrong. I continue eating meat not because I am deceiving myself but because whatever suffering my dietary preference causes falls outside the conventions of responsibility by which I presently live.[19] Second, the vegetarian historian would err even more egregiously if he supposed that we carnivores, in order to sustain our self-deceptions, busy ourselves with projects to alleviate human suffering as a means (conscious or not) of putting animal suffering out of mind. My indifference to animal suffering may depend on seeing only the end product of the butcher's work, but it does not depend on my all too infrequent efforts to alleviate human suffering. The vegetarian historian's error in imputing self-deception to us, his humane but unrepentantly carnivorous ancestors, is duplicated when we impute self-deception to the abolitionists on account of their failure to extend help to wage slaves.

Now let us proceed to a more elaborate exercise designed to show how inescapable conventions are in the allocation of moral responsibility, and how the conventions themselves change in time. Let us call this the "case of the starving stranger." As I sit at my desk writing this essay, and as you, the reader, now sit reading it, both of us are aware that some people in Phnom Penh, Bombay, Rangoon, the Sahel, and elsewhere will die next week of starvation. They are strangers; all we know about them is that they will die. We also know that it would be possible for any one of us to sell a car or a house, buy an airline ticket, fly to Bombay or wherever, seek out at least one of those starving strangers, and save his life, or at the very least extend it. We could be there tomorrow, and we really could save him. Now to admit that we have it in our power to prevent this person's death by starvation is to admit that our inaction—our preference for sitting here, reading and writing about moral responsibility, going on with our daily routine—is a necessary condition for the stranger's death. But for our refusal to go to his aid, he would live.

This means that we are causally involved in his death. Our refusal to give aid is one of the many conditions that, together, make up what John Stuart Mill called the cause "philosophically speaking" of this evil event. Now to say that we are causally involved is, of course, not to say that our failure to act is "the cause" of his death: it is only one among many conditions, and not every condition is properly regarded as "the cause." But the troubling fact remains that *but for* our inaction, this evil event would not occur.[20]

Why do we not go to his aid? It is not for lack of ethical maxims teaching us that it is good to help strangers. Presumably we all subscribe to the Golden Rule, and certainly if we were starving we would hope that some stranger would care enough to drop his daily routine and come to our aid. Yet we sit here. We do not do for him what we would have him do for us. Are we hypocrites? Are we engaged in self-deception? Do we in any sense *intend* his death?

I think not—unless, of course, we wish to stretch the meaning of intention way beyond customary usage, so that it indiscriminately lumps together premeditated murder with a failure to avail ourselves of an opportunity to do good. There is much more to say about the way we arrive at judgments of both causation and intention, but for my purposes it is enough to observe that the limits of moral responsibility have to be drawn somewhere and that the "somewhere" will always fall far short of much pain and suffering that we could do something to alleviate. What is crucially important to see is that we never include within our circle of responsibility all those events in which we are causally involved. We always set limits that fall short of our power to intervene. Whatever limits we do set can therefore always be challenged and made to look arbitrary or "selective" by insistent questioning—for they are finally nothing more than conventions. Good reasons can be given for preferring some conventions to others, but there is no escaping convention itself and even a degree of arbitrariness in our choice of which to accept. The necessity for being selective is built into the nature of the problem. Even the person who tries to extend his limits to encompass all those events in which he is causally involved will, in his futile efforts to save all the starving strangers in the world, have to choose whether to go first to Bombay or Calcutta and whether to begin with person X or person Y. These choices will appear no less arbitrary and reprehensible (at least to the stranger not chosen) than the convention that permits you and me to exclude this predictable consequence of our inaction from the category of intention, and to sit here with only a pin-prick of guilt as we contemplate our involvement in the stranger's death.[21]

Curiously, our feeling of responsibility for the stranger's plight, though nowhere near strong enough to move us to action, is probably stronger today than it would have been before the airplane. If William Wilberforce had faced this question in 1800, he at least could have begged off on the grounds that the sea voyage to India was long and costly and he might die en route. This suggests that new technology—using that word broadly to refer to all means of accomplishing our ends, including new institutions and political organizations that enable us to attain ends otherwise out of reach—can change the moral universe in which we live. Technological innovation can perform this startling feat, because it supplies us with new ways of acting at a distance and new ways of influencing future events and thereby imposes on us new occasions for the attribution of responsibility and guilt. In short, new techniques, or ways of intervening in the course of events, can change the conventional limits within which we feel responsible enough to act. Imagine that we have at our disposal an as yet uninvented technology, far more advanced than the airplane, that will enable us to save the starving stranger with minimal expenditure of time and energy, no disruption of our ordinary routine. If we could save him by just reaching out to press a button, then a failure to act would become indefensible. What convention previously enabled us to regard as an acceptably incidental concomitant of our inaction would then be transformed into heinous neglect or even—arguably—an intention to do harm. No convention could save us from responsibility then. And notice that this drastic change in our operative sense of responsibility could be brought about without any change at all in our ethical convictions. All of our ideas, every abstract formulation of moral obligation could remain the same; the only change needed to get us over the threshold of action is an expansion of the range of opportunities available to us for shaping the future and intervening in other lives. The latter point constitutes an especially telling objection to those who believe that humanitarianism can be explained merely by pointing to the proliferation of sermons and other texts on the importance of love and benevolence.

These "ways of intervening in the course of events" and "opportunities for shaping the future" play such an important role in the history of moral responsibility and will occupy such a prominent place in my analysis that they deserve a distinctive label. The word "technique" carries misleading connotations—of superficialities of style, on the one hand, and of highly organized bodies of scientific knowledge, on the other. What we need is a word that suggests the full range of practical know-how about cause-and-effect connections, from that required to put a man on the moon, at the upper end of the scale, to that needed to get in a harvest on time or mobilize the manpower and material needed to run a blacksmith's shop, at the lower and much more important end of the scale.

The philosopher Douglas Gasking not only suggested a suitably homely name in his essay "Causation and Recipes" but also explained why this category of practical formulas for getting things done is so important. The very idea of causation, in its most fundamental or primitive sense, is, according to Gasking, "essentially connected with our manipulative techniques for producing results." Not science but plain *recipe* knowledge, or technique in its most inclusive sense, is the wellspring of causal thinking. "A statement about the cause of something," wrote Gasking, "is very closely connected with a recipe for producing it or preventing it."[22] Although one can think of science as an elaboration of recipe knowledge, resulting from the substitution of open-ended inference-licenses for recipes, it is what Gasking called the "producing-by-means-of relation" that underlies causal thinking, and this relation emerges from man's most basic efforts to sustain life.

> Men discovered that whenever they manipulated certain things in certain ways in certain conditions certain things happened. When you hold a stone in your hand and make certain complex movements of arm and fingers the stone sails through the air approximately in a parabola. When you manipulate two bits of wood and some dry grass for a long time in a certain way the grass catches fire. When you squeeze an egg, it breaks. When you put a stone in the fire it gets hot. Thus men found out how to produce certain effects by manipulating things in certain ways: how to make an egg break, how to make a stone hot, how to make dry grass catch fire, and so on.[23]

What makes recipe knowledge important for the historian trying to understand the rise of humanitarianism is that neither causal perception nor feelings of moral responsibility can exist in the absence of appropriate recipes. One simply cannot see a human act (or omission) "A" as the cause of event "E" unless one possesses a recipe for producing events *like* "E" by means of acts (or omissions) *like* "A." And where the very possibility of causal perception is lacking, there can be no feelings of moral responsibility. By the same token, other things remaining equal, an enhancement of causal perception by the introduction of new or more far-reaching recipes can extend moral responsibility beyond its former limits.

Armed with this understanding of the dependence of moral conventions on recipe knowledge and causal perception, we can find in the case of the starving stranger many clues and research suggestions for the historian who wants to explain the origins of humanitarian sensibility. Although the clues point strongly in the direction of capitalism, they do not point toward class interest. To extract these clues, we will formalize the case of the starving stranger, recasting it as a set of preconditions that must exist before people will go to the aid of strangers.

There are four preconditions to the emergence of humanitarianism as a historical phenomenon. First and most obvious, we must adhere to ethical maxims that make helping strangers the right thing to do, before we can feel obliged to aid them. If our ethical convictions permit us to ignore the suffering of people outside our own family or clan, then there can be no basis whatever for the emergence of those activities and attitudes that we call humanitarian. Although adherence to appropriate maxims is indispensable, the case of the starving stranger shows that it is not enough by itself to provoke humane behavior. The Golden Rule alone provides a sufficient ethical basis for our deciding right now to get up and go to Ethiopia, yet we remain seated.

A second precondition, also illustrated in the case of the starving stranger, is that we must perceive ourselves to be causally involved in the evil event. Once again, being causally involved does not mean that we regard ourselves as "the cause"; only that we recognize our refusal to act as a necessary condition without which the evil event would not occur. Along with this prerequisite goes the third. We cannot regard ourselves as causally involved in another's suffering unless we see a way to stop it. We must perceive a causal connection, a chain of cause-and-effect links, that begins with some act of ours as cause and ends with the alleviation of the stranger's suffering as effect. We must, in short, have a technique, or *recipe*, for intervening—a specific sequence of steps that we know we can take to alter the ordinary course of events. As long as we truly perceive an evil as inaccessible to manipulation—as an unavoidable or "necessary" evil—our feelings of sympathy, no matter how great, will not produce the sense of operative responsibility that leads to action aimed at avoiding or alleviating the evil in question.

Although the possession of such recipes sets the stage for going to the stranger's aid, even this is not enough. Today you and I have a recipe for getting to Ethiopia and preventing starvation, we admit that our failure to go is a necessary condition for the stranger's death, and we all subscribe to the Golden Rule. Yet here we sit.

The fourth precondition, the one that finally gets us into a psychological frame of mind in which *some* of us will feel compelled to act, is this: the recipes for intervention available to us must be ones of sufficient ordinariness, familiarity, certainty of effect, and ease of operation that our failure to use them would constitute a suspension of routine, an out-of-the-ordinary event, possibly even an intentional act in itself.[24] Only then will we begin to feel that our inaction is not merely one among many conditions necessary for the occurrence or continuation of the evil event but instead a significant contributory *cause*.

To say that our refusal to aid the stranger assumes causal status only when it appears extraordinary against a background of ordinary recipe usage is to base ourselves securely in the existing literature on the philosophy and psychology of causal attribution, for that literature continually reaffirms that abnormality is the principal criterion that prompts us to single out certain events, acts, or conditions as causal.[25] The main reason you and I can go about our daily routine and not be overwhelmed with guilt about the stranger's plight is that the only recipe we have for going to his aid is far more exotic and more difficult to implement than the recipes we customarily use in everyday life. It involves a causal connection between his life and ours that is much more indirect, remote, and tenuous than the ones we habitually employ, so we do not regard our failure to act on the recipe as abnormal. None of us habitually liquidates major assets and departs on a moment's notice for the remotest parts of the globe in the pursuit even of selfish ends. If in our everyday routines we normally employed recipes as exotic as this one, then our failure to use it would begin to look extraordinary, and would therefore begin to assume causal status. And, once we begin to perceive our inaction as a cause of the stranger's suffering, then the psychological pressure to do something in his behalf can grow irresistible.[26]

These preconditions drawn from the case of the starving stranger help clarify both the way in which revolutions in moral sensibility ought to be conceived and the way in which they are to be explained. First, we ought to construe major alterations of sensibility such as the rise of abolitionism as the result of shifts in the conventional boundaries of moral responsibility. Thus, what emerged in the century after 1750 was not, in the first instance at least, either a new configuration of class interests or a novel set of values geared to the hegemony of a rising class. Instead, the principal novelty was an expansion of the conventional limits of moral responsibility that prompted people whose values may have remained as traditional (and as unrelated to class) as the Golden Rule to behave in ways that were unprecedented and not necessarily well suited to their material interests. What happened was that the conventional limits of moral responsibility observed by an influential minority in society expanded to encompass evils that previously had fallen outside anyone's operative sphere of responsibility. The evils in question are of course the miseries of the slave, which had always been recognized but which before the eighteenth century had possessed the same cognitive and moral status that the misery of the starving stranger in Ethiopia has for us today.[27]

The question historians need to answer is why events such as the death of the starving stranger sometimes move out of the morally indifferent category of "unintended consequences," for which no one feels any operative sense of responsibility, and become matters for which certain people feel acutely responsible. Here lies the second lesson to be drawn from our list of prerequisites: once revolutions in moral sensibility are understood to result from shifts in the conventional boundaries of moral responsibility, the task of explanation can be seen to consist in finding the historical developments that exerted an outward, expansionary pressure on those conventional limits. Our set of preconditions also suggests what successful explanations might look like by alerting us to the intimate relationship between feelings of responsibility and perceptions of causal involvement. It suggests that the limiting conventions by which people live are a function of the range of events in which they perceive themselves to be causally involved, either by commission or omission and, further, that the range of events in which they perceive themselves to be involved is shaped by the number and the "power" or "reach" of the recipes for intervention that they and the people around them habitually use. What expands a person's horizons of causal involvement, and hence potentially expands also his or her limits of moral responsibility, is the routine employment of recipes of great complexity or temporal extension. So what the historian needs to look for are historical factors that give people heightened confidence in recipes they already have or encourage them to develop new recipes, or more complex recipes, or recipes that reach farther into the future. Every new recipe, or increase in the "reach" or complexity of recipes, extends the horizons of causal perception and thereby broadens the sphere within which a person may *potentially* feel himself to be the cause of an unnecessary evil.

The word "potentially" requires special attention. We are not concerned with individual episodes of human kindness and decency—which I assume can occur anywhere, anytime—but with a sustained, collective pattern of behavior in which substantial numbers of people regularly act to alleviate the suffering of strangers. That, I take it, is what we mean by the emergence of a new humanitarian sensibility in the eighteenth century. Our aim, then, is to specify the minimum conditions that must be satisfied before this collective phenomenon can begin. Not all people who experience these conditions will become humanitarian reformers. In fact, most will not, and to account for those few who do, we would have to look beyond the limits of this explanatory scheme to conventional biographical and historical details about the teachings to which they were exposed, their personal temperaments, the depth of their religious faith, their courage, and so on.

Although the form of explanation suggested here does not pretend to explain why certain individuals become humanitarian reformers and others do not, it does alert us to the distinctiveness of the moral experience of people who are equipped with a large repertoire of far-reaching recipes. Because such people feel comparatively confident of their ability to intervene in the course of events and to shape the future at will, they are the prime candidates for the first historical appearance of that heightened feeling of causal involvement that is a prerequisite for humanitarianism. With the capacity to intervene goes the possibility of feeling obliged to take responsibility—but only the possibility. Many people, whose large endowment of recipe knowledge gives them the capacity to intervene, will not do so, or will do so only for the sake of self-aggrandizement, but some unusually sensitive individuals will be "trapped," as it were, by their broadened horizons of causal involvement and feel compelled to go to the aid of strangers for whose misery they would previously have felt no more than passive sympathy. The explanatory approach recommended here does not pretend to plumb the mysteries of individual sensitivity or compassion. It does, however, offer a way to understand why even the most scrupulous and compassionate men and women did not feel obliged to go to the aid of suffering slaves before the middle of the eighteenth century.[28]

Far from transforming acts of conscience into subtle reflexes of more fundamental drives, this explanatory approach permits us to give the humanitarian reformers full credit for their moral insight, their courage in the face of adversity, and their tenacity in uprooting entrenched institutions. They were consummate interpreters of a new moral universe. Yet it also enables us to see that their new interpretation was called forth by changes in the social and economic conditions of life and that, once the stage was set, similar measures almost certainly would have been carried out by other individuals if not by Wilberforce, Garrison, Phillips, and all the other formidable men and women who actually did the job. One need not pretend that human beings are uncaused causes in order to admire them.

Capitalism and the Origins of the Humanitarian Sensibility, Part 2

Having set forth the limitations of the social control thesis and explored the implications of the case of the starving stranger, we can now proceed to the third and final stage of the argument, a brief sketch—no more—of an alternative way to formulate the relationship between capitalism and the origins of the humanitarian sensibility. As the reader will recall, the thesis to be maintained here is that the crucial links between capitalism and humanitarianism stem not from the rise of the bourgeoisie per se but from its most characteristic institution, the market, and they are bonds created not by class interest but by the subtle isomorphisms and homologies that arise from a cognitive style common to economic affairs, judgments of moral responsibility, and much else.

This is not to deny that some effects of the attack on slavery furthered bourgeois interests. The consequences of the antislavery movement that Davis called "hegemonic" are real enough, but we have not been given any adequate reason to think they were produced by class interest, by a desire for hegemony, or by any other form of intention, conscious or unconscious. They belong mainly to the category of unintended consequences. "Hegemonic" exaggerates their purposefulness, and the term "self-deception" is not capable of clarifying their status. None of these conclusions require us to give up the most important contribution of Marxian historiography: the suggestion that the humanitarian impulse emerged when and where it did because of its kinship with those social and economic changes that we customarily denominate as "the rise of capitalism." The task now is to specify the nature and extent of that kinship.

First published in *American Historical Review* 90 (June 1985): 547–66.

One could argue in the spirit of Norbert Elias that the kinship is very strong indeed, that the practices we label "capitalistic" and the acts we identify as "humanitarian" are simply different manifestations of a single cultural complex, or "form of life." Elias's brilliant account of the shifting "thresholds of embarrassment" and "standards of affective control" that have regulated manners during European man's long ascent up the ladder of the "civilizing process" provides immensely suggestive insights into the present subject. One cannot help being amused by Elias's description of the gradual elaboration of rules and taboos affecting the polite way to spit, expel gas, blow one's nose, defecate, and lift morsels of food into one's mouth. But the boundaries between polite and impolite, permissible and impermissible, that operate in these comparatively trivial matters are not unlike the conventions that determine whether knowledge of a starving stranger will produce only passive sympathy or a flood of emotion and expressive action. Indeed, Elias devoted a chapter to the shift of boundaries that made brutality, one of the uncomplicated "pleasures of life" in the medieval period, deeply horrifying (though still titillating) to more modern sensibilities.[1] Incongruous though the thought may seem, the boundaries we observe today between good and bad manners could prove to be seamlessly interwoven both with the "capitalist" conventions that authorize the individual to adopt a comparatively high level of aggressiveness in economic affairs and with the "humanitarian" conventions that inhibit us from taking pleasure in (or even remaining indifferent to) the agony of others. Perhaps, as Elias said, "The question why men's behavior and emotions change is really the same as the question why their forms of life change."[2]

Although the explanatory approach recommended here converges with that of Elias, it is less holistic and more concerned with identifying specific mechanisms of change. It does not treat capitalism and humanitarianism as two expressions of a single form of life but does argue that the emergence of a market-oriented form of life gave rise to new habits of causal attribution that set the stage for humanitarianism. Before proceeding with the development of this form of explanation, however, we must pause to consider a possibility at the opposite end of the spectrum from Elias's holism — the possibility that there is no kinship at all between capitalism and humanitarianism. The idea that humanitarianism arose from or depended in any way on the marketplace, with its notoriously lax ethical standards, will seem perversely counterintuitive to many readers, and for good reason. The face of the market that we all know best, regardless of our political preferences, is the grim visage that warns "Caveat emptor!" Buyer beware! How, the skeptic may ask, can an institution that explicitly foreshortens or confines within narrow, formal limits the responsibility of each person for his fellowman be said to have extended anyone's sense of moral responsibility? That the market has faces other than this most familiar one is the principal argumentative burden of the following pages. Let us begin, however, by conceding the full force of the classical indictment.

Consider the rules of the marketplace as they were embodied in the Anglo-American law of contract at its zenith in the nineteenth century. The rules assume that everyone will put his own interests first and withhold even customary or neighborly levels of concern for everyone else. The seller charges what the market will bear, not what the buyer can afford to pay. In negotiating a contract, the parties deal at what the law calls "arm's length," each relying on his own skill and judgment, neither owing any fiduciary duties to the other. As they maneuver for advantage and work out the terms on which their carefully limited cooperation will proceed, the parties are neither obliged to volunteer relevant information nor entitled to expect others to do so. The deal is sealed by agreement. Differences of bargaining power, mistakes, pressures of time, ignorance of pertinent facts, subjective intentions are all beside the point, for these pressures are deemed to be a normal part of life in the marketplace. Unless the voluntariness of the agreement can be undercut by demonstrating force, threat, or fraud, each party can be compelled by law to carry out its part of the bargain, no matter how unjust the agreed-upon exchange of goods and services may appear to be.[3] In all of this there is undeniably a license for callousness, for the implicit assumption is that the individual is not only the sole proper judge of his own needs and interests but also their sole proper guarantor.

The most rigorous students of the market on the eve of industrialization, the political economists, by no means conceded that it was exclusively a force for moral indifference, but both friends and foes of capitalism often read into technical analyses of wage and price movements a very simple message: since the laws of supply and demand automatically transmute each individual's self-interest into the greater good of the greater number, no one need be concerned with the public interest. Once this lesson with its time bomb of antitraditional implications was incorporated into common sense, the very possibility of moral obligation was placed in doubt; the burden of proof henceforth rested on those who wished to deny that "everything is permitted." If we couple this familiar line of argument with the rich nineteenth-century folklore about avaricious landlords and piratical factory owners, and then add to that combination the metahistorical imagery of a class of me-first bourgeois individualists displacing a feudal aristocracy still enmeshed in a traditional web of clientage and patronage relations, we will indeed scarcely see how the coming of capitalism could have expanded the conventional boundaries of moral responsibility. And yet it did.

After nearly two centuries of criticism of market society, it is easy to forget how brutal life could be before the profit motive ruled supreme and how moderate, in the long perspective of human history, the capitalist's license for aggression really is. The paternalist code that required the lord to care for his dependents provided no basis whatsoever for systematically going out of one's way to aid strangers, and, even in the eighteenth century, Elias's "civilizing process" had made so little headway that most people could, like their medieval ancestors, still ignore a cry of "Help! Help!" without any feeling of distress.[4] As for the fabled greed of the capitalist, one can only say again what has been said so many times: although plentiful in the marketplace, greed is not the capitalist's distinguishing feature. As Max Weber put it:

> The impulse to acquisition, pursuit of gain, of money, of the greatest possible amount of money, has in itself nothing to do with capitalism. This impulse exists and has existed among waiters, physicians, coachmen, artists, prostitutes, dishonest officials, soldiers, nobles, crusaders, gamblers, and beggars. One may say that it has been common to all sorts and conditions of men at all times and in all countries of the earth, wherever the objective possibility of it is or has been given. It should be taught in the kindergarten of cultural history that this naive idea of capitalism must be given up once and for all. Unlimited greed for gain is not in the least identical with capitalism, and is still less its spirit. Capitalism *may* even be identical with the restraint, or at least a rational tempering, of this irrational impulse.[5]

The capitalist marketplace is a scene of perpetual struggle, and its tendency to inject calculations of least cost into every sphere of life can, indeed, stunt the human spirit. But contrary to romantic folklore, the marketplace is not a Hobbesian war of all against all. Many holds are barred. Success ordinarily requires not only pugnacity and shrewdness but also restraint.

The market presents another face—perhaps equally unsmiling but suggesting quite different conclusions—as soon as we think of it as the abolitionists and their generation often did: as an agency of social discipline or of education and character modification. Adam Smith's "invisible hand" was, after all, not merely an economic mechanism but also a sweeping new mode of social discipline that displaced older, more overt forms of control precisely because of its welcome impersonality and the efficiency with which it allocated goods and resources. The spread of competitive relationships not only channeled behavior directly, encouraging people through shifting wage and price levels to engage in some activities and disengage from others, but also provided an immensely powerful educational force, capable of reaching into the depths of personal psychology. The market altered character by heaping tangible rewards on people who displayed a certain calculating, moderately assertive style of conduct, while humbling others whose manner was more unbuttoned or who pitched their affairs at a level of aggressiveness either higher or lower than the prevailing standard.

The autonomous power of the market to shape character is often underestimated because of the stress Weber and more recent scholars have placed on the reverse of this phenomenon: the inability of the market to flourish where it lacks an ample supply of self-disciplined individuals, already made alert to the promptings of the invisible hand by inward-turning, self-monitoring habits like those taught by the Protestant sects. But on this point Weber was explicit: capitalism in Europe needed the personality-transforming power and sweeping recruitment capacity of religion only in order to breach the walls of traditionalism and gain a dominant position. Once the market has a secure foothold, said Weber, it no longer needs the support of religious doctrine because it independently "educates and selects the economic subjects it needs through a process of economic survival of the fittest."[6] Weber recognized an obvious and nonvicious circularity in the relationship between institutions and individual character: the institution of the market could not sustain itself without large numbers of "economic men," and, in turn, the proportion of these men to the population and the esteem in which they were held depended largely on the framework of opportunity and affirmation that the market established.

The form of life that the market both presupposed and encouraged is, of course, too complex to be adequately described in this essay, but at the expense of some oversimplification, we can think of the process in terms of two "lessons" taught (and simultaneously presupposed) by the market. The lessons were closely interwoven: the first taught people to keep their promises; the second taught them to attend to the remote consequences of their actions. Those who learned these lessons well and who could take for granted the existence of many others imbued with the same lessons were the first to cross the threshold into a new moral universe, one in which the horizons of causal perception were sufficiently wide, and the techniques routinely employed in everyday tasks sufficiently complex and future oriented, that failing to go to the aid of a suffering stranger might become an unconscionable act.[7]

Consider first the lesson of promise keeping. In the long history of human morality, there is no landmark more significant than the appearance of the man who can be trusted to keep his promises. The norm of promise keeping (observed often in the breach, as all norms are) is so basic to the form of life that prevails today that we take it for granted, forgetting how recently it came into being and at what cost, in terms of instinctual renunciation, this stage of the "civilizing process" was attained. Ironically, it was Friedrich Nietzsche — whom no one will accuse of being a friend of capitalism (or, for that matter, of humanitarianism or anything else requiring instinctual renunciation) — who gave the most eloquent testimony to the importance of this historical moment. He began the second essay of *On the Genealogy of Morals* with these words: "To breed an animal *with the right to make promises* — is this not the paradoxical task that nature has set itself in the case of man? Is it not the real problem regarding man?" Keeping promises can only occur to a human animal who has developed the capacity to remember what he once willed, and memory, argued Nietzsche, is diametrically opposed to animal good health. Forgetfulness, he contended (in passages strongly suggestive of Freud on repression), is "a form of *robust* health," without which man can experience "no happiness, no cheerfulness, no hope, no pride, no *present*." That, in spite of this, man has to a great extent become an animal with the right to make promises seemed to Nietzsche a "remarkable" achievement, a "tremendous labor" of self-overcoming, in view of the strength of the forces opposing such a development. Promise keeping requires

> a desire for the continuance of something desired once, a real *memory of the will*: so that between the original "I will," "I shall do this" and the actual discharge of the will, its *act*, a world of strange new things, circumstances, even acts of will may be interposed without breaking this long chain of will. But how many things this presupposes! To ordain the future in advance in this way, man must first have learned to distinguish necessary events from chance ones, to think causally, to see and anticipate distant eventualities as if they belonged to the present, to decide with certainty what is the goal and what [are] the means to it, and in general be able to calculate and compute. Man himself must first of all have become *calculable, regular, necessary,* even in his own image of himself, if he is to be able to stand security for *his own future,* which is what one who promises does![8]

Contemptuous though he was of asceticism, "bad conscience," and all the other signs of "morbid softening and moralization through which the animal 'man' finally learns to be ashamed of all his instincts," Nietzsche's attitude toward this basic phase of renunciation was decidedly respectful. In fact, the "ripest fruit" of this tremendous cultural process is what he called the "sovereign individual," who, precisely because he has earned the right to make promises, cannot but be aware of his "mastery over circumstances, over nature, and over all more short-willed and unreliable creatures." [9]

> The proud awareness of the extraordinary privilege of *responsibility*, the consciousness of this rare freedom, this power over oneself and over fate, has in his case penetrated to the profoundest depths and become instinct, the dominating instinct. What will he call this dominating instinct, supposing he feels the need to give it a name? The answer is beyond doubt: this sovereign man calls it his *conscience*.[10]

Set aside for a moment the surprising resemblance between the abolitionists and Nietzsche's "sovereign individual," with his terrific conscience and extraordinarily extended sense of responsibility; let us dwell, instead, on the relationship between more ordinary levels of self-overcoming and the rise of capitalism. Here Nietzsche allows us to make a crucial point. Historically speaking, capitalism requires conscience and can even be said to be identical with the ascendancy of conscience. This "tremendous labor" of instinctual renunciation on which promise keeping rests — a labor that even Nietzsche, a reckless critic of renunciation, felt obliged to endorse and make the starting point for his "sovereign individual" (one whose freedom would continue to be conditioned by his promises) — is an absolute prerequisite for the emergence of possessive individualism and market society. The individual cannot be said to possess his capacity to perform labor at some future time, or to be free to dispose of his labor to others for due compensation, until he is "self-possessed" — until, in other words, he can overcome his "healthy" forgetfulness and feel obliged to act on long chains of will.[11] And in the reciprocal manner that always holds between institutions and character, the practices and traits of personality that the market presupposes as a condition of its existence, it also induces and perpetually reinforces.

Conscience and promise keeping emerged in human history, of course, long before capitalism. Moreover, promise keeping is not merely a free-standing psychological trait but a cultural practice, deeply embedded in a fabric of social relationships and dependent in part on an effectively institutionalized threat of force in the event of noncompliance. But it was not until the eighteenth century, in western Europe, England, and North America, that societies first appeared whose economic systems depended on the expectation that most people, most of the time, were sufficiently conscience-ridden (and certain of retribution) that they could be trusted to keep their promises. In other words, only then did promise keeping become so widespread that it could be elevated into a general social norm. Only to the extent that such a norm prevails can economic affairs be based on nothing more authoritative than the obligations arising out of promises. And a growing reliance on mutual promises, or contractual relations, in lieu of relations based on status, custom, or traditional authority comes very close to the heart of what we mean by "the rise of capitalism."

Both the growing force of the norm of promise keeping and its synchronization with the spread of market relations are clearly inscribed in the history of the law of contract. A contract is, of course, an exchange of promises, and as such the law of contract provides us with a direct measure of the centrality of promise keeping in society. But the significance of the rising trajectory that we can trace in the history of Anglo-American contract law is not limited to this, for, in addition to being an exchange of promises, every contract is also an ensemble of mutually contingent recipes.[12] When people enter into contractual relations, each commits himself to bring to pass some designated future event, usually without bothering to spell out the intricate but taken-for-granted sequence of mundane cause-and-effect connections that he plans to rely on. Although the documents supporting contractual agreements ordinarily specify little more than the desired outcome, the very fact that the parties have contracted together signifies two things: a tacit claim by each promisor that he possesses the recipe knowledge necessary for producing the desired outcome and a tacit expression of faith by each promisee that the promisor's recipes do exist and can be expected to work. Contract law, therefore, supplies not only evidence of the growing force of conscience in market society but also evidence about the growing fund of recipe knowledge on which perceptions of causal involvement and moral responsibility necessarily rest.

The historical record shows that the norm of promise keeping attained only recently the ascendancy we take for granted today. In England before the twelfth century, promises exchanged by private individuals were generally beneath the notice of the king's courts. In that century and the next, a few contractual relationships gained legal sanction through writs of covenant, debt, and detinue. The rigidity and limited scope of these forms of pleading led to their growing circumvention by actions of trespass, or what today would be called torts or wrongs, and by the early seventeenth century a subspecies of trespass, the action of assumpsit (meaning "undertaking," or assumption of responsibility for bringing an event to pass), had developed into a general remedy for breaches of contract.[13] Extensive though the early development of contract law was, it pales in comparison to what happened in the last decades of the eighteenth century, when the hitherto gradual reorientation of English life to the market accelerated dramatically. So great was the corresponding leap of the law that as late as 1765, when Blackstone published his *Commentaries,* contract law played (by comparison to its later role) a "very small part in the legal scheme," amounting to little more than "an appendage to the law of property."[14]

In the decades following 1770, as contract law disentangled itself from property law and grew explosively, swiftly subsuming property law and much else within its widening province, a subtle shift occurred in the grounds of promissory liability, one that gave still greater impetus to the prodigious enlargement in the sphere of legally enforceable promises then under way. Traditionally, liability had rested on a combination of promise and consideration. Promise alone, the mere fact of a voluntary and deliberate declaration of intent to do something, was not enough. What made a promise binding was consideration, proof that there had been "adequate motivating circumstances" — such as a fee or other concrete benefit — to induce the promisor to give his promise. Since judge and jury determined the adequacy of consideration, this doctrine left an opening for judicial discretion and for communal standards of "just price" and fairness that imposed severe constraints on the kinds of contractual relations individuals were able to form.[15]

In decline, yet still surprisingly vigorous in Blackstone's day, these constraints gave way completely in the last decades of the eighteenth century and early decades of the nineteenth (the entire process in America lagging a couple of decades behind England). As Anglo-American law entered the "Age of Contract," it simultaneously shifted toward a pure "will" or "consensus theory" of liability according to which obligation arose less from consideration than from the naked will of the contracting parties — the very *nuda voluntas* that traditional law had rejected. Originating as a kind of tort, contract now took on its modern status as the antithesis of tort: obligations created not by law but by private agreement. Traditionally, the courts had been willing to enforce a promise only when the circumstances inducing the defendant to give it (the consideration) were so strong that he was in a sense obliged to perform the act in question whether or not he had promised to do so. A much wider range of promises became binding, as the courts abandoned any attempt to evaluate the circumstances underlying an uncoerced declaration of intention. Now that intent was a sufficient ground of obligation, a promisor could be made to perform, or pay damages in lieu of performance, even if he backed out of his contract before the promisee had relied, to his detriment, on the promise given. Even if the promisor had not yet received any of the benefits that the contract called for, he could he held liable. For the first time the law strained to make promisors generally liable for whatever expectations their promises created. Never before had promises counted for so much in human affairs, and never before had the penalties for being short-willed and unreliable been so severe.[16]

It is not merely coincidental that humanitarianism burst into bloom in the late eighteenth century just as the norm of promise keeping was being elevated to a supreme moral and legal imperative. It is obvious that the new stress on promise keeping contributed to the emergence of the humanitarian sensibility by encouraging new levels of scrupulosity in the fulfillment of ethical maxims. If one's customers and trading partners were increasingly conceded the right and actual power to invoke legal penalties for one's failure to live up to one's promises, what of the obligations created by one's covenant with God? The Golden Rule took on a new operational significance for pious men like John Woolman not simply because of an upwelling of piety. Also, the spread of market transactions changed the backdrop against which scrupulosity was measured: imposed on everyday affairs was an unprecedentedly high standard of conscientious performance.[17]

What of Caveat emptor? We have seen that the code of the marketplace encouraged contracting parties to treat each other in an unneighborly way, coldly and suspiciously—as strangers, in fact—and it is well known how devastating the consequences of this market-induced callousness could be, especially in relations between employers and employees. But even as the market shrank the conventional limits of moral responsibility in this respect, it was expanding them in others.

In the Age of Contract, those who engaged in market transactions *were*, more often, strangers, people who shared no tie of blood, faith, or community. Such people would not have dared to do business with one another but for the growing assurances provided them by the law and other market-oriented institutions that promises would be kept—even promises made to a stranger. For example, the dominance in the transatlantic trade that Jewish and Quaker merchants of New York and Newport enjoyed because of their ability to trust fellow believers in faraway ports broke down in the 1750s precisely because the norm of promise keeping had by then gained such force that the "arm's length" variety of trust needed to do overseas business was no longer confined to fellow members of persecuted sects.[18] Nor was the extension of trust to strangers the only way in which a promise-keeping form of life raised standards of scrupulosity. As Lord Kames, Scottish moral-sense philosopher and sessions judge, observed in his *Principles of Equity* (1767), "Contracts and promises are not confined to commercial dealings: they serve also to make benevolence a duty, independent of any pecuniary interest. . . . For it is remarkable in human nature, that though we always sympathize with our relations, and with those under our eye, the distress of persons remote and unknown affects us very little."[19] What made the customary level of indifference for the fate of strangers seem "remarkable" to Kames was the routinization of the norm of promise keeping in everyday affairs. And, of course, once indifference had become remarkable, it had potentially become unconscionable as well.

But scrupulosity is not enough. The case of the starving stranger shows us that even scrupulous adherence to ethical maxims need not lead to humane action. No matter how hard people strive to live up to moral codes, they have no occasion for feeling causally implicated in the sufferings of a stranger until they possess techniques capable of affecting his condition. Even then their response is not likely to go beyond passive sympathy unless the relevant techniques are so familiar that not to use them would stand out as an abnormality, a suspension of expected levels of carefulness. So in order to link capitalism with humanitarianism, we need to show not only that the market induced a higher level of conscientiousness but also that it expanded the range of causal perception and inspired people's confidence in their power to intervene in the course of events. Here lies the significance of the fact that contracts are both promises and mutually contingent recipes, for, as we saw in our hypothetical case, new ways of acting on the world, new recipes for producing desired events, are what push people over the threshold separating passive sympathy and humane action.

The explosive growth of contract law in the century following 1770 gives us a useful measure of the increasing frequency of recipe usage and the burgeoning fund of recipe knowledge available to the merchants, manufacturers, artisans, and improving farmers of England and America in these years. Not only was the fund of knowledge growing but recipes of increasing complexity and unprecedented temporal extension were being employed. In the early development of English law, suits for breach of contract typically involved simple undertakings like the conveyance of a cow across a river or the construction of a cottage, but by the end of the eighteenth century we find extremely complex transactions, often requiring the coordination of an intricate sequence of activities by people far removed from one another in space and time.[20] The variety of goals that private citizens pursued and the range of means available for pursuing them were clearly on the rise. In view of what we have learned from the case of the starving stranger, this is exactly the sort of development that we would expect to give some people such a strong conviction of their ability to intervene at will in the course of events that passivity would, for them, begin to appear abnormal and, hence, blameworthy. By the middle of the nineteenth century, this conviction was strong enough in the mind of an abolitionist like O. B. Frothingham that, although the evils of pauperism still struck him as "providential," something growing "out of the inevitable condition of things," the miseries of the slave no longer seemed beyond the reach of reform. Slavery, he wrote, is "an institution which the conscious will of man has built up, and which the same will, faithfully exerted, might . . . abolish in a year, a month, a week, a day. . . . Pauperism, from its nature involves no direct Guilt. Slavery is essential Guilt."[21]

The breathtaking confidence of the Age of Enlightenment is too well known to need any review here. Countercurrents of doubt and skepticism notwithstanding, doctrines of automatic progress enjoyed greatest currency during the century following 1750. Neither before nor since has European man felt so sure that merely by daring to use his own reason he might make himself master of both nature and fate. The supreme sense of individual and collective potency that prevailed in these decades made all existing institutional constraints seem malleable and contributed powerfully to the creation of a situation in which slavery could be challenged and other humanitarian reforms set in motion. To trace all the sources of this outburst of exaggerated pride in man's role as a causal agent, capable of shaping the future to his own will, would lead us far afield — for example, into the history of science and mechanical invention. But one important source lies close at hand in the market and in the impetus it gave to the accumulation and elaboration of manipulative techniques for the conduct of everyday affairs. It was not only the exotic achievements of Newtonian science or dramatic labor-saving devices like the steam engine that underwrote Enlightenment optimism but also the buoyancy supplied by a surge of homely recipes for getting things done.

By its very nature, the market encouraged the production of recipe knowledge. As the prime mover of a promise-keeping form of life, the market established a domain within which human behavior was cut loose from the anchor of tradition and yet simultaneously rendered as stable and predictable as "long chains of will" could make it. The combination of changeability and foreseeability created powerful incentives for the development of a manipulative, problem-solving sort of intelligence. As early as 1697, Daniel Defoe gave the name "projectors" to the distinctively future-oriented and knowledge-possessing men whose form of life was most closely attuned to the dynamics of market competition.

If industry be in any business rewarded with success, 'tis in the merchandizing part of the world, who indeed may be more truly said to live by their wits than any [other] people whatsoever. All foreign negoce [*sic*], tho' to some 'tis a plain road by the help of custom, yet it is in its beginning all project, contrivance, and invention. Every new voyage the merchant contrives is a project, and ships are sent from port to port, as markets and merchandizes differ, by the help of strange and universal intelligence; wherein some are so exquisite, so swift, and so exact, that a merchant sitting at home in his counting-house, at once converses with all parts of the known world. This, and travel, makes a true-bred merchant the most intelligent man in the world, and consequently the most capable, when urg'd by necessity, to contrive new ways to live.

Himself an exemplar of "the Projecting Humour that now reigns," Defoe devoted most of his *Essay Upon Projects* to no fewer than thirteen elaborate and ambitious plans for the improvement of national life, including a modernization of the banking system, construction of a national system of paved highways, establishment of nationwide pension and casualty insurance plans, a military academy, a college for women, and a "Fool's House" where the mentally incompetent would be sheltered from ridicule and exploitation.[22] As a recent student of economic thought and ideology in seventeenth-century England observed, "The extension of the market through individual initiative also worked to activate the participants' imaginative powers." Once the market had become a crucial regulator of human activity, dispensing rewards and providing valuable information, it could not but encourage "long-range planning through rational calculations."[23]

Not only raw intelligence—a *capacity* for envisioning the future and solving the problems it presented—but also solutions themselves took on added value under the market's aegis. Being imitative creatures, we humans solve most of our problems by adapting the techniques that have worked in the past to the different, yet partly similar, circumstances we now face. So the market's thirst for foresight and mental resourcefulness could not have been slaked without a quantum leap in the production, proliferation, circulation, and preservation of recipe knowledge. The extent and almost infinite variety of this homey sort of knowledge defies description, yet its importance can hardly be exaggerated. This expanding fund of ever more complex and powerful recipes for the conduct of daily affairs is what satisfied the critical preconditions for the emergence of the humanitarian sensibility.

The growing preoccupation of English and American courts with contractual litigation after 1770 mirrors the increasing density of recipe usage in the society outside the courtroom and thus reveals the power of the market to push outward the limits of causal perception and involvement. But contracts not only mirror recipe usage, they are themselves a singularly important kind of recipe for the mobilization of manpower and knowledge. When contracting parties commit themselves to bring certain designated events to pass, they fix the future with regard to those events, thereby providing each other with a significantly stabilized environment in which to operate. By making its own behavior predictable, each party to a contract enables the others to depend on it, and to incorporate its promised future performance into their own recipes as one ingredient. The result is a magnification of personal power, a way of doing collaboratively what no individual could do alone. Once the norm of promise keeping gained the legal sanction and the position of cultural ascendancy implied by the "will theory" of liability, the recipe of "contracting together" could become a powerful tool for shaping the future.

Among all the new techniques that flourished under the encouragement of the market, none did more to stretch people's sense of personal power — and therefore to extend their sense of causal involvement in other lives — than contractualism itself. And among all the sources of the humanitarian sensibility, none was more important than the contribution made by a promise-keeping form of life: a heightened sense of personal effectiveness created by the possession and use of powerful recipes — recipes made powerful in part by the growing calculability of a market society that tethered each ego to its own past intentions with "long chains of will," even as this society liberated each ego from traditional constraints on personal ambition. Nietzsche got the paradox right: by becoming sufficiently "calculable," "regular," and "necessary" to stand security for his own future, European man extended his sovereignty over nature and fate. And with every outward shift of the perimeter of sovereignty, the sphere within which conscience and responsibility potentially operated had to expand as well.

The promise-keeping aspect of the form of life spawned by the market did a great deal to satisfy the critical preconditions for the emergence of humanitarianism. But this was not the only contribution that the market made to the humanitarian sensibility. In fact, promise keeping can be regarded as only one particular manifestation of a still more fundamental lesson the market taught: to attend to the remote consequences of one's acts. The two lessons were so closely entangled that in discussing the first we have already touched on the second, but the second was taught in every phase of market life — not just in the making of contracts.

The force of the market's second lesson is evident in the special place assigned to the idea of principle during the entrepreneurial phase of capitalism. As the legal scholar P. S. Atiyah observed, the "Age of Contract" was also an

"Age of Principle." Since the term could refer to rules of moral conduct as well as to lawlike uniformities of nature, it bridged the widening chasm between nature and morality. "There were principles of political economy, principles of ethics and morality, principles of jurisprudence, principles of political behaviour, principles of commercial behaviour; there were also Men of Principle; and there was the contrast between Principle and Expediency."[24] No doubt Atiyah was correct to argue that the search for principles was sparked by the decay of traditional authority and the need for an alternative foundation flexible enough for a society of self-governing individuals. But more to the present point, the person who firmly grasped correct principles was one fit to prosper in a market society.

The defining characteristic of the "man of principle," the moral paragon of a promise-keeping, market-centered form of life, was his willingness to act on principle no matter how inconvenient it might be. Comparatively speaking, he cared little for the short-term consequences of his actions and was firmly convinced that in the long run, adherence to the highly generalized maxims of conduct that he called principles would produce the most desirable outcomes. His was a calculus of utility that assigned such low weight to immediate consequences and such high value to remote ones that he could seem at times to be above utilitarian considerations altogether. What gave him the assurance to do this was, initially, his faith in the principle he adhered to—a recipe, let us note, of a very general and overarching character, such as "Time is money" or "Never go back on your word." Armed with his principles, gaze fixed on the remote good they assured him he would receive, the man (or woman) of principle was a formidable character in history, if also a rigid and uncompromising one. The abolitionists were notoriously men and women of principle, and, as we noted earlier, they bear more than a passing resemblance in this regard to Nietzsche's "sovereign individual." Once again Nietzsche saw exactly what was required. In order to preserve the connection between an original "I will" and the actual "discharge of the will" at a later time, the man of principle must, like the sovereign individual, "see and anticipate distant eventualities as if they belonged to the present." He must, in other words, devote such close attention to the remote consequences of the various choices before him that he lives partly in the future.

To satisfy this *cognitive* precondition for the moral stature that goes with conscience and the right to make promises, one thing further is required: that man learn, as Nietzsche said, to "think causally."[25] Since thinking causally consists of linking present choices to consequences more or less remote in time by the use of recipes that map a route from one to the other, what crucially distinguishes the man of principle from all "more short-willed and unreliable creatures" is a preoccupation with the remote consequences of his actions— a preoccupation made possible by his possession of far-reaching recipes and "principles" and a form of life that validates his trust in them.

Earnest people with a bent toward self-control have existed in all human societies, and their personality traits have often enjoyed the endorsement of religion. But through most of recorded history, people imbued with these traits could not be at all certain that their earthly rewards would be measurably superior to the rewards accruing to less disciplined personality types. Scrupulous attention to remote consequences brings little advantage when life is either fixed by tradition or so lacking in fixity that it defies prediction. With the development of a market economy came a sweeping endorsement of self-control and all the traits that accompany it, in the form of palpable benefits that no one could ignore. Although the growth of political stability and economic abundance played an important part, it was mainly the disciplinary force of the market that provided the intricate blend of ceaseless change, on the one hand, and predictability, on the other, in which a preoccupation with remote consequences paid off most handsomely. Every recipe postulates a causal regularity, and the farther a recipe reaches into the future, or the more complex the qualitative transformations it calls for, the greater the risk that it will fail. The man of principle, who tries to live by recipes of the most extended and risky sort, can thrive only under conditions like those that prevailed in the early entrepreneurial phase of capitalism, when the future was at once open enough to the individual to be manipulable and yet closed enough to be foreseeable.

The premium the market paid for accurate forecasts was readily visible to anyone routinely involved in market transactions. Where direct experience with the market was lacking, the same lesson, suitably draped in a moral and religious vocabulary, was driven home by numerous Victorian moralists. Anticipating the remote consequences of one's actions was thought to require not only concentrated attention but also self-restraint and a capacity to delay gratification that the middle class found lamentably lacking in criminals, paupers, madmen, children—not excepting their own—and others who became objects of humanitarian concern. "Want of Reflection," declared John Burt, a typical prison reformer, "is preeminently the characteristic of the criminal. The habit is always wanting, often the capacity for it defective."[26]

The missionary zeal of the middle class to disseminate to each rising generation and to all "dependent classes" its own habit of deferring immediate gratification for the sake of remote and principled rewards is well known. Teaching people the virtues of reflection and close attention to the distant consequences of their actions came to be regarded as a universal key to social progress, whether in the education of children, the "moral treatment" of the insane, the cultivation of self-reliance in paupers (through plans like those of Samuel Gridley Howe), or the widely imitated incentive schemes of Alexander Maconochie, which were intended to produce the same effect among prisoners.[27] Early-nineteenth-century moral reformers felt that their crusade was succeeding, and, though they may have claimed credit for lessons that the market found its own ways to teach, there seems little reason to doubt that the character traits of the English and American populations did shift in these years. John Stuart Mill spoke as if the crucial battles had already been won when he claimed in 1835 that "the commonest person lives according to maxims of prudence founded on foresight of consequences. . . . The whole course of human life is founded upon the fact" that many consequences can be foreseen.[28] Although Herbert Spencer thought a severe regimen of prison discipline was appropriate for people "who dwell only in the present, the special, the concrete [and] who do not recognize the contingencies of the future," he favored comparatively mild treatment for the prison inmates of England, where liberal political institutions presupposed a population already habituated to "weighing distant results and being chiefly guided by them."[29]

Today it is obvious that Spencer and the Victorian middle class for whom he spoke greatly overestimated the universality of the values that a newly emergent form of life made supreme and underestimated the resistance to those values that would soon come not only from other classes but also from the sons and daughters of the middle class. But it should be equally obvious that the very possibility of feeling obliged to go to the aid of a suffering stranger — whether his suffering was that occasioned by chattel slavery or by what the observer interpreted as slavery to sin — was enormously heightened by the emergence of a form of life that made attention to the remote consequences of one's acts (or omissions) an emblem of civilization itself. On this issue Spencer and Nietzsche agreed: people who "dwell only in the present" live in a world that cannot sustain "bad consciences" or acute sensations of moral responsibility. To acknowledge this is not to say that all those who learned to dwell partly in the future became abolitionists. Clearly, most people equipped with the wide causal horizons that go with powerful recipes either devoted themselves to the new opportunities for self-aggrandizement that the market also opened up or, at best, tended their own gardens, abiding by traditional conventions of moral responsibility. But some of these long-willed people were bound to discover that traditional conventions confining their responsibility to family and neighbors were no longer compatible with the extended causal recipes they employed in everyday affairs. Attributing to themselves far-reaching powers of intervention, they also found themselves exposed to sensations of guilt and responsibility that their predecessors, no matter how conscientious, had not experienced.

What, then, did capitalism contribute to the freeing of the slaves? Only a *precondition,* albeit a vital one: a proliferation of recipe knowledge and consequent expansion of the conventional limits of causal perception and moral responsibility that compelled some exceptionally scrupulous individuals to attack slavery and prepared others to listen and comprehend. The precondition could have been satisfied by other means, yet during the period in question, no other force pressed outward on the limits of moral responsibility with the strength of the market. Since capitalism supplied only a precondition, no one need be surprised that the subsequent history of capitalist societies has not been greatly distinguished by humanitarian achievements. The argument presented here is not that markets breed humane action but that in the particular historical circumstances of late-eighteenth-century Anglo-American culture, the market happens to have been the force that pushed causal perception across the threshold that had hitherto made the slaves' misery (and much other human suffering) seem a necessary evil. One would no more expect markets continually to elevate the morality of the population than one would expect oxygen — in the absence of which ignition cannot occur — always to produce fire. Then, too, there is reason to fear that still another face of the market has prevailed in the later stages of capitalism, one that gave far less support to the humanitarian sensibility.[30]

The early Quaker abolitionist John Woolman supplies a fittingly concrete concluding illustration of the process we have been discussing. Familiar with the extensive libraries and busy countinghouses of family friends in nearby Philadelphia, Woolman, at age twenty-one, left his father's farm to keep books and tend store. Soon he opened his own retail store, learned the tailor's trade, and supplemented his earnings by keeping an orchard, teaching, drafting wills and legal documents, and conducting land surveys. "The increase of business became my burden," he later said, "for though my natural inclination was toward merchandise, yet I believed Truth required me to live more free from outward cumbers."[31] Giving up his store at age thirty-six, Woolman spent the rest of his life traveling widely as an itinerant Quaker minister, displaying everywhere a remarkable gift for challenging the morality of slaveholding without offending slaveholders.

The order of Woolman's thoughts in his classic 1746 essay, "Some Considerations on the Keeping of Negroes," corresponds closely to the stages I contend anyone would have had to undergo as he moved intellectually from a world in which slave misery provoked only the passive sympathy we feel today for starving strangers to a world in which remaining passive in the face of such misery seemed unconscionable. Woolman began with convention. Although the "customs" governing the extent of our duty to care for our fellowmen seem as deeply fixed in the nature of things as "the natural produce of a soil," said Woolman, the highest wisdom requires us to "forgo" these customs and adhere to God's "infallible standard: Truth." Conceding that God may have favored "us" over Negroes, Woolman insisted that it was not with any design that we exploit them or be indifferent to their fate. God's love is universal, and ours should imitate His. The "natural affection" that we tend to confine to our own immediate family is only a "branch of self-love," and it neither distinguishes us from inferior creatures nor satisfies our Savior's injunction to love all of mankind. The criterion by which we should test our conduct is known to us all: "How should I approve of this conduct were I in their circumstance and they in mine?" (198–203).[32]

Then Woolman addressed two anticipated objections. The first was that the Golden Rule does not really require care for strangers. This he countered with a passage from Leviticus: "The stranger that dwelleth with you shall be as one born amongst you, and thou shalt love him as thyself." The second was the slaveowner's plea that, having made an investment and undertaken risk, he was now entitled to the slave's labor. Here Woolman responded that the master's property in the slave is "wrong from the beginning. . . . If I purchase a man who hath never forfeited his liberty, the natural right of freedom is in him" (203, 204).[33]

Having called existing conventions of moral responsibility into question and pointed to an accepted ethical maxim that, if acted upon, would require radical changes of conduct, Woolman then graciously conceded the fallibility of human understanding and even a kind of limited relativity of values. This concession is extremely revealing within the framework of explanation developed here, because it is based on his clear recognition that many people in his society were virtually incapable of perceiving their acts or omissions as significant contributory causes of the slave's plight.

> While we have no right to keep men as servants for term of life but that of superior power, to do this with design by their labour to profit ourselves and our families I believe is wrong. But I do not believe that all who have kept slaves have therefore been chargeable with guilt. If their motives thereto were free

from selfishness and their slaves content, they were a sort of freemen, which I believe hath sometimes been the case.

Whatever a man does in the spirit of charity, to him it is not sin; and while he lives and acts in this spirit, he learns all things essential to his happiness as an individual. *And if he doth not see that any injury or injustice to any other person is necessarily promoted by any part of his form of government, I believe the merciful Judge will not lay iniquity to his charge. Yet others who live in the same spirit of charity from a clear convincement may see the relation of one thing to another and the necessary tendency of each; and hence it may be absolutely binding on them to desist from some parts of conduct which some good men have been in.* (211; emphasis added)

From Woolman's perspective, the slaveholder's conduct was not immoral as long as he failed to see "the relation of one thing to another and the necessary tendency of each." To persist after being convinced of these causal connections was another matter, and, of course, convincing slaveholders that their conduct had more distant consequences than they recognized was Woolman's lifework. If the points he addressed in his essay are any reflection of the arguments he heard as he traveled around the country meeting with slaveholders, the slaveholders' principal defense against Woolman's gentle prodding was the remoteness of their responsibility, as mere owners of slaves, for the undoubted misery inflicted on the slave by the person who enslaved him. Historians have treated this defense as a cynical dodge, but Woolman took it very seriously. The geographical remoteness of the scene of initial enslavement, argued Woolman, was no defense: "Great distance makes nothing in our favour. To willingly join with unrighteousness to the injury of men who live some thousands of miles off is the same in substance as joining with it to the injury of our neighbours." Nor was temporal remoteness any defense: "Can it be possible for an honest man to think that with view to self-interest we may continue slavery to the offspring of these unhappy sufferers, merely because they are the children of slaves—and not have a share of this guilt?" (233, 235).

It was, however, not only spatial and temporal remoteness with which Woolman had to contend. The misery of slaves seemed remote to his listeners in a more fundamental way. The crucial novelty of Woolman's own perspective—the element of his thinking that set him far apart from most of his audience in the 1740s but that, when more widely shared a century later, helped swell antislavery ranks—was his recognition of the causal relationship that exists in market societies between supply and demand.

Whatever nicety of distinction there may be betwixt going in person on expeditions to catch slaves, and buying those with a view to self-interest which others have taken, it is clear and plain to an upright mind that such distinction is in words, not in substance; for the parties are concerned in the same work and have a necessary connection with and dependence on each other. *For were there none to purchase slaves, they who live by stealing and selling them would of consequence do less at it.* (234; emphasis added)

How natural that a man who was both a devout Quaker, vigorously striving for a clear conscience in worldly affairs, and a skillful "projector," attentive to the remote consequences of his acts and familiar with the intricate web of mutual dependencies that the market establishes between buyers and sellers, should be among the first to see the seemingly civilized and law-abiding slave-owner as engaged in essentially "the same work" as the barbaric slave stealer. Woolman, writing thirty years before Adam Smith's *Wealth of Nations* put talk of supply and demand on everybody's lips, was ahead of his time and knew better than to be angry when his contemporaries failed to perceive the "dependence" and "necessary connection" that seemed so obvious to him. The idea that by owning a slave (or even a product of slave labor) one helped constitute the demand without which suppliers of slave labor could not stay in business gained plausibility in the decades ahead, as more and more people came to share in the form of life Woolman and other Quakers adopted so early.[34]

Within little more than one long lifetime after Woolman wrote, slavery, an ancient institution from which millions of people profited, directly or indirectly, was completely overthrown in North America and the British Empire. In spite of the enormous interests at stake, the rarity, even among abolitionists, of notions of racial equality, and the availability in England and America of a political-legal culture strongly oriented to the defense of property rights, surprisingly few people were willing to defend those who owned property in slaves. Thus, an institution, which, had it been evaluated in purely technical terms, might have represented a solution to the problems of labor discipline that modernizers everywhere confronted, was abruptly abandoned.[35] This astounding reversal of fortunes does not testify to the importance of "interests," which could as easily be said to have favored the opposite outcome, or to the autonomous power of high ideals, which are, in themselves, compatible with many levels of passivity and activism. What it shows instead is the force of the conventions that govern causal perception and moral responsibility, without which we would not know what our interests are or what it means to be responsible.

CHAPTER TEN

Responsibility, Convention, and the Role of Ideas in History

> It is commonplace — we are all Marxists to this extent — that our own society places unrecognized constraints upon our imaginations. It deserves, then, to become a commonplace that the historical study of the ideas of other societies should be undertaken as the indispensable and the irreplaceable means of placing limits on those constraints.
>
> — Quentin Skinner, "Meaning and Understanding in the History of Ideas" (1969)

The "unrecognized constraints" upon imagination of which Quentin Skinner wrote were those of convention.[1] History is, indeed, one means of bringing such constraints to light, as many besides Marxists can confidently attest. By reading between the lines of a historical text, alert to what is not being said because the author felt able to take it for granted, we become aware of differences in the conventions that shape our own thinking and those that prevailed in other eras.[2] Awareness of such differences cannot liberate us from convention — nothing can — but it can earn us a saving measure of maneuvering room vis-à-vis the seductive illusions of originality, intellectual self-sufficiency, and transparency of communicative intent that the present always holds out to us. An awareness of the role that convention plays in our own lives is no guarantee of wisdom, but without it we have no hope of interpreting the discursive

---

Parts of this essay draw on three previous essays of mine on humanitarianism and antislavery that first appeared in the *American Historical Review* between 1985 and 1987. Those essays now appear together with vigorously critical rejoinders by David Brion Davis and John Ashworth in *The Anti-slavery Debate: Capitalism and Abolitionism as a Problem in Historical Interpretation*, ed. Thomas Bender (Berkeley: University of California Press, 1992). Reviews of the Bender volume include Seymour Drescher, in *History and Theory* 32 (1993): 311–29, and Morton J. Horwitz, "Reconstructing Historical Theory from the Debris of the Cold War," *Yale Law Journal* 102 (1993): 1287–92. An important comment on and extension of the argument appears in David Eltis, "Europeans and the

280

practices of other times and places on their own terms. Denying our own dependence on convention, we mistake our own ways for universal ways and experience the Other as an imperfect approximation of ourselves, always obstinately falling short of the good, as currently and locally understood.

Insofar as the history of ideas[3] succeeds in exposing the operation of convention, it unavoidably highlights the limitations of reason, but it need not do so in a mood either of iconoclasm or of despair. Hans-Georg Gadamer's chillingly fatalistic assertion that "the self-awareness of the individual is only a flickering in the closed circuits of historical life" contrasts sharply with Skinner's guarded optimism.[4] A critic of Enlightenment excess who remains loyal to its central traditions, Skinner urges us to explore convention's shadowy domain of unconscious habit, presupposition, prejudgment, and prejudice neither to discredit reason, nor to belabor its shortcomings, but in hopes of strengthening its claims within a more defensible perimeter. When successful, a history that aims at elucidating the operations of convention equips us with some of the elementary cognitive tools we need in order to shape our own destiny. It does this even as it complicates our picture of life and gives us a degree of immunity against the "terrible simplifiers," as numerous in our generation as in any other. The prophylactic value of the history of ideas is perhaps greatest at a time such as the present, when the prevailing currents set strongly in the direction of social history. Insofar as harnessing the past to present politics is taken to be history's paramount virtue, and group interests defined in terms of race, class, and gender are believed to constitute a three-tiered royal road to historical understanding, social historians will not tarry long over convention, finding in it little more than a reflex of interest.

Without suggesting that all historians should be historians of ideas, or even that historians of ideas are always sensitive to the workings of convention, my aim in what follows is to set forth some of the problems and possibilities of such an approach through examination of a single example, the "idea" of responsibility. Far from thinking that the approach exemplified here is the wave of the future, or that aspiring young historians will find it an expedient career

Rise and Fall of African Slavery in the Americas: An Interpretation," *American Historical Review* 98 (Dec. 1993): 1399–423. Another essay by Seymour Drescher, "The Long Goodbye: Dutch Capitalism and Antislavery in Comparative Perspective," *American Historical Review* 99 (Feb. 1994): 44–69, is also relevant. I have received valuable advice about this essay—often taking the form of vigorous dissent from its conclusions—from Don Morrison, David Nirenberg, Larry Temkin, and Martin Wiener. What I say here has undoubtedly been influenced by all these critics and commentators, but of course they bear no responsibility for my views, and this essay is not meant as a response to any of them.

choice, I believe on the contrary that the history of ideas will continue to be uphill sledding in a discipline most of whose members will, in all likelihood, continue to define themselves by their discomfort in the presence of "ideas." Possession of a Ph.D. in history is no guarantee of sensitivity to anachronism, any more than it is proof against parochialism or epistemological naiveté. As long as historians continue to flee from theory, confuse description with explanation, and make a fetish of accumulating redundant empirical detail, the approach set forth here will seem to most members of the profession an unduly abstract and exotic enterprise. That means, however, that those who do adopt such an approach will do so out of conviction, not conformist expediency, and in that lies the principal strength of the history of ideas today.

My debt to Quentin Skinner is already apparent. In the interest of brevity, my plan here is to hoist myself up on the shoulders of two other scholars, neither of them historians, who have had penetrating things to say about the conventions that had to prevail before "responsibility" could take on its present range of meanings. The first is Friedrich Nietzsche, who had no qualms at all about asserting the priority of convention over reason, just so long as he secured recognition that both were subordinate to the "will to power." The second is the philosopher Bernard Williams, whose recent book, *Shame and Necessity*, addresses (among other issues) a classic problem: the puzzling absence from ancient Greek culture, in spite of its undeniable philosophical sophistication, of any conception of responsibility capable of sustaining an attack on slavery. Although the judicious balance Williams strikes between the claims of reason and the force of convention has much to commend it, I shall argue that certain amendments might yield a still more satisfying formulation.

"Responsibility" is a word of surprisingly recent coinage. Like "individualism" and "altruism," French imports that entered the English language only in the 1830s, "responsibility" plays such a central role in the form of life we inhabit today that it is not easy to imagine how our ancestors ever got along without it. Yet the word is as young as the United States, its first recorded usage having occurred in 1788, during the debate over the Constitution. Federalist paper 63, written by James Madison, speaks of frequent elections as a means of ensuring "a due responsibility in the government to the people," and notes that "responsibility, in order to be reasonable, must be limited to objects within the power of the responsible party."[5] "Responsibilité" first appeared in France at about the same time.

Although born under political auspices, the word's meaning has never been confined to politics. This is not surprising—although the abstract noun "responsibility" was new in 1788, the adjective "responsible" was not. No counterpart either to the noun or to the adjective existed in classical Latin, but "responsible" or its equivalents existed in French as early as the thirteenth century, in English by the end of the sixteenth century, and in German by the middle of the seventeenth century. These dates considerably lengthen the word's lineage, yet even they seem surprisingly recent, given the primal quality of the values and practices to which the word refers. Once coined, "responsibility" was easily assimilated to philosophical controversies that had been begun in other terms, such as "free will," "accountability," "answerability," and "imputability." Richard McKeon found the earliest philosophical treatment of responsibility in 1859, when Alexander Bain mentioned it only to recommend an alternative, "punishability." Bain contended that "a man can never be said to be responsible, if you are not prepared to punish him when he cannot satisfactorily answer the charges against him." John Stuart Mill agreed, declaring in 1865 that "responsibility means punishment." By the 1880s, L. Lévy-Bruhl was using the term in a more ambitious way that made it a touchstone for moral inquiry of all kinds, but precisely because the term could be so easily substituted for older alternatives, McKeon concludes that its introduction did little to alter the course of philosophical debate.[6]

The element of continuity should not be exaggerated, however. What is most intriguing about the comparatively short etymological lineage of "responsible" and "responsibility" is the thought that our conceptions of morality and human agency, in which these terms figure so prominently today, may be less a timeless feature of human nature and more the product of changing historical conditions than is commonly recognized. No one would argue that the consequentiality of human choice only began to be noticed in 1788, but it puts no strain on common sense to suggest that the emergence of a new word signifies something new in the lives of those who use it. At the very least we might say that a relationship between persons and events that had hitherto been a comparatively compartmentalized matter, discussed in other terms by theologians and philosophers, took on in these years a sufficiently novel prominence or centrality in everyday political and civil affairs to prompt the adoption of a new word, one sufficiently attractive that it came into wide use, eventually displacing established alternatives. Praise and blame obviously were not new in 1788, but conventions governing their imputation may well have been changing—possibly in response to rising standards of accountability in government, triggered by democratic revolutions in America and France; or more broadly in response to an escalating sense of human agency, fostered not only by political events but also by economic development and the accelerating pace of technological innovation in societies increasingly oriented to the market.

Developments of this kind, originating far outside the usual orbit of the history of ideas, alter everyday social practices and expectations and thus are liable to change the tacit conventions by which people live and assign meaning to their lives. It was to just such conventions that Quentin Skinner called attention, but for reasons that differ from mine in one significant way. He was concerned about the danger of misunderstanding historical texts through failure to grasp the context of social and linguistic conventions in which they were written. "An understanding of conventions, however implicit," he argued, is a "necessary condition for an understanding of all sorts of speech act[s]." Texts written in the past obviously pose special problems of interpretation because the passage of time threatens to disrupt the shared conventions on which both author and reader rely: "The success of any act of communication necessarily depends on at least a mutual intuiting by Speaker and Audience of a whole complex of conventions, social as well as linguistic, about what can and cannot be stated, what sorts of meanings and allusions can be expected to be understood without having to be explicitly stated . . . and in general what criteria for the application of any given concept . . . are conventionally accepted as applying in that given situation and society."[7]

When we shift our attention to the subject of this essay, the history of responsibility, sensitivity to the role of convention can help us avert another kind of misunderstanding, one that concerns not the intended meaning of *texts* but the ethical import of *actions* (and, equally important, *omissions to act*). If the rules for imputing praise, blame, and responsibility (or, to speak generically, moral liability for the consequences of one's acts and omissions) have indeed varied in time, as few historians will doubt and the recent emergence of the very word "responsibility" strongly suggests, then obviously there is a danger that we historians will unwittingly project into the past our own attributive conventions, supposing them to be universal, when in truth they are of recent vintage and therefore not simply or straightforwardly applicable to people who lived prior to their ascendancy.

Although my argument is addressed to the danger of misunderstanding acts and omissions rather than texts, in other ways it closely parallels Skinner's. Thus Skinner warned that

> the historians of our own past still tend [perhaps because our own past looks more familiar than a primitive society] to be much less self-aware than the

social anthropologists have become about the danger that an application of familiar concepts and conventions may actually be self-defeating if the project is the understanding of the past. The danger in both types of study is . . . that Audience at time two will "understand" Speaker at time one to have intended to communicate something which Speaker at time one might not or even could not have been in a position at time one to have had as his intention."[8]

The parallel danger concerning action and responsibility is that we will retrospectively condemn past actors for failing to live up to a set of obligations that, although familiar and normative in our era, may not have been in place at the time the actors lived. In ethical acts as in communicative acts, the passage of time breeds misunderstanding by occluding past conventions, creating, as it were, a vacuum into which the conventions of our own day rush with a specious appearance of naturalness.

Skinner focused all his attention on the single sin of anachronism, the better to catechize his readers on rules suitable for its avoidance. But we would do well to remember that anachronism is the twin of ethnocentrism. These two primordial sins against cosmopolitan understanding mark, respectively, the diachronic and synchronic axes between which the entire universe of human affairs is suspended. It makes little difference whether we describe the sin in question as a failure to acknowledge the force of convention, developing through time, or a failure to acknowledge the force of culture, varying from one human community to another. The temporally varying "social and linguistic conventions" to which Skinner called attention are, after all, seamlessly interwoven with the multiple levels of meaning that anthropologist Clifford Geertz was evoking when he called for "thick description." Geertz said that in order to make sense of human conduct we must pay close attention to "webs of significance," "stratified hierarch[ies] of meaningful structures," "piled-up structures of inference and implication," and "socially established structures of meaning." These are the elements of which culture is comprised, and culture is nothing other than convention, frozen at a moment in its development. To be sure, "culture" has in recent decades become for historians as well as anthropologists the more familiar term; some may even think of it as the more inclusive and interesting category, of which convention is only a particular (and perhaps oppressive) part. But "culture" in this non-evaluative, anthropological sense is a twentieth-century neologism that has not yet displaced "convention" in the vocabulary of philosophers. For both Skinner's purposes and mine, "convention" is the more generic and therefore the more resonant and inclusive category.[9]

All three projects have much in common. Geertz worried about "thin descriptions," culturally myopic and therefore incapable of detecting any difference between involuntary tics and meaningful winks. Skinner worried about an anachronistic way of reading texts, one that highlighted "perennial problems" only to lose sight of the shifting meanings that words acquire as language games change from one generation to the next. Transposing their concerns to the realm of ethics, I worry about a facile moralism that, in trying to create a more "usable" past, disregards (usually inadvertently) historical changes in the way human beings have allocated praise, blame, and responsibility. All three of us preach against complacency and warn that convention's grip is too often underestimated, even by professional historians.

One last caveat is in order. If being oblivious to the role of convention has its dangers, so of course do exaggerations of convention's force. This is true in ethnography and textual criticism as well as ethics, but the danger is especially acute in ethics because the very idea of moral responsibility implies the existence of obligations that overleap narrow boundaries of place and time. Exaggerating the force of convention reduces morality to the will-o'-the-wisp of social conformity, depriving it of any legitimate force of its own and allowing it no purchase beyond the borders of a particular community at a moment in time. The classic defense against this danger is to invoke, not mere conventions — things of human creation — but absolute standards that are said to be timeless and universal, having their being outside human history altogether. Denying, as it must, history's first lesson of change, this maneuver gets historians nowhere. But neither will it do to run to the opposite extreme, saying that the rules of human conduct change with every passing breeze and are wholly contingent on time, place, and situation. Between the local and the universal there is much middle ground, well suited to human habitation. The trick in achieving balance is to give the devil of convention his due, without abandoning the claims of reason. Balancing acts are, of course, easier to recommend than to perform, but that is no argument for stepping off the wire into the void.[10]

Although Friedrich Nietzsche cared little for balance, he deserves our attention because no one has explored with greater insight the conventions and presuppositions underlying modern concepts of responsibility. He opened the second essay of *On the Genealogy of Morals* with an eloquent tribute to responsibility. "To breed an animal *with the right to make promises*," he asked, "is this not the paradoxical task that nature has set itself in the case of man? Is it not the real problem regarding man?" Keeping promises is a habit that can only be formed by a human animal that has developed the capacity to remember what it once willed and then act on that memory rather than immediately felt wants. Memory, argued Nietzsche, is a precondition of responsible conduct, yet it obstructs the fulfillment of this moment's desires and is in that sense diametrically opposed to animal good health. Forgetfulness, he contended (in passages strongly suggestive of Freud on repression), is "a form of *robust* health," without which man can experience "no happiness, no cheerfulness, no hope, no pride, no *present*."[11]

However formidable the obstacles, humans have to a great extent become animals with the right to make promises. This seemed to Nietzsche a "remarkable" achievement, a "tremendous labor" of self-overcoming. Spelling out the cognitive and psychological elements of responsible conduct to show how much was at stake, he put causal thinking at the center of the drama.[12] Keeping promises presupposes not only memory, linking past to present, but also a causal imagination that construes the present as a staging ground for the construction of the future. Promise keepers must not only suspend present impulse and remember what they once willed, but also know how a desired future state of the world can be produced by action undertaken in the present. Promise keeping, Nietzsche wrote, requires

> a desire for the continuance of something desired once, a real *memory of the will*: so that between the original "I will," "I shall do this" and the actual discharge of the will, its *act,* a world of strange new things, circumstances, even acts of will may be interposed without breaking this long chain of will.
>
> But how many things this presupposes! To ordain the future in advance in this way, man must first have learned to distinguish necessary events from chance ones, to think causally, to see and anticipate distant eventualities as if they belonged to the present, to decide with certainty what is the goal and what [are] the means to it, and in general be able to calculate and compute. Man himself must first of all have become *calculable, regular, necessary,* even in his own image of himself, if he is to be able to stand security for *his own future,* which is what one who promises does!
>
> This precisely is the long story of how *responsibility* originated. (58–59)

Scornful of asceticism, "bad conscience," and all the other signs of "morbid softening and moralization through which the animal 'man' finally learns to be ashamed of all his instincts," Nietzsche nonetheless had immense respect for the early phase of instinctual renunciation that made responsibility possible. He likened the acquisition of causal thinking and calculability to the evolutionary emergence of amphibians. Just as the first animals to give up the buoyancy of the sea had to fight instinct every step of the way and learn by trial and error how to carry themselves erect on land, so in the development of responsibility human animals who were "well adapted to the wilderness, to war, to prowling, to adventure," suddenly found all their instinctual drives "disvalued" and had to rely on "consciousness," their "weakest and most fallible organ!" (67, 84).

The "ripest fruit" of this stupendous development was what Nietzsche called the "sovereign individual," who, having earned the right to make promises, could not but be aware of his "mastery over circumstances, over nature, and over all more short-willed and unreliable creatures." "The proud awareness of the extraordinary privilege of *responsibility,* the consciousness of this rare freedom, this power over oneself and over fate, has in his case penetrated to the profoundest depths and become instinct, the dominating instinct. What will he call this dominating instinct, supposing he feels the need to give it a name? The answer is beyond doubt: this sovereign man calls it his *conscience*" (59–60). Ironically, it was this great historical drama—the advent of the responsible, conscientious, sovereign individual, an "animal soul turned against itself" so as to become worthy of "divine spectators"—that inspired Nietzsche's grandiose fantasies about the coming of an overman, a still higher and more godlike specimen of humanity who would exercise his will to power without guilt, thereby rescuing Europe from self-loathing and rendering the choice between good and evil obsolete (85).

Alexander Bain had linked responsibility to punishment and called attention to the metonymic character of the word. Just as "crown" can stand for royalty and "miter" for episcopacy, so he believed that "response" had come to stand for something more complex: the practice of allowing accused criminals, before being punished, to answer the charges against them. Nietzsche, for whom responsibility was, in the first instance at least, a cultural phenomenon rather than a philosophical concept, assigned a more creative role to pain. Etymological evidence persuaded him that punishing offenders because they could have acted differently was a late and subtle form of judgment that would have made little sense to our ancestors. Long before notions of voluntariness and just deserts appeared on the scene, punishment was an expression of unbridled rage, channeled only by a crude equivalence presumed to exist between money and pain. Nietzsche believed that in primitive times, creditors unable to collect debts were compensated by being given license to inflict bodily harm on the debtor, the degree of harm corresponding to the size of the debt. The delight of inflicting pain, he thought, "constituted the great festival pleasure" of primitive man; turned inward and directed against one's own "natural inclinations," the infliction of pain became the source of all the "good" things on which we moderns pride ourselves, including reason and responsibility. "We modern men are the heirs of the conscience-vivisection and self-torture of millennia" (95, 66, 62).[13]

Nietzsche dramatized—some would say overdramatized—the historicity of responsibility while leaving its chronology wholly indeterminate. Some stages of the (highly conjectural) developmental process he described would have had to occur in prehistoric times, others early in the Christian era, still others much more recently. The most radical of historicists, he was no historian and cared not at all about dates. Since today we still lack anything even remotely approaching a history of responsibility, no one can specify when the various elements of this form of life came into play, or how fully it has been embraced by different peoples at different times and places. We have only a few scattered landmarks to help us get our temporal bearings.

Max Weber, who read and respected Nietzsche, took the Protestant Reformation of the sixteenth century to be the great watershed between "traditional" and "rational" (or modern) ways of life in Europe. If Weber was right, the ascetic values that largely define responsible conduct in Western culture today were initially cultivated in monasteries and oriented to otherworldly goals, but they were carried into the marketplace of everyday life and evolved in close conjunction with capitalism from the time of the Reformation forward. Any thought of a link between capitalism and rising standards of responsibility may seem paradoxical, yet Weber's point was sound: Even though market economies live by the rule of Caveat emptor and deliberately shrink responsibility in some dimensions (e.g., the limited-liability corporation), they also depend on a norm of promise keeping and cannot thrive without an ample supply of calculating, self-disciplined "economic men" (and women), alert to their interests and acutely attentive to the remote consequences of their conduct. It is among people of just this consequentialist cast of mind that perceptions of responsibility are most likely to flourish.[14] My assumption is not that the market elevates morality, but that the form of life the market fosters may entail the heightened sense of agency and enlarged causal horizon without which Nietzsche's "long-willed" sovereign individual cannot function, whether for good or evil. The expansive causal imagination that enables the entrepreneur confidently to assume responsibility for constructing a profitable future is no less necessary for ambitious projects of humanitarian reform than for brutal schemes of self-aggrandizement.

Recent research by social historians suggests that, as a cultural and psychological phenomenon, the ethic of responsibility had not achieved dominion at all levels of European society even as late as the mid-nineteenth century.

Middle-class moralists of the Victorian era no doubt indulged their own hunger for amour-propre and underestimated the degree to which responsible conduct presupposes economic security, but they were probably not wrong to sense in working-class culture an attitude more fatalistic and more tolerant of irresponsibility than that of their own class. Evangelical Protestants in England certainly felt that they were fighting an uphill battle as they tried to inculcate habits of foresight, repression of impulse, and delay of gratification in working-class populations.[15] "Thinking causally" and anticipating "distant eventualities as if they belonged to the present" are not built into human nature. These traits are no less historical than the rational forms of acquisitiveness that Weber associated with the market and traced back to the worldly asceticism of the early Protestants. Such traits helped constitute the cultural phenomenon that Nietzsche thought so momentous, but the triumph of responsibility may have been more recent than either Nietzsche or Weber recognized—if, indeed, it is complete even today.

Nowhere has the developmental chronology of responsibility been more vigorously debated than in the case of ancient Greece. If there is ample room for disagreement about the timing and the uneven spread of the ethic of responsibility in modern European societies, there has until recently been nearly a consensus about its absence from the world of Homer. In a passage that rivals Nietzsche in eloquence, the Italian writer Roberto Calasso expresses a widespread view when he describes Homer's world as one in which people and events were threaded together by a logic very different from our own.

> Whenever their lives were set aflame, through desire or suffering, or even reflection, the Homeric heroes knew that a God was at work. . . . They were more cautious than anybody when it came to attributing to themselves the origins of their actions. . . . The moderns are proud above all of their responsibility, but in being so they presume to respond in a voice that they are not even sure is theirs. The Homeric heroes knew nothing of that cumbersome word *responsibility*, nor would they have believed in it if they had. For them, it was as if every crime were committed in a state of mental infirmity. But such infirmity meant that a God was present and at work. What we consider infirmity they saw as "divine infatuation" (átë). . . . Thus a people obsessed with the idea of hubris were also a people who dismissed with the utmost skepticism an agent's claim actually to *do* anything.[16]

Calasso's eloquence skates on the edge of exaggeration. Different from us though the ancients were, they did not regard one another merely as playthings of the gods or straws in the wind of fate. For the most part, they saw each other as authentic actors and assigned praise and blame accordingly. True, as Calasso says, they left many an opening for divine intervention, but they were not in this respect wholly different from the Christians who came after them, who also found it difficult to reconcile human accountability with divine strength. From Pelagius in the fifth century to Arminius in the seventeenth, devout Christians quarreled about responsibility for sin and salvation in a world ruled by a God whose power was immense—so immense that incautious commentators could make it seem to crowd human responsibility out of the picture altogether, depriving humans of any rationale for doing good and threatening to make God the author even of sin. How could one construe human choice as effective without seeming to limit the limitless sovereignty of God? To that question the response of Aquinas was that "in all things that operate God is the cause of their operating"—yet he never meant to suggest that God's hand guided that of the assassin or the thief. The orthodox formulation, which Aquinas helped devise, was that "providence does not exclude freedom of the will," but words like these only papered over the problem that would finally break the Christian church in two.[17] When Luther and Calvin attacked "good works" and denied that the will could be free, they were recommending in regard to the paramount issue of salvation an attitude similar to that which Calasso says the Greeks displayed in all aspects of life: "skepticism [about] an agent's claim actually to *do* anything."

The difference between the Greeks and ourselves is neither the number of gods they had to accommodate nor the fact that some of their beliefs were contradictory. The past two centuries of secular social thought show that, even in the absence of any god, speculation about freedom and fate never escapes contradiction for long. Rather, the difference lies in the absence or the seeming immaturity in Greek culture of concepts such as decision, will, intention, and guilt. In the passage above, Calasso echoes Nietzsche in giving the ancients credit for a certain profundity about the limits of human mastery, a profundity that is easily mistaken for superficiality. Yet even Nietzsche gave some credence to the widespread impression that, when all is said and done, there is something childlike and premoral about the ancients. In its boldest form, the idea is that with a few exceptions such as Plato, Aristotle, Socrates, and some versions of the character Antigone, the Greeks were indeed children in a Piagetian tale of moral development, in which we moderns figure as the adults.[18]

This "progressivist" scenario has come under sharp attack from Bernard Williams. In *Shame and Necessity* (1993) he argues on the contrary that "many of the most basic materials of our ethical outlook are present in Homer . . .

what the critics find lacking are not so much the benefits of moral maturity as the accretions of misleading philosophy." Although Homer lacked words for "intention" and "decide," the "idea is there," says Williams. Williams concedes that it makes some sense to speak of ancient Greece as a "shame culture," but he challenges the usual distinction between shame and guilt, suggesting that internalized fear of shame functioned among the ancients in much the same way that the interior goad of guilt is said to operate in more modern psyches. At the heart of his dissatisfaction with the progressivist account are its tacitly Kantian assumptions about the nature of morality. The main thing he thinks moderns find missing in Greek thought is Kant's radical distinction between autonomy and heteronomy, which he considers religious in inspiration and largely illusory in practice. Insofar as the Greeks refused to think of morality as adherence to laws disclosed either by reason or divine illumination, Williams thinks they were not immature, but wise.[19]

Although he does not deny the existence of important differences, Williams highlights the similarity of modern and ancient thinking about human responsibility by suggesting that all judgments of responsibility consist of some combination of four elements: *cause, intention, state,* and *response.* "These are the basic elements of any conception of responsibility." Williams believes that these elements were as apparent to Homer as they are to us, and although Homer combined them in ways that are unfamiliar to us (and often unsuited to the world we now live in), we have no grounds for considering our ways superior. "There is not, and there never could be, just one appropriate way of adjusting these elements to one another" (55).

The first of the four elements, causation, is primary. "Without this," as Williams says, "there is no concept of responsibility at all" (56). Human beings act, and their acts alter an existing state of affairs. Sometimes the alteration is intended, sometimes not. Either way, some may welcome the new state of affairs, but others may deplore it, and when it is deplored a demand may arise for some response from the originating actor. This may be a demand that the actor makes upon himself, or the demand may be made by others, or both. When the new state of affairs is welcomed, the question becomes one of praise rather than blame. In any event, there will be interest in the actor's intentions, if for no other reason than to understand what has happened.

These are, Williams admits, "banalities," but "universal" ones, present in any historical or cultural setting. His central point is that although any judgment of responsibility must include these four elements (giving reason some purchase on human conduct *across* boundaries of time and place), there is no one right way of relating them. There are many ways of connecting intention and state with response; many ways of deciding what qualifies as a cause. All four elements are vulnerable to various sorts of skeptical objections, and each is elastic enough to shrink or expand with circumstances (55). Thus in matters of "strict liability," modern tort law does not require the defendant to intend or really even to cause the harm in order to be held liable, but merely to be well situated to prevent it. If pragmatic policy considerations can induce us moderns to shrink two of the four building blocks of responsibility this much, we should not be surprised to find in the thinking of the ancients a similar elasticity in the service of their quite different needs and purposes.

Williams's four-part scheme of analysis is illuminating, and it helps him earn one of the conclusions he aimed at, namely, that when it comes to "underlying conceptions" the difference between us and the Greeks may not be as great as the progressivists suppose. But he also wanted to dispel the idea that their moral reasoning was inferior to our own, and to do that, he knew he needed to present a "philosophical description of an historical reality" (4). Here his success is less complete, for reasons that have to do with the diverging motives of history and philosophy. In his effort to demonstrate the conceptual continuity of responsibility across the ages, Williams empties its constituent elements of any particular content and soars to a high level of abstraction that, although appropriate to most philosophical questions, makes it exceedingly difficult to keep in focus the lived experience of actual historical actors. From this altitude, there is little possibility of understanding how conceptions of responsibility change.

Consider slavery, for example. Few differences between us and the Greeks feel more profound than our repugnance for slavery and their unquestioning acceptance of it. Williams's abstract categories leave us no adequate way of registering this profound difference. Repugnance for slavery and acceptance of slavery entail two very different assessments of responsibility for the suffering of others. For Williams, however, all such judgments merely rearrange the same four elements: "adjustments" vary while "underlying conceptions" remain the same. This will not do. It terminates inquiry just as things become interesting. A comparably premature termination of inquiry would occur if one were to say that, since poker and bridge are just different ways of arranging the same fifty-two-card deck, the two games really come to the same thing. On the contrary: Having chosen to compare poker and bridge, one must look beyond the games' reliance on a common deck of cards and focus on the different rules by which they are played. Likewise, if one wishes to take the historicity of responsibility seriously, as Williams does, then one must recognize that nineteenth-century abolitionists and fifth-century B.C. Greek philosophers were playing the game of responsibility very differently. One must then ask what could have produced such a profound change in the rules.

It is revealing that when Williams tackles the problem of change most directly, in his examination of Aristotle's decidedly premodern views on slavery, his timeless four-element conception of responsibility disappears from sight. There is no evidence that Aristotle or anyone else in the ancient world ever felt sufficiently responsible for the suffering of slaves to challenge the institution of slavery. That slaves suffered was common knowledge: To be enslaved, as Williams observes, was to the ancients "the very paradigm of bad luck" or "disaster." But the justice of slavery was seldom discussed, much less questioned, and although Aristotle distinguished himself by considering it worthy of discussion, the conclusions he reached are notoriously ambivalent and inconsistent. He was content to regard some people as "natural slaves." He knew that some actual slaves did not belong in the category of "natural slave," and the enslavement of such persons was therefore in his view "against nature" and "not just." One might think that this remark goes some distance toward closing the gap between ancient and modern, but Williams is quick to admit that the appearance is deceiving. Aristotle, like his contemporaries, perceived in the master-slave relation an implacable necessity that we moderns can only strain to understand. Saying that slavery was "not just," says Williams, was not the same thing for Aristotle and his contemporaries as calling it "unjust." Having summed up the difference between Aristotle's time and ours in terms of a difference (apparent to them but not to us) between "not just" and "unjust," Williams then fails, in my view, to translate that baffling distinction into terms intelligible to a modern mind (123, 116).[20]

Here is what he says: "Slavery, in most people's eyes, was not just, but necessary. Because it was necessary, it was not, as an institution, seen as unjust either: to say that it was unjust would imply that ideally, at least, it should cease to exist, and few if any, could see how that might be. If as an institution it was not seen as either just or unjust, there was not much to be said about its justice, and indeed it has often been noticed that in extant Greek literature there are very few discussions at all of the justice of slavery" (117). I have no quarrel with Williams's principal point. It is indeed self-indulgent of us to formulate the difference between the ancients and ourselves simply as a matter of their "immaturity." I also think he is onto something important when he asserts that Aristotle and his contemporaries construed slavery in such a way that its existence seemed necessary and its abolition almost literally unthinkable. But Williams's distinction between "not just" and "unjust" cannot carry the weight of his argument, and his ad hoc way of accounting for the ancients' perception of necessity is not adequate to the task he set himself.

Consider each of these two points in turn. In the passage quoted above, Williams credits the Greeks with understanding that slavery was "not just," while reserving for us moderns the view that slavery is both "not just" and also "unjust." What the ancients could have meant by distinguishing between "not just" and "unjust" is never made clear. Perhaps Williams does not think it can be.[21] At one point in the passage quoted above, he identifies the modern opinion that slavery is unjust with the view that "ideally, at least, it should cease to exist." Taken by itself, this phrase seems to imply that the crucial difference between us and Aristotle is that we possess a higher *ideal* of justice that was not available to him. The ambiguous conclusion of Williams's sentence casts doubt on this construal, however, and it is precisely the sort of interpretation he rejected in earlier pages. His stress on the universality and timelessness of the four basic elements constituting judgments of responsibility is but one example of his repeated claim that differences between us and the Greeks "*cannot* best be understood in terms of a shift in basic ethical conceptions of agency, responsibility, shame, or freedom" (7; emphasis added).

In subsequent pages, Williams unambiguously reasserts his central claim: The crucial difference between past and present does *not* lie in the ancients' ideals or basic conceptions of justice, which were similar to ours. Instead, the difference lies in their comparative inability to imagine any course of action that would bring about the practical implementation of those ideals. Their bland acceptance of slavery is attributable, then, to what Quentin Skinner might have called "constraints upon imagination," rather than immaturity of judgment or a failure of moral insight as such. The crux of the matter for Williams is that the ancients drew differently the line that defines where the domain of necessity leaves off and human agency begins. In their eyes, slavery, though not just, was irremediable. That is a matter of social psychology rather than philosophy; a matter of the limits they perceived to their own collective power of reshaping the world, rather than a flawed understanding of what justice would, in principle, require.

Here nuance becomes vital, and Williams should be allowed to speak for himself:

Most people did not suppose that because slavery was necessary, it was therefore just; this, as Aristotle very clearly saw, would not be enough, and a further argument would be needed, one that he hopelessly tried to find. *The effect of the necessity was, rather, that life proceeded on the basis of slavery and left no space, effectively, for the question of its justice to be raised.*

Once the question is raised, it is quite hard not to see slavery as unjust, indeed as a paradigm of injustice, in the light of considerations basically available to the Greeks themselves. . . . We, now, have no difficulty in seeing slavery as unjust: we have economic arrangements and a conception of a society of citizens with which slavery is straightforwardly incompatible. This may stir a reflex of cultural self-congratulation, or at least satisfaction that in some dimensions there is progress. *But the main feature of the Greek attitude to slavery, I have suggested, was not a morally primitive belief in its justice, but the fact that considerations of justice and injustice were immobilised by the demands of what was seen as social and economic necessity. That phenomenon has not so much been eliminated from modern life as shifted to different places.*

We have social practices in relation to which we are in a situation much like that of the Greeks with slavery. We recognise arbitrary and brutal ways in which people are handled by society, ways which are conditioned, often, by no more than exposure to luck. We have the intellectual resources to regard the situation of these people, and the systems that allow these things, as unjust, but are uncertain whether to do so, partly because we have seen the corruption and collapse of supposedly alternative systems, partly because we have no settled opinion on the question about which Aristotle tried to contrive a settled opinion, how far the existence of a worthwhile life for some people involves the imposition of suffering on others. (124–25; emphasis added)

In a nutshell, Williams's strategy is to insist on continuity between the Greeks and ourselves at the level of abstract ideals of what justice requires, while conceding that they differ greatly from us in perceptions of necessity and possibility. So necessary did the existence of slavery (and presumably many other features of their society) seem to the ancients, so far beyond the reach of human will did these arrangements appear to lie, that no cognitive "space" was left, effectively, for the question of justice even to be raised. Although he conspicuously avoids using the term, perhaps because of its religious connotations, what he is saying is that the ancients perceived slavery as a *necessary evil*.

This is fine as far as it goes, but it does not go far enough. To say, as Williams does, that "considerations of justice and injustice were immobilised by the demands of what was seen as social and economic necessity" is indiscriminately to lump Aristotle together with thousands of slaveowners who sincerely believed, even in the midst of the American Civil War, that their entire way of life, as admirable as any other, depended on the perpetuation of slavery. Necessity is the first resort even of the lowest scoundrel. Williams needs to credit

Aristotle with more than this tendentious and self-serving sort of "necessity" in order to make good on his claim that the ancients' moral judgment was not inferior to our own. If the constraints that kept Aristotle from seeing in slavery anything worse than a "necessary evil" boiled down to nothing more than this — an ideological blind spot or "immobilisation" induced by the inconvenience of doing without slave labor — then surely in this regard we moderns would be entitled to feel morally superior, and the progressivist interpretation that Williams wishes to deflate would instead be vindicated.

Williams's cryptic observation that perceptions of necessary evil have not been "eliminated" in modern times, only "shifted to different places," is extremely promising, but it begs for further elaboration. He is of course right to insist that we moderns, too, have our "necessary evils." But that must not be allowed to obscure an even more important fact: The domain of necessity is perceived to be far less extensive today than it was in Aristotle's day. Its shrinkage is a dramatic difference between past and present. In that difference, I suspect, lies the grain of truth behind the persistent, but finally implausible progressivist intuition that we, the contemporaries of Adolf Hitler, Joseph Stalin, and Pol Pot, are as a group more mature moral reasoners than the author of the *Nicomachean Ethics*.

How do "necessary evils" such as slavery come to seem remediable, thus shrinking the domain of necessity and expanding the realm within which the imperatives of responsibility can operate? My principal complaint is that Williams fails to address this question. To answer it, we need a way of thinking about responsibility that candidly acknowledges its historicity without either abandoning reason or falling back on naive notions of moral progress. Such an approach need not run to the Nietzschean extreme of obliterating distinctions between good and evil, but neither can it embrace a linear narrative of ever-closer approximations to some moral law or ideal of conduct that stands outside human history and above convention. We need to admit that moral judgment is only partly systematic (leaving room for equally competent reasoners sometimes to reach conflicting conclusions) and to recognize that, even at its most systematic, moral deliberation takes place within a given framework of assumptions, the possession of which is essentially a matter of "luck," for which individual reasoners deserve little or no personal credit. To be sure, individuals differ greatly, both in their insight into the requirements of morality and in their courage to do what is required. But even the boldest of moral innovators can do no more (it is, after all, a great deal) than revise, extend, rearrange, and apply to new situations an array of conventions that they acquire through inheritance.

No philosopher in the analytic tradition has done more than Williams to take "luck" into philosophical account, and his insistence that past and present differ less in formal prescriptions than in the perceived limits of human agency puts us on the right track.[22] In the remainder of this essay, I will propose amending his formulation in two ways: by stressing (even more than he already has) the dependence of all judgments of responsibility on perceptions of causal efficacy, and by noting that causal perception, in turn, cannot avoid being largely a matter of social convention, subject to all the vicissitudes of historical change. As we have seen, Williams understands full well that a perception of causal relationship between a person's act or omission and an altered state of affairs is the seed crystal without which judgments of responsibility cannot even begin to take shape. To that I would add only that causation is also the linchpin between history and morality, enabling us to understand why evils once thought to be necessary come to seem remediable as historical developments reconfigure the perceptual universe within which moral actors operate.

Consider a truism of moral philosophy, "Ought implies can." To say that "ought implies can" is, obviously, to say that we do not hold people responsible for doing what they cannot do. Less obviously, the truism also means that our sense of what people are responsible for extends no farther than our causal perception — that is, our way of sifting through the virtual infinity of consequences flowing from a person's acts and omissions, classifying only a small fraction as truly *belonging* to the actor in a morally relevant way and thus qualifying for praise or blame. At most, we hold people responsible only for evils over which we believe they have significant causal influence — ones about which they "can" do something. Even this is only an outer limit, a prerequisite that is necessary (but not sufficient) for blameworthiness, for there are many evils that people obviously *could* do something to alleviate for which we do not hold them responsible.

Convention enters crucially into what we think people "can" do, and because it does, the dependence of "ought" on "can" carries with it the further implication that convention necessarily plays a large role in moral judgment. Cause-and-effect relations pervade our thinking at every level, from high theory to the most mundane affairs of everyday life. They constitute, as a British philosopher put it, the "cement [or glue] of the universe."[23] Virtually everything we do, from checking a book out of the library to calming a frightened child, draws on our fund of knowledge about the relation of present acts to future states of the world — the relation, in other words, of cause to effect. But those relations are not given as such in raw experience; causal relationships are something we *impute* to the people, events, and things around us, and we do so in ways shaped by social convention.

To illustrate the role of convention, imagine that a great earthquake has just occurred, such as the one that struck Mexico City in 1985. In a strictly physical sense, I undoubtedly "can" stop writing this essay, board a flight to Mexico City, and help save at least one stranger's life by lifting debris and performing other emergency tasks. If I took literally the well-nigh universal rule of reciprocity, "Do unto others what you would have them do unto you," this seems to be the only acceptable thing to do, for if I were pinned beneath a collapsed building, I would certainly want others to drop their daily routines and come to my aid. Yet I continue writing instead of going to the aid of the stranger, and no one accuses me of violating the Golden Rule. Why not? *But for* my inaction, the stranger would live. Why am I not deemed blameworthy for this death, which is undeniably among the consequences that flow from my failure to go to his aid? The answer is clear. I am not held responsible for this lamentable consequence of my inaction because, by the prevailing conventions of my time and place, this "can" is not real, not operative. Mexico City is "too far away"; going there would disrupt my life "too much."[24]

Too far and too much by what measure? Convention supplies the measure. Convention authorizes me to say I "cannot" help the stranger, at least not in this direct way, even though, in a purely physical sense, I undoubtedly possess the means of doing so. This shared, tacit understanding that converts the "can" of physical ability into the "cannot" of acceptable moral practice, need not be arbitrary—it may be loosely related to considerations of relative cost, for example—but I am not persuaded that its rational elements could ever be strong enough to anchor it against tides of change or lift it up out of the category of convention altogether. The existence of such conventions is nothing to regret. In the absence of convention, prescriptions such as the Golden Rule would either have to be ignored altogether, or taken literally, which would set standards so high that no one, no matter how scrupulous and compassionate, could live up to them. The world brims over with suffering strangers who, but for our inaction, would undeniably be better off; we cannot literally do for every suffering Other what we would have Others do for us.[25]

If ought implies can, and "can" is conventional in this sense, then it follows inexorably that our understanding of moral responsibility—of what we "ought" to do—is deeply embedded in social practice and cannot avoid being influenced, at least in broad outline, by the material circumstances, the historical experiences, and, especially, the technological capabilities of the society in which we live. As our collective circumstances, experiences, and capabilities change, we should expect the conventions of moral responsibility to change as well, though not in any simple or automatic manner. The easiest way to illustrate the point is to imagine a dramatic change in what we "can" do. The invention of technology that would permit us to travel to Mexico City, or any other scene of disaster, instantaneously and at trivial expense would be very likely to alter the conventions governing moral responsibility in our society—making my failure to go to the aid of the earthquake victim morally unacceptable, at least in some quarters. Any change that stretches our causal horizons and expands the sphere within which we feel we "can" act has the potential to transform what we hitherto perceived as "necessary evils" into remediable ones. And once an evil is perceived as remediable, some people (not all, certainly) will be exposed to feelings of guilt and responsibility for suffering that previously was viewed with indifference or, at most, aroused only passive sympathy—like the sympathy the ancient Greeks felt for those who had the misfortune to be enslaved, or which the reader and I feel today for distant earthquake victims who are "too far away" to help.[26]

This is the sort of development that I believe paved the way for "modern" or "humane" or "responsible" attitudes toward slavery and many other cruel and exploitative practices. My understanding parallels Williams's at some levels while diverging at others. He is right that we moderns have nothing to teach the ancients about the requirements of justice, abstractly considered. He is also right to insist that the ancients owe us no apologies for lacking the heightened sense of agency that has prompted Europeans since the eighteenth century to perceive in slavery an evil both unjust *and* unnecessary. But these strengths of Williams's analysis need to be supplemented with a fuller acknowledgment that the element of causation, although universally present in judgments of responsibility, plays a role that is historically contingent, depending as it must on conventional understandings of what people "can" do. Of the four elements that Williams says are universal features of all judgments of responsibility, causation is the most historical; the one most likely to vary with changes in people's everyday practices, material circumstances, and technological capabilities. As causal conventions change, so must perceptions of freedom and fate, possibility and necessity. And as evils previously regarded as necessary are brought perceptually and conceptually within the reach of remedial action, people whose basic conceptions of justice may not differ from those of their ancestors may nonetheless feel obliged to act in unprecedented ways. Because the causal imagination feeds on awareness that things could be other than they are, the high rate of change and technological innovation in modern societies fosters an expansive sense of agency (and correspondingly shrunken domain of necessity) that was unthinkable in Aristotle's day.

This is not to give technology (even in the very capacious and wholly un-mechanical sense of the word intended here) credit for being an autonomous force or unilinear process in history. Nor is it to credit technology with being a force for the moral betterment of mankind—every expansion of causal horizons creates new opportunities for doing evil as well as good. It is merely to recognize that (a) people cannot feel responsible enough to do anything about ending suffering as long as they cannot imagine any practicable course of action that will reliably lead to that outcome, and (b) imagining complex, far-reaching courses of moral reform comes easiest to those who in their every-day affairs routinely witness or take part in projects that are comparably far reaching in their effects. Whether the projects are motivated by altruism or selfish interests is not decisive; what is important is that the projects be far-reaching—not solely in a spatial sense but also in temporal scope and in the number and complexity of the qualitative transformations necessary to their accomplishment.

At the scene of a bloody accident we expect less of laypeople than of physicians, who have the knowledge and skills to intervene in ways that it would be reckless for a layperson to attempt. By the same token, responsibility for all manner of institutionalized injustice weighs heaviest on people who have been acculturated to accept change as natural, to pride themselves on their demonstrated mastery of fate, and routinely to participate in or witness ambitious projects aimed at distant goals—again, "distant" not only in space or time but also in the number and complexity of the cause-and-effect linkages necessary to their attainment. From such experience comes a person like Oskar Schindler: undistinguished in moral character, perhaps, but bold, worldly-wise, and thus equipped with such wide causal horizons that he may, under the pressure of circumstance, feel responsible for the performance of humane feats of which other, more sensitive moralists would be incapable.

One reason for thinking that this feature of modern life accounts for changed attitudes toward slave suffering is the startling recency of the humanitarian phenomenon. Individual Good Samaritans go back as far as human memory. Organized efforts to rescue kinsmen or fellow believers from slavery were common in medieval Europe. But sustained movements collectively dedicated to the relief of suffering strangers—people sharing no tie of blood, faith, or common citizenship—and aiming at the demolition of the institutional arrangements that held them down, are a phenomenon of the recent past. No slave society of which we have historical knowledge lacked voices recognizing that slaves suffered: Aristotle knew it, Aquinas knew it, Locke knew it even as he wrote slavery into the Fundamental Constitutions of Carolina. Yet no serious opposition to the institution of slavery developed before the eighteenth century. In the entire history of responsibility, there is no fact more sobering or revealing than this. *For two millennia after Aristotle, the suffering of slaves continued to be perceived as nothing worse than a regrettable but necessary evil.* The first people to go farther and condemn the institution outright were isolated religious zealots of the sixteenth and seventeenth centuries, all but forgotten by history and dismissed by their contemporaries as misfits. With the single exception of Jean Bodin in the sixteenth century, even Europe's most insightful moralists and philosophers did no more than acknowledge that slavery was ethically problematical—until the middle decades of the eighteenth century.[27] Then, in little more than a century, slavery was suddenly transformed from a troubling but readily defensible institution into a self-evidently intolerable relic of barbarism, noxious to decent people everywhere. On a historical scale of reckoning, this reversal of opinion occurred overnight.

Most of those who attacked slavery were fired by religious indignation, but the Christian doctrines they hurled at slaveowners had for centuries been thought compatible with slaveholding. We do not demean the abolitionists' labors, without which emancipation would never have been achieved, by entertaining the possibility that their crusade was made possible (not *produced*, but *made possible*) by changes in the material circumstances and technological capabilities of the society in which they lived. The historical developments that set the stage for new attitudes toward suffering and servitude lay outside the realm of "ideas," in political and especially economic changes that greatly expanded the horizon within which deliberate human action routinely took place. The upshot, I suggest, was an outward shift in the conventions governing perceptions of causation, necessity, and moral responsibility, such that what had hitherto appeared to be "necessary evils" began to seem remediable.

Before substantial numbers of people could feel outraged by the very existence of slavery and take action to uproot it, they had to be able to impute to themselves historically unprecedented powers of intervention, and they had to perceive hierarchical social arrangements and institutional structures, not as reflections of God's will or manifestations of nature's own order, but as contingent, malleable phenomena open to human influence and correction. In other words, the conventionally defined domain of necessity—the domain comprising events that are not construed as the consequence of any human choice, act, or omission—had to shrink. Not until slavery's evil appeared remediable would anyone, even so thoughtful a person as Aristotle, feel responsible for doing anything about it. And not until human agency seemed expansive enough to challenge even such ancient and interest-bound institutions as slavery would people feel the need for the new word "responsibility," the adoption of which was eloquent testimony to the ever-wider range of consequences that by the 1780s were being traced back to human choice rather than to traditional founts of necessity such as God, Chance, Fate, Fortune, Luck, or Nature.

Here we come full circle. My speculation is that the coinage of the word "responsibility" in the late eighteenth century was one straw in the wind, registering the onset of a major upheaval in the conventions governing causal attribution in Western culture. That speculation having been ventured, it is important to notice in closing that the upheaval, if such it is, is still under way — and gaining momentum. The philosopher Hans Jonas puts his finger on its deepest sources and reminds us that its consequences are by no means entirely encouraging. Like the shell of an exploding star, responsibility swiftly expands in all directions under the continuing impulse of man's growing technological virtuosity and ever-higher expectations of self-mastery and control of nature. But as it expands, obliterating perceptions of necessity wherever it reaches, the shell grows thin and brittle. A day may come when, overextended, it collapses back upon itself.

"Modern technology," warns Jonas, "informed by an ever-deeper penetration of nature and propelled by the forces of market and politics, has enhanced human power beyond anything known or even dreamed of before." "It is a power over matter, over life on earth, and over man himself; and it keeps growing at an accelerating pace. Its unfettered exercise for about two centuries now has raised the material estate of its wielders and main beneficiaries, the industrial 'West,' to heights equally unknown in the history of mankind. . . . But lately, the other side of the triumphal advance has begun to show its face, disturbing the euphoria of success with threats that are as novel as its welcomed fruits." [28]

Although expanding horizons of responsibility helped doom slavery and brought succor to untold numbers of suffering strangers who otherwise would have met with nothing better than passive sympathy, the continuation of this process is not an unmixed blessing. We have become keenly aware in recent decades that the explosion of technological innovation that propels this outward sweep of human responsibility has horrific dangers of its own, such as nuclear holocaust and ecological catastrophe. We also know that staggering ethical dilemmas lie just around the corner, as human agency penetrates still

deeper into nature, unravels genetic codes, and trembles on the brink of creating life itself. In spite of all the publicity devoted to threats such as these,
they are not the only ones we have to fear. The most serious may stem from
the overdevelopment of the idea of responsibility itself.

Every time technical ingenuity makes new inroads against the given and the
necessary, responsibility becomes more expansive, more tenuous, and more
susceptible to the ancient charge of hubris. Many commentators have sensed
in modern culture a growing arbitrariness, as expanding causal horizons paradoxically make us seem responsible for everything in principle and nothing
in particular. As the realm of the given shrinks toward the vanishing point,
evils begin to appear "necessary" only insofar as fragile conventions dignify
our reluctance to disrupt our lives for the sake of rendering aid. Under these
conditions, responsibility itself is transformed from a concrete relation with
specific applications into a diffuse quality that floats freely through all relations, ready to be imputed manipulatively to anyone, anytime, for anything.
One wonders which is worse, the paralysis that comes from acknowledging
that we are, through omission, causally complicit in evils all over the world, or
the cynicism that comes from knowing that only those evils that win the lot-
tery of politics stand any chance of actually being remedied.

Other observers have noted that the ethical maxims of the past increasingly fail us because they evolved in contexts dramatically different from the
one in which we now operate.[29] The goods and evils that our ancestors tried
to attain or avoid were close at hand, proximate both in space and time. As
Jonas says, "The effective range of action was small, the time span of foresight, goal-setting, and accountability was short, control of circumstances was
limited. The long run of consequences was left to chance, fate, or providence.
Ethics accordingly was of the here and now. . . . The agent and the 'other' of
his action [shared] a common present. . . . No one was held responsible for
the unintended later effects of his well-intentioned, well-considered, and well-
performed act. The short arm of human power did not call for a long arm of
predictive knowledge."[30]

Now, as Jonas says, "all this has decisively changed. Modern technology
has introduced actions of such novel scale, objects, and consequences that the
framework of former ethics can no longer contain them." We saw that Calasso
credited the wisdom and modesty of the ancient Greeks for their having "dismissed with the utmost skepticism an agent's claim actually to *do* anything,"
but it should now be apparent that their "modesty" was inseparable from the
constricted causal imagination instilled in them by a technologically limited

form of life, one unequipped with the expansive sense of agency required to sustain the view that the suffering of the slave was anything worse than a necessary evil. One can only wonder what will pass for wisdom and modesty in the world of the future, in which, as Jonas says, the "lengthened reach" or "causal pregnancy" of our technological deeds will put responsibility at "the center of the ethical stage," with "no less than man's fate for its object." [31] What counts as "hubris" as we approach a condition in which necessity evaporates and all problems appear in principle to be soluble, if only enough resources are dedicated to them? The possibilities for both good and ill are incalculable — but among them is the possibility that the supposed beneficiaries of modernity's widening gyre of freedom and responsibility will rebel and do whatever it takes to reinstate the reign of necessity rather than bear the rising burden of guilt and frustration that goes with boundless causal horizons.

The question for historians (perhaps of no great moment in the larger scheme of things) is how we are to avoid letting history become Voltaire's "bag of tricks played upon the dead." Throughout the modern era, conventions of responsibility have not only been in motion, they have moved at an accelerating pace, a state of affairs that make the danger of arbitrary and anachronistic judgment more acute than ever. Under conditions such as these, it seems obvious that all historians, not just those specializing in the history of ideas, owe it to their audience to suspend judgment long enough to specify as clearly as they can the conventions by which their subjects lived. But achieving that goal will be hard, for it goes against the grain of the historical profession as now constituted, both intellectually and institutionally.

Conventions are not empirical entities that can be weighed or counted; they will not be found in the archives filed under "C." Controversies about them will seem frustratingly inconclusive, and the profession's favorite myth — that historian's quarrels turn on hard facts rather than imponderable issues of interpretation — will become harder and harder to sustain. Ferreting out conventions will require skills of logical inference and imagination that have never figured prominently in either the recruitment or the training of historians. Taking conventions into account will complicate the stories historians tell and incur the wrath of all those — not only defenders of the status quo, but also its critics — who have a vested interest in using the past to serve present interests predictably. Skeptics who see nothing to gain from acknowledging the force of convention are numerous, both inside and outside the profession. Some of the most vociferous naysayers will be those who construe convention as an ancillary reflex of group interest. In their eyes, powerful elites, well versed in the arts of "social control" and "cultural hegemony," find it no harder to imbue subject populations with convenient conventions than to select ready-made clothing out of a mail-order catalog.

Quentin Skinner observed more than twenty years ago that "it is the limit of our imaginative grasp as well as our lack of information that makes the past a foreign country, just as it is imaginative grasp as well as control of information that makes the historian." When Skinner wrote those words he was none too sanguine that historians would come to grips with the foreignness of the past. Still greater pessimism seems warranted today, for little has changed. Just as in 1970, most historians today still believe that it is "best not to think about their subject but merely to do it, as if these were self-evidently separate activities."[32] After two decades of talk about the importance of context and the desirability of "thick description," historians have scarcely begun to scale the barriers to understanding that shifting conventions throw in their path. Nor are they likely to do so as long as they are more concerned to use the past than to understand it. To be sure, we reconstruct the past for our sake, not its own, but understanding it in its own terms is the indispensable prerequisite for honest use.

CHAPTER ELEVEN

A Brief Excursus on Formalism

Is it possible, in spite of everything I have said to the contrary, that the comparative insensitivity of the abolitionists to the needs of wage labor was the result of class interest, just as Davis and Ashworth argue? Of course. Interest can never be ruled out. There is no human act so incontrovertibly disinterested that it cannot be construed as self-interested by one's enclosing it within a suitable interpretive framework.[1] But the ease with which any sophomore can perform this trick should make us wonder about its value. Trying to explain events without referring to interests would be absurd, but we can take note of the infinite elasticity of the concept and the obsessiveness of our reliance on it and then develop a certain skepticism in the presence of those of every political persuasion who take it to be the sole proper terminus of explanation.

Let us consider a concrete example of an abolitionist who displayed the "selectivity" that Davis and Ashworth, for all their differences, both construe as a sure sign of bias induced by class interest — an abolitionist, that is, who regarded the suffering of slaves as a far more urgent and acute problem than the suffering of immiserated wage laborers. The example is one my critics ought to find congenial, for it lends itself readily to an interpretation in terms of

This is an extract from a reply I wrote to two criticisms of "Capitalism and the Origins of the Humanitarian Sensibility [parts 1 and 2]" (see chapters 8 and 9 of this volume). My critics were David Brion Davis and John Ashworth. Their criticisms and my reply were originally published together in the *American Historical Review* 92 (Oct. 1987). A few years later, when Thomas Bender gathered together all the elements of the controversy and published them as *The Antislavery Debate: Capitalism and Abolitionism as a Problem in Historical Interpretation* (Berkeley: University of California Press, 1992), Davis and Ashworth supplied new rejoinders to my reply. By that time, the controversy had reached, if not passed, the point of diminishing returns, and the last thing I wanted to do then — or now — is reopen it. Although most of my 1987 reply would be informative only to readers who are already familiar with the Davis and Ashworth essays that triggered it, the class interest. My aim is not to show that such an interpretation is flatly erroneous — no such demonstration could ever succeed, in my view — but rather to display in a specific case the tendency of explanation-by-interest to terminate inquiry prematurely.

My example is the American abolitionist Wendell Phillips, whose views are especially pertinent because, in spite of his patrician origins, he ultimately came to believe something quite close to what Davis and Ashworth assume that all abolitionists would always have believed if their judgment had not been clouded by class interest. In 1871, when Phillips presided over a Labor Reform convention that declared war on the entire system of wage labor, alleging that it "enslaves" the workingman and "demoralizes" and "cheats" both him and his employer, he construed the problems of labor in a way that is basically familiar to us today — that is, in a way that sees through the formal liberty of abused wageworkers and situates their problems on a continuum with those of chattel slaves, acknowledging differences in degree, perhaps, but not in kind.[2]

But of course Phillips had not always thought that it made sense to compare wage earners and slaves, much less to lump their problems together as variations on the single theme of labor exploitation. Before the Civil War, like most humanitarian reformers of his generation, he had found the very idea of "wages slavery" to be "utterly unintelligible," at least in the American context. In a remarkable statement in 1847, he acknowledged that manufactured articles were often the products of "unrequited labor" and that complaints against capital and monopoly were well justified in England and Europe, but he insisted that the situation was different in America. Between the free laborers of the North and the slaves of the South, he drew a distinction so drastic as to stagger the imagination of any twentieth-century reader:

> Except in a few crowded cities and a few manufacturing towns, I believe the terms "wages slavery" and "white slavery" would be utterly unintelligible to an audience of laboring people, as applied to themselves. There are two prominent

section on formalism reproduced here can stand on its own. It presupposes only that the reader is familiar with the broad contours of my argument in "Capitalism and the Origins of the Humanitarian Sensibility," especially my contention that Davis's interpretation of antislavery is flawed by its overreliance on the concept of interest and underestimation of the power of convention to define the limits within which ethical judgment operates. As a free-standing piece, this discussion of formalism provides a useful lead into the next essay in this volume, "Persons as Uncaused Causes," which I was writing at about the same time. The extract that appears here is roughly the concluding sixth of the 1987 reply. I have expanded the original text at some points and revised it at others. The additions and revisions are meant to clarify the position I originally articulated, not alter it.

points which distinguish the laborers in this country from the slaves. First, the laborers, as a class, are neither wronged nor oppressed: and secondly, if they were, they possess ample power to defend themselves, by the exercise of their own acknowledged rights. Does legislation bear hard upon them? Their votes can alter it. Does capital wrong them? Economy will make them capitalists. Does the crowded competition of cities reduce their wages? They have only to stay at home, devoted to other pursuits, and soon diminished supply will bring the remedy. . . . To economy, self-denial, temperance, education, and moral and religious character, the laboring class, and every other class in this country, must owe its elevation and improvement.[3]

These are the words of a person who defines the self and its relation to the world in a manner that is extremely formalistic by present standards. Phillips in 1847 seems not to have recognized any distinction between the form of freedom and its substance. He seems to have believed that a person who is physically and legally unconstrained is as free as any human being ever can be. Some of what he said resembles twentieth-century laissez-faire conservatism, but the resemblance is largely spurious, and even a reckless conservative today would be unlikely to assert in public, as Phillips unhesitatingly did, that workers need only practice "economy" in order to become capitalists in their own right, or that low wages can be raised by staying at home, or that self-denial, the ballot box, and good character form a sure path to advancement. These assertions are shot through with implications of a strongly formalist character, and everything turns on what we make of this alien element in Phillips's thinking.

The more alien an idea is, the easier it is to dismiss as ideology, but if we resist that temptation and take what Phillips said as an expression of the way the world once looked to an acute and certainly conscientious observer, we immediately discover that his attitude in 1847 toward wage labor is not at all perplexing—once we grant him his formalist premises. No matter how unrealistic we may think these premises, once adopted, they lead naturally and consistently to the conclusion that "wages slavery" is a contradiction in terms.

The cast of Phillips's mind will not be unfamiliar to students of Victorian culture in England and America. He wrote as if a normal, healthy, adult self was an uncaused cause, a pure point of origin, a kind of cornucopia, if you will, in which purposeful activity arose out of nothing and surged into the world. To be a person, in this view, was only incidentally to be a material body, caught up in nature's endless fabric of cause-and-effect relations and fully subject to all the natural processes of growth, disease, and decay. Although persons originate much and alter the world by their every act and decision, they are the consequence of very little, other than the design of their creator.

The heart of personhood lay in the will, and the will, though not necessarily supernatural, was uncanny. The self formed a pure point of origin through its mysterious capacity of "willing," of almost magically transmuting the evanescent, inward, and private experience of desire and choice into the concrete, outward, and public phenomenon of action. More mysterious still, the resulting external acts produced consequences that corresponded with, or satisfied, the internal desires—or, at least, could do so if the will allowed itself to be guided by the dictates of reason and knowledge.

The self's ability to trigger causal chains and set events in motion meant that it was very much *in* the world, and yet, because it was always the producer, never merely the product of any antecedent chain of natural causation, it was not quite *of* this world. Every merely natural cause is a transitive link in a chain and can be construed both as the cause of what it produces and as the effect of some link antecedent to it—which, in turn, can be seen as the effect of some cause still more remote, and so on indefinitely. But the self in the act of willing was seen as a new, nontransitive, causal beginning, independent of everything but the First Cause and His providential order—a very special sort of dependence that even predestinarians insisted did not dilute in the least the self's responsibility for whatever it willingly did.[4] In the world of formalism, the self's every act was deemed voluntary insofar as will was in it, and scarcely anything other than direct physical coercion was thought capable of displacing the will and emptying an act of its voluntary character.

Formalism assigned such a high level of autonomy to the will that the context within which the will fixed on particular paths and goals faded into the distant background, making nearly all deliberate acts appear voluntary. Circumstances, the stuff of environmentalist interpretations of behavior, counted for very little in judging what the self was responsible for. The self was responsible for whatever its activity led to, almost without regard to the circumstances surrounding choice and action. The formalist had no difficulty in recognizing that the will actively assessed its environment and inclined toward one act rather than another *in light* of various circumstantial factors, but to assign these factors causal significance and treat them as the explanation of what the self did would have been to deprive the self of the uncaused character that made it what it was. The cause (and therefore the explanation) of what people did was their choosing to do it, not the circumstances surrounding the choice. We of the twentieth century impute to circumstances a power to mold and induce choice—virtually to cause it and certainly to shed explanatory light upon it—that mere circumstances could not possess in a formalist's eyes.

These are the conventional premises defining selfhood and governing the allocation of praise, blame, and responsibility that I believe Phillips and most members of his generation shared in the 1840s. They account for what we perceive as his curious insensitivity to the plight of exploited wageworkers and the poor even as he did everything in his power to alleviate the suffering of slaves. From our (not necessarily superior) vantage point, Phillips and his contemporaries were oblivious to an entire range of environmental factors that powerfully influence conduct yet leave people formally free to do as they please. Where we see a deceptive form of freedom, lacking substance, they saw a large and sunlit realm of authentically voluntary choice.

To a person who sees the world as Phillips did in 1847, the difference between a free worker and a slave is a matter not of degree but of quality. Phillips imputed to free workers—a class "neither wronged nor oppressed" and equipped with "ample power to defend themselves"—a degree of autonomy so great that their problems were not commensurable with those of slaves. Free workers, unlike slaves, were masters of their own fate. Even by our twentieth-century standards, there is an irreducible element of voluntariness in even the most fated of contractual arrangements: The free worker can, at a cost, always refuse the employment contract. For a formalist, the perceived cost approximates zero because the conditions impelling the employee to accept undesirable conditions of work are assigned little weight.

Because wage earners were thought free to rise or fall to whatever social position corresponded to their inner merit, those who found themselves in a state of misery had little besides themselves to blame. Formalist assumptions did not prevent decent people like Phillips from feeling passive sympathy for a pauper or playing the Good Samaritan in particular cases by "lending a hand" to a person "down on his luck." But there could be no general attack on the institution of wage labor or any systematic attempt to reform the institution (indeed, the institution of wage labor could not even be perceived in a causal role), as long as reformers saw the world through lenses that made most of the poor appear to be deeply complicitous in their own suffering. Because formalists perceived the causes of suffering to lie largely in the victim's own apparently unimpeded choices (ultimately, in defects of the will), the only general remedy for their misfortunes was to help them perfect the arts of self-mastery and educate them about the predictable consequences of their actions. The lessons of "economy," "self-denial," "temperance," and "education" thus stood at the head of Phillips's list of priorities. We must struggle to appreciate that, to him and to most members of his generation, this thin gruel was not only an adequate prescription for social improvement but a trenchant identification of what on formalist premises were the vital nutrients of progressive change.

Although on formalist assumptions immiserated wage earners were the cause of their own misery, slaves could not possibly be cast in the same causal role.[5] The status of chattel property shrinks to the vanishing point every hint of voluntariness, making the slave the perfect victim, a person whose misery even to formalists is untainted by any suspicion of complicity. It is for this reason that the concern for slavery displayed by Phillips's generation of reformers could be more wholehearted and vehement than their reaction to most other forms of suffering. To one who makes little or no distinction between formal and substantive freedom, legally free workers bear a large measure of responsibility for their own plight, but the suffering of slaves, being wholly involuntary, is the responsibility of everyone who has any power to stop it.

Clearly, then, the different treatment Phillips accorded to slaves and wage laborers in the 1840s resulted not from a discrete bias against wage laborers, as the explanatory schemes of Davis and Ashworth require, but from a system of conventional assumptions that colored Phillips's and his generation's thinking about all human conduct, including their own. I contend that those conventions, contrary to the assumptions of Davis and Ashworth, say more about the staying power of religion than about the innovative cunning of economic interest under capitalism.

This is not the place to sort out all the intricate connections among religion, formalism, and the rise of capitalism. Nor is there space here to delve into all the sources of that great nineteenth-century upheaval in the conventions governing causal attribution that would eventually put both religion and formalism on the defensive and pave the way for even ex-formalists like Phillips to embark upon antiformalist critiques of free labor.[6] For present purposes, it should be enough to observe that in the long run, nothing could have been more toxic to the assumptions of formalism than the culture of the market itself. As the century progressed, the market insinuated itself ever more deeply into the social fabric, tending always to exert outward, expansive pressures on the causal horizons of those caught up in its web. One effect, for observers as morally earnest and intellectually agile as Phillips, was a gradual loss of confidence in the classical Christian image of the self as an uncaused cause.

Phillips's abandonment of formalist assumptions in the 1870s made him a harbinger of what intellectual historians have long called the "revolt against formalism."[7] Social theorists and intellectuals of all political stripes in England, the United States, and Europe displayed during the 1880s, 1890s, and early 1900s a growing readiness to doubt the autonomy of the self and to shift explanatory weight to matters of circumstance. Not coincidentally, these years also witnessed the birth of the modern social scientist, whose watch-

word was not autonomy but interdependence and who found the springs of
conduct neither in the soul nor in conscious choice, but in instinct and environment.[8] The hugely successful claim to professional authority that social
scientists made in the last third of the century hinged upon assigning causal
status to circumstantial factors that had hitherto been assigned little weight
in the explanation of human conduct, but seemed too obvious to ignore in
a world increasingly oriented to market transactions. Although many of the
early social scientists were active in church affairs and sought to ally social
science with traditional aspirations for Christian brotherhood and communal
solidarity, the mode of explanation they championed was deeply at variance
with the ancient Christian hope of weaning oneself from the snares of this
world and becoming something more than a mere "creature of circumstance."

That formalist assumptions about personhood should lose credibility and
be displaced by a far less flattering image of the self just as industrial capitalism
was reaching maturity, makes no sense on Davis's and Ashworth's premises,
which treat formalist assumptions about personhood as an ideological prop,
brought into existence by capitalism and sustained by bourgeois interests. But
the concomitance of capitalism's triumph and formalism's retreat should not
surprise us. The culture of the market is one that for better or worse frankly
embraces what Immanuel Kant called "heteronomy," which is to say, a state
of contingency and circumstantiality so pervasive that autonomy is out of the
question.

The most elementary premise of a market-oriented life is that every self
perpetually seeks its own interest and aims at gratification, not through spiritual transcendence, but by being scrupulously attentive to the ever-shifting
circumstantial pressures and inducements generated by supply and demand.
Under market auspices it is not God who is my shepherd and ensures that I
shall not want, but the invisible hand. The world of the market, like that of
the social scientist, is a seamless web of reciprocally interacting influences in
which no cause is uncaused, no self autonomous, no choice beyond explanation in terms of situational pressures and preconditions. In such a world — our
world today, like it or not — even the acts of the most willing self can be construed as consequences of circumstance. Voluntariness no longer signals a new
causal beginning, but only one more effect of circumstantial pressures and inducements that are susceptible to manipulation by powerful interests. In such
a world, there is no longer any great difficulty in seeing the immiserated but
formally free laborer as a victim of circumstances beyond his or her control.
And since free laborers are authentic victims, whose own choices cannot adequately account for their plight, their misery becomes — like that of the chattel

slave — the responsibility of anyone who has the power to stop it. The world the market makes, in short, is one in which the extravagant formalism that Phillips displayed in 1847 can no longer reign supreme; it must compete on increasingly unfavorable terms against rival modes of explanation.

It is true, as Davis says, that formalism, like opposition to slavery, "cannot be divorced from the vast economic changes" of the eighteenth and nineteenth centuries.[9] Nothing can be divorced from economic changes as profound as these, but that is not the point at issue. The pivotal questions concern the nature and consistency of the relationship between capitalism and formalism. I have no doubt that formalistic habits of mind traditionally cultivated by the Christian churches helped insulate early-nineteenth-century entrepreneurs against the barbs of conscience and public opinion as they drove hard bargains with workers too needy, as the young Phillips put it, to "stay at home," waiting for wages to rise. But formalism long antedated capitalism, and it had a multitude of effects, many of which powerfully obstructed the path of capital. We trivialize formalist convictions and misrepresent their origin in treating them as a simple reflex of economic interest.

Instead of construing Phillips's formalism in the 1840s as the telltale imprint of unconsciously intended class interest (Davis), or false consciousness (Ashworth), we might more plausibly interpret it simply as a fairly predictable outcome of his Christian upbringing. No doubt the formalist habits of mind long encouraged by Christian teachings sometimes coincidentally facilitated capitalist interests, especially in the early nineteenth century, before the invisible hand became an iron fist, as it had by the end of the century. But it is vital to recognize that a far deeper and more fateful affinity exists between market culture and *anti*formalist modes of thinking. This will be a bitter pill to swallow for readers who pride themselves on their antiformalist convictions, imagining them to arise from personal discernment, compassion, and conscience. But a far more likely source of the prevailing antiformalism among intellectuals of our era is the marketplace itself, whose atmosphere of subjective valuation and pervasive contingency all of us breathe every day.[10]

Most implausible of all is the assumption, shared not only by Davis and Ashworth but by many other historians of modern society, that wherever we encounter formalism we are looking at an ideological reflex of class interest. The formalist cast of mind was not anything capitalism brought into existence. Six hundred years before Phillips was born and long before anything worth calling capitalism appeared on the scene, Thomas Aquinas was already defining the outer perimeter of voluntary action no less extravagantly than Phillips did in the 1840s. In an image that Hobbes would borrow four hundred years later, and that Aristotle had employed more ambivalently a millennium and a half earlier, Aquinas, the great codifier of Christian doctrine, insisted that even a man at sea, who chooses to throw his possessions overboard rather than risk death in a storm, is acting voluntarily. "*That which is done through fear is voluntary*," said Aquinas. "*The will cannot be compelled to act . . . violence cannot be done to the will.*" [11] If acts undertaken in fear of death are not excluded from the "voluntary," then nothing is. No maxim of conservative jurisprudence in the Age of Contract affirmed formalism any more confidently or sanctified promissory obligations any more wholeheartedly than this formula, drafted by a medieval cleric expanding upon Aristotle.

We sense how truly alien to our own experience the perspective of classical Christian formalism is when we see how literally Aquinas believed that the willing self was a new causal beginning, a pure point of origin, whose acts had no explanation apart from choice itself. Ignoring all the circumstantial factors that (for us, at least) shape the will and tailor life's opportunities to the imperatives of a particular social order — to all the factors, in other words, that create a gap between the form and the substance of freedom — Aquinas denied that there was anything at all outside the self, anywhere in God's created universe, that could move the will, other than its own object (the "apprehended good") and the gentle art of persuasion. From this perspective, attenuated but by no means extinguished in the Christianity of Wendell Phillips's youth, harsh circumstances could never relieve a normal, healthy adult from responsibility for whatever labor arrangements he or she might willingly enter into, no matter how dangerous or unrewarding the labor, no matter how bleak the alternatives. One's will, be it sound or flawed, was believed to be the source from which one's entire life and fate unfolded, for the will was immune to any this-worldly force more violent than the sweet murmurings of persuasion.

> Now it is a law of providence that everything is moved by its proximate cause. . . . But the proximate moving cause of the will is the apprehended good, which is its object, and the will is moved by it as sight is by color. Therefore no created substance can move the will except by means of the apprehended good — in so far, namely, as it shows that a particular thing is good to do; and this is *to persuade*. Therefore no created substance can act on the will, or cause our choice, except by way of persuasion. [12]

We are the heirs today of a revolt against formalism that bore fruit in the years 1880–1920, thereby inaugurating the modern era in social thought. [13] To expect people who lived prior to this intellectual watershed to share our anti-formalist conceptions of freedom and responsibility is to project into an age different in important ways from ours the deceptively familiar features of our own world. It is also to underestimate the genuine historical novelty of anti-formalism, one prophetic stream of which first struggled into existence in the thought of Owen, Fourier, Marx, Engels, and a small cadre of others, who were the first to criticize the highly abstract and autonomous characterization of the self and its relation to the world that came to be known in the nineteenth century as "individualism." To find that the abolitionists defined freedom for-malistically and were therefore more sympathetic to slaves (whose lack of in-dependence made them perfect victims) than to impoverished wageworkers (whose formally defined freedom meant that they always bore substantial re-sponsibility for their own misery) is merely to reaffirm that the likes of Owen and Marx were truly harbingers of a new age who construed the world in ways that were profoundly unconventional—which is to say culturally unavailable to most people of their era.

Given the antiquity of formalism and its centrality in the Christian tradi-tion, the question we need to ask about Wendell Phillips is not why he "selec-tively" attacked slavery and ignored the plight of wage laborers in 1847, but why, a few decades later, he and many others abandoned the premises of for-malism and adopted a far less robust concept of the self that put the entire problem of responsibility and reform in a dramatically new light. As long as we are mesmerized by the idea of interest, this question cannot even come up.

If we asked Davis and Ashworth why Phillips changed his mind between 1847 and 1871, we would likely receive an answer that treats twentieth-century antiformalist assumptions not as anything mediated by convention or emer-gent in history but simply as, well, the way things really are and always have been. Davis's answer would presumably explain how Phillips managed to stop deceiving himself about formalistic assumptions that, unconsciously, in his heart of hearts, he had always known were unrealistic. Ashworth—perhaps after hesitating momentarily at the thought of a change of values without any corresponding change in the interests they supposedly "grew" from—would presumably strive to show how Phillips managed to break the grip of "false consciousness" and began seeing things in their true light. From both van-tage points, Phillips's initial opinion seems to require explanation, since it was an error, but his later opinion would apparently not merit an explanation be-cause, when people give up error for truth, there is nothing to explain.

In contrast, if we take the role of conventions seriously, put the overworked concept of interest on hold, and abstain from pressing the all-too-human claim that our own views bear the unmistakable stamp of reality, Phillips's change of perspective between 1847 and 1871 can be seen as a revealing incident in a cultural transformation of far-reaching significance. To recognize the tendency of explanation by interest to terminate inquiry prematurely is not to abandon it as a mode of explanation, but merely to recognize the existence of other modes that in particular cases may prove more fruitful. To scold our ancestors for not being antiformalists like us and then to add insult to injury by attributing their formalism to class interest is to succumb to just that form of parochialism that knowledge of history should help us to overcome.

CHAPTER TWELVE

Persons as Uncaused Causes

John Stuart Mill, the Spirit of Capitalism, and the "Invention" of Formalism

> During the later returns of my dejection, the doctrine of what is called Philosophical Necessity weighed on my existence like an incubus. I felt as if I was scientifically proved to be the helpless slave of antecedent circumstances; as if my character and that of all others had been formed for us by agencies beyond our control, and was wholly out of our own power. I often said to myself, what a relief it would be if I could disbelieve the doctrine of the formation of character by circumstances.
>
> —John Stuart Mill, *Autobiography* (1873)

> For, behold, this is what it is to be human . . . a creature with a will, at once bound and free.
>
> —Pope Gregory I

We humans obviously were not cut out to understand the problem of free will and determinism. That does not prevent us from trying. Year after year, generation after generation, the books and essays issue forth, not only those that address the problem directly (shelved under "theology" and "philosophy"), but also those bearing labels such as "history," "social science," "hermeneutics," "structuralism," or "deconstruction" that become entangled in its coils

The original version of this essay was prepared for the conference "The Culture of the Market," sponsored by the Murphy Institute of Political Economy, Tulane University, in March 1990. Jonathan Riley commented on the paper at the conference, and I am indebted to him for several changes, none of which are likely to persuade him. Richard Teichgraeber, Director of the Murphy Institute, provided useful advice, as did Marilyn Brown, Alan Kahan, Wilfred McClay, and Martin Wiener. Later versions of the essay benefited from the comments of Stefan Collini, John Daly, more or less inadvertently. Many a proud discovery amounts to nothing more than an unwitting echo of Pelagius or Augustine; few authors find anything more profound to say than Gregory I, who candidly admitted defeat.[1] To be in the grip of convictions about freedom and fate that are at once compelling and irreconcilable is evidently part of what it means to be human.

The famous "dejection" or "mental crisis" that John Stuart Mill experienced as a young man can serve as a reminder that the conundrums of freedom and fate are not exclusively philosophical but are also psychological. Whatever else it may be, freedom is in the first instance a matter of perception. To be "free" instead of determined is to perceive oneself, or one's choices and actions, as causes instead of effects, as origins that reach creatively into the future, rather than terminations foreordained by antecedent events. It is, at least provisionally, to perceive oneself as an uncaused cause. Yet after Darwin it is no longer clear how there can be any such thing as an uncaused cause. Thus we stumble over the problem of freedom every time we attribute causal status to ourselves, other persons, things, conditions, or events—which is to say we are always stumbling over the problem, for attributing causation is a game we humans play incessantly.[2]

Like all games, the game of causal attribution has rules, but they do not cover all situations, they remain open to dispute, and they often are observed in the breach. Even when played by the rules, the game is afflicted by all the infirmities that predictably characterize human thinking about freedom and fate. Still, like other norms, the rules of causal attribution prevail on the whole and in the main, loosely governing the way the game is played, even when the players are not conscious of them and are quite incapable of putting them into words. It is by means of this rule-bound game that we construct and sustain, moment by moment, the cultural universe in which we live. To know how people play the game of causal attribution is to know nearly all there is to know about their form of life, for the web of cultural meanings in which we human beings suspend ourselves is largely made up of cause and effect relations. But for our perception of causal connection, experience would collapse into a heap of unrelated bits and pieces. Causation, as one British philosopher put it, is the "cement," or glue, that holds our world together.[3] We play the game, organizing our experience into meaningful configurations, every time

Thomas Grey, Charles Lockhart, Bruce Mazlish, and Carole Pateman. Having acknowledged their influence, I do not hesitate to claim responsibility for any blame or praise the essay may attract—thus providing a homey illustration of the intransitivity that authorship (indeed, life itself) presupposes. The essay also appears in *The Culture of the Market: Historical Essays,* ed. Thomas L. Haskell and Richard F. Teichgraeber III (Cambridge: Cambridge University Press, 1993), 441–502.

we connect one element to another causally—every time we feel proud for the good we have done, or guilty for the bad; every time we praise others for what they have accomplished, or blame them for their failings; every time we welcome the punishment of a criminal, or rejoice at the vindication of an innocent person; every time we curse our fate or thank our lucky stars; every time we explain events by saying, "This happened because of that," or "This produced that," or "She made it," or "He did it," or "I've got the flu."

We cannot fry an egg, drive to work, please a lover, or explain why we are late without drawing on our knowledge of causal relations. Tacit imputations of causation are what enable us to make the distinctions we depend upon every day between innocence and complicity, originality and imitation, spontaneity and deliberateness, exploitation and just compensation, accident and design. Perceptions of causal relations permeate everything we think, say, or do, and it could not be otherwise, for the rules of causal attribution are, after all, the rules of change itself; of being and nonbeing, of how things come into, and go out of, existence. All our judgments, moral and factual alike, depend upon deciding what is cause, what is effect. Nothing could be more fundamental, or more paradoxical.

Much of our confusion about freedom and fate stems from the fact that the rules that govern the game of causal attribution are themselves in play. They change; they, too (within limits), come into and go out of existence, and thus different eras, different cultures, or even different factions within a single culture may play the game differently. This essay will touch upon such a change, one of such immense scale that we might better describe it as an upheaval, and one that is intimately associated (as cause? as effect?) with the rise of market culture.

Our focal point is the experience of one man, the philosopher John Stuart Mill, who, in 1826, at the age of twenty, was temporarily paralyzed by the fear that, despite all appearances to the contrary, he was a passive "stock or stone," destitute of emotional vitality, incapable of originating action, merely a "helpless slave of antecedent circumstances"—a being whose freedom to choose and think and act was, in his own eyes, empty and merely formal.[4] The mental crisis occupies a large place in Mill's *Autobiography* and has attracted the attention of many scholars, but none, I think, have taken Mill literally enough. He himself described his crisis as a matter of causal attribution. So persuaded was he of the force of circumstances in shaping character that he found it impossible, for a time, to cast himself in a causal role. He came to regard himself as literally inconsequential, as devoid of agency, incapable of having effect. What dejected him, he said, was the fear that, all subjective appearances to the contrary, everything he did and thought originated not with him, but in the antecedent circumstances that had made him the person he was.

On his own account, in other words, the crisis arose out of the *transitivity* of cause-and-effect relationships, the fact that anything we call a "cause" (including even the voluntary choices and actions of apparently free human agents) can upon logical reflection be regarded as the *effect* of prior causes, thereby compromising its causal status. How we distinguish one link in a chain or network of cause-and-effect connections and construe it as "the cause" of subsequent events (a construal that always requires us to exclude from consciousness another set of reflections that would instead construe it as an effect of antecedent events) is one of the abiding problems in the philosophy of causal attribution, and one that holds immense practical significance for the interpretation of human affairs. Indeed, in this regard the rules of the attributive game, by allocating causation between the self and the circumstances that impinge upon it, quite literally constitute personhood. Whatever else the self may be, it is at least that shadowy region where the influence of environing circumstances seems to leave off and awareness of conscious choice and action seems to begin. Insofar as the rules of the game prompt us to see the relation between environing circumstance and human action in an intransitive light, we experience the self as an uncaused cause, a pure point of origin, a kind of cornucopia in which purposeful activity arises out of nothing and surges into the world. When on the contrary we construe that relation in a more transitive light, as Mill did in the depths of his dejection, fate expands at the expense of freedom, and the very existence of the self can be placed in jeopardy.

Since a person can be regarded as free only to the extent that he or she is construed as causally efficacious, the problem of transitivity is the classic problem of freedom and fate, recast in psychological and attributive rather than philosophical terms.[5] As Gregory I observed so long ago, depending on the angle of view taken, the human will can always be seen as either "bound" (a product of external and antecedent circumstances), or "free" (not merely one link among others in a causal chain originating elsewhere, but an *origin* of such chains). Compelling evidence can be cited for either view, and the choice between them can be momentous, but to fully embrace the truth of one, as Mill found, is to negate the equally compelling truth of the other.

Although previous writers have not been unaware that Mill talked about the crisis in terms of causal attribution, they have seen little significance in the terms he chose. Several have treated his causal language as an intellectualization of something more visceral: the young man's Oedipal rebellion against his father, James Mill, whose Draconian project for educating his children could hardly help leaving them feeling that they had been "formed . . . by agencies beyond our control." Without denying in the least the father's dominance, the son's rebellion, or even the overtones of sexual rivalry that a Freudian interpretation would give to their relationship, I contend that the younger Mill got it right the first time: his problem was first and foremost the transitivity of causation. His progenitor's domineering ways presented that problem in such an acute manner that it could not be evaded, but the problem was not confined to James Mill, or to domineering fathers generally. Compelled by his father's intrusiveness to grapple with the problem of transitivity, the young man was among the first to discover that the resources supplied by market culture are not well suited to that task.

It was not accidental, I shall argue, that the young man who underwent this crisis was raised in a family whose spiritual history so closely corresponds to the momentous trajectory that Max Weber traced from a pious "Protestant ethic" in the seventeenth century, to a utilitarian and secular ethic, highly conducive to capitalism, by the end of the eighteenth. Nor was it accidental, I believe, that this especially acute episode of anxiety about freedom and consequentiality should have occurred in the world's most advanced market economy just as it was setting forth on the rocky road to full-scale industrial capitalism. Least of all is it incidental that this youth, who feared in 1826 that his self might be swallowed up in a sea of circumstantiality, only a few years earlier had been euphorically confident of his power to outwit fate and construct a future of his own choosing. John Stuart Mill's youthful oscillation between the extremes of voluntaristic euphoria and fatalistic dejection was, I believe, precisely the experience that enabled him to become, as a mature adult, one of the principal intellectual architects of a new market-oriented form of life, one that subtly and profoundly altered ancient boundaries between freedom and fate in Western culture.

In later years Mill wrote influentially on the logic of science, rescued utilitarianism from the eccentricities of Jeremy Bentham, pioneered in the fledgling discipline of political economy, and wrote such cornerstones of the Liberal tradition as "On Liberty" and "On the Subjugation of Women." Although we customarily associate Max Weber's famous thesis with those who truck and trade in the marketplace, there is a broader sense, recognized by Weber, in which the utility-maximizing "Spirit of Capitalism" found in John Stuart Mill its most sophisticated exemplar. In saying this, I do not forget Mill's respect for socialism or mistake him for an uncritical admirer of the market. My point is simply that in the grand narrative Weber told of Europe's journey away from traditional contentment-with-things-as-they-are toward the obsessive rationalization of the "iron cage," capitalism and socialism figure not as antitheses, but as parallel tracks leading to the same destination.[6]

That such an astute observer, and one so well placed to discern the innermost tendencies of a market-oriented form of life, should have chosen to make the story of his youthful "mental crisis" the central event of his *Autobiography* tells us something important about the precariousness of selfhood and the evanescence of the experience of freedom in the culture of capitalism. And that, in turn, can tell us something important about an upheaval in the conventions of causal attribution that began more than two centuries ago and that continues to shake the foundations of Western culture today.

Mill's mental crisis embodies in psychological miniature an attributive predicament that by the end of the nineteenth century had assumed the proportions of a culture-wide malaise. We live today in a culture that is perpetually riven by seemingly unresolvable disputes between "formalists" and "antiformalists," between those who construe persons as autonomous agents, only intransitively related to the circumstances of their lives, and those who construe persons transitively, as products of a circumstantial setting that profoundly influences everything they think or do, quite literally making them the persons they are. For convenience, I speak of two fixed and opposed poles, but in truth "formalism" and "antiformalism" are inherently relative, constantly in motion, and very much matters of degree. One generation's bold new antiformalism has often become the next generation's stale formalism; both can reside uncomfortably in a single troubled mind; each calls the other into being by labeling and condemning it.

Ancient though the dilemmas of freedom and fate undoubtedly are, it is only in the form of life spawned by the market that the rules of the attributive game become so elastic and unstable that every event is open to multiple interpretations, ranging from "formalistic" ones, which construe thinkers and actors as uncaused causes, to "deep," "structural," or "radical" ones, which treat conscious choice and perception as reflexes of underlying realities. Market culture on this interpretation creates a world of depths and surfaces, in which politics involves not only a clash of interests but also a struggle between incommensurable modes of interpretation, each professing allegiance to its own distinctive pattern of causal attribution and incredulous of all alternatives. To intellectuals, those members of the culture who specialize in interpretive virtuosity, no cause is uncaused, no choice spontaneous, no act uninterested, no person unselfish, no interpretation immune to the charge of formality. As an uncommonly articulate eyewitness to the early stages of the upheaval that produced this disturbing situation, and an early victim of the fears it aroused, John Stuart Mill deserves our close attention.

Before examining Mill's own account of his mental crisis, we should take note of a quirk of perspective that threatens to mislead us about his role in history. When Oliver Wendell Holmes, John Dewey, Thorstein Veblen, Charles Beard, and other American intellectuals embarked upon their highly successful "revolt against formalism" at the beginning of this century, they pointed to John Stuart Mill as a prime exemplar of the brittle formalities they hoped to sweep away.[7] Like the Foucauldians and Derrideans of the 1980s, the antiformalists of Dewey's generation armed themselves with a broadly historicist critique of reason, but (again like their "postmodern" counterparts) their historicism was no guarantee of sensitivity to the historicity of the debate in which they were engaged. In choosing Mill as their target, they displayed ironically short historical memories, for in his own day Mill and his utilitarian friends were for good reason regarded as "philosophic radicals," who delighted in unmasking formalities and demonstrating that behind all fine words and high ideals the real motor of human affairs was interest. Interest itself they understood to be the conscious trace of an inborn urge to maximize pleasure and minimize pain, not much less mechanical in its operation than the tendency of plants to turn away from shadow and toward light. "Interest" has been a rallying cry of antiformalists ever since—when we discount the reasons people give for their choices and insist instead upon the driving force of interest, we depict them as creatures of circumstance, actors whose conduct becomes all too predictable once their needs and wants, their most urgent contingencies and dependencies, have been identified.[8]

   That Mill could be construed by his own generation as a militant antiformalist and by the next generation as virtually the inventor of formalism says something, of course, about his ambivalence, and the ambivalence that must be felt by anyone who thinks deeply on these issues. It says still more about the succession of ever more militant versions of antiformalism that cascaded down through the nineteenth century, each triumphantly relabeling its predecessors "formalistic." This was, after all, the century that began with Kant and ended with Nietzsche. It began, that is, with a philosophy that profoundly subverted common sense by conceding that reason, forever imprisoned within the circumstances of its own structure, could never achieve certainty about things-in-themselves, and it ended with Nietzsche, who dismissed all talk of a world beyond the phenomenal and construed reason itself in a radically transitive light, as nothing more than sheep's clothing for the dark cunning of the will.

More important for my immediate purposes, however, Mill's reputation for antiformalism in his own generation and formalism in the next says worlds about the singularity of his moment in history. He was one of the first post-Christian theorists of human agency, and among all such theorists he was perhaps the very first to strive for a complete and balanced view of the matter.[9] Unlike Helvétius and La Mettrie and other materialists of the previous century, who, in the face of stiff resistance, were content to score polemical points against the monolithic voluntarism of the Church, Mill did not feel embattled and did not bother to attack (or defend) any religious conception of the relation between persons and circumstances. "I was brought up from the first," he said, "without any religious belief, in the ordinary acceptation of the term. . . . I am thus one of the very few examples, in this country, of one who has, not thrown off religious belief, but never had it: I grew up in a negative state with regard to it." Growing up in no faith at all was sufficiently eccentric in Mill's youth that his father, James Mill, an agnostic and an outspoken champion of candor and free speech, advised his son to hide his unbelief from the world, a pretense that the boy found vexatious but prudent. By the time the younger Mill wrote his *Autobiography* in the 1850s, candid avowals of unbelief had become acceptable in intellectual circles, but this was a dramatic change: he called it a "great advance in liberty of discussion . . . one of the most important differences between the present time and that of my childhood."[10]

As a distinctively secular thinker, one of the principal lessons that Mill drew from his youthful mental crisis and then developed in his mature philosophy was that in matters bearing on freedom and fate, the only safe ground lay in the middle. The extreme positions lying to either side were untenable—"free will" because it imputed to mankind an implausible capacity for transcendence, and "determinism" because it led to the fatalism and paralysis that Mill knew all too well from firsthand experience. To define the problem this way, as a matter of seeking a *via media* between rejected extremes, is the distinctive feature of the secular worldview that Western intellectuals adopted as religion lost its grip on their world. As we shall see, the Christian framework that had once reigned supreme and that during Mill's lifetime still retained the loyalty of most of his contemporaries, defined the problem in a quite different way, which did not attach any particular premium to a middle path. Although for believers it safeguarded the integrity of the self more effectively than any secular scheme is ever likely to do, it also paradoxically allowed for a much fuller acknowledgment of the role played by circumstantiality.

Mill may well strike us today as he struck Dewey's generation, as excessively formal. He certainly could never have said with Gadamer that "the self-awareness of the individual is only a flickering in the closed circuits of historical life."[11] Yet Mill's thought is far more akin to our own than that of Coleridge or others among his contemporaries whose allegiance to Christian conceptions of the soul and Providential modes of interpretation remained intact. However we may differ from him, he shares our secular assumptions, and in the broad sweep of history that makes him one of us. To see how differently the problem of transitivity was dealt with in the Christian era and how pioneering Mill's treatment of it was, consider the contrast between his attitude toward circumstantiality and that of Martin Luther, writing three centuries earlier in an era of uncompromised faith.

Luther published *The Bondage of the Will* in 1525 as a refutation of Erasmus. In it the world is depicted as a cosmic contest between adversaries of such stupendous power that no thought of human freedom could plausibly arise. "All Christians know," wrote Luther, "that there are in the world two kingdoms at war with each other. In the one, Satan reigns. . . . In the other kingdom Christ reigns. His kingdom continually resists and wars against that of Satan; and we are translated into His kingdom, not by our own power, but by the grace of God, which delivers us from this present evil world and tears us away from the power of darkness." Human autonomy being out of the question in such a world, the only issue was which master to serve, which army to join. "The knowledge and confession of these two kingdoms, ever warring against each other with all their might and power, would suffice by itself to confute the doctrine of 'free will,' seeing that we are compelled to serve in Satan's kingdom if we are not plucked from it by Divine power. The common man, I repeat, knows this, and confesses it plainly enough by his proverbs, prayers, efforts and entire life."[12]

Given the necessity of submitting either to Satan or to God, a variety of radical situatedness became not only acceptable to Luther, but the proper goal of life. The abandonment of any pretense to autonomy or intransitivity was all to the good, just so long as one could be sure that it was the hand of God in which one was situated. Autonomy thus held no appeal for Luther, and, still more surprising in modern eyes, circumstantiality held no terror.

I frankly confess that, for myself, even if it could be, I should not want "free will" to be given to me, nor anything to be left in my own hands to enable me to endeavor after salvation; not merely because in face of so many dangers, and adversities, and assaults of devils, I could not stand my ground and hold fast my "free will" (for one devil is stronger than all men, and on these terms no man could be saved); but because, even were there no dangers, adversities, or devils I should still be forced to labour with no guarantee of success, and to beat my fists at the air. If I lived and worked to all eternity, my conscience would never reach comfortable certainty as to how much it must do to satisfy God. Whatever work I had done, there would still be a nagging doubt as to whether it pleased God, or whether he required something more. The experience of all who seek righteousness by works proves that; and I learned it well enough myself over a period of many years, to my own great hurt. But now that God has taken my salvation out of the control of my own will, and put it under the control of His, and promised to save me, not according to my working or running, but according to His own grace and mercy, I have the comfortable certainty that He is faithful and will not lie to me, and that he is also great and powerful, so that no devils or opposition can break him or pluck me from Him.[13]

The contrast between Mill and Luther could not be more striking. Mill was terrorized by the thought that he was the "helpless slave of antecedent circumstances," but Luther welcomed the bondage of his will and drew strength from the thought that his every choice and act originated not in him, but in antecedent circumstances that had been willed by (or were identical with) his ever active, omnipotent Creator. Mill and Luther played the game of causal attribution by very different rules, and the heart of the difference was Mill's inability to believe in a Divine Being whose essence was precisely that He was the cause of everything, including the circumstances in which the self was situated.

To put the matter in terms that are highly anachronistic (and theologically indelicate) but nonetheless instructive for secular, twentieth-century people such as ourselves, we might say that the whole point of theology—of speculations about a Being who is understood to be the Creator and First Cause of all that exists—is to confront the problem of causal transitivity in the most thoroughgoing way and take the sting out of it once and for all. To conceive of one's self as snugly nestled in the palm of a beneficent God, and to feel that the active will of the omnipotent Creator manifests itself in all one's acts and choices, is, after all, an experience of radical situatedness—but not a displeasing or debilitating one. In effect, religion resolves the problem of transitivity and banishes the terrors that circumstantial determination arouses by first conceding that the self is not an uncaused cause, but then by simultaneously insisting that what the self is the effect of, what it owes its existence to, is neither the endless and aimless interweavings of natural causal processes, nor the banalities of happenstance, but the First Cause Himself. "If we cannot be uncaused causes," religionists as much as say, "let us be the unmediated effects of the First Cause." If our lives must be seen in part as the unwitting products of a particular circumstantial setting, let us divinize the circumstances that hold us in thrall by construing ourselves as the creatures of a loving Creator, and life's setting itself as the instrument by which His will be done.[14]

The quintessentially causal language in which God was customarily addressed—"Maker," "Father," "First Cause," "Prime Mover," "Creator"—says much about the game of causal attribution that prevailed in the Christian era. Insofar as people felt in their lives the active presence and power of such a supremely causal entity, the question of transitivity simply could not arise in its modern form. As long as persons and their choices were understood to be the products of God's will, evidence of transitivity could only flatter their self-esteem, for it was a token of their Godliness, their intimate proximity to the First Cause. As Mill's contemporary Samuel Coleridge put it,

> In the Bible each agent appears and acts as a self-subsisting individual: each has a life of its own, and yet all are one life. The elements of necessity and free-will are reconciled in the higher power of an omniscient Providence, that predestinates the whole in the moral freedom of the integral parts. Of this the Bible never suffers us to lose sight. The root is never detached from the ground. It is God everywhere: and all creatures conform to his decrees, the righteous by performance of the law, the disobedient by the sufferance of the penalty.[15]

Insofar as God's omnipotence was understood to extend "everywhere," crowding out the influence of mere mundane circumstances, or divinizing them, harnessing them to His ends, even the most insistent contingencies could not pose any threat to the integrity of the self or undermine the self's suitability for praise and blame. Mill's dejection arose precisely from the fear that his motives were not truly his, having been created by circumstances beyond his control. On Coleridge's interpretation, Mill's fear was misplaced. That a person's motives did not arise *de novo* from his or her understanding, but were the products of antecedent circumstances, did not bother Coleridge in the least, because he was confident that what stood behind the understanding of the faithful was a beneficent God. "The understanding may suggest motives, may avail itself of motives, and make judicious conjectures respecting the probable consequences of actions," said Coleridge. "But the Knowledge taught in the Scriptures *produces* the motives. . . . Strange as this will appear to such as forget that motives can be causes only in a secondary and improper sense . . . motives themselves are effects, the principle of which, good or evil, lies far deeper."[16]

Danger lay not in admitting the situatedness of the self, but only in getting the situation wrong—mistaking the hand of Satan for that of God. The anxious balancing act between autonomy and dependence that makes Mill seem to us familiar today could not begin until the First Cause had faded, for only then could circumstantiality take on its present appearance as a debilitating miasma that, if not kept at arm's length, threatens to engulf the self. Virtually everyone today takes it for granted, as Mill did in his mature writing, that the extreme positions on either side of the debate are to be avoided. What we want today, and what each of us optimistically imagines himself or herself to have achieved, is an understanding of the relation between persons and circumstances that "does justice" to both autonomy and dependence, that "balances" the opposing claims of agency and structure, of free will and determinism— that, in the astute words of Michael Sandel, avoids both the "radically disembodied subject" toward which formalism tends, and the "radically situated subject" toward which antiformalism tends.[17] We agree, in other words, that persons are neither independent of their circumstances nor seamlessly interwoven with them and that the relation between self and circumstance is neither wholly intransitive nor wholly transitive. Able to agree about little else, we carve out a "middle path" and wonder why everyone else's "middle path" fails to correspond with our own.[18] No one, let it be noticed, no matter how sensational their structuralist rhetoric (e.g., "the author is dead") admits personally to being a mere "creature of circumstance," undeserving of either credit or blame for anything that happens in the world. Today even the most reckless secular antiformalist will admit, at least when pressed, that the very idea of personhood seems to require some degree of autonomy, for if the self were nothing more than an empty conduit through which environmental forces surged, unhindered and unchanged, it would be literally inconsequential, incapable of having effect in the world, and thus no proper self at all.[19] It was precisely the loss of this autonomy, and fear that he was, indeed, a "radically situated subject," incapable of truly originating anything, unsuitable either for praise or blame, that plunged the young John Stuart Mill into such deep despair.

Indispensable though some saving residue of autonomy is to our sense of balance, we seem unable to justify our intuitions about it. We wonder if autonomy is but a pale substitute for "soul." Jon Elster speaks for us all when he confesses that "I can offer no satisfactory definition of autonomy."

> Just as there are persons known for their judgement, there are persons that apparently are in control over the processes whereby their desires are formed, or at least are not in the grip of processes with which they do not identify them-

selves. Yet the identity and even the existence of such persons is much more controversial than in the case of judgement. . . . One might fear that when the list of non-autonomous processes of desire formation is extended, as it has been in the past, and surely will be in the future, it will come to gobble up all our desires, leaving nothing to autonomy.[20]

Most of us muddle along, steering clear of all obvious exaggerations of either freedom or fate, only vaguely aware of our residual reliance on a notion of autonomy that we are not at all sure how to defend. It is some comfort to know that in this respect we share a good deal with our pre-Christian ancestors in fifth-century Athens. One of the central preoccupations of ancient Greek thought, Martha Nussbaum eloquently observes, was a hope at once "splendid and equivocal":

> However much human beings resemble lower forms of life, we are unlike, we want to insist, in one crucial respect. We have reason. We are able to deliberate and choose, to make a plan in which ends are ranked, to decide actively what is to have value and how much. All this must count for something. If it is true that a lot about us is messy, needy, uncontrolled, rooted [like a growing plant] in the dirt and standing helplessly in the rain, it is also true that there is something about us that is pure and purely active, something that we could think of [as Plato did] as being "divine, immortal, intelligible, unitary, indissoluble, ever self-consistent and invariable."

Much as secular Western intellectuals strive today for a *via media* between rejected extremes, so the Greeks, on Nussbaum's interpretation, tried to balance "the pursuit of self-sufficiency" and the "effort to banish contingency from human life" against their own "vivid sense of the special beauty of the contingent and the mutable." Their "love for the riskiness and openness of empirical humanity," Nussbaum explains, found poignant expression in "recurrent stories about gods who fall in love with mortals."[21]

Christianity told a less equivocal story, about a God who monopolized causal potency throughout the universe and assumed human form only in order to redeem the faithful and rescue them from mortality itself. Not content to leave the "splendid hope" a plaything of fate or capricious gods, Christians conceived of a God whose irresistible influence extended everywhere and pervaded mundane affairs, domesticating and divinizing them for the benefit of His followers. Protestants went even farther than traditional Christians by accentuating the Augustinian theme of predestination and stressing Providential modes of interpretation. Theirs was a world in which fortune and fate were regarded as words of the heathen. Everything that happened happened because God willed it to happen, if not directly then indirectly through the gift of moral freedom bestowed on those whom He predestined for salvation.

The gradual decay in the West of the ancient practice of construing the events of this world as the effects of divine will is the most dramatic change in the game of causal attribution that history records. "Secularization," the opaque and uninformative label customarily given to this change, heralded the emergence of a new attributive game in which the self, no longer sheltered from the random play of undivinized circumstance, would be obliged to abandon time-honored assumptions about its place in the world and devise new strategies suitable for a temporally and causally boundless universe. Unable to construe the events of this world as effects set in motion by the First Cause, Mill found himself unable also to share Luther's calm acceptance of "radical situatedness," for when inquiry into the sources of the self cannot find any sure stopping place in the Creator, the chains of causal linkage run off to infinity, and the "splendid hope" of freedom is in perpetual danger of being swallowed up by fate. If Mill's struggles to reconceive the relation between self and world do not win the approval of twentieth-century readers because they seem half-hearted and residually "formal," it is not because we have found any satisfactory solution to the dilemmas he confronted.

Max Weber was onto something important when he identified the rise of capitalism with changes in religious sensibility. Indeed, I suspect that the relation between religion and economic change is even more intimate than he imagined. The change in religious sensibility that figures most prominently in Weber's thesis is the development within Christianity of an ethic of worldly asceticism, culminating in the Protestant Reformation. The inculcation of this ethic by Protestant divines, said Weber, unintentionally recruited large numbers of people into the self-monitoring, calculating, deliberate mode of life— a preparation for the life of "economic man"—without which the market's capacity for allocative efficiency could never have been fully realized. The discipline of supply and demand had little impact on people incapable of self-restraint or inattentive to economic self-interest. No reader of *The Protestant Ethic and the Spirit of Capitalism* could fail to recognize the importance of the Protestant ethic, but it is easy to overlook another change of religious sensibility that is logically just as important to Weber's argument. That change is secularization. Weber did not explore secularization or try to explain it, but simply asserted it as a ready-made explanation for the otherwise puzzling conjunction that made up his title: How did the "Protestant Ethic" evolve into the "Spirit of Capitalism"? Weber's none too illuminating answer was secularization, which drained the Protestant ethic of its original purpose of glorifying God, and thus left behind a dry husk of habit, devoid of religious meaning, which obliged its adherents to labor diligently in their callings; to strive always to maximize their assets, whether personal or material; and to do so as an end in itself, neither having nor seeming to require any higher justification. As we turn now to the first part of the story leading up to Mill's mental crisis, it is important to recall that he embodied both of the changes in religious sensibility that Weber referred to: he was both an heir to the Protestant ethic and the architect of a form of life that was distinctively both economic and secular.

James Mill, who was raised in the church and trained as a Scotch Presbyterian preacher, took care to instruct his children in ecclesiastical history. His son remembered being encouraged "to take the strongest interest in the Reformation, as the great and decisive contest against priestly tyranny for liberty of thought." But the elder Mill ultimately repudiated the religion he was licensed to preach and threw aside even deism on the moral grounds that any all-powerful being would have to be regarded as the author of unspeakable evils. The most important religious lesson that John Stuart Mill remembered learning from his father was agnostic. That lesson took just the form one would predict of a person who had once expected to see the hand of God in all the events of this world, but who found that mode of causal attribution impossible to sustain and therefore had to adapt to another, in which certain questions, once answerable in terms of divine will, no longer could even be asked. The lesson, explicitly causal, was this: "The manner in which the world came into existence was a subject on which nothing was known [and] . . . the question 'Who made me?' cannot be answered." [22]

In the absence of a benign First Cause, the question "Who [or what] made me?" tugs at the lid of a Pandora's box full of transitive possibilities. That question would haunt Mill during his "mental crisis," but during the years of his youth leading up to that event, he seems to have been preoccupied with another question, equally causal, but pointing, as it were, in exactly the opposite direction: *What can I make, or do?* The latter question, which casts the self in the role of maker instead of thing made, cause instead of effect, disembodied subject instead of situated object, had about it in Mill's lifetime an aura of novelty and excitement and open-ended hopefulness that we jaded denizens of the twentieth century can scarcely imagine. It was the question on which utilitarianism was built, and it was a question that in the very asking tended to draw a veil over its increasingly alarming counterpart in the game of causal attribution, "Who [or what] made me?"

Under the tutelage first of his father — "The last of the eighteenth century," as the son later called him (213) — and then Jeremy Bentham, the younger Mill was led to believe that the horizons of what was called "human improvement" were in his lifetime expanding in every direction, opening up a bright new world of possibilities for human mastery after millennia of abject acquiescence in fate. Futile though reason might be when inquiring into first causes and the origins of selfhood (Who made me?), an agnostic of the Millian variety saw no reason for dismay. What mattered was one's ability cogently to assess the circumstances of the present and chart a course toward a desirable future (What can I make?). The paramount question was not about the past, but about the future, not what made the self, but what sort of world the self could make. And as to the world's plasticity, and the power and creativity of the self to use reason instrumentally to bring about future states of the world by actions taken in the present — as to all these matters pertaining to human agency, the younger Mill was taught to have no doubts at all. About his ability to help make a new and better world, he was initially as confident as a proper Scotch Presbyterian would have been about tracing the origins of *his* highest self back to the amazing and undeserved grace of the Creator, thus answering unequivocally the question, "Who made me?"

But just as a shadow of doubt always accompanied the scrupulous Presbyterian's confidence that his true self had been molded by the hand of God, so the younger Mill's confidence in his own capacity to make a better world was subtly undercut from the beginning. As is well known, his father, James Mill, enthusiastically embraced the environmentalism of Locke, Hartley, and the French philosophes, and took it to justify, or rather require, an unprecedented extension of parental responsibility for the education of the young. Of all the enlightened doctrines that James Mill stood for, none was more fundamental to his thinking, according to his son, than that which taught "the formation of all human character by circumstances, through the universal Principle of Association, and the consequent unlimited possibility of improving the moral and intellectual condition of mankind by education" (111). The wonder, from our retrospective vantage point, is that the generations of reformers that embraced this doctrine so enthusiastically construed it entirely as a measure of their own "unlimited" power and responsibility to shape the future — not as an unsettling reminder that their own character was susceptible to similar shaping forces and their own autonomy no more than a fragile hope. The result of the doctrine in James Mill's case was an educational regime for his son so aggressive that although its explicit lesson may have been free agency, it also conveyed a tacit message of a very different kind.

The younger Mill's instruction began with Greek at age three and proceeded at breakneck pace from *Aesop's Fables,* the first Greek text he read, to Plato's dialogues, including the *Theætetus,* which he read (finding it "totally impossible" to understand) by the age of seven. The boy's schoolday began before breakfast—he accompanied his father on walks through the countryside, telling him of the books he had read and taken notes on the day before: Xenophon on Socrates; the histories of Robertson, Hume, and Gibbon; McCrie's *Life of John Knox,* Sewall's and Rutty's histories of the Quakers; accounts of Drake and Cook and the great voyages, among many others. "He was fond of putting into my hands books which exhibited men of energy and resource in unusual circumstances, struggling against difficulties and overcoming them" (9, 11). The day continued at James Mill's writing table, where he cleared a space for his son and, although hard at work on his own *History of India*—and "one of the most impatient of men"—allowed himself to be interrupted every time the boy came to a Greek word that he did not know (9). Latin training commenced at age eight; Aristotle's *Organon* was tackled at twelve; and at age thirteen, a "complete course" of political economy, including the recently published work of David Ricardo, a friend of the family (13, 21, 31).

John Stuart Mill looked back upon this "unusual and remarkable" education with gratitude for the "advantage of a quarter of a century" that it gave him over his contemporaries, but his gratitude was mixed, as we can well imagine, with a good deal of ambivalence about the intensity of his father's influence over him (5, 33). Convinced of the power of circumstances and the plasticity of character, the elder Mill set out to fashion for his son a character that would be autonomous and creative in the highest degree. The son's subsequent career suggests that the father's project substantially succeeded. But the means to that end required that he lay siege to the child, annihilating today's autonomy for the sake of tomorrow's. "Whether I was more a gainer or a loser by his severity," John Stuart Mill later "hesitate[d]" to say, but he was sure that "the element which was chiefly deficient in his moral relation to his children, was that of tenderness" (53). "I was constantly meriting reproof by inattention, inobservance, and general slackness of mind in matters of daily life" (39). Standards seem to have been deliberately set impossibly high: "He was often, and much beyond reason, provoked by my failures in cases where success could not have been expected" (31). Other children were kept away, lest their influence intrude upon the father's. "Extreme vigilance" was exercised to prevent the boy from hearing himself praised. "From his own intercourse with me, I could derive none but a very humble opinion of myself; and the standard of comparison he always held up to me, was not what other people did, but what a man could and ought to do" (35).

John Stuart Mill never forgot the place in Hyde Park where he and his father were walking when, at age fourteen, as the boy was about to leave the household for the first time, his father explained to him "that whatever I knew more than others, could not be ascribed to any merit in me, but to the very unusual advantage which had fallen to my lot, of having a father who was able to teach me, and willing to give the necessary trouble and time" (37). When some years later a friend, impressed by his sensitivity to poetry, admitted that at first Mill had seemed to him "a 'made,' or manufactured man," there can be little doubt about who Mill thought, or feared, his maker might be (163).

Still, the overt message of his early education was not to fret about ultimate origins or the grounding of selfhood, but instead to take his place confidently in the ranks of those fighting for the improvement of mankind. In that mission Jeremy Bentham rapidly assumed a tutorial status higher even than that of his father. Although Mill's education under his father had already been one long "course of Benthamism," when he read for himself the first pages of Bentham's *Traité de Législation* at age fifteen, the principle of utility "burst upon me with all the force of novelty."

> The reading of this book was an epoch in my life; one of the turning points in my mental history. . . . The feeling rushed upon me, that all previous moralists were superseded, and that here indeed was the commencement of a new era in thought. . . . Under the guidance of the ethical principle of Pleasurable and Painful Consequences, followed out in the method of detail introduced into these subjects by Bentham, I felt taken up to an eminence from which I could survey a vast intellectual domain, and see stretching out into the distance intellectual results beyond all computation. As I proceeded farther, there seemed to be added to this intellectual clearness, the most inspiring prospects of practical improvement in human affairs.

The elevated language of Mill's recollections, when he looked back on that moment from middle age, soars still higher:

> When I laid down the last volume of the *Traité*, I had become a different being. The "principle of utility," understood as Bentham understood it, and applied in the manner in which he applied it through these three volumes, fell exactly into its place as the keystone which held together the detached and fragmentary component parts of my knowledge and beliefs. I now had opinions; a creed, a doctrine, a philosophy: in one among the best senses of the word, a religion; the inculcation and diffusion of which could be made the principal outward purpose of a life. (69)

There is no more striking textual specimen than this of the limitless confidence so characteristic of late-eighteenth- and early-nineteenth-century reformers, as their causal horizon billowed outward and brought within what seemed easy reach of instrumental reason an immense range of opportunities for doing good — "opportunities" that had hitherto seemed impossibly remote and intractable, and therefore not really opportunities at all. In this heady experience lies the origin of the humanitarian sensibility: with every new opportunity came new responsibilities, new sources of guilt, new occasions for the commission of evil through omitting to do good.[23] The heightened sense of agency struck the young Mill with all the force of a religious conversion, supplying him at one stroke with an identity and a mission in life — a "religion," he did not hesitate to call it. That sense of power had been centuries in preparation, but what crystallized it for him was Bentham's daring delineation of cause-and-effect linkages suitable for the use of reform-minded legislators aiming at the reengineering of man and society. No wonder the shock of recognition left the boy feeling whole for the first time, a "different being," viewing the world from on high, intellectually in command of a vast domain. He knew how powerfully circumstances could shape character. After all, Bentham's recipes for altering individual and social character by manipulating the circumstances of people's lives differed only in scale and scope of ambition from the ones Mill's father had employed so successfully in making him the singularly well educated person he was.

The word "utilitarianism" was given its modern signification in the winter of 1822–23, when Mill, a boy of sixteen, formed the idea of a fortnightly gathering of young disciples in the home of Bentham, who lived nearby and was his father's close associate. Mill christened it the "Utilitarian Society," borrowing the unfamiliar term from a novel about a Scotch clergyman who warned his parishioners not to "leave the Gospel and become utilitarians" (81). The society continued to meet until 1826, when Mill turned twenty and the "mental crisis" struck.

During the three and a half years between John Stuart Mill's discovery of Bentham and his breakdown, there was little to suggest that his father's project had been anything but successful. In 1823 the precocious lad was given a sinecure in the East India Company, working as a clerk under the direct supervision of his father in the office of the Examiner of East India Correspondence. Though still in his teens, his letters and articles on parliamentary affairs, defects of the law, and religious freedom began appearing in such Liberal and quasi-radical periodicals as the *Traveller* and the *Morning Chronicle.* Bentham took him on for a year as editor (and in some passages co-author) of the five-volume *Rationale of Judicial Evidence,* in Mill's mature opinion "one of the richest" of all Bentham's productions (119). The creation of the *Westminster Review* as the quasi-official organ of the "philosophical radicals" gave

Mill a receptive vehicle for his views, and he became its most prolific contributor. It was, he observed, "a time of rapidly rising Liberalism," and the *Review* "made a considerable noise in the world . . . [giving] a recognized *status* . . . to the Benthamic type of radicalism, out of all proportion to the number of its adherents" (101).

At an age when most people are still struggling to escape adolescence, Mill was associating with an increasingly illustrious set of friends and engaging in public debates with experienced orators twice or thrice his age. He was already a full-fledged political intellectual with a growing reputation and a brilliant future. Yet the chapter of his *Autobiography* in which he recounts his early publishing exploits in the *Westminster Review* is titled "Youthful Propagandism," and in retrospect he credited himself with little originality and only the appearance of self-possession. He took pains to note that although Bentham was the chief intellectual inspiration of the radicals, his father "exercised a far greater personal ascendancy": it was his father's opinions "which gave the distinguishing character to the Benthamic or utilitarian propagandism of the time." He gave his father credit for having "perfect command over his great mental resources," and he had never met anyone who "could do such ample justice to his best thoughts in colloquial discussion." The elder Mill's opinions "flowed from him in a continuing stream," and the younger Mill could conceive of himself as no more than a "channel" through which his father's energy poured into the world—a metaphor that in its perfect passivity says much about the young man's inability to cast himself successfully in the role of a genuinely creative causal agent (105). The same message is conveyed by his admission that during these years the common complaint against Benthamite radicals, that they were "mere reasoning machine[s], . . . [was] not altogether untrue of me" (111).

The utilitarian philosophy that so intoxicated the young John Stuart Mill was, from the neo-Kantian perspective of Max Weber, simply the "spirit of capitalism" in its most systematic, intellectualized aspect. Utilitarianism and the "spirit of capitalism" are nearly synonyms in Weber's vocabulary; they refer to the same dry husk of habit left behind when the Protestant ethic lost its anchorage in Christian piety. He spoke, for example, of the religious roots of the Protestant ethic dying out and "giving way to utilitarian worldliness," and of the "great religious ethic of the seventeenth century" bequeathing a pharisaically good conscience to its "utilitarian successor." Near the end of *The Protestant Ethic and the Spirit of Capitalism,* acknowledging the study's limitations, Weber said that in order to complete it, one would have to trace the emergence of secular rationalism through all the areas of ascetic religion, from the "medieval beginnings of worldly asceticism to its dissolution into pure utilitarianism."[24]

In Mill's day, utilitarianism was less a philosophy than a celebration and technical elaboration of human consequentiality. Its roots lay in the heightened sense of worldly agency that the Protestant ethic cultivated. Consider the words of Benjamin Franklin, another heir of the Protestant ethic whose utilitarian cast of mind is well known, and who served as Weber's prime exemplar of the "Spirit of Capitalism."

> Remember, that *time* is money. He that can earn ten shillings a day by his labour, and goes abroad, or sits idle, one half of that day, though he spends but sixpence during his diversion or idleness, ought not to reckon *that* the only expense; he has really spent, or rather thrown away, five shillings besides. . . .
>
> Remember, that *credit* is money. If a man lets his money lie in my hands after it is due, he gives me the interest. . . .
>
> He that kills a breeding-sow, destroys all her offspring to the thousandth generation. He that murders a crown, destroys all that it might have produced, even scores of pounds. . . .
>
> He that loses five shillings, not only loses that sum, but all the advantage that might be made by turning it in dealing, which by the time that a young man becomes old, will amount to a considerable sum of money. (48–50)

"That this is the spirit of capitalism which here speaks in characteristic fashion," wrote Weber in *The Protestant Ethic*, "no one will doubt, however little we may wish to claim that everything which could be understood as pertaining to that spirit is contained in it" (51). There is indeed little reason to doubt that Franklin's words embody the spirit of capitalism. What may be more surprising, in spite of Weber's routine association of utilitarianism with the spirit of capitalism, is the thought that these same words also express vital elements of the worldview that the younger Mill embraced when he embarked on a career of idealistic utilitarian and humanitarian reform. The suggestion seems at first glance counterintuitive. Capitalists, after all, pursue self-interest. Humanitarian reformers aim at altruistic ends, and over the course of the past two centuries it has often been private property and its bourgeois possessors that have blocked reform. What concern is it of the idealistic reformer that "time is money," or that lost shillings and dead breeding-sows entail what economists call "opportunity costs"?

Although Benjamin Franklin addressed his advice to young tradesmen who wanted to get rich, and Jeremy Bentham addressed his to legislators who presumably aspired to the greatest good for the greatest number, the two men's advice is crucially similar in what it presupposes about human agency. The two men played by the same rules of causal attribution. Both took for granted an audience whose members were alert to opportunity and confident of their ability to intervene in the course of human affairs and thereby to shape events to their own will. Both writers aimed to inculcate in their readers still greater alertness and self-confidence. The advice of both men embodied a novel attitude toward time, one that radically annexed the future to the present and made it malleable in the hands of the deliberate, farsighted actor. For Franklin and Bentham, as for James Mill and John Stuart Mill, the future is not something distant and inexorable that happens to us, regardless of our choices, but something that in large measure we are already creating, moment by moment, both by our actions and by our omissions to act in the present. So immediate is the future's relation to the present, so certain is the actor's capacity to shape it by embarking *now* on the preferred course of action, that the design and production of the future becomes a duty. To allow an unintended future to come about is to be careless, to betray a norm of responsibility.

Although Weber never spoke in terms of causal attribution, his highest ambition in *The Protestant Ethic* was to trace the historical emergence of this sense of duty, for he was convinced that this was the principal contribution that religion made to the rise of capitalism. Granting the force of Kurnberger's gibe that capitalists "make tallow out of cattle and money out of men," Weber nonetheless sharply distinguished the spirit of capitalism from acquisitiveness per se, and focused instead on a "peculiarity of this philosophy of avarice . . . above all the idea of a duty of the individual toward the increase of his capital, which is assumed as an end in itself."

> Truly what is here preached is not simply a means of making one's way in the world, but a peculiar ethic. The infraction of its rules is treated not as foolishness but as forgetfulness of duty. That is the essence of the matter. . . .
>
> And in truth this peculiar idea, so familiar to us to-day, but in reality so little a matter of course, of one's duty in a calling, is what is most characteristic of capitalistic culture, and is in a sense the fundamental basis of it. It is an obligation which the individual is supposed to feel and does feel toward the content of his professional activity, no matter in what it consists, in particular no matter whether it appears on the surface as a utilization of his personal powers, or only of his material possessions (as capital). (51, 54)

The altruistic Benthamite reformer and the calculating, leather-aproned shopkeeper cherished different goals, but both lived with one foot in the future and both displayed a heightened sense of causal agency that carried with it new obligations. Some of these new obligations were moral, some merely prudential. A person who felt obliged to honor the precept that "time is money" might, of course, fulfill that obligation entirely in prudential, self-serving ways. But once habituated to the idea that future and present are so closely and predictably related that it would be a breach of obligation to pass up any opportunity to make capital grow, some people were bound to transpose that future-oriented dutifulness into the moral sphere, and to conclude that it was a still greater breach of obligation to pass up opportunities to "do good" in a larger, more public sense. The sense of duty is the same in both cases, and so is the logic of causal attribution: the person who passes up opportunities, however slight, to make money must bear responsibility for the earnings forgone. Similarly, the person who passes up opportunities to do good—even indirect ones, like signing petitions and taking all the other complex steps necessary to uproot an institution as deeply entrenched as slavery—must bear responsibility for the continued existence of evil.

Morally, of course, there is a vital contrast between people whose felt obligation toward the future extends only to matters of self-interest and those whose concerns embrace the public interest as well. But what was historically novel in the period 1750–1850 was the perception of the future as plastic and the self as able, even duty-bound, to shape it. Thus for our purposes the businessman who mined the future for profit and the reformer who sculpted it in hopes of improving mankind had more in common with each other than either had with the people Weber called "traditionalists," who, because they ordinarily felt incapable of controlling the future—and certainly acknowledged no duty to do so—perceived themselves to be living in a different sort of world.

Weber, keenly aware of the artificiality of ideal types, but also cognizant of their heuristic indispensability, characterized the world of traditionalism as the reversed mirror image, as it were, of the "spirit of capitalism." The traditionalist saw in tradition an adequate guide to conduct, failed to see present acts and choices as having any very close or reliable instrumental relationship to the future, and displayed an attitude of resignation toward whatever life might bring. From this perspective, not intrinsically any less respectable in Weber's eyes than the one that prevails today, the present appeared to be an extension of the past, moving inexorably toward an unknowable destination under the influence of forces that dwarfed human volition. Since traditionalists did not view their present as a staging ground for the production of the future, they seldom encountered the most distinctive features of modern life, "opportunities," those curious temporal interfaces that permit us almost magically to reach through time, as it were, and secure particular futures by actions we take in the present. The very idea of an "opportunity" presupposes a predictable instrumental relation between present actions and future events that played little part in the traditional imagination. Thus the traditionalist laborer, when offered higher piece rates for getting the harvest in on time, instead quit working as soon as his or her customary wage was earned, leaving the crop to rot on the vine (59–60). "A man does not 'by nature' wish to earn more and more money," observed Weber, "but simply to live as he is accustomed to live and to earn as much as is necessary for that purpose. Wherever modern capitalism has begun its work of increasing the productivity of human labour by increasing its intensity, it has encountered the immensely stubborn resistance of this leading trait of pre-capitalistic labour" (60).[25]

Before Adam Smith's "invisible hand" could allocate goods and resources in its relentless but singularly efficient manner, there had to exist in the population substantial numbers of "economic men," people of a calculating and manipulative frame of mind, who did not take tradition as their guide and were not content with things as they always had been. They had to be alert to opportunity, attentive to the subtle disciplinary pressures created by changes in prices and wages, and willing to alter their modes of conduct so as to maximize every advantage. Weber recognized full well that capitalism had existed in isolated enclaves long before the Protestant Reformation. He also recognized that the market itself, by rewarding some character types and penalizing others, encouraged the development of the utility-maximizing sort of person that its efficient operation demanded. But he did not believe that the market by itself could ever have created—out of a population militantly averse to change and ideologically well armed against the *auri sacra fames*—sufficiently large numbers of "economic men" to account for the massive transformation of the western European economy that did, in fact, occur in the centuries following the Reformation.

> Thus the capitalism of to-day, which has come to dominate economic life, educates and selects the economic subjects which it needs through a process of economic survival of the fittest. But here one can easily see the limits of the concept of selection as a means of historical explanation. In order that a manner of life so well adapted to the peculiarities of capitalism could be selected at all, i.e. should come to dominate others, it had to originate somewhere, and not in isolated individuals alone, but as a way of life common to whole groups of men. This origin is what really needs explanation. (55)

What made the traditionalist's transformation into "economic man" so difficult to explain was that the traditionalist's most distinctive trait, his comparative blindness to opportunity, ruled out an entire range of explanations.

Ordinarily we explain what people do by showing that they had something to gain from it, that they were acting on interest, responding to incentives. But to speak of "gain," "interests," and "incentives" is to presuppose that the actor perceives opportunity as we do. Having defined traditionalists as people insensitive to the existence of opportunity, Weber obviously could not say that they adopted a radically new, opportunity-perceiving style of life because of the opportunities such a life offered. The emergence of "economic man" would be no puzzle at all if one could assume that opportunities for personal enrichment (or public improvement) were fixed facts with uniform and transparent meanings, sure to be grasped as such in any and all cultural settings. But Weber knew that this was not the case. Traditional society condemned the pursuit of Mammon, viewed change of all kinds with deep suspicion, and was populated by people whose understanding of the relationship between present and future discouraged perceptions of opportunity. Why had all this changed? Why would such people have ever abandoned their tradition-oriented way of life and adopted one of perpetual busy-ness and self-aggrandizement? What had induced the cognitive shift necessary to the emergence of "opportunity"? From our retrospective vantage point, it is all too easy to say that the prospect of a higher standard of living should have been more than enough to lure people out of traditional ways of life, which usually entailed penury, if not grinding poverty. But the prospect of affluence, even supposing it could have been brought into focus, could not have had any leverage on people who were traditionalists in the specific sense Weber so carefully defined—that is, who were *unresponsive* to incentives and *genuinely content* to do as they had always done. How, then, can we account for the change?

As is well known, Weber found in religion a solution to the puzzle. Although traditional culture prized stability and discouraged people from even recognizing the existence of material incentives for changing their lives, that culture did a great deal to sensitize them to religious incentives. In the intensely religious atmosphere of the sixteenth and seventeenth centuries, the one opportunity to shape the future that was deeply etched in the minds of all who were exposed to the teachings of the Church was that of salvation. For the sake of eternal life, Weber suggested, perhaps even traditionalists would abandon tradition, give up a life of satisfaction with things as they had always been, and embark upon a life of restless striving and ceaseless self-advancement.

For the purposes of the present argument, what is most important about Weber's thesis is his suggestion that the heightened sense of personal agency and obligation to grasp opportunity and construct the future that characterized the capitalist entrepreneur (and, by extension, altruistic reformers such as John Stuart Mill) was originally inculcated, paradoxically, by a religious doctrine that was stunningly deterministic. One of Weber's principal achievements in *The Protestant Ethic* was his demonstration that the logical implications of predestination, which undoubtedly pointed in the direction of fatalism and resignation to the will of God, were massively overshadowed by the psychological implications, which pointed in just the opposite direction.[26] The language of causal attribution developed in the preceding pages helps reinforce Weber's point. By reviving the Augustinian theme of predestination and hammering home the Protestant message of God's omnipotence and the utter impotence of the natural man to accomplish anything at all toward his own salvation, Calvin, like Luther before him, was carrying out a thoroughgoing divinization of the circumstances underpinning human existence. Calvin's human subject was, with a vengeance, "radically situated," for without an infusion of divine grace the natural man was wholly incapable of merit, and even the saint was understood to be dependent at every instant upon his Maker's gratuitous and undeserved mercy. In the words of a latter-day Calvinist, Jonathan Edwards, "The constant exercise of the infinite power of God is necessary to keep bodies in being."[27] To adopt the Protestant conviction that man was saved by "faith alone" was to insist on the transitivity of all cause-and-effect relations not originating directly in God, and to come very close to depicting God, not merely as the First Cause, but as the sole authentic cause in the universe. Nonetheless, for Calvin as for Luther, the resulting bondage to circumstance was sweet and liberating because the circumstances that shaped the conduct and personhood of the elect were understood to be the very substance of God's grace.[28]

Who was elect? Everything hinged on this. No scrupulous Calvinist could ever be sure of the answer. But as Weber showed in his discussion of the "doctrine of proof," believers were encouraged to look for signs of election in their everyday affairs, their "calling," and it was in this search that the "economic man" was forged. God in his inscrutable wisdom had predestined some to eternal life and others to an eternity of suffering. Convinced that the ways of God were inaccessible to human reason, but convinced also that the smallest and homeliest detail of everyday existence might signal the will of an omnipotent and ever active Being, believers anxiously examined the trajectory of their daily experience in hopes of catching glimpses of divine favor. Since God's grace was all that kept even the saints from sinking into the bottomless corruption of the natural world, any success in holding oneself upright had to be attributed only proximately to oneself and ultimately to God.

The logical impossibility of ascertaining one's own state of grace with certainty made self-surveillance all the more important and supplied believers with an unparalleled psychological incentive to become self-conscious, self-monitoring agents, who conceived of their lives as careers extending from past to present to future and who constantly adjusted their conduct so as to bring about the closest possible fit between present intentions and future conse- quences — all the while crediting whatever success they might achieve to an in- fusion of divine Grace. "Only a life guided by constant thought could achieve conquest over the state of nature," Weber observed. What Calvin demanded of his followers was "constant self-control" and a "systematic rational ordering of the moral life as a whole." Under the leadership of the Protestant reform- ers, Christian asceticism "slammed the door of the monastery behind it" and "strode into the market-place of life," seeking to discipline the spontaneity of the impulses and to penetrate the routine of everyday life with its methodi- cal rigor. And the vital step in fashioning a new form of life that would allow people to live in the world, but be neither of nor for this world, was to per- suade them to "act upon [their] constant motives" [29] — or, as we might say, to *intentionalize* their lives, acting always in such a way as to render their ex- perience, insofar as possible, a product (proximately, of course) of their own God-fearing intentions rather than of tradition, chance, accident, or the will of other human beings. Only persons bent upon the intentionalization of their lives and equipped with the recipe knowledge that that end presupposes can construe the production of the future as a duty, and thereby fulfill the vital prerequisite without which Weber doubted that modern capitalism could have come into being in Europe. In their campaign to humble all rivals to God's causal omnipotence, Protestants declared fortune and fate to be words of the heathen and construed their own agency in a radically transitive light, as the inexorable unfolding of a divine plan formed outside time. But in so doing they unintentionally created a niche in traditional culture within which, with- out incurring the sanctions either of conscience or of community, they could act for all the world as if they were duty-bound to pursue opportunities, re- spond to material incentives, make their own lives, and even become, for all practical purposes, "self-made men."

That a doctrine logically so deterministic, and so candidly designed to rid the universe of all agents but One, could in psychological practice sharpen the boundaries of personhood and powerfully heighten people's sense of re- sponsibility for the conduct of their own lives will always remain paradoxical, notwithstanding all Weber's elucidations. The paradox is testimony to the im- mensely different configuration that the problem of relating persons to their circumstances had under religious auspices as compared with its configuration today, when with some brave exceptions it is only the uneducated who continue to construe the world as a stage cunningly designed by God for the enactment of a drama of redemption. Among intellectuals living in the wake of Darwin—and in the wake of all the social and economic changes of the nineteenth and twentieth centuries that conspired palpably to reinforce Darwin's message of endless flux and contingency—design has disappeared from the universe and the circumstantial setting of human existence seems beyond any possibility of divinization.

We have seen the fruitfulness of Weber's insight that the psychological implications of a belief system need not correspond to its logical implications; that a doctrine pointing logically toward fatalism and resignation can, in practice, foster the most intense sort of activism. What Mill's mental crisis suggests is that the reverse is also true: a doctrine whose logical implications highlight the power of humans to make the world what they will, can, in practice, induce feelings of inconsequentiality and a beleaguered sense of self. Just as predestination can lead in practice to a keen awareness of all the respects in which the world depends upon the self, so the doctrine of utility, in spite of its overt celebration of the boundlessness of human agency, can lead to an oppressive sensitivity to all the respects in which the self depends upon the world. The truth of the proposition is plainly evident in the relation between James Mill and his son. It was an expansive sense of agency and a corresponding alertness to opportunity and feeling of obligation to superintend his son's education that led the father to intrude upon the boy's life, depriving him of every semblance of autonomy and leaving him convinced that he was "a 'made,' or manufactured man." The relation between father and son illustrates in miniature the peculiar dynamics of freedom and fate in the wider culture, for insofar as actors inhabit the same world, and are exposed to the consequences of one another's actions, the agency of one cannot fail to intrude upon and undermine the autonomy of the others. In the world of proliferating technique and technological innovation that the market fosters, every new capacity to act breeds feelings of incapacity in those who are acted upon, and every expansion of causal horizons renders more fragile the perceptions of intransitivity upon which autonomy depends. Far from being a polar opposition, the relation between freedom and fate begins to take on the ominous appearance of an identity.

The fifth chapter of the *Autobiography* is devoted to the "mental crisis" and the "important transformations in my opinions and character" that Mill attributed to it. He began his account of the crisis by recalling its "origin," the euphoria that swept over him upon reading Bentham. That he should thus identify his dejection and paralysis with the voluntaristic enthusiasm that immediately preceded it is a matter of considerable significance within the present interpretive framework, and a point to which we shall want to return. "From the winter of 1821, when I first read Bentham," he wrote, "I had what might truly be called an object in life; to be a reformer of the world. My conception of my own happiness was entirely identified with this object . . . my whole reliance was placed on this."

> This did very well for several years, during which the general improvement going on in the world and the idea of myself as engaged with others in struggling to promote it, seemed enough to fill up an interesting and animated existence. But the time came when I awakened from this as from a dream. It was in the summer of 1826. I was in a dull state of nerves, such as everybody is occasionally liable to; unsusceptible to enjoyment or pleasurable excitement; one of those moods when what is pleasure at other times, becomes insipid or indifferent; the state, I should think, in which converts to Methodism usually are, when smitten by their first "conviction of sin." (137)

Mill was keenly aware that his experience, although on his view wholly secular, conformed rather closely to a pattern etched by centuries of Christian teachings about conversion and spiritual rebirth. The pursuit of happiness on which his "whole reliance" had hitherto been placed lost its dreamlike charm; pride and self-confidence gave way to the anguish and self-revulsion of the sinner; and life quite literally lost the only point it could have on utilitarian premises. The question, *What can I make, or do?* no longer entranced him:

> In this frame of mind it occurred to me to put the question directly to myself, "Suppose that all your objects in life were realized; that all the changes in institutions and opinions which you are looking forward to, could be completely effected at this very instant: would this be a great joy and happiness to you?" And an irrepressible self-consciousness distinctly answered "No!" At this my heart sank within me: the whole foundation on which my life was constructed fell down. All my happiness was to have been found in the continual pursuit of this end. The end had ceased to charm, and how could there ever again be any interest in the means? I seemed to have nothing left to live for. (139)

No longer inspired by visions of the better world that he and other friends of human improvement could make through their own expansive agency, his "whole foundation" collapsed, and the question his father and Jeremy Bentham had taught him not to ask, "Who made me?" pressed in upon him as never before. A cloud settled over his life that neither sleep nor his favorite books was able to dispel. "I carried it with me into all companies, into all occupations."

Feeling that his distress was neither interesting nor respectable, and that he deserved no sympathy, he spoke to no one about it. Although it would have been natural, he said, to turn to his father for advice, he was "the last person" to approach in a "case such as this." "Everything convinced me that he had no knowledge of any such mental state as I was suffering from, and that even if he could be made to understand it, he was not the physician who could heal it. My education, which was wholly his work, had been conducted without any regard to the possibility of its ending in this result; and I saw no use in giving him the pain of thinking that his plans had failed, when the failure was probably irremediable, and at all events, beyond the power of *his* remedies" (139).

The Oedipal overtones of the episode are unmistakable. Mill himself attributed his cure in part to the poetic inspiration of Wordsworth, in part to his formulation of the balanced, nonfatalistic view of liberty and necessity that he eventually set forth in his *System of Logic*, but also in part to a flood of tears mysteriously triggered by a passage he happened to read in Marmontel's *Memoirs*. The passage described the death of a father, the plight of his wife and children, and the daring resolution of his son, a "mere boy," to "supply the place of all that they had lost."

> A vivid conception of the scene and its feelings came over me, and I was moved to tears. From this moment my burthen grew lighter. The oppression of the thought that all feeling was dead within me, was gone. I was no longer hopeless: I was not a stock or a stone. I had still, it seemed, some of the material out of which all worth of character, and all capacity for happiness are made. Relieved from my ever present sense of irremediable wretchedness, I gradually found that the ordinary incidents of life could again give me some pleasure. . . . Thus the cloud gradually drew off, and I again enjoyed life: and though I had several relapses, some of which lasted many months, I never again was as miserable as I had been. (*Autobiography,* 145)

There is no reason to challenge Bruce Mazlish's conclusion that "the 'dejection' of Mill's experience, the 'depressing and paralyzing' nature of that experience, was intimately connected to his feeling that he had been 'made,' *completely determined,* by his father." How his own character had been formed became for this dutiful son "*the* most pressing and constant question of his life," and one that could not fail to implicate the man who had fathered him and so minutely superintended his education.[30] Freud's understanding of "overdetermination" leaves ample room for us to construe Mill's later writings on liberty and necessity both as worthy philosophical efforts in their own right and as manifestations of a deeply rooted personal need to come to terms with the suffocating influence of his father. The only mistake would be to think that the dread "incubus" of "Philosophical Necessity" was for Mill merely a surrogate for his domineering progenitor. The possibilities that choice is a subjective illusion, that human action is fully determined by the conditions in which it occurs, that the self originates nothing and is, in truth, inconsequential — these possibilities define a dread-inspiring state of mind, quite apart from whatever amplification they may receive from Oedipal associations. Being conceived is, after all, the most elemental form of being caused, or "made," and thus biological descent raises in microcosm all the problems of transitivity.

Mill's own efforts to trace the sources and explain the consequences of his crisis veered somewhat erratically between emotional and intellectual planes of interpretation. At the emotional level he treated his dejection as a result of impoverished feelings. His emotional reaction to Marmontel's *Memoirs* seemed relevant to him, of course, not because he recognized any sexual rivalry with his father, but simply because his tears reassured him that all feeling was not dead within him, that he was "not a stock or a stone" (16).[31] The Romantic reaction against the Enlightenment that Mill reported was "streaming in upon me" at the time supplied him with a ready-made interpretation of melancholia as the result of impoverished feelings, and laid the blame for impoverished feelings squarely on the analytical habits of mind that his father and Bentham had so assiduously cultivated in him (169). The identification of good psychic health with the exercise of, or "being in touch with," the emotions was not then the cliché it has since become, but it was already sufficiently commonplace that Mill took pains to note that he had "always before received with incredulity" what he now came to accept: "that the habit of analysis has a tendency to wear away the feelings" (141).

Mill never entirely abandoned the associationist framework of Locke and Hartley, according to which analysis was the indispensable means of detecting false associations, separating ideas that had come to be associated only through accident or prejudice. By analytically sifting out false associations we attain "our clearest knowledge of the permanent sequences in nature; the real connexions between Things . . . natural laws." These laws, in turn, "cause our ideas of things that are joined together in Nature, to cohere more and more closely in our thoughts" (141, 143). Mill's crisis persuaded him that the analytical habit, however "favourable to prudence and clearsightedness," was a "perpetual worm at the root both of the passions and of the virtues." His father, using the familiar instruments of praise and blame, reward and punishment, had striven to make the good of mankind the object of the boy's existence by contriving to associate feelings of happiness with everything promoting the general good. But to no avail.

My education, I thought, had failed to create these feelings in sufficient strength to resist the dissolving influence of analysis, while the whole course of my intellectual cultivation had made precocious and premature analysis the inveterate habit of my mind. I was thus, as I said to myself, left stranded at the commencement of my voyage, with a well equipped ship and a rudder, but no sail. . . . The fountains of vanity and ambition seemed to have dried up within me, as completely as those of benevolence. . . . There seemed no power in nature sufficient to begin the formation of my character anew, and create in a mind now irretrievably analytic, fresh associations of pleasure with any of the objects of human desire. (143)

Thomas Carlyle's first great essay, "Signs of the Times," appeared in the *Edinburgh Review* in 1829, during the "later stages" of Mill's dejection. It was a tirade against the very philosophy in which Mill had been trained and a trenchant commentary on the implications of that philosophy for the psychology of human agency. When Carlyle condemned the "Age of Machinery" and lamented a generation "grown mechanical in head and heart," one of his principal targets was the British associationist tradition from Locke to Bentham, and the danger he identified with that tradition was precisely that of drowning human agency in a sea of circumstantiality. "The Philosopher of this age," he argued, "is not a Socrates, a Plato, a Hooker, or Taylor, who inculcates on men the necessity and infinite worth of moral goodness, the great truth that our happiness depends on the mind which is within us; but a Smith, a De Lolme, a Bentham, who chiefly inculcates the reverse of this, — that our happiness depends entirely on external circumstances; nay, that the strength and dignity of the mind within us is itself the creature and consequence of these." [32]

Although Carlyle's early writings at first struck Mill as a "haze of poetry and German metaphysics," their "wonderful power" eventually made a "deep impression." [33] The first meeting of the two men took place in 1831, shortly after Mill's recovery. In composing the account of his crisis that appears in the *Autobiography,* Mill seems to have relied extensively on Carlylean language. After all, Carlyle, by attacking "Mechanism" and identifying it closely with the "doctrine of circumstances," held out to Mill a very appealing interpretation of his mental crisis, one that lifted it out of the realm of accident and personal idiosyncrasy and gave it a cultural, or even cosmic, dimension. In words that must have seemed full of resonance to the young man in his misery, Carlyle declared that "our favourite Philosophers have no love and no hatred; they stand among us not to do, nor to create anything, but as a sort of Logic-mills, to grind out the true causes and effects of all that is done and created." In the eyes of such philosophers, complained Carlyle, not only precocious youngsters with domineering fathers, but even history's greatest and most heroic

figures were "simply so many mechanical phenomena, caused or causing."[34]
Identifying utilitarianism with a leaden stress on circumstantiality, and linking
it closely to Adam Smith and the pursuit of profit, Carlyle depicted the antiformalist world of the Benthamites as a seamless web of causal contingency, inimical to passion, corrosive of all high values, and unfit for human habitation.
In doing so, he described the very symptoms Mill was then experiencing, and
traced those symptoms straight to the market-bred dilemma of transitivity:

> The infinite, absolute character of Virtue has passed into a finite, conditional
> one; it is no longer a worship of the Beautiful and Good; but a calculation of
> the Profitable. Worship, indeed, in any sense, is not recognized among us, or is
> mechanically explained into Fear of pain, or Hope of pleasure. . . .
>   By arguing on the "force of circumstances," we have argued away all force
> from ourselves; and stand leashed together, uniform in dress and movement,
> like the rowers of some boundless galley. . . . Practically considered, our creed
> is Fatalism; and, free in hand and foot, we are shackled in heart and soul with
> far straiter than feudal chains. Truly may we say, with the Philosopher, "the
> deep meaning of the Laws of Mechanism lies heavy on us"; and in the closet,
> in the marketplace, in the temple, by the social hearth, encumbers the whole
> movements of our mind, and over our noblest faculties is spreading a night-
> mare sleep.[35]

Perceptive though Carlyle's diagnosis was, his prescription for a cure
amounted to little more than an obstinate refusal to accept the disturbing
message of circumstantiality to which consciousness exposed him. Here again,
Mill seems to have followed Carlyle's lead. Of the two great lessons that Mill
drew from his crisis, the first was a theory of life that he himself acknowledged
had "much in common with . . . the anti-self-consciousness theory of Carlyle"
(145). As if in repudiation of the Calvinist imperative to constantly monitor
experience and adjust conduct to make life, insofar as possible, a product of
one's own deliberate intentions, Mill now sang the praises of serendipity, spontaneity, and unconsciousness. "Ask yourself whether you are happy and you
cease to be so," he observed. "The only chance is to treat, not happiness, but
some end external to it, as the purpose of life. Let your self-consciousness, your
scrutiny, your self-interrogation, exhaust themselves on that; and if otherwise
fortunately circumstanced, you will inhale happiness with the air you breathe,
without dwelling on it or thinking about it . . . or putting it to flight by fatal
questioning. This theory now became the basis of my philosophy of life" (147).
    Although elements of the "anti-self-consciousness theory" were already ap-
parent in "Signs of the Times," Carlyle developed the theme more fully in

"Characteristics," published in 1831, which continued his attack on "Utilitarianism, or Radicalism, or the Mechanical Philosophy, or by whatever name it is called," and identified it with a larger "fever of Skepticism [that] must needs burn itself out" (102, 100). Noting that in all departments of life the "Voluntary and the Conscious" bear only a small proportion to the "Involuntary and Unconscious," Carlyle opted wholeheartedly for the latter, contending that unconsciousness was a sign of "wholeness" and "right performance" (75, 73, 77). "Boundless as is the domain of man, it is but a small fractional proportion of it that he rules with Consciousness and by Forethought," he argued. Rhetorically he asked "is it the skillful anatomist that cuts the best figure at the Sadler Wells? or does the boxer hit better for knowing that he has a *flexor longus* and a *flexor brevis?*" (71).

What Carlyle wanted from life was what he found missing from the literature of the age, "spontaneous devotedness to the object, being wholly possessed by the object, what we can call Inspiration" (86). For him, as for Mill, the "choking incubus" (103) that drained away all possibility of spontaneity was an all too acute awareness of the causal force of circumstance in a setting that resisted every effort at divinization. "Freewill no longer reigns unquestioned and by divine right," he observed, "but like a mere earthly sovereign, by expediency, by Rewards and Punishments: or rather, let us say, the Freewill, so far as may be, has abdicated and withdrawn into the dark, and a spectral nightmare of a Necessity usurps its throne" (74). Unlike Karl Marx, who warned of the formalist fantasies of autonomy and self-sufficiency the market might foster, Carlyle warned of a market-bred attentiveness to circumstance and preoccupation with contingency that threatened to eviscerate the very idea of freedom and induce a kind of self-inflicted paralysis.

> Never since the beginning of Time was there, that we hear or read of, so intensely self-conscious a Society. . . .
> Truly it may be said, the Divinity has withdrawn from the earth; or veils himself in that wide-wasting Whirlwind of a departing Era, wherein the fewest can discern his goings. Not Godhead, but an iron, ignoble circle of Necessity embraces all things; binds the youth of these times into a sluggish thrall, or else exasperates him into a rebel. Heroic Action is paralysed; for what worth now remains unquestionable with him? (83, 92)

The second lesson that Mill drew from his crisis followed from the first. In order to silence the nagging voice of consciousness and restore unity to a self that seemed intolerably divided and becalmed on a glassy sea of disenchantment, he concluded that one must cultivate the feelings, the region of elemental and spontaneous energies, the source of the "winds" without which even the best-equipped ship could not sail. He vowed to give "its proper place, among the prime necessities of human well-being, to the internal culture of the individual. . . . The maintenance of a due balance among the faculties, now seemed to me of primary importance. The cultivation of the feelings became one of the cardinal points in my ethical and philosophical creed" (147).

Coleridge and Harriet Taylor would become Mill's chief guides in matters of feeling, but here, too, the influence of Carlyle seems unmistakable. In "Signs of the Times," Carlyle had distinguished the "inward" or "Dynamical" province from the "Mechanical" or "outward" one. The former he identified with "the primary, unmodified forces and energies of man, the mysterious springs of Enthusiasm, Poetry, Religion" (42). He conceded that excessive cultivation of the "Dynamical province" could lead to "idle, visionary, impracticable courses" and even to "Superstition and Fanaticism," but he insisted that undue cultivation of the Mechanical—although "productive of many palpable benefits"—would prove to be equally pernicious because of its tendency to destroy "Moral Force . . . the parent of all other Force." The good life, then, required a balanced cultivation of both the inward and the outward dimensions of life, and since the present age exceeded all others in its development of the Mechanical, the time had come to cultivate the Dynamical, even if it meant a diminished role for the intellect—even, indeed, if it meant loss of consciousness (46). "If in any sphere of man's life, then in the Moral sphere, as the inmost and most vital of all, it is good that there be wholeness; that there be unconsciousness, which is the evidence of this. Let the free, reasonable Will, which dwells in us, as in our Holy of Holies, be indeed free, and obeyed like a Divinity, as is its right and effort: the perfect obedience will be the silent one" (73).

Still dejected and desperate for a renewed sense of spontaneity, Mill first came upon the poetry of Wordsworth in the autumn of 1828 and recorded the occasion as an "important event" in his life (149). What made Wordsworth's poems "a medicine for my state of mind," he said, "was that they expressed, not mere outward beauty, but states of feeling, and of thought coloured by feeling, under the excitement of beauty. They seemed to be the very culture of the feelings, which I was in quest of." The delights of reading Wordsworth reassured him that human beings had access to a "source of inward joy, of sympathetic and imaginative pleasure" which could never be exhausted. Here was a "perennial source of happiness" that would continue to give life a purpose, even when all the goals of utilitarian reform had been achieved, even "when all the greater evils in life shall have been removed" (151).

Here, indeed, was a solution of sorts to the crisis itself, for the strength of his response to Wordsworth convinced Mill that by reading poetry, listening to music, and otherwise cultivating the inward, "Dynamical" world of the feelings, he might safely continue the very practice on which he blamed his dejection—his analytical mode of inquiry. "The delight which these poems gave me, proved that with culture of this sort, there was nothing to dread from the most confirmed habit of analysis" (153). By counterbalancing inward and outward culture, he felt that he could fill his slack sails and yet also keep his bearings. The irony of "cultivating" the emotions as a deliberate, instrumental means of achieving spontaneity seems to have escaped him.

Thus, in the end, the great lessons Mill learned from his crisis required him not to repudiate his original self, or to disavow the father who had played such a large role in fashioning it, but only to supplement that original self with a greater openness and sensitivity to the emotive dimension of life. For the remainder of his life, Mill prided himself on his balanced appreciation of the emotional and the intellectual. Indeed, straddling fences, embracing both sides of issues that lesser thinkers regarded as irreconcilable, became one of his trademarks as a thinker. Although raised as a utilitarian and always ready to bring the principle of utility to bear on new questions, he would never again give his sole allegiance to utility or any other principle or system; although moved by Romanticism, and deeply indebted to it for the interpretive framework in which he cast his mental crisis, no one would ever mistake him for a Romantic. In the great debate between the eighteenth and the nineteenth centuries, he adopted Goethe's motto of "many-sidedness," acknowledging truths on both sides and marveling at the "blind rage with which the combatants rushed against one another" (171). Far from giving up his "early opinions"— "in no essential part of which I at any time wavered"—he claimed in the end that all the new thinking he did under the pressure of his dejection "only laid the foundation of these [early opinions] more deeply and strongly" while clarifying their effect (175). In resolving the crisis, he had moved a "great distance" from his father's "tone of thought and feeling" (189). For better or worse, however, John Stuart Mill was still his father's son, and he knew it.

Mill was proud of his resolution of the crisis and believed that others might benefit from knowledge of it. Accordingly it forms the pivotal event of the *Autobiography*, overshadowing even the story of his unconventional and transformative relationship to Harriet Taylor. What seems to have pleased him most is the tense philosophical reconciliation between liberty and necessity that he first presented in his *System of Logic* and then briefly summarized in the *Autobiography*. It was in connection with this—a recapitulation, as it were, of the ultimate meaning for posterity of John Stuart Mill's mental crisis — that he wrote the passage that stands at the head of this essay, which can now be reproduced in full:

> During the later returns of my dejection, the doctrine of what is called Philosophical Necessity weighed on my existence like an incubus. I felt as if I was scientifically proved to be the helpless slave of antecedent circumstances; as if my character and that of all others had been formed for us by agencies beyond our control, and was wholly out of our own power. I often said to myself, what a relief it would be if I could disbelieve the doctrine of the formation of character by circumstances; and remembering the wish of Fox respecting the doctrine of resistance to governments, that it might never be forgotten by kings, nor remembered by subjects, I said that it would be a blessing if the doctrine of necessity could be believed by all *quoad* the characters of others, and disbelieved in regard to their own. I pondered painfully on the subject, till gradually I saw light through it. I perceived, that the word Necessity, as a name for the doctrine of Cause and Effect applied to human action, carried with it a misleading association; and that this association was the operative force in the depressing and paralyzing influence which I had experienced. I saw that though our character is formed by circumstances, our own desires can do much to shape those circumstances; and that what is really inspiriting and ennobling in the doctrine of freewill, is the conviction that we have real power over the formation of our own character; that our will, by influencing some of our circumstances, can modify our future habits or capabilities of willing.

Assuring his readers that this formulation was not an abandonment of the doctrine of circumstances, but rather "that doctrine itself, properly understood," he drew a sharp distinction between the doctrine of circumstances and "Fatalism," and discarded altogether the misleading word "Necessity." Thus stripped of its thorns, the heritage impressed upon him by Bentham and his father — "the last of the eighteenth century" — could be embraced once again, both for its truth and its goodness.

> The theory [of circumstances] which I now for the first time rightly apprehended, ceased altogether to be discouraging, and besides the release to my spirits, I no longer suffered under the burthen, so heavy to one who aims at being a reformer in opinions, of thinking one doctrine true, and the contrary doctrine morally beneficial. The train of thought which had extricated me from this dilemma, seemed to me, in after years, fitted to render a similar service to others; and it now forms the chapter on Liberty and Necessity in the concluding Book of my *System of Logic*. (175, 177)

Mill's confidence that other people had experienced something like his crisis, and would want to know how he had extricated himself from it, was surely correct. Yet any reader who turns from the *Autobiography* to the *System of Logic*, hoping for further illumination, is likely to be disappointed. Even when spelled out fully, Mill's resolution of the problem of transitivity seems less than decisive.

Although uncomfortable with the connotations of the word "necessity," Mill made clear in his ultimate formulation that his own position in the long controversy dating back to Pelagius was much closer to "Necessity" than to "Free Will." In the *System of Logic* he rejected completely the Christian doctrine handed down from Aquinas, that the will, unlike other phenomena, is determined not by its antecedents, but solely by itself.[36] The question he set himself was how to reconcile necessity—the view that the will is determined by character, and character by circumstance—with our subjective sense of freedom. Some people, he argued, imagine that the predictability of our conduct is, in itself, enough to destroy our feeling of freedom. But predictability need not conflict at all with our sense of freedom, he contended, once we see the significance of Hume's discovery that "there is nothing in causation but invariable, certain, and unconditional sequence."[37] Since in both material and mental matters, there is no "intimate connexion," no "peculiar tie," or "mysterious constraint" linking cause and effect, we can acknowledge the predictability of our conduct in the eyes of those who know us well, and admit even the corollary of strict causal regularity in human affairs, without undermining our feeling of freedom. These concessions to necessity did not bother Mill, because they successfully skirted the principal danger he wished to avoid, namely, the implication that we are ever "compelled, as by a magical spell, to obey any particular motive" (838).

What Mill was most eager to conserve was the primordial insight of asceticism: the possibility of authentically opposing one's own motives, of the self standing in genuine opposition to itself and thus participating in its own making. In stark opposition to the ascetic possibility stood fatalism. "A fatalist believes, or half believes (for nobody is a consistent fatalist), not only that whatever is about to happen, will be the infallible result of the causes which produce it, (which is the true necessitarian doctrine,) but moreover that there is no use in struggling against it; that it will happen however we may strive to prevent it." And in the *System of Logic*, unlike the *Autobiography*, he specifically identified fatalism with the followers of Robert Owen.[38]

> In the words of the sect which in our own day has most perseveringly inculcated and most perversely misunderstood this great doctrine . . . , [man's] charac-

ter is formed *for* him, and not *by* him; therefore his wishing that it had been formed differently is of no use; he has no power to alter it. But this is a grand error. He has, to a certain extent, a power to alter his character. Its being, in the ultimate resort, formed for him, is not inconsistent with its being, in part, formed *by* him as one of the intermediate agents. His character is formed by his circumstances (including among these his particular organization); but his own desire to mould it in a particular way is one of those circumstances, and by no means one of the least influential. (840)

Although this argument earned the voluntarist conclusion it aimed at — that "we are exactly as capable of making our own character, *if we will,* as others are of making it for us" — Mill knew that it could not carry the day. He continued: "Yes (answers the Owenite), but these words, 'if we will,' surrender the whole point: since the will to alter our own character is given us, not by any efforts of ours, but by circumstances which we cannot help; it comes to us either from external causes, or not at all" (840). Faced with an infinite regression, Mill slipped out of the mode of demonstrative argument and appealed to considerations that in the hands of William James and John Dewey would come to be known as "pragmatic." In a spirit closely akin to that which James would later adopt in his famous essay "The Will to Believe," Mill observed that "to think that we have no power of altering our character, and to think that we shall not use our power unless we desire to use it, are very different things, and have a very different effect on the mind" (841). Having no doubt that the conditions of human existence could only grow worse if people lost confidence in the possibility of improving their character, Mill opted for the conclusion that would do the most good. However far beyond proof the authenticity of freedom might remain, all risk of error was overwhelmed by the desirability of believing in it. Without ever overcoming the danger of infinite regression or proving that our efforts at self-reform really originate with the self, Mill was content in the end merely to observe how inconvenient it would be to accept the contrary conclusion. In so doing, he tacitly conceded that on secular premises the problem of transitivity was insoluble, even as he insisted that life could (and should) go on as if it were.

Mill did not associate his mental crisis with Owen or with socialism. He mentioned the Owenites only once in the *Autobiography,* and that single mention occurs in the chapter preceding the one devoted to his mental crisis. Obviously the "doctrine of the formation of character by circumstances" was not anything he learned from Owen, for it had been his father's guiding principle. Still, the timing of his encounter with the Owenites is intriguing, for it occurred in 1825, the year before the onset of the mental crisis. A group of Owenites calling themselves the Cooperative Society were holding weekly public debates in Chancery Lane when Mill and his circle of brilliant young intellectuals in the Utilitarian Society heard about them and began attending. "Some one of us started the notion of going there in a body and having a general battle," he wrote, and the result was a *"lutte corps-a-corps"* between Owenites and political economists that continued for three months and drew large audiences, including many from the Inns of Court. Distinguished orators spoke on each side. Mill regarded one of his own opponents, Connop Thirlwall, later a bishop and a famous historian, as the best speaker he ever heard. Mill called it a "perfectly friendly dispute" and stressed that the two sides had "the same objects in view," but acknowledged that the Owenites regarded the political economists as their most "inveterate opponents" (127, 129).

It is of course appropriate that Mill, exemplar of the Spirit of Capitalism, should battle Owen, the first Socialist—and even more appropriate, given the present interpretive framework, that the battle should have revolved around the suitability of the self for causal attribution. Because the debate between capitalism and socialism has been under way now for the better part of two centuries, and the affairs of the entire globe have hinged upon it, the issues that initially sparked the debate have long since been lost to view beneath layers of impassioned rhetoric and the accumulated debris of discarded theoretical epicycles. The supersession of Owenite socialism by the Marxian variety, with its celebration of proletarian revolution and ponderous, quasi-mystical Teutonic vocabulary, has obscured the simple question about causal attribution and transitivity with which the great debate began: "Who [or what] made me?"[39]

That, after all, was the question Owen was tacitly asking and answering in 1813, when he published *A New View of Society; or, Essays on the Principle of the Formation of the Human Character,* the text that launched the socialist movement in England. He took direct aim at the widespread but erroneous notion that "each individual man forms his own character, and that therefore he is accountable for all his sentiments and habits, and consequently merits reward for some, and punishment for others." This exaggerated view of human responsibility was, Owen asserted, the "true and sole origin of evil." Although he regarded the presumption of individual autonomy as "the Evil Genius of the world" and an "error that carries misery in all its consequences," he was optimistic that its days were numbered.

> This error cannot much longer exist; for every day will make it more and more evident THAT THE CHARACTER OF MAN IS, WITHOUT A SINGLE EXCEPTION, ALWAYS FORMED FOR HIM; THAT IT MAY BE, AND IS CHIEFLY,

CREATED BY HIS PREDECESSORS; THAT THEY GIVE HIM, OR MAY GIVE
HIM HIS IDEAS AND HABITS, WHICH ARE THE POWERS THAT GOVERN AND
DIRECT HIS CONDUCT. MAN, THEREFORE, NEVER DID, NOR IS IT POSSIBLE
HE EVER CAN, FORM HIS OWN CHARACTER.[40]

Transitivity was not a problem for Owen or his followers, for they cheerfully
and naively accepted the "radical situatedness" of the self, seeing no more danger in it than Luther had (on wholly different premises) three centuries earlier.
Putting "society" in the place that God once occupied as the first cause and
creator of man, they waved farewell to individual autonomy and moral responsibility without so much as a backward look. Protestant divines had always
taken great pains to show that God's overruling Providence in no way lessened
human moral responsibility, but Owen failed even to acknowledge the problem.[41] He was sure that "all goodness, wisdom, and happiness" would accrue to
mankind with recognition of the great truth that "all the faculties of humanity
are created for the individual, without his consent or knowledge; that these
faculties are well or ill cultivated from birth *for* the individual, *by society;* and
that society alone should be responsible for the inferior or superior, good or
bad, cultivation of every one."[42] The question why, given the complete transitivity of all human choices, anyone *ought* to seek justice, or *ought* to oppose
evil, troubled Owen not at all. His followers did not hesitate to draw the "very
obvious deduction," namely, "that virtue and vice were equally necessitated,
and [that] the ascription of merit or demerit to the agent who manifested
the operation of this unchangeable and uncontrollable law, was a *non sequitur,* and an injustice."[43] Unable to divinize the circumstances in which the self
was sunk (a project that Auguste Comte actually undertook with his "religion
of Humanity"), the Owenites offered as a substitute the socialization of those
circumstances in a distant, rational future, a strategy on which the revolutionary varieties of socialism did not significantly improve.[44] It should not surprise
us that Owen attacked "all the existing false religions of the world" more bit-
terly than he did either the property-owning classes or the social system that
worked to their advantage. Nor should it surprise us that the initial resistance
to Owenite socialism came not from the owners of property so much as from
outraged religionists, to whom it seemed sacrilegious for human society to be
assigned the causal status hitherto belonging to God.[45]

If the importance of Mill's struggle to make sense of transitivity was lost on
the Owenites, his efforts were also unsatisfactory to traditional Christians. The
latter were more likely than the Owenites to appreciate what was at stake, but
in their eyes Mill's attempt to rescue the self failed because it conceded far too
much to a world of circumstantiality, unredeemed by any hint of divine pur-

pose. Of all the Protestant denominations the Unitarians were most eager to assimilate new learning, most willing to water down the supernatural element in Christianity, and most likely to welcome sophisticated defenses of voluntarism. Yet the leading Unitarian in England, James Martineau, found little to admire in the "middle" path Mill had struck between freedom and fate. From the vantage point of even the most avant-garde religionists, Mill was, like Owen or Bentham, an antiformalist radical, whose conception of the self practically snuffed out autonomy and left human beings mere creatures of circumstance.

> Our author's whole picture of man exhibits him as a natural product, shaped by the scene on which he is cast; and he rejects every theory without exception which has been set up in psychology, in logic, in morals, to vindicate the autonomy of human reason and conscience. . . .
>
> If, in his aim to supplement Bentham, our author yielded to an idealistic impulse, he remained true, in what he retained in the great utilitarian, to the materialistic tendencies of the school. The inward side of ethics is made, in every aspect, dependent on the outward. Do we ask what determines the moral quality of actions? we are referred, not to their spring, but to their consequences. Do we inquire how we came by our moral sentiments? by contagion, we are told, of other people's approbation and disapprobation, not by any self-reflective judgment of our own. Do we seek for the adequate sources of a man's guilt or goodness? we are presented with an enumeration of the external conditions which made his character, like his health, just what it is.[46]

John Stuart Mill, it should now be clear, did not invent formalism. What he "invented" (or reinvented, in view of its antiquity) was a precarious balancing act that enabled him to maintain a modicum of poise in the midst of an unprecedented upheaval in the conventions governing causal attribution. The balance he struck appeared excessively formal to a few of his most radical contemporaries, such as the Owenites, but insufficiently so to many more, who, like James Martineau, complained that Mill treated mankind merely as "a natural product, moulded by surrounding pressures." Eager though Mill was to reaffirm the ascetic possibility of the self standing in genuine opposition to itself, Martineau's complaint was precisely that Mill had left too little room for "self-formation, the evolution from within towards an unrealized type of perfection."[47]

In the eyes of believers, Mill's formulation of the problem of freedom and fate could not satisfy, for in truth it left the self open and exposed to the same process of disenchantment that Scottish philosopher Thomas Reid had observed at work on natural objects in the eighteenth century. "As philosophy advances," wrote Reid, "life and activity in natural objects retires, and leaves them dead and inactive. Instead of moving voluntarily, we find them to be moved necessarily; instead of acting, we find them to be acted upon; and nature appears as one great machine, where one wheel is turned by another, and that by a third; and how far this necessary succession may reach, the philosopher does not know." [48] The perceptions of transitivity that lay at the heart of this process of disenchantment would, by the end of the nineteenth century, no longer be confined to natural objects, and Max Weber saw as perceptively as anyone of his generation what it would mean for disenchantment to overtake and pervade the entire world of self and society.

Weber showed in the Protestant ethic thesis that a doctrine pointing logically toward fatalism can, in psychological practice, foster voluntarism. Mill's mental crisis, as we have seen, suggests that the reverse is also true: a doctrine that is logically enabling can, in practice, carry psychological implications that are paralyzing. On the face of things it seems extremely paradoxical that a radically heightened sense of agency should, in and of itself, lead to a radically constricted one, yet Mill thought this was true in his own case. His Benthamite euphoria did not merely precede his dejection, but was its "origin," he said. On his own associationist premises, reinforced, as we have seen, by Carlyle's vitalistic derogation of self-consciousness, Mill had no way of accounting for this sudden transmutation of voluntaristic euphoria into fatalistic depression except by invoking what he himself had always regarded as a cliché, the idea that analytical thinking eroded the feelings. An account more plausible to twentieth-century minds comes into view as soon as we step outside Mill's own associationist framework and think in terms of causal attribution.

Environmentalist arguments of the sort that Mill and the utilitarians subscribed to have always carried paradoxical implications about human agency. If the character of human beings is a product of their environment, then human beings have the power to change their character by changing their environment. But this accession of power is ironically drained of content because consistency requires us to acknowledge that we who act to shape a new future are no less malleable than those we act upon. Our present power over the future implies an equivalent power of the past over the present, thus raising Mill's question of transitivity: how can we know that our apparent power over the future is anything more than the power of the accumulated past, acting through us, its unwitting and deluded agents? As long as we think only of our power over the future, environmentalism is an enabling doctrine that flatters the self and promises ever higher levels of mastery. But if, as environmentalism assumes, all events of this world are sewn together by relations of contingency, then, being consistent, we cannot well deny that we ourselves, and all our present acts and choices, are the effects of equally compelling environmental contingencies for which we deserve neither blame nor credit. Environmentalism leaves no secure space for uncaused causes. If we allow our gaze to drift away from the happy panorama that unfolds when we think about our power over the future, and think instead about the past influences of which we, even in the act of willing, are passive effects, the implications of environmentalism are hideously reversed and become deeply unflattering to the self and its sense of autonomy.

Since environmentalism is a style of causal attribution, the same paradox can be put in another way that highlights the role of knowledge. The optimism of the environmentalist, who gazes into the future and is gratified to think of the new world he or she can make, presupposes knowledge of a host of necessary causal connections between present acts and future states of the world. Without "recipe knowledge" charting causal linkages between present acts and future events, we could perceive no opportunities for reform or control. The more ample the fund of recipe knowledge, the farther into the future it reaches, and the more certain the connections it discloses between cause and effect, the more expansive the actor's sense of agency, the broader the actor's causal horizon, and the more gratifying the prospect.

But human beings are not only causes, they are also effects. They not only gaze into the future and ponder what effects their acts and omissions might one day have, they also (sometimes) look over their shoulders at the past and ask themselves, "Of what am I the effect?" or, in Mill's vocabulary, "Who made me?" In this second sphere of causal attribution the motive is explanatory rather than pragmatic. And when it comes to explaining how we got to be who we are, the ample fund of far-reaching causal recipes that seemed so enabling, as long as it was confined to the pragmatic sphere, blows up in our face. The psychological significance of our knowledge of causal relations reverses as we pass from one sphere to the other. In the pragmatic, future-facing sphere of causal attribution (What can I make?), the more certain the connection between cause and effect, the more powerful we feel, for in that sphere we cast ourselves in the role of cause and welcome necessity, since it assures us that our recipes will work. But in the retrospectively oriented explanatory sphere where we cast ourselves in the role of effect (What made me?), the more necessary the connection, the less basis we have for feeling that our acts truly originate with us. The very element that in the pragmatic sphere assured us that our choices would be effectual, in the explanatory sphere undermines the authenticity of choice itself. In the pragmatic sphere, the richer and more complex our knowledge of causal relations becomes, the finer our control over the future appears to be; but in the explanatory sphere, the richer and more complex our knowledge, the greater the perceived force of circumstance in our lives, the more contingent our existence seems, and the less original and consequential we feel. Freedom and fate, then, are not the north and south poles of human possibility, defining by their remoteness from each other the most extreme of oppositions. Instead, if Mill's experience is any guide, in our culture they are two sides of a single coin, separated by only the coin's thickness and about equally likely, once put in motion, to land facing up.

Capitalism puts the coin in motion. It does so by fostering a form of life in which technique proliferates explosively because, as Weber showed, people feel duty-bound to "intentionalize" their experience, perpetually struggling to minimize unintended outcomes and achieve technical mastery over the future. Although the intentionalizing motive has its roots in religious doctrine, what sustains it in a mature economy is not religion, but the competitive discipline of supply and demand. Weber is easy to misunderstand on this point. The power of the market to produce the kinds of people and practices it needs is easily underestimated because Weber was eager to show that religion was no mere reflex of economic change and that the market could not flourish until Calvinism had provided it with an ample supply of self-monitoring "economic men." But Weber knew full well that capitalism needed the personality-transforming power and sweeping recruitment capacity of religion only in order to breach the walls of traditionalism and gain a dominant position. Once it prevails, he recognized, the market no longer needs the support of religion because it independently "educates and selects the economic subjects which it needs through a process of economic survival of the fittest."[49] In the circular manner that often holds between institutions and character, the practices and traits of personality that the market presupposes as a condition of its existence, it also induces and perpetually reinforces. And insofar as those traits and practices aim at the production of an intended future, the market cannot fail to encourage habits of remote causal attribution.

The "economic man" initially fostered by religion and then continually re-created and reinforced by the market itself cannot do the work cut out for him unless he has wide causal horizons and an ample fund of techniques, or "recipe knowledge," linking present acts to future outcomes. For such a person, as we have seen, the present must be construed as a staging ground for the production of the future, and the instrumental relation between present acts and future outcomes must appear so certain, so necessary, that failure to attend to the production of a desirable future will be interpreted as a breach of obligation. He must think causally: and since thinking causally consists in linking present choices to consequences more or less remote in time by techniques or recipes that map a route from one to the other, the market man (or woman) must be both a voluntarist and a virtuoso of technique, attentive to the remote consequences of behavior and acutely conscious of ways in which the world can be bent to one's will. The market by its very nature encouraged the production, proliferation, circulation, and preservation of recipe knowledge. As Joyce Appleby observed in her study of economic theory and ideology in seventeenth-century England, the extension of the market worked to "activate the participants' imaginative powers" and stimulate "long-range planning through rational calculations."[50] The most distinctive feature of the character induced by the market, then, is its habit of remote causal attribution, its readiness to perceive its own choices as the cause of distant events — "distant" not only in time and space but also in terms of the counterintuitive qualitative transformations involved in their production. To say all this is merely to unfold the implications of Franklin's quintessential formulation of the Spirit of Capitalism, "Time is money" — three deceptively simple words that neatly collapse "then" into "now," "there" into "here," and one qualitative order of things, "time," into another, "money."

Yet, as we have just seen, human beings do not spend all their lives in the future-oriented, pragmatic sphere of causal attribution. And when they shift their attention to the retrospective, explanatory sphere, the one in which we ask, "Who [or what] made me?" the psychological implications of their market-induced habit of remote causal attribution can take on a very different meaning. Both the entrepreneur and the humanitarian reformer feel lifted up to a commanding eminence, as Mill did, by their possession of far-reaching recipe knowledge; but the causal knowledge that sustains a vaulting sense of agency in the pragmatic mode, merely highlights the inescapable dependence of self on world when one shifts into the explanatory mode. Having learned in the everyday, pragmatic world of the marketplace to think in terms of extended chains of causal linkage, and having learned in particular to distrust proximate causal attribution because of its superficiality, its failure to take into account the full range of future events that are within the power of the will to shape and anticipate, the modern self plays by rules of causal attribution that can, when transposed into the explanatory sphere, promote feelings of powerlessness and inconsequentiality more extreme, one suspects, than anything felt by our ancestors in traditional society, who never dared imagine that they could command the future or escape the past. Although it is only human to be in the grip of contradictory convictions about freedom and fate, there is reason to believe that the form of life spawned by the market exacerbates the contradiction.

Perhaps that should not surprise us, for we have always known that capitalism allows the individual unprecedented liberty to do as he or she pleases, but only on the unspoken condition that each individual be exposed to the relentless, if "invisible," discipline of supply and demand, which ensures — at least in theory — that what truly pleases will also conform in the long run to the harsh dictates of allocative efficiency. C. B. Macpherson expressed the paradox succinctly. "The market makes men free; it requires for its effective operation that all men be free and rational; yet the independent rational decisions of each man produce at every moment a configuration of forces which confronts each man compulsively. All men's choices determine, and each man's choice is determined by, the market."[51]

Consistency being among the most ephemeral of human motives, most of us do not find it difficult to compartmentalize our lives, reserving our far-flung causal horizons for pragmatic matters, where they make us feel good, and excluding such perceptions from explanatory inquiries, where they can be so troublesome. John Stuart Mill, among the most consistent of men, was at greater risk than most of us. But in a world shaped by market discipline, remote causal attribution is always a live option even when it does not prevail, and the "radical" or "deep" forms of explanation and perception to which it gives rise can never be ruled out of court. Nor should we want them to be. Indeed, we might observe that the market, by creating a culture in which every human act or event is susceptible to multiple interpretations depending on whether its causes are construed to lie on the "surface" or to be more "deeply" situated, creates also the possibility of a class of people specializing in "deep" explanation. Would it be too much to suggest that for the past century or two there has existed such a class, known ever since the Dreyfus affair of the 1890s as the "intellectuals"? And to suggest also that the politics of market societies have for the past century been largely a contest between those who see the plight of the poor and the downtrodden to be a product of deep-lying structural conditions over which the victims have no control, and those who, on the contrary, see them more nearly as free agents, deeply complicit in their own difficulties? Different modes of causal attribution, and thus of explanation, create the principal political chasms that divide us.

Certainly from Mill's day down to our own, the smugness of the self-made man — the person who imagines that his or her comfortable situation in life owes much to personal merit and little to luck, circumstance, or communal nurturance — has helped knit together political and cultural radicals in a common campaign to "make paste" of the bourgeoisie: to expose the formalist pretensions not only of bourgeois politics and economics but also of law, science, art, and religion, and thereby to roll back ideological mystification and pave the way for a more authentic life, one that acknowledges the precariousness of personhood and takes into account the inescapable "situatedness" of us all. The defining characteristic of the "self-made man" is his evident imperviousness to Mill's troubling insight that causation may be transitive; that even one's freest choices and most creative acts may be the effects of causal factors lying outside the self. And, in turn, the most distinctive and emblematic characteristic of the modern literary or humanist intellectual has been disdain for, and knowing superiority to, those who imagine themselves to be "self-made"—or, to speak generically, superiority to the formalist, the person who exaggerates autonomy and underestimates the role that circumstances play in shaping the way people think and act and become who they are.

Among intellectuals today it is widely assumed that formalism thrives in market societies for all the same reasons that ideologies of individualism do. Liberalism, individualism, and formalism seem to go together and to be mutually reinforcing. The reason seems obvious: class interest. The bourgeoisie stands to gain by relaxing the bonds of community, celebrating the entrepreneurial autonomy of its own members, and pretending that everyone in liberal society, whether rich or poor, enjoys the same extensive liberty to think and do whatever they please. The ideological functions of formalism seem plainly evident in the classic case of the "free" laborer who, unlike the slave, the serf, or the apprentice, is physically unconstrained and legally free to sell his or her labor to the highest bidder, but who discovers how empty formal freedom is when he or she tries to negotiate a favorable wage contract with a supposed "equal," the wealthy factory owner. Inequalities of bargaining power make all the difference, and those inequalities cannot come into focus as long as they are seen through the distorting lenses of formalism.[52] Still other layers of antecedent circumstance come into view as we extend our gaze back into the past, noticing that the worker belongs to a class deprived of access to the means of production by an enclosure movement or by other, still earlier, forms of primitive accumulation. Formalism, by magnifying autonomy and shrinking circumstance, is thus said to veil the dominance of the ruling class, to legitimate the exploitation of wage labor, and to establish the structural conditions that confine choice within safe channels and define the status quo. As Mill's contemporary Karl Marx put it in *The German Ideology*, "In imagination, individuals seem freer under the dominance of the bourgeoisie than before, because their conditions of life seem accidental; in reality, of course, they are less free, because they are more subjected to the violence of things."[53]

There are important elements of truth in this classic scenario, just as there are in the ancient suspicion that, in the end, all of us are indeed "creatures of circumstance," notwithstanding all our "splendid hope" to the contrary. Yet if the interests of the ruling class under capitalism are so well served by formalism, it is not at all easy to understand why, over a period during which capitalism has marched from victory to victory, formalism has been forced to beat one retreat after another. Nor is it easy to understand, if the circumstance of class interest has exerted such a powerful influence over the thought and experience of the formalists, how antiformalist intellectuals (most of whose origins have been bourgeois) have managed to exempt themselves from its power. In the present context the question of consistency must arise. Have antiformalists themselves been entirely free of illusions of self-creation and autonomy, as they have embarked, generation after generation, on the exhilarating and manifestly self-affirming project *pour épater la bourgeoisie*? In attacking formalism, have radicals been struggling against the tide and striking at the soft underbelly of the enemy, as they have believed? Or could it be that in adopting the posture of antiformalism they have unwittingly been riding in the swift central current of cultural transformation, echoing and even amplifying the very market forces they set out to master, occupying, as it were, an attributive niche that the market itself carved out for them? These questions about the relation between capitalism and formalism take on special significance today, when the emancipatory aspirations that once accompanied the critique of bourgeois culture seem in some quarters to have evaporated, leaving behind a residue of antiformalist *ressentiment* (often masked as *jouissance*) that aims merely at the "deconstruction" of any and all construals of reality—as if hunting down settled convictions were a self-justifying activity, even after all hope of arriving at superior convictions (truer, more realistic, more just) has been given up.

The question becomes, What sort of culture does the market foster? The one sketched by Marx, in which interest prompts people (nonradicals, at least) habitually to mistake formal freedom for the real thing and impute to themselves and others a degree of autonomy that the world cannot actually supply? Or the one that Mill sensed in the depths of his despair and that was most memorably characterized by Carlyle—a culture organized around the habit of remote causal attribution, in which even the greatest freedoms to which humans can plausibly aspire are apt to seem, at least to sensitive souls, unreal and unsatisfying (merely "formal"), thereby stimulating an appetite for sensations of spontaneity, self-sufficiency, and authenticity more intense than any society can satisfy?

These are ambitious questions, and I do not claim to answer them decisively. The principal argumentative burden of the preceding pages has been simply that the relation between capitalism and formalism is more complex than the conventional story would have it, and that the conventional story errs most grievously in supposing that "interest" is the only way economic developments can influence consciousness. The market teaches not one, but many lessons. Some of course serve the interests of those who benefit most from the market's existence; but others cut against the grain of interest, creating, for instance, the very possibility of perceiving the beneficiaries of the market as a "ruling class," whose authority stems neither from nature nor God, but merely from mutable circumstances of the sort that human beings can hope to understand and influence.

It will not do to say either that the market fosters formalism, or that it fosters antiformalism: what it fosters is precisely the debate between the two. The market makes possible the emergence of a game of causal attribution whose rules are sufficiently indeterminate that every event has both "formal" and "deep" interpretations, and which therefore allows for the emergence of rival elites, each committed to its own mode of explanation. Knowing this does not discredit either elite. Having once sampled the explanatory fruits of remote causal attribution, one finds that there is no turning back. Those of us who take what used to be called the "life of the mind" seriously cannot rest content with a mode of explanation that we regard as superficial; nor can we set in advance any fixed limits on how deep explanation should run. But neither are we obliged to succumb to the illusion that depth always equals truth. The commonsense explanations yielded by "proximate" causal attribution are inescapable and can never be rendered wholly obsolete by their deeper rivals. "Deep" explanations deliver nothing more than another perspective, shaped like all other perspectives by the perceiver's time, place, and situation. Thus when we set about the destructive work of stripping away the masks that shelter someone else's self from the world, we should do so in the full knowledge that we, too, rely on a conception of self that, when stripped of all claims to autonomy, ceases to exist. Perhaps the most obvious lesson to draw from John Stuart Mill's mental crisis is simply that although our claims of autonomy vary in degree and in kind, in the end (in practice, even if not in rhetoric) we are all "formalists," all claimants to an autonomy we cannot conclusively justify. To play the game of causal attribution is to construe at least one self, one's own, intransitively. What life would be like in the absence of that game, I find it impossible to imagine.

NOTES

INTRODUCTION History, Explanatory Schemes, and Other Wonders of Common Sense

1. The citations reflect my grasp of the literature at the time the various essays were written; there would be no point in bringing them up to date. Nor has the language of the early essays been revised to accord with the new gender conventions of the 1980s, whereby such words as "mankind," "man," and "he" are no longer permitted to stand for both sexes.

2. Thomas Carlyle, *A Carlyle Reader: Selections from the Writings of Thomas Carlyle*, ed. G. B. Tennyson (New York: Modern Library, 1969), 59.

3. Controversies breed strange bedfellows. Militantly antipositivist though they are, narrativists such as Hayden White and Louis Mink borrow a plank from their opponents' platform when they contend that insofar as knowledge of the past is mediated — even by something so elementary and inescapable as narrative form — it cannot be faithful to its object. Positivists, who claim to possess knowledge that unproblematically corresponds to the real, have no need of mediated knowledge, but antipositivists cannot do without it. That is why centrists such as Thomas Kuhn, Richard Rorty, Max Weber, and William James have neither aspired to unmediated knowledge nor thought that its absence is anything to lament. The candidly acknowledged artifice of "ideal types," in Weber's case, and "paradigms," in Kuhn's, exemplifies the untroubled acceptance of mediating devices that is characteristic of the centrist position in current debates. Once narrativism turns radical and construes narrative form itself as a distorting influence, "reality" has tacitly been placed beyond any possibility of human experience. To such arguments one can only respond as David Carr has, by asking "What is it that narrative . . . is supposed to distort?" ("Narrative and the Real World: An Argument for Continuity," *History and Theory* 25 [1986]: 121). See also Louis O. Mink, "Narrative Form as a Cognitive Instrument," in his *Historical Understanding*, ed. Brian Fay, Eugene O. Golob, and Richard T. Vann (Ithaca: Cornell University Press, 1987), 182–203; and Hayden White, *Metahistory: The Historical Imagination in Nineteenth-Century Europe* (Baltimore: Johns Hopkins University Press, 1973), and *The Content of the Form: Narrative Discourse and Historical Representation* (Baltimore: Johns Hopkins University Press, 1987).

4. Mink, "Narrative Form as a Cognitive Instrument," 182.

5. *The Emergence of Professional Social Science: The American Social Science Association and the Nineteenth-Century Crisis of Authority* (Urbana: University of Illinois Press, 1977).

6. Bernard Williams, *Shame and Necessity* (Berkeley: University of California Press, 1993), 56.

7. Carl G. Hempel, "The Function of General Laws in History" (1942), in *Theories of History,* ed. Patrick Gardiner (New York: Free Press, 1959), 344–55.

8. Hans Kellner, *Language and Historical Representation: Getting the Story Crooked* (Madison: University of Wisconsin Press, 1989), 299–300. The reduction of causation and much else to linguistic phenomena is asserted most uncompromisingly by Kellner's mentor, Hayden White: "Once the world of phenomena is separated into two orders of being (agents and causes on the one hand, acts and effects on the other), the primitive consciousness is endowed, *by purely linguistic means alone,* with the conceptual categories (agents, causes, spirits, essences) necessary for the theology, science, and philosophy of civilized reflection" (*Metahistory,* 35).

9. Mink, "Narrative Form as a Cognitive Instrument," 187.

10. J. L. Mackie, *The Cement of the Universe: A Study of Causation* (Oxford: Oxford University Press, 1974).

11. "'Objectivity' in Social Science," in Max Weber, *Sociological Writings,* ed. Wolf Heydebrand (New York: Continuum, 1994), 254 (emphasis added).

12. Hempel, "Function of General Laws in History," 348.

13. This discussion of the *Challenger* tragedy was written in haste, without benefit of a library. Inadequate though it is as an account of the tragedy, it succinctly serves its didactic purpose here, which is to present a set-piece illustration of the kinds of attributive judgments that are involved in explaining an event. Just as this text goes to press, Diane Vaughan's extraordinary historical ethnography of the *Challenger* launch decision arrives in my hands, too late to be utilized. Although the book is framed as a sociological study about the way mistakes occur in corporate organizations, it is also a splendid case study that exhibits the full complexity of explanation by causal attribution. Diane Vaughan, *The Challenger Launch Decision: Risky Technology, Culture, and Deviance at NASA* (Chicago: University of Chicago Press, 1996).

14. H.L.A. Hart, after distinguishing between the different approaches to causation taken by Hume and Mill, credits the latter with laying bare "a problem scarcely mentioned before in the history of philosophy: are there any principles governing the selection we apparently make of one of a complex set of conditions as the cause?" H.L.A. Hart and A. M. Honoré, *Causation in the Law* (London: Oxford University Press, 1959), 16. Hart and Honoré's chapter 1, "Causation and Common Sense," remains an invaluable point of departure for all discussion of the attributive mode of causal reasoning.

CHAPTER 1   Were Slaves More Efficient?

1. Robert William Fogel and Stanley L. Engerman, *Time on the Cross,* vol. 1, *The Economics of American Negro Slavery* (Boston: Little, Brown, 1974), 192, reviewed in *New York Review of Books,* May 2, by C. Vann Woodward. My understanding of the issues has been sharpened by friendly correspondence with Professor Engerman and by the assistance of Rice University colleagues too numerous to name.

2. Evsey D. Domar, "On the Measurement of Technological Change," *Economic Journal* 71 (Dec. 1961): 709–29; "On the Measurement of Comparative Efficiency," in *Comparison of Economic Systems: Theoretical and Methodological Approaches,* ed.

A. Eckstein (Berkeley: University of California Press, 1971), 229; Moses Abramovitz, "Resource and Output Trends in the United States Since 1870," *American Economic Review, Papers and Proceedings* 46 (May 1956): 5–23.

3. Fogel and Engerman, *Time on the Cross,* vol. 2, *Evidence and Methods: A Supplement,* 131, 138 (emphasis added). The market value of the nation's agricultural output was taken from estimates by Marvin W. Towne and Wayne D. Rasmussen, "Farm Gross Product and Gross Investment in the Nineteenth Century," in *Trends in the American Economy in the Nineteenth Century: Studies in Income and Wealth,* vol. 24 (Princeton: Princeton University Press, 1960), 255–312. Fogel and Engerman describe their initial procedure for calculating regional output as follows: "The allocation of crops [to the two regions] was based on census data regarding the physical product of each crop. Thus in the case of wheat, for example, the Towne-Rasmussen value of national wheat output in 1860 was $151.0 million. According to the 1860 census, the southern and northern shares of national wheat output were 22.4 and 73.2 percent, respectively. Therefore the value of southern wheat output in 1860 was measured as $33.8 million, while that of the North was $110.5 million" (131).

Clearly output is expressed in market value. The authors refine their initial output figures by adjusting for three sources of possible bias (133–35). None of the adjustments serves to free the index from its dependence on consumer demand. For their final computation the authors use different physical output data for the South, but still weight it with prices taken from the Towne-Rasmussen article (138).

4. Fogel and Engerman, *Time on the Cross,* 1: 210.

5. Some economists have recognized that the index does not discriminate between two different aspects of efficiency, one reflecting producer performance per se, the other reflecting producer responsiveness to consumer demands. Abram Bergson distinguishes between "efficiency in the sense of realization of production possibilities" and efficiency in the sense of "the degree of optimality of the output structure." He acknowledges that the index measures "performance in the two spheres together." In short, part of the index's test of efficiency is whether producers select the optimal mix of outputs, given a certain demand structure. But this supposes that all producers are equally capable of responding to demand. This is a valid assumption in many cases, but it is absurd to suggest that Massachusetts farmers flunked any test of optimality by failing to grow cotton. Edward F. Denison also has recognized the need to take into account the effect of demand pressure upon fluctuations in productivity. See Bergson, "Comparative Productivity and Efficiency in the Soviet Union and the United States," in *Comparison of Economic Systems,* ed. Eckstein, 195; and Denison, *Why Growth Rates Differ: Postwar Experience in Nine Western Countries* (Washington, D.C.: Brookings Institution, 1967), 273–276. In a forthcoming review essay in the *Journal of Economic History,* Paul A. David and Peter Temin make the same point (see chap. 2, note 7).

6. *Time on the Cross,* 1: 209. Subsequent page references are cited parenthetically in the text.

7. Stuart Bruchey, ed. and comp., *Cotton and the Growth of the American Economy, 1790–1860: Sources and Readings* (New York: Harcourt, Brace and World, 1967), tables 1A, 2A, and 2B.

8. A. W. Silver, *Manchester Men and Indian Cotton, 1847–1872* (Manchester: Manchester University Press, 1966), 32, 9, 227.

9. E. R. J. Owen, *Cotton and the Egyptian Economy, 1820–1914* (London: Oxford University Press, 1969), 50, 31, 199–202; J. A. Todd, *The World's Cotton Crops* (London: A. and C. Black, 1924), 239–49.

10. Todd, *The World's Cotton Crops,* 98, 395.

11. Gavin Wright, "An Econometric Study of Cotton Production and Trade, 1830–1880," *Review of Economics and Statistics* 53 (May 1971): 111. I do not claim that planters conspired to control prices. I claim only that the South enjoyed such competitive leeway that it might have realized a profit even if its labor force was neither diligent nor well managed.

12. *Time on the Cross,* 1: 194.

13. Ibid., 196.

14. This is not to say that cotton demand is the only point on which Fogel and Engerman's efficiency calculation can be challenged. The "efficiency" gap also rests on their dubious assumption that the quality of northern farmland was 2.5 times higher per acre than southern farmland. Nor do they consider the possibility that slavery made its chief contribution to "efficiency" by repelling free yeoman farmers, thus reducing land prices and the level of capital investment in southern agriculture. See also the extensive critique of their labor and land indices by David and Temin in a forthcoming issue of the *Journal of Economic History.* If the calculations of David and Temin are correct, the "efficiency" gap may not only be reduced, but reversed.

CHAPTER 2   The True & Tragical History of *Time on the Cross*

1. Stanley Elkins, *Slavery: A Problem in American Institutional and Intellectual Life,* 2d ed. (Chicago: University of Chicago Press, 1968).

2. R. W. Fogel, "The Specification Problem in Economic History," *Journal of Economic History* 27 (Sept. 1967): 283–308.

3. Fogel's railroad book stirred up a valuable discussion of the nature and role of causal attribution in historical scholarship, but his substantive conclusion that the railroad was dispensable is regarded with considerable suspicion by cliometricians. For a sampling of reservations and objections, see Paul A. David, "Transport Innovation and Economic Growth: Professor Fogel On and Off the Rails," *Economic History Review* 22 (Dec. 1969): 506–25; Meghnad Desai, "Some Issues in Econometric History," *Economic History Review* 21 (Apr. 1968): 1–16; Stanley Lebergott, "United States Transport Advances and Externalities," *Journal of Economic History* 26 (Dec. 1966): 437–61; Harry N. Scheiber, "On the New Economic History and Its Limitations: A Review Essay," *Agricultural History* 41 (Oct. 1967): 383–95; Peter D. McClelland, "Railroads, American Growth, and the New Economic History: A Critique," *Journal of Economic History* 28 (Mar. 1968): 102–23; Alexander Gerschenkron, "The Discipline and I," *Journal of Economic History* 27 (Dec. 1967): 454–58.

4. Fogel, "From the Marxists to the Mormons," *Times Literary Supplement,* June 13, 1975, 670.

5. *New York Times,* May 2, 1974.

6. Gutman, "The World Two Cliometricians Made: A Review-Essay of F + E = T/C," *Journal of Negro History* 60 (Jan. 1975): 53–227. The many typographical errors in this printing have been corrected in the book.

7. The chapters by David and Temin are revisions of "Slavery: The Progressive Institution?" *Journal of Economic History* 34 (Sept. 1974): 739–83, and "Capitalist Masters, Bourgeois Slaves," *Journal of Interdisciplinary History* 5 (Winter 1975): 445–57.

8. A shorter version of Wright's paper appears in the *Explorations in Economic History* collection, as does a criticism by Richard Vedder of Fogel and Engerman's calculation of the rate of expropriation.

9. Robert William Fogel and Stanley L. Engerman, *Time on the Cross*, vol. 1, *The Economics of American Negro Slavery* (Boston: Little, Brown, 1974), 116; Sutch, "The Treatment Received by American Slaves," *Explorations in Economic History* 12 (Fall 1975): 25–30, in manuscript; *Reckoning with Slavery*, chap. 6 (emphasis added).

10. William K. Scarborough, "New Direction or False Direction? A Critique of the 'New Economic History'" (Rochester conference paper); Gutman, *Slavery and the Numbers Game*, 66–69; Sutch, "The Treatment Received by American Slaves," 20–24, in manuscript; *Reckoning with Slavery*, chap. 2.

11. Sutch, "The Treatment Received by American Slaves," 17–20, in manuscript; Gutman, *Slavery and the Numbers Game*, 69–77; *Reckoning with Slavery*, chap. 2.

12. Gutman, *Slavery and the Numbers Game*, 140–52; Sutch, "The Treatment Received by American Slaves," 113–17, in manuscript; *Reckoning with Slavery*, chap. 4; Edward Shorter, "Protein, Puberty, and Premarital Sexuality: American Blacks vs. French Peasants" (Rochester conference paper); Peter Laslett, "The Slave Family Household in the Old South" (Rochester conference paper). Although the text adjacent to the bar graph says that the graph is based on first surviving children, the graph itself is mislabeled, and Gutman shows (ibid.) that Fogel, in a widely delivered prepublication paper, lost track of the distinction. Even if the graph was what it purports to be, Fogel and Engerman's interpretation of it would be odd: they claim it shows a "relative shortage of births in the late-teen ages," but actually it shows more births in this age category (fifteen to nineteen years old) than any other, and no basis is given for comparison with other populations (*Time on the Cross*, 1: 137–38).

13. Sutch, "The Treatment Received by American Slaves," 87, in manuscript; *Reckoning with Slavery*, chap. 3. Sutch also shows that Fogel and Engerman miscalculated the rate of slave sales, so the probabilities given here are too low.

14. Gutman, *Slavery and the Numbers Game*, 18–19. (Gutman miscalculates the rate of lynching, but the point of his argument is entirely sound.) *Reckoning with Slavery*, chap. 2.

15. *Time on the Cross*, 1: 49.

16. Sutch, "The Treatment Received by American Slaves," 85–104, in manuscript; Gutman, *Slavery and the Numbers Game*, 102–40; *Reckoning with Slavery*, chap. 3.

17. "Were Slaves More Efficient? Some Doubts about *Time on the Cross*," *New York Review of Books*, Sept. 19, 1974, 38–42 (included in this volume).

18. There is one narrowly circumscribed sense in which consumer behavior is relevant to productive efficiency: namely, the producer, in order to be efficient, must choose to produce those goods for which demand is greatest. We would not call "efficient" the entrepreneur who tries to manufacture and sell ice at the North Pole, no matter how much ice he produces, because there is no demand for his product. But responsiveness to demand is a proper criterion of producer efficiency only on the presupposition that competing producers are equally able to respond. We judge the antebellum Mas-

sachusetts farmer *unlucky* because his soil and climate were unsuitable for cotton — not inefficient.

19. Domar, "On Total Productivity and All That," *Journal of Political Economy* 70 (Dec. 1962): 559, cited by Harold Woodman, "The Old South and the New History" (Rochester conference paper).

20. David, "One Potato, Two Potato, Sweet Potato Pie: Clio Looks at Slavery and the South" (Rochester conference paper); Stanley Lebergott, review of *Time on the Cross,* in *American Political Science Review* 69 (June 1975): 697–700; Woodman, "The Old South and the New History"; Jay Mandle, "Strength and Growth in a Plantation Economy: An Appraisal of *Time on the Cross*" (Rochester conference paper); Frank Tipton Jr. and Clarence Walker, review of *Time on the Cross,* in *History and Theory* 14 (1975): 91–121.

21. Fogel, "From the Marxists to the Mormons," 667–70.

22. I am obliged to James H. Blackman, Program Director for Economics, National Science Foundation, for this information.

23. The trustees said they were "not disposed to put aside" the recommendations of their anonymous award jury, but some of them felt compelled to announce that "had the choice of prize winners been theirs alone, the decisions with respect to [*Time on the Cross*] would have been different or postponed pending further supporting evidence." A spokesman explained that the trustees believed that the book represented "thorough and honest scholarship," but thought the authors' methods "may require further study before full value can be placed on the book's findings." This misses the critics' point altogether, for it is not so much the method as the authors' abuse of it that is at issue. *Washington Post,* May 2, 1975.

CHAPTER 3 Power to the Experts

1. Paul Goodman, "The New Reformation," in *Beyond the New Left,* ed. Irving Howe (New York: McCall, 1970), 86.

2. Ibid.

3. The professions themselves, of course, long antedate what Bledstein calls the "culture of professionalism." In Italy a strong professional class emerged alongside the universities in the thirteenth and fourteenth centuries. In England the word "profession" was in use as early as the fourteenth century to refer to particular orders of monks and nuns; by the sixteenth century it was applied to other vocations, especially law, medicine, and the military. For broad surveys of professional life in Europe and America, see Carlo Cipolla, "The Professions: The Long View," *Journal of European Economic History* 2 (Spring 1973): 37–52; William J. Bouwsma, "Lawyers and Early Modern Culture," *American Historical Review* 78 (Apr. 1973): 303–27; and Samuel Haber, "The Professions and Higher Education in America: A Historical View," in *Higher Education and the Labor Market,* ed. Margaret S. Hill (New York: McGraw-Hill, 1974).

4. Emile Durkheim, *The Division of Labor in Society,* trans. George Simpson (New York: Macmillan, 1933), 43.

5. Emil Lederer and Jacob Marschak, "Der neue Mittelstand," *Grundriss der Sozialökomik,* sec. 9, pt. 1 (Tübingen, 1926), cited in C. Wright Mills, *White Collar: The American Middle Classes* (New York: Oxford University Press, 1951), 359.

6. Mills, *White Collar,* ix.

7. Ralf Dahrendorf, *Class and Class Conflict in Industrial Society* (Stanford: Stanford University Press, 1959), 52, 56.

8. Readers of Bledstein's account, having been led to think of the university and the professions as institutions brought into existence by, and for the sake of, the middle class, will be surprised to discover that as late as 1900, near the terminal date of Bledstein's study, only 3.9 percent of the college-age population was attending (let alone graduating from) college. Moreover, even by the generous standards of the census taker, only 4.3 percent of the work force in that year could be classified as "professional or technical" (Fritz Machlup, *The Production and Distribution of Knowledge in the United States* [Princeton: Princeton University Press, 1962], 78; Daniel Bell, *The Coming of Post-Industrial Society* [New York: Basic Books, 1976], 134).

Not until well into the twentieth century did the major part of the middle class benefit from attendance at the university that this very class is said to have created for its own advancement. College-educated professional people were too small a part of the late-nineteenth-century middle class to stand for the whole, and the number who exerted significant influence over the development of the university or the professions was smaller still.

CHAPTER 4   Professionalism versus Capitalism

1. A list of books and articles questioning or denouncing the myth of professional disinterestedness would have to include most of what has been written on the professions since 1960. The traditional celebratory view lives on, however, in the work of Paul Halmos, *The Personal Service Society* (New York: Schocken Books, 1970).

2. This search, conducted with the help of Megan Seaholm, covered the *American Journal of Sociology, American Sociological Review, Social Forces,* and *Annals of the American Academy of Political and Social Science* through 1940. Professions and professionalization were not subjects of great interest to sociologists before the late 1930s. What sociologists did have to say on the subject in these years presupposed both a strong kinship between university professors and nonacademic professionals, and the moral superiority of all professionals to businessmen. The closest thing I could find to an article hostile to the professions was published by the *American Journal of Sociology* in 1915 with a special note from the editor disclaiming any responsibility for the "largely partisan opinions" of the author, Hubert Langerock, a correspondent for the European Socialist Press Service. See "Professionalism: A Study in Professional Deformation," *American Journal of Sociology* 21 (July 1915): 3–44. When *Annals* devoted its May 1922 issue to several dozen articles on professional ethics, it was giving voice to a short-lived movement of academics and nonacademic professionals that had first taken shape in the form of the Inter-Professional Conference, held in Detroit in 1919. Architects, chemists, dentists, doctors, engineers, nurses, and other professional people gathered for the purpose of discovering "how to liberate the professions from the domination of selfish interest, both within and without the professions, to devise ways and means of better utilizing the professional heritage of knowledge and skill for the benefit of society, and to create relations between the professions looking toward that end." See *Annals* 101 (May 1922): 13. It was for this volume that Robert M. MacIver wrote the often republished essay "The Social Significance of Professional Ethics." Although Mac-

Iver denied that "business men are in fact selfish while professional men are altruistic," he then proceeded to adopt Tawney's conception of function, crediting professionals with recognition of their duty to serve the public and warning businessmen that they must learn to do the same. Not until Talcott Parsons's seminal essay, "The Professions and Social Structure," *Social Forces* 27 (May 1939), was the premise of professional disinterestedness attacked in a thorough and internally consistent manner. That Parsons should be the author of this pivotal contribution to the scholarship of the professions is exceedingly ironic, for today he is remembered as the fountainhead of a school of sociology that has often been criticized for being too friendly to the professions, and too accepting, in particular, of their claim to disinterestedness. Recent scholars have not been wrong to characterize Parsons's view as friendlier than their own, perhaps friendlier than the facts will warrant. But if we take a long view of the matter, fully cognizant of the context within which Parsons wrote, what ought to impress us about his conception of the professions is not the lingering element of affection that one does indeed find there, but rather the comparatively cool, clinical detachment that he brought to phenomena previous scholars had warmly and uniformly endorsed. Far from initiating a celebratory tradition in the sociology of the professions, Parsons broke with just such a tradition and set the stage for the still more critical treatment that rose up in the 1960s and 1970s to challenge his own comparatively neutral views.

3. A. M. Carr-Saunders and P. A. Wilson, *The Professions* (London: Frank Cass, 1964 [1933]), 497.

4. Eric Hobsbawm, "The Fabians Reconsidered," in his *Labouring Men: Studies in the History of Labour* (Garden City, N.Y.: Doubleday, 1967), 295–320; Harold Perkin, *The Origins of Modern English Society, 1780–1880* (Toronto: University of Toronto Press, 1972); Alvin Gouldner, *The Future of the Intellectuals and the Rise of the New Class* (New York: Continuum, 1979); Barbara Ehrenreich and John Ehrenreich, "The Professional-Managerial Class," in *Between Labour and Capital,* ed. Pat Walker (London: Harvester Press, 1979), 5–45; George Konrad and Ivan Szelenyi, *Intellectuals on the Road to Class Power,* trans. Andrew Arato and R. E. Allen (New York: Harcourt Brace Jovanovich, 1979).

5. Gouldner, *Future of the Intellectuals,* 31.

6. See Gouldner's conception of the "culture of critical discourse" (*Future of the Intellectuals,* 28–47 and passim).

7. Philip Rieff, *The Triumph of the Therapeutic: Uses of Faith after Freud* (London: Chatto and Windus, 1966).

8. Karl Polanyi, *The Great Transformation* (Boston: Beacon Press, 1944). One of the many strengths of Magali Sarfatti Larson's *The Rise of Professionalism: A Sociological Analysis* (Berkeley: University of California Press, 1977) is her demonstration of the importance of Polanyi's thesis to students of professionalization.

9. Polanyi, *Great Transformation,* 192, 152, 145.

10. Thomas L. Haskell, *The Emergence of Professional Social Science: The American Social Science Association and the Nineteenth-Century Crisis of Authority* (Urbana: University of Illinois Press, 1977), chap. 4; Sheldon Rothblatt, *The Revolution of the Dons: Cambridge and Society in Victorian England* (London: Faber and Faber, 1968). The *locus classicus* of the movement to establish authority is Matthew Arnold, *Culture and Anarchy* (Cambridge: Cambridge University Press, 1932 [1869]).

11. Tawney numbered the Archbishop of Canterbury among his closest friends and confided to his commonplace book in 1913 that his commitment to equality rested on religious grounds: "It is only when one contemplates the infinitely great that human differences appear so infinitely small as to be, negligeable [*sic*]. . . . What is wrong with the modern world is that having ceased to believe in the greatness of God, and therefore the infinite smallness (or greatness—the same thing!) of *man*, it has to invent or emphasize distinctions between *men*" (*R. H. Tawney's Commonplace Book*, ed. J. M. Winter and D. M. Joslin [Cambridge: Cambridge University Press, 1972], 53, 54). See also Ross Terrill, *R. H. Tawney and His Times: Socialism as Fellowship* (Cambridge, Mass.: Harvard University Press, 1973), 61.

12. R. H. Tawney, *Equality* (New York: Harcourt, Brace, 1931), 271.

13. *Commonplace Book*, 82–83.

14. Terrill, *Tawney and His Times*, 170.

15. *Commonplace Book*, 120.

16. R. H. Tawney, *The Acquisitive Society* (New York: Harcourt, Brace, 1920), 8, 11. Subsequent page references are cited parenthetically in the text.

17. *Commonplace Book*, 39, 143.

18. Tawney, *Acquisitive Society*, 94–95.

19. Raymond Williams, *Culture and Society, 1780–1950* (Garden City, N.Y.: Doubleday, 1960); Perkin, *Origins of Modern English Society;* Martin Wiener, *English Culture and the Decline of the Industrial Spirit, 1850–1980* (Cambridge: Cambridge University Press, 1981); Rothblatt, *Revolution of the Dons.*

20. Perkin, *Origins of Modern English Society*, 265–66.

21. Arnold quoted in Wiener, *English Culture and the Decline of the Industrial Spirit*, 16, 38.

22. Perkin, *Origins of Modern English Society*, 258, 408–54; see also Wiener, *English Culture and the Decline of the Industrial Spirit.*

23. Rothblatt, *Revolution of the Dons*, 87, 272, 258. The professional ideal was also inculcated in the reformed public schools: see Daniel Duman, "The Creation and Diffusion of a Professional Ideology in 19th Century England," *Sociological Review* 27 (Feb. 1979): 113–38.

24. Hobsbawm, "The Fabians Reconsidered," 308–9, 315.

25. Tawney, *Acquisitive Society*, 161, 184.

26. Tawney, *Equality*, 248; *Acquisitive Society*, 170.

27. Tawney, *Acquisitive Society*, 176–77.

28. Haskell, *Emergence of Professional Social Science*, 229; Steven J. Diner, *A City and Its Universities: Public Policy in Chicago, 1892–1919* (Chapel Hill: University of North Carolina Press, 1980). The strongest case yet made for the kinship of "Progressive" reformers throughout the West appears in James T. Kloppenberg, *Uncertain Victory: Social Democracy and Progressivism in European and American Thought, 1870–1920* (New York: Oxford University Press, 1986), which I read in manuscript.

29. See Hobsbawm, "The Fabians Reconsidered," 310. On the founding of the American Economic Association, see Haskell, *Emergence of Professional Social Science*, chap. 8; and Mary O. Furner, *Advocacy and Objectivity: A Crisis in the Professionalization of American Social Science, 1865–1905* (Lexington: University Press of Kentucky, 1975). On the *Methodenstreit*, see Joseph A. Schumpeter, *History of Economic Analysis*

(New York: Oxford University Press, 1954); Albion Small, *Origins of Sociology* (Chicago: University of Chicago Press, 1924); Carl Menger, *Problems of Economics and Sociology,* ed. L. Schneider (Urbana: University of Illinois Press, 1963); R. S. Howey, *Rise of the Marginal Utility School, 1870–1889* (Lawrence: University of Kansas Press, 1960); R. D. Collison Black, A. W. Coats, and C. D. W. Goodwin, eds., *The Marginal Revolution in Economics: Interpretation and Evaluation* (Durham, N.C.: Duke University Press, 1977); Jurgen Herbst, *The German Historical School in American Scholarship: A Study in the Transfer of Culture* (Ithaca: Cornell University Press, 1965); Fritz Ringer, *Decline of the German Mandarins: The German Academic Community, 1890–1933* (Cambridge, Mass.: Harvard University Press, 1969).

30. Steven Lukes, *Emile Durkheim: His Life and Work, A Historical and Critical Study* (New York: Harper and Row, 1972), 320.

31. Emile Durkheim, *Professional Ethics and Civic Morals,* trans. Cornelia Brookfield (London: Routledge and Kegan Paul, 1957), 11. Subsequent page references are cited parenthetically in the text.

32. Terence J. Johnson, *Professions and Power* (London: Macmillan, 1972), 41–61.

33. Durkheim displayed little interest in either the solidarism of Léon Bourgeois or administrative syndicalism, contemporary movements close to his own position; see Lukes, *Durkheim: His Life and Work,* 338–41, 350–54, 536–38.

34. Ibid., 334–43; Philip Rieff, ed., *On Intellectuals: Theoretical Studies, Case Studies* (Garden City, N.Y.: Doubleday, 1970), 87n.

35. Haskell, *Emergence of Professional Social Science,* and "Professionalization as Cultural Reform," *Humanities in Society* 1 (Spring 1978): 103–14; Robert H. Wiebe, *The Search for Order, 1877–1920* (New York: Hill and Wang, 1967); Samuel P. Hays, *The Response to Industrialism, 1885–1914* (Chicago: University of Chicago Press, 1957); Burton J. Bledstein, *The Culture of Professionalism: The Middle Class and the Development of Higher Education in America* (New York: Norton, 1976); Diner, *A City and Its Universities;* George M. Fredrickson, *The Inner Civil War: Northern Intellectuals and the Crisis of the Union* (New York: Harper and Row, 1965); T. J. Jackson Lears, *No Place of Grace: Antimodernism and the Transformation of American Culture, 1880–1920* (New York: Pantheon, 1981); Peter Dobkin Hall, *The Organization of American Culture: Private Institutions, Elites, and the Origins of American Nationality* (New York: New York University Press, 1982); and the essays by Bender, Hall, and Ross in *The Authority of Experts: Studies in History and Theory,* ed. T. L. Haskell (Bloomington: Indiana University Press, 1984).

36. Thorstein Veblen, *The Higher Learning in America: A Memorandum on the Conduct of Universities by Business Men* (New York: Hill and Wang, 1957 [1918]), 31.

37. Ibid., 145, 23, 19; Thorstein Veblen, "The Place of Science in Modern Civilization," in his *Veblen on Marx, Race, Science and Economics* (New York: Capricorn, 1969 [1919]), 18–22. On Veblen's instinctivism, see T. L. Haskell, "Veblen on Capitalism: Intellectual History In and Out of Context," *Reviews in American History* 7 (1979): 553–60, and "Reply" [to John Diggins, "The Problem of Contextualism in Intellectual History"], *Newsletter of the Intellectual History Group* (Spring 1981): 27–32.

38. Thorstein Veblen, *The Engineers and the Price System* (New York: Viking, 1947 [1921]); *Higher Learning in America,* 7, 25, 9, 8.

39. Durkheim, *Professional Ethics,* 23–24.

40. Lukes, *Durkheim: His Life and Work,* 487n.

41. *Commonplace Book,* 42.

42. Charles Sanders Peirce, *Collected Papers,* ed. Charles Hartshorne and Paul Weiss (Cambridge, Mass.: Harvard University Press, 1931–60), VI-290. In the custom of Peirce scholars, my references to Peirce's writings will be to volume and paragraph of the *Collected Papers.* Thus VI-290 means volume six, paragraph 290. Subsequent citations are in parentheses in the text.

43. My discussion of Peirce in the following pages is both an extension and a revision, in part, of my earlier statement in *Emergence of Professional Social Science,* 237–39.

44. A useful introduction to current debate over Peirce among Continental writers, such as Habermas, Apel, and Gadamer, is supplied by Margareta Bertilsson, *Towards a Social Reconstruction of Science Theory: Peirce's Theory of Inquiry, and Beyond,* Lund Studies in Sociology (Lund: Bokcafeet, 1978).

45. See also C. Wright Mills, *Sociology and Pragmatism: The Higher Learning in America,* ed. I. L. Horowitz (New York: Payne-Whitman, 1964), 159.

46. Bertilsson, *Towards a Social Reconstruction of Science Theory,* 64, 68.

47. John E. Smith, "Community and Reality," in *Perspectives on Peirce,* ed. Richard J. Bernstein (New Haven: Yale University Press, 1965), 118.

48. Haskell, *Emergence of Professional Social Science,* chaps. 4 (on the Lazzaroni), 7 (merger of ASSA and Johns Hopkins), 8 (founding of the Historical and Economic Associations). Further references to the Lazzaroni will be found in ibid., 69–74.

49. I am much indebted to the essay on Peirce by R. Jackson Wilson, *In Quest of Community: Social Philosophy in the United States, 1860–1920* (London: Oxford University Press, 1968), 48. See also Karl-Otto Apel, *Charles S. Peirce: From Pragmatism to Pragmaticism,* trans. J. M. Krois (Amherst: University of Massachusetts Press, 1981), xvi; and Apel, *Toward a Transformation of Philosophy,* trans. G. Adey and D. Frisby (London: Routledge and Kegan Paul, 1980), especially "The Communication Community as the Transcendental Presupposition for the Social Sciences" and "The *a priori* of the Communication Community and the Foundations of Ethics." Still another relevant discussion is Jakob Liszka, "Community in C. S. Peirce: Science as a Means and as an End," *Transactions of the Charles S. Peirce Society* 14 (Fall 1978): 305–21.

50. After writing these words, I was pleased to discover that Nicholas Rescher, in an argument not intended to stress the relation of Peirce's conception to liberal political theory or the ethos of capitalism, also likens Peirce's view of the self-correcting operation of scientific inquiry to the free market mechanism that determines the price of commodities. See his *Peirce's Philosophy of Science: Critical Studies in His Theory of Induction and Scientific Method* (Notre Dame, Ind.: University of Notre Dame Press, 1978), 15.

51. Wilson, *In Quest of Community,* 57n.

52. Rescher, *Peirce's Philosophy of Science,* 51–52, 41–42. See also Apel, *Peirce,* 157, where he speaks of Peirce's community as "an open society of critics."

53. Max Weber, *The Protestant Ethic and the Spirit of Capitalism,* trans. Talcott Parsons (New York: Scribners, 1958), 17 (emphasis deleted).

54. Larson, *Rise of Professionalism,* 9. To be more exact, Larson believes that the opposition to the market voiced by professionals was largely a matter of "appearances"

and "ideological self-conceptions," and therefore she hesitates to treat professionalization in the nineteenth century as an authentic manifestation of Polanyi's countermovement. I do not hesitate because I believe that most professionals were sincere, but
deeply ambivalent about the ways of the marketplace. Their ambivalence, far from dis-
qualifying them, seems to me to confirm their membership in the movement Polanyi
describes.

CHAPTER 5   The Curious Persistence of Rights Talk
in the Age of Interpretation

   1. It is sometimes assumed that rights stand partly in opposition to morality, since
they are claims made by individuals against the group, while moral rules restrain individual liberty for the sake of the public interest or the collective will of the community.
I would argue, on the contrary, that every right for one person implies duties for others,
and indeed that rights are the principal means by which duty is smuggled back into
cultures dominated by the rhetoric of individualism. On the correlativity of rights and
duties, see Joel Feinberg, "The Nature and Value of Rights," *Journal of Value Inquiry* 4
(Winter 1970): 243–57.
   2. Michel Foucault and Hayden White are the most obvious exceptions, but neither
would care to be known as a member of the profession. Michel Foucault, *Discipline
and Punish: The Birth of the Prison,* trans. A. Sheridan (New York: Pantheon, 1977);
Hayden White, *Metahistory: The Historical Imagination in Nineteenth-Century Europe*
(Baltimore: Johns Hopkins University Press, 1973).
   3. Carl L. Becker, "What Are Historical Facts?" in *The Philosophy of History in Our
Time: An Anthology,* ed. H. Meyerhoff (Garden City, N.Y.: Doubleday, 1959), 120–37;
Charles A. Beard, "Written History as an Act of Faith," ibid., 140–51. Here and elsewhere, I employ the word "historicism" as it is commonly used in contemporary philosophical and literary discourse. Historians should be warned that it bears no simple or
straightforward relation to the practice of their craft, which is, from a radical historicist
point of view, quaintly positivistic in its assumption that one can make sense of the past
and arrive at interpretations of it that possess intersubjective validity. Among literary
critics and philosophers, the word often functions as a synonym for the irreducible incoherence of raw experience and, consequently, the futility of reason. Tempting though
it may seem to historians to invoke special privileges in the definition of the term, those
usages are sanctioned by long custom. The moderate form of historicism I am trying to
advance is a descendant of the "via media" that James T. Kloppenberg describes in his
remarkably comprehensive account of social thought and philosophy at the turn of the
century. See James T. Kloppenberg, *Uncertain Victory: Social Democracy and Progressivism in European and American Thought, 1870–1920* (New York: Oxford University Press,
1986); Friedrich Meinecke, *Historism: The Rise of a New Historical Outlook,* trans. J. E.
Anderson (London: Routledge and Kegan Paul, 1972); Maurice Mandelbaum, *History,
Man and Reason: A Study in Nineteenth-Century Thought* (Baltimore: Johns Hopkins
University Press, 1971); Morton White, *Social Thought in America: The Revolt Against
Formalism* (Boston: Beacon Press, 1957); H. Stuart Hughes, *Consciousness and Society:
The Reorientation of European Social Thought, 1890–1930* (New York: Knopf, 1958).
   4. Allan Bloom, *The Closing of the American Mind: How Higher Education Has*

Failed Democracy and Impoverished the Souls of Today's Students (New York: Simon and Schuster, 1987); Leo Strauss, *Natural Right and History* (Chicago: University of Chicago Press, 1953).

5. Strauss, *Natural Right and History*, 1–2.

6. It is true, however, that historicism has been hostile to the idea of rights and that Germany has been exceptionally hospitable to historicism. In spite of his mainly liberal convictions, even Max Weber had little use for the idea of human rights, which he called "an extreme rationalist fantasy." See Stephen P. Turner and Regis A. Factor, *Max Weber and the Dispute over Reason and Value: A Study in Philosophy, Ethics, and Politics* (London: Routledge and Kegan Paul, 1984), 66. On the influence of the German historical school in America, see Laurence R. Veysey, *The Emergence of the American University* (Chicago: University of Chicago Press, 1965); and Jurgen Herbst, *The German Historical School in American Scholarship: A Study in the Transfer of Culture* (Ithaca: Cornell University Press, 1965). On the "crisis of democratic theory" that Strauss erroneously thought began in the 1930s and 1940s, see Edward A. Purcell Jr., *The Crisis of Democratic Theory: Scientific Naturalism and the Problem of Value* (Lexington: University Press of Kentucky, 1973).

7. Harris E. Starr, *William Graham Sumner* (New York: Holt, 1925), 72, 64. "Rights is the child of the law; from real law come real rights; but from imaginary laws, from 'laws of nature,' come imaginary rights. . . . Natural rights is simple nonsense; natural and imprescriptable rights (an American phrase), rhetorical nonsense, nonsense upon stilts." Bentham quoted in Maurice Cranston, "Are There Any Human Rights?" *Daedalus* 112 (Fall 1983): 4. Garry Wills, *Inventing America: Jefferson's Declaration of Independence* (New York: Doubleday, 1978), 181–92.

8. Ronald Dworkin, *Taking Rights Seriously* (Cambridge, Mass.: Harvard University Press, 1977), 184.

9. Strauss, *Natural Right and History*, 2–3.

10. Ibid., 26–27.

11. For a typically acid attack on Strauss, and a useful guide to the large literature that details the real flaws and tendentiousness of his work, as well as that of his notoriously loyal, but often able, followers, see M. F. Burnyeat, "Sphinx without a Secret," *New York Review of Books*, May 30, 1985, 30–36.

12. Strauss, *Natural Right and History*, 5; Clifford Geertz, *The Interpretation of Cultures: Selected Essays* (New York: Basic Books, 1973), 28–29. Clifford Geertz, "Anti Anti-Relativism," *American Anthropologist* 86 (June 1984): 263–78, is a typically agile and charming performance, well worth everyone's reading, but it evades all the serious issues.

13. Richard Rorty, *Philosophy and the Mirror of Nature* (Princeton: Princeton University Press, 1979), 10.

14. Michel Foucault, *Power/Knowledge: Selected Interviews and Other Writings, 1972–77*, ed. Colin Gordon (New York: Pantheon, 1980), 80; Richard Wolin, "Foucault's Aesthetic Decisionism," *Telos* 67 (Spring 1986): 71–86.

15. Only people of angelic patience and much time on their hands read Jacques Derrida, *Of Grammatology*, trans. G. C. Spivak (Baltimore: Johns Hopkins University Press, 1974). The rest of us read Jonathan Culler, *On Deconstruction* (Ithaca: Cornell University Press, 1982). For an account of the radical wing of historicism that is singu-

larly lucid and remarkable for its combination of sympathy and critical detachment, see Allan Megill, *Prophets of Extremity: Nietzsche, Heidegger, Foucault, Derrida* (Berkeley: University of California Press, 1985). Also valuable are David Hollinger, "The Knower and the Artificer," *American Quarterly* 39 (Spring 1987): 37–55; Frederick Crews, "The House of Grand Theory," *New York Review of Books*, May 29, 1986, 36–42; Quentin Skinner, ed., *The Return of Grand Theory in the Human Sciences* (Cambridge: Cambridge University Press, 1985); Gerald Graff, *Literature Against Itself: Literary Ideas in Modern Society* (Chicago: University of Chicago Press, 1979); Richard J. Bernstein, *Beyond Objectivism and Relativism: Science, Hermeneutics, and Praxis* (Philadelphia: University of Pennsylvania Press, 1983).

16. Friedrich Nietzsche, *On the Genealogy of Morals and Ecce Homo*, trans. Walter Kaufmann and R. J. Hollingdale (New York: Random House, 1969), 77, 80.

17. Ibid., 76.

18. Strauss, *Natural Right and History*, 167.

19. Nietzsche, *On the Genealogy of Morals*, 119.

20. "Symposium on Critique of Rights," *Texas Law Review* 62 (May 1984): 1363–617.

21. Alasdair MacIntyre, *After Virtue: A Study in Moral Theory*, 2d ed. (Notre Dame, Ind.: University of Notre Dame Press, 1984), 2. Subsequent page references are cited parenthetically in the text.

22. For a related criticism, see Richard J. Bernstein, "Nietzsche or Aristotle? Reflections on Alasdair MacIntyre's *After Virtue*," *Soundings* 67 (Spring 1984): 6–29; and Alasdair MacIntyre, "Bernstein's Distorting Mirrors: A Rejoinder," ibid., 30–41.

23. Of course we may be living on borrowed time.

24. If, as often happens, the relativist exempts his or her own views and values from the general claim that thought is situationally determined, then, I take it, we would be fools to continue the conversation.

25. David Hume, *A Treatise of Human Nature, Being an Attempt to Introduce the Experimental Method of Reasoning into Moral Subjects*, vol. 1, *Of the Understanding*, in *The Philosophical Works [of David Hume]*, ed. Thomas Hill Green and Thomas Hodge Grose (Aalen: Scientia, 1964), 548–49.

26. Insofar as rights spell out the implications of personhood, a recent collection on "the category of the person" provides much food for thought. In an examination of the effort by Marcel Mauss and other Durkheimians to write the sociology of the fundamental Aristotelian (actually Kantian) categories, Steven Collins advances a conception of "human predicaments" that blends durability and contingency in extremely suggestive ways. Collins rejects the ahistorical, a priori, categories of Kant and yet acknowledges the existence of nonmetaphysical categories that are so deeply rooted in the human condition that they do not vary significantly between cultures or across time. "If we assume, as I think we can, that there is a set of basic predicaments which define what it is to be human, then they will neither vary cross-culturally nor develop historically. As to their origin, we may claim, with Durkheim, that insofar as some of them are inextricably linked with the existence of society (as, for instance, personhood) they may be said to arise from the empirical fact of society, but to be given in this way a priori to individuals. Insofar as some predicaments may be at the mercy of a variety of non-universal, perhaps historical, factors, they may be said (i) to originate empirically, (ii) to vary cross-culturally . . . and (iii) to develop historically." This lays out a

spectrum of possibilities well suited to a conventionalist conception of rights. Steven Collins, "Categories, Concepts or Predicaments? Remarks on Mauss's Use of Philosophical Terminology," in *The Category of the Person: Anthropology, Philosophy, History*, ed. Michael Carrithers, Steven Collins, and Steven Lukes (Cambridge: Cambridge University Press, 1985), 70, 73.

27. Mark Tushnet, "An Essay on Rights," *Texas Law Review* 62 (May 1984): 1363–403, esp. 1366.

28. Ibid., 1370, 1371, 1363.

29. The technological innovation imagined by Tushnet would solve one problem only to create others, and I certainly do not find anything cheerful in the prospect of unwanted fetuses being brought to term mechanically and then set out for adoption. It is only for limited argumentative purposes that I take this imaginary case as a point of departure.

30. Thomas L. Haskell, "Capitalism and the Origins of the Humanitarian Sensibility [parts 1 and 2]," *American Historical Review* 90 (Apr. 1985): 339–61, (June 1985): 547–66. (Both essays are included in this volume.)

31. For an expression of such fears that I read only after this essay was written, see David Brion Davis, "Reflections on Abolitionism and Ideological Hegemony," *American Historical Review* 92 (Oct. 1987): 797–812; and Thomas L. Haskell, "Convention and Hegemonic Interest in the Debate over Antislavery: A Reply to Davis and Ashworth," ibid., 829–78.

32. Cranston, "Are There Any Human Rights?" 6.

33. John Rawls, "Kantian Constructivism in Moral Theory," *Journal of Philosophy* 77 (Sept. 1980): 515–72. See John Rawls, *A Theory of Justice* (Cambridge, Mass.: Harvard University Press, 1971); Robert Nozick, *Anarchy, State, and Utopia* (Oxford: Basil Blackwell, 1974); H. L. A. Hart, "Between Utility and Rights," in *The Idea of Freedom: Essays in Honour of Isaiah Berlin*, ed. Alan Ryan (Oxford: Oxford University Press, 1979), 77–98; Dworkin, *Taking Rights Seriously*.

34. Rawls, "Kantian Constructivism," 519.

35. Michael J. Sandel, *Liberalism and the Limits of Justice* (Cambridge: Cambridge University Press, 1982). See also Thomas Nagel, "Rawls on Justice," in *Reading Rawls: Critical Studies on Rawls' A Theory of Justice*, ed. Norman Daniels (New York: Basic Books, 1975); and Milton Fisk, "History and Reason in Rawls' Moral Theory," ibid.

36. Thomas S. Kuhn, *The Structure of Scientific Revolutions*, 2d ed. (Chicago: University of Chicago Press, 1970); and "Notes on Lakatos," in *PSA 1970, in Memory of Rudolph Carnap*, ed. Roger C. Buck and Robert S. Cohen, Boston Studies in the Philosophy of Science, no. 8 (Dordrecht: Reidel, 1971), 144.

37. Although he does not share my sense of urgency, Allan Megill provides much justification for it in his *Prophets of Extremity*.

38. Thomas S. Kuhn, "Rhetoric and Liberation" (manuscript prepared for the symposium "Rhetoric in the Human Sciences," University of Iowa, Mar. 28, 1984), 1, 7–8. The paper Kuhn responded to was published as Richard Rorty, "Solidarity or Objectivity?" in *Post-Analytic Philosophy*, ed. John Rajchman and Cornel West (New York: Columbia University Press, 1985), 3–19. A slightly different strategy for reestablishing the possibility of objectivity within a historicist approach was suggested by Donald Davidson: "In giving up dependence on the concept of an uninterpreted reality, some-

thing outside all schemes and science, we do not relinquish the notion of objective truth—quite the contrary. Given the dogma of a dualism of scheme and reality, we get conceptual relativity, and truth relative to a scheme. Without the dogma, this kind of relativity goes by the board. Of course truth of sentences remains relative to language, but that is as objective as can be. In giving up the dualism of scheme and world we do not give up the world, but re-establish unmediated touch with the familiar objects whose antics make our sentences and opinions true or false." Donald Davidson, "On the Very Idea of a Conceptual Scheme," in his *Inquiries into Truth and Interpretation* (Oxford: Oxford University Press, 1984), 199–214. A comparable strategy is developed by Bernstein, *Beyond Objectivism and Relativism.* For an eloquent defense of objectivity, see Thomas Nagel, *The View from Nowhere* (New York: Oxford University Press, 1986).

CHAPTER 6   Objectivity Is Not Neutrality

1. Eugene Genovese and Elizabeth Fox-Genovese do not hesitate, for example, to speak of "Braudel's great and anti-Marxist work"—and then follow through on what might otherwise be an empty gesture with a close and critical analysis of that work. I look forward to the day when spokespersons for other movements can treat their opponents with similar detachment. Elizabeth Fox-Genovese and Eugene D. Genovese, *Fruits of Merchant Capital: Slavery and Bourgeois Property in the Rise and Expansion of Capitalism* (New York: Oxford University Press, 1983), 188.

2. Friedrich Nietzsche, *On the Genealogy of Morals and Ecce Homo,* trans. Walter Kaufmann and R. J. Hollingdale (New York: Random House, 1969). See especially the third essay of *On the Genealogy of Morals,* titled "What is the Meaning of Ascetic Ideals?"

3. Geoffrey Galt Harpham, *The Ascetic Imperative in Culture and Criticism* (Chicago: University of Chicago Press, 1987), xi, xii.

4. Thomas Nagel, *The View from Nowhere* (New York: Oxford University Press, 1986), 4–6, 68.

5. Nietzsche, *On the Genealogy of Morals,* 87.

6. Nagel, *View from Nowhere,* 71.

7. Although in other respects people attracted to "postmodernism" are often especially eager to give the subjective element its due, they tend not to take seriously detachment, self-restraint, self-denial, or any of the other subjective experiences of *self versus self* upon which asceticism builds. No wonder: Postmodernism typically presupposes a self too vaporous to resist anything, least of all its own all-consuming desires. From the postmodernist standpoint, the self is not a discrete agent that takes *cognizance* of circumstances, and selects a course of action *in light* of them; instead its "situatedness" is so thoroughgoing that, like the electrified gas inside a neon tube, it can only conform to the shape of its circumstantial container and respond on cue as environing forces surge irresistibly through it. Thus Stanley Fish, in a candid, if characteristically reckless, essay titled "Critical Self-Consciousness, or Can We Know What We're Doing?" derides the idea that there is any emancipatory potential in striving to become more self-aware: "To be in a situation (as one always is)," says Fish, "is already to be equipped with an awareness of possible goals, obstacles, dangers, rewards, alternatives, etc., and nothing is or could be aided by something called 'self-consciousness.'" Consciousness is ex-

haustively determined by situation: the first lesson of antifoundationalism, Fish says, is precisely that "being situated means that one cannot achieve a distance on one's beliefs." His root assumption is straightforwardly fatalistic: our subjective experience of freedom to choose between options is simply an illusion. "Freedom, in whatever shape it appears, is another name for constraint" (*Doing What Comes Naturally: Change, Rhetoric, and the Practice of Theory in Literary and Legal Studies* [Durham, N.C.: Duke University Press, 1989], 466, 467, 459). It is ironic that although Fish has little use for the idea of objectivity and Nagel defends it, Fish's error, as seen from Nagel's standpoint, is precisely that Fish is trying too hard to "be objective." Fish, that is, gives no credence at all to the "internal" (subjective) view, according to which our own power to bring one event rather than another into existence seems quite indisputable, and instead he tries once and for all to substitute for that view the "external" (objective) one, according to which the real causes of our acts may well lie outside our deceptively vivid experience of conscious choice. Nagel, in contrast, accords to some subjective experience a status no less real than that derived from the "view from nowhere." In his words, "the seductive appeal of objective reality depends on a mistake. It is not the given. Reality is not just objective reality. Sometimes, in the philosophy of mind but also elsewhere, the truth is not to be found by traveling as far away from one's personal perspective as possible" (Nagel, *View from Nowhere*, 27. See also 114–15).

8. Throughout this essay I have, for purposes of argument, accepted the conventional wisdom that our Victorian forebears really expected through self-annihilation to be transported into the realm of truth. In fact, my guess is that a more sensitive contextual reading would show that they were less naive than we like to think. The important book that has come to epitomize conventional wisdom on this point is Richard Rorty, *Philosophy and the Mirror of Nature* (Princeton: Princeton University Press, 1979).

9. For Nietzsche's sincere admiration for the human capacity for promise keeping and other basic renunciatory traits, see the second essay of *On the Genealogy of Morals*, especially 57–61 and 84–85. Walter A. Kaufmann's *Nietzsche: Philosopher, Psychologist, Antichrist*, 3d ed. (Princeton: Princeton University Press, 1968), develops the theme of self-overcoming at length.

10. I find it difficult to imagine that a person so narrowly committed would, as a matter of fact, succeed in entering sympathetically into the thought of another, even for polemical purposes, but the assertion still holds—if he or she *did* succeed, there would be no other reason to deny the objectivity of the performance.

11. Nietzsche, *On the Genealogy of Morals*, 119.

12. Ibid.

13. Novick is insistent about the virtual identity of objectivity and neutrality. Thus when one of the profession's founders, Hermann Eduard von Holst, the prominent German historian who established the department at the University of Chicago, tried to disentangle the idea of objectivity from that of neutrality, Novick complains of the "elusiveness" and "ambiguity" of his language: "Von Holst, with no apparent sense of inconsistency, could profess 'the objectivity of the historian,' of the 'cool, unbiased student' aiming at the 'stern historical truth,' and yet praise Woodrow Wilson for being 'no votary of that exaggerated, nay, impossible *objektivität*, which virtually amounts to a denial of his right to hold any political or moral opinion as to the events and men he is treating of. But he has no thesis to prove. With unimpeachable honesty and un-

deviating singleness of purpose he strives—as Ranke puts it—"simply to say how it was."' The elusiveness and ambiguity in von Holst's usage was characteristic" (25-26). Von Holst's statement is no model of clarity about the relationship between objectivity and neutrality, but it does make it clear that, even among the founding generation, the necessity of distinguishing between the two was recognized. That is a fact with which Novick never comes to terms.

14. For three quite different, though related, accounts of the movement I have in mind, each assigning it different causes and chronologies, see Alasdair MacIntyre, *After Virtue: A Study in Moral Theory,* 2d ed. (Notre Dame, Ind.: University of Notre Dame Press, 1984); Philip Rieff, *The Triumph of the Therapeutic: Uses of Faith after Freud,* with a new preface (Chicago: University of Chicago Press, 1987); and T. J. Jackson Lears, *No Place of Grace: Antimodernism and the Transformation of American Culture, 1880-1920* (New York: Pantheon, 1981).

15. A culture that acknowledges no significant difference between "You *ought* to do/believe *x*" and "I *want* you to do/believe *x*"—the former an invocation of objective obligation, the latter a report of merely subjective desires—is, I believe, in serious trouble. But there is, in my view, no help to be had outside the sphere of history and convention. After three centuries of inquiry into the basis of moral judgment it appears that no ultimate, metaphysical foundations are to be found—in nature, divine will, or anywhere else. Admitting that moral judgment cannot be based on timeless absolutes, universally applicable and utterly independent of human consciousness and practice, does not mean, however, that we must set morality adrift and leave it at the mercy of whimsy and fashion. Thomas Kuhn has shown how authoritative science remains even when we admit the social, conventional quality of scientific understanding and give up the claim that scientists aim at correspondence with eternal verities: *The Structure of Scientific Revolutions,* 2d ed. (Chicago: University of Chicago Press, 1970). Similarly, the most sophisticated proponents of moral realism today do not try to rally faith in supposedly self-evident absolutes or claim that moral rules are independent of cultural conditioning; they admit the historicity and even the conventionality of our ethical thinking and seek to reestablish grounds for obligation on that more modest base. Moral realists have been fighting an uphill battle for a long time, but there is no lack of able voices: see, in addition to MacIntyre's *After Virtue,* Peter Railton, "Moral Realism," *Philosophical Review* 95 (1986): 163-207; the essays by Simon Blackburn and John McDowell in *Morality and Objectivity: A Tribute to J. L. Mackie,* ed. Ted Honderich (Boston: Routledge and Kegan Paul, 1985); and Derek Parfit, *Reasons and Persons* (New York: Oxford University Press, 1984). I have discussed these issues at greater length in "The Curious Persistence of Rights Talk in the 'Age of Interpretation,'" *Journal of American History* 74 (1987): 984-1012 (included in this volume), and "Convention and Hegemonic Interest in the Debate over Antislavery: A Reply to Davis and Ashworth," *American Historical Review* 92 (Oct. 1987): 829-78.

16. Of the two paragraphs he says: "Although radically compressed, this is, I think, a fair summary of the original and continuing objectivist creed—an ideal to be pursued by individuals, policed by the collectivity." He concedes that over the past century the concept has been modified—objectivists are less confident that they can purge themselves of values and preconceptions; more likely to ground objectivity in social mecha-

nisms, as opposed to individual qualities; more tolerant of hypotheses; more willing to think of truth seeking as a matter of "tacking" toward reality, or proceeding dialectically, as opposed to brick making and wall building. "But," he concludes, "despite these recent modifications, older usages remain powerful, and perhaps even dominant" (2).

17. Novick also likens objectivity to the Christian myth of the redemptive death of Christ and the Marxist myth of the emancipatory potential of the proletariat. In a footnote apologizing for his use of the neologisms "objectivism" and "objectivist," he observes that "it would be very difficult to write several hundred pages on the belief in the divinity of Christ, and on believers, without 'Christianity' and 'Christians' " (3n).

18. Novick closes the chapter with an interesting discussion of the rise during the 1970s of so-called public history, many of whose practitioners work not in universities, but for government agencies and private firms. In spite of dramatic differences, these practitioners often share with those of black history and women's history a suspicion of traditional universalistic values (510–21).

19. For a powerful reaffirmation of universalistic values and a painstaking demolition of arguments for routinely treating racial identity as a positive criterion of merit, see Randall L. Kennedy, "Racial Critiques of Legal Academia," *Harvard Law Review* 102 (1989): 1745–819. Kennedy is especially insightful about the dynamics of blame and guilt that often shape the interactions of black scholars and white scholars, and has very telling things to say about the long-term dangers those dynamics pose for the black community.

20. C. Vann Woodward, "The Siege," *New York Review of Books,* Sept. 25, 1986, 10.

21. Thomas L. Haskell and Sanford Levinson, "Academic Freedom and Expert Witnessing: Historians and the *Sears* Case," *Texas Law Review* 66 [special issue on academic freedom] (June 1988): 1629–59; Alice Kessler-Harris, "Academic Freedom and Expert Witnessing: A Response to Haskell and Levinson," ibid. 67 (1988): 429–40; Thomas L. Haskell and Sanford Levinson, "On Academic Freedom and Hypothetical Pools: A Reply to Kessler-Harris," ibid. 67 (June 1989): 1591–604.

22. The *sic* notations appear in his text. Judging from the terms Novick uses to describe the argumentative constraints that tripped up Kessler-Harris—an "impossible situation," a matter of "format," "the rules of the game," a "narrowly posed question"—he erroneously supposes that some arcane legal technicality limited her freedom of expression. On the contrary, these constraints stemmed directly from one of the law's most elemental safeguards: that defendants are innocent until proven culpable. The EEOC, as plaintiff, had the burden of showing not only that employer discrimination was one possible explanation for the different hiring rates of men and women (which no one doubted), but that it was a better explanation than that advanced by the defendant. Both the original judge and the appeals court decided in favor of Sears.

23. He leaves no doubt at all, if one disregards his passing suggestion, relegated to a footnote, that Kessler-Harris's criterion of causation was "exactly" that which the philosopher R. G. Collingwood expounded: the cause of an event is whatever factor we can "do something about" (506n). The suggestion oversimplifies Collingwood's point, which was already notoriously oversimple: see the criticisms of Collingwood in H. L. A. Hart and A. M. Honoré, *Causation in the Law* (London: Oxford University Press, 1959), 31–34. If this were the sole criterion of causal attribution, it would make no sense to

treat earthquakes, lightning, and floods as causes of anything; many agonizing moral questions would evaporate; and many of the law's complex rules of criminal and civil liability would become unintelligible.

24. Rosenberg quoted in Haskell and Levinson, "Academic Freedom and Expert Witnessing," 1653 (emphasis added).

25. Ibid., 1630–632, 1635–36.

26. "When committed scholars enter the legal arena, they uphold the highest academic standards when the circumstances allow; when circumstances don't, they fudge" (507).

27. Speaking of the conflicting pressures of feminism and scholarship in the Sears case, he says, "Of all the illusions in which we seek refuge, none is more pathetic than that which holds out the prospect of satisfactorily resolving irreconcilable claims" (510). But he does not tell us what he finds unsatisfactory about Rosenberg's resolution of those supposedly "irreconcilable" claims. Her choice was not whether to be a feminist or a scholar, but whether, as both a feminist and a scholar, to bow to the momentum of the movement, or to blow the whistle on an ill-conceived feminist project. The fact that her blowing of the whistle incurred the wrath of other movement members does not testify to the irreconcilability of scholarship and political commitment, but only to the tension between them and the need for courage.

28. For a claim that, instead of being read out of the profession, what leftist historians presently face is the responsibility of running it (now that demoralized liberals have unaccountably let control of it slip out of their own hands), see Jonathan M. Wiener, "Radical Historians and the Crisis in American History, 1959-1980," *Journal of American History* 76 (1989): 399–434.

29. For a sample of the conflict in literary circles, see Frederick Crews, "The Parting of the Twins," *New York Review of Books*, July 20, 1989, 39–44, and subsequent letters to the editor, ibid., Sept. 28, 1989, or any issue of the journal *Critical Inquiry*.

30. Denis Donoghue, "The Strange Case of Paul de Man," *New York Review of Books*, June 29, 1989, 37.

31. "I, too, aspire to see clearly, like a rifleman, with one eye shut; I, too, aspire to think without assent. This is the ultimate violence to which the modern intellectual is committed. Since things have become as they are, I, too, share the modern desire not to be deceived. . . . This is the unreligion of the age, and its master science. . . . The systematic hunting down of all settled convictions represents the anti-cultural predicate upon which the modern personality is being reorganized" (Rieff, *Triumph of the Therapeutic*, 13).

32. Sun Tzu, *The Art of War*, trans. and intro. by Samuel B. Griffith, foreword by B. H. Liddell Hart (New York: Oxford University Press, 1963), 96–97.

33. Jean-François Lyotard, *Peregrinations: Law, Form, Event* [The Wellek Library Lectures at the University of California, Irvine] (New York: Columbia University Press, 1988), 45–46.

34. Ibid., 46.

35. Ibid., 47–48, 51.

36. Donoghue, "The Strange Case of Paul de Man," 37. Is it wrong of me to expect an author's rhetoric about "theoretical" matters to have a bearing on his or her practice?

Stanley Fish would say it is. Fish (a Milton scholar who is no doubt conversant with the rhetorical strategies employed by Puritan divines to ward off the seemingly fatalistic implications of predestination) has repeatedly argued that theory neither has nor needs to have any consequences for everyday practice. For Fish the inconsequentiality of anti-foundationalist theory (the "truth" of which he does not doubt) is a corollary of the self's radical situatedness and its consequent inability to achieve detachment. His often repeated thesis is that "being situated not only means that one cannot achieve a distance on one's beliefs, but that one's beliefs do not relax their hold because one 'knows' that they are local and not universal. This in turn means that even someone . . . who is firmly convinced of the circumstantiality of his convictions will nevertheless experience those convictions as universally, not locally, true. It is therefore not surprising but inevitable that at the end of every argument, even of an argument that says there can be no end, the universalist perspective will reemerge as strongly as ever" (*Doing What Comes Naturally*, 467). There is an important kernel of truth in what Fish says, yet we are left wondering why, if antifoundationalism is without consequences, anyone finds it illuminating or worth arguing about. One also wonders if it is wise to engage in conversations with people who feel entitled, for all practical purposes, to regard their own beliefs as universally valid, while regarding everyone else's as unfounded and parochial. For parallel Puritan arguments, see Perry Miller's classic essay, "The Marrow of Puritan Divinity," in his *Errand into the Wilderness* (New York: Harper and Row, 1956), 48–98.

37. As John Dunn put it in a context that is similar, though not identical, "maps are maps, not regrettably ineffectual surrogates for physical environments" (*Political Obligation in Its Historical Context: Essays in Political Theory* [Cambridge: Cambridge University Press, 1980], 14).

CHAPTER 7   Justifying Academic Freedom in the
Era of Power/Knowledge

1. College attendance ratios appear in Fritz Machlup, *The Production and Distribution of Knowledge in the United States* (Princeton: Princeton University Press, 1962), 78. On the development of the modern American university, see Richard Hofstadter and Walter Metzger, *The Development of Academic Freedom in the United States* (New York: Columbia University Press, 1955); Laurence R. Veysey, *The Emergence of the American University* (Chicago: University of Chicago Press, 1965); Hugh Hawkins, *Pioneer: A History of the Johns Hopkins University, 1874–1889* (Ithaca: Cornell University Press, 1960); Thomas Bender, *Intellect and Public Life: Essays on the Social History of Academic Intellectuals in the United States* (Baltimore: Johns Hopkins University Press, 1993); Dorothy Ross, *Origins of American Social Science* (Cambridge: Cambridge University Press, 1991); Burton J. Bledstein, *The Culture of Professionalism: The Middle Class and the Development of Higher Education in America* (New York: Norton, 1976); and Thomas L. Haskell, *The Emergence of Professional Social Science: The American Social Science Association and the Nineteenth-Century Crisis of Authority* (Urbana: University of Illinois Press, 1977).

2. Lorraine Daston, "The Ideal and the Reality of the Republic of Letters in the Enlightenment," *Science in Context* 4 (Autumn 1991): 367–86.

3. The reforms of the nineteenth century were made possible by a long and rich tradition of academic freedom, carefully developed in the classic work by Hofstadter and Metzger, *Development of Academic Freedom.*

4. The term "community of the competent" is Francis E. Abbot's, who was a member of the Metaphysical Club, where Charles Peirce and William James worked out the basic ideas of pragmatism in the 1870s. Stow Persons, *Free Religion: An American Faith* (New Haven: Yale University Press, 1947), 31, 125–29; Philip P. Wiener, *Evolution and the Founders of Pragmatism* (New York: Harper and Row, 1965), 41–48.

5. Karl-Otto Apel, *Charles S. Peirce: From Pragmatism to Pragmaticism,* trans. J. M. Krois (Amherst: University of Massachusetts Press, 1981), xvi; and Apel, *Toward a Transformation of Philosophy,* trans. G. Adey and D. Frisby (London: Routledge and Kegan Paul, 1980).

6. An early pioneer was Friedrich August Wolf, founder of a famous seminar in classical studies at Halle in the 1780s, who borrowed the ideology of cultivation (*Bildung*) from Humboldt and used it, paradoxically, to elevate research above teaching so as to achieve a level of authority that pedagogy alone could not supply. See Anthony J. La Vopa, "Specialists Against Specialization: Hellenism as Professional Ideology in German Classical Studies," in *German Professions, 1800–1950,* ed. Geoffrey Cocks and Konrad H. Jarausch (New York: Oxford University Press, 1990), 27–45.

7. The inadequacies of the economic monopoly model are developed more fully in my "Professionalism *versus* Capitalism: R. H. Tawney, Emile Durkheim, and C. S. Peirce on the Disinterestedness of Professional Communities," in *The Authority of Experts: Studies in History and Theory,* ed. Thomas L. Haskell (Bloomington: Indiana University Press, 1984), 180–225 (included in this volume). On the "culture of critical discourse" fostered by these communities, see Alvin Gouldner, *The Future of the Intellectuals and the Rise of the New Class* (New York: Continuum, 1979).

8. Brennan quoted in William W. Van Alstyne, "Academic Freedom and the First Amendment in the Supreme Court of the United States: An Unhurried Historical Review," *Freedom and Tenure in the Academy: The Fiftieth Anniversary of the 1940 Statement of Principles,* William Van Alstyne, special editor, *Law and Contemporary Problems* 53 (Summer 1990): 114.

9. Michel Foucault, *Power/Knowledge: Selected Interviews and Other Writings 1972–77,* ed. Colin Gordon (New York: Pantheon, 1980). In *Discipline and Punish,* Foucault's formulation took this practical form: "Instead of treating the history of penal law and the history of the human sciences as two separate series [that merely have effects on one another, my aim is to] see whether there is some common matrix or . . . single process of 'epistemological-juridical' formation; in short, [to] make the technology of power the very principle both of the humanization of the penal system and of the knowledge of man" (Foucault, *Discipline and Punish: The Birth of the Prison,* trans. Alan Sheridan [New York: Pantheon, 1977], 23). The problem is that in making the "technology of power" the "*very principle*" of humanitarian reform and knowledge of man, one reduces knowledge and justice to power. Or, to take him at his word, Foucault does not *reduce* one to the other, but argues for their simultaneous production in a "single process," which blurs the opposition between them just as surely as reduction would. Blurring that opposition means obscuring the difference between education and indoctrination, scholarship and propaganda, history and fiction, right and might, consent

and coercion, and so on, tending to make these and other classic oppositions, as I put it above, "two sides of a single coin."

10. Committed Foucauldians will remind us that distinguishing between power and disinterested knowledge can itself be construed as an exercise in power. Indeed it can. Once one accepts the proposition that power is the only game in town, power relations can and will be teased out of anything at all. The same could be said for sex, religion, or any number of other grand obsessions. Any master key, once subscribed to, will seem to open all locks. The dangers of reducing everything to power relations are twofold. First, making power the master category obscures a vital distinction between force and persuasion that is constitutive for liberal politics. Second, unlike sex, religion, and other interpretive obsessions, the presumption that power is the master motive is a classic example of the self-fulfilling prophecy. He who insists upon construing dancing as sex by other means is merely a bore; but he who construes scholarship as politics by other means provokes in others the very motives he imputes to them, no matter how unjust the original imputation.

11. Mary O. Furner, *Advocacy and Objectivity: A Crisis in the Professionalization of American Social Science, 1865–1905* (Lexington: University Press of Kentucky, 1975), 234.

12. Ibid., 235.

13. Ibid., 235–36.

14. James C. Mohr, "Academic Turmoil and Public Opinion: The Ross Case at Stanford," *Pacific Historical Review* 39 (Feb. 1970): 39–61; Furner, *Advocacy and Objectivity*, 238.

15. Ross quoted in Furner, *Advocacy and Objectivity*, 238.

16. Ibid., 239–41.

17. Ibid., 245; Hofstadter and Metzger, *Development of Academic Freedom*, 442–43.

18. Furner, *Advocacy and Objectivity*, 246, 251, 252–53.

19. Small quoted in Hofstadter and Metzger, *Development of Academic Freedom*, 443.

20. Holmes quoted in Van Alstyne, "Academic Freedom and the First Amendment," 98, 84. Even today, of course, the legal protections of the First Amendment extend only to public institutions, but I assume that that has been far enough to decisively influence the culture of the private sphere as well.

21. The kinship of professors and professionals was especially close in the case of the social science disciplines, which received unprecedented prominence in the modern American university and provided the most frequent setting for academic-freedom controversies. The pioneering members of the American Social Science Association, which began meeting in 1865 and spawned the AHA in 1884 and the AEA in 1885, were forward-looking professionals who considered the social sciences to be elaborations of a professional division of labor that extended far beyond the university and defined the wisdom and knowledge necessary for exercising leadership in a merit-based liberal democracy. See Haskell, *Emergence of Professional Social Science*, 100–110. Stephen Bann brings out the intimate dependence of the historians' mode of discourse on that deployed by physicians, lawyers, and ministers. See Bann, "History and Her Siblings: Law, Medicine and Theology," in his *The Inventions of History: Essays on the Representation of the Past* (Manchester: Manchester University Press, 1990), 12–32.

22. These words appear in the three-page brochure sent out by the "committee on

organization" in November 1914, announcing the founding session to be held in January. The passage continues: "The general purposes of such an Association would be to facilitate a more effective cooperation among the members of the profession in the discharge of their special responsibilities as custodians of the interests of higher education and research in America; to promote a more general and methodical discussion of problems related to education in higher institutions of learning; to create means for the authoritative expression of the public opinion of college and university teachers; and to maintain and advance the standards and ideals of the profession." AAUP Archives, Washington, D.C., file marked "A. O. Lovejoy 1914," also published in *Bulletin of the AAUP* 2 (Mar. 1916): 11–13.

23. I follow the lead of Walter Metzger in stressing the tension between two definitions of academic freedom, the "professional" and the "constitutional" (the latter deriving from the First Amendment); see Metzger, "Profession and Constitution: Two Definitions of Academic Freedom in America," *Texas Law Review* 66 (June 1988): 1265–322. For a somewhat divergent view, see David M. Rabban, "A Functional Analysis of 'Individual' and 'Institutional' Academic Freedom under the First Amendment," in *Freedom and Tenure in the Academy,* ed. Van Alstyne, 227–301.

24. On this point, the charter document of the AAUP, the 1915 Report on Academic Freedom and Tenure, is explicit: "It is, in short, not the absolute freedom of utterance of the individual scholar, but the absolute freedom of thought, of inquiry, of discussion and of teaching, of the academic profession, that is asserted by this declaration of principles." AAUP, "General Report of the Committee on Academic Freedom and Academic Tenure (1915)," included as Appendix A of *Freedom and Tenure in the Academy,* ed. Van Alstyne, 404–5. Subsequent page references are cited parenthetically in the text.

25. This and the next paragraph borrow from my introduction to *The Authority of Experts,* x–xi.

26. H. Stuart Hughes, *Consciousness and Society: The Reorientation of European Social Thought, 1890–1930* (New York: Knopf, 1958), chap. 2; James T. Kloppenberg, *Uncertain Victory: Social Democracy and Progressivism in European and American Thought, 1870–1920* (New York: Oxford University Press, 1986).

27. The 1915 report also presented "practical proposals" calling for faculty representation on committees considering reappointment; judicial hearings and formulation of explicit grounds in cases of dismissal; and permanent tenure for all positions above the grade of instructor after ten (not seven) years of service. The practical nuts and bolts underpinning academic freedom were further developed in a second landmark AAUP document, which continues to enjoy something approaching constitutional status today, the 1940 Statement of Principles on Academic Freedom and Tenure. By that date, although as many as half of all colleges and universities may have still been appointing faculty on an annual basis, hiring practices had become sufficiently uniform at the leading institutions that the AAUP made a bid to install tenure as the keystone of academic freedom. It called for permanent tenure for all academics after a probationary period normally not exceeding seven years, and allowed for termination only at retirement, upon demonstration of adequate cause, or because of extraordinary financial exigencies. The 1940 statement, which of course does not have the force of law, was a compromise jointly written by teachers in the AAUP and administrators in the American Association of Colleges. The premier association of administrators, the

American Association of Universities, has never endorsed the 1940 principles, although its member institutions probably uphold them at least as scrupulously as other schools. See Walter P. Metzger, "The 1940 Statement of Principles on Academic Freedom and Tenure," in *Freedom and Tenure in the Academy*, ed. Van Alstyne, 1–77.

28. Habermas, *Legitimation Crisis* (Boston: Beacon Press, 1975), 107–8.

29. For a fuller discussion of the two Peirces and the theme of professionalization, see my *Emergence of Professional Social Science*, and "Professionalism *versus* Capitalism," 208 (included in this volume). On Peirce's influence at Harvard, see Bruce Kuklick, *The Rise of American Philosophy: Cambridge, Massachusetts, 1860–1930* (New Haven: Yale University Press, 1977).

30. Kuhn, *The Structure of Scientific Revolutions*, 2d ed. (Chicago: University of Chicago Press, 1970); Rorty, *Philosophy and the Mirror of Nature* (Princeton: Princeton University Press, 1979); Fish, *Is There a Text in This Class? The Authority of Interpretive Communities* (Cambridge, Mass.: Harvard University Press, 1980), and "Anti-Professionalism," in Fish, *Doing What Comes Naturally: Change, Rhetoric, and the Practice of Theory in Literary and Legal Studies* (Durham, N.C.: Duke University Press, 1989), chap. 11.

31. Stephen Toulmin never mentions Peirce, but presents an account of knowledge that is comparably community oriented, in *Human Understanding: The Collective Use and Evolution of Concepts* (Princeton: Princeton University Press, 1972). An explosion of interest in Peirce is under way today; among many recent publications, most relevant is C. J. Misak, *Truth and the End of Inquiry* (Oxford: Oxford University Press, 1991).

32. Charles Sanders Peirce, *Collected Papers*, ed. Charles Hartshorne and Paul Weiss (Cambridge, Mass.: Harvard University Press, 1931–60), V-317 (reference is to volume and paragraph; subsequent citations are in parentheses in the text). This and the next two paragraphs are drawn (more or less verbatim) from my essay "Professionalism versus Capitalism," chap. 4 of this volume.

33. Smith, "Community and Reality," in *Perspectives on Peirce*, ed. Richard J. Bernstein (New Haven: Yale University Press, 1965), 118.

34. Kuhn, *Structure of Scientific Revolutions*, 205–6, 170–72.

35. For Kuhn's ambivalence, see ibid., 121, 126, 170–73. Rorty, *Philosophy and the Mirror of Nature*, 10; Richard Rorty, *Consequences of Pragmatism: Essays, 1972–1980* (Minneapolis: University of Minnesota Press, 1982), xiv, 96–98. In an unpublished 1984 paper titled "Rhetoric and Liberation," Kuhn, commenting on a paper by Rorty titled "Solidarity or Objectivity?," expressed his dissent from Rorty's sweeping rejection of objectivity and warm embrace of solidarity as an adequate standard of correct belief. Kuhn warned of a "profound misconception of the human condition, a misconception here manifest in an insufficient respect for the intrinsic authority of language. . . . I said I would speak as Cassandra, and I have been doing so. What I fear are attempts to separate language or discourse from the real and to do so in the name of freedom." Rorty's paper was published in *Post-Analytic Philosophy*, ed. John Rajchman and Cornel West (New York: Columbia University Press, 1985), 3–19.

36. Rorty, *Consequences of Pragmatism*, 169–70. On the issue of edification versus verification, see Lovejoy, "On Some Conditions of Progress in Philosophical Inquiry," *Philosophical Review* 26 (Mar. 1917): 131–38; and Daniel J. Wilson, *Arthur O. Lovejoy and the Quest for Intelligibility* (Chapel Hill: University of North Carolina Press, 1980), 92.

37. Lovejoy, "On Some Conditions of Progress," 130, 159–60.

38. Ibid., 160.

39. Lovejoy, *The Thirteen Pragmatisms and Other Essays* (Baltimore: Johns Hopkins University Press, 1963), 79–112.

40. Lovejoy, "On Some Conditions of Progress," 131.

41. Ibid., 150, 133, 132, 151–52.

42. Stefan Collini, ed., *Interpretation and Overinterpretation: Umberto Eco with Richard Rorty, Jonathan Culler, Christine Brooke-Rose* (Cambridge: Cambridge University Press, 1992), 12, 19.

43. Clifford Geertz, *The Interpretation of Cultures: Selected Essays* (New York: Basic Books, 1973), 29.

44. See, for examples, Richard J. Bernstein, *Beyond Objectivism and Relativism: Science, Hermeneutics, and Praxis* (Philadelphia: University of Pennsylvania Press, 1983), 36, 69, 71; Hilary Putnam, *Realism with a Human Face,* ed. James Conant (Cambridge, Mass.: Harvard University Press, 1990), 21–22; and Jürgen Habermas, *Postmetaphysical Thinking: Philosophical Essays,* trans. William Mark Hehengarten (Cambridge, Mass.: MIT Press, 1992), chap. 5, "Peirce and Communication."

45. Rorty, *Consequences of Pragmatism,* 160, 173. The order of the quoted passages has been altered. See other comments about Peirce, ibid., 160–61, xlv.

46. The passage is worth quoting at greater length. Notice that neither literally nor in spirit did Dewey put the word "truth" in quotation marks. Rorty's proto-Nietzschean Dewey is not easily detected in passages such as this. "It is clear that . . . any attack, or even any restriction, upon academic freedom is directed against the university itself. To investigate truth; critically to verify fact; to reach conclusions by means of the best methods at command, untrammeled by external fear or favor, to communicate this truth to the student; to interpret to him its bearing on the questions he will have to face in life—this is precisely the aim and object of the university. To aim a blow at any one of these operations is to deal a vital wound to the university itself. The university function is the truth function. At one time it may be more concerned with the tradition or transmission of truth, and at another time with its discovery. . . . The one thing that is inherent and essential is the idea of truth" (Dewey, "Academic Freedom," *Educational Review* 23 [1902]: 3; reprinted in *The American Concept of Academic Freedom in Formation: A Collection of Essays and Reports,* ed. Walter P. Metzger [New York: Arno Press, 1977]).

47. Dewey's speech appears in *Science,* n.s., 41 (Jan. 29, 1915): 150.

48. This famous line of Peirce's is given a place of honor in a recent ringing defense of free speech. See Jonathan Rauch, *Kindly Inquisitors: The New Attacks on Free Thought* (Chicago: University of Chicago Press, 1993), vii.

49. Rorty sometimes uses the term "community of inquiry" as a near synonym for culture or society: "We can always enlarge the scope of 'us' by regarding other people, or cultures, as members of the same community of inquiry as ourselves—by treating them as part of the group among whom unforced agreement is to be sought" (Rorty, *Objectivity, Relativism, and Truth: Philosophical Papers* [Cambridge: Cambridge University Press, 1991], 1: 38).

50. Ibid., 38, 41, 88.

51. Rorty, *Contingency, Irony, and Solidarity* (Cambridge: Cambridge University Press, 1989), 51–52.

52. Rorty is not the first to see in the values of the academic community a way of life suitable for the larger society. For similar gestures at the turn of the century by R. H. Tawney and Emile Durkheim, see my essay "Professionalism versus Capitalism," in this volume.

53. What I have in mind is something corresponding roughly to the "moderate realism" Mary B. Hesse proposes for science, which steers a middle course between instrumentalism and the "strong realism" of, say, Plato. "Such a moderate realism of scientific knowledge turns out to be particular rather than general, local rather than universal, approximate rather than exact, immediately describable and verifiable rather than theoretically deep and reductive. It is not the theoretical frameworks as such that validate the claim of science to be a distinctive and reliable body of knowledge, but rather the way they are used to further the feedback method of successful prediction and control" ("Models, Metaphors and Truth," in *Knowledge and Language,* vol. 3, *Metaphor and Knowledge,* ed. F. R. Ankersmit and J. J. A. Mooij [Dordrecht: Kluwer, 1993], 49–66). Along similar lines, one thinks of Stephen Toulmin's comment that "questions of 'rationality' are concerned, precisely, not with the particular intellectual doctrines that a man—or a professional group—adopts at any given time, but rather with the conditions on which, and the manner in which, he is prepared to criticize and change those doctrines as time goes on" (*Human Understanding,* 84).

54. For an amusing and trenchant response to this imperial prospect, see David A. Hollinger, "Giving at the Office in the Age of Power/Knowledge," *Michigan Quarterly Review* 29 (Winter 1990): 123–32.

55. I am obliged to David Rabban for this succinct formulation of the problem.

56. Fish, *Is There a Text in This Class?.*

57. Fish, *Doing What Comes Naturally,* 207, 201. Subsequent page references are cited parenthetically in the text.

58. Fish quotes Magali Sarfatti Larson, *The Rise of Professionalism: A Sociological Analysis* (Berkeley: University of California Press, 1977), 221–22.

59. These three quotations, all concerned with the Critical Legal Studies movement, come from three different articles. The immediate context of the first is a discussion of the work of Mark Kelman; of the last two a discussion of the work of Roberto Unger. Since Kelman and Unger are members of the same movement, bringing the passages together does not, I think, deprive them of an appropriate context.

60. Fish, "There's No Such Thing as Free Speech and It's a Good Thing, Too," *Boston Review* 17 (Feb. 1992): 3, also published in *Debating PC: The Controversy over Political Correctness on College Campuses,* ed. Paul Berman (New York: Dell, 1992), and Stanley Fish, *There's No Such Thing as Free Speech and It's a Good Thing, Too* (New York: Oxford University Press, 1994). Subsequent page references are cited parenthetically in the text.

61. Fish presents his own position as an alternative to "First Amendment absolutism," but his dismissive attitude toward the "fighting words" test puts him in opposition to many non-absolutists, such as myself, who are worried about the growing censoriousness of the academic left, but who also believe that the most abusive and persistent hate speech should be punished.

62. Philip Rieff, *The Triumph of the Therapeutic: Uses of Faith after Freud* (Chicago: University of Chicago Press, 1987), 61.

63. This is not the place to spell out the way these assumptions operate in the work

of Foucault and other recent writers, but many readers will recognize them as the foundational assumptions, as it were, of anti-foundationalism. Even so sympathetic a reader as Charles Taylor rejects what he calls Foucault's "case for the invasion of everyday understanding by relations of power," formidable though he admits it is. "Only if we could show that relations of domination, and the strategies which create and sustain them, have totally invaded the world of everyday self-understanding could we adopt the narrow, neo-Clausewitzian interpretation [according to which intellectual debate is war by other means] and make all dominant ideas the outcome of conflicts which centre on war and the struggle for power" ("The Hermeneutics of Conflict," in *Meaning and Context: Quentin Skinner and His Critics*, ed. James Tully [Princeton: Princeton University Press, 1988], 226). For telling second thoughts about the supposed boundlessness of interpretation (by an influential early advocate of the reader's power to "produce" the meaning of a text), see Umberto Eco's contribution to Stefan Collini, ed., *Interpretation and Overinterpretation*.

64. Fish, "There's No Such Thing," 26.

65. Louis Menand, "The Future of Academic Freedom," *Academe* 79 (May–June 1993): 13.

66. Bender, *Intellect and Public Life*, 142–43.

67. Rorty, *Objectivity, Relativism, and Truth*, 2. For a brilliant commentary on Rorty's use of the concept of "ethnocentrism" and related issues, see David Hollinger, "How Wide the Circle of the 'We'? American Intellectuals and the Problem of the Ethnos Since World War II," *American Historical Review* 98 (Apr. 1993): 317–37.

68. Alexis de Tocqueville, *Democracy in America*, trans. H. Reeve (New York: Schocken Books, 1961), 1: 309–12. Some of the language of this paragraph is drawn from my *Emergence of Professional Social Science*, 75.

69. A case in point is the conduct of feminist historians, outraged that one of their number had chosen to testify as an expert witness for Sears and against the EEOC in a case involving charges of sexual discrimination. For an account of the case and citations to the substantial literature it spawned, see Thomas L. Haskell and Sanford Levinson, "Academic Freedom and Expert Witnessing: Historians and the *Sears* Case," *Texas Law Review* 66 [special issue on academic freedom] (June 1988): 1629–59; Alice Kessler-Harris, "Academic Freedom and Expert Witnessing: A Response to Haskell and Levinson," *Texas Law Review* 67 (1988): 429–40; Haskell and Levinson, "On Academic Freedom and Hypothetical Pools: A Reply to Alice Kessler-Harris," *Texas Law Review* 67 (June 1989): 1591–604. For more on internally originated pressure for orthodoxy, see David M. Rabban, "Does Academic Freedom Limit Faculty Autonomy?" *Texas Law Review* 66 (June 1988): 1405–430.

70. Brewster, "On Tenure," *AAUP Bulletin* 58 (1972): 381, 382. See also Fritz Machlup, "On Some Misconceptions Concerning Academic Freedom," in *Academic Freedom and Tenure*, ed. L. Joughin (Madison: University of Wisconsin Press, 1967). Both are cited in Rabban, "Does Academic Freedom Limit Faculty Autonomy?"

71. Hayden White, "The Politics of Historical Interpretation: Discipline and De-Sublimation," in his *The Content of the Form: Narrative Discourse and Historical Representation* (Baltimore: Johns Hopkins University Press, 1987), 58–82. Subsequent page references are cited parenthetically in the text.

72. It is easy to underestimate White's radicalism here. His doubts are not confined

to overconfident varieties of historiography that claim to settle "scientifically" matters generally recognized as debatable. His doubts extend to any account cast in narrative form that claims to represent the real. Narrative form, on his view, distorts the mere meaningless sequence of reality, imparting to it the "odor of the ideal." It does so, moreover, in the service of a "moralizing impulse" that inevitably seeks to authorize a particular social order. See "The Value of Narrativity in the Representation of Reality," in *The Content of the Form*, 21, 24, 13. White quotes Roland Barthes's unequivocal claim that "historical discourse is in its essence a form of ideological elaboration," without either embracing or rejecting it ("The Question of Narrative in Contemporary Historical Theory," in ibid., 36).

73. Hayden White, *Metahistory: The Historical Imagination in Nineteenth-Century Europe* (Baltimore: Johns Hopkins University Press, 1973), xii. For a powerful reconsideration by a scholar who has long admired White and still credits him with setting the terms of debate, see Lionel Gossman, "Towards a Rational Historiography," *Transactions of the American Philosophical Society* 79, pt. 3 (1989).

74. This is not an insignificant concession, for if we can know that some interpretations are completely beyond the pale, that would imply the existence of a nonrelative standard enabling us to assess degrees of plausibility rationally. White does not pause to consider this line of thought.

75. Carlo Ginzburg, "Just One Witness," in *Probing the Limits of Representation: Nazism and the "Final Solution,"* ed. Saul Friedlander (Cambridge, Mass.: Harvard University Press, 1992), 93.

76. This appears also to be the judgment of Martin Jay, who, in the concluding section of his own very sympathetic commentary on White's paper, acknowledges that the entire *raison d'être* of scholarly discourse is placed in jeopardy by White's analysis: "Although it would be foolish to assume that the uncoerced consensus of opinion, which is the *telos* of the discursive process, can be more than a regulative ideal never to be fully realized, it is still the case that scholars striving to convince each other live by it. However complicated the process may be made by the interference of nondiscursive elements, however inconclusive the outcome always is, the professional institutionalization of communicative rationality means that 'effectiveness' [an allusion both to White's essay and to Ginzburg's criticism of it] can be more than merely a neutral description of what the majority believes is true or right. It may, to be sure, sometimes be little more than that, but there is no reason to despair of a more compelling alternative. Indeed, otherwise the entire raison d'être of scholarly discourse is undone" ("Of Plots, Witnesses, and Judgments," in *Probing the Limits of Representation*, 106).

77. Ash quoted in Lionel Gossman, "Towards a Rational Historiography," 68.

CHAPTER 8 Capitalism and the Origins of the
Humanitarian Sensibility, Part 1

1. David Brion Davis, *The Problem of Slavery in Western Culture* (Ithaca: Cornell University Press, 1966).

2. For the touchstone of what has become a large body of literature, see Eric Williams, *Capitalism and Slavery* (Chapel Hill: University of North Carolina Press, 1944). Also see C. L. R. James, *The Black Jacobins: Toussaint L'Ouverture and the San Domingo*

Revolution (New York: Vintage, 1963); Roger Anstey, "Capitalism and Slavery: A Critique," *Economic History Review,* 2d ser., 21 (1968): 307–20; Eugene Genovese, "Materialism and Idealism in the History of Negro Slavery in the Americas," in Laura Foner and Eugene Genovese, eds., *Slavery in the New World: A Reader in Comparative History* (Englewood Cliffs, N.J.: Prentice-Hall, 1969), 238–55; Christine Bolt and Seymour Drescher, eds., *Anti-Slavery, Religion, and Reform: Essays in Memory of Roger Anstey* (Hamden, Conn.: Archon, 1980); and James Walvin, ed., *Slavery and British Society, 1776–1846* (Baton Rouge: Louisiana State University Press, 1982). Additional major contributions to the controversy by Anstey, Davis, Drescher, and Temperley are cited below.

3. Lecky quoted in David Brion Davis, *The Problem of Slavery in the Age of Revolution, 1770–1823* (Ithaca: Cornell University Press, 1975), 353.

4. Foucault, *Discipline and Punish: The Birth of the Prison,* trans. Alan Sheridan (New York: Pantheon, 1977), 82.

5. Anstey, *The Atlantic Slave Trade and British Abolition, 1760–1810* (Atlantic Highlands, N.J.: Humanities Press, 1975); and Drescher, *Econocide: British Slavery in the Era of Abolition* (Pittsburgh: University of Pittsburgh Press, 1977).

6. Temperley, "Capitalism, Slavery, and Ideology," *Past and Present* 75 (1977): 105. I wrote the first draft of this essay before reading Temperley's article, but his aim in many ways parallels my own. And I certainly share Temperley's view that the question to answer is "how could a philosophy which extolled the pursuit of individual self-interest have contributed, in the absence of any expectation of economic gain, to the achievement of so praiseworthy an object as the abolition of slavery" (117). I am not convinced, however, that a full answer to this question can be gotten by examining capitalism as an ideology. Also see Temperley, "Anti-Slavery as a Form of Cultural Imperialism," in Bolt and Drescher, *Anti-Slavery, Religion, and Reform,* 335–50. In his later article, Temperley stressed the convergence of nationalism, an accelerating pace of economic growth, and notions of naturally or divinely ordained progress, factors that mesh closely with the somewhat more abstract argument I present here.

7. Although Weber's treatment of the relationship between ideas and interest in *The Protestant Ethic and the Spirit of Capitalism* seems to me the best model we have, I have not tried to conform to it here. Weber used the concept of elective affinities in very diverse ways. See Weber, *The Protestant Ethic and the Spirit of Capitalism,* trans. Talcott Parsons (New York: Scribners, 1958, 1976); and Richard Herbert Howe, "Max Weber's Elective Affinities: Sociology within the Bounds of Pure Reason," *American Journal of Sociology* 84 (1978): 366–85. Also see Weber, "Religious Ethics and the World," in Guenther Roth and Claus Wittich, eds., *Economy and Society: An Outline of Interpretive Sociology,* trans. Ephraim Fischoff et al. (New York: Bedminster Press, 1968), 2: 577.

8. Davis, *Slavery in the Age of Revolution,* 379. Subsequent page references are cited parenthetically in the text.

9. As Davis said: "The antislavery movement, like [Adam] Smith's political economy, reflected the needs and values of the emerging capitalist order. Smith provided theoretical justification for the belief that all classes and segments of society share a natural identity of interest. The antislavery movement, while absorbing the ambivalent emotions of the age, was essentially dedicated to a practical demonstration of the same reassuring message" (350).

10. Although in my opinion he finally skirted its inescapably reductive implications, Raymond Williams fully concurred that the social control explanation cannot do without intention; Williams, "Base and Superstructure in Marxist Cultural Theory," *New Left Review* 82 (1973): 3–16. Speaking of formulations like Georg Lukacs's that stress the "totality" of social practices rather than a layered image of base and superstructure, Williams said, "It is very easy for the notion of totality to empty of its essential content the original Marxist proposition." The danger, wrote Williams, is that of "withdrawing from the claim that there is any process of determination. And this I, for one, would be very unwilling to do. Indeed, the key question to ask about any notion of totality in cultural theory is this: whether the notion of totality includes the notion of intention. . . . Intention, the notion of intention, restores the key question, or rather the key emphasis." In order for an interpretation to be called "Marxist," Williams believed it should at least depict the "organization and structure [of society] . . . as directly related to certain social intentions, intentions by which we define the society, intentions which in all our experience have been the rule of a particular class" (7). My complaint, of course, is not that Davis, by relying on a soft form of intention, has veered too far from any "original proposition" but that he has clung to a greater degree of intention than he seems comfortable with, and a greater degree than the evidence can substantiate. The rival scheme of explanation I advocate retains the claim that there is a "process of determination" but deliberately abandons the claim of intentionality.

11. On the two traditions in Marxist historiography, see Richard Johnson, "Edward Thompson, Eugene Genovese, and Socialist-Humanist History," *History Workshop* 6 (1978): 79–100. On Gramsci, see Walter L. Adamson, *Hegemony and Revolution: A Study of Antonio Gramsci's Political and Cultural Theory* (Berkeley: University of California Press, 1980), chap. 6; James Joll, *Antonio Gramsci* (New York: Viking, 1977), chap. 9; Thomas R. Bates, "Gramsci and the Theory of Hegemony," *Journal of the History of Ideas* 36 (1975): 351–66; and Antonio Gramsci, *Selections from the Prison Notebooks of Antonio Gramsci,* ed. Quintin Hoare and Geoffrey Nowell Smith (New York: International Publishers, 1972).

12. Davis, *Slavery in the Age of Revolution,* 349; Hauser quoted in William A. Muraskin, "The Social Control Theory in American History: A Critique," *Journal of Social History* 9 (1976): 566.

13. "For I can assure you that it is quite possible, and highly probable indeed, that the dreamer does know what his dream means: *only he does not know that he knows it and for that reason thinks he does not know it*" (Freud, *Introductory Lectures on Psychoanalysis,* trans. James Strachey [New York: Norton, 1977], 101). Freud likened the hidden knowledge to a person's name that we know but cannot recall. His proof of the existence of such knowledge was, of course, hypnosis, and free association was the means of bringing it to light. Also see ibid., 103, 110, 113.

14. Ibid., 106, 273–85.

15. Davis's claim that abolitionism was a "selective response to labor exploitation" is an echo of the criticism that radical labor leaders, such as William Cobbett, Richard Oastler, and Bronterre O'Brien, leveled against the abolitionists in their own time. What remains unclear, in spite of much recent discussion of the relation between abolitionism and the labor movement, is the exact basis of the labor critique. Did labor leaders have a more advanced humanitarian perspective that really assigned equal importance

to all varieties of exploitation, whether of slave or free labor (as Davis himself did)? Or did they simply assign a higher priority to the problems of wage laborers (nearby and racially similar) than to those of enslaved laborers (far away and racially different)? To what extent was the workingman's criticism of abolitionism a pragmatic tactic for drawing attention to his own cause rather than a considered judgment of the equivalence of exploitation in the two cases? These are not easy questions to answer for the period before the 1840s, and they become easy then only in the case of a few extreme figures, like Marx and Engels, whose perspective clearly embraced (albeit abstractly) a wider world of suffering than did that of the abolitionists. Moreover, as we shall see in the first of two hypothetical exercises, even if we conclude that labor spokesmen really did "transcend" the limiting conventions of the day, this would not justify us in thinking that it would have been easy for their contemporaries to follow suit, or that their contemporaries would have done so but for self-deception. On labor and abolition, see Patricia Hollis, "Anti-Slavery and British Working-Class Radicalism in the Years of Reform," in Bolt and Drescher, *Anti-Slavery, Religion, and Reform,* 295–315; Eric Foner, "Abolitionism and the Labor Movement in Ante-bellum America," in ibid., 254–71; Jonathan A. Glickstein, " 'Poverty is not Slavery': American Abolitionists and the Competitive Labor Market," in Lewis Perry and Michael Fellman, eds., *Antislavery Reconsidered: New Perspectives on the Abolitionists* (Baton Rouge: Louisiana State University Press, 1979), 195–218; Marcus Cunliffe, *Chattel Slavery and Wage Slavery: The Anglo-American Context, 1830–1860* (Athens: University of Georgia Press, 1979); and Betty Fladeland, " 'Our Cause Being One and the Same': Abolitionists and Chartism," in Walvin, *Slavery and British Society.* In *Slavery and British Society,* see the essays by Drescher and Walvin that stress the great popularity of the abolitionist cause in England, even outside middle-class ranks.

16. Raymond Williams's comments on intentionality, quoted in note 10 (above), are pertinent here as well.

17. Freud, *Introductory Lectures on Psychoanalysis,* 40–41, 61.

18. I pass hastily over a deep abyss — the glib assumption so characteristic of modern scholarship that a person's "interests" are readily identifiable and constitute a complete explanation of his conduct. In fact, the term is utterly elastic. There is no human choice that cannot be construed as self-interested. As a limiting case, consider a situation in which persons A and B happen on a burning house; person A dives into the flames to save the screaming occupants while B refuses to endanger himself. B's selfishness is plain to see, but A's conduct can also be understood to reflect "enlightened" self-interest. The difference, one can argue, is simply that in A's subjective scheme of valuation, physical safety counts for less than social approbation. So he, like B, pursues what interests him most. (There is even a perspective from which one might prefer B's plainly selfish act to A's, on the grounds that B at least did not strive for the potentially "hegemonic" pleasure of achieving moral supremacy over another.) Needless to add, I am deeply troubled by any perspective on human affairs that obscures the radical moral superiority of A's choice over B's. The breathtaking scope of the metatheoretical issues at stake here is evident in the pivotal role that debates over the very possibility of altruistic action in a Darwinian universe have had in recent discussions of evolutionary theory and sociobiology. See Arthur L. Caplan, ed., *The Sociobiology Debate: Readings on Ethical and Scientific Issues* (New York: Harper and Row, 1978), 213–26, 254, 308.

19. A defender of the self-deception argument might ask how I can claim to know whether I am deceiving myself or not, to which the appropriate reply is that, in the absence of any possibility of empirical demonstration, my claim, based on introspection, has at least as much merit as any opposing claim.

20. Mill, as quoted in H. L. A. Hart and A. M. Honoré, *Causation in the Law* (London: Oxford University Press, 1959), 16. Hart's analysis is the foundation of much of what I say here, though I am strongly attracted to Joel Feinberg's amendments to Hart's excessively voluntarist perspective. See Feinberg, "Causing Voluntary Actions," in his *Doing and Deserving: Essays in the Theory of Responsibility* (Princeton: Princeton University Press, 1970), 152–86. It is noteworthy that much of Hart's magisterial volume is an inquiry into "the principles governing the selection we apparently make of one of a complex set of conditions as the cause" and that when he inaugurated that inquiry it was "a problem scarcely mentioned before in the history of philosophy" (Hart and Honoré, *Causation in the Law,* 16).

21. Among these sheltering conventions are those that permit us to feel that we have done our part by making donations to charitable organizations, or by committing ourselves to a political movement that, if it should triumph, would, we trust, alleviate the suffering in question. The latter route to a good conscience is especially vulnerable to the charge of self-delusion, and neither of these routes can seem anything but arbitrary and "selective" from the standpoint of the stranger who starves next week. Yet these are the best choices available to us. Surely it is better to send an annual check to CARE, or even merely to adopt a political rhetoric that condemns maldistribution of wealth, than to do nothing at all. How much better remains far more open to question than any of us like to think.

22. Gasking, "Causation and Recipes," *Mind* 64 (1955): 483. Also see Hart and Honoré, *Causation in the Law,* 26, 29, 69.

23. Gasking, "Causation and Recipes," 486, 482.

24. The fourth precondition is not that we must have an ordinary, familiar, and certain recipe specifically tailored to the specific task at hand but that our ordinary, familiar, and certain recipes must be sufficiently like what is needed to inspire confidence that the task can be accomplished with only moderate adjustments of the available and proven means.

25. "The notion, that a cause is essentially something which interferes with or intervenes in the course of events which would ordinarily take place, is central to the common-sense concept of cause, and at least as essential as the notions of invariable or constant sequence so much stressed by Mill and Hume" (Hart and Honoré, *Causation in the Law,* 27). Hart also assigned a special place to voluntary acts, but Feinberg argued that these are so often perceived as causal only because of their "abnormality": "*The more expectable human behavior is, whether voluntary or not, the less likely it is to 'negative causal connection'* [that is, to be seen as a cause rather than as the effect of some more remote cause]" ("Causing Voluntary Actions," 165). Also see N. R. Hanson, "Causal Chains," *Mind* 64 (1955): 309: "We tend to be very selective about the sorts of things of which we ask, 'What is its cause?' This question is usually asked only when we are confronted with a breach of routine."

26. Recipe knowledge stems from many sources. Because my aim in this essay is to link humanitarianism to the market, the recipe knowledge of immediate interest is that

which originated in market transactions. But no recipe knowledge was more critical for the development of humanitarianism and antislavery than that which originated in the special religious and political experience of the Quakers. Howard Temperley noted that, in the course of their struggles against tithe bills and other injurious legislation, Quakers by the 1730s had already mobilized quarterly, monthly, and local meetings into "a political machine of remarkable strength and sophistication . . . [combining] central direction with constituency action. Long before anyone else, Quakers had become adept at using a broad range of techniques designed to exert extraparliamentary pressure, including mass petitioning, lobbying, drawing up voting lists, and obtaining pledges" (Temperley, "Anti-Slavery," in Patricia Hollis, ed., *Pressure from Without: In Early Victorian England* [London: Edward Arnold, 1974], 31). Quakers were not only adept at manipulating public opinion and Parliament but also knew more than anyone else about shaping the traits of individual character, a kind of recipe knowledge that was presupposed by the penitentiary and the "moral treatment" of the insane. See Richard T. Vann, *The Social Development of English Quakerism, 1655–1755* (Cambridge, Mass.: Harvard University Press, 1969), chap. 1, and pp. 167–79, 204–8.

27. A section of *Las Siete Partidas,* thirteenth-century legal guidelines that influenced later legislation in Spain and Spanish America (both of which accepted the institution of slavery), declared that "slavery is the most evil and the most despicable thing which can be found among men, because man, who is the most noble and free creature, among all the creatures that God made, is placed in the power of another" (Herbert S. Klein, "Anglicanism, Catholicism, and the Negro Slave," in Ann J. Lane, ed., *The Debate over Slavery: Stanley Elkins and His Critics* [Urbana: University of Illinois Press, 1971], 142).

28. In fact, this mode of explanation is perfectly compatible with the assumption that such individual personality traits as compassion and scrupulosity were as evident before 1750 as after. If being "good" consists—as I think it must, for the most part—of scrupulous adherence to the ethical maxims of one's culture (such as the Golden Rule), within the operational limits prescribed by convention and the availability of techniques for intervention, then it makes perfectly good sense to say that people did not become "better" after 1750; they just adapted their conduct to a new set of conventions and capabilities. The argument thus does not rest on any assumption of moral progress, as that term is ordinarily understood, though it does assume that post-1750 conventions of responsibility embrace a wider range of suffering humanity and are in that sense superior to earlier ones.

CHAPTER 9 Capitalism and the Origins of the Humanitarian Sensibility, Part 2

1. Elias, *The Civilizing Process: The History of Manners,* trans. Edmund Jephcott (New York: Urizen Books, 1978), chap. 10.

2. Ibid., 205.

3. P. S. Atiyah, *The Rise and Fall of Freedom of Contract* (Oxford: Clarendon Press, 1979), 402–4.

4. The minstrel Bertran de Born sang joyfully of hearing the cry "Help! Help!" and seeing "the dead pierced by the wood of the lances decked with banners." As late as the sixteenth century the king and queen of France celebrated Midsummer Day in Paris

by joining a festive throng to burn alive one or two dozen cats (Elias, *Civilizing Process*, 193, 203). The gruesome agonies inflicted on the regicide Damiens in 1757 supply the opening scene for Michel Foucault's *Discipline and Punish: The Birth of the Prison*, trans. Alan Sheridan (New York: Pantheon, 1977), 3–6. Trial by ordeal was not abolished until the Fourth Lateran Council met in 1215, and the use of judicial torture as a means of eliciting confessions in cases of serious crime continued on the Continent (though seldom in England) from the thirteenth century until the last half of the eighteenth. In central Europe it lingered on even into the nineteenth century. See John H. Langbein, *Torture and the Law of Proof: Europe and England in the Ancien Regime* (Chicago: University of Chicago Press, 1977).

5. Weber, *The Protestant Ethic and the Spirit of Capitalism*, trans. Talcott Parsons (New York: Scribners, 1958), 17; Edward P. Thompson, "The Transforming Power of the Cross," in his *The Making of the English Working Class* (New York: Knopf, 1966); Bernard Semmel, *The Methodist Revolution* (New York: Basic Books, 1973); and Paul E. Johnson, *A Shopkeeper's Millennium: Society and Revivals in Rochester, N.Y., 1815–1837* (New York: Hill and Wang, 1978).

6. Weber, *Protestant Ethic*, 55. For the history of the expectation, widespread from the sixteenth to the eighteenth century, that capitalism would bring political harmony by taming the passions and infusing a wholesome discipline into the population, see Albert O. Hirschman, *The Passions and the Interests: Political Arguments for Capitalism before Its Triumph* (Princeton: Princeton University Press, 1977).

7. On my use of the term "techniques" and the preconditions for the appearance of the humanitarian sensibility, see the "case of the starving stranger" in my "Capitalism and the Origins of the Humanitarian Sensibility, Part 1," 251–58 (this volume).

8. Nietzsche, *On the Genealogy of Morals and Ecce Homo*, trans. Walter Kaufmann and R. J. Hollingdale (New York: Random House, 1969), 57–59.

9. Ibid., 67, 59–60. Nietzsche's admiration is sincere: "The existence on earth of an animal soul turned against itself, taking sides against itself, was something so new, profound, unheard of, enigmatic, contradictory, *and pregnant with a future* that the aspect of the earth was essentially altered. Indeed, divine spectators were needed to do justice to the spectacle that thus began and the end of which is not yet in sight" (85). Now that the ladder of renunciation had been arduously climbed, of course, Nietzsche was inexplicably confident that his new model man could kick it away and simply levitate.

10. Ibid., 60.

11. C. B. Macpherson, *The Political Theory of Possessive Individualism: Hobbes to Locke* (London: Oxford University Press, 1962), 48: "If a single criterion of the possessive market society is wanted it is that man's labour is a commodity, i.e. that a man's energy and skill are his own, yet are regarded not as integral parts of his personality, but as possessions, the use and disposal of which he is free to hand over to others for a price."

12. For my use of the term "recipe" and the role that recipe knowledge plays in establishing the background against which causal attribution and judgments of moral responsibility are made, see "Capitalism and the Origins of the Humanitarian Sensibility, Part 1," 253–57 (this volume).

13. A. W. B. Simpson, *A History of the Common Law of Contract: The Rise of the Action of Assumpsit* (Oxford: Clarendon Press, 1975), 4, 199, 215–18, 281–316.

14. Atiyah, *Rise and Fall of Freedom of Contract*, 102. On parallel developments in

America, see Morton J. Horwitz, *The Transformation of American Law, 1780–1860* (Cambridge, Mass.: Harvard University Press, 1977), chap. 6. Also see Grant Gilmore, *The Death of Contract* (Columbus: Ohio State University Press, 1974). Although Horwitz's book is extremely valuable, it falls victim (as Atiyah's does not) to the usual weaknesses of the social control mode of explanation: an exaggeration of the role played by class interest, based on the assumption that only interest can link base with superstructure.

15. Simpson, *History of the Common Law of Contract,* 323; Atiyah, *Rise and Fall of Freedom of Contract,* 139–49.

16. Atiyah, *Rise and Fall of Freedom of Contract,* 139–49, 194–205, 208, 212–16; and Horwitz, *Transformation of American Law,* 160, 174, 180–86, 200–201.

17. I discuss Woolman more fully in the closing pages of this essay.

18. Daniel Snydacker, "Traders in Exile: Quakers and Jews of New York and Newport in the New World Economy, 1650–1776" (Ph.D. diss., Johns Hopkins University, 1982).

19. Henry Home, Lord Kames, *Principles of Equity,* 2d ed. (Printed for A. Millar, London, and A. Kincaid and J. Bell, Edinburgh, 1767), 16–17. These words appear in Kames's "Preliminary Discourse: Being an Investigation of the Moral Laws of Society," which was not included in any other edition of *Principles of Equity.*

20. Simpson, *History of the Common Law of Contract,* 204, 249; Atiyah, *Rise and Fall of Freedom of Contract,* 219–26.

21. Frothingham quoted in Jonathan A. Glickstein, "'Poverty is not Slavery': American Abolitionists and the Competitive Labor Market," in Lewis Perry and Michael Fellman, eds., *Antislavery Reconsidered: New Perspectives on the Abolitionists* (Baton Rouge: Louisiana State University Press, 1979), 199. Frothingham also predicted that pauperism, "in all its dismal shapes, with all its terrible sorrows, . . . will be outgrown as man becomes more wise and powerful" (ibid.). Yet another outward shift in the horizon of causal involvement not unlike what Frothingham predicted can perhaps be observed in Wendell Phillips's change of opinion on wage labor. Before the Civil War he dismissed the term "wage slavery" as "utterly unintelligible" but by 1871 had declared his opposition to the entire wage system. Phillips quoted in Daniel T. Rodgers, *The Work Ethic in Industrial America, 1850–1920* (Chicago: University of Chicago Press, 1978), 32.

22. Defoe, *An Essay Upon Projects* (Menston, Eng.: Scolar Press, 1969), 7–8, 24. The earliest entry in the Oxford English Dictionary for "project" in the sense of "a plan, scheme, purpose, something proposed for execution," is dated 1601.

23. Joyce Oldham Appleby, *Economic Thought and Ideology in Seventeenth-Century England* (Princeton: Princeton University Press, 1978), 246, 84. Also see her comments on the importance of calculating equivalencies and on the power of abstraction (245, 247, 93). She noted that Defoe's demarcation of the period after 1680 as a "projecting age" is justified by the rapid economic growth and great surge of inventions that took place in these years (164–65). Seymour Drescher observed that the abolitionists "represented that portion of European society most completely mobilized for living with the sense of individual power, responsibility, and insecurity that flowed from the market" (Drescher, *Econocide: British Slavery in the Era of Abolition* [Pittsburgh: University of Pittsburgh Press, 1977], 183).

24. Atiyah, *Rise and Fall of Freedom of Contract,* 345–46.

25. Nietzsche, *On the Genealogy of Morals,* 58.

26. Burt quoted in George Combe, *Remarks on the Principles of Criminal Legislation and the Practice of Prison Discipline* (London: Simpkin, Marshall, 1854), 64 (emphasis deleted).

27. Michael Katz, writing of school reformers, said "the control of the passions coincided with another goal, especially necessary for social mobility but usually expressed in rather different terms: the ability to plan for the future. 'Forming plans for a distant future,' individuals 'rise nearer and nearer to a spiritual existence.' Ideally the parents and, if not, the school had to teach this lesson: substitute future for immediate gratification. . . . Restraint it was that separated the child from the adult. Men, claimed one writer, 'act from principle . . . the restraints of society are felt. They can see remote consequences. But children act from the impulses of their natures quickened by the objects around them.' Thus restraint was the personality characteristic central to education" (Katz, *The Irony of Early School Reform: Educational Innovations in Mid-Nineteenth-Century Massachusetts* [Cambridge, Mass.: Harvard University Press, 1968], 121). Also see Brian Harrison, *Drink and the Victorians: The Temperance Question in England, 1815–1872* (Pittsburgh: University of Pittsburgh Press, 1971); Blake McKelvey, *American Prisons: A History of Good Intentions* (Montclair, N.J.: P. Smith, 1977), 36–38; David J. Rothman, *The Discovery of the Asylum: Social Order and Disorder in the American Republic* (Boston: Little, Brown, 1971); Michael Ignatieff, *A Just Measure of Pain: The Penitentiary and the Industrial Revolution* (New York: Pantheon, 1978); Andrew Scull, *Museums of Madness: The Social Organization of Insanity in Nineteenth-Century England* (New York: St. Martin's Press, 1979); Andrew Scull, "Moral Treatment Reconsidered: Some Sociological Comments on an Episode in the History of British Psychiatry," *Psychological Medicine* 9 (1979): 421–28; Martin Wiener, ed., *Humanitarianism or Control? A Symposium on Aspects of Nineteenth-Century Social Reform in Britain and America, Rice University Studies* 67 (1981); and Harold Schwartz, *Samuel Gridley Howe: Social Reformer, 1801–1876* (Cambridge, Mass.: Harvard University Press, 1956), chap. 6.

28. Mill quoted in Atiyah, *Rise and Fall of Freedom of Contract,* 432.

29. Spencer, "Prison Ethics," in his *Essays Moral, Political, and Aesthetic* (New York: n.p., 1888), 216–17.

30. Here I have in mind Philip Rieff, *The Triumph of the Therapeutic: Uses of Faith after Freud* (New York: Harper and Row, 1966), and T. J. Jackson Lears, *No Place of Grace: Antimodernism and the Transformation of American Culture, 1880–1920* (New York: Pantheon, 1981).

31. Woolman, *The Journal and Major Essays of John Woolman,* ed. Phillips P. Moulton (New York: Oxford University Press, 1971), 53. Subsequent page references are cited parenthetically in the text.

32. The Golden Rule first appears in the sixth paragraph of Woolman's essay; this version, later in the book, is in a passage that Woolman drew from the works of a London Quaker, Alexander Arscott. Sydney James observed that for Quakers "even launching a business without adequate training and credit was a case of failure to do 'unto all men, as we would they should do unto us'" (*A People Among Peoples: Quaker Benevolence in Eighteenth-Century America* [Cambridge, Mass.: Harvard University Press, 1963], 32).

33. Woolman's inclusion of the proviso that the slave never forfeited his liberty indi-

406 Notes to Pages 279–81

cates that he was familiar with the work of the natural rights philosophers. See Richard
Tuck, *Natural Rights Theories: Their Origin and Development* (New York: Cambridge
University Press, 1979).

34. In his journal, Woolman recorded his anxiety about accepting hospitality from
slaveholders, because it enabled him to save his own money and thereby made him
party to their oppression of slaves. He cleared his conscience by carrying small silver
coins with him that he paid to the slaves of the household, either directly or through
their masters (*Journal and Major Essays*, 59–61). Although recipe knowledge and an
awareness of the "necessary connection" between events is a precondition for the emergence of the humanitarian sensibility, these things are by no means sufficient in themselves to produce that sensibility. Daniel Defoe, a disappointed investor in the Royal
African Company, is a case in point. Like Woolman, he conceived of the slave trade as
part of a network of cause-and-effect relationships. But from this he drew in 1713 the
conclusion that the slave trade was indispensable to England's prosperity: "The case
is as plain as cause and consequence: Mark the climax. No African trade, no negroes;
no negroes no sugars, gingers, indicoes [*sic*] etc; no sugars etc no island; no islands
no continent; no continent no trade" (quoted in Peter Earle, *The World of Defoe* [Lon-
don: Weidenfeld and Nicolson, 1976], 131). Defoe's involvement with the slave trade was
brought to my attention by Seymour Drescher.

35. Stanley Engerman brought this possibility to my attention.

CHAPTER 10   Responsibility, Convention, and the Role of
Ideas in History

1. Quentin Skinner, "Meaning and Understanding in the History of Ideas," in
Meaning and Context: Quentin Skinner and His Critics, ed. James Tully (Princeton:
Princeton University Press, 1988), 67. This influential essay originally appeared in *His-
tory and Theory* 8 (1969): 3–53.

2. For an intriguing effort to convert this art of "reading between the lines" into a
science of presuppositions — and call it "metaphysics" — see R. G. Collingwood, *An Essay on Metaphysics* (London: Oxford University Press, 1940), chaps. 4–7. The most revealing presuppositions of all are those that underwrite common sense. As Louis Mink,
a careful reader of Collingwood, put it, "Nothing is more wonderful than common
sense. . . . The common sense of an age, we recognize when we compare that age with
others, may well be for different times and places beyond the limits of comprehension
or even of fantasy. A primary reason for this is that common sense of whatever age has
presuppositions which derive not from universal human experience, but from a shared
conceptual framework, which determines what shall count as experience for its com-
municants" ("Narrative Form as a Cognitive Instrument," in *The Writing of History:
Literary Form and Human Understanding,* ed. R. H. Canary and H. Kozicki [Madison:
University of Wisconsin Press, 1978], 129).

3. The label "history of ideas" is sometimes contrasted with "intellectual history"
on the one hand and "cultural history" on the other. No such distinction is intended
here. In the passage quoted at the head of the essay, Skinner uses "history of ideas" to
stand indiscriminately for a variety of approaches, and for the sake of consistency I follow suit.

4. Hans-Georg Gadamer, *Truth and Method* (New York: Seabury Press, 1975), 245.

The implications of Gadamer's position are spelled out in characteristically candid fashion by Stanley Fish, "Critical Self-Consciousness, or Can We Know What We're Doing?" in his *Doing What Comes Naturally: Change, Rhetoric, and the Practice of Theory in Literary and Legal Studies* (Durham, N.C.: Duke University Press, 1989), 437–67.

5. Richard McKeon, "The Development and the Significance of the Concept of Responsibility," *Revue Internationale de Philosophie* 11 (1957): 6–8, 23. Relying on the OED, McKeon credits Alexander Hamilton with first use of the term (in Federalist 64) and dates it 1787. In fact, Madison used the term in Federalist 63, which appeared in 1788. See Bernard Bailyn, comp., *The Debate on the Constitution* (New York: Library of America, 1993), pt. 2, 317.

6. McKeon, "Concept of Responsibility," 6–8, 23.

7. Skinner, "Conventions and the Understanding of Speech Acts," *Philosophical Quarterly* 20 (1970): 135, 137. Here and elsewhere, in quoting from this article, I have spelled out Skinner's shorthand notation. Thus, instead of "S" and "A," I use "Speaker" and "Audience," and instead of t_1 and t_2, I use "time one" and "time two."

8. Ibid., 136.

9. Clifford Geertz, "Thick Description: Toward an Interpretive Theory of Culture," in *The Interpretation of Cultures: Selected Essays* (New York: Basic Books, 1973), 5, 7, 12.

10. These obviously are far-reaching philosophical issues, but since the entire pragmatic tradition from Charles Peirce to Richard Rorty might be described as an effort to chart a middle path between the extremes of "History" and "Reason," perhaps I will be forgiven the parochialism of confining myself to a few recent North American texts: James T. Kloppenberg, *Uncertain Victory: Social Democracy and Progressivism in European and American Thought, 1870–1920* (New York: Oxford University Press, 1986); Robert B. Westbrook, *John Dewey and American Democracy* (Ithaca: Cornell University Press, 1991); Richard Rorty, *Philosophy and the Mirror of Nature* (Princeton: Princeton University Press, 1979); and Richard J. Bernstein, *Beyond Objectivity and Relativism: Science, Hermeneutics, and Praxis* (Philadelphia: University of Pennsylvania Press, 1983). For an uncritical embrace of contingency, see Barbara Herrnstein Smith, *Contingencies of Value: Alternative Perspectives for Critical Theory* (Cambridge, Mass.: Harvard University Press, 1988). For excess in the opposite direction, see Allan Bloom, *The Closing of the American Mind: How Higher Education Has Failed Democracy and Impoverished the Souls of Today's Students* (New York: Simon and Schuster, 1987). For unusually trenchant commentaries on these and related problems, see David Hollinger, "How Wide the Circle of the 'We'? American Intellectuals and the Problem of the Ethnos Since World War II," *American Historical Review* 98 (Apr. 1993): 317–37, and "Postethnic America," *Contentions* 2 (1992): 79–96. Also relevant is my essay, "The Curious Persistence of Rights Talk in the Age of Interpretation" (chap. 5 in this volume).

11. Friedrich Nietzsche, *On the Genealogy of Morals and Ecce Homo*, trans. Walter Kaufmann and R. J. Hollingdale (New York: Random House, 1969), 57–58. Subsequent page references are cited parenthetically in the text.

12. This is not to suggest that Nietzsche took causality at face value. On the contrary, he ultimately reduced it to "fear of the unfamiliar." For a useful discussion, see Walter A. Kaufmann, *Nietzsche: Philosopher, Psychologist, Antichrist*, 3d ed. (Princeton: Princeton University Press, 1968), 263–64.

13. McKeon, "Concept of Responsibility," 6–7.

14. Max Weber, *The Protestant Ethic and the Spirit of Capitalism,* trans. Talcott Parsons (New York: Scribners, 1976), 154. For a fuller account of the implications of Weber's analysis for causal attribution and perceptions of responsibility, see my essay "Persons as Uncaused Causes: John Stuart Mill, the Spirit of Capitalism, and the 'Invention' of Formalism" (chap. 12 in this volume).

15. To cite only the best-known authority, and one who had no sympathy whatever with the Evangelicals' project, see Edward P. Thompson, *The Making of the English Working Class* (New York: Knopf, 1963), chap. 11.

16. Roberto Calasso, *The Marriage of Cadmus and Harmony,* trans. Tim Parks (New York: Knopf, 1993), 93–94.

17. *Basic Writings of St. Thomas Aquinas,* ed. Anton C. Pegis (New York: Random House, 1945), 2: 121, 134.

18. Here I paraphrase Bernard Williams, *Shame and Necessity* (Berkeley: University of California Press, 1993), 77. His principal target is A. H. Adkins, *Merit and Responsibility: A Study in Greek Values* (Oxford: Oxford University Press, 1960).

19. Williams, *Shame and Necessity,* 21, 33. Subsequent page references are cited parenthetically in the text.

20. Skinner stresses that the historian who tries to reconstruct the meaning of a text has not completed the job until the text is translated into terms intelligible to modern minds. Showing that the text is convention-governed is not enough. "It will be necessary, in short, if it is to be said that [the historian] has *understood* [the text] at all, that he should be capable of rendering into terms that make sense [by the standards of the present] of the meaning and force of [the author's] utterance [as understood by the author's contemporaries]." Skinner concedes that translation will sometimes prove to be impossible. Skinner, "Conventions and the Understanding of Speech Acts," 136–37.

21. My puzzlement about Williams's distinction between "unjust" and "not just" may reflect nothing more than my inadequate socialization into a way of speaking conventional among philosophers, one that reserves the word "unjust" for remediable evils and rejects in principle the notion of natural or cosmic injustice. If so, my sole remaining difference with Williams is his failure to address the key *historical* question of why perceptions of necessity change, converting necessary evils into remediable ones. I am obliged to Larry Temkin for bringing this possibility to my attention.

22. Bernard Williams, *Moral Luck* (Cambridge: Cambridge University Press, 1981); and *Ethics and the Limits of Philosophy* (Cambridge, Mass.: Harvard University Press, 1985). In the latter volume, see especially chapter 10, "Morality, the Peculiar Institution."

23. J. L. Mackie, *The Cement of the Universe: A Study of Causation* (Oxford: Oxford University Press, 1974).

24. For a fuller development of this line of argument, see my "Capitalism and the Origins of the Humanitarian Sensibility [parts 1 and 2]" (chaps. 8 and 9 in this volume).

25. The point I am making about the unavoidable role of convention in judgments of responsibility parallels the illustration Geertz famously used to make his own point about the importance of "thick description" (which he, in turn, borrowed from the philosopher Gilbert Ryle). A wink, Geertz observed, is much more than a twitch of the eye muscles, and any analyst who fails to grasp the difference—which resides not in the physical movement itself, but in the culturally defined meanings assigned to that event by a particular community—will be a very poor student of human affairs. In

the case of the suffering earthquake victim, the corresponding error would be to lump together as if ethically indistinguishable all failures to render aid, whether by the victim's next-door neighbors or by strangers living thousands of miles away. An analyst who appreciated the "thickness" of the conventions governing responsibility would not make this mistake, recognizing that not all who could, in principle, render aid are under equal obligations to do so. All of us who *could* go to the stranger's aid are, indeed, causally implicated in the prolongation of his suffering: it is undeniably true that *but for* our inaction, his suffering would be relieved. But only those of us falling within conventionally defined limits of proximity and ease of intervention will actually be vulnerable to allegations of irresponsibility. The conventions of responsibility always *and inevitably* fall short of much suffering that we could alleviate if we wanted to badly enough. Acknowledging convention's force does not prevent us from calling conventions morally wrong when they underestimate our real power to render aid.

26. Williams made a similar point when he likened the ancient attitude toward slavery to modern attitudes toward social injustices of a comparatively intractable kind: those about which we lack any remedy sufficiently familiar, "cost effective," and certain of success to justify confidence. The recent debacle of United Nations–sponsored humanitarian aid in Somalia might be taken as an example of misplaced confidence in our powers of intervention. Some would point to the absence of intervention in the Bosnian or Rwandan nightmares as examples of the opposite error.

27. David Brion Davis, *The Problem of Slavery in Western Culture* (Ithaca: Cornell University Press, 1966).

28. Hans Jonas, *The Imperative of Responsibility: In Search of an Ethics for the Technological Age,* trans. Hans Jonas, with David Herr (Chicago: University of Chicago Press, 1984), ix.

29. Alasdair MacIntyre, *After Virtue: A Study in Moral Theory,* 2d ed. (Notre Dame, Ind.: University of Notre Dame Press, 1984), 10.

30. Jonas, *Imperative of Responsibility,* 5–6.

31. Ibid., x.

32. Skinner, "Conventions and the Understanding of Speech Acts," 137, 138.

CHAPTER 11   A Brief Excursus on Formalism

1. Haskell, "Capitalism and the Origins of the Humanitarian Sensibility, Part 1," 351 n. 32 (see chap. 8, note 18, in this volume).

2. Wendell Phillips, *Speeches, Lectures, and Letters,* 2d ser. (Boston: Lee and Shepard, 1894), 152. I presume a good deal in saying that "we" agree with Phillips in seeing through formalism. The "we" I have in mind applies to academic intellectuals in the humanities.

3. Phillips quoted in John R. Commons et al., eds., *A Documentary History of American Industrial Society* (New York: Russell and Russell, 1958), 7: 220–21. See also Daniel T. Rodgers, *The Work Ethic in Industrial America, 1850–1920* (Chicago: University of Chicago Press, 1978), 32; and Richard Stott, "British Immigrants and the American 'Work Ethic' in the Mid-Nineteenth Century," *Labor History* 26 (Winter 1985): 86–102.

4. "Man is entirely, perfectly and unspeakably different from a mere machine, in that he has reason and understanding, and has a faculty of will, and so is capable of

volition and choice; . . . so that he has liberty to act according to his choice, and to do what he pleases . . . [and so is fully worthy of] praise . . . [or] punishment" (Jonathan Edwards, *Freedom of the Will* [New Haven: Yale University Press, 1957], 370).

5. Here I may understate the extravagance (in our eyes) of the formalist concept of voluntariness, for at a more abstract level the question of whether people could ever be thought to have voluntarily renounced their freedom and chosen to become slaves was taken very seriously by several generations of rights theorists, beginning in the early sixteenth century. At a more prosaic level, one of the principal rationales for the legitimacy of slaveowning construed the slave as originally a captive in war, who might well choose slavery over death. See Richard Tuck, *Natural Rights Theories: Their Origin and Development* (New York: Cambridge University Press, 1979), 3, 49, 54, 100; and David Brion Davis, *The Problem of Slavery in Western Culture* (Ithaca: Cornell University Press, 1966), 117–20.

6. My essay, "Persons as Uncaused Causes," chapter 12 of this volume, is a preliminary exploration of these developments.

7. Morton White, *Social Thought in America: The Revolt Against Formalism* (Boston: Beacon Press, 1957). White was concerned only with the United States, but James T. Kloppenberg has shown strong parallels between developments in this country, England, Germany and France, in *Uncertain Victory: Social Democracy and Progressivism in European and American Thought, 1870–1920* (New York: Oxford University Press, 1986).

8. Thomas L. Haskell, *The Emergence of Professional Social Science: The American Social Science Association and the Nineteenth-Century Crisis of Authority* (Urbana: University of Illinois Press, 1977); Dorothy Ross, *Origins of American Social Science* (Cambridge: Cambridge University Press, 1991).

9. Davis, "Reflections on Abolitionism and Ideological Hegemony," *American Historical Review* 92 (Oct. 1987): 806.

10. For more on the connection between antiformalism and market culture, see "Persons as Uncaused Causes," chapter 12 of this volume.

11. Emphasis added. Aquinas and Aristotle, unlike Hobbes, recognized that the seafarer's act is of a "mixed kind" and that there is a sense in which it is involuntary. But both assigned clear priority to the sense in which it is voluntary, just as Hobbes did. *Basic Writings of St. Thomas Aquinas,* ed. Anton C. Pegis (New York: Random House, 1945), 2: 234, 231; *The Nichomachean Ethics of Aristotle,* trans. D. P. Chase (New York: E. P. Dutton, 1911), bk. 3, 44–45; Thomas Hobbes, *Leviathan* (chap. 22), in *British Moralists, 1650–1800,* ed. D. D. Raphael (Oxford: Clarendon Press, 1969), 1: 55.

12. Aquinas, *Summa Contra Gentiles,* bk. 3, chap. 88, *Basic Writings,* 2: 168–69.

13. In addition to White, *Social Thought in America,* see H. Stuart Hughes, *Consciousness and Society: The Reorientation of European Social Thought, 1890–1930* (New York: Knopf, 1958); Talcott Parsons, *The Structure of Social Action: A Study in Social Theory with Reference to a Group of Recent European Writers* (New York: McGraw-Hill, 1937); Kloppenberg, *Uncertain Victory;* and Haskell, *Emergence of Professional Social Science.*

CHAPTER 12   Persons as Uncaused Causes

1. See Peter Brown, *The Body and Society: Men, Women, and Sexual Renunciation in Early Christianity* (New York: Columbia University Press, 1988), 434.

2. Needless to say, when I refer to causal attribution as a game, I mean to stress its conventional and rule-bound character, not any lack of seriousness. My interest in causal attribution was first sparked by Fritz Heider, "Social Perception and Phenomenal Causality," *Psychological Review* (Nov. 1944): 358–74, and much influenced by H. L. A. Hart and A. M. Honoré, *Causation in the Law* (London: Oxford University Press, 1959), and Joel Feinberg, "Causing Voluntary Actions," in his *Doing and Deserving: Essays in the Theory of Responsibility* (Princeton: Princeton University Press, 1970), 152–86.

3. J. L. Mackie, *The Cement of the Universe: A Study of Causation* (Oxford: Oxford University Press, 1974).

4. John Stuart Mill, *Autobiography and Literary Essays,* ed. John M. Robson and Jack Stillinger, vol. 1 of *Collected Works of John Stuart Mill,* ed. John M. Robson (Toronto: University of Toronto Press, 1981), 1: 175.

5. To construe the question as one of causal attribution is, of course, to construe it in terms other than those actually employed by most of the principal contributors to the great controversy over freedom and fate. There is some risk in this strategy, some danger of forcing diverse perceptions into a Procrustean mold, but there are also certain advantages, especially when the contributor's own language approximates that of causal attribution as closely as Mill's obviously does. In a recent study notable for its commodious coverage and strict reporting of the actual language of the debate, John R. Reed observed that "after all, during the nineteenth century, though men had many models of the self from which to choose, in the end they were forced to make only a few central decisions. Either the self was coherent and directed from within, or it lacked integrity and depended upon external energy" (*Victorian Will* [Athens: Ohio University Press, 1989], 24).

6. As H. Stuart Hughes wrote, Weber's framework of analysis emphasized the continuity of capitalism and socialism: "Viewed in the context of the rationalization or bureaucratization of living, the distinction between capitalism and socialism ceased to be of major importance" (*Consciousness and Society: The Reorientation of European Social Thought, 1890–1930,* rev. ed. [New York: Vintage, 1977], 318).

7. Morton White, *Social Thought in America: The Revolt Against Formalism* (Boston: Beacon Press, 1957), 14, 21–27.

8. Macauley's skepticism about the explanatory power of "interest" is worth recalling. In his criticism of James Mill's *Essay on Government,* Macauley called it but a "truism" that men act always from self-interest. "This truism the Utilitarians proclaim with as much pride as if it were new, and as much zeal as if it were important. But in fact, when explained, it means only that men, if they can, will do as they choose. When we see the actions of a man, we know with certainty what he thinks his interest to be. But it is impossible to reason with certainty from what *we* take to be his interest to his actions. . . . [It is idle] to attribute any importance to a proposition, which, when interpreted, means only that a man had rather do what he had rather do. If the doctrine that men always act from self-interest, be laid down in any other sense than this—if the meaning of the word self-interest be narrowed so as to exclude any one of

the motives which may by possibility act on any human being, — the proposition ceases to be identical; but at the same time it ceases to be true" (T. B. Macauley, "Mill's Essay on Government: Utilitarian Logic and Politics" [1829], in *Utilitarian Logic and Politics: James Mill's Essay on Government, Macauley's Critique and the Ensuing Debate*, ed. Jack Lively and John Rees [Oxford: Oxford University Press, 1978], 124–25).

9. David Hume has perhaps the best claim to being first, and was no doubt a deeper thinker than Mill, yet he never displayed Mill's concern to develop a complete and balanced view of the subject. See Hume, *Inquiries Concerning Human Understanding and Concerning the Principles of Morals*, ed. L. A. Selby-Bigge, 3d ed., revised by P. H. Neddich (Oxford: Clarendon Press, 1975 [1777]), 92.

10. John Stuart Mill, *Autobiography*, 41, 45, 47.

11. Hans-Georg Gadamer, *Truth and Method* (New York: Seabury Press, 1975), 245.

12. Martin Luther, *The Bondage of the Will*, ed. J. I. Packer and O. R. Johnston (n.p.: Fleming H. Revell, 1957), 312.

13. Ibid., 313–14.

14. Calvin went even farther than Luther in divinizing the circumstantial setting of life. "The providence of God, as it is taught in scripture, is opposed to fortune and fortuitous accidents," wrote Calvin. "If any one falls into the hands of robbers, or meets with wild beasts; if by a sudden storm he is shipwrecked on the ocean; if he is killed by the fall of a house or a tree; if another, wandering through deserts, finds relief for his penury, or, after having been tossed about by the waves, reaches the port, and escapes, as it were, but a hair's breadth from death, — carnal reason will ascribe all these occurrences, both prosperous and adverse, to fortune. But whoever has been taught from the mouth of Christ, that the hairs of his head are all numbered (Matt. x:30), will seek further for a cause, and conclude that all events are governed by the secret counsel of God" (*Institutes of the Christian Religion*, excerpted in *European Origins of American Thought*, ed. David D. Van Tassel and Robert W. McAhren [Chicago: Rand McNally, 1969], 4–5). As Michael Walzer observes, "In Calvinist thought nature ceased altogether to be a realm of secondary causation, a world whose laws were anciently established and subject to God's will only in the extraordinary case of a miracle. Providence no longer consisted in law or in foresight: 'providence consists in action.' The eternal order of nature became an order of circumstantial and particular events, the cause of each being the immediate, active (but inscrutable) will of God. . . . 'no wind ever rises or blows, but by the special command of God.'" Walzer notes that although Calvin's God "required an obedience so precise and total as to be without precedent in the history of tyranny, he also freed men from all sorts of alternative jurisdictions and authorities" (*Revolution of the Saints: A Study in the Origins of Radical Politics* [New York: Athenaeum, 1969], 35 [quoting Calvin], 152).

15. Samuel Taylor Coleridge, *Lay Sermons*, ed. R. J. White, vol. 6 of *Collected Works* (n.p.: Routledge and Kegan Paul and Princeton University Press, 1972), 31–32.

16. Ibid., 21.

17. Michael J. Sandel, *Liberalism and the Limits of Justice* (Cambridge: Cambridge University Press, 1982), 21.

18. James T. Kloppenberg, *Uncertain Victory: Social Democracy and Progressivism in European and American Thought, 1870–1920* (New York: Oxford University Press, 1986), 26–28.

19. As Joel Feinberg argues, the key question in the debate between free will and determinism is not *whether* we are "plugged into" nature, but *how:* "If the determining influences are filtered through our own network of predispositions, expectations, purposes, and values, if our own threshold requirements are carefully observed, if there is no jarring and abrupt change in the course of our natural bent, then it seems to me to do no violence to common sense for us to claim the act as our own, even though its causal initiation be located in the external world. In short, the more like an easy triggering of a natural predisposition an external cause is, the less difficulty there is in treating its effects as a voluntary action" ("Causing Voluntary Actions," 172).

20. Jon Elster, *Sour Grapes: Studies in the Subversion of Rationality* (Cambridge: Cambridge University Press, 1983), 21.

21. Martha Nussbaum, *The Fragility of Goodness: Luck and Ethics in Greek Tragedy and Philosophy* (Cambridge: Cambridge University Press, 1986), 2 (quoting Plato, *Phaedrus*), 3.

22. John Stuart Mill, *Autobiography,* 45; see also 41, 43. Subsequent page references are cited parenthetically in the text.

23. For a more extensive discussion of these points, see my "Capitalism and the Origins of the Humanitarian Sensibility [parts 1 and 2]" (chaps. 8 and 9 in this volume).

24. Max Weber, *The Protestant Ethic and the Spirit of Capitalism,* trans. Talcott Parsons (New York: Scribners, 1976), 176, 183. Subsequent page references are cited parenthetically in the text.

25. For the significance of "recipe knowledge," see my "Capitalism and the Origins of the Humanitarian Sensibility, Part 1," 253–58 (this volume).

26. "Fatalism is, of course, the only logical consequence of predestination. But on account of the idea of proof the psychological result was precisely the opposite" (Weber, *Protestant Ethic,* 232n).

27. Quoted in Perry Miller, *Jonathan Edwards* (New York: Dell, 1967), 91.

28. One could argue that Weber's insight into the psychological dynamics of predestination was incomplete. The doctrine had not one, but two faces: threatening and consoling. It threatened irrevocable damnation but also offered assurance that the circumstantial setting of life was, in spite of all appearances to the contrary, an instrument of divine purpose. Weber assumed that the doctrine struck fear into the hearts of adherents and drove them in sheer terror to cling to the idea of the calling as one's only spiritual life raft. But predestination could have been a comforting doctrine for people already disturbed by the eruption of contingency in their lives and eager to believe that even the most disruptive events reflected the will of God. An interpretation of predestination stressing its tendency to divinize the circumstances of human existence and thereby assure people that they were not mere "creatures of circumstance" would reinforce Michael Walzer's suggestion, *contra* Weber, that the effect of predestination was less to induce anxiety than to "confirm and explain in theological terms perceptions men already had of the dangers of the world and the self" (*Revolution of the Saints,* 308).

29. Weber, *Protestant Ethic,* 118, 126, 119.

30. Bruce Mazlish, *James and John Stuart Mill: Father and Son in the Nineteenth Century* (New York: Basic Books, 1975), 227, 404.

31. The absence of any mention of his mother in the *Autobiography* only fuels twentieth-century suspicions of denial.

32. Thomas Carlyle, *A Carlyle Reader: Selections from the Writings of Thomas Carlyle*, ed. G. B. Tennyson (New York: Modern Library, 1969), 34, 37, 40–41.

33. John Stuart Mill, *Autobiography*, 181, 183. Speaking of Carlyle's early articles, Mill also observed that "for a long time I saw nothing in these (as my father saw nothing in them to the last) but insane rhapsody" (169). Mill did not deem himself a competent judge of Carlyle, whom he regarded as a "poet" and a "man of intuition," and he credited Harriet Taylor with "interpreting" Carlyle for him (183).

34. *A Carlyle Reader*, 46–47. The passage continues: "Speak to any small man of a high, majestic Reformation, of a high majestic Luther; and forthwith he sets about 'accounting' for it; how the 'circumstances of the time' called for such a character, and found him, we suppose, standing girt and road-ready, to do its errand; how the 'circumstances of the time' created, fashioned, floated him quietly along into the result; how, in short, this small man, had he been there, could have performed the like himself!" (47).

35. *A Carlyle Reader*, 46, 51. Subsequent page references are cited parenthetically in the text.

36. "Now it is a law of providence that everything is moved by its proximate cause. . . . But the proximate moving cause of the will is the apprehended good, which is its object, and the will is moved by it as sight is by color. Therefore no created substance can move the will except by means of the apprehended good—in so far, namely, as it shows that a particular thing is good to do; and this is *to persuade*. Therefore no created substance can act on the will, or cause our choice, except by way of persuasion" (Aquinas, *Summa Contra Gentiles*, bk. 3, chap. 88, *Basic Writings of St. Thomas Aquinas*, ed. Anton C. Pegis [New York: Random House, 1945], 2: 168–69).

37. John Stuart Mill, *A System of Logic, Ratiocinative and Inductive: Being a Connected View of the Principles of Evidence and the Methods of Scientific Investigation*, vol. 8 of *The Collected Works*, ed. J. M. Robson (Toronto: University of Toronto Press and Routledge and Kegan Paul, 1974), 837. Subsequent page references are cited parenthetically in the text.

38. The masthead of the Owenite periodical (more or less weekly) *The New Moral World* carried the motto "The Character of Man is Formed for Him and not by Him."

39. On the supersession of Owenism by Marxism, see Gregory Claeys, *Machinery, Money and the Millennium: From Moral Economy to Socialism* (Cambridge, Eng.: Polity Press, 1987), 156–83.

40. Robert Owen, *A New View of Society; or, Essays on the Principle of the Formation of the Human Character* (Glencoe, Ill.: Free Press, n.d. [3d ed., 1817]), 90–92. The passage was repeated over and over in Owenite literature, and usually printed in boldface.

41. Luther, for example, held that "necessity does not destroy moral responsibility" (*Bondage of the Will*, 185).

42. Robert Owen, *The Revolution in the Mind and Practice of the Human Race: or the Coming Change from Irrationality to Rationality* (Clifton, N.J.: A. M. Kelley, 1973 [1849]), 144.

43. *The New Moral World: or Gazette of the Universal Community of Rational Religionists*, n.s., 48:6 (Sept. 21, 1839): 753.

44. Gertrude Lenzer, ed., *Auguste Comte and Positivism: The Essential Writings* (New York: Harper and Row, 1975).

45. Robert Owen, *The Life of Robert Owen* (London: Frank Cass, 1967 [1857]), 1: 159–64 (quotation on 160).

46. James Martineau, *Essays, Reviews, and Addresses* (London: Longman's Green, 1891), 3: 520, 527.

47. Ibid., 527.

48. Reid quoted in Mill, *A System of Logic,* 358.

49. Weber, *Protestant Ethic,* 55.

50. Joyce Oldham Appleby, *Economic Thought and Ideology in Seventeenth-Century England* (Princeton: Princeton University Press, 1978), 246, 84.

51. C. B. Macpherson, *The Political Theory of Possessive Individualism: Hobbes to Locke* (London: Oxford University Press, 1962), 106.

52. For a brilliant reassertion of this insight, and an attempt to disentangle it from the categories of traditional Marxist analysis, see William Reddy, *Money and Liberty in Modern Europe: A Critique of Historical Understanding* (Cambridge: Cambridge University Press, 1987), especially chap. 3, "Growth of the Liberal Illusion."

53. Karl Marx, *The German Ideology,* excerpted in *The Marx-Engels Reader,* ed. Robert C. Tucker (New York: Norton, 1972), 163.

INDEX

Abbot, Francis E., 390 n.4
abnormality, criterion for attribution of causation, 20–21, 256–57, 401 n.25
Abraham, David, 160
Abrams v. United States, 183
academic freedom, and disciplinary autonomy, 184–85
Addams, Jane, 228
After Virtue (MacIntyre), 126–33
American Association for the Advancement of Science (AAAS), 191
American Association of University Professors (AAUP), 60, 175, 178; likened to ABA, AMA, 184; and Ross case, 182, 184
American Bar Association (ABA), 184
American Economic Association (AEA), 177, 179, 182, 184
American Historical Association (AHA), 165, 177, 184
American Medical Association, 184
American Philosophical Association (APA), 195, 204
Amnesty International, 122, 124, 213
Andrews, E. Benjamin, 183
Anstey, Roger, 236
antiformalism, 227, 232, 329; harbingers of, 316; succession of more militant forms, 324. *See also* formalism
antifoundationalism, foundational assumptions of, 212–13
antirealism, 201–2
Apel, Karl-Otto, 177
Appleby, Joyce Oldham, 363
Aquinas, Saint Thomas, 302, 355; quoted, 291, 315

Aristotle, 233, 291, 302; formalist assumptions of, 314–15; views on slavery discussed by Bernard Williams, 294–97
Arnold, Matthew, 185
asceticism: as defense of a principal goal of J. S. Mill's doctrine on freedom and fate, 355–56, 359; objectivity a facet of, 148–51; presupposed by Victorian founders of modern university, 190
Ash, Timothy Garton, 222–23
Ashworth, John, 307
Association for the Study of Negro Life and History, 162
associationism, 348, 349
Atiyah, P. S., 272–73
attributive mode of causal reasoning. *See* causal reasoning
Augustine, Saint, 319, 330
authority, 175, 186–87
Autobiography (J. S. Mill), 323, 325, 337
autonomy: Elster on difficulty of defining, 329–30; as required by idea of personhood, 329

Bagehot, Walter, 196
Bain, Alexander, 283, 288
Barclay, David, 243
Beard, Charles, 116, 153, 324
Becker, Carl, 116, 154
Bender, Thomas, 214
Bentham, Jeremy, 119, 333, 338–40, 359, 360
Berger, Peter, quoted, 245
Bernstein, Richard, 198
Black Family in Slavery and Freedom (Gutman), 162

Library of Congress Cataloging-in-Publication Data

Haskell, Thomas L., 1939–
Objectivity is not neutrality : explanatory schemes in history / Thomas L. Haskell.
p. cm.
Includes bibliographical references (p.) and index.
ISBN 0-8018-5681-7 (alk. paper)
1. United States — Historiography.   2. Objectivity.   I. Title.
E175.H38   1998
973'.072 — dc21   97-18956
                                                  CIP